PRINCIPLES OF THE ENGLISH
LAW OF OBLIGATIONS

Keith
Jone

CW01082626

PRINCIPLES OF THE ENGLISH LAW OF OBLIGATIONS

Edited by

PROFESSOR ANDREW BURROWS QC, FBA, DCL

Professor of the Law of England, University of Oxford, Fellow of All Souls College

CONTRIBUTORS

Andrew Burrows QC FBA DCL

John Davies

Ewan McKendrick QC

Donal Nolan

Charles Mitchell

OXFORD

UNIVERSITY PRESS

OXFORD
UNIVERSITY PRESS

Great Clarendon Street, Oxford, OX2 6DP,
United Kingdom

Oxford University Press is a department of the University of Oxford.
It furthers the University's objective of excellence in research, scholarship,
and education by publishing worldwide. Oxford is a registered trade mark of
Oxford University Press in the UK and in certain other countries

Published in the United States of America by Oxford University Press
198 Madison Avenue, New York, NY 10016, United States of America

British Library Cataloguing in Publication Data
Data available

Library of Congress Control Number: 2015949399

ISBN 978–0–19–874623–2

EDITOR

Professor Andrew Burrows QC, FBA, DCL
Professor of the Law of England, University of Oxford,
Fellow of All Souls College

CONTRIBUTORS

Professor Andrew Burrows
QC FBA DCL
All Souls College Oxford

Mr John Davies
Brasenose College Oxford

Professor Ewan McKendrick QC
University of Oxford

Professor Charles Mitchell
University College London

Mr Donal Nolan
Worcester College Oxford

INTRODUCTION

This book essentially reproduces the chapters in *English Private Law* which are concerned with the law of obligations, namely contract, tort and equitable wrongs, unjust enrichment, and remedies. *English Private Law* seeks to provide a high-quality overview of the rules and principles that constitute English private law and the intention in producing a student paperback edition is to make particular parts of that work more accessible to students. The benefit of such an overview is that it enables students to see the overall picture of the law and hence to understand how its various parts may be regarded as fitting together in a coherent whole.

The authors are acknowledged experts in their respective subject areas and their brief has been to produce as clear, simple and accurate an overview as possible of the relevant rules and principles. What one has here, therefore, is the product of many years of learning in each particular area.

It is believed that all students studying for law degrees or on law conversion courses will find this book invaluable.

English private law is best viewed as concerned with the rights which, one against another, people can realize in courts. Those rights may be helpfully divided according to who the rights can be enforced against (the question of 'exigibility'). Some rights can be demanded only from the person against whom they first arise or against someone who stands in that person's shoes and thus represents her. Some rights are, by contrast, more widely demandable and, of those, some follow things and can be demanded from any person in whose hands the thing is found. When names are added, this makes a division between rights *in rem*—that is, proprietary rights—whose exigibility depends on the location of a thing; and rights *in personam*—that is, personal rights—which are rights exigible only against the person against whom they originally arise or that person's representatives.[1] Rights realizable in court are therefore proprietary or personal. As personal rights correlate with obligations, the category of all personal rights is called the law of obligations.

The law of obligations is itself structured according to the main causative events of personal rights, namely contract, wrongs and unjust enrichment. This book also includes the law concerned with the realization of those rights in court (ie the law on judicial remedies).

It is important to appreciate that, with the exception of changing the chapter numbers and making corresponding amendments to the cross-references, this book essentially replicates the relevant parts of *English Private Law* which stated the law as at 30 January 2013. However, some light updating has been undertaken to reflect developments up until 30 April 2015 (and it has been assumed for the purposes of the updating that the Consumer Rights Act 2015 is in force although at the time of writing that is not so).

The reference 'EPL' refers to the main work *English Private Law*, edited by Andrew Burrows (OUP, 3rd edn, 2013).

Chapter 1 of this book correlates to EPL chapter 8, chapters 2–3 to EPL chapters 17–18, and chapter 4 to EPL chapter 21.

---

[1] It must not be allowed to escape notice that the subdivision of rights between *in rem* and *in personam* is not exhaustive. A category which is omitted is the category of rights which are good against all people but do not follow any *res*. All of these are superstructural rights which manifest themselves in the wrongs which infringe them. Thus the right to bodily integrity is protected through the torts which are committed against the body, and the right to reputation is protected by the torts of defamation. Such primary rights are 'superstructural' in that they provide the superstructure over the wrong: every wrong is the infringement of a primary right. Not every primary right is a right *in rem*. A primary right can be *in rem*, *in personam* (say, from contract), or, to give the residue a name, 'purely superstructural'.

CONTENTS

TABLE OF CASES

Table of UK Statutes

TABLE OF LEGISLATION

TABLE OF UK STATUTORY
INSTRUMENTS

1

CONTRACT: IN GENERAL

A. Introduction

(1) Agreement

1.01 A contract is an agreement which is either enforced by law or recognized by law as affecting the rights and duties of the parties. Usually, but not necessarily,[1] such an agreement arises from an exchange of promises: eg one by a seller to deliver goods and one by a buyer to pay for them. The concept of a contract as an agreement is, however, subject to two significant qualifications.

(a) The objective test

1.02 First, in determining whether an agreement has come into existence, the law normally applies an 'objective' test: if A so conducts himself as to induce B reasonably to believe that A has agreed to terms proposed by B, then A will generally be bound by those terms even though he may not in fact have intended to agree to them.[2] The law adopts this principle because, in the case put, B could be seriously prejudiced if A were allowed to avoid liability by showing that he had no such actual intention. The principle therefore does not apply where B knows that, in spite of the objective appearance, A had no intention of agreeing to B's terms.[3]

(b) Restrictions on freedom of contract

1.03 Secondly, there are many practical and legal restrictions on the principle of 'freedom of contract'. The *practical* restrictions arise where persons (often private consumers) contract with commercial suppliers for goods or services to be supplied on the latter's standard terms.[4] There is obviously room for argument on the question whether, in such cases, the customer has not agreed at all to these terms (of which he may be ignorant) or whether he has agreed to them reluctantly, or has simply taken his chance of them, whatever they may be. Similar questions of degree can arise from *legal* restrictions: eg, where a person is prohibited from refusing to contract with another on specified grounds, such as the other's age, disability, gender reassignment, marriage and civil partnership, race, religion or belief, sex or sexual orientation.[5] In such cases, the resulting relationship is generally nevertheless regarded as contractual because its other terms depend on agreement. But some relationships are the result of such a degree of legal compulsion as wholly to lose any consensual nature. There is, eg, no contract where a person's property is compulsorily acquired against his will, even though he receives compensation,[6] or where medicines are supplied to a person under the National Health Service, even though he pays a prescription charge.[7]

(2) The 'Expectation Interest'

1.04 Our concern here will be with the requirements of a legally enforceable agreement; with factors which, even where these requirements are satisfied, further restrict the legal effectiveness of agreements; with the parties by and against whom contracts can be enforced; and with the legal effects of failure in performance. One such effect is to give rise to certain judicial

---

[1] Not in the case of a unilateral contract (para 1.07).

[2] *Smith v Hughes* (1871) LR 6 QB 597, 607; *RTS Flexible Systems Ltd v Molkerei Alois Müller GmbH & Co (UK Production)* [2010] UKSC 14, [2010] 1 WLR 753, at [45] and see 1.05.

[3] See 1.05, 1.145.

[4] See section D for legal controls of such terms.

[5] See Equality Act 2010, ss 4–12.

[6] *Sovmots Investments Ltd v Secretary of State for the Environment* [1977] QB 411, 443, aff'd without reference to this point [1979] AC 144.

[7] See *Pfizer Corp v Ministry of Health* [1965] AC 512.

remedies, discussed in Chapter 4, but one aspect of this topic is of such importance to the nature of contract as a legal and commercial institution that it must be mentioned here. A civil wrong commonly gives the victim the right to compensation for having been made worse off by its commission; but the law of contract goes further in compensating him for the wrongdoer's failure to make him better off. It protects the victim's *expectation interest* or, as it is sometimes termed, 'performance interest':[8] eg by awarding a buyer the difference between the price which he has agreed to pay to the seller and the higher market value of the goods when they should have been, but were not, delivered.[9] The law of tort also sometimes awards damages for 'loss of expectations': eg for loss of expected earnings in personal injury cases. But these expectations generally exist independently of the wrong which impairs them, while the law of contract protects expectations which owe their very existence to the agreement for breach of which the action is brought. It does so in order to provide a legal framework for, and hence to promote stability in, many spheres of commercial activity.

B. Constituent Elements

(1) Agreement

(a) Reaching agreement: offer and acceptance

(i) Offer

Definition. The process by which parties reach agreement is usually[10] analysed into the **1.05** acceptance by one party of an offer made by the other. An offer is an expression of willingness to contract on the terms stated in it as soon as those terms are accepted by the party to whom the statement is made.[11] Under the objective test,[12] a statement by A can be an offer if it induces B reasonably to believe that A intended to be bound by it on acceptance,[13] even though A had no such intention.[14] A will not, however, be so bound if B knew that A had no such intention;[15] nor, probably, if B simply had no view on this question.[16] An offer may be made either expressly or by conduct[17] but probably not by mere inactivity since this, standing alone, is normally equivocal and so unlikely to induce one party to believe that the other intends to be bound.[18]

Offer and invitation to treat. An offer must be distinguished from an invitation to make **1.06** an offer, known in law as an 'invitation to treat': eg, an owner of property who wishes to sell it may invite offers for it at or about a specified price.[19] In such a case, the offer (if any) will

---

[8] See, eg, D Friedmann 'The Performance Interest in Contract Damages' (1995) 111 LQR 628.

[9] Sale of Goods Act 1979, s 51(3).

[10] There are exceptional cases in which this analysis is hard to apply: eg multipartite agreements, as in *The Satanita* [1895] P 248, aff'd sub nom *Clarke v Dunraven* [1897] AC 59; cf *Gibson v Manchester CC* [1978] 1 WLR 520, 523, reversed [1979] 1 WLR 294.

[11] eg *Storer v Manchester CC* [1974] 1 WLR 1403.

[12] See 1.02.

[13] See *Centrovincial Estates plc v Merchant Investor Assurance Co Ltd* [1983] Commercial LR 158; *Moran v University of Salford The Times*, 23 November 1993.

[14] *The Splendid Sun* [1981] 1 QB 694.

[15] *Ignazio Messina & Co v Polskie Linie Oceaniczne* [1995] 2 Lloyd's Rep 566, 571.

[16] *The Hannah Blumenthal* [1983] 1 AC 854 as interpreted in *The Leonidas D* [1985] 1 WLR 925; contrast *The Golden Bear* [1987] 1 Lloyd's Rep 330, 341; *The Multitank Holsatia* [1988] 2 Lloyd's Rep 486, 492.

[17] *Hart v Mills* (1846) 15 LJ Ex 200.

[18] *The Splendid Sun*, n 14, as explained in *The Hannah Blumenthal*, n 16; for a statutory solution of the problem that arose in these cases, see Arbitration Act 1996, s 41(3).

[19] *Gibson v Manchester CC* [1979] 1 WLR 294.

be made to the owner, not by him. In borderline cases, the distinction between an offer and an invitation to treat can be hard to draw (depending as it does on the elusive criterion of intention) and in some situations of common occurrence the law has reduced this difficulty by laying down prima facie rules on the point. For example, the display of price-marked goods for sale in a shop or an indication on a website of their availability is usually no more than an invitation to treat, the offer coming from the customer when he indicates that he wishes to buy.[20] Similarly, at an auction sale no offer is made by putting the goods up for auction: the offer is made by the bidder and is accepted by the auctioneer, usually on the 'fall of the hammer'.[21] Newspaper advertisements that goods are for sale are likewise not offers;[22] but an advertisement of a reward (eg for the return of lost property) is commonly regarded as an offer,[23] presumably because no further bargaining is expected to result from it. Advertisements relating to the sale or supply of goods can also give rise to contractual liability to buyers who deal as consumers.[24]

(ii) Acceptance

1.07 Concept. Assuming that an offer has been made, an agreement comes into existence when the offer is accepted either expressly (by words of acceptance) or by conduct. Usually, the acceptance, as well as the offer, contains a promise and the resulting contract is then bilateral: eg where A has in his offer promised to deliver goods and B in his acceptance to pay for them. There may also be a unilateral contract where A makes a promise but B does not: eg where A promises B to pay him £100 for walking from London to York, and B does so without making any promise.[25]

1.08 Correspondence of acceptance with offer. The acceptance must correspond with the offer: eg, an offer to sell something for £1,000 is not accepted by a reply stating that the offeree will pay £800.[26] Such a reply rejects the original offer (so that the offeree can no longer accept it)[27] and it also amounts to a new offer which the original offeror can accept. These rules govern the so-called 'battle of forms' in which each party sends to the other a previously prepared form setting out the terms on which he is prepared to deal. Normally the contract, if any, will be on the terms of the last document in the series which the recipient may accept by conduct (eg by rendering the requested services);[28] but it is also possible for the sender of the last document to indicate his acceptance of terms set out in the other party's earlier document[29] or, in an exceptional case, for a court to find that the terms of the parties' contract are to be found in the standard terms of neither party.[30]

1.09 'Communication' of Acceptance. The general rule is that an acceptance has no effect unless it is 'communicated' to the offeror[31] or to an agent of his who is authorized to receive it.[32] The rule exists to protect the offeror from the hardship of being bound without knowing

---

[20] *Pharmaceutical Society of GB v Boots Cash Chemists Ltd* [1952] 2 QB 795.
[21] Sale of Goods Act 1979, s 57(2); *British Car Auctions Ltd v Wright* [1972] 1 WLR 1519.
[22] *Partridge v Crittenden* [1968] 1 WLR 1204.
[23] cf *Carlill v Carbolic Smoke Ball Co* [1893] 1 QB 256.
[24] See, eg, Sale of Goods Act 1979, s 14(2D); Consumer Rights Act 2015, s 9(5).
[25] See *Great Northern Rly v Witham* (1873) LR 9 CP 16, 19.
[26] cf *Tinn v Hoffmann & Co* (1873) 29 LT 271.
[27] See 1.18; *Jones v Daniel* [1894] 2 Ch 332.
[28] *BRS v Arthur V Crutchley Ltd* [1967] 2 All ER 285; *Tekdata Interconnections Ltd v Amphenol Ltd* [2009] EWCA Civ 1209, [2010] 1 Lloyd's Rep 357.
[29] *Butler Machine Tool Co Ltd v Ex-Cell-O Corp (England) Ltd* [1979] 1 WLR 401.
[30] *GHSP Incorporated v AB Electronic Ltd* [2010] EWHC 1828 (Comm), [2011] 1 Lloyd's Rep 432; *Transformers and Rectifiers Ltd v Needs Ltd* [2015] EWHC 269 (TCC).
[31] *Holwell Securities Ltd v Hughes* [1974] 1 WLR 155, 157.
[32] *Henthorn v Fraser* [1892] 2 Ch 27, 33.

that his offer has been accepted. It follows that the rule does not apply where it is the offeror's 'own fault that he did not get it'[33] (the acceptance): eg if the acceptance is typed out on his telex machine during business hours and simply not read by him or any of his staff.[34] It is also possible for the offeror expressly or impliedly to waive the requirement of communication. This is commonly the position in the case of an offer of a unilateral contract since the offeror in such a case does not expect advance notice of the offeree's intention to do the required act.[35]

Posted acceptance.   An acceptance contained in a letter sent by post could, in theory, take   **1.10** effect at a variety of points, ranging from the time of posting to that of actual communication to the offeror. What is usually called the general rule of English law is that the acceptance takes effect as soon as it is posted.[36] There may therefore be a contract even though the acceptance is lost in the post;[37] and the contract is made at the time of posting[38] even though the acceptance is delayed in the post.[39] Such loss or delay can prejudice either party who may act on his belief that there is, or is not, a contract; and the posting rule favours the offeree on the not altogether convincing ground that the offeror, by starting negotiations by post, takes the risk of loss or delay in the post.[40] The rule applies only where it is reasonable to use the post as a means of communication[41] and it may be excluded by the terms of the offer.[42] It does not apply to 'instantaneous' communications, eg by telephone, fax, or telex,[43] since where these are used the acceptor will often know at once that his attempted communication has failed, and so be able to retrieve the situation. The application of the rule to acceptances by email[44] or in website trading[45] should depend on whether their failure is likewise immediately apparent to the acceptor.

The most important practical consequence of the posting rule is that a posted acceptance pre-   **1.11** vails over a previously posted but as yet uncommunicated withdrawal of the offer.[46] But the rule, being one of convenience, will not apply where it would lead to 'manifest inconvenience and absurdity'.[47] It would not, eg, apply where the acceptance was lost or delayed as a result, not of an accident in the post, but of the acceptor's carelessness in misdirecting the acceptance.[48] The loss or delay could also be caused by the carelessness of the offeror: eg where he had failed in the offer to give his correct address. In all such cases the resulting loss should

---

[33] *Entores v Miles Far East Corp* [1955] 2 QB 327, 332.
[34] *The Brimnes* [1975] QB 929; for messages received out of business hours, see *The Pamela* [1995] 2 Lloyd's Rep 249, 252.
[35] *Carlill's* case, n 23.
[36] *Henthorn v Fraser*, n 32; *Adams v Lindsell* (1818) 1 B & Ald 681.
[37] *The Household Fire and Carriage Accident etc Insurance Co Ltd v Grant* (1879) 4 Ex D 216.
[38] *Potter v Sanders* (1846) 6 Hare 1.
[39] *Dunlop v Higgins* (1848) 1 HLC 381.
[40] *Household etc Insurance Co Ltd v Grant*, n 37, at 223; the negotiations may in fact have been started by the *offeree*, where he receives a counter-offer.
[41] See *Henthorn v Fraser*, n 32.
[42] *Holwell Securities Ltd v Hughes* [1974] 1 WLR 155.
[43] *Entores* case, n 33; *Brinkibon Ltd v Stahag Stahl etc* [1983] 2 AC 34.
[44] It is likely that communication by email will be held to be instantaneous so that it does not fall within the scope of the postal rule: *Thomas v BPE Solicitors (a firm)* [2010] EWHC 306 (Ch), at [86].
[45] The Electronic Commerce (EC Directive) Regulations 2002, SI 2002/2013 state that communications in this medium are 'received' when the addressee is 'able to access them' (reg 11(2) (c)); but this does not necessarily answer the question when the contract is made. For judicial consideration of the issue, see *Chwee Kin Keong v Digilandmall.com Pte Ltd* [2004] SGHC 71, [2004] 2 SLR 594, aff'd [2005] 1 SLR 502.
[46] *Byrne & Co v Leon van Thienhoven & Co* (1880) 5 CPD 344; see 1.17.
[47] *Holwell Securities* case, n 42, at 161.
[48] *Korbetis v Transgrain Shipping BV* [2005] EWHC 1345 (QB), at [15] (fax message sent to wrong number).

fall on the party responsible for the defect in the communication. It is a more open question whether the posting rule should preclude an acceptor who had posted his acceptance from relying on a subsequently posted withdrawal which reached the offeror before or together with the acceptance.[49] The better view is that the posting of the acceptance should curtail the offeree's power to withdraw his acceptance,[50] just as it curtails the offeror's power to withdraw his offer.[51] For if it did not have this effect the offeree could, on a fluctuating market, in practice secure an option at no charge to himself and to the possible prejudice of the offeror.

1.12 **Distance contracts.** A consumer who has entered into a 'distance contract' (such as the one made by an exchange of letters or emails) for the supply of goods or services by a commercial supplier has the 'right to cancel' the contract within a specified period.[52] The underlying assumption is that a contract has first come into existence under the rules stated in 1.10 and 1.11; the supplier has no corresponding right to cancel.

1.13 **Stipulated mode of acceptance.** The offeror may for his own protection stipulate in the offer that it must be accepted in a specified way: eg by a letter sent by first class post. The general rule is that an acceptance sent in another way is not effective[53] and amounts at most to a counter-offer. The rule is subject to an exception where the method adopted is from the offeror's point of view just as efficacious as the prescribed method.[54] It also does not apply in the increasingly common situation in which the terms of the offer are contained in a form drawn up by the offeree: eg in an application for credit. In such a case the stipulation as to the mode of acceptance exists for the benefit of the *offeree* and may be waived by him.[55]

1.14 **Silence.** An offer may specify that it may be accepted simply by failing to reply to it; but as a general rule such 'silence' does not bind the offeree.[56] The reasons for this rule are that it would be undesirable to put an offeree who did not wish to accept the offer to the trouble and expense of rejecting it; and that the offeree's 'silence' is generally equivocal, not giving rise to an inference of intention to accept 'save in the most exceptional circumstances'.[57] Where such circumstances give rise to an 'obligation to speak',[58] the offeree may be bound by silence: eg where he has solicited the offer and then failed to reply to it in circumstances leading the offeror reasonably to believe that it has been accepted.[59] Action by the offeror, to the knowledge of the offeree, in reliance on the belief that the offer had been accepted may also estop the offeree from denying that he has accepted the offer.[60] The rule that 'silence' does not bind the offeree does not mean that his acceptance must be expressed in words. An offer may be accepted by conduct[61] and the offeror may waive the normal requirement of

---

[49] Contrast *Wenckheim v Arndt* (NZ) (1873) 1 Jurists Report 73 with *Morrison v Thoelke* 155 So 2d 889 (1963).

[50] *Korbetis* case, n 48.

[51] See *Byrne & Co v Leon van Thienhoven & Co*, n 46.

[52] Consumer Contracts (Information, Cancellation and Additional Charges) Regulations 2013, SI 2013/3134, reg 29; for exceptions, see regs 34(3), 34(9), 35(5) and 36(4).

[53] *Financings Ltd v Stimson* [1962] 1 WLR 1184.

[54] *Manchester Diocesan Council for Education v Commercial & General Investments Ltd* [1970] 1 WLR 241.

[55] See *Robophone Facilities v Blank* [1966] 1 WLR 1428; *Carlyle Finance Ltd v Pallas Industrial Finance Ltd* [1999] 1 All ER (Comm) 659.

[56] *Felthouse v Bindley* (1862) 11 CBNS 869.

[57] *The Leonidas D* [1985] 1 WLR 925, 927.

[58] *The Agrabele* [1985] 2 Lloyd's Rep 496, 509 (reversed on other grounds [1987] 2 Lloyd's Rep 275); *Re Selectmove* [1995] 1 WLR 474, 478; cf *Vitol SA v Norelf Ltd* [1996] AC 800.

[59] eg *Rust v Abbey Life Insurance Co Ltd* [1979] 2 Lloyd's Rep 334.

[60] cf *Spiro v Lintern* [1973] 1 WLR 1002, 1011.

[61] See 1.07; *Roberts v Hayward* (1828) 3 C & P 432.

communication of such acceptance.[62] 'Conduct' here refers to some action on the part of the offeree: mere inaction does not suffice, save in the exceptional situations already described.[63] The general rule that 'silence' does not amount to an acceptance exists for the protection of the offeree. It is therefore arguable that the rule should not protect the offeror: ie that he should be bound where he has by the terms of the offer induced the offeree to believe that the latter's failure to reply would give rise to a contract.[64]

Acceptance in ignorance of offer. A person may, without knowing of an offer, do an act **1.15** apparently amounting to an acceptance of it: eg give information not knowing that a reward has been offered for it. In such a case, there is no agreement and hence no contract.[65] Giving the information with knowledge of the offer can, however, amount to an acceptance even though it was given primarily[66] (though not if it was given exclusively)[67] with some motive other than that of claiming the reward. There is also no contract where two persons make identical cross-offers, neither knowing of the other's when he makes his own.[68] There may be an agreement in such a case, but the rule avoids the uncertainty resulting from the fortuitous nature of the agreement.

Acceptance in case of unilateral contract. In the case of a unilateral contract,[69] the offer **1.16** can be accepted by doing the required act (eg walking to York); there is no need to give advance notice of acceptance to the offeror. It is probable that part performance (eg walking part of the way to York) can also amount to an acceptance and will have this effect where it gives rise to a clear inference of intention to accept.[70] A purported withdrawal of the offer at this stage would then be a breach of contract except where on its true construction the offer reserved a right of withdrawal to the offeror at any time before full performance.[71] Even where the withdrawal was wrongful, the full sum promised would not be due till the offeree had completed performance of the stipulated act[72] (ie walked all the way to York).

(iii) Termination of offer

Withdrawal. Events may happen after an offer has been made which bring it to an end, so **1.17** that it can no longer be accepted. One such event is the withdrawal of the offer, the general rule being that an offer can be withdrawn at any time before acceptance.[73] The offeree must also, in general, have notice of the withdrawal so that an offer is not withdrawn merely by the offeror's acting inconsistently[74] with it: eg by disposing of its subject matter to a third party. The notice must actually reach the offeree: mere posting of it does not suffice. Thus if, after a withdrawal has been posted but before it has reached the offeree, the latter posts an acceptance, a contract is concluded even though there was at no stage any agreement between the

---

[62] See 1.09.

[63] *The Leonidas D*, n 57.

[64] This possibility was doubted in *Fairline Shipping Corp v Adamson* [1975] QB 180, 189 (where, however, the offer did *not* expressly provide for acceptance by silence).

[65] *R v Clarke* (1927) 40 CLR 227, 233; *Tracomin SA v Anton C Nielsen* [1984] 2 Lloyd's Rep 195, 203.

[66] cf *Carlill v Carbolic Smoke Ball Co* [1893] 1 QB 256.

[67] *R v Clarke*, n 65.

[68] *Tinn v Hoffmann & Co* (1873) 29 LT 271, 278.

[69] See 1.07.

[70] *Errington v Errington* [1952] 1 KB 290, 295; *Soulsbury v Soulsbury* [2008] EWCA Civ 969, [2008] Fam 1, at [49]–[50].

[71] Cf *Luxor (Eastbourne) Ltd v Cooper* [1941] AC 108, 124.

[72] See *Daulia Ltd v Four Millbank Nominees Ltd* [1978] Ch 231, 238; *Harvela Investments Ltd v Royal Trust of Canada (CI) Ltd* [1986] AC 207, 224.

[73] *Routledge v Grant* (1828) 4 Bing 653.

[74] *Stevenson, Jacques & Co v McLean* (1880) 5 QBD 343.

parties.[75] The rule is based on the consideration of convenience that no offeree could safely act in reliance on his acceptance (eg by selling on the subject matter) if he were subject to the risk that an effective withdrawal might at the time of acceptance have been in the post. The requirement of 'communication' may be displaced by the conduct of the offeree: eg if he simply failed to read a withdrawal sent to his address[76] or if he had moved after receipt of the offer without notifying the offeror. It also does not literally apply to offers made to the public (eg of rewards for information): such an offer can be withdrawn by taking reasonable steps to bring the withdrawal to the attention of the class of persons likely to have seen the offer.[77]

1.18 **Rejection.** Rejection terminates an offer;[78] and a counter-offer amounts to a rejection of the original offer[79] which can then no longer be accepted. A mere enquiry whether the offeror is prepared to vary the terms of the offer (eg by reducing his price) may, however, amount, not to a counter-offer, but to a mere 'request for information'. The distinction between such a request and a counter-offer turns on the intention of the offeree, as reasonably understood by the offeror.[80]

1.19 It seems that a rejection terminates an offer only when communicated: there is no ground of convenience for holding that it should have this effect when posted. Hence it remains open to the offeree after posting a rejection to accept the offer by an overtaking communication. But once the rejection has reached the offeror, he should not be bound[81] by an acceptance which was posted while the rejection was still in the post but reached him only after the rejection had done so.

1.20 **Lapse of time.** An offer which is expressed to last only for a specified time cannot be accepted after the end of that time. If no such time is specified, the offer lapses at the end of a reasonable time.[82] What is a reasonable time depends on such facts as the nature of the subject matter and the means used to communicate the offer. On a similar principle, an offer which provides that it is to terminate on the occurrence of some event cannot be accepted after that event has happened. Such a term may be implied so that, eg, an offer to buy goods cannot be accepted after they have been seriously damaged.[83]

1.21 **Death.** Death of either of the parties makes it impossible for them to reach agreement, but this should not be an absolute bar to the creation of a contract. To hold that it was such a bar could cause hardship: eg where A made a continuing offer to guarantee loans to be made by B to C and B then made such a loan after, and in ignorance of, A's death.[84] Conversely, where it was the offeree who died, the offeror would not normally be prejudiced if the offer were accepted by the offeree's personal representatives. Death of either party should terminate an offer only if it was one to enter into a contract which, by reason of its 'personal' nature, would be discharged by such death.[85]

1.22 **Supervening incapacity.** Supervening personal incapacity[86] can arise where one of the parties becomes mentally ill. That party would not be bound by an acceptance made after his

---

[75] *Byrne & Co v Leon van Thienhoven* (1880) 5 CPD 344.
[76] cf *Eaglehill Ltd v J Needham (Builders) Ltd* [1973] AC 992, 1011; *The Brimnes* [1975] QB 929.
[77] *Shuey v US* 92 US 73 (1875).
[78] *Tinn v Hoffmann & Co* (1873) 29 LT 271, 278.
[79] *Hyde v Wrench* (1840) 3 Beav 334.
[80] *Stevenson, Jacques & Co v McLean*, n 74; *Gibson v Manchester CC* [1979] 1 WLR 294, 302.
[81] ie under the rule stated in 1.10.
[82] *Ramsgate Victoria Hotel Co Ltd v Montefiore* (1866) LR 1 Ex 109.
[83] *Financings Ltd v Stimson* [1962] 1 WLR 1184.
[84] See *Coulthart v Clementson* (1879) 5 QBD 42.
[85] See 1.443.
[86] For supervening corporate incapacity, see EPL ch 3.

disability had become known to the other party or after his property had become subject to the control of the court; but the other party would be so bound.[87]

(b) Vagueness, uncertainty, and incompleteness

Vagueness.   Even where an agreement has been reached, its terms may be too vague to give rise to a contract.[88] The courts here must guard against, on the one hand, the danger of imposing on the parties terms to which they have not agreed and, on the other, that of striking down agreements intended to be binding but drafted (perhaps deliberately) in loose terms so as to withstand the stresses of changing economic circumstances. In pursuit of the latter aim, they can resolve apparent vagueness by reference to trade custom or usage[89] or to the standard of reasonableness;[90] or by disregarding meaningless or self-contradictory phrases.[91] They can also impose on the parties, or on one of them the duty to resolve the uncertainty.[92]   **1.23**

Failure to specify vital terms.   An agreement may lack certainty because it fails to specify a vital term or vital terms of the alleged bargain,[93] such as the date on which a lease is to commence[94] or the price to be paid for goods or the remuneration to be paid for services.[95] But if the court is satisfied that the parties nevertheless intended to enter into a binding contract it will, where possible, give effect to that intention so that (eg) a reasonable price or remuneration must be paid.[96] Even where no contract has come into existence, such remuneration may also be due on restitutionary principles to a person who has rendered services in the belief that there was a contract.[97]   **1.24**

Terms to be agreed.   Parties may not wish to bind themselves over the course of a long-term agreement to fixed prices or other terms and may therefore stipulate that such terms are 'to be agreed' from time to time. If the court is satisfied that the parties intended to be bound at once, it may uphold the agreement[98] and require the points left outstanding to be negotiated in good faith;[99] but it will not do so where it concludes that the parties intended to be bound only when the outstanding point was settled.[100] The agreement would then be merely one to negotiate, and even an express agreement to this effect is 'too uncertain to be enforced'.[101] Nor, in a case of this kind, can a term be implied requiring the parties to negotiate 'in good faith' since the requirement of good faith is, in such a case, 'inherently inconsistent with   **1.25**

---

[87] This follows from the rules stated in 1.278.

[88] *G Scammell & Nephew Ltd v Ouston* [1941] AC 251.

[89] *Shamrock SS Co v Blue Star Line* (1899) 81 LT 413.

[90] *Hillas & Co Ltd v Arcos Ltd* (1932) 147 LT 503. Contrast *Baird Textile Holdings Ltd v Marks & Spencer plc* [2001] EWCA Civ 274, [2002] 1 All ER (Comm) 737, where there were no objective criteria for determining what was 'reasonable'.

[91] *Nicolene Ltd v Simmonds* [1953] QB 543.

[92] *David T Boyd & Co v Louis Louca* [1973] 1 Lloyd's Rep 209; *Scammell v Dicker* [2005] EWCA Civ 405, [2005] 3 All ER 838, at [31].

[93] *Barbudev v Eurocom Cable Management Bulgaria EOOD* [2012] EWCA 548, [2012] 2 All ER (Comm) 963.

[94] *Harvey v Pratt* [1965] 1 WLR 1025.

[95] *May & Butcher v R* [1934] KB 17n.

[96] Sale of Goods Act 1979, s 8(2); Supply of Goods and Services Act 1982, s 15(1).

[97] *Peter Lind & Co Ltd v Mersey Docks & Harbour Board* [1972] 2 Lloyd's Rep 234; *Whittle Movers Ltd v Hollywood Express Ltd* [2009] EWCA Civ 1189, [2009] 2 CLC 771.

[98] eg *Foley v Classique Coaches Ltd* [1934] 2 KB 1.

[99] *Petromec Inc v Petroleo Brasileiro SA Petrobas* [2005] EWCA Civ 891; [2006] 1 Lloyd's Rep 121, at [115]–[121].

[100] eg *May & Butcher Ltd v R* [1934] 2 KB 17n; *Barbudev v Eurocom Cable Management Bulgaria EOOD* [2012] EWCA 548, [2012] 2 All ER (Comm) 963.

[101] *Courtney & Fairbairn Ltd v Tolaini* [1975] 1 WLR 297, 301.

the position of a negotiating party',[102] who must be free to advance his own interests in the negotiations.

1.26 Ways of resolving uncertainty. An agreement which leaves open matters such as the price is nevertheless binding if it lays down some *standard* (such as 'market value') for resolving the uncertainty;[103] or if it provides some *machinery* for this purpose: eg that the price is to be fixed by the valuation of a third party. If the third party fails to make the valuation, the agreement is avoided;[104] but this result will not follow where the part of the machinery which fails to work is 'subsidiary and incidental':[105] eg where it relates only to the method of appointing the valuer.[106]

1.27 Stipulation for execution of formal document. The parties to an agreement may stipulate for it to be embodied in a formal document. The agreement may then be regarded as incomplete, or as not intended to be legally binding, until the execution of such a document.[107] Alternatively, the document may be intended only as a formal record of an already binding agreement.[108] The distinction between these two categories depends on the purpose of the stipulation in each case.[109]

1.28 Agreements for the sale of land by private treaty are usually expressed to be made 'subject to contract'. Such an agreement is incomplete until the terms of the formal contract are agreed;[110] but even after this has been done the agreement is not legally binding until there has been an 'exchange of contracts'.[111] Each party must sign a document containing all the expressly agreed terms;[112] and the requirement of 'exchange' prima facie means that each party must then hand the document signed by him to the other, or send it to him by post.[113] The reason why before 'exchange' there is no contract is not that there is any uncertainty as to the agreed terms: it is that, before then, neither party intends to be legally bound. The law on this point has been criticized[114] as it enables a party to go back on the agreement with impunity; and the criticism has led to mitigations of the requirement: eg by allowing 'exchange' to take place by telephone.[115] A party's freedom to go back on the agreement may also be restricted by the doctrine of proprietary estoppel;[116] and, as a practical matter, by a collateral

---

[102] *Walford v Miles* [1992] 2 AC 128, 138; *Shaker v Vistajet Group Holding SA* [2012] EWHC 1329 (Comm), [2012] 2 Lloyd's Rep 93. When deciding whether or not an obligation to act in 'good faith' or to use 'reasonable (or best) endeavours' is enforceable, it is important to have regard to the object intended to be procured by the good faith actions or the reasonable (or best) endeavours, as the case may be: *Jet2.com Ltd v Blackpool Airport Ltd* [2012] EWCA Civ 417, [2012] 2 All ER (Comm) 1053. Thus a time limited obligation to seek to resolve a dispute by friendly negotiations has been held to be enforceable: see *Emirates Trading Agency LLC v Prime Mineral Exports Pte Ltd* [2014] (Comm), [2015] 1 WLR 1145.

[103] *Brown v Gould* [1972] Ch 53; cf *Hillas & Co Ltd v Arcos Ltd* (1932) 147 LT 503. Contrast *Willis Management (Isle of Man) Ltd v Cable and Wireless plc* [2005] EWCA Civ 806, [2005] 2 Lloyd's Rep 597, where the standard (of fairness) was expressed to be the subject of further negotiations.

[104] Sale of Goods Act 1979, s 9(1); *Gillatt v Sky Television Ltd* [2000] 1 All ER (Comm) 461.

[105] *Re Malpass* [1985] Ch 42, 50.

[106] *Sudbrook Trading Estate Ltd v Eggleton* [1983] 1 AC 444.

[107] *BSC v Cleveland Bridge & Engineering Co Ltd* [1984] 1 All ER 504.

[108] *Rossiter v Miller* (1878) 3 App Cas 1184.

[109] The distinction may not be an easy one to draw. Contrast, eg, *Everton Football Club Co Ltd v Sail Group Ltd* [2011] EWHC 126 (QB) and *Tryggingstfelagio Foroyar P/F v CPT Empresas Maritimas SA (The M/V Athena)* [2011] EWHC 589 (Admlty), [2011] 1 CLC 425.

[110] *Winn v Bull* (1877) 7 Ch D 29.

[111] *Chillingworth v Esche* [1924] 1 Ch 97; *Eccles v Bryant & Pollock* [1948] Ch 93.

[112] Law of Property (Miscellaneous Provisions) Act 1989, ss 2(1), (3).

[113] See *Commission for the New Towns v Cooper (Great Britain) Ltd* [1995] Ch 259, 289, 293, 295.

[114] *Cohen v Nessdale Ltd* [1981] 3 All ER 118, 128 (affd [1982] 2 All ER 97).

[115] *Domb v Isoz* [1980] Ch 548.

[116] See *A-G of Hong Kong v Humphreys Estate (Queen's Gardens) Ltd* [1987] AC 114, 124, 127–128 and see 1.62.

contract (known as a 'lock-out' agreement) by which he can bind himself for a fixed period not to deal in relation to the land with anyone else.[117]

(c) Conditional agreements

A conditional agreement is one the operation of which depends on an event which is not certain to occur. The condition is *contingent* where the event is one which neither party undertakes to bring about and *promissory* where it is the performance by one party of his undertaking. A condition is *precedent* (or suspensive) if the obligation subject to it is not to accrue until the event occurs; it is *subsequent* (or resolutive) if on the occurrence of the event an obligation is discharged.

1.29

An agreement subject to a contingent condition precedent may before the event occurs have no binding force at all;[118] but it is also possible for such an agreement, on its true construction, to impose some degree of obligation even before then. One possibility is that, so long as the event can still occur within the specified time, neither party can withdraw;[119] though once it becomes clear that the event can no longer so occur, the obligation is discharged.[120] A second possibility is that before the event occurs neither party must prevent its occurrence,[121] or at least that he must not deliberately[122] or wrongfully[123] do so; though no such duty would normally rest on a party where the condition was his 'satisfaction' with the subject matter or the other party's performance.[124] A third possibility is that one party must make reasonable efforts to bring about the event (eg the grant of an export licence where the contract was 'subject to' such licence).[125] A party who is in breach of one of the *subsidiary* obligations here described is liable in damages for that breach[126] even though, by reason of the non-occurrence of the event, the *principal* obligations (eg to buy and sell) have not accrued.[127]

1.30

(2) Consideration

(a) Introduction

(i) Nature of the doctrine

Gratuitous and onerous promises. In English law agreements or promises have contractual force only if they are either made in a deed or supported by some 'consideration'. The doctrine of consideration is based on the idea of *reciprocity*: in order to be entitled to enforce a promise as a contract, the promisee must have given 'something of value in the eye of the law'[128] in exchange for the promise. An informal gratuitous promise is therefore not binding as a contract.[129] The reasons for this rule are that such promises may be rashly made,[130]

1.31

---

[117] *Pitt v PHH Asset Management Ltd* [1994] 1 WLR 327.

[118] *Pym v Campbell* (1856) 6 E & B 370, 374.

[119] *Smith v Butler* [1900] 1 QB 694.

[120] *Total Gas Marketing Ltd v Arco British Ltd* [1998] 2 Lloyd's Rep 209, 215; *Jameson v CEGB* [2000] 1 AC 455, 478: a condition precedent may then operate as a condition subsequent.

[121] *Mackay v Dick* (1881) 6 App Cas 251.

[122] *Blake & Co v Sohn* [1969] 1 WLR 1412.

[123] See *Thompson v Asda-MFI Group plc* [1988] Ch 241.

[124] *Lee-Parker v Izzet (No 2)* [1972] 1 WLR 775; cf Sale of Goods Act 1979, s 18 r 4; for a possible qualification, contrast *The John S Darbyshire* [1977] 2 Lloyd's Rep 457, 464 ('subject to bona fides') with *Stabilad Ltd v Stephens & Carter Ltd (No 2)* [1999] 2 All ER (Comm) 651, 662 (no 'obligation to act in good faith').

[125] *Re Anglo-Russian Merchant Traders and John Batt (London) Ltd* [1917] 2 KB 679.

[126] eg *Malik v CETA Ltd* [1974] 2 Lloyd's Rep 279.

[127] *Little v Courage Ltd* (1995) 70 P & CR 469, 475 (rejecting the doctrine of fictional fulfilment of the condition in such cases).

[128] *Thomas v Thomas* (1842) 2 QB 851, 859.

[129] *Re Hudson* (1885) 54 LJ Ch 811.

[130] *Beaton v McDivitt* (1998) 13 NSWLR 162, 170.

that their enforceability might prejudice third parties (such as creditors or dependants of the promisor)[131] and that the claims of a gratuitous promisee are thought to be less compelling than those of one who has given value for the promise. English law does provide a fairly simple mechanism for making gratuitous promises enforceable: an individual can do this by making the promise in a signed and witnessed document which states on its face that it is intended to be a deed.[132] Such formal requirements provide some safeguard against the dangers (listed above) of giving contractual force to *informal* gratuitous promises.

1.32 The concept of a gratuitous promise covers not only the simple case of a promise by A to make a gift of money or property, but also the case of a promise to provide some other facility to B, such as the loan of a book or to render some service, without reward. In the first of these situations, A would be under no contractual liability if he later refused to make the loan;[133] and in the second he would similarly be under no such liability for simple *non-feasance*, ie for failure to engage in the promised course of action.[134] A might, indeed, be liable in tort for *misfeasance* if he began to render the service and was negligent in performing it and so caused loss to B.[135] Mere *non-feasance* does not generally give rise to such liability in tort.[136] It may exceptionally do so where the circumstances impose on A a 'duty to act';[137] but such a duty will not arise merely because A has made a gratuitous promise. Consideration for A's apparently gratuitous promise may, however, be provided by B's making a counter-promise: eg where a legal relationship (such as that of carrier and passenger) has arisen as a result of A's beginning to perform a promise to give B free rides on A's vehicles, and B has promised A not to sue A for negligence in the performance of the carriage operation.[138]

(ii) Definition

1.33 **Benefit and detriment.** The notion of reciprocity underlies the often repeated definition of consideration as being *either* a detriment to the promisee (in that he gives value) *or* a benefit to the promisor (in that he receives value).[139] Where the contract is bilateral, each party will make and receive a promise and the requirement of consideration must be satisfied in relation to *each of these promises*. It is wrong to think of the consideration *for the contract*. In a contract of sale, eg, it is a detriment for the seller to part with goods, so that he thereby provides consideration for the buyer's promise to pay the price, even though that price exceeds the value of the goods.

1.34 The twin notions of 'benefit' and 'detriment' have lent themselves to a good deal of judicial manipulation. On the one hand, judges have sometimes regarded any benefit or detriment *which could be detected by the court* as consideration, even though the performance in question was not so regarded by the parties;[140] and in this way they have 'found' or 'invented'

---

[131] *Eastwood v Kenyon* (1840) 11 A & E 438, 451.

[132] Law of Property (Miscellaneous Provisions) Act 1989, s 1; for the rules governing the execution of deeds by companies incorporated under the Companies Acts, see Companies Act 2006, s 46; Regulatory Reform (Execution of Deeds and Documents) Order 2005, SI 2005/1906.

[133] Though the borrower would be liable for failure to perform any promise to return the book in good condition: *Bainbridge v Firmstone* (1838) 8 A & E 743.

[134] *Argy Trading & Development Co Ltd v Lapid Developments Ltd* [1977] 1 WLR 444; *The Zephyr* [1985] 2 Lloyd's Rep 529, 538.

[135] *Wilkinson v Coverdale* (1793)1 Esp 75; cf *Hedley Byrne & Co Ltd v Heller & Partners Ltd* [1964] AC 465.

[136] *Customs & Excise Commissioners v Barclays Bank plc* [2006] UKHL 28, [2007] 1 AC 181, at [39].

[137] *White v Jones* [1995] 2 AC 207, 261.

[138] *Gore v Van der Lann* [1967] 2 QB 31.

[139] eg *Currie v Misa* (1875) LR 10 Ex 153, 162; the *Argy* case, n 134, at 455; the *Gore* case, n 138, at 42; *Edmonds v Lawson* [2000] QB 501.

[140] eg 1.43, at n 171; *The Alev* [1989] 1 Lloyd's Rep 138, 147; cf *Shadwell v Shadwell* (1860) 9 CBNS 159, 174.

consideration for promises which a lay person might regard as gratuitous.[141] Conversely, they have sometimes regarded acts or promises which were benefits or detriments *in fact* as not having this characteristic *in law*: eg because the performance rendered or promised was *already legally due*.[142] In such (and some other) situations, the courts have refused to give contractual force to promises which are not, in any realistic sense, gratuitous; they have done so on many disparate grounds of policy, using the doctrine of consideration as a substitute for other, then imperfectly developed,[143] doctrines.

Mutual promises.   When *performance* by one of the parties would satisfy the requirement of consideration,[144] a *promise* to render that performance generally has the same effect: hence a promise by a seller to deliver goods in a month's time given in exchange for the buyer's promise to pay on delivery is an immediately binding contract. Difficulty can, however, arise where one of a pair of mutual promises is, for some reason, not binding in law. Sometimes, such a promise cannot be consideration for a counter-promise: eg, a promise by A to pay B a pension cannot be enforced if the sole consideration provided for it is B's promise not to compete with A and that promise is invalid for restraint of trade.[145] But the position is different where the law invalidates B's promise for the protection of a class of which B is a member: eg, where B is a minor. Then B's promise can constitute consideration for a counter-promise made by A;[146] and the same is true where B's promise has been procured by A's fraud.[147] The law relating to defective promises as consideration cannot be logically deduced from the requirement of consideration; it is based rather on the policy of the rule which, in each case, makes the promise defective.   **1.35**

Mutual promises, though sufficient, are not necessary to satisfy the requirement of consideration. Thus in the case of a unilateral contract performance, and even part performance, of the required act (such as walking to York)[148] can constitute consideration.   **1.36**

Effects of promises unsupported by consideration.   An informal promise that is not supported by consideration has no contractual force; but it does not follow that such a promise has no legal effects. In particular, the law may, in circumstances to be discussed later in this chapter, place restrictions on the revocability of some such promises.[149] It may even protect the promisee's expectation interest,[150] though only as a matter of discretion and not (as in the case of a promise supported by consideration) as of right.   **1.37**

(b) Adequacy

The requirement of consideration means that *some* value must be given for a promise; but as a general rule the law is not concerned with the question whether 'adequate' value has been given:[151] the doctrine of consideration is not intended as a price control mechanism. It follows that a promise to pay £1,000 in exchange for a peppercorn or one to convey valuable property for £1 can be binding as a contract. The consideration in such a case is said to be   **1.38**

---

[141] Although it should be noted that the proposition that the courts have power to 'invent' consideration is not one that is universally accepted.

[142] eg 1.47, at n 184; 1.58.

[143] eg the doctrine of duress before the development discussed in 1.203.

[144] Not if performance would *not* satisfy the requirement: eg if a debtor in the cases discussed in 1.58 made a *promise* of part payment of a debt.

[145] *Wyatt v Kreglinger & Fernau* [1933] 1 KB 793.

[146] See 1.272.

[147] See 1.176.

[148] See 1.07.

[149] See 1.52, 1.53, 1.60, 1.62.

[150] See 1.64, at n 267.

[151] *Westlake v Adams* (1858) CBNS 248, 265; *Midland Bank & Trust Co Ltd v Green* [1981] AC 513.

'nominal' and normally suffices, though there are situations in which a disposition for such a consideration could prejudice third parties and therefore lack validity.[152] In such cases, a 'nominal' consideration must be distinguished from one which is merely inadequate; and it is submitted that a consideration is, for such purposes, 'nominal' if, as a matter of common sense, it is obviously of no more than token value.[153]

1.39   The general rule stated in 1.38 is well established; but the law is not insensitive to the problem of unequal bargains, so that the general rule is subject to exceptions to be discussed elsewhere in this chapter.[154] Conversely, a gratuitous promise supported by a nominal consideration may not deserve the same degree of protection as one supported by substantial consideration. For this reason equity will not aid a 'volunteer', ie a person who has given either no or no substantial consideration.[155] There are also special statutory rules which protect third parties (such as creditors of the promisor) where only nominal or inadequate consideration has been given for the promise.[156]

(c) Past consideration

1.40   The consideration for a promise must be given in exchange for it and this requirement is not satisfied where the consideration consists of something done before the promise was made. Such 'consideration' is said to be 'past' and, in general,[157] bad in law.[158] In applying this rule, the courts apply a functional, rather than a strictly chronological, test.[159] A manufacturer's guarantee may be given shortly after the customer has bought the goods but the consideration provided by the customer is not regarded as past if his purchase and the giving of the guarantee were substantially a single transaction because the customer had been led to believe that he was buying guaranteed goods.[160] A past act can also be good consideration for a promise if it was done at the request of the promisor on the understanding that payment would be made for it and if such payment would (had it been promised in advance) have been legally recoverable.[161] This rule covers the case in which services are rendered on a commercial basis but the rate of payment is fixed only after they have been rendered. Where, on this principle, a past *act* can constitute consideration, the same is true of a past *promise*.[162]

(d) Consideration must move from promisee

1.41   The consideration for a promise must be provided by the promisee[163] who therefore cannot enforce the promise if the whole of the consideration for it was provided by a third party: eg if A promised B to pay him £1,000 if C rendered some service to A and C did so. Consideration need not, however, move to the promisor.[164] Accordingly, the requirement of

---

[152]   eg Insolvency Act 1986, ss 238, 339, 423.

[153]   See *Westminster CC v Duke of Westminster* [1991] 4 All ER 136, 146 (reversed in part on another ground (1992) 24 Housing LR 572); for a different view, see the *Midland Bank* case, n 151, at 532.

[154]   See 1.208 and 1.242, and 3.73–3.75.

[155]   *Jefferys v Jefferys* (1841) Cr & Ph 138. The rule prevents the enforcement of a gratuitous *promise* but does not affect the validity of *a completed gift*: *Pennington v Waine* [2002] EWCA Civ 227; [2002] 1 WLR 2075.

[156]   See n 152.

[157]   For exceptions, see Bills of Exchange Act 1882, s 27(1)(b); Limitation Act 1980, s 27(5).

[158]   *Eastwood v Kenyon* (1840) 11 A & E 438; *Re McArdle* [1951] Ch 669.

[159]   See, eg, *Classic Maritime Inc v Lion Diversified Holdings Berhad* [2009] EWHC 1142 (Comm), [2010] 1 Lloyd's Rep 59, at [43]–[46].

[160]   A 'consumer guarantee' within the Consumer Rights Act 2015, s 30 binds the guarantor by force of the Act (s 30(3)); there is no requirement of consideration.

[161]   *Re Casey's Patents* [1892] 1 Ch 104, 115–116.

[162]   *Pao On v Lau Yiu Long* [1980] AC 614.

[163]   *Thomas v Thomas* (1842) 2 QB 851, 859; *Pollway Ltd v Abdullah* [1974] 1 WLR 493, 497.

[164]   *Re Wyvern Developments Ltd* [1974] 1 WLR 1097.

consideration is satisfied where the promisee at the promisor's request confers a benefit on a third party,[165] or suffers some detriment (such as giving up his job),[166] without thereby conferring any direct benefit on the promisor. By statute a person who is not a party to a contract can sometimes enforce a term in the contract against the promisor even though the claimant has not provided any consideration for the promise;[167] but consideration in such cases still has to be provided *by the promisee.*

(e) The value of consideration

(i) Sentimental motives

Consideration must be of 'value in the eye of the law'.[168] The requirement is not satisfied by merely sentimental motives, so that 'natural affection of itself is not a sufficient consideration'.[169]   **1.42**

(ii) Illusory consideration

A promise has no contractual force where the consideration for it is merely illusory. On this   **1.43**
principle, a promisee could not enforce a promise if the alleged consideration for it was a counter-promise from him which was known to be impossible to perform; or if it was one to do an act which he would have done anyway, even if the promise had not been made; or if it was one to refrain 'from a course of action which it was never intended to pursue';[170] or if his counter-promise left performance entirely to his discretion (ie it was one to do something 'if I feel like it'.)[171] Since, however, consideration need not be adequate, acts or omissions of even trifling value can satisfy the requirement of consideration,[172] at least if they were so regarded by the parties.

(iii) Compromises and forbearances

Where A has a legal claim against B of uncertain value, and promises to give up that claim in   **1.44**
return for B's promise to pay him an agreed sum, there is generally no difficulty with regard to consideration: the consideration for B's promise to make the payment is A's giving up of his claim, while the consideration for A's promise to give up the claim is B's making the payment. The requirement of consideration for B's promise is satisfied even where A makes no *promise* to B but simply forbears in fact from pursuing his claim,[173] so long as it is clear that A's forbearance was induced by B's promise (typically to make a payment to A).[174] The requirement is likewise satisfied if the claim which A gives up, or promises to give up, is one which is *doubtful* in law (since in such a case its relinquishment involves a possibility of detriment to A and of benefit to B);[175] and the same is true where the claim is *clearly bad* in law, so long as A honestly believed it to be a good claim, seriously intended to prosecute it and did not conceal from B any facts which would exonerate B.[176] There may be no detriment to A

---

[165] *Bolton v Madden* (1873) LR 9 QB 55.

[166] *Jones v Padavatton* [1969] 1 WLR 328.

[167] Contracts (Rights of Third Parties) Act 1999, s 1; 1.303.

[168] See 1.31, n 128.

[169] *Bret v JS* (1600) Cro Eliz 756.

[170] *Arrale v Costain Civil Engineering Ltd* [1976] 1 Lloyd's Rep 98, 106.

[171] See *Firestone Tyre & Rubber Co Ltd v Vokins & Co Ltd* [1951] 1 Lloyd's Rep 32; *Stabilad Ltd v Stephens & Carter Ltd* [1999] 2 All ER (Comm) 651, 659.

[172] *Chappell & Co Ltd v Nestlé Co Ltd* [1960] AC 87.

[173] *Alliance Bank v Broom* (1864) 2 Dr & Sm 289.

[174] *Wigan v English & Scottish Law Life Assurance Association* [1909] Ch 291; and see *Combe v Combe* [1951] 2 KB 215, where the requirement of inducement was not satisfied.

[175] *Haigh v Brooks* (1839) 10 A & E 309.

[176] *Cook v Wright* (1861) 1 B & S 559; *Callisher v Bischoffsheim* (1870) LR 5 QB 449.

(or benefit to B) in A's giving up a claim which he was bound to lose, but the law will uphold the agreement in order to encourage reasonable compromises. This reasoning, however, does not apply where the claim is *known* by A (and perhaps by B) to be bad, so that B's promise has no contractual force where the sole[177] consideration provided for it by A is his giving up a 'claim' of this kind.[178]

(f) Existing duties

1.45 A may, before any promise is made to him by B, already be under a legal duty to do an act (or to abstain from doing something). It is arguable that A's merely doing what he was already legally bound to do cannot *in law* be a detriment to him; and, indeed, that to allow A in such a case to enforce B's promise would lead to the undesirable result of encouraging A to refuse to perform his original duty unless some added inducement were held out to him and so of supporting a form of duress. On the other hand, performance by A in such cases may *in fact* benefit B;[179] and where no element of duress is involved, the law is now moving towards the position that A's performance of (or promise to perform) an existing duty can amount to consideration for B's promise.

(i) 'Public' duty

1.46 The above conflict of principles is well illustrated by cases in which A's existing duty is a 'public duty', ie one imposed by the general law rather than by contract. Obviously, a person does not provide consideration merely by forbearing to commit a crime;[180] nor should a public officer be able to enforce a promise for doing nothing more than his duty as such.[181] But where there are no such grounds of public policy for refusing enforcement, the prevailing view is that the performance of a 'public' duty can constitute consideration.[182] There is no such doubt in the case where the promisee does more than he is required by the pre-existing duty to do; in such a case the promisee clearly provides consideration.[183]

(ii) Duty imposed by contract with promisor

1.47 The law at one time took the view that the mere performance by A of a duty owed by him under a pre-existing contract with B was no consideration for a promise by B to A. Hence a promise to sailors that, if they completed the voyage for which they had signed on, they would be paid higher wages than those specified in their original contract was held not to be enforceable by the sailors.[184] More recently, however, it has been held that the performance of such a duty did constitute consideration, so that a promise by a building contractor to pay a subcontractor more than the originally agreed sum was held binding in the absence of any circumstances amounting to duress on the subcontractor's part. The consideration was said to consist of the *factual benefit* obtained by the contractor from the actual performance of the

---

[177] Not where there is also other consideration: *The Siboen and The Sibotre* [1976] 1 Lloyd's Rep 293, 334.

[178] *Poteliakhoff v Teakle* [1938] 2 KB 816 (gambling debt; such debts are now legally enforceable by virtue of Gambling Act 2005, s 335 (1)).

[179] cf 1.34.

[180] *Brown v Brine* (1875) 1 Ex D 5.

[181] *Morgan v Palmer* (1824) 2 B & C 729, 736.

[182] *Ward v Byham* [1956] 1 WLR 496, 498.

[183] *Glasbrook Bros Ltd v Glamorgan CC* [1925] AC 270.

[184] *Stilk v Myrick* (1809) 2 Camp 317. For a more modern statement of the rule see *WRN Ltd v Ayris* [2008] EWHC 1080 (QB), [2008] IRLR 889, at [46]. Slightly more equivocal is the decision of the Court of Appeal in *Attrill v Dresdner Kleinwort Ltd* [2011] EWCA Civ 229, [2011] IRLR 613 and see also *Attrill v Dresdner Kleinwort Ltd* [2013] EWCA Civ 394, [2013] 3 All ER 607, at [95].

subcontractor's work.[185] Consideration may also be provided by A's doing *more* than he was obliged to do by his original contact with B.[186]

(iii) Duty imposed by contract with a third party

Performance of a duty owed by A to X under a contract between them can constitute consideration for a promise made by B to A. If, eg, A contracts with a shipowner X to unload goods belonging to B from the ship, the performance of that duty can be consideration for B's promise to A not to make any claim against A in respect of damage done to the goods by A while unloading them;[187] for although A is already bound by his contract with X to do the work he confers a factual benefit on B by doing it. On the same principle, a *promise* to perform such a duty can constitute consideration, eg where A is indebted to the X company and promises B, a shareholder in that company, to pay the debt, that promise can be consideration for a counter-promise made by B to A.[188]

1.48

(g) Rescission and variation

Our concern here is with cases in which parties to a contract agree either to release each other from further performance (rescission) or to alter the terms of the contract (variation). So far as variation is concerned, the question whether performance from A of his part of the original contract constitutes consideration for a new promise by B has already been discussed;[189] our present concern is with the question whether there is consideration for B's promise to be content with some performance *other* than that originally promised by A.

1.49

(i) Rescission

Rescission gives rise to no difficulty with regard to consideration where each party has, and agrees to give up, outstanding rights against the other. In such cases the rescission generates its own consideration, but this would not be true where one party (A) promised to release the other (B) and B made no counter-promise to A; or if only A had outstanding rights under the contract because B had broken the contract but A had not done so. Rescission after breach by only one party requires separate consideration;[190] in technical language there must (in general)[191] be not only an 'accord' but 'satisfaction': ie a payment, or promise of payment, from the party in breach.[192]

1.50

(ii) Variation

Where a 'variation' amounts to a rescission of the old contract followed by the making of a new one on different terms, the case is governed by the principles stated in 1.50. Where the parties agree to vary a contract in a way that is *capable* of benefiting either party (eg where they agree to vary the length of a lease,[193] the time of performance,[194] or the currency of payment)[195] the requirement of consideration is again satisfied, unless the variation is in fact

1.51

---

[185] *Williams v Roffey Bros & Nicholls (Contractors) Ltd* [1991] 1 QB 1. See also *Forde v Birmingham City Council* [2009] EWHC 12 (QB), [2009] 1 WLR 2732, at [89]. The reasoning would not apply where A had threatened not to perform the original contract and this threat amounted to duress: see *South Caribbean Trading v Trafigura Beheer BV* [2004] EWHC 2676 (Comm), [2005] 1 Lloyd's Rep 128, at [109].

[186] *Hanson v Royden* (1867) LR 3 CP 47; *The Atlantic Baron* [1979] QB 705.

[187] *The Eurymedon* [1975] AC 154.

[188] *Pao On v Lau Yiu Long* [1980] AC 614.

[189] See 1.47.

[190] *Atlantic Shipping Co Ltd v Louis Dreyfus & Co* [1922] 2 AC 250, 262.

[191] For an exception, see Bills of Exchange Act 1882, s 62.

[192] *British-Russian Gazette Ltd v Associated Newspapers Ltd* [1933] 2 KB 616, 643.

[193] *Fenner v Blake* [1900] 1 QB 426.

[194] *South Caribbean* case, n 185.

[195] *WJ Alan & Co Ltd v El Nasr Export & Import Co* [1972] 2 QB 189.

made wholly for the benefit of one.[196] Even where the variation is not supported by a consideration of the kind just described, it may (on proof of the requisite contractual intention) be enforceable as a separate contract, collateral to the main transaction.[197] The cases which give rise to difficulty are those in which the variation can confer a legal benefit on only one of the parties. Sometimes, such a variation has no contractual force unless that party provides some separate consideration for the other's promise: this is, eg, true where a creditor promises to accept part payment of a debt in full settlement.[198] In other cases, however, it is arguable that a variation which can confer a *legal* benefit on only one party is supported by consideration if it *in fact* also confers a benefit on the other.[199]

(iii) Common law waiver

1.52 A variation which has no contractual force for want of consideration (or for some other reason) may nevertheless have limited legal effects as a 'waiver'. This word is used in many senses[200] and sometimes means no more than 'rescission' or 'variation'. It is also used to describe the legal effects of arrangements which fall short of contractually binding variations and which will here be called 'forbearances'. The party *requesting* such a forbearance cannot refuse to accept performance varied in accordance with it;[201] nor if such performance is rendered and accepted can either party claim damages on the ground that the performance was not in accordance with the original contract.[202] The difficult cases are those in which the party *granting* the forbearance then wants to go back on it and enforce the contract in accordance with its original terms: eg where a buyer who had said that he would accept late delivery then insisted on the originally agreed delivery date. Under the common law doctrine of waiver, he cannot peremptorily take this course;[203] but such a waiver differs from a contractually binding variation in that the party granting it can generally retract it on giving reasonable notice to the other party.[204] The distinction between such a waiver and a contractually binding variation was said to depend on the elusive criterion of the intention of the parties;[205] and it led to the paradoxical position that the more a party tried to bind himself the less he was likely to succeed; for a binding variation required consideration while a waiver did not.

(iv) Equitable forbearance (or promissory estoppel)

1.53 Equity provided a more satisfactory approach to the problem of variations not supported by consideration in concentrating on the conduct of the party granting the forbearance and its effect on the other party. It developed the principle sometimes referred to as 'promissory estoppel' because it is in some respects[206] analogous to the doctrine of estoppel by representation, though it more closely resembles[207] the common law doctrine of waiver in the sense

---

[196] *Vanbergen v St Edmund's Properties Ltd* [1933] 2 KB 233.
[197] *Brikom Investments Ltd v Carr* [1979] QB 467.
[198] See 1.58.
[199] On the analogy of the *Williams* case, see 1.47.
[200] *The Laconia* [1977] AC 850, 871.
[201] *Hickman v Haynes* (1875) LR 10 CP 598.
[202] *Ogle v Vane* (1868) LR 3 QB 272.
[203] *Hartley v Hymans* [1920] 3 KB 475.
[204] *Charles Rickards Ltd v Oppenhaim* [1950] 1 KB 616.
[205] *Stead v Dawber* (1839) 10 A & E 57.
[206] But not in all: in particular, estoppel by representation was based on a representation of *existing fact*: *Jorden v Money* (1854) 5 HLC 185, while a representation of *intention* or a *promise* suffices for the purpose of the doctrine of 'promissory estoppel'; the former doctrine operates with permanent effect while the latter is only suspensive: para 1.54; and the former doctrine prevents a party from denying *facts*, while the latter prevents him from denying the *legal effects* of a promise which is proved or admitted to have been made.
[207] In the respects stated in n 206.

of forbearance. The equitable doctrine applies where one party to a contract by words or conduct makes a clear and unequivocal representation which leads the other 'to suppose that the strict rights arising under the contract will not be enforced or will be kept in suspense or held in abeyance'.[208] The party making the representation will then not be allowed to enforce those rights 'where it would be inequitable for him to do so having regard to the dealings which have thus taken place between the parties'.[209] The effects of a promise under this doctrine differ in three respects from those of a variation supported by consideration.

First, the equitable doctrine normally only *suspends* the rights under the original contract: **1.54** they can normally be reasserted on giving reasonable notice.[210] This is one respect in which promissory estoppel resembles waiver (in the sense of forbearance).[211] It extinguishes rights only where subsequent events make it impossible for the promisee to perform the original obligation[212] or make it highly inequitable to require him to do so.[213]

Secondly, the equitable doctrine applies only where it would be 'inequitable' for the promisor **1.55** to go back on his promise. This will normally be the position where the promisee has acted in reliance on the promise so that it is no longer possible to restore him to the position in which he was before he so acted.[214] But even where the promisee has so acted other circumstances may justify the promisor in going back on the promise (even without due notice): eg, a creditor's promise to give his debtor extra time to pay may be revoked on the ground that another creditor is about to levy execution on the debtor's property.[215]

Thirdly, in English law the doctrine merely prevents the enforcement of existing rights: it 'does **1.56** not create new causes of action where none existed before'.[216] It thus does not apply in cases of the kind discussed in 1.47, in which the effect of a variation is to *increase* the obligations of one party by his promise to make extra payments to the other. This position is sometimes described by saying that the doctrine operates as a shield and not as a sword;[217] but the metaphor is apt to mislead for the doctrine can assist a claimant no less than a defendant: eg where it prevents the defendant from relying on a defence that would have *destroyed the claimant's original cause of action*.[218] What the doctrine cannot do is to prevent a defendant from relying on the point that, apart from the promise, the claimant's original cause of action *never existed at all*.

(v) Distinguished from estoppel by convention

'Estoppel by convention' arises where parties 'act on an assumed state of facts or law…shared **1.57** by both or made by one and acquiesced in by the other'.[219] A party then cannot go back on that assumption if it would be 'unconscionable'[220] for him to do so and if the parties

---

[208] *Hughes v Metropolitan Rly* (1877) 2 App Cas 439, 448.
[209] *Hughes v Metropolitan Rly* (1877) 2 App Cas 439, 448.
[210] *Tool Metal Manufacturing Co Ltd v Tungsten Electric Co Ltd* [1955] 1 WLR 761; *The Kanchenjunga* [1990] 1 Lloyd's Rep 391, 399.
[211] See 1.52.
[212] *Birmingham & District Land Co v London & North-Western Rly Co* (1888) 40 Ch D 268.
[213] *Ogilvy v Hope-Davies* [1976] 1 All ER 683.
[214] *Maharaj v Chand* [1986] AC 898.
[215] *Williams v Stern* (1879) 5 QBD 409.
[216] *Combe v Combe* [1951] 2 KB 215; contrast, in the United States, Restatement 2d, *Contracts*, § 90; and, in Australia, *Waltons Stores (Interstate) Ltd v Maher* (1988) 164 CLR 387.
[217] *Combe v Combe*, n 216, at 224.
[218] eg by lapse of time: *The Ion* [1980] 2 Lloyd's Rep 245.
[219] *The Indian Endurance (No 2)* [1998] AC 878, 913.
[220] *Amalgamated Investment & Property Co Ltd v Texas Commerce Bank International* [1982] QB 84; *The Vistafjord* [1988] 2 Lloyd's Rep 343; *ING Bank NV v Ros Roca SA* [2011] EWCA Civ 353, [2012] 1 WLR 472.

have conducted themselves on the basis of the shared assumption.[221] It follows from these requirements that no such estoppel arises where each party spontaneously makes a different mistake and there is no subsequent conduct of the party alleged to be estopped from which his acquiescence in the other's mistaken assumption could be inferred.[222] Estoppel by convention is distinct[223]from 'promissory estoppel'[224] from which it differs in two ways. The first difference lies in its requirements: it can arise without any 'clear and unequivocal' representation.[225] The second difference lies in its nature or effect: it prevents a person from denying that a promise *has been made*, while 'promissory estoppel' is concerned with *the legal effects* of a promise which is shown or admitted to have been made.[226] Where the assumed promise would, had it been made, have been unsupported by consideration, both doctrines can operate in the same case: estoppel by convention to prevent a party from denying that the promise has been made, and promissory estoppel to determine its legal effects.[227] It seems that estoppel by convention resembles promissory estoppel[228] and estoppel by representation[229] in that it cannot give rise to new rights.[230]

(h) Part payment of a debt

(i) General common law rule

1.58 The general common law rule is that a creditor who promises to accept part payment of a debt in full settlement is not bound by that promise. In *Foakes v Beer* [231] the House of Lords held that a creditor who had made such a promise was nevertheless entitled to recover the balance: there was no consideration for the creditor's promise as the debtor had, in return for it, done no more than he was already bound to do. The rule may once have served the useful purpose of protecting the creditor against the too ruthless exploitation by the debtor of his position as a potential defendant in litigation. But it is also open to the objection that this protective function is now more satisfactorily performed by the concept of duress;[232] and that voluntary part payment may often be a benefit to the creditor. In cases of the kind discussed in 1.47 a similar factual benefit has been held to satisfy the requirement of consideration; but in the present context such reasoning would be inconsistent with *Foakes v Beer*, which is open to challenge only in the Supreme Court.[233]

(ii) Common law exceptions

1.59 The rigour of the common law rule is mitigated by many exceptions. The rule applies only to 'liquidated' claims, ie to claims for a fixed sum such as the agreed price for goods or services. Where the claim is 'unliquidated' so that its value is uncertain, no difficulty with respect

---

[221] *The Captain Gregos (No 2)* [1990] 2 Lloyd's Rep 395, 400.

[222] *The August P Leonhardt* [1985] 2 Lloyd's Rep 28.

[223] Although the distinction is not always an easy one to draw, as demonstrated by *ING Bank NV v Ros Roca SA* [2011] EWCA Civ 353, [2012] 1 WLR 472, which Carnwath LJ analysed as a case of estoppel by convention, while Rix LJ preferred to invoke promissory estoppel.

[224] See 1.53.

[225] *Troop v Gibson* (1986) 277 EG 1134.

[226] cf 1.53, n 206. In the cases cited in n 220, the promises (if made) would unquestionably have been supported by consideration.

[227] eg (apparently) in *Troop v Gibson*, n 225.

[228] See 1.56.

[229] See 1.202.

[230] *See Johnson v Gore Wood & Co* [2002] 2 AC 1, 40; *Smithkline Beecham plc v Apotex Europe Ltd* [2006] EWCA Civ 658, [2007] Ch 71, at [109]–[112].

[231] (1884) 9 App Cas 605. For a modern affirmation of the rule see *Collier v P & M J Wright (Holdings) Ltd* [2007] EWCA Civ 1329, [2008] 1 WLR 643.

[232] See 1.203.

[233] See *Re Selectmove Ltd* [1995] 1 WLR 474.

to consideration arises out of an agreement fixing its amount.[234] The same is true where the claim is in good faith disputed[235] and where there is some variation (other than in the amount of payment) of the debtor's performance: eg where part payment is made before the due day, or in a different currency, or accompanied by the delivery of a small chattel;[236] or where the debtor confers some benefit (other than the mere fact of voluntary part payment) on the creditor, even though the debtor is already bound by the contract to do this.[237] Consideration may also be provided by the debtor's forbearing to enforce a cross-claim which he has against the creditor.[238] The rule also does not apply where a number of creditors enter into a composition agreement with each other and with the debtor to accept a dividend in full settlement: there is consideration in the benefit which each creditor gets in being assured of some payment and this 'moves' from the debtor in that his co-operation is needed for the operation of the agreement.[239] The rule also does not apply where the part payment is made by a third party to whom the creditor makes a promise not to sue the debtor for the balance.[240] The reason for this rule is that the court will not allow the creditor to break his contract with the third party by suing the debtor for the balance.[241] The debtor may also be entitled to enforce this contract under the Contracts (Rights of Third Parties) Act 1999.[242] An agreement between debtor and creditor to accept part payment in full settlement may finally take effect as a collateral contract, though for this purpose some separate consideration moving from the debtor is required.[243]

(iii) Equitable evasion

The equitable doctrine of 'promissory estoppel' had been established before *Foakes v Beer*[244] **1.60** but was not in that case thought to be applicable to cases in which a debtor paid part of a debt in reliance on the creditor's promise to accept such payment in full settlement. But in the later *High Trees*[245] case it was said at first instance that the doctrine could apply to such a promise, in that case to one by the lessor of a block of flats to reduce the rent for so long as wartime difficulties of subletting continued. This view is at first sight in direct conflict with *Foakes v Beer* but it was nevertheless developed further in *Collier v P & M J Wright (Holdings) Ltd*.[246] There Arden LJ stated that if a debtor offers to pay part only of what he owes, the creditor voluntarily accepts that offer and in reliance on that acceptance the debtor makes the promised part payment, then the creditor is bound to accept that sum in full and final satisfaction of the whole debt.[247] On this analysis the right of the creditor to recover the balance of the debt is not simply in suspension; it is extinguished. This principle has the potential substantially to limit, if not undermine, the decision in *Foakes* insofar as it provides that a debtor who pays (as distinct from one who merely promises to pay) the promised part of the debt will be entitled to rely upon promissory estoppel for the purpose of defeating a claim brought by the creditor to recover the unpaid balance of the debt.

---

[234] *Wilkinson v Byers* (1834) 1 A & E 106.
[235] *Cooper v Parker* (1855) 15 CB 822.
[236] See *Pinnell's* case (1602) 5 Co Rep 117a; and 1.51.
[237] See the *Anangel Atlas* case [1990] 2 Lloyd's Rep 526.
[238] *Brikom Investments Ltd v Carr* [1979] QB 467.
[239] *Good v Cheesman* (1831) 2 B & Ad 328.
[240] *Hirachand Punamchand v Temple* [1911] 2 KB 330.
[241] The court may even restrain the creditor from doing so: *Snelling v John G Snelling Ltd* [1973] 1 QB 87.
[242] See 1.304. In the present context it is the debtor who is the 'third party' for the purpose of the 1999 Act.
[243] *Brikom Investments Ltd v Carr* [1979] QB 467.
[244] ie in *Hughes v Metropolitan Rly* (1877) 2 App Cas 439; 1.53.
[245] [1947] KB 130, *per* Denning J.
[246] [2007] EWCA Civ 1329, [2008] 1 WLR 643.
[247] [2007] EWCA Civ 1329, [2008] 1 WLR 643, at [42]. The judgment of Longmore LJ is rather more circumspect.

1.61   The equitable doctrine applies only where it is 'inequitable' for the promisor to go back on his promise. It will generally be inequitable for a creditor to seek to resile from a voluntary promise to accept part payment, once the debtor has made the promised payment. However, in other circumstances it may not be inequitable for the creditor to go back on his promise. So, eg, it would not generally be inequitable for a creditor to go back on his promise where the debtor had failed to pay the agreed smaller amount.[248] It has also been suggested that the court could take into account the debtor's conduct in procuring the creditor's promise: eg, where the debtor had secured the promise by taking undue advantage of the creditor's urgent need for an immediate payment.[249] Such cases are, however, more appropriately dealt with under the now expanded notion of duress,[250] than under some vague notion of promises obtained 'improperly' but in circumstances falling short of duress.[251]

(i) Proprietary estoppel

(i) Nature and scope

1.62   The doctrine of proprietary estoppel applies to many situations[252] with only one of which we are here concerned. This arises where the owner of property (usually land) makes a representation or promise to another person that the latter has, or will be granted, legally enforceable rights in or over the property, and the latter acts to his detriment in reliance on that representation or promise.[253] The landowner may then be estopped from denying the existence of those rights or compelled to grant them even though his promise was not binding as a contract, eg, for want of consideration. Illustrations of the doctrine are provided by family arrangements by which a parent (A) promises a child (B) that, if B will build a house on A's land, then A will give the land to B[254] or allow B to stay there for B's life.[255] A may then be precluded from revoking the promise after B has built the house. In such cases, A would be unjustly enriched if he were allowed freely to revoke the promise, but detrimental reliance by B can also give rise to the estoppel even though it does not lead to any improvement of A's land[256] or to any other enrichment of A.[257]

(ii) Requirements

1.63   The promise must induce the promisee to believe that legally enforceable rights have been or will be created in his favour.[258] It follows that a promise which expressly disclaims an intention to be legally bound (such as one made 'subject to contract' or expressly reserving the promisor's power to revoke) will not normally give rise to a proprietary estoppel.[259] The rights to which the promise refers must, in general, be rights in or over the property of the promisor[260] and it is an open question whether the doctrine can apply in relation to property

---

[248]   cf *Re Selectmove* [1995] 1 WLR 474, 481.

[249]   *D & C Builders Ltd v Rees* [1966] 2 QB 617, *per* Lord Denning MR.

[250]   See 1.203.

[251]   *Pao On v Lau Yiu Long* [1980] AC 614, 643.

[252]   So many that the doctrine has been called 'an amalgam of doubtful utility': *Amalgamated Investment & Property Co Ltd v Texas Commerce International Bank Ltd* [1982] QB 84, 103.

[253]   The leading modern cases are *Yeoman's Row Management Ltd v Cobbe* [2008] UKHL 55, [2008] 1 WLR 1752 and *Thorner v Major* [2009] UKHL 18, [2009] 1 WLR 776.

[254]   *Dillwyn v Llewelyn* (1862) 4 De GF & J 517.

[255]   *Inwards v Baker* [1965] 2 QB 29.

[256]   eg *Campbell v Griffin* [2001] EWCA Civ 990, [2001] WTLR 981; *Jennings v Rice* [2002] EWCA Civ 159, [2003]1 FCR 501 (personal services).

[257]   eg *Crabb v Arun DC* [1976] Ch 179.

[258]   See *Coombes v Smith* [1986] 1 WLR 808.

[259]   *A-G of Hong Kong v Humphrey Estates (Queen's Gardens)* [1987] 1 AC 114.

[260]   See *Western Fish Products Ltd v Penwith DC* [1981] 2 All ER 204; for an exception see *Salvation Army Trustee Co v West Yorks Metropolitan CC* (1981) 41 P & CR 179 (promise relating to promisee's land so closely linked with one relating to promisor's land as to form in substance one transaction).

other than land. The promisee must have relied on the promise to his detriment;[261] and the detriment must be so substantial as to make it unconscionable[262] for the promisor to go back on the promise.[263] The promisee must have an expectation of a 'certain interest in land'[264] and his reliance must relate to some specific property:[265] without such a limitation the doctrine could lead to the enforceability of any gift promise on which the promisee had relied and this would be fundamentally inconsistent with the doctrine of consideration. Before the promisee has acted in reliance on the promise, the promisor can revoke it;[266] and he may be entitled to do so even after such action in reliance if the parties can, in spite of it, be restored to their original positions.

(iii) Effects

Proprietary estoppel can give rise to a variety of legal effects: it can take the form of ordering **1.64** the promisor to convey the land to the promisee,[267] or of entitling the promisee to a right of occupation for life,[268] or of giving him a licence for a specified period[269] or one terminable on reasonable notice,[270] or of giving him a charge over the property[271] or of a monetary adjustment in respect of the improvements made by the promisee to the promisor's land.[272] Although the remedy is thus 'extremely flexible,'[273] the courts will, in fashioning it, adopt a 'principled approach'.[274] In particular, they will take into account the terms of the promise, the extent of the promisee's reliance on it and the proportion between that reliance and the promisee's expectation.[275] Where, eg, the remedy is by way of an award of money, the test of proportionality means that the promisee will recover such sum as is reasonable in the light of his reliance, even though the amount may fall short of his expectations.[276] This test may, however, be displaced by the subsequent conduct of the promisor in seeking to go back on the promise.[277] The court can also order the *promisee* to pay compensation as a condition of his getting title to the land if it is clear to both parties that the promisor did not intend to give up his title gratuitously;[278] and it may deny any remedy at all where, on balance, greater injustice would be caused by enforcing the promise than by allowing the promisor to go back on it.[279]

---

[261] The requirements of 'reliance' and 'detriment' are often 'intertwined': *Henry v Henry* [2010] UKPC 3, [2010] 1 All ER 988, at [55].

[262] However, unconscionable behaviour will not, of itself, suffice to establish a proprietary estoppel; *Yeoman's Row Management Ltd v Cobbe* [2008] UKHL 55, [2008] 1 WLR 1752.

[263] *Gillett v Holt* [2001] 2 Ch 210, 239; *Jennings v Rice* [2002] EWCA Civ 159, [2003] 1 FCR 501, at [21], [42].

[264] *Yeoman's Row Management Ltd v Cobbe* [2008] UKHL 55, [2008] 1 WLR 1752, at [18].

[265] *Layton v Martin* [1986] 2 Financial LR 227; contrast (perhaps) *Re Basham* [1986] 1 WLR 1498, 1508.

[266] eg if in the cases cited in nn 254 and 255 the promise had been revoked before any building work had been done.

[267] *Dillwyn v Llewelyn*, n 254.

[268] *Inwards v Baker*, n 255.

[269] *Tanner v Tanner* [1975] 1 WLR 1346.

[270] *Canadian Pacific Railway v R* [1931] AC 414.

[271] *Kinane v Mackie-Conteh* [2005] EWCA Civ 45, [2005] WTLR 345, at [33].

[272] *Gillett v Holt* [2001] Ch 210 (combining monetary compensation with an order to convey part of the land).

[273] *Roebuck v Mungovin* [1994] 2 AC 224, 235.

[274] *Jennings v Rice*, n 263, at [43].

[275] *Jennings v Rice*, n 263, at [36], [56].

[276] As in *Jennings v Rice*, n 263.

[277] *Pascoe v Turner* [1979] 1 WLR 431, 439; *Gillett v Holt* [2001] Ch 210, 235.

[278] *Lim Teng Huan v Ang Swee Chuan* [1992] 1 WLR 113.

[279] *Sledmore v Dalby* (1996) 72 P & CR 196.

(j) Irrevocable offers

1.65   An offer can be withdrawn at any time before it has been accepted;[280] and this is so even though the offeror has promised not to withdraw it for a specified period.[281] In some commercial contexts, this position is well understood and accepted: eg, in the case of share options the grantee expects to provide consideration for the option (unless it is granted by deed). In others, the rule may fail to give effect to the reasonable expectation of the offeree: eg where an offer from a subcontractor to supply materials to a builder is expressed to be 'firm' for a specified period and the builder then on the basis of the offer enters into a commitment with his customer.[282] In such a context, the rule by which such 'firm' offers are freely revocable has been criticized;[283] and the rule is subject (in the interests of commercial convenience) to an exception where payment under a contract (usually for the sale of goods) is to be made by an irrevocable letter of credit to be issued by the buyer's bank. Notification of the credit by that bank normally takes the form of a promise to pay the seller against tender of specified documents; and the commercial understanding is that the bank is bound on such notification, even before the seller can be said to have provided consideration for the bank's promise by performing, or beginning to perform, his part of the contract of sale. The law accepts this position, probably by way of exception to the requirement of consideration.[284]

(3) *Contractual Intention*

(a) Nature of the requirement

1.66   An agreement is not (even if the requirement of consideration is satisfied)[285] binding as a contract if it was made without any intention of creating legal relations.

(b) Proof of contractual intention

1.67   In deciding whether the present requirement is satisfied, the courts distinguish between implied agreements and express ones. The former are approached on the basis that 'contracts are not lightly to be implied'[286] and that the burden of proof on the issue of contractual intention is on the party alleging the existence of the contract.[287] But where the claim is based on an express agreement made in a commercial context, it is up to the other party to disprove such intention. As 'the onus is a heavy one'[288] and as the courts in such cases apply an objective test,[289] the requirement of contractual intention is (in relation to express agreements) significant only in the somewhat exceptional situations described in 1.68 to 1.71.

---

[280] See 1.17.

[281] *Dickinson v Dodds* (1876) 2 Ch D 463.

[282] For a way of avoiding the difficulty, see the Canadian case of *Northern Construction Co Ltd v Gloge Heating & Plumbing* (1984) 6 DLR (4th) 450.

[283] Law Commission Working Paper 60, *Firm Offers* (1975).

[284] See *Hamzeh Malas & Sons v British Imex Industries Ltd* [1958] 2 QB 127; *The American Accord* [1983] 1 AC 168, 183.

[285] See eg *R v Civil Service Appeal Board, ex p Bruce* [1988] ICR 649, 655, 659 (aff'd on other grounds [1989] ICR 171).

[286] *Blackpool & Fylde Aero Club v Blackpool BC* [1990] 1 WLR 1195, 1202.

[287] *Baird Textile Holdings Ltd v Marks & Spencer plc* [2001] EWCA Civ 274, [2002] 1 All ER (Comm) 737 (burden not discharged); *Modahl v British Athletics Federation* [2001] EWCA Civ 1447, [2002] 1 WLR 1192 (burden discharged).

[288] *Edwards v Skyways Ltd* [1964] 1 WLR 349, 355.

[289] *Kingswood Estate Co Ltd v Anderson* [1963] 2 QB 169.

(c) Illustrations

Contractual intention is most obviously negatived by an express provision: eg, by an 'honour **1.68**
clause' which states that the agreement is not to be a 'legal agreement',[290] or by the words
'subject to contract' in an agreement for the sale of land,[291] or by the terms of a 'letter of
comfort'.[292] Vagueness in the agreed terms (even if not such as to show that no agreement
was ever reached)[293] may also negative the existence of an intention to be bound.[294] On this
ground it has been held that there was no contractual liability for sales talk in promotional lit-
erature stating that a manufacturer's product was 'foolproof';[295] though more precise claims
(eg that the product would last for seven years) have been held to have contractual force.[296]

Social and domestic agreements (such as those resulting from acceptance of an invitation to **1.69**
dinner) are not normally contracts;[297] and the same is true of many agreements made within
the family circle which relate to the normal running of the household.[298] This may be true
even where the parties are living apart, eg, because one party to a marriage is temporarily
working abroad.[299] A further reason why such agreements have no legal effect is that they
may leave performance largely to the discretion of the promisor;[300] and this factor may negative contractual intention even in a commercial context.[301]

A collective agreement between a trade union and an employer or an association of employers **1.70**
is, by statute, 'conclusively presumed not to have been intended by the parties to be a legally
enforceable contract' unless it is in writing and expressly provides that it is intended to be
legally enforceable.[302]

Contractual intention may be negatived by many other disparate factors. These include **1.71**
the nature of the relationship between the parties,[303] the fact that the agreement was a

---

[290] *Rose & Frank Co v JR Crompton & Bros Ltd* [1925] AC 455.
[291] See 1.28.
[292] *Kleinwort Benson Ltd v Malaysian Mining Corp* [1989] 1 WLR 379; *Associated British Ports v Ferryways NV* [2009] EWCA Civ 189, [2009] 1 Lloyd's Rep 595.
[293] See 1.23.
[294] eg *Baird Textile* case, n 287. In more recent cases the courts have tended to be slow to conclude that the parties did not intend to be bound (see, eg, *Barbudev v Eurocom Cable Management Bulgaria EOOD* [2012] EWCA 548, [2012] 2 All ER (Comm) 963), particularly where they have signed the document said to contain the contractual terms (*Dhanani v Crasnianski* [2011] EWHC 926 (Comm), [2011] 2 All ER (Comm) 799).
[295] *Lambert v Lewis* [1982] AC 225 (aff'd [1982] AC 268, 271 on other grounds). Such statements are also probably too vague to impose liability to consumers under the Consumer Rights Act 2015, s 9(5) ('specific characteristics' claimed by seller of goods in advertising).
[296] cf *Shanklin Pier Ltd v Detel Products Ltd* [1951] 2 KB 854.
[297] *Balfour v Balfour* [1919] 2 KB 571, 578.
[298] *Gage v King* [1961] 1 QB 188. However, a court may be willing to find the existence of an intention to be bound where a husband and wife enter into an 'agreement to share the ownership or tenancy of the matrimonial home, bank accounts, savings or other assets': *Granatino v Radmacher* [2010] UKSC 42, [2011] 1 AC 534, at [142].
[299] *Balfour v Balfour*, n 297.
[300] *Gould v Gould* [1970] 1 QB 275; cf *Vaughan v Vaughan* [1953] 1 QB 762, 765.
[301] *Taylor v Brewer* (1813) 1 M & S 290; *Re Richmond Gate Property Co Ltd* [1965] 1 WLR 335; *Carmichael v National Power plc* [1999] 1 WLR 2042. But a promise containing a substantial discretionary component will have contractual force where the law requires the discretion to be exercised 'rationally and in good faith': (see *Horkulak v Cantor Fitzgerald International* [2004] EWCA Civ 1287, [2005] ICR 402 at [48] and *Commerzbank AG v Keen* [2006] EWCA Civ 1536, [2006] 1 WLR 872, at [59] (employee's discretionary bonus)).
[302] Trade Union and Labour Relations (Consolidation) Act 1992, s 179(1) and (2); cf at common law, *Ford Motor Co v AEF* [1969] 2 QB 403.
[303] eg, that between a church and a minister of religion appointed by it: contrast *President of the Methodist Conference v Parfitt* [1984] QB 368 (no intention to create legal relations) with *Percy v Board of National Mission of the Church of Scotland* [2005] UKHL 73, [2006] 2 AC 28 (where such an intention was found to

sham,[304] that it was believed simply to give effect to an already existing right (so that there was no intention to make a *new* contract)[305] and that the promissory statement was made in jest or anger.[306] The relevant factors cannot be neatly classified since the question of contractual intention is, in the last resort, one of fact in each case.

(4) Form

(a) General

1.72 To say that a contract must be in a certain form means that its conclusion must be marked or recorded in a specified manner, typically (in modern legal systems) in writing. The requirement, where it exists, must normally[307] be satisfied in addition to those of agreement, consideration and contractual intention. Formal requirements promote certainty by making it relatively easy to tell when a contract has been made, what type of contract it is and what its terms are. They also act as a safeguard against entering into a contract rashly; and they help to protect the weaker party to a contract by ensuring that he is provided with a written record of its terms. These functions of form are well illustrated by the elaborate formal requirements that protect the debtor under regulated consumer credit agreements.[308] On the other hand, formal requirements may be time-consuming, clumsy and a source of technical pitfalls. Contrary to popular belief, the general rule is that contracts can be made informally, by word of mouth. Exceptions to this general rule now all owe their existence to legislation relating to particular types of contracts. These exceptions cannot be stated in detail here; but two topics of general interest call for discussion.

(b) Types of formal requirements

1.73 Formal requirements vary considerably in their stringency. At one extreme, the requirement is satisfied only by a deed: this is the position with regard to leases of land for more than three years.[309] A second requirement is that the contract must be *made in writing*: this is the position with regard to regulated consumer credit agreements[310] and to most contracts for the sale of interests in land.[311] A third requirement is that there must be a *note or memorandum in writing*: this requirement exists in relation to contracts of guarantee.[312] This requirement can be satisfied by a document coming into existence after the contract was made: for this reason it is said that the contract need not be in writing but only *evidenced in writing*. Such a requirement exists also for policies of marine insurance.[313] A fourth requirement is that

---

exist). Each case must ultimately be judged on its own facts (*E v English Province of Our Lady of Charity* [2012] EWCA Civ 938, [2012] 4 All ER 1152, at [29]).

[304] *The Ocean Enterprise* [1997] 1 Lloyd's Rep 449, 484.

[305] *The Aramis* [1989] 1 Lloyd's Rep 213; *Judge v Crown Leisure Ltd* [2005] EWCA Civ 571, [2005] IRLR 823.

[306] *Licences Insurance Corporation and Guarantee Fund (Ltd) v Lawson* (1896) 12 TLR 501.

[307] In the case of a deed, the formal requirement can operate as a *substitute* for consideration.

[308] Consumer Credit Act 1974, ss 55, 60, 61. A consumer credit agreement is a 'regulated credit agreement' if it falls within the definition set out in s 8(3) of the Act.

[309] Law of Property Act 1925, s 52.

[310] Consumer Credit Act 1974, s 61.

[311] Law of Property (Miscellaneous Provisions) Act 1989, s 2(1) and (3).

[312] Statute of Frauds 1677, s 4, repealed so far as it related to certain other contracts by Law Reform (Enforcement of Contracts) Act 1954. The courts have experienced considerable difficulty in distinguishing between a guarantee (which is subject to the formal requirement) and an indemnity (which is not): see generally *Actionstrength Ltd v International Glass Engineering In.Gl.EN.SpA* [2003] UKHL 17, [2003] 2 AC 541 and *Yeoman Credit Ltd v Latter* [1961] 1 WLR 828, 835.

[313] Marine Insurance Act 1906, s 22.

one party must supply to the other certain written particulars: eg, an employer must give his employee a document setting out the principal terms of the contract,[314] and under some leases the landlord must give the tenant a rent book setting out specified particulars.[315]

(c) Electronic communications

The formal requirements described above can generally be satisfied by electronic communica- **1.74** tions and signatures:[316] eg where a contract is made on a website or by an exchange of emails. An EC Directive requires member states to ensure that contracts can be made by electronic means,[317] but this requirement does not extend to contracts for the sale of interests in land or to contracts of guarantee.

(d) Effect of non-compliance

Failure to comply with a formal requirement varies according to the nature of the require- **1.75** ment and the terms of the legislation imposing it.

One possibility is that the legislation may make the contract 'void'[318] or that the contract **1.76** simply fails to come into existence. The latter consequence follows from failure to comply with the formal requirements for the making of a contract for the sale of an interest in land;[319] though the hardship that can result from this position (eg to a purchaser who has partly performed or otherwise acted in reliance on the contract) can sometimes be mitigated by the use of such legal devices as constructive trust,[320] proprietary estoppel,[321] rectifica- tion[322] or the enforcement of a term of a collateral contract.[323]

A second possibility is that the contract comes into existence but fails to produce all the **1.77** consequences that it would have produced if the required form had been used. For example, if a lease for over three years were in writing but not made by deed, it would be 'void for the purpose of conveying or creating a legal estate'[324] but nevertheless enforceable between the parties as an agreement for a lease.[325]

---

[314] Employment Rights Act 1996, s 1.

[315] Landlord and Tenant Act 1985, s 4.

[316] Clicking on a website button would not necessarily satisfy the requirement of 'signature'. If it did, the protective function of formal requirements (1.72) could be considerably impaired.

[317] Directive 2000/31 EC, Art 9. Parts of the Directive (but not Art 9) are implemented by The Electronic Commerce (EC Directive) Regulations 2002, SI 2002/2013.

[318] Bills of Sale Act 1878 (Amendment) Act 1882.

[319] See n 311.

[320] See Law of Property (Miscellaneous Provisions) Act 1989, s 2(5); *Yaxley v Gotts* [2000] Ch 162, 193; *Herbert v Doyle* [2010] EWCA Civ 1095, [2011] 1 EGLR 119.

[321] The extent to which proprietary estoppel can perform this role is presently unclear. In *Thorner v Major* [2009] UKHL 18, [2009] 1 WLR 776, at [99] Lord Neuberger stated that proprietary estoppel could have a role to play, whereas in *Yeoman's Row Management Ltd v Cobbe* [2008] UKHL 55, [2008] 1 WLR 1752, at [29] Lord Scott inclined to the opposite view. Proprietary estoppel (or, for that matter, the constructive trust) is unlikely to be invoked by the courts where the parties have not implemented their intention to make a formal document setting out the terms on which one party is to acquire an interest in property, the parties have failed to reach agreement with sufficient clarity on the property to be acquired, or they did not expect their agreement to be immediately binding (*Herbert v Doyle* [2010] EWCA Civ 1095, [2011] 1 EGLR 119, at [57]).

[322] Law of Property (Miscellaneous Provisions Act 1989, s 2(4); 1.153.

[323] eg *Record v Bell* [1991] 1 WLR 853. In order to be enforceable in this way, the agreement must be freestanding, separate from the contract for the sale or other disposition of an interest in land: *Keay v Morris Homes (West Midlands) Ltd* [2012] EWCA Civ 900, [2012] 1 WLR 2855.

[324] Law of Property Act 1925, s 52.

[325] *Walsh v Lonsdale* (1882) 21 Ch D 9.

1.78 A third possibility is that *one* party's right to enforce the contract may be restricted. For example, an improperly executed regulated consumer credit agreement cannot be enforced against the debtor without an order of the court.[326] In deciding whether to make such an order the court has, in effect, a wide discretion which can prevent the debtor from relying on unmeritorious defences based on technical slips.[327] Where no enforcement order is made, the debtor is not liable to make restitution to the creditor in respect of benefits received under the agreement.[328]

1.79 A fourth possibility is that the contract is valid but cannot be enforced (by action) against the party who has not signed a note or memorandum of it. This is the position with regard to contracts of guarantee.[329] As the contract is not void the party who has not signed it is not entitled to the return of money paid or property transferred by him under it.[330]

1.80 A fifth possibility, laid down for policies of marine insurance, is that the contract is not admissible in evidence unless it complies with the formal requirements.[331]

1.81 A final possibility is that failure to comply with the formal requirement, though amounting to a criminal offence, does not affect the validity of the contract. This is the position where a landlord should have, but has not, provided his tenant with a rent book: the landlord can nevertheless sue for rent.[332]

(e) Formal requirements for rescission and variation

1.82 A contract which is subject to a formal requirement can nevertheless be rescinded informally[333] (unless the rescinding agreement amounts itself to a contract which is subject to a formal requirement). An attempt to vary such a contract may amount to a rescission followed by the making of a new contract. In that case, the rescission is effective but the new contract is subject to the formal requirement.[334] If the attempt is a mere variation (eg by the addition or deletion of a term)[335] it is ineffective and each party can sue (and sue only) on the original contract.[336]

C. Contents

(1) Express Terms

(a) Ascertainment and meaning

1.83 The express terms of a contract are those set out in the words used by the parties. The meaning of these words is determined objectively.[337] Declarations of subjective intent are inadmissible.[338] When seeking to ascertain the meaning of a disputed term, a court can

---

[326] Consumer Credit Act 1974, s 65.
[327] Consumer Credit Act 1974, s 127.
[328] *Dimond v Lovell* [2002] AC 384, 398.
[329] See n 312.
[330] *Thomas v Brown* (1876) 1 QBD 714.
[331] Marine Insurance Act 1906, s 22.
[332] *Shaw v Groom* [1970] 2 QB 504.
[333] See *Morris v Baron & Co* [1918] AC 1.
[334] *Morris v Baron & Co* [1918] AC 1.
[335] For the distinction between such a variation and a rescission, see *British and Beningtons Ltd v NW Cachar Tea Co* [1923] AC 48, 68.
[336] *Goss v Nugent* (1833) 5 B & Ad 58.
[337] *Investors Compensation Scheme Ltd v West Bromwich Building Society* [1998] 1 WLR 896, 912–913.
[338] *Investors Compensation Scheme Ltd v West Bromwich Building Society* [1998] 1 WLR 896, 912–913.

draw upon a wide range of materials (the so-called 'matrix of fact'),[339] although evidence of the parties' prior negotiations[340] and of their conduct subsequent to the making of the contract[341] are generally inadmissible. The courts will not lightly conclude that something has gone wrong with the language used by the parties[342] and will generally give to the parties' words their natural and ordinary meaning, particularly where the parties had access to legal advice and could be expected to choose their words carefully.[343] However, the courts are not obliged to adopt the natural and ordinary meaning of the words used and, exceptionally, eg in the case of a badly drafted contract,[344] they can depart from that meaning in order to give effect to the objective intention of the parties. Further, a court can adopt this approach as a matter of interpretation: it is not necessary for them to resort to rectification for this purpose.[345] When considering the alternative possible meanings of a disputed term, the court should[345a] consider which interpretation is the more commercially sensible and can generally be expected to adopt the more, rather than the less, commercial construction.[346]

(b) Incorporation by reference

A contractual document may incorporate the terms of another document. Most commonly **1.84** this is done by express reference in the first document to the second (eg by reference in a contract to terms settled by a trade association). Such incorporation may also be effected without express reference if the court is satisfied that the parties intended to incorporate the second document in the first.[347] Since the incorporated document may be one of considerable length and complexity, it is possible for some of its terms to conflict with those of the incorporating document. The court must then resolve the inconsistency and will be inclined to give primacy to the document actually drawn up by the parties, this being likely to express their predominant intention.[348] The requirements for the incorporation of standard terms drawn up *by one of the parties* are discussed below.[349]

---

[339] *Prenn v Simmonds* [1971] 1 WLR 1381, 1383–1384. The range of admissible material is broad, but not limitless: *Bank of Credit and Commerce International v Ali* [2001] UKHL 8, [2002] 1 AC 251, at [39].

[340] *Chartbrook Ltd v Persimmon Homes Ltd* [2009] UKHL 38, [2009] 1 AC 1101. Such evidence may, however, be admissible for the purpose of establishing that 'a fact which may be relevant as background was known to the parties' or to support a claim for rectification or estoppel (see also *Oceanbulk Shipping and Trading SA v TMT Asia Ltd* [2010] UKSC 44, [2011] 1 AC 662, at [40]).

[341] *James Miller & Partners Ltd v Whitworth Street Estates (Manchester) Ltd* [1970] AC 583, 603, 606. Such evidence is admissible where the contract is oral (*Maggs (t/a BM Builders) v Marsh* [2006] EWCA Civ 1058, [2006] BLR 395) and for the purpose of establishing an estoppel.

[342] *Chartbrook Ltd v Persimmon Homes Ltd* [2009] UKHL 38, [2009] 1 AC 1101, at [15]. The mere fact that the term as drafted has unintended consequences does not mean that something has gone wrong with the language: *Prophet plc v Huggett* [2014] EWCA Civ 1013, [2014] IRLR 797.

[343] *Scottish Widows Fund and Life Assurance Society v BGC International* [2012] EWCA Civ 607.

[344] *Multi-Link Leisure Developments v North Lanarkshire Council* [2010] UKSC 47, [2011] 1 All ER 175.

[345] Although it would be open to a court to resort to rectification (on which see 1.158) if it was appropriate to do so. The relationship between interpretation and rectification is now a 'close' one, but the two doctrines remain distinct and have their own separate requirements (*Oceanbulk Shipping and Trading SA v TMT Asia Ltd* [2010] UKSC 44, [2011] 1 AC 662, at [44], *Cherry Tree Investments Ltd v Landmain Ltd* [2012] EWCA Civ 736, [2013] Ch 305, at [98] and *Tartsinis v Navona Management Co* [2015] EWHC 57 (Comm), at [13]).

[345a] There is no obligation on the part of the court to do so (*Edgworth Capital (Luxembourg) Sarl v Ramblas Investments BV* [2015] EWHC 150 (Comm), at [34]).

[346] *Rainy Sky SA v Kookmin Bank* [2011] UKSC 50, [2011] 1 WLR 2900, at [23].

[347] *Jacobs v Batavia & General Plantations Trust Ltd* [1924] 1 Ch 287, aff'd [1924] 2 Ch 329.

[348] See *Adamastos Shipping Co Ltd v Anglo-Saxon Petroleum Co Ltd* [1959] AC 133.

[349] See 1.95–1.97.

(c) The parol evidence rule

1.85 This rule states that where a contract has been reduced to writing, then 'parol evidence' (ie evidence extrinsic to the document) cannot be used to add to, vary or contradict the written instrument.[350] The purpose of the rule is to promote commercial certainty by holding the parties bound by the writing and by it alone.[351] On the other hand, the rule is capable of leading to injustice where parties have in fact agreed to terms not set out in the document; and the courts have mitigated such injustice by recognizing exceptions to the rule or by limiting its scope.

(d) Qualifications

1.86 The rule relates only to evidence as to the *content* of the contract, so that extrinsic evidence can be used to challenge its *validity*,[352] eg for lack of consideration; or to establish some vitiating factor such as mistake.[353] On a similar principle, evidence can be admitted to show that the contract is subject to a contingent condition precedent not stated in the written document.[354]

1.87 Extrinsic evidence can be used to elucidate the meaning of the document: eg to explain vague or ambiguous terms[355] or to identify the subject matter[356] or to make it clear which party was buyer and which seller.[357] But where the document names the parties, evidence is not admissible to contradict it to show that one of the named parties was someone else.[358] Where a contract of sale is in writing, the buyer cannot enforce an oral undertaking as to quality; but he may be entitled to rely on a statement in it as a misrepresentation if it contains a false statement of fact,[359] or as overriding an exemption clause in the written contract.[360]

1.88 The rule excludes evidence of *express* terms but not evidence showing that a term ought to be implied[361] (or evidence negativing a usual implication).[362] Evidence of *custom* may also be used for this purpose,[363] so long as it does not *contradict* the written contract;[364] but this restriction does not apply where custom is used simply to show that words in the contract bore a special (customary) meaning.[365]

1.89 It may be possible to show that parties have made two contracts relating to the same subject matter: one in writing and the other oral. Evidence of the oral contract is then admissible to prove the second (or 'collateral') contract,[366] even (it seems) if it to some extent contradicts the written contract.[367] Such a collateral contract must, however, satisfy the

---

[350] *Jacobs v Batavia & General Plantations Trust Ltd* [1924] 1 Ch 287, 295.
[351] *AIB Group plc v Martin* [2001] UKHL 63, [2002] 1 WLR 94, at [4].
[352] *Kleinwort Benson Ltd v Malaysian Mining Corp* [1989] 1 WLR 379, 392.
[353] *Roe v RA Naylor Ltd* (1918) 87 LJKB 958, 964.
[354] *Pym v Campbell* (1856) 6 E & B 370.
[355] *Bank of New Zealand v Simpson* [1900] AC 182.
[356] *Macdonald v Longbottom* (1859) 1 E & E 977.
[357] *Newell v Redford* (1867) LR 3 CP 52.
[358] *Shogun Finance Ltd v Hudson* [2003] UKHL 62, [2004] 1 AC 919, at [49].
[359] Misrepresentation Act 1967, s 1(a).
[360] See 1.107.
[361] *Gillespie Bros & Co v Cheney Eggar & Co* [1896] 2 QB 59.
[362] *Burgess v Wickham* (1863) 3 B & S 669.
[363] *Hutton v Warren* (1836) 1 M & W 466, 475.
[364] *Palgrave Brown & Son v SS Turid (Owners)* [1922] AC 397.
[365] *Smith v Wilson* (1832) 3 B & Ad 728.
[366] *Mann v Nunn* (1874) 30 LT 526.
[367] *City & Westminster Properties (1934) Ltd v Mudd* [1959] Ch 129; but see *Angell v Duke* (1875) 32 LT 320; *Henderson v Arthur* [1907] KB 10.

normal requirements for contract formation such as those of consideration and contractual intention.[368]

The law distinguishes between documents intended only as informal memoranda[369] and those intended to be complete or exhaustive records of what has been agreed. Extrinsic evidence is excluded only where the document is of the latter kind;[370] and if a document appears to a reasonable person to fall into this category, a presumption arises that the document was indeed an exclusive record.[371] Evidence of extrinsic terms (though in fact agreed) will then be excluded unless the party relying on them can show that the other did not regard the document as such a record. **1.90**

(2) Implied Terms

(a) Terms implied in fact

A term will be implied in fact if it is one which the parties must have intended to include because it was 'so obvious that it goes without saying' so that, if an 'officious bystander' were to suggest its inclusion as an express term, they would immediately accept the suggestion.[372] It is also often said that the term must be 'necessary to give such business efficacy as the parties must have intended';[373] but this seems to be no more than a practical test for determining what the parties must have intended, under the 'officious bystander' test. Although different language has been used to express the test to be applied by the courts when seeking to imply a term in fact, the expressions have all been said to be aspects of the same question, namely whether the proposed implied term would spell out in express words what the instrument, read against the relevant background, would reasonably be understood to mean.[374] It is not sufficient for the term to satisfy the standard of reasonableness,[375] and the courts will not 'improve the contract which the parties have made for themselves'.[376] They will also refuse to imply a term where one party simply did not know the facts on which the alleged implication was to be based;[377] and, generally, where it is not clear that *both* parties would have agreed to the implication.[378] Occasionally, indeed, they may imply a term, even though one party would *not* have agreed to it, on the ground that an intention to incorporate it must be *imputed* to that party; but this power is to be 'sparingly and cautiously used' and only where the implication is 'strictly necessary'.[379] **1.91**

(b) Terms implied in law

Many of the obligations arising out of certain types of special contracts are said to be based on 'implied terms': in certain circumstances it is, eg, an 'implied term' of a contract for the sale of goods that the goods are fit for the particular purpose for which the buyer requires them;[380] **1.92**

---

[368] *Heilbut, Symons & Co v Buckleton* [1913] AC 30.
[369] eg *Allen v Pink* (1838) 4 M & W 140.
[370] *Hutton v Watling* [1948] Ch 398.
[371] *Gillespie Bros & Co v Cheney Eggar & Co* [1896] 2 QB 59, 62.
[372] *Shirlaw v Southern Foundries (1926) Ltd* [1939] 2 KB 206, 227 (affd [1940] AC 701).
[373] *Luxor (Eastbourne) Ltd v Cooper* [1941] AC 108, 137.
[374] *Attorney General of Belize v Belize Telecom Ltd* [2009] UKPC 10, [2009] 2 All ER 1127, at [21].
[375] *Liverpool City Council v Irwin* [1977] AC 239; *Mediterranean Salvage & Towage Ltd v Seamar Trading & Commerce Inc (The Reborn)* [2009] EWCA Civ 531, [2009] 2 Lloyd's Rep 639, at [15]; *Marks and Spencer plc v BNP Paribas Securities Services Trust Co (Jersey) Ltd* [2014] EWCA Civ 603.
[376] *Trollope & Colls Ltd v NW Metropolitan Hospital Board* [1973] 1 WLR 601, 609.
[377] *Spring v NASDS* [1956] 1 WLR 585, 599.
[378] eg *Shell UK Ltd v Lostock Garages Ltd* [1976] 1 WLR 1187.
[379] *Equitable Life Assurance Society v Hyman* [2002] 1 AC 408, 459.
[380] Sale of Goods Act 1979, s 14(3).

and an implied term of a contract of employment that the employer will take reasonable care not to endanger the employee's health.[381] Many such terms are implied even though the 'officious bystander' test is not satisfied so that the implication is not based on the court's view as to the common intention of the parties.[382] That intention is relevant only to the extent that it may be open to the parties to exclude the term in question by express contrary agreement.[383] Nor are such terms subject to the 'business efficacy' test as applied to terms alleged to be implied in fact: a contract of sale may well have such efficacy without the implication referred to above.[384] Terms implied in law are 'legal incidents of [particular] kinds of contractual relationships';[385] in deciding whether such terms ought to be implied, the courts are concerned with considerations of 'justice and policy';[386] and to this extent the tests of reasonableness and fairness are relevant to an implication of this kind.[387]

(c) Terms implied by custom or usage

1.93 Where persons deal in a particular market, a custom of that market may be implied into their contract unless the custom is inconsistent with the express terms of the contract or with terms implied otherwise than by custom. In cases of such inconsistency the custom is said to be 'unreasonable'; eg, a custom allowing an agent to sell his own goods to his principal is unreasonable as it is in conflict with his duty to the principal to buy as cheaply as possible.[388] The question of reasonableness is one of law and where the custom is reasonable it binds both parties whether they knew of it or not.[389] Terms may similarly be implied by usage of the trade in which the contracting parties were engaged.[390]

D. Standard Terms

1.94 The terms of many contracts are set out in standard forms prepared by or for one party and presented to the other. The practice has the advantages of saving time and creating standard patterns of dealing so as to enable parties to know what sorts of risks they will have to bear and cover by insurance. On the other hand, it has also been used by commercial suppliers of goods and services to exploit and abuse superior bargaining power, especially in contracts with consumers. It is this aspect of the subject which has engaged the attention of courts and legislatures, initially in cases involving terms which excluded or limited the supplier's liability, but also in cases in which terms conferred certain unduly advantageous rights on him.

(1) Exemption Clauses at Common Law

(a) Incorporation

(i) Signature

1.95 The first method of incorporating an exemption clause in a contract is to get the party to be bound by it to sign the document in which it is contained. If that document is one which

---

[381] *Johnstone v Bloomsbury Area Health Authority* [1992] QB 333.
[382] *Liverpool City Council v Irwin* [1977] AC 239.
[383] For some legislative restrictions on the right so to exclude certain implied terms, see 1.112 and 1.113.
[384] At n 380; see the *Liverpool City Council* case, n 382, at 255.
[385] *Mears v Safecar Securities Ltd* [1983] QB 54, 78.
[386] *The Star Texas* [1993] 2 Lloyd's Rep 445, 452; *Crossley v Faithful & Gould Holdings* [2004] EWCA Civ 293, [2004] 4 All ER 447, at [36].
[387] See *Re Charge Card Services* [1989] Ch 497, 513.
[388] *Robinson v Mollett* (1875) LR 7 HL 802.
[389] *Reynolds v Smith* (1893) 9 TLR 494.
[390] *British Crane Hire Corp v Ipswich Plant Hire Ltd* [1975] QB 303.

could reasonably have been expected to contain contractual terms,[391] the signer is then prima facie[392] bound by it even though he did not read it[393] and even though he was incapable of understanding it.[394]

(ii) Notice

The document containing the exemption clause, or incorporating it by reference,[395] may **1.96** simply be handed to the party to be bound. The clause then becomes part of the contract only if reasonable steps to bring it to the attention of that party have been taken by the other.[396] This depends first on whether the document was intended to have contractual force (so that a term printed on a mere receipt for payment will not be incorporated);[397] and secondly on whether the steps taken to give notice were in all the circumstances sufficient to bring the existence of the term to the attention of the other party.[398] If the clause is an unusual one, the party relying on it must take steps to 'make it conspicuous'.[399] If reasonable steps are taken, the clause is incorporated though not read by the other party.[400] The steps must be taken at or before the time of contracting, not at some later time.[401]

(iii) Course of dealing

Where parties have entered into a series of contracts on terms incorporating an exemption **1.97** clause, that clause may be incorporated into a particular contract even though, when making it, the steps required to incorporate it are, by some oversight, not taken.[402] For this purpose there must be a regular course of dealing (not just a small number of transactions within a long time-span);[403] and it must be *consistent*.[404] A term may also be implied by custom or usage[405] even though there is no course of dealing *between the parties*.

(b) Construction

(i) General

An exemption clause will generally be construed strictly against the party at whose instigation **1.98** it was included in the contract and who now seeks to rely on it: eg, a clause stating that 'no warranty … *is* given' has been held not to excuse a supplier of goods for breach of a collateral undertaking *previously* given.[406] The rule is less rigorously applied to clauses which merely *limit* liability since it is less 'inherently improbable'[407] that a party will agree to a limitation than to a total exclusion of the other's liability.

---

[391] *Grogan v Robin Meredith Plant Hire* [1996] CLC 1127.
[392] Subject to defences such as *non est factum*: see 1.149.
[393] *L'Estrange v F Graucob Ltd* [1934] 2 KB 394; criticized in *McCutcheon v David MacBrayne Ltd* [1964] 1 WLR 125, 133. In the case of a signed document, there is no need to satisfy the requirement of notice (1.96); unless, perhaps, the term in question is 'particularly onerous or unusual': *Ocean Chemical Transport Inc v Exnor Craggs Ltd* [2000] 1 Lloyd's Rep 446, 454.
[394] *The Luna* [1920] P 22.
[395] As in *Thompson v London, Midland & Scottish Rly* [1930] 1 KB 41.
[396] *Parker v South Eastern Rly* (1877) 2 CPD 416.
[397] *Chapelton v Barry UDC* [1940] 1 KB 532.
[398] *Parker v SE Rly*, n 396.
[399] *Crooks v Allen* (1879) 5 QBD 38, 40; *J Spurling Ltd v Bradshaw* [1956] 1 WLR 461, 466.
[400] *Thompson v LM & S Rly*, n 395; cf *O'Brien v MGN Ltd* [2001] EWCA Civ 1279, [2002] CLC 33 (rules governing newspaper competition).
[401] *Olley v Marlborough Court* [1949] 1 KB 532.
[402] *Hardwick Game Farm v Suffolk Agricultural, etc Association* [1969] 2 AC 31, 90, 104, 105, 113, 130.
[403] *Hollier v Rambler Motors (AMC) Ltd* [1972] 2 QB 71.
[404] *McCutcheon v David MacBrayne Ltd* [1964] 1 WLR 125.
[405] See 1.93.
[406] *Webster v Higgins* [1948] 2 All ER 127.
[407] *Ailsa Craig Fishing Co Ltd v Malvern Fishing Co* [1983] 1 WLR 964, 970.

(ii) Negligence

1.99 Legislation now restricts a party's power to exclude liability for negligence;[408] and even where it remains possible to do so 'clear words'[409] must be used for this purpose. The most obvious way of satisfying this requirement is to refer expressly to 'negligence'. Such a reference is normally essential where there is a realistic possibility[410] that the party relying on the clause can be made liable without negligence. 'General words' (containing no such reference) are then prima facie construed to cover only his strict liability;[411] though this rule of construction can be displaced by words which clearly show that negligence liability is to be covered.[412] Even the prima facie rule does not apply where the party's *only* liability is for negligence so that then general words *can* cover negligence[413] unless they are construed merely as a warning that the party in question is not liable for loss caused without his negligence.[414]

(iii) Seriousness of breach

1.100 **Fundamental breach.** Before exemption clauses were subjected to legislative control,[415] the courts were reluctant to allow a party to rely on an exemption clause where his breach was a particularly serious one; and to this end they developed the so-called doctrine of fundamental breach. According to one view, this made it impossible as a matter of law to exclude liability for such breaches. This 'substantive doctrine' may once have been a useful device for protecting consumers; but it is no longer needed for this purpose now that legislation has intervened, and it was, in any event, not restricted to the consumer context. The House of Lords has accordingly rejected the substantive doctrine and has held that the doctrine of fundamental breach is no more than a rule of construction.[416] As such, the rule amounts to a presumption that general words in an exemption clause will not normally cover certain very serious breaches; but the presumption can be overcome if the words are sufficiently clear.[417]

1.101 **Scope of the rule.** One group of cases in which the rule applies is that in which there has been a breach of a 'fundamental term', ie of one so central to the purpose of the contract that any breach of it turns the performance rendered into one essentially different from that promised. The example often given is that of a seller who promised to deliver peas and instead delivered beans:[418] exemption clauses have been construed not to cover the breach of such a term.[419] Whether such a breach has been committed depends on the nature of the

---

[408] See 1.112 and 1.113.

[409] *Gillespie Bros Ltd v Roy Bowles Transport Ltd* [1973] QB 400, 419.

[410] *Smith v South Wales Switchgear Ltd* [1978] 1 WLR 165, 178.

[411] *Canada Steamship Lines Ltd v R* [1952] AC 192, 208. However, the principles laid down by the Privy Council in *Canada Steamship* should not be applied 'mechanistically' and should be regarded as 'no more than guidelines': *Mir Steel UK Ltd v Morris* [2012] EWCA Civ 1397, [2013] 2 All ER (Comm) 54, at [35] and *Greenwich Millennium Village Ltd v Essex Services Group plc* [2014] EWCA Civ 960, [2014] 1 WLR 3517.

[412] *Joseph Travers & Sons Ltd v Cooper* [1915] KB 73.

[413] *Alderslade v Hendon Laundry* [1945] KB 189.

[414] *Hollier v Rambler Motors (AMC) Ltd* [1972] 2 QB 71.

[415] See 1.109 et seq.

[416] *Suisse Atlantique Société d'Armement Maritime v Rotterdamsche Kolen Centrale NV* [1967] 1 AC 361; *Photo Production Ltd v Securicor Transport Ltd* [1980] AC 827; *George Mitchell (Chesterhall) Ltd v Finney Lock Seeds Ltd* [1983] 2 AC 803.

[417] *AstraZeneca UK Ltd v Albemarle International Corporation* [2011] EWHC 1574 (Comm), [2011] 2 CLC 252, in this respect declining to follow the decision of Gabriel Moss QC in *Internet Broadcasting Corporation v MAR LLC* [2009] EWHC 844 (Ch), [2009] 2 Lloyd's Rep 265 that there is a presumption against a clause being construed so as to cover a deliberate, repudiatory breach of contract.

[418] *Chanter v Hopkins* (1838) 4 M & W 399, 404.

[419] eg *Andrews Bros (Bournemouth) Ltd v Singer & Co Ltd* [1934] 1 KB 17.

performance promised and the extent to which that rendered differed from that promised.[420] In contracts for the carriage of goods by sea, the term as to the route to be taken is regarded as fundamental,[421] so that *any*[422] 'deviation' from that route (even if it has not caused the loss) deprives the carrier of the benefit of exemption clauses. This special rule is said to be based on the possibility of the cargo owner's losing his insurance cover in consequence of the deviation[423] and on the consequent need to protect his rights against the carrier.[424] The rule has been extended to land carriage[425] and to storage contracts.[426]

In a second group of cases, the courts have been concerned with the *manner* of the breach. These cases construe exemption clauses so as not to apply to *deliberate* breaches;[427] they are based on the assumption that 'the parties never contemplated that such a breach should be excused or limited'.[428] This reasoning was, eg, applied to cases of misdelivery of goods by bailees to persons known not to be entitled to them.[429] **1.102**

In a third group of cases, the rule of construction applies (irrespective of the nature of the term broken or of the manner of breach) because of the practical *consequences* of the breach. It may, eg, apply to delays in performance which are particularly serious by reason of their extent,[430] or to defects in goods which make the goods practically useless to their acquirer[431] even though they do not make the thing delivered *totally* different from that promised.[432] **1.103**

Nature and the effects of the rule. Breaches of the kinds described in 1.101 to 1.103 will be covered by an exemption clause only if the clause 'most clearly and unambiguously'[433] so provides. There is 'a strong, though rebuttable, presumption'[434] that the parties did not intend to cover such breaches. The presumption being rebuttable, it follows that a breach of the most serious kind can be covered, eg, by a clause referring expressly to 'fundamental breach'[435] and even by general words if the court is satisfied that they were intended to, and on their true construction did, cover the serious breach that occurred.[436] There may, however, be limits to this approach: the courts may refuse to give effect to a clause which gives so much protection to a supplier as to enable him to supply the specified subject matter or whatever he chooses (eg seeds or sawdust) so as to turn his promise into 'no more than a statement of intent'.[437] The **1.104**

---

[420] See the *George Mitchell* case, n 416; delivery of defective seed not breach of a fundamental term in a contract for the sale of 'seed'.

[421] *Joseph Thorley Ltd v Orchis Steamship Co Ltd* [1907] KB 660; *Hain Steamship Co v Tate & Lyle Ltd* (1936) 41 Com Cas 350.

[422] *Suisse Atlantique* case, n 416, at 423.

[423] See Marine Insurance Act 1906, s 46.

[424] *Hain SS Co* case, n 421, at 354.

[425] *London & North-Western Rly v Neilson* [1922] 2 AC 263.

[426] *Woolf v Collis Removal Services* [1948] 1 KB 11, 15.

[427] *The Cap Palos* [1921] P 458.

[428] *Suisse Atlantique* case, n 416, at 435.

[429] *Alexander v Railway Executive* [1951] 2 KB 882; *Sze Hai Tong Bank Ltd v Rambler Cycle Co Ltd* [1959] AC 576.

[430] *Suisse Atlantique* case, n 416.

[431] eg *Yeoman Credit Ltd v Apps* [1962] 2 QB 508; *Farnsworth Finance Facilities Ltd v Attryde* [1970] 1 WLR 1053.

[432] As in the cases cited in n 431.

[433] *Ailsa Craig Fishing Co Ltd v Malvern Fishing Co Ltd* [1983] 1 WLR 964, 966.

[434] *Suisse Atlantique* case, n 416, at 432.

[435] See *The Antwerpen* [1994] 1 Lloyd's Rep 213.

[436] As in the cases cited in n 416.

[437] *The TFL Prosperity* [1984] 1 WLR 48, 59.

transaction in such a case might not be a contract at all on the ground that the supplier's promise was an illusory one.[438]

1.105 A breach of the kind here under discussion normally gives the injured party a right to damages and a right to terminate the contract.[439] A clause which in terms excludes only the right to damages does not affect that party's right to terminate;[440] but he cannot, by exercising that right, bring the contract to an end retrospectively and so get rid of the clause so far as it relates to loss suffered before termination.[441] Even liability for prospective loss would continue to be excluded or limited by a clause which on its true construction covered such loss.[442] Conversely, where the injured party elects not to terminate, but to affirm, the contract, he continues to be bound by a clause limiting the damages to which he is entitled by reason of the breach.[443]

1.106 The rule of construction applies to clauses which limit or exclude liability; but there is less need to apply it to clauses which fix damages in advance[444] since these may benefit either party; and this is true also of arbitration clauses.[445] The rule also does not seem to apply to clauses which specify a party's duty in such a way that his failure to achieve a particular result is not a breach at all.[446]

(c) Other common law limitations

1.107 At common law, a party cannot rely on an exemption clause if he has misrepresented its contents to the other party[447] or if he has at the time of contracting given an express undertaking which is inconsistent with the clause.[448] An exemption clause is also ineffective to the extent that it purports to exclude liability for a party's own fraud[449] or for breach of fiduciary duty[450] or for breach of certain requirements of procedural fairness known as the rules of 'natural justice'.[451] There is also some support for the view that exemption clauses may be invalid (at least in extreme cases) for unreasonableness.[452] But the need for such a development has been reduced by legislation subjecting some exemption clauses to a requirement of reasonableness;[453] and it is also open to the objection that it could extend this requirement to situations from which the legislature had excluded it.

---

[438] *Firestone Tyre & Rubber Co Ltd v Vokins & Co Ltd* [1951] 1 Lloyd's Rep 32, 39. The court may avoid such a conclusion by giving a 'restricted meaning' to apparently wide words: *Mitsubishi Corp v Eastwind Transport Ltd* [2004] EWHC 2924 (Comm), [2005] 1 All ER (Comm) 328, at [29].

[439] See 1.359–1.384.

[440] See the *Suisse Atlantique* case, n 416.

[441] *Photo Production Ltd v Securicor Transport Ltd* [1980] AC 827. There may be an exception in the deviation cases (regarded as *sui generis* in this case at 845) to the rule stated in the text above.

[442] This must follow from the rejection (see n 416) of the 'substantive' doctrine of fundamental breach.

[443] *Photo Production* case, n 441, at 849.

[444] As in the *Suisse Atlantique* case, n 416.

[445] *Woolf v Collis Removal Service* [1948] KB 11.

[446] See *GH Renton & Co v Palmyra Trading Corp* [1957] AC 149.

[447] *Curtis & Chemical Cleaning & Dyeing Co Ltd* [1951] 1 KB 805.

[448] *Couchman v Hill* [1947] KB 554; *Harling v Eddy* [1951] 2 KB 739.

[449] *S Pearson & Son Ltd v Dublin Corp* [1907] AC 351, 353, 362. It is an open question whether a party can exclude liability for the fraud of his own agent; and, even if this can be done, the intention to exclude such liability must be expressed 'in clear and unmistakable terms': *HIH Casualty & General Insurance Ltd v Chase Manhattan Bank* [2003] UKHL 6, [2003] 1 All ER (Comm) 349, at [16]; cf [24], [82], [92] and [122].

[450] *Gluckstein v Barnes* [1900] AC 240.

[451] *Lee v Showmen's Guild* [1952] 2 QB 329.

[452] *Thompson v London, Midland & Scottish Rly* [1930] 1 KB 41, 56.

[453] See 1.113.

(2) Other Standard Terms at Common Law

The problems raised by standard terms are not confined to exemption clauses, though these **1.108** have been the main subject of judicial activity in this field. They can arise also where standard terms confer rights on their proponent: eg the right to unexpectedly high payments to be made by a hirer of goods on failing to return them at the agreed time.[454] The restriction on the efficacy of these clauses is likely to lie in the high degree of notice generally required to incorporate them into the contract.[455] Some such terms are also subject to legislative control.[456]

(3) Legislative Limitations on Effectiveness

Legislative limitations on the effectiveness of standard terms often take the form of simply **1.109** depriving such terms of legal validity; but other techniques will also be considered in 1.129 to 1.131.

(a) The Unfair Contract Terms Act 1977

(i) Terminology

The Act generally applies only to terms affecting 'business liability', ie liability arising from **1.110** acts done or to be done by a person (B) in the course of a business, or from the occupation of business premises.[457] The Act no longer encompasses contracts concluded between a trader and a consumer.[458] Many provisions of the Act strike at terms which 'exclude or restrict liability'. This expression is not defined but is expanded so as to include provisions imposing short time limits or excluding a remedy[462] (but not an arbitration clause).[463] Clauses which do not in so many words exclude or restrict liability may have this effect in substance.[464] The Act generally leaves the parties free to define their *duties*; but it does limit a party's ability to exclude or restrict his duty of care giving rise to liability in negligence[465] and the duties arising out of the statutorily implied terms in contracts for the sale of goods.[466] Even apart from these provisions, the courts will not allow a party to 'emasculate'[467] the Act by drafting what is in substance an exemption clause in terms which purport to define his duty.

(ii) Structure of the Act

The Act distinguishes between terms which are simply ineffective and those which are **1.111** ineffective unless the party relying on them shows[468] that they satisfy the requirement of reasonableness.

Ineffective terms.   A term by which B seeks to exclude or restrict his liability for death **1.112** or personal injury resulting from negligence;[469] is ineffective, as is a term by which a seller or supplier purports to exclude or restrict liability in respect of an undertaking as

---

[454] As in *Interfoto Picture Library Ltd v Stiletto Visual Programmes Ltd* [1989] QB 433.
[455] See 1.96, n 399; *Interfoto* case, n 454, *per* Dillon LJ.
[456] See 1.113, n 482 and 1.119.
[457] Unfair Contract Terms Act 1977, s 1(3).
[458] Such contracts now fall within the scope of the Consumer Rights Act 2015, on which see 1.119–1.124.
[Footnotes 459–461 have been deleted in the paperback edition.]
[462] Unfair Contract Terms Act 1977, s 13(1).
[463] Unfair Contract Terms Act 1977, s 13(2).
[464] eg *Phillips Products Ltd v Hyland* [1987] 1 WLR 659.
[465] See the references in Unfair Contract Terms Act 1977, s 13(1) to s 2.
[466] See the references in Unfair Contract Terms Act 1977, s 13(1) to ss 6 and 7.
[467] *Smith v Eric S Bush* [1990] 1 AC 831, 848.
[468] Unfair Contract Terms Act 1977, s 11(5).
[469] Unfair Contract Terms Act 1977, s 2(1).

to title.[470] There is much other legislation which invalidates exemption clauses in specific contracts.

1.113 **Terms subject to reasonableness requirement.** These include[473] terms by which B seeks to exclude or restrict his liability for negligence giving rise to loss or damage other than death or personal injury;[474] terms purporting to exclude or restrict liability for breach of the statutorily implied terms in contracts for the supply of goods where the acquirer does *not* deal as consumer;[475] and other contracts on B's written standard terms of business[476] by which B seeks to exclude or restrict liability for his own breach,[477] or claims to be entitled to render a performance substantially different from that reasonably expected of him[478] or no performance at all[479] (though a provision entitling one party to refuse to make a payment because of the other's failure to perform[480] appears not to fall within this provision).

1.114 The Act seeks in two ways to reduce the uncertainty to which a judicially administered reasonableness requirement can give rise. First, it provides that the question whether the requirement is satisfied is to be determined by reference to the time of contracting.[483] Secondly, it lays down guidelines for determining the reasonableness of terms which limit a party's liability to a specified sum of money[484] and further guidelines where the contract is one for the supply of goods.[485] These statutory guidelines are not an exhaustive list of factors to be taken into consideration for the present purpose.[486] An appellate court will not reverse a decision on the issue of reasonableness merely because it disagrees with the decision;[487] but it may do so where the decision was based on a wrong principle of law.[488] Terms incorporated after negotiation between parties 'of equal bargaining power'[489] are unlikely to be struck down for unreasonableness; but even between such parties a term may be unreasonable if it was not the subject of negotiations between them[490] and would (if valid) have affected 'matters which the parties would have regarded as fundamental'.[491]

1.115 **Partly effective terms.** The Act throughout provides that specified liabilities cannot be excluded or restricted 'by reference' to certain terms. It follows that if, eg, a contract for the sale of goods contained a term excluding liability for 'any breach', then the term

---

[470] Unfair Contract Terms Act 1977, s 6(1) and see also s 7(3A).
[Footnotes 471–472 have been deleted in the paperback edition.]
[473] See also Misrepresentation Act 1967, s 3; and 1.189.
[474] Unfair Contract Terms Act 1977, s 2(2).
[475] Unfair Contract Terms Act 1977, ss 6(3), 7(3), 7(4).
[476] Unfair Contract Terms Act 1977, s 3(1).
[477] Unfair Contract Terms Act 1977, s 3(2)(a).
[478] Unfair Contract Terms Act 1977, s 3(2)(b)(i).
[479] Unfair Contract Terms Act 1977, s 3(2 (b)(ii).
[480] eg one making an obligation 'entire': see 1.369.
[Footnotes 481–482 have been deleted in the paperback edition.]
[483] Unfair Contract Terms Act 1977, s 11(1); contrast the common law rule under which the efficacy of an exemption clause depends on the *effects* of the breach: see 1.103.
[484] Unfair Contract Terms Act 1977, s 11(4).
[485] Unfair Contract Terms Act 1977, s 11(2) and Sch 2.
[486] *Smith v Eric S Bush* [1990] 1 AC 831, 838.
[487] *George Mitchell (Chesterhall) Ltd v Finney Lock Seeds Ltd* [1983] 2 AC 803, 810.
[488] *Granville Oil & Chemicals Ltd v Davies Turner & Co Ltd* [2003] EWCA Civ 570, [2003] 1 All ER (Comm) 819.
[489] *Watford Electronics Ltd v Sanderson* [2001] EWCA Civ 317, [2001] 1 All ER (Comm) 696, at [55]; *Air Transworld Ltd v Bombardier Inc* [2012] EWHC 243 (Comm), [2012] 1 Lloyd's Rep 349, at [133].
[490] *Balmoral Group Ltd v Borealis (UK) Ltd* [2006] EWHC 1900 (Comm), [2006] 2 Lloyd's Rep 629, at [423].
[491] *Bacardi-Martini Beverages Ltd v Thomas Hardy Packaging Ltd* [2002] EWCA Civ 549, [2002] 2 All ER (Comm) 335, at [26]; *Britvic Soft Drinks Ltd v Messer UK Ltd* [2002] EWCA Civ 548, [2002] 2 All ER (Comm) 321, at [26].

would not protect the seller from liability for breach of his implied undertaking as to title,[492] but it could protect him from liability for late delivery (subject only to common law restrictions). Similarly, if a single term were severable, the party in breach might be prevented by the Act from relying on one part of it while another might satisfy the requirement of reasonableness or be unaffected by the Act's provisions.[493] But the court will not *modify* the term actually included so as to allow the party in breach to rely, eg, on a reasonable *limitation*, where the term provided for an unreasonable *exclusion*, of liability.[494]

(iii) Restrictions on evasion

Secondary contract.   Section 10 of the Act provides that a person is not bound by a contract   **1.116**
depriving him of rights under 'another contract' so far as 'these rights extend to the enforcement of another's liability' which the Act 'prevents' that other from excluding or restricting. The section does not apply where parties to a contract by which an earlier contract containing terms which would be subject to the Act renegotiate those terms or settle disputes under the earlier contract by subsequent agreement.[495] Its purpose is to deal with the situation in which a term in a contract between A and B provides that B is not to exercise rights against C under a separate contract between B and C if such a term, had it been in the contract between B and C, would have been ineffective under the Act.[496]

Choice of law clauses.   The Act[497] prevents a party from evading its provisions by a   **1.117**
term 'imposed' mainly for this purpose which provides that the contract is to be governed by the law of a foreign country containing no provisions similar to those to be found in the Act.

(iv) Scope

Many contract terms fall outside the scope of the 1977 Act because they are not covered   **1.118**
by any of its provisions. This is particularly so now that the Consumer Rights Act 2015 has taken contracts between a trader and a consumer out of the 1977 Act and into the new regime enacted by the 2015 Act. A number of other contracts are excepted from specified provisions of the Act. These include contracts of insurance, any contract 'so far as it relates to the creation transfer or termination' of an interest in land,[498] and (to a more limited extent) charterparties and (other) contracts for the carriage of goods by sea.[499] The Act does not apply to contracts for the international supply of goods,[500] to contractual provisions authorized or required under other legislation or certain international conventions,[501] or to contract governed by English law by virtue only of a choice of law clause.[502]

---

[492]   See s 6(1)(a).
[493]   *RW Green Ltd v Cade Bros Farms* [1978] 1 Lloyd's Rep 602.
[494]   *George Mitchell* case, n 487, at 816; *Stewart Gill Ltd v Horatio Meyer & Co Ltd* [1992] QB 600.
[495]   *Tudor Grange Holdings Ltd v Citibank NA* [1992] Ch 53, 65–67.
[496]   *Tudor Grange* case, n 495, at 65–67.
[497]   Unfair Contract Terms Act 1977, s 27(2); Contracts (Applicable Law) Act 1990, s 1 and Sch 1 art 5 (2) and (4); and see 1.128.
[498]   Unfair Contract Terms Act 1977, Sch 1 para 1.
[499]   Unfair Contract Terms Act 1977, Sch 1 para 2.
[500]   Unfair Contract Terms Act 1977, s 26(1), on which see *Trident Turboprop (Dublin) Ltd v First Flight Couriers Ltd* [2009] EWCA Civ 290, [2010] QB 86 and *Amiri Flight Authority v BAE Systems plc* [2003] EWCA Civ 1447, [2004] 1 All ER (Comm) 385.
[501]   Unfair Contract Terms Act 1977, s 29.
[502]   Unfair Contract Terms Act 1977, s 27(1).

(b) The Consumer Rights Act 2015

(i) General

1.119 Part 2 of the Consumer Rights Act 2015 gives effect to an EC Council Directive on Unfair Terms in Consumer Contracts.[503] It applies to a contract between a trader[504] and a consumer[505] and is central provision is that an 'unfair term of a consumer contract is not binding on the consumer.'[506] Thus unfair terms, including exclusion and limitation of liability clauses, contained in a contract between a trader and a consumer are now regulated by this Act and not by the Unfair Contract Terms Act 1977. Consumer notices are also included within Part 2 to the extent that the notice relates to rights or obligations as between a trader and a consumer or purports to exclude or restrict a trader's liability to a consumer.[507]

(ii) Terminology

1.120 The Act defines a '*consumer*' as an individual acting for purposes that are wholly or mainly outside that individual's trade, business, craft or profession.[508] Thus a company cannot be a consumer for the purposes of the Act. A *trader* is defined as 'a person acting for purposes relating to that person's trade, business, craft or profession, whether acting personally or through another person acting in the trader's name or on the trader's behalf.'[509]

1.121 The restriction previously found in the statutory predecessors to Part 2 of the 2015 Act that the controls apply only[510] to terms which have not been 'individually negotiated'[511] has been removed from the 2015 Act so that terms which have been individually negotiated between a trader and a consumer are now within the scope of the legislation. It is, however, less likely that such terms will be found to be unfair, although there is obviously no guarantee that they will survive a challenge under the Act.

(iii) Unfairness and good faith

1.122 An unfair term is one which is 'contrary to the requirement of good faith' (ie, of 'fair and open dealing')[512] and 'causes a significant[513] imbalance in the parties' rights and obligations arising under the contract, to the detriment of the consumer'.[514] To reduce the uncertainty resulting from these requirements, account is to be taken[515] of 'the nature of the subject matter of the contract' (eg the fact that the goods were second-hand), of 'all the circumstances existing when the term was agreed' (eg the fact that the consumer had examined the goods) and 'all

---

[503] Council Directive (EEC) 93/13 OJL 95/29. This is the third occasion on which this has been done. The first is to be found in the Unfair Terms in Consumer Contracts Regulations 1994 (SI 1994/3159) which were revoked by the Unfair Terms in Consumer Contracts Regulations 1999 (SI 1999/2083) which in turn were revoked by the Consumer Rights Act 2015.

[504] A term defined in s 76(2) and 2(1) of the Act.

[505] A term defined in s 76(2) and 2(3) of the Act.

[506] Consumer Rights Act 2015, s 62(1).

[507] ibid s 61(4).

[508] ibid, s 2(3).

[509] ibid, s 2(2).

[510] Unfair Terms in Consumer Contracts Regulations, 1999 (SI 1999/2083), regs 3(1), 4(1) and 5(1).

[511] ibid, reg 5(1).

[512] *Director General of Fair Trading v First National Bank* [2001] UKHL 52; [2002] 1 AC 481 at [17], where openness is said to refer to the way in which terms are set out and fairness to their substance.

[513] The need for the imbalance to be 'significant' was emphasized in *Office of Fair Trading v Ashbourne Management Services Ltd* [2011] EWHC 1237 (Ch); [2011] All ER (D) 276 (May), [174].

[514] Consumer Rights Act 2015, s 62(4). The fact that the term in question was included at the consumer's suggestion may show that there was no such 'imbalance': *Bryen & Langley Ltd v Boston* [2005] EWCA Civ 973; [2005] BLR 508. But this conclusion is not inevitable, particularly where the adviser did not inform the consumer of the drawbacks of the clause: *Harrison v Shepherd Homes Ltd* [2011] EWHC 1811 (TCC); [2011] All ER (D) 140 (Jul).

[515] Consumer Rights Act 2015, s 62(5).

of the other terms of the contract or of any other contract on which it depends' (eg the fact that a supplier undertook more extensive duties than were imposed by the general law could justify the imposition of a short time limit). Further guidelines are in effect provided by a long and elaborate list of examples[516] of terms which '*may* be regarded as unfair'.[517] The list is 'indicative and non-exhaustive'[518] so that a term of a kind included in it is only prima facie unfair, and a term may be unfair although it is not included in the list.

A term of a consumer contract may not be assessed for fairness under section 62 of the Act to the extent that '(a) it specifies the main subject matter of the contract, or (b) the assessment is of the appropriateness of the price payable under the contract by comparison with the goods, digital content or services supplied under it'.[519] The scope of this exclusion has proved to be problematic[520] and the amendments made by the 2015 Act are intended to clarify the law. The central point to grasp is that the legislation is not intended as a mechanism of quality or price control:[521] with regard to such *core provisions*, they recognize the parties' freedom of contract. This is, however, true only where terms of this kind are 'transparent and prominent'.[522] An obscurely worded price term enabling the supplier unexpectedly to increase a price prominently stated elsewhere in the contract could therefore be subject to the requirement of fairness. The courts have also been generally reluctant to give too wide a scope to the concept of a 'core term' since, if they do so, the object of the Regulations will be 'plainly frustrated'.[523] Hence while a term specifying the price payable by the consumer would not fall within the scope of the Act', one specifying the consequences of his failure to pay that price would be subject to the Act.[524] In relation to the 'appropriateness' of the price it should be noted that the exclusion relates only to a comparison with the goods, digital content or services supplied under the contract. Thus the price term is not excluded from the Act as such; it is only excluded from certain forms of assessment. In other words, the term is excluded from certain forms of assessment (namely on grounds of price/quality ratio) but can be subject to challenge on other grounds (eg on the ground that it is unfair because of its other, discriminatory effects).[525] **1.123**

A trader cannot by a term of a consumer contract or by a consumer notice exclude or restrict liability for death or personal injury resulting from negligence.[526] However, this does not extend to any contract so far as it is a contract of insurance, any contract so far as it relates to the creation or transfer of an interest in land or affect the validity of any discharge or indemnity given by a person in consideration of the receipt by that person of compensation in settlement of any claim that person has.[527] **1.123A**

(iv) Excepted terms

The Act does not apply to terms which reflect (1) certain 'mandatory statutory or regulatory provisions'[528] such as terms which a contract is required under other legislation to contain,[529] **1.124**

---

[516] ibid, Sch 2, Part 1.
[517] ibid, s 63(1).
[518] ibid.
[519] ibid, s 64(1).
[520] Contrast the decision of the House of Lords in *DirectorGeneral of Fair Trading v First National Bank*, n 512 with the decision of the Supreme Court in *Office of Fair Trading v Abbey National plc* [2009] UKSC 6; [2010] 1 AC 696.
[521] *DirectorGeneral of Fair Trading v First National Bank*, n 512 above, at [12].
[522] Consumer Rights act 2015, s64(2).
[523] *Director General of Fair Trading v First National Bank* (n 512 above) at [52].
[524] ibid.
[525] *Office of Fair Trading v Abbey National plc* [2009] UKSC 6; [2010] 1 AC 696, at [41].
[526] Consumer Rights Act 2015, s 65(1).
[527] ibid s 66(1) and (2).
[528] ibid, s 73(1)(a).
[529] eg see para 1.130.

or (b) 'the provisions or principles of international conventions to which Member States or the EU is a party'.[530]

(v) Excluded contracts

1.125 'Contracts of employment or apprenticeship' are excluded from the Act.[531] Otherwise, the definition of a consumer contract is a broad one and would appear to be apt to include a contract of insurance,[532] contracts for the supply of intellectual property (such as contracts to license the use of computer software) and to contracts for the sale of interests in land (though they would not apply to a contract for the sale of a dwelling by one private home-owner to another since neither party to such a sale would act as a trader).

(vi) Drafting and interpretation

1.126 The Act requires that a trader ensure that 'any written term of a contract is 'transparent'[533] and a term is transparent for this purpose if it is 'expressed in plain and intelligible language and it is legible'.[534] Failure to comply with this requirement is not stated to make the term even prima facie unfair; nor does the requirement extend to oral contracts. If there is doubt about the meaning of a written term (and even 'plain, intelligible language' can have more than one meaning) the interpretation most favourable to the consumer is generally [535] to prevail.[536]

(vii) Effect of unfairness

1.127 An unfair term in a contract to which the Act applies is 'not binding on the consumer'.[537] However, this does not prevent the consumer from relying on the term if he chooses to do so.[538] Hence if it is an exemption clause the consumer will be able to enforce rights under the contract as if the term had not been included; if it purports to confer rights on the other party, those rights will not arise; and if effect has been given to them restitution may have to be ordered. The rest of the contract, however, continues to bind *both* parties so far as it is practicable to give effect to the rest of the contract without the unfair term.[539] Thus the consumer is not relieved from liability for the price merely because the contract contains an unfair exemption clause.

(viii) Choice of law clauses

1.128 The consumer cannot be deprived of the protection of the Act by a choice of law clause subjecting the contract to the law of a country or territory other than an EEA State which, but for such a clause, would not apply to it.[540]

(4) Other Legislative Control Techniques

1.129 Simply to deprive standard terms of legal validity might not be an effective way of controlling their abuse, especially in contracts between commercial suppliers and consumers. Legislation therefore makes use of other techniques of control.

---

[530] Consumer Rights Act 2015, s 73(1)(b).
[531] Consumer Rights Act 2015, s 61(2).
[532] An inference which derives support from 93/13/EEC, note 503 above, Recital 19.
[533] Consumer Rights act 2015, s 68(1)
[534] Consumer Rights Act 2015, s 68(2).
[535] Except in injunction proceedings under paragraph 3 of Schedule 3 to the Act: s 69(2).
[536] ibid, s 69(1).
[537] Consumer Rights Act 2015, s 62(2).
[538] ibid s 62(3).
[539] ibid, s 67.
[540] ibid, s 64.

One possibility is to control the contents of a contract by requiring certain terms to be included **1.130** in it. Extensive use of this technique is made in the consumer credit field where, eg, the debtor must be given a 'cooling off' period[549] and has the right to earn certain rebates on making early payments.[550] A term inconsistent with such provisions is void.[551] Variants of this technique are to require specified information to be given to a party who deals as consumer[552] and to subject contracts to a kind of supervised bargaining: eg in certain leases covenants by the landlord can be excluded only by a court order made with the consent of both parties.[553]

A second possibility is to invoke the intervention of an outside body, usually but not invari- **1.131** ably[554] a public authority, to exercise a form of administrative control. The Consumer Rights Act 2015 imposes on the Competition and Markets Authority and certain other bodies a duty to consider complaints that any contract term drawn up for general use is unfair and to ask the court to restrain such use by injunction.[556] Such 'pre-emptive challenges'[557] by public authorities may well be more effective than private litigation as a means of controlling standard contract terms which are unfair to consumers.

E. Mistake

The cases on mistake as a vitiating factor fall into two main groups.[558] In the first, the parties **1.132** make the same mistake: eg both think that the subject matter exists when it does not. Here they reach agreement but the mistake *nullifies* consent, ie deprives their agreement of legal effect. In the second, they make different mistakes: eg one thinks that they are contracting about one thing and the other about another. Here they are at cross-purposes and do not reach agreement so that the mistake *negatives* consent. The feature which is common to the two situations is that the mistake must be *fundamental* so that a party cannot rely on a 'mistake' which has led him merely to make a bad bargain. The law has to strike a difficult balance between the hardship of holding a mistaken party to his bargain and the uncertainty which could result from too great a readiness to grant relief on the ground of mistake. While the common law has stressed the need for certainty, equity has been more ambivalent. For many years it was somewhat more ready to relieve the mistaken party, but more recent authority has reduced the scope of such equitable relief.[559]

(1) Mistakes Nullifying Consent

(a) Fundamental mistake at common law

(i) *Types of mistake*

In general. A mistake will most obviously nullify consent where it relates to the *existence* **1.133** of the subject matter of the contract.[560] It can equally have this effect where it relates to the

---

[Footnotes 541–548 have been deleted in the paperback edition.]

[549] Consumer Credit Act 1974, ss 67, 68.

[550] Consumer Credit Act 1974, ss 94, 95, 99, 100.

[551] Consumer Credit Act 1974, s 173.

[552] eg Consumer Contracts (Information, Cancellation and Additional Charges) Regulations 2013, SI 2013/3134, Part 2.

[553] Landlord and Tenant Act 1985, ss 11, 12.

[554] See Consumer Rights Act 2015, Sch 3 para 8(1)(k) (Consumers' Association).

[Footnote 555 has been deleted in the paperback edition.]

[556] s 70, Schedules 3 and 5.

[557] *Director General of Fair Trading v First National Bank* [2001] UKHL 52, [2002] 1 AC 481, at [33].

[558] *Bell v Lever Bros Ltd* [1932] AC 161, 217.

[559] See 1.139, 1.148.

[560] eg *Galloway v Galloway* (1914) 30 TLR 531; and see 1.136.

identity of the subject matter,[561] that is, where both parties believe that they are dealing with X when they are actually dealing with Y. The same is again true where the parties mistakenly believe that performance is possible (either physically[562] or legally)[563] when it is not; and perhaps even when it is commercially impossible, in the sense that the commercial object which both parties had in mind cannot be achieved.[564]

1.134 **Mistake as to quality.** If one party *undertakes* that the subject matter has a quality that it lacks, that party is normally in breach (and the other may not be bound to perform).[565] If, however, both parties simply assume that the thing has the quality which it lacks then, in general, the mistake is not regarded as fundamental.[566] It will be so regarded only if it is 'as to the existence of some quality which makes the thing without the quality essentially different from the thing as it was believed to be'.[567] This requirement has been very strictly interpreted. In *Bell v Lever Bros Ltd*[568] a contract was made to pay £50,000 to two employees for termination of their service agreements and it was held that this contract was not made void for mistake when it was discovered that the service agreements could have been summarily terminated for breach of duty, without compensation. Similarly, if a picture were sold at a high price in the belief that it was an old master when it was a modern copy, then the buyer would have no remedy for mistake.[569] On the other hand, there would be such a remedy if table napkins were bought as relics of Charles I when they were Georgian;[570] and where a policy on the life of X was sold in the belief that X was alive when in fact he was dead so that the policy was worth more than the price paid for it.[571] The various cases and examples given above are not easy to reconcile;[572] but the principle that runs through them is that a mistake as to quality will not generally be regarded as fundamental unless the quality in question is so important to the parties that they use it to *identify* the subject matter. In the example of a modern copy bought and sold as an old master, it is, indeed, hard to accept that the mistake is not fundamental on this principle; but the example is an unrealistic one since such a sale is likely either to contain a warranty or to involve conscious risk-taking, in which case there would be no scope for mistake.[573]

1.135 **Mistake of law.** It used to be thought that the validity of a contract was not affected by a mistake of 'law', as opposed to one of 'fact'.[574] But this distinction was hard to draw and even harder to justify. It was first relaxed, at least in equity, by treating as a mistake of 'fact' one as to 'private right' even though it was based on a mistake of law, eg as to the construction

---

[561] More commonly, this type of confusion will *negative* consent (see 1.141).

[562] cf *Sheik Bros Ltd v Ochsner* [1957] AC 136.

[563] *Bell v Lever Bros Ltd* [1932] AC 161, 218; *Norwich Union Fire Insurance Society Ltd v Price* [1934] AC 455, 463; *The Great Peace* [2002] EWCA Civ 1407, [2003] QB 697, at [126]–[128].

[564] *Griffith v Brymer* (1903) 19 TLR 434.

[565] *Gompertz v Bartlett* (1853) 2 E & B 849.

[566] *Scott v Littledale* (1858) 8 E & B 815; *Harrison & Jones v Bunten & Lancaster* [1953] 1 QB 646.

[567] *Bell v Lever Bros Ltd* [1932] AC 161, 218; *Kennedy v Panama Royal Mail Co* (1867) LR 2 QB 580, 588 expresses a somewhat wider view.

[568] [1932] AC 218; cf *The Great Peace*, n 563 (ship chartered to render salvage services to another under a mistake as to the position of the former ship, making her less useful than expected, but not useless, for rendering the services).

[569] *Bell v Lever Bros Ltd* [1932] AC 161, 266; cf *Leaf v International Galleries* [1950] 2 KB 86, 89.

[570] See *Nicholson & Venn v Smith-Marriott* (1947) 177 LT 189.

[571] *Scott v Coulson* [1903] 2 Ch 249; cf *Associated Japanese Bank (International) Ltd v Crédit du Nord SA* [1989] 1 WLR 255.

[572] eg *Bell v Lever Bros Ltd* [1932] AC 161 is hard to reconcile with *Scott v Coulson*, n 571.

[573] *Deutsche Morgan Grenfell Group plc v Inland Revenue Commissioners* [2006] UKHL 49, [2007] 1 AC 558, at [27].

[574] *British Homophone Ltd v Kunz* (1935) 152 LT 589, 593; *Solle v Butcher* [1950] 1 KB 671.

of a document.[575] The distinction was later rejected in the context of restitution claims[576] and it no longer applies in the present context.[577] The validity of a contract can therefore be challenged on the ground of mistake of law, so long as the mistake is 'fundamental'.[578] But a challenge on this ground will fail where the parties were merely in doubt as to the point in question[579] (as opposed to being mistaken about it), or where they took the risk[580] that the law on the point might not be as they had supposed it to be. Such factors may, eg, lead to the rejection of the challenge where the impugned contract was a compromise of a disputed claim.[581]

(ii) Effects of the mistake

At common law, the starting principle is that a fundamental mistake makes the contract void;[582] but this rule may be displaced if, on its true construction, the contract provides that one party or even both are to be bound in spite of the mistake.[583] In the case of a contract for the sale of goods, eg, the contract will usually be void if the goods without the knowledge of either party had perished when the contract was made;[584] but it is in principle possible for either party to accept the risk of such a mistake: ie, for the seller to *undertake* that the goods are in existence[585] or for the buyer to promise to pay even though they are not. A party may, even in the absence of such an undertaking, be liable on the ground that he was at fault in inducing the other party to make the mistake.[586]

1.136

(b) Mistakes for which equity gives relief

(i) Types of mistake

Developments to be discussed in 1.139 have curtailed equitable relief for mistake but have left open the availability of at least one such form of relief, to be discussed in 1.138. For this purpose, the mistake need not be 'fundamental' in the narrow common law sense. In this way, equity to some extent mitigates the hardship to the mistaken party that may result from the narrow common law definition of a fundamental mistake; but in doing so it puts at risk the certainty which that definition is meant to promote. To mitigate this risk, the mistake must be a serious one,[587] so that a mere mistake as to 'the expectations of the parties'[588] (eg as to the development potential of land) will not suffice even in equity.

1.137

(ii) Effects of mistake

Refusal of specific performance. Even though the contract is valid at law because the mistake is not fundamental, equity may refuse specific performance,[589] leaving the claimant

1.138

---

[575] *Cooper v Phibbs* (1867) LR 2 HL 1049; cf *Allcard v Walker* [1896] 2 Ch 369 (mistake as to contractual capacity).
[576] *Kleinwort Benson Ltd v Lincoln City Council* [1999] 2 AC 349.
[577] *Brennan v Bolt Burdon* [2004] EWCA Civ 1017, [2005] QB 303, at [10], [17], [26]; cf at [60].
[578] See *Shamil Bank of Bahrain v Beximco Pharmaceuticals* [2004] EWCA Civ 19, [2004] 2 Lloyd's Rep 1, at [59]–[60], where the mistake was not fundamental.
[579] *Brennan's* case, n 577, at [19], [23], [36].
[580] *Brennan's* case, n 577, at [22], [23], [31], [39].
[581] *Brennan's* case, n 577, at [12], [51], [63], [64].
[582] *Associated Japanese Bank* case, n 571, at 268.
[583] cf Marine Insurance Act 1906, Sch 1 r 1 ('Lost or not lost' clause).
[584] Sale of Goods Act 1979, s 6; cf *Couturier v Hastie* (1856) 5 HLC 673 (where only the liability of the buyer was in issue); *Barrow, Lane & Ballard Ltd v Philips & Co Ltd* [1929] 1 KB 574, 582.
[585] *McRae v Commonwealth Disposals Commission* (1951) 84 CLR 377.
[586] *McRae v Commonwealth Disposals Commission* (1951) 84 CLR 377, 408; *Associated Japanese Bank* case, n 571, at 268.
[587] *William Sindall plc v Cambridgeshire CC* [1994] 1 WLR 1016, 1041.
[588] *Amalgamated Investment & Property Co Ltd v John Walker & Sons Ltd* [1977] 1 WLR 164, 172.
[589] *Jones v Rimmer* (1880) 14 Ch D 588.

to his remedy in damages. It may also order specific performance on terms, eg where land is sold under a mistake as to area, on the terms that the price is varied.[590] There is no scope for such equitable relief where the contract is *void* at common law. It can then simply be disregarded by the parties, though a court order may be necessary to restore them to their original positions.[591]

1.139 **No rescission on terms.** At one time, there was considerable support in the authorities for the view that a contract which was not void because the mistake was not fundamental in the narrow common law sense[592] could be rescinded in equity by the mistaken party,[593] on whom terms could in turn be imposed to ensure that justice was done to the other party.[594] The exercise of this power to rescind could, no doubt, 'on occasion be the passport to a just result'.[595] But no satisfactory way was ever found of reconciling it with the common law rule applied in *Bell v Lever Bros Ltd*[596] or with the interests of certainty which that rule was intended to promote. To restore doctrinal consistency, the Court of Appeal in *The Great Peace*[597] held that there was no longer any power to rescind a contract for mistake in equity where the contract was valid at law because the mistake was not 'fundamental' in the common law sense.

(2) Mistakes Negativing Consent

1.140 A mistake which puts the parties so seriously at cross-purposes as to negative consent will impair the validity of a contract only in a number of somewhat exceptional situations, to be discussed in 1.146.

(a) Types of mistake

(i) As to subject matter

1.141 Consent is negatived where one party intends to deal with one thing and the other with a different one: eg if a seller intends to sell the cargo on ship A and the buyer to buy that on ship B.[598] If the parties are merely at odds as to the quality of the goods intended by both, consent will not normally be negatived since a mistake as to quality is not usually fundamental.[599]

(ii) As to the person

1.142 Consent is negatived if one party (A) to the alleged contract makes a fundamental mistake about the other (B). Usually B is an impecunious rogue who makes some pretence about himself to induce A to give him credit; and between these parties it makes little difference whether the mistake is fundamental so as to make the contract void;[600] for, even if this is not the case, A will be entitled to rescind the contract for fraud.[601] But the point is crucial if B has resold the subject matter to C, a purchaser in good faith: if the mistake was fundamental, no title will pass to B and hence none to C,[602] while if the mistake was not fundamental B will acquire a voidable

---

[590] *Aspinalls to Powell and Scholefield* (1889) 60 LT 595.
[591] As in *Cooper v Phibbs* (1867) LR 2 HL 149.
[592] See 1.134.
[593] eg, *Magee v Pennine Insurance Co Ltd* [1969] QB 507.
[594] eg, *Solle v Butcher* [1950] 1 KB 671.
[595] *West Sussex Properties Ltd v Chichester District Council*, 28 June 2000, at [42].
[596] [1932] AC 161; 1.134.
[597] [2002] EWCA Civ 1407, [2003] QB 697.
[598] *Raffles v Wichelhaus* (1864) 2 H & C 906, as explained in *Smith v Hughes* (1871) LR 6 QB 597.
[599] See 1.134.
[600] As B will be aware of the mistake, it is *operative*: see 1.146.
[601] See 1.175, 1.176.
[602] For criticism of this position, see Law Revision Committee, 12th Report (1966) Cmnd 2958, para 15; *Shogun Finance Ltd v Hudson* [2003] UKHL 62, [2004] 1 AC 919, at [5], [60], [84].

title and A could not avoid this against C. For this purpose, A's mistake is fundamental if it is one as to the *identity* of B: ie if A deals with B in the belief that B is X;[603] but it is not normally fundamental if A's mistake is merely as to an *attribute* of B: eg if A deals with B in the mistaken belief that B is a person of substance to whom credit can safely be given.[604] A mistake as to an attribute would be fundamental only if it related to *the* attribute by which A had identified B: eg if he had identified B as 'the wife of X'.[605] The distinction between the last two situations may in practice be hard to draw, particularly where A and B are in each other's presence when the contract is made. Prima facie they will then be taken to have identified each other by the ordinary process of sight and hearing;[606] but it may be possible to show that A identified B in some other way, eg as residing in a specified house.[607] Where the contract is in writing, the difficulty of determining whether a mistake is as to an identifying attribute is mitigated in the sense that the question, who the parties to the contract are, then turns on the construction of the contractual document; and prima facie they are the persons described as such in that document.[608]

(iii) As to terms

Consent may be negatived by a mistake as to the terms of the contract: eg where a seller **1.143** intended to sell goods at a specified price per *piece* and the buyer to buy for the same price per *pound*.[609] There is some support for the view that a mistake as to terms need not be fundamental, so that, while consent is not negatived by a mistake as to the existence of a non-fundamental quality, it will be negatived by a mistake as to the existence of a *warranty* of that same quality.[610]

(b) Mistake must induce contract

The mistake has no effect on the contract unless it relates to a point of commercial signifi- **1.144** cance to the mistaken party and induces him to enter into the contract. If A buys goods from a shop believing it to be owned by B when it had just been sold by B to C, A's mistake is fundamental, but it will in most cases not matter to A so long as he in fact gets the goods he wanted to buy. The mistake will induce the contract only if A had some special reason for wanting to deal with B: eg that B owed him money which A intended to set off against the price of the goods.[611]

(c) Effects of mistake

(i) At common law

Contract generally valid. Where mistake negatives consent, the validity of the contract is **1.145** not affected if, as is generally the case, A has so conducted himself as to induce B reasonably to believe that A was agreeing to B's terms.[612] If, eg, at an auction A bids for one lot when he thinks that he is bidding for another, then it follows from the objective principle[613] that he cannot rely on his mistake even though it is fundamental and has induced the contract.

---

[603] *Cundy v Lindsay* (1878) 3 App Cas 459.
[604] *King's Norton Metal Co Ltd v Edridge, Merrett & Co Ltd* (1894) 14 TLR 98.
[605] *Lake v Simmons* [1927] AC 487.
[606] *Phillips v Brooks* [1919] 2 KB 243; *Lewis v Averay* [1972] QB 198.
[607] *Ingram v Little* [1961] 1 QB 31, doubted in the *Shogun* case, n 602, at [87], [110], [185].
[608] *Shogun Finance Ltd v Hudson*, n 602; alternatively, A had there intended to deal only with X and had made a mistake as to an identifying attribute of the person (B) who had posed as X.
[609] *Hartog v Colin & Shields* [1939] 3 All ER 566.
[610] *Smith v Hughes* (1871) LR 6 QB 597; and see n 616.
[611] *Boulton v Jones* (1857) 2 H & N 564; A should then be required to assign to C the debt owed by B to A.
[612] *Centrovincial Estates plc v Merchant Investors Assurance Co Ltd* [1983] Commercial LR 158.
[613] See 1.02.

1.146 **Contract exceptionally void.** A mistake which negatives consent is *operative* (so as to make the contract void) only in three exceptional situations to which the objective principle does not apply. These are (1) where there is such *perfect ambiguity* (eg as to the subject matter) that a reasonable person would have no ground for believing that the parties intended to deal with one of two things rather than with the other;[614] (2) where the mistake of one party is *known* to the other;[615] and (3) where that mistake is negligently induced by the other party. In the third, and possibly in the second, of these cases, the mistake may operate against the party who negligently induced (or knew of) the other party's mistake, but not against the latter party.[616]

(ii) In equity

1.147 **Bar to specific performance.** Where the contract is not void at law because the mistake is *not fundamental*, equity can refuse specific performance in accordance with the principles already discussed.[617] The contract may also be valid at law under the objective principle where the mistake, though fundamental, is *not operative*: eg where a buyer at an auction by mistake bids for the wrong lot.[618] Specific performance may then be refused (or ordered only on terms)[619] if, but only if, 'hardship amounting to injustice'[620] would result from an unconditional grant of the remedy.[621]

1.148 **No rescission.** Where a mistake has, or is alleged to have, negatived consent, the contract may nevertheless be valid at law for one of two reasons. The first is that the mistake is *not fundamental*; and in cases of this kind the former view, that the contract could be rescinded in equity,[622] can no longer stand after *The Great Peace*.[623] That case was, indeed, concerned with a mistake alleged to have *nullified* consent; but its reasoning (that doctrinal coherence would be destroyed and certainty undermined by allowing contracts which were valid at law to be rescinded in equity for a mistake which was not fundamental)[624] applies as much to mistakes alleged to have negatived consent.[625] The second reason why a mistake alleged to have negatived consent may not affect the validity of the contract is that the mistake, though fundamental, was *not operative*. In such a case, rescission in equity would seriously undermine the objective principle and is therefore not available.[626] Refusal of specific performance[627] is not open to the same objection since it does not deprive the claimant of his remedy at law.

---

[614] *Raffles v Wichelhaus* (1864) 2 H & C 906, as explained in *The Great Peace* [2002] EWCA Civ 1407, [2003] QB 697, at [29].

[615] As in *Cundy v Lindsay* (1878) 3 App Cas 459; 1.140.

[616] Where a seller knew of the buyer's mistaken belief as to the existence of an undertaking as to quality, the seller could (on the objective principle) be treated as if he had given the undertaking and be precluded by his breach of it from enforcing the contract. This is a second possible explanation of *Smith v Hughes*, n 610.

[617] See 1.138, n 589.

[618] See 1.145.

[619] *Baskomb v Beckwith* (1869) LR 8 Eq 100.

[620] *Tamplin v James* (1879) 15 Ch D 215, 221.

[621] As in *Malins v Freeman* (1836) 2 Keen 25.

[622] See *Torrance v Bolton* (1872) 8 Ch App 118, perhaps now explicable as a case of misrepresentation.

[623] [2002] EWCA Civ 1407; [2003] QB 697.

[624] See 1.139.

[625] *Statoil ASA v Louis Dreyfus Energy Services LP* [2008] EWHC 2257 (Comm), [2008] 2 Lloyd's Rep 685, at [97]–[105].

[626] *Riverlate Properties Ltd v Paul* [1975] Ch 133.

[627] See 1.147, n 621.

(3) Documents Mistakenly Signed

(a) Doctrine of 'non est factum'

A person who signs a contractual document is generally bound by it whether he reads it **1.149**
or not; but long ago[628] the law recognized a special defence available to illiterate persons
who executed deeds which had been incorrectly read over to them. This was the defence of
'non est factum' (it is not my deed); it was later extended to persons who could read and
explained on the ground that 'the mind of the signer did not accompany the signature'.[629]
But this extension gave rise to the danger of conflict with the objective principle, particularly where A was by the fraud of B induced to sign a document (such as a guarantee of
B's bank overdraft) apparently containing a contract between A and C. To reduce the risk
of prejudice to C, the law has restricted the scope of the doctrine in the ways described in
1.150 to 1.152.

(b) Restrictions

The doctrine is not normally available to adults of normal attainments and capacity. It **1.150**
applies only in favour of persons who can have 'no real understanding' of the document
'whether . . . from defective education, illness or innate incapacity';[630] and of those who have
been tricked into signing the document.[631]

The doctrine is restricted by a rule closely analogous to the requirement that a mistake must **1.151**
be 'fundamental'.[632] It applies only where the difference between the document signed and
the document as it was believed to be is a 'radical' or 'essential' or 'fundamental' or 'substantial' one.[633]

The defence is not available to a person who was careless in signing the document.[634] **1.152**
Although the standard of care seems to be subjective,[635] the burden of disproving carelessness
lies on the signer and is not easy to discharge.[636]

(4) Mistakes in Recording Agreements

(a) Remedy of rectification

The equitable (and hence discretionary)[637] remedy of rectification is available where there has **1.153**
been a mistake, not in the *making*, but in the *recording* of a contract: it brings a document
into line with the earlier agreement.[638] A crucial point is that 'Courts of equity do not rectify
contracts; they may and do rectify instruments'.[639] A document which accurately records
a prior agreement thus cannot be rectified merely because that agreement was made under
some mistake:[640] if rectification were available in such a case, the remedy would subvert the
rules which limit the kinds of mistake which can invalidate contracts.

---

[628] *Thoroughgood's case* (1584) 2 Co Rep 9a.
[629] *Foster v Mackinnon* (1869) LR 4 CP 704, 711.
[630] *Saunders v Anglian Building Society Ltd* [1971] AC 1004, 1016.
[631] *Saunders' case*, n 630, at 1025.
[632] See 1.133, 1.134, 1.141, and 1.142.
[633] *Saunders' case*, n 630, at 1017, 1019, 1021, 1026, 1034.
[634] *Saunders' case*, n 630; *United Dominions Trust v Western* [1976] QB 513 (document containing blanks).
[635] Since a reasonable person cannot normally rely on the defence.
[636] *Saunders' case*, n 630, esp at 1023.
[637] Rectification claims also tend to be 'highly fact specific': *Daventry District Council v Daventry & District Housing Ltd* [2011] EWCA 1153, [2012] 1 WLR 1333, at [2].
[638] *Murray v Parker* (1854) 19 Beav 305; *Allnutt v Wilding* [2006] EWHC 1905, [2006] BTC 8040, at [16].
[639] *Mackenzie v Coulson* (1869) LR 9 Eq 369, 375; *The Olympic Pride* [1980] 2 Lloyd's Rep 67, 72.
[640] cf *Frederick E Rose (London) Ltd v William H Pim Jr & Co Ltd* [1953] 2 QB 450.

(b) Requirements

1.154 The mistake must normally be that of both parties.[641] If, eg, a lease provided for a monthly rent of £1,000, it could not be rectified merely because the landlord intended the rent to be £2,000 since this would impose on the tenant a liability to which he had not agreed or appeared to agree. Rectification could be ordered in such a case only if the tenant was guilty of fraud, or knew of the landlord's mistake or wilfully shut his eyes to it and sought to take advantage of it.[642] Nor, in the absence of such facts, can the tenant be forced to choose between having the lease rectified or rescinded[643] since this course would deprive him of the protection of the objective principle.

1.155 Rectification is available if the document fails accurately to record a prior agreement or (even less stringently) a 'continuing common intention', and 'some outward expression of accord'.[644] The test to be applied when seeking to identify the intention of the parties has been held to be an objective one,[645] albeit the test may require 'refinement'[646] and may also take account of 'some subjective evidence of intention or understanding'.[647] Rectification can be ordered even though there was no prior binding contract: eg because the prior agreement was not intended to be legally binding before execution of the document. There must, however, be clear evidence of the prior agreement, since the court has to guard against the danger of imposing on a party terms to which he had not agreed.[648]

(c) Restrictions

1.156 Rectification may be barred by lapse of time or the intervention of third party rights.[649] The remedy is not barred by impossibility of restoring the pre-contract position;[650] for its purpose is not to undo what has been done but to give effect to the parties' agreement.[651]

1.157 Rectification is not available where other machinery is provided by law for correcting mistakes: eg where a mistake has been made in drawing up a settlement which is binding by virtue of a court order.[652]

1.158 A claim for rectification of a document may be accompanied by one as to its construction. The claimant should then put forward both claims in the proceedings; for if judgment is given against him on the point of construction his rectification claim will be barred if it could have been, but was not, made in those proceedings.[653] The courts can 'correct' errors in the expression of a document by the application of the principles applicable to the interpretation of contracts.[654] Although the rules which govern the remedy of rectification differ from the

---

[641] *Faraday v Tamworth Union* (1916) 86 LJ Ch 436.
[642] *Garrard v Frankel* (1862) 30 Beav 445, 451; *Blay v Pollard & Morris* [1930] 1 KB 628, 633; *Commission for the New Towns v Cooper* [1995] Ch 259, 277.
[643] *Riverlate Properties Ltd v Paul* [1975] Ch 133.
[644] *Joscelyne v Nissen* [1970] 2 QB 86, 98.
[645] *Chartbrook Ltd v Persimmon Homes Ltd* [2009] UKHL 38, [2009] 1 AC 1101, at [48]–[66].
[646] *Daventry District Council v Daventry & District Housing Ltd* [2011] EWCA 1153, [2012] 1 WLR 1333, at [104].
[647] *Daventry District Council v Daventry & District Housing Ltd* [2011] EWCA 1153, [2012] 1 WLR 1333, at [104]; *Tartsinis v Navona Management Co* [2015] EWHC 57 (Comm), at [87]–[99].
[648] *Fowler v Fowler* (1859) 4 De G & J 250, 265; *The Olympic Pride* [1980] 2 Lloyd's Rep 67, 73.
[649] *Bloomer v Spittle* (1872) LR 13 Eq 427; *Beale v Kyte* [1907] 1 Ch 564; *Smith v Jones* [1954] 1 WLR 1089; cf 1.181.
[650] Contrast 1.182.
[651] eg *Cook v Fearn* (1878) 48 LJ Ch 63.
[652] *Mills v Fox* (1887) 37 Ch D 153.
[653] *Crane v Hegeman-Harris Co Inc* [1939] 4 All ER 68.
[654] *Nittan (UK) Ltd v Solent Steel Fabrication Ltd* [1981] 1 Lloyd's Rep 633. This process was referred to as 'corrective interpretation' by Arden LJ in *Cherry Tree Investments Ltd v Landmain Ltd* [2012] EWCA Civ 736, [2013] Ch 305, at [38].

principles applicable to the interpretation of contracts,[655] the relationship between the two is nevertheless close.[656]

F. Misrepresentation

A person who has been induced to enter into a contract by certain kinds of misleading state- **1.159** ments will, where certain general requirements are satisfied, have remedies by way of damages or rescission or both. Sometimes these remedies (or one of them) are available also for mere nondisclosure.

(1) The Representation

The starting point for this discussion is that the representation must be one of *existing fact*. **1.160** This requirement is, however, much modified, as the contrast between such and certain other kinds of representation will show.

(a) Statements of opinion or belief

Some kinds of sales talk (such as a description of land as 'fertile and improveable')[657] are so **1.161** vague as to have no legal effect. Even a more precise statement (such as one that land could support 2,000 sheep)[658] is not a ground for relief if the representor had (as the representee knew) no personal knowledge of the relevant facts. A statement of opinion or belief can, however, give rise to liability if the maker professed to have special knowledge or skill with regard to the matter stated;[659] or if the statement by implication contained a representation that the person making it held the belief stated.[660]

(b) Statements as to the future

A person who promises to do something and then breaks that promise is liable for breach of **1.162** contract if the promise had contractual force. If it had no such force, he is not liable for misrepresentation unless, when he made the promise, he had no intention of performing it; for in that case he would be misrepresenting his present state of mind, which is 'as much a fact as the state of his digestion'.[661] A person who makes a statement of expectation or belief may similarly by implication state that he holds the belief on reasonable grounds,[662] or at least honestly.[663]

---

[655] *Daventry District Council v Daventry & District Housing Ltd* [2011] EWCA 1153, [2012] 1 WLR 1333, at [198].

[656] *Oceanbulk Shipping and Trading SA v TMT Asia Ltd* [2010] UKSC 44; [2011] 1 AC 662, at [44]. There does, however, remain a distinct role for rectification to play: *Cherry Tree Investments Ltd v Landmain Ltd* [2012] EWCA Civ 736, [2013] Ch 305, at [98]. Contrast *Tartsinis v Navona Management Co* [2015] EHWC 57 (Comm), [13] where Leggatt J stated that interpretation and rectification are 'very different exercises' which it is important to keep 'separate'.

[657] *Dimmock v Hallett* (1866) LR 2 Ch App 21.

[658] *Bissett v Wilkinson* [1927] AC 177.

[659] *Esso Petroleum Co Ltd v Mardon* [1976] QB 801; cf *MCI Worldcom International Inc v Primus Communications plc* [2004] EWCA Civ 957, [2004] 2 All ER (Comm) 833, at [30].

[660] *Brown v Raphael* [1958] Ch 636, 641; contrast *Harlingdon and Leinster Enterprises v Christopher Hull Fine Art Ltd* [1991] 1 QB 564.

[661] *Edgington v Fitzmaurice* (1885) 29 Ch D 459, 482; cf, in criminal law, Fraud Act 2006, s 2(3).

[662] *The Mihalis Angelos* [1971] 1 QB 164, 194, 205.

[663] *Economides v Commercial Union Assurance Co plc* [1998] QB 587; cf Marine Insurance Act 1906, s 20(5).

(c) Statements of law

1.163 It was formerly said that a misrepresentation of law (as opposed to one of fact) gave rise to no claim for compensation.[664] But the distinction between the two kinds of misrepresentation has not survived the rejection by the House of Lords of a similar distinction in the context of a restitution claim for the recovery of money paid under a mistake.[665] The reasoning of this decision is regarded as being of general application,[666] so that relief is now available for misrepresentation of law in the same way as it is for misrepresentations of fact.[667]

(2) Other Conditions of Liability

(a) Unambiguous

1.164 A representation may be capable of bearing two meanings, one true and the other false. There is then no liability in damages for deceit if the representee understood the representation in the former (true) sense.[668] Even if he understood it in the latter (false) sense, the representor is so liable only if he intended it to be so understood:[669] ie not if he honestly intended it to bear the true meaning.[670]

(b) Materiality

1.165 The representation must, in general, be material, ie it must relate to a matter which would influence a reasonable person in deciding whether, or on what terms, to enter into the contract.[671] This does not mean that it must, in all the circumstances, be reasonable for the representee to rely on the representation. It might not be reasonable for him to do this where he had, but did not take, an opportunity of discovering the truth; but this is not of itself a bar to relief.[672] Exceptionally, there is no requirement of materiality where the representation is fraudulent;[673] where the requirement is excluded by a term of the contract;[674] or where the claim is not one for misrepresentation inducing the claimant to enter into a contract with the defendant but is one for breach of a duty of care arising out of an antecedent contract between these parties.[675]

(c) Reliance

1.166 There is no relief for misrepresentation if the representee did not rely on the representation: eg because he knew the truth.[676] The same result follows if the representation never came to his attention;[677] but a representation made by A to B can give C a ground for relief against A if A intended the representation to be (and it was) repeated by B to C, or where this should

---

[664] *Rashdall v Ford* (1866) LR 2 Eq 750; *Beattie v Ebury* (1872) LR 7 Ch App 693; *André & Cie SA v Ets Michel Blanc* [1979] 2 Lloyd's Rep 427, 434.

[665] *Kleinwort Benson Ltd v Lincoln CC* [1999] 2 AC 349; cf 1.135; and, in criminal law, Fraud Act 2006, s 2(3).

[666] *Pankhania v Hackney LBC* [2002] EWHC 2441 (Ch), at [68], approved in *Brennan v Bolt Burden* [2004] EWCA Civ 1017, [2005] QB 303, at [11].

[667] If the representee had taken his own legal advice on the point, his claim would fail for want of reliance on the misrepresentation; see 1.166.

[668] *Smith v Chadwick* (1884) 9 App Cas 187.

[669] *The Siboen and the Sibotre* [1976] 1 Lloyd's Rep 293, 318.

[670] *Akerhielm v De Mare* [1959] AC 789.

[671] *Mc Dowell v Fraser* (1779) 1 Dougl 260, 261; *Traill v Baring* (1864) 4 DJ & S 318, 326; Marine Insurance Act 1906, s 20(2).

[672] See 1.166.

[673] *Smith v Kay* (1859) 7 HLC 750.

[674] *London Assurance v Mansell* (1879) 11 Ch D 363, 368 (basis of contract clauses in insurance proposal).

[675] See *Bristol & West Building Society v Mothew* [1998] Ch 1, 10–11.

[676] *Eurocopy plc v Teesdale* [1992] BCLC 1067.

[677] *Ex p Biggs* (1859) 28 LJ Ch 50.

have been foreseen by A.[678] Reliance is normally negatived where the representee made his own investigations into the matter;[679] but this rule does not apply to cases of fraud[680] since so to apply it would put a premium on skilful deception. The fact that the representee had, but failed to take, an opportunity of discovering the truth is not, of itself, a ground for denying relief;[681] but where it was reasonable for the representee to make use of that opportunity and he failed to do so relief will be denied if the representation was not fraudulent.[682] Relief may be given to a representee who was induced to enter into the contract both by the representation and by other factors,[683] unless these other factors were such decisive inducements that he would have entered into the contract even if he had known the truth.[684]

(3) Damages

(a) Fraud

A person who suffers loss as a result of being induced by a false statement to enter into a contract can recover damages in tort for deceit if he can show that the person making the statement *either* knew that it was false *or* had no belief in its truth *or* made it recklessly, not caring whether it was true or false.[685] He need not establish an intention to cause loss or other bad motive:[686] an 'intention to deceive' suffices even though there is no 'intention to defraud'.[687]

1.167

(b) Negligence at common law

There is liability in tort where a misrepresentation is made carelessly, in breach of a duty to take reasonable care that the representation is accurate. Such a duty arises when there is a 'special relationship' between the parties;[688] the requirements of such a relationship are discussed elsewhere in this book.[689] The duty can, and often does, arise where the misrepresentation does not induce the representee to enter into a contract with the representor.[690] But it can arise also where the representation does induce such a contract: eg between prospective lessee and lessor.[691] Such commercial relationships will not be 'special' (so as to give rise to a duty of care at common law) if it is reasonable for the representor to assume that the representee has acted on his own judgment or advice; but even in such a case the representor can be subject to the statutory liability in damages discussed in 1.169.

1.168

---

[678] *Pilmore v Hood* (1838) 5 Bing NC 97; *Smith v Eric S Bush* [1990] 1 AC 831; cf *Clef Aquitaine SARL v Laporte Materials (Barrow) Ltd* [2001] QB 488, where B's rights under the contract were transferred to C.

[679] *Redgrave v Hurd* (1881) 20 Ch D 1, 14; *McInerny v Lloyds Bank Ltd* [1974] 1 Lloyd's Rep 246, 254.

[680] *S Pearson & Son Ltd v Dublin Corporation* [1907] AC 351.

[681] *Redgrave v Hurd*, n 679.

[682] *Smith v Eric S Bush*, n 678; cf *Peekay Intermark Ltd* [2006] EWCA Civ 386, [2006] 2 Lloyd's Rep 511 (no relief for a misrepresentation corrected by the terms of the contractual document signed, but not read, by the representee). To this extent, the rule in *Redgrave v Hurd*, n 679, seems now to be qualified.

[683] *Edgington v Fitzmaurice* (1885) 29 Ch D 459; *Standard Chartered Bank v Pakistan National Shipping Corp (No 2)* [2002] UKHL 43, [2003] 1 AC 959, at [14]–[15].

[684] *JEB Fasteners Ltd v Mark S Broom & Co* [1983] 1 All ER 583; *Raiffeisen Zentralbank Osterreich AG v Royal Bank of Scotland plc* [2010] EWHC 1392 (Comm), [2011] 1 Lloyd's Rep 123, at [170].

[685] *Derry v Peek* (1889) 14 App Cas 337; on similar facts see now Financial Services and Markets Act 2000, s 90. For criminal liability, see Fraud Act, 2006.

[686] *Polhill v Walter* (1832) 3 B & Ad 114.

[687] *Standard Chartered Bank v Pakistan National Shipping Corp* [1995] 2 Lloyd's Rep 365, 375; *Standard Chartered Bank v Pakistan National Shipping Corp (No 2)* [2000] 1 Lloyd's Rep 218, 221, reversed on another ground [2003] 1 AC 959.

[688] *Hedley Byrne & Co Ltd v Heller & Partners Ltd* [1964] AC 465.

[689] See ch 2.

[690] eg in *Hedley Byrne's* case, n 688.

[691] *Esso Petroleum Co Ltd v Mardon* [1976] QB 801.

(c) Misrepresentation Act 1967, section 2(1)

1.169 This subsection creates a statutory liability in damages 'where a person [A] has entered into a contract after a misrepresentation has been made to him by another party [B] thereto'. The statutory cause of action is based on negligence[692] but is in at least two respects more favourable to A than common law liability for negligence: it arises although there is no 'special relationship' between A and B; and the burden is on B to prove that, up to the time the contract was made, he believed on reasonable grounds that the facts represented were true. In deciding whether B had discharged this burden, the court would have regard to the means at his disposal for discovering the truth.[693] The subsection provides that, if B would have been liable had the misrepresentation been made fraudulently, then 'he shall be so liable' even though it was not so made. One consequence of this 'fiction of fraud' is that the measure of damages is derived from the tort of deceit,[694] not the tort of negligence, although the courts have not consistently invoked the analogy of deceit in the interpretation of the subsection.[695] A claimant who has a right to redress under Part 4A of the Consumer Protection from Unfair Trading Regulations 2008[695a] is not entitled to recover damages under section 2(1) in respect of conduct constituting the misrepresentation.[695b]

(d) Breach of contract

(i) Term of main contract

1.170 A pre-contract statement may be a 'mere' representation, inducing the contract, or one of its terms. In the latter case, the person making the statement is considered to undertake that it was true and will therefore, if it is untrue, be liable in damages for breach, irrespective of negligence. Where the statement is set out in the contractual document, it will normally on its true construction[696] be a term, but the intention to guarantee its truth may be negatived by express contrary provision or by other circumstances. Where the statement is not set out in any contractual document, the question whether it has contractual force depends on the intention (objectively ascertained) of its maker.[697] Factors relevant to the ascertainment of this intention include the wording of the statement,[698] its importance to the representee[699] and the relative abilities of the parties to determine its truth: eg a statement as to the age of a car is more likely to be a term when made by a dealer[700] than when made by a private seller.[701]

(ii) Collateral contract

1.171 It may be impossible for a statement to take effect as a term of the contract induced by it: eg because it fails to comply with formal requirements or because of the parol evidence rule.[702] The statement may nevertheless take effect as a collateral contract[703] if the representor had the

---

692 *South Australia Asset Management Corp v York Montague Ltd* [1997] AC 191, 216.

693 See *Howard Marine & Dredging Co Ltd v A Ogden & Sons (Excavations) Ltd* [1978] QB 574.

694 *Royscot Trust Ltd v Rogerson* [1991] 2 QB 297; *Cheltenham Borough Council v Laird* [2009] EWHC 1253 (QB), [2009] IRLR 621, at [524]; *Yam Seng Pte Ltd v International Trade Corporation Ltd* [2013] EWHC 111 (QB), [2013] 1 All ER (Comm) 321, at [206].

695 *Gran Gelato Ltd v Richcliff (Group) Ltd* [1992] Ch 560, where the analogy was drawn with the tort of negligence in concluding that the defence of contributory negligence was applicable to a claim under the subsection.

695a SI 2008/1277.

695b Misrepresentation Act 1967, s 2(4) which also applies to a claim for damages under s 2(2).

696 *Behn v Burness* (1863) 1 B & S 751, 754.

697 *Howard Marine* case, n 693, at 595.

698 *Hummingbird Motors Ltd v Hobbs* [1986] RTR 276 (statement expressly one of belief only).

699 *Bannerman v White* (1861) 10 CBNS 855; contrast *Oscar Chess Ltd v Williams* [1957] 1 WLR 370.

700 Cf *Dick Bentley Productions Ltd v Harold Smith (Motors) Ltd* [1965] 1 WLR 623.

701 *Oscar Chess* case, n 699.

702 See 1.75 and 1.85.

703 *De Lassalle v Guildford* [1901] 2 KB 215; *Esso Petroleum Co Ltd v Mardon* [1976] QB 801.

requisite contractual intention[704] and if consideration was provided by the representee. The latter requirement will usually[705] be satisfied by his entering into the main contract.

(e) Damages in lieu of rescission

Before 1967, rescission was the only remedy for a wholly innocent misrepresentation and **1.172** might provide an unduly drastic solution, especially where the misrepresentation related to a relatively minor matter.[706] Section 2(2) of the Misrepresentation Act 1967 therefore gives the court a discretion to uphold the contract[707] and award damages 'in lieu of rescission' where the representee would be entitled to rescind a contract made after a misrepresentation had been made to him otherwise than fraudulently. The subsection gives no *right* to damages, and a claim for damages under it cannot be combined with one for rescission.[708] Its wording also suggests that such a claim cannot be made after the right to rescind has been lost;[709] but the policy reasons for barring this right scarcely justify this restriction on the discretion to award damages under section 2(2).[710]

(f) Content of the right to damages

Damages for deceit, for negligence at common law and under section 2(1) of the **1.173** Misrepresentation Act 1967[711] are damages in tort and are intended to put the representee into the position in which he would have been if the tort had not been committed; while damages for a misrepresentation having contractual force are damages for breach of contract and are intended to put the representee into the position in which he would have been if the contract had been performed.[712] If, eg, he is induced to buy a thing by a misrepresentation as to a quality which it lacks, his damages in tort will be the difference between the price he paid for the thing and its actual value (assessed prima facie but not invariably [713] at the date of the transaction),[714] while in contract they will be the difference between the thing's actual value and the value that it would have had, if the representation had been true.[715] In addition the representee may be entitled to consequential loss which in contract can include profits which he would have made from the thing if the representation had been true; in tort he can at most recover the profit that an alternative investment would have yielded.[716] Consequential loss is recoverable only if it is not too remote and the test of remoteness is more favourable to the claimant in tort than it is in contract[717] (particularly if the defendant is,[718] or is treated as if he were,[719] guilty of fraud). Damages in lieu of rescission under section 2(2) of the 1967 Act

---

[704] *Heilbut Symons & Co v Buckleton* [1913] AC 30, 47.

[705] Except, perhaps, where the representee was already bound to enter into the main contract: see 1.47.

[706] *William Sindall plc v Cambridgeshire CC* [1994] 1 WLR 1016, 1036, 1043.

[707] For refusal to exercise the discretion, see *Highland Insurance Co v Continental Insurance Co* [1987] 1 Lloyd's Rep 109.

[708] Rescission does not bar a claim for damages under s 2(1).

[709] cf *The Lucy* [1983] 1 Lloyd's Rep 188, 201–202; contrast *Zanzibar v British Aerospace (Lancaster House) Ltd* [2000] 1 WLR 2333.

[710] *Thomas Witter Ltd v T B P Industries Ltd* [1996] 2 All ER 573, 591.

[711] *F & H Entertainment Ltd v Leisure Enterprises Ltd* (1976) 240 EG 455.

[712] *Twycross v Grant* (1877) 2 CPD 496, 504; *South Australia Asset Management Corp v York Montague Ltd* [1997] AC 191, 216.

[713] *Smith New Court Securities Ltd v Scrimgeour Vickers (Asset Management) Ltd* [1997] AC 254.

[714] *Twycross v Grant*, n 712; cf *Clef Aquitaine SARL v Laporte Materials (Barrow) Ltd* [2001] QB 488, where the seller's misrepresentation related to the price at which he sold similar goods to other buyers and the damages in tort were the extra amount which the buyer was thus induced to pay.

[715] eg Sale of Goods Act 1979, s 53(3).

[716] *East v Maurer* [1991] 1 WLR 461.

[717] *The Heron II* [1969] 1 AC 350.

[718] *Doyle v Olby Ironmongers Ltd* [1969] 2 QB 158, 167.

[719] *Royscot Trust Ltd v Rogerson* [1991] 2 QB 297 as to which see n 694.

are *sui generis* and may be restricted to the amount by which the value of what the representor received exceeds that of what he gave in return.[720]

(g) Indemnity

1.174 There is no right to damages for a wholly innocent misrepresentation having no contractual force; nor, where rescission is ordered or upheld, or (arguably) where the right to rescind has been lost, is there any discretion to award damages in lieu.[721] The court may, however, as part of the process of rescission, order the representor to pay an 'indemnity'. Such an order may be made in respect, not only of payments made by the representee to the representor, but also of sums spent by the representee in performing his other obligations under the contract.[722] An indemnity is distinct from damages in that it is not available in respect of loss suffered in consequence of acts which the representee did in reliance on the contract without being required under it to do them.[723]

(4) Rescission

(a) Rescission for misrepresentation

(i) Option to rescind

1.175 Misrepresentation gives the representee the option to avoid the contract.[724] If he exercises the option, the contract is 'wipe(d)...out altogether'[725] so that each party is released from his obligations under the contract and the representee is entitled to recover what he has given, on terms of restoring what he has received, under it.[726]

(ii) Contract not void

1.176 Unlike mistake, which can make a contract void,[727] misrepresentation makes the contract voidable by the representee. Hence if A is induced by some fraud of B (not inducing a fundamental mistake) to sell and deliver goods to B, then B can transfer a good title to C if C buys the goods from B in good faith before A has rescinded the contract.[728] By contrast, if the fraud does lead to a fundamental mistake B, and hence C, will acquire no title to the goods.[729]

(iii) Modes of rescission

1.177 Under the rule stated in 1.176 it is crucial to know when the contract has been rescinded. This question can give rise to difficulties since rescission can be effected either by taking legal proceedings (which may be needed to work out the consequences of rescission) or extra-judicially: eg by retaking goods obtained by fraud[730] or by giving notice to the representor.[731] Obviously no such steps can be taken where the representor has absconded with goods

---

[720] See *William Sindall v Cambridgeshire CC* [1994] 1 WLR 1016, 1038, 1044.
[721] See 1.172.
[722] *Newbigging v Adam* (1886) 34 Ch D 582; and see (1888) 13 App Cas 308.
[723] *Whittington v Seale-Hayne* (1900) 82 LT 49.
[724] *Clough v London & North Western Rly* (1871) LR 7 Ex 26, 34; *Redgrave v Hurd* (1881) 20 Ch D 1.
[725] *The Kanchenjunga* [1990] 1 Lloyd's Rep 391, 398.
[726] See 1.182.
[727] See 1.136 and 1.146.
[728] *White v Garden* (1851) 10 CB 919; *Lewis v Averay* [1972] 1 QB 198.
[729] *Cundy v Lindsay* (1878) 3 App Cas 459; 1.142.
[730] *Re Eastgate* [1905] 1 KB 465, doubted on another point in *Re Goldcorp Exchange Ltd* [1995] 1 AC 74, 103.
[731] eg *Reese Silver Mining Co v Smith* (1869) LR 4 HL 64.

obtained by fraud. In one such case, giving notice to the police was held to suffice,[732] with the unfortunate result of depriving a good faith purchaser of the goods.[733] This rule seems to be designed to protect victims of fraud and so not to apply where the misrepresentation was negligent or wholly innocent.

(b) Termination for breach

A breach of contract may entitle the victim to terminate the contract; generally he can do **1.178** so only if the breach is a sufficiently serious one.[734] Since such termination is based on a defect in the performance, as opposed to one in the formation, of a contract, it does not (like rescission for misrepresentation) retrospectively annul the contract; hence it does not deprive the injured party of his right to damages for the breach.[735] The two processes overlap where a misrepresentation which has induced a contract then becomes one of its terms. The right to rescind for misrepresentation[736] survives such incorporation,[737] though if the matter to which the misrepresentation relates is only slight, then the court may, under section 2(2) of the Misrepresentation Act 1967, uphold the contract and award damages in lieu.[738] If the untruth of the incorporated representation is such as to give rise to a right to rescind for breach, the injured party can either rescind for misrepresentation or terminate for breach. He will usually take the latter course since this can (unlike the former) be combined with a claim for damages for breach and is probably not subject to the court's discretion under section 2(2).

(c) Misrepresentation as a defence

A person who has been induced by a misrepresentation to enter into a contract can, to the **1.179** extent that he has not performed his part, rely on the misrepresentation as a defence to an action on the contract.[739] This defensive stance is sometimes regarded as a form of rescission but it is not in all respects governed by the same rules as the process of a representee's claiming the return of what he gave under the contract. To make good such a claim, he must restore what he received under the contract;[740] but there is no such requirement where the victim of a fraudulent representation simply relies on it as a defence to a claim by the representor.[741] This somewhat harsh rule is probably meant to deter fraud[742] and there is no authority to support it where the representation is negligent or wholly innocent.

(d) Limits to rescission

Rescission is a source of potential hardship to (a) third parties and (b) the representor. Of the **1.180** restrictions on the scope of the remedy (to be discussed below) the first is designed to avoid the former, and the others the latter, type of hardship.

---

[732] *Car & Universal Finance Co Ltd v Caldwell* [1965] 1 QB 525; contrast, in Scotland, *Macleod v Ker* 1965 SC 253.

[733] For criticism, see Law Revision Committee, 12th Report, para 16 (Cmnd 2958, 1966).

[734] For this requirement, and the exceptions to it, see 1.365 et seq.

[735] See 1.427.

[736] A mere breach of a promise gives no such right: see 1.162.

[737] Misrepresentation Act 1967, s 1(a).

[738] See 1.172.

[739] *Redgrave v Hurd* (1881) 20 Ch D 1.

[740] See 1.182.

[741] *Feise v Parkinson* (1812) 4 Taunt 640, 641; Marine Insurance Act 1906, s 84(1) and (3)(a); *Berg v Sadler & Moore* [1937] 2 KB 158. For the position where rescission for *duress* takes the form of simply relying on this factor as a defence, see *Halpern v Halpern* [2007] EWCA Civ 291; [2007] 2 Lloyd's Rep 56.

[742] *South Australia Asset Management Corp v York Montague Ltd* [1997] AC 191, 215.

(i) Third party rights

1.181 Once an innocent third party has for value acquired an interest in the subject matter of a contract induced by the misrepresentation, the contract cannot be rescinded so as to deprive him of that interest.[743]

(ii) Restitution impossible

1.182 Except in the situation described in 1.179, a person seeking to rescind a contract must restore what he has received under it. Where he has received money, restitution need not be in specie: he simply restores an equivalent sum.[744] The difficult cases are those in which some benefit other than money has been received and cannot be fully or literally restored.

1.183 **Changes in subject matter made by representee.**   The right to rescind is barred if the representee has disposed of the subject matter or so diminished its value as no longer to be able to make substantial restitution.[745] But if he can make substantial, though not precise, restitution, he can rescind on restoring the subject matter with an allowance for the diminution in value[746] and (even if there is no such diminution) for any benefits derived by him from his use of the thing.[747] Diminution in value is not a bar to rescission if it occurs in the course of a reasonable test of the accuracy of the representation.[748]

1.184 **Changes in subject matter made by representor.**   Where the misrepresentation is that of the buyer, and the seller wishes to rescind, changes made by the buyer do not as a matter of law bar the seller's right to rescind[749] (though they might deprive him of any interest in exercising it). If the seller wishes to rescind, he will have not only to repay the price but also to make an allowance in respect of the buyer's other expenses if incurred in the performance of the contract,[750] though not if they were incurred for some other reason and did not benefit the representee.[751]

1.185 **Other deterioration or decline in value.**   Deterioration or decline in value does not bar the right to rescind where it is due either to the very defect in the subject matter which it was represented not to have or to some external cause: eg to a fall in the market value of shares[752] or to damage to goods caused by a third party.[753]

(iii) Affirmation

1.186 The right to rescind for misrepresentation is lost if, with knowledge of the truth, the representee affirms the contract. Affirmation may be express or inferred from conduct, such as retaining goods or shares[754] or remaining in occupation of land.[755] Failure to rescind in

---

[743] See 1.176 and cf 1.210.

[744] The same may be true of other fungibles: *Smith New Court Securities Ltd v Scrimgeour Vickers (Asset Management) Ltd* [1997] AC 254, 264.

[745] *Clarke v Dickson* (1858) El Bl & El 148; *Lagunas Nitrate Co v Lagunas Syndicate* [1899] 2 Ch 392.

[746] *Erlanger v New Sombrero Phosphate Co* (1878) 3 App Cas 1218.

[747] *Hulton v Hulton* [1917] 1 KB 813, 826.

[748] cf *Head v Tattersall* (1871) LR 7 Ex 7, 12.

[749] *Spence v Crawford* [1939] 3 All ER 271.

[750] *Spence v Crawford* [1939] 3 All ER 271.

[751] cf *Mackenzie v Royal Bank of Canada* [1934] AC 468.

[752] *Armstrong v Jackson* [1917] 2 KB 822.

[753] *Head v Tattersall* (1871) LR 7 Ex 7.

[754] eg *United Shoe Machinery Co of Canada v Brunet* [1909] AC 330; *Western Bank of Scotland v Addie* (1867) LR 1 Sc & Div 145.

[755] *Kennard v Ashman* (1894) 10 TLR 213.

ignorance of the truth does not amount to affirmation and will not of itself bar the right to rescind for misrepresentation.[756]

(iv) Lapse of time

The right to rescind for innocent misrepresentation is barred by lapse of time, which begins **1.187** to run when the contract was made or perhaps when the representee ought, acting reasonably, to have discovered the truth.[757] Where the representation is fraudulent, lapse of time is not itself a bar to rescission though it may, after discovery of the truth,[758] be evidence of affirmation.[759]

(v) Misrepresentation Act 1967, section 2(2)

This subsection gives the court a discretion to declare the contract subsisting and to award **1.188** damages in lieu of rescission. The discretion may be exercised even where none of the above bars to rescission has arisen; but if such a bar has arisen the court has no discretion: it *must* refuse to allow rescission.

(5) Excluding Liability for Misrepresentation

At common law, liability for misrepresentation can be excluded,[760] subject to the restrictions **1.189** discussed in section D. But under section 3 of the Misrepresentation Act 1967 the requirement of reasonableness (as stated in the Unfair Contract Terms Act 1977) applies to terms by which one party to a contract purports to exclude or restrict[761] his liability to the other[762] for misrepresentation inducing the contract.

(6) Non-disclosure

(a) General rules

A misrepresentation need not be made in so many words: it may be inferred from conduct **1.190** (as in the stock case of papering over the cracks)[763] or from stating a misleading half-truth.[764] But where no representation, express or implied, has been made, the general rule is that there is no civil liability either on a seller for failing to disclose facts which reduce,[765] or on a buyer for failing to disclose facts which increase,[766] the value of the subject matter.[767] The rule is based on the difficulty of specifying which of the many facts known to each party and affecting the bargain would need to be disclosed.

---

[756] It may bar the right to rescind for misrepresentation by lapse of time: see 1.187; or the right to rescind for breach: see 1.389.

[757] See *Leaf v International Galleries* [1950] 2 KB 86.

[758] *Aaron's Reefs Ltd v Twiss* [1896] AC 273, 287.

[759] *Clough v London & North Western Rly* (1871) LR 7 Ex 26, 35.

[760] *Toomey v Eagle Star Insurance Co Ltd (No 2)* [1995] 2 Lloyd's Rep 88.

[761] The courts have experienced some difficulty in deciding when a clause 'excludes or restricts' liability for this purpose: see *Raiffeisen Zentralbank Osterreich AG v Royal Bank of Scotland plc* [2010] EWHC 1392 (Comm), [2011] 1 Lloyd's Rep 123, at [310]; *Axa Sun Life Services plc v Campbell Martin Ltd* [2011] EWCA Civ 133, [2011] 2 Lloyd's Rep 1.

[762] Section 3 of the 1967 Act would not apply where the representation induces a contract with a third person, as in *Smith v Eric S Bush* [1990] AC 831. Section 2(2) of the 1977 Act could apply in such a case, but only where the liability in question was 'business liability'; there is no such requirement in s 3 of the 1967 Act.

[763] See *Gordon v Selico Co Ltd* (1986) 278 EG 53.

[764] *Nottingham Patent Brick & Tile Co v Butler* (1886) 16 QBD 778.

[765] *Ward v Hobbs* (1878) 4 App Cas 13.

[766] *Smith v Hughes* (1871) LR 6 QB 587, 604; but there is criminal liability for certain kinds of 'insider dealing' under Criminal Justice Act 1993, Part V.

[767] For defects constituting a source of *danger* see 1.197.

(b) Exceptional cases

1.191 Some duty of disclosure exists in the situations described in 1.192 to 1.199. In these situations, a person need generally disclose only facts that he (or his agent)[768] knows at the time of contracting, though the duty in certain cases ceases before that point.[769] It may also extend after that point, especially where the contract itself imposes the duty of disclosure.[770]

1.192 **Change of circumstances.** A representation about the subject matter of negotiations may be true when made but be wholly falsified by a radical change of circumstances before the contract is made. That change must then be disclosed,[771] at least if the interval between the representation and the conclusion of the contract is not so long as to make it unreasonable for the representee still to rely on the representation.[772] The same rule probably applies where the representation is one of an intention which is later changed,[773] unless the intention originally stated is such as is intrinsically likely to be changed.[774]

1.193 **Utmost good faith.** In certain types of contracts (known as contracts *uberrimae fidei*) there is a duty to disclose material facts on the ground that one party is typically in a much better position than the other to know such facts. The prime example is the contract of insurance where 'the insurer knows nothing and the...[insured] knows everything'.[775] Hence the latter must, in general,[776] disclose all such facts as a prudent insurer would take into account in deciding whether or on what terms to accept the risk.[777] The insurer is under a reciprocal duty to disclose facts material to the risk known to him but not to the insured.[778]

1.194 Certain agreements between members of a family for settling disputes as to family property are likewise contracts *uberrimae fidei*.[779]

1.195 **Limited duty of disclosure.** Contracts under which there is a more limited duty of disclosure than that just described include contracts of suretyship, in which the creditor must disclose unusual facts which the surety would not normally expect,[780] and contracts for the sale of land, in which the vendor must disclose unusual defects of title which a prudent purchaser would not be expected to discover.[781] There are also certain requirements of disclosure in relation to compromises of invalid claims and exemption clauses.[782]

---

[768] *Blackburn, Low & Co v Vigors* (1887) 12 App Cas 531.

[769] *Cory v Patton* (1872) LR 7 QB 304 (insurance binding before contract as a matter of business).

[770] *Phillips v Foxall* (1872) LR 7 QB 666 (fidelity bond); *The Star Sea* [2001] UKHL 1, [2003] AC 469; in such cases, the non-disclosure does not *induce* the contract, but is a *breach* of it: see 1.201.

[771] *With v O'Flanagan* [1936] Ch 575; cf *The Kriti Palm* [2006] EWCA Civ 1601, [2007] 1 All ER (Comm) 667, at [383], [440].

[772] cf *Argy Trading Development Co Ltd v Lapid Developments Ltd* [1977] 1 WLR 444, 461–2.

[773] *Traill v Baring* (1864) 4 DJ & S 318.

[774] *Wales v Wadham* [1977] 1 WLR 199, disapproved on another ground in *Livesey v Jenkins* [1985] AC 424 (intention not to remarry).

[775] *Rozanes v Bowen* (1928) 32 Lloyd's List Rep 98, 102.

[776] There are exceptions: eg facts which the insurer knows or which diminish the risk need not be disclosed: *Carter v Boehm* (1766) 3 Burr 1905, 1910. See also Consumer (Disclosure and Representations) Act 2012.

[777] *Lambert v Co-operative Insurance Society Ltd* [1975] 2 Lloyd's Rep 485; Marine Insurance Act 1906, s 18(2); *Pan Atlantic Insurance Co Ltd v Pine Top Insurance Co* [1995] AC 501.

[778] *Carter v Boehm*, n 776, at 1909.

[779] *Greenwood v Greenwood* (1863) 2 DJ & S 28.

[780] *Levett v Barclays Bank plc* [1995] 1 WLR 1260. Typically the contract will be one of suretyship if the surety is selected by the debtor but it may be one of insurance if he is selected by the creditor and so is likely to know less than the creditor about the debtor's creditworthiness: see *Trade Indemnity Co Ltd v Workington Harbour Board* [1937] AC 1.

[781] *Rignall Developments Ltd v Halil* [1988] Ch 190; *William Sindall plc v Cambridgeshire CC* [1994] 1 WLR 1016, 1023.

[782] See 1.44; *Curtis v Chemical Cleaning and Dyeing Co Ltd* [1951] 1 KB 805, 809.

Relationship of parties.   A duty of disclosure may arise because there is a 'fiduciary' rela-   **1.196**
tionship between the parties: eg that of principal and agent.[783] Commonly such a duty is
one which arises in the *performance* of a contract; but its breach may also *induce* a further
contract[784] and it is with this aspect of the duty that the present discussion is concerned.

Latent defects.   A seller is under no duty to disclose latent defects which merely affect   **1.197**
the value of the subject matter; but he may be liable in negligence for failing to warn the
buyer of a defect which is a source of danger and causes personal injury or damage to other
property.[785]

Custom.   A duty of disclosure may be imposed by a trade or market custom.[786]   **1.198**

Legislation.   Extensive duties of disclosure are imposed by statute in relation to listing of   **1.199**
securities and to company prospectuses.[787]

(c) Effects of non-disclosure

Cases of 'non-disclosure' can be divided into those of *inferred representation* in which a repre-   **1.200**
sentation is inferred from conduct or from failure to correct a representation falsified by later
events; and those of *pure non-disclosure* in which the law provides a remedy though no such
inference can be drawn. In cases of inferred representation, the injured parties' remedies by
way of damages and rescission are the same as those for express misrepresentation. In cases
of pure non-disclosure the remedies are sometimes by way of rescission only: this is the position in contracts of insurance;[788] and sometimes by way of damages only: this is the position
where the statutory duty described in 1.199 is broken.[789] The distinction between the two
groups of cases is also relevant for the purposes of the Misrepresentation Act 1967, where the
phrase 'misrepresentation made'[790] seems to cover cases of inferred representation but not
those of pure non-disclosure.

It is further necessary to distinguish between non-disclosure which *induces* the making of a   **1.201**
contract and non-disclosure which amounts to a *breach* of a contract after it has been made.[791]
In the latter case, the right to terminate is governed by the rules which apply to termination
for breach.[792] Such termination differs from rescission for an inducing non-disclosure in two
ways: it does not retrospectively annul the contract[793] and it is generally available only where
the breach is a serious one.[794]

---

[783] eg *Armstrong v Jackson* [1917] 2 KB 822; cf *Item Software (UK) Ltd v Fassihi* [2004] EWCA Civ 1244,
[2005] ICR 450 (company director); *Conlon v Sims* [2006] EWCA Civ 1749, [2007] 3 All ER 802, at [127]–
[128] (prospective partners).

[784] *Sybron Corporation v Rochem Ltd* [1984] Ch 112.

[785] *Hurley v Dyke* [1979] RTR 265, 303.

[786] *Jones v Bowden* (1813) 4 Taunt 847.

[787] Financial Services and Markets Act 2000, s 80.

[788] *Banque Keyser Ullmann SA v Skandia (UK) Insurance Co Ltd* [1990] 1 QB 65, 779–781, aff'd on this
point [1991] 2 AC 249, 288.

[789] *Re South of England Natural Gas Co* [1911] 1 Ch 573.

[790] In s 2(1) and (2).

[791] cf n 770.

[792] *The Star Sea* [2001] UKHL 1, [2003] AC 439.

[793] See 1.422, 1.424; and cf 1.174, 1.177 for an exception in the case of fraudulent insurance claims, see
The Star Sea, n 792, at [62].

[794] See 1.365, 1.366.

(7) Estoppel by Representation

1.202 A person who makes a precise and unambiguous representation of fact may be 'estopped' (ie prevented) from denying its truth if the person to whom it was made was intended to act in reliance on it and did so act to his detriment.[795] Such an estoppel does not give rise to a cause of action[796] but only to a defence: eg it could provide a tenant with a defence to an action for breach of covenant to repair without making the landlord liable in damages for disrepair. It could, however, make the landlord liable for wrongfully ejecting the tenant for alleged breach of covenant to repair, the tenant's cause of action in such a case being based on the lease and not on the representation.[797]

G. Improper Pressure

(1) Duress

1.203 At common law, a contract made under duress is voidable[798] by the victim of the duress. Duress may take one of three forms: duress of the person,[799] duress of goods[800] and economic duress.[801] There are two principal components to any duress claim. The first is the application of illegitimate pressure.[802] A threat may be illegitimate because either the threat[803] or what is threatened is legally wrongful,[804] albeit pressure need not be unlawful for it to be regarded as illegitimate.[805] A threat to break a contract can, but will not necessarily, amount to the application of illegitimate pressure.[806] On the other hand, mere 'commercial pressure'[807] or a threat to exercise contractual rights[808] will not generally be regarded as illegitimate. Second, the illegitimate pressure must have caused the party subject to the pressure to enter into the contract. In the case of duress of the person it suffices that the pressure was a cause of the decision to enter into the contract.[809] But in the case of economic duress, the pressure must either have been a 'but for'[810] or a 'significant'[811] cause of the decision to

---

[795] *Low v Bouverie* [1891] 3 Ch 82; *Woodhouse AC Israel Cocoa Ltd v Nigerian Produce Marketing Co* [1982] AC 741.

[796] *Low v Bouverie*, n 795, at 101.

[797] cf in an analogous context, *Coventry, Sheppard & Co v The Great Eastern Rly Co* (1883) 11 QBD 776.

[798] *Pao On v Lau Yiu Long* [1980] AC 614, 634; *The Universe Sentinel* [1983] 1 AC 366, 383, 400; *Borrelli v Ting* [2010] UKPC 21, at [34] (contract held to be 'invalid'). The contract is not *void*.

[799] *Barton v Armstrong* [1976] AC 104.

[800] *Astley v Reynolds* (1731) 2 Str 915. The decision in *Skeate v Beale* (1840) 11 Ad & E 983, in which it was held that the unlawful detention of another's goods does not constitute duress, is unlikely to be followed today: *The Evia Luck (No 2)* [1992] 2 AC 152, 165.

[801] *The Siboen and the Sibotre* [1976] 1 Lloyd's Rep 293; *Pao On v Lau Yiu Long*, n 798; *The Universe Sentinel*, n 798; *The Evia Luck (No 2)*, n 800; *DSDN Subsea Ltd v Petroleum Geo-Services ASA* [2000] BLR 530; *R v Attorney-General for England and Wales* [2003] UKPC 22.

[802] *The Universe Sentinel*, n 798.

[803] *The Universe Sentinel* [1983] 1 AC 366, 401 (blackmail).

[804] *The Universe Sentinel* [1983] 1 AC 366, 383.

[805] *Progress Bulk Carriers Ltd v Tube City IMS LLC* [2012] EWHC 273, [2012] 1 Lloyd's Rep 501, at [42].

[806] *Kolmar Group AG v Traxpo Enterprises Pty Ltd* [2010] EWHC 113 (Comm), [2010] 2 Lloyd's Rep 653, at [92].

[807] *Pao On v Lau Yiu Long*, n 798.

[808] *CTN Cash & Carry Ltd v Gallagher* [1994] 4 All ER 714; *Alf Vaughan & Co Ltd v Royscot Trust plc* [1999] 1 All ER (Comm) 856.

[809] *Barton v Armstrong*, n 799: the threat must be a reason for the decision or present in the claimant's mind.

[810] *Kolmar Group AG v Traxpo Enterprises Pty Ltd*, n 806, at [92]

[811] *The Evia Luck (No 2)*, n 800, at 165; *Huyton SA v Peter Cremer GmbH & Co Inc* [1999] 1 Lloyd's Rep 620, 636–637.

enter into the contract. When considering whether the pressure was a sufficient cause of the decision to enter into the contract, the court will have regard to the reasonableness of the alternatives open to the party subject to the pressure.[812]

(2) Undue Influence

(a) The forms which undue influence may assume

A contract may be set aside on the ground that one party entered into it under the undue **1.204** influence of another. Undue influence may take different forms. Traditionally, a distinction was drawn between actual and presumed undue influence but the significance of this distinction has diminished in recent years.[813] The cases can be placed along a spectrum. At one end, there are cases akin to common law duress in which the influence which one party has exerted over the other takes the form of the application of pressure.[814] At the other end of the spectrum are cases in which the law presumes that there is a relationship of influence between the parties and puts the onus on the party in the position of influence to rebut the presumption that undue influence has been exercised.[815] To make good a case of undue influence it is generally insufficient to establish that one party was reliant or dependent upon the other. It is usually[816] necessary to go further and establish that the party against whom relief is sought took unfair advantage of the other party or otherwise unfairly exploited his position of influence.[817]

(b) Actual undue influence

Equity gives relief where, though no threat has been made, undue influence has been exer- **1.205** cised by one party over the other.[818] The party claiming relief must show that the influence existed and that its exercise brought about the transaction;[819] he need not show that the transaction was to his manifest disadvantage.[820]

(c) Presumed undue influence

Equity also gives relief where the relationship between two persons is such as to give rise to **1.206** a 'presumption of undue influence'.[821] This arises where the party seeking to impugn the transaction establishes[822] that the transaction 'calls for explanation': eg, because it is a substantial transfer of property (as opposed to a moderate Christmas gift[823]) or a guarantee by A of B's business debts. The effect of establishing these facts is to give rise to 'a rebuttable evidential presumption of undue influence'[824] to the effect that 'in the absence of a satisfactory

---

[812] *B & S Contracts and Design Ltd v Victor Green Publications Ltd* [1984] ICR 419.
[813] Especially after the decision of the House of Lords in *Royal Bank of Scotland v Etridge (No 2)* [2001] UKHL 44, [2002] 2 AC 773 (hereafter 'the *Etridge* case').
[814] *Williams v Bayley* (1866) LR 1 HL 200; the *Etridge* case, n 813, at [8].
[815] The *Etridge* case, n 813, at [9].
[816] But it may not be necessary in all cases: *Pesticcio v Huet* [2004] EWCA Civ 372, [2004] WTLR 699.
[817] *R v Attorney-General for England and Wales* [2003] UKPC 22, at [21]; *National Commercial Bank (Jamaica) Ltd v Hew* [2003] UKPC 51, at [29]–[31].
[818] *Williams v Bayley* (1866) LR 1 HL 200.
[819] *Howes v Bishop* [1909] 2 KB 390.
[820] *CIBC Mortgages v Pitt* [1994] AC 200; the *Etridge* case, n 813, at [12].
[821] *Barclays Bank plc v O'Brien* [1994] 1 AC 180, 189; the *Etridge* case, n 813, at [16]. The following account is based mainly on the speech of Lord Nicholls (with which Lords Bingham at [3] and Clyde at [91] agreed).
[822] The *Etridge* case, n 813, at [13], [14].
[823] The *Etridge* case, n 813, at [24], [156].
[824] The *Etridge* case, n 813, at [16], [153], [194].

explanation, the transaction can only have been procured by undue influence'.[825] It will then be up to B to rebut the presumption.[826] A common way of rebutting the presumption is to show that A was independently[827] and competently[828] advised; it can also be rebutted by other evidence that A's will was not 'overborne'[829] or that the transaction was a result of the exercise by the claimant of 'full, free and informed thought'.[830]

1.207   The fact that A reposed trust and confidence in B can be established in one of two ways. First, it can be established by showing that the relationship between them belonged to a group in which 'the law presumes irrebuttably'[831] that B had influence over A: eg where the relationship is that of parent and child,[832] trustee and beneficiary[833] or solicitor and client.[834] The effect of this irrebuttable presumption is merely that the influence *exists*. It is not of itself a ground for relief: eg, a moderate Christmas gift from a child to its parent would not be invalid since it would not 'call for explanation'.[835] A second way of establishing that A reposed trust and confidence in B is to show that this was in fact the position. This possibility covers a wide range of situations which 'cannot be listed exhaustively'.[836] It applies to the relationship of husband and wife (or other cohabitants) living together.[837] Such persons normally repose trust and confidence in each other,[838] but even a substantial gift by A to B, or a guarantee by A of B's business debts will not normally[839] 'call for explanation' since, between such persons, transactions of this kind can plausibly be accounted for by motives of affection or joint interest.[840] The restricted scope of the 'evidential presumption' in such cases reflects the point that the influence often leads to a transaction with a bank which has lent money on the security of the couple's home who then have a common interest in resisting the enforcement of the security. There is, however, a 'minority of cases'[841] in which the husband has taken advantage of the wife's 'vulnerability';[842] the law will then protect the wife against such conduct,[843] though it is not clear whether it will do so on the ground of actual[844] or of presumed[845] undue influence.

---

[825] The *Etridge* case, n 813, at [14]; eg *Randall v Randall* [2004] EWHC 2285, [2005] WTLR 119.

[826] *Allcard v Skinner* (1887) 36 Ch D 145.

[827] *Inche Noriah v Shaik Allie Bin Omar* [1929] AC 127; for the position between the victim and a third party, see 1.210.

[828] See *Pesticcio v Hurst* [2004] EWCA Civ 372, [2004] WTLR 699.

[829] The *Etridge* case, n 813, at [162].

[830] *Hackett v Crown Prosecution Service* [2011] EWHC 1170 (Admin). The presumption will not be rebutted by demonstrating that there was a reasonable explanation for the transaction (*Smith v Cooper* [2010] EWCA Civ 722, [2010] 2 FCR 551).

[831] The *Etridge* case, n 813, at [18].

[832] *Bullock v Lloyd's Bank* [1995] Ch 317.

[833] *Ellis v Barker* (1871) LR 7 Ch App 104; *Thomson v Eastwood* (1877) 2 App Cas 215.

[834] *Wright v Carter* [1903] 1 Ch 27.

[835] The *Etridge* case, n 813, at [14].

[836] The *Etridge* case, n 813, at [10]; for illustrations, see *Tate v Williamson* (1866) LR 2 Ch App 55 (financial adviser and dissolute client); *O'Sullivan v Management Agency & Music Ltd* [1985] QB 428 (manager and unknown song-writer who later became a celebrity).

[837] *Howes v Bishop* [1909] 2 KB 390; *Barclays Bank plc v O'Brien* [1994] 1 AC 180, 198.

[838] The *Etridge* case, n 813, at [45], [159].

[839] The *Etridge* case, n 813, at [30].

[840] The *Etridge* case, n 813, at [159]; hence in the *Etridge* case two members of the House of Lords rejected or doubted the existence of any presumption in the husband and wife cases.

[841] The *Etridge* case, n 813, at [37].

[842] The *Etridge* case, n 813, at [36]; cf at [163].

[843] *Barclays Bank v Coleman* [2001] QB 20, aff'd in the *Etridge* case, n 813.

[844] The *Etridge* case, n 813, at [130].

[845] The *Etridge* case, n 813, at [291].

(d) Unconscionable bargains

Even in the absence of actual or presumed undue influence, equity sometimes gave relief **1.208**
against bargains regarded as 'unconscionable' because one party had exploited some weakness
of the other.[846] On this ground sales of 'reversions' by 'expectant heirs' could be set aside
for simple undervalue, though this is no longer of itself a ground for relief.[847] According
to one view, 'inequality of bargaining power' is similarly a ground for giving relief to the
weaker party;[848] but the prevailing view is that relief is not *generally* available on this ground
alone.[849] There are, however, a number of *specific* instances in which the abuse of superior
bargaining power is a ground for relief under legislation[850] or judge-made rules.[851]

(e) Bars to relief

(i) General

Relief on equitable grounds discussed in 1.204 to 1.207 is, like rescission for misre- **1.209**
presentation,[852] barred by inability to make restitution,[853] affirmation,[854] lapse of time[855] and
the intervention of third party rights. Only the last of these bars calls for further discussion.

(ii) Third party rights

Relief for undue influence may be sought against a third party: eg, where A is induced by such **1.210**
influence exerted by B to mortgage A's house as security for a business debt owed by B to C,
or to guarantee such a debt. A can then set the transaction aside against C if C either knew of
the undue influence or was 'put on enquiry'.[856] This (not strictly accurate)[857] phrase means
that C is under a duty to take reasonable steps[858] to reduce the risk of A's entering into the
transaction as a result of undue influence (or other vitiating factor). Whether C is under such
a duty depends on two factors. The first is the nature of the transaction. For example, the duty
arises where A guarantees B's business debts to C,[859] but not where C makes a joint loan to
A and B, since on its face the latter may, while the former does not, benefit A.[860] The second
factor is the relationship between A and B. In many of the decided cases, A was B's wife,[861]
but the duty can also arise where A is B's husband,[862] where they are unmarried cohabitants

---

[846] *Evans v Llewellin* (1787) 1 Cox CC 333; *Cresswell v Cresswell* [1978] 1 WLR 255 n; *Strydom v Vendside Ltd* [2009] EWHC 2130 (QB), at [36].

[847] *Aylesford v Morris* (1873) LR 8 Ch App 484; *Nevill v Snelling* (1880) 15 Ch D 679; Law of Property Act 1925, s 174.

[848] *Lloyds Bank Ltd v Bundy* [1975] QB 326, 339, *per* Lord Denning MR.

[849] *Pao On v Lau Yiu Long*, n 798, at 634; *National Westminster Bank plc v Morgan* [1985] AC 686, 708.

[850] See, eg, Consumer Credit Act 1974, ss 140A and 140B (relief for individual debtor under a consumer credit agreement whose relationship with the creditor is 'unfair' to the debtor), on which see *Plevin v Paragon Finance Ltd* [2014] UKSC 61, [2014] 1 WLR 4222.

[851] eg, 1.242 (restraint of trade).

[852] See 1.181–1.187.

[853] ie substantial restitution: see the *O'Sullivan* case, n 836. cf *Halpern v Halpern* [2007] EWCA Civ 291; [2007] 2 Lloyd's Rep 56, a case of alleged duress in which it seems to be assumed that such cases are not governed by the special rule (stated in 1.179) which applies where rescission for *fraud* takes the form of simply relying on this vitiating factor as a defence.

[854] *Mitchell v Homfray* (1882) 8 QBD 587.

[855] *Allcard v Skinner* (1887) 36 Ch D 145, 187.

[856] The *Etridge* case, n 813, at [44].

[857] The *Etridge* case, n 813, at [41].

[858] The *Etridge* case, n 813, at [54].

[859] The *Etridge* case, n 813, at [48], [47].

[860] The *Etridge* case, n 813, at [48].

[861] This was the position in the situations under review in the *Etridge* case, n 813.

[862] The *Etridge* case, n 813, at [47].

(whether hetero- or homosexual)[863] or where they are in some other relationship of trust and confidence.[864] The duty may extend to all cases in which A acts as surety for B's debts on a non-commercial basis.[865] Where the duty arises, C must communicate directly[866] with A to the effect that C will require a solicitor acting for A (who may also act for B and C)[867] to confirm to C that the solicitor has, at a meeting with A at which B was not present, explained to A the nature and effects of the document embodying the transaction.[868] If C takes these steps, C is normally entitled to rely on the solicitor's confirmation that the transaction has been duly explained to A.[869] Failure to take these steps is not itself a ground for relief: it does not dispense with A's need to make a case of actual or presumed undue influence.

H. Illegality

1.211 The law refuses to give full legal effect to contracts which are illegal (or affected by illegality) because they are contrary either to law or to public policy.

(1) Contracts Contrary to Law

(a) Making of contract forbidden by law

1.212 A contract is illegal if the mere making of it amounts to a criminal offence, such as a criminal conspiracy.[870] A contract to finance another person's litigation in return for a share in the proceeds formerly amounted to the crime of champerty. Such a contract remains illegal even after the abolition of criminal liability for champerty;[871] but legislation now in many cases validates agreements in writing for the payment by a client to a person who provides him with advocacy or litigation services of a 'conditional fee', payable only if the litigation ends in the client's favour.[872]

1.213 Where legislation prohibits the making of a contract without rendering it criminal, the contract is illegal only if in the court's view this was the purpose of the legislation.[873] If the legislation declares the contract to be merely void, it will not be illegal.[874]

---

[863] *Barclays Bank plc v O'Brien* [1994] 1 AC 180, 196. The rule presumably applies where A and B are civil partners within the Civil Partnership Act 2004.

[864] eg *Crédit Lyonnais Bank Nederland NV v Burch* [1997] 1 All ER 144.

[865] The *Etridge* case, n 813, at [87].

[866] The *Etridge* case, n 813, at [79].

[867] The *Etridge* case, n 813, at [73], [74], [79].

[868] The *Etridge* case, n 813, at [66], [76], [79].

[869] The *Etridge* case, n 813, at [56].

[870] *Scott v Brown* [1892] 2 QB 724.

[871] *Re Thomas* [1894] 1 QB 747; Criminal Law Act 1967, ss 13, 14; *Trendtex Trading Corp v Crédit Suisse* [1982] AC 679; *Callery v Gray* [2001] EWCA Civ 1117, [2001] 1 WLR 2112, aff'd [2002] UKHL 28, [2002] 1 WLR 2000.

[872] Courts and Legal Services Act 1990, ss 58 and 58A; Conditional Fee Agreements Regulations 2000, SI 2000/692; for an account of the history of legislative changes in this branch of the law see *Callery v Gray*, n 871. 'Contingency fee' agreements, by which the legal adviser is remunerated by a share of the proceeds of litigation, remain illegal: *Callery v Gray* [2001] EWCA Civ 117, at [6].

[873] See *Harse v Pearl Life Assurance Co Ltd* [1904] 1 KB 558; cf *Fuji Finance Inc v Aetna Life Insurance Co Ltd* [1997] Ch 173.

[874] Marine Insurance Act 1906, s 4(1); *Re London County Commercial Reinsurance Office Ltd* [1922] 2 Ch 67.

(b) Object of contract contrary to law

A contract having as its object the commission of a crime will often be illegal on the ground **1.214** that it amounts to a criminal conspiracy.[875] It may be illegal even where there is no such conspiracy: eg where the offence is one of strict liability and is committed without guilty intent.[876] On an analogous principle, a contract is illegal if one party to the other's knowledge intended to use the subject matter for an illegal purpose.[877]

A contract for the commission of a civil wrong is illegal if both parties share a guilty intent **1.215** (eg to defraud creditors).[878] But the contract is not illegal if both parties act in good faith;[879] and if only one has a guilty intent, the contract can be enforced by the other.[880] However, the commission of a tort which does not have dishonesty as an essential element, will not fall within the definition of illegality for this purpose.[880a]

(c) Method of performance contrary to law

An offence may be committed in the method of performing a contract which is lawful in **1.216** itself: eg where a carrier of goods by sea overloads his ship. In one such case,[881] it was held that this did not make the contract illegal as the purpose of the legislation which had been contravened was to impose a fine for the prohibited *conduct* and not to prohibit the *contract* (as the carrier's consequent loss of freight would far exceed the fine for the offence).

A contract subject to a licensing or similar requirement is illegal if it is performed[882] (or **1.217** intended to be performed)[883] without the requisite licence. This is also true where legislation requires a person to be licensed to carry on a specified kind of business and expressly or impliedly prohibits contracts made in the course of such a business without the licence.[884] The result of holding the contract invalid could, however, be to prejudice persons of the very class which the licensing requirement was meant to protect; and by statute the illegality does not (in certain cases) deprive such persons of their rights under the contract.[885]

(d) Performance contingent on unlawful act

A promise to pay a person money on his committing an unlawful act is illegal on the principle that a person should not profit from his own wrong; though the application of this rule **1.218** to a case[886] in which it prevented the estate of an insolvent person from recovering under his life insurance policy on his committing suicide (then a crime) is controversial.[887] The principle is qualified in relation to promises to indemnify a person against criminal liability: the promisee cannot enforce such a promise if he committed the crime with guilty intent,[888]

---

[875] See 1.212.
[876] For such cases, see 1.251.
[877] *Langton v Hughes* (1813) 1 M & S 593.
[878] *Mallalieu v Hodgson* (1851) 16 QB 689; *Birkett v Acorn Business Machines Ltd* [1999] 2 All ER (Comm) 429.
[879] Sale of Goods Act 1979, s 12 makes this assumption.
[880] See *Clay v Yates* (1856) 11 H & N 73.
[880a] *Les Laboratoires Servier v Apotex Inc* [2014] UKSC 55, [2015] AC 430, at [28].
[881] *St John Shipping Corp v Joseph Rank Ltd* [1957] 1 QB 267.
[882] eg *J Dennis & Co Ltd v Munn* [1949] 2 KB 327.
[883] eg *Bigos v Bousted* [1951] 1 All ER 92.
[884] *Bedford Insurance Co Ltd v Instituto de Resseguros do Brasil* [1985] 1 QB 966.
[885] Financial Services and Markets Act 2000, ss 26(1), 27(1).
[886] *Beresford v Royal Exchange Assurance* [1938] AC 586.
[887] Since enforcement would have benefited only the wrongdoer's creditors and not the wrongdoer himself.
[888] *Colburn v Patmore* (1834) 1 CM & R 73.

but he probably can enforce it if the offence was one of strict liability and was innocently committed.[889]

1.219   A promise to indemnify a person for civil liability incurred without guilty intent (eg one in an insurance policy against liability for negligence) is valid; indeed a promise of this kind may be implied in law.[890] By contrast, a promise to indemnify a person against liability for an intentional wrong (such as deceit) is illegal.[891] The same is generally true of a promise to indemnify a person against civil liability arising out of his deliberate commission[892] of a crime;[893] but not if the crime was committed without guilty intent.[894] In the case of motor accidents, the *victim* of even deliberate criminal conduct has in certain circumstances rights against the offender's insurer[895] or the Motor Insurers' Bureau.[896]

(2) Contracts Contrary to Public Policy

(a) Introductory

1.220   Contracts are contrary to public policy if they have a clear tendency[897] to bring about a state of affairs which the law regards as harmful. This is an inherently flexible notion, varying in content with changing social and economic conditions. It is therefore a source of uncertainty and of the danger that it could enable courts to invalidate any contracts of which they strongly disapproved. For this reason, the courts have become reluctant to 'invent a new head of public policy',[898] particularly where the allegedly harmful tendency raises issues on which Parliament might be expected to legislate.[899] But they retain a creative role 'where the subject matter is "lawyer's law"':[900] eg in extending existing 'heads'[901] and even in occasionally inventing new ones.[902] They also sometimes invalidate contracts or terms on what are essentially public policy grounds without explicitly mentioning the doctrine.[903]

1.221   The following paragraphs will describe most of the types of contracts which are contrary to public policy. Given its complexity, separate consideration will be given to the doctrine of restraint of trade.

(b) Types of contracts contrary to public policy

(i) Sexual immorality

1.222   A contract is contrary to public policy if its object is to promote sexual immorality. This phrase here refers to extra-marital sexual intercourse so that a contract to procure such intercourse is

---

[889]   eg *Osman v J Ralph Moss Ltd* [1970] 1 Lloyd's Rep 313.

[890]   *Betts v Gibbin* (1834) 1 A & E 57; *The Nogar Marin* [1988] 1 Lloyd's Rep 412, 417.

[891]   *Brown Jenkinson & Co Ltd v Percy Dalton (London) Ltd* [1957] 2 QB 621.

[892]   Not where the deliberate act is that of the defendant's employee, for which the defendant is vicariously liable: *Lancashire CC v Municipal Mutual Insurance Ltd* [1997] QB 897.

[893]   *Gray v Barr* [1971] QB 554; *Charlton v Fisher* [2001] EWCA Civ 112; [2002] QB 578.

[894]   *Gardner v Moore* [1984] AC 548, 560.

[895]   Third Parties (Rights against Insurers) Act 1930, to be replaced by Third Parties (Rights against Insurers) Act 2010.

[896]   *Hardy v MIB* [1964] 2 QB 743; *Gardner v Moore* [1984] AC 548, 560–561.

[897]   *Fender v St John Mildmay* [1938] AC 1, 13.

[898]   *Janson v Driefontein Consolidated Mines Ltd* [1902] AC 481, 491.

[899]   *D v NSPCC* [1978] AC 171, 235; *McFarlane v Tayside Health Board* [2000] 2 AC 59, 100–101.

[900]   *D v NSPCC*, n 899, at 235.

[901]   eg in cases such as *Nagle v Feilden* [1966] 1 QB 633.

[902]   eg *Neville v Dominion of Canada News Ltd* [1915] 3 KB 556; *Johnson v Moreton* [1980] AC 37.

[903]   eg in some of the rules of construction applied to exemption clauses: see 1.100.

illegal,[904] as also is a contract which indirectly promotes it, such as one to let a brougham to a prostitute to enable her to attract customers.[905] However, now that extra-marital 'cohabitation, whether heterosexual or homosexual, is widespread'[906] agreements between persons who so cohabit in stable relationships are no longer illegal and can give rise to a variety of legal consequences,[907] including contracts if the requirement of contractual intention[908] is satisfied. This is, a fortiori, true where parties of the same sex have entered into a civil partnership under the Civil Partnership Act 2004.

(ii) Freedom of marriage

A promise not to marry or to pay a sum of money in the event of the promisor's marriage is invalid as a restraint of marriage.[909] The rule does not apply where the contract may merely deter a person from marrying without containing a promise not to marry: eg to a contract to pay an allowance until marriage.[910] It may also not apply where the restraint was limited in time or otherwise reasonable.   **1.223**

To prevent the arranging of marriages from being commercialized, contracts by which one person undertakes for a fee to find a spouse for another (known as marriage brokage contracts) are contrary to public policy,[911] even though their harmful tendencies are far from clear.   **1.224**

(iii) Protecting marriage

Three rules reflect the principle that an agreement tending to weaken the marriage bond is invalid, albeit these rules are now more flexible than they were in former times.   **1.225**

First, the common law rule was that a promise made by someone who was already married to marry someone after the death of his or her spouse was not enforceable by a party who knew that the promisor was married at the time at which the promise was made.[912] However, this rule is now largely of historical interest, given the abolition of the action for breach of promise of marriage[913] albeit that certain rights in property remain effective 'where an agreement [between them] to marry is terminated'.[914] These rights can be enforced by a party to the agreement who was already married when it was made;[915] and it follows a fortiori that they can also be enforced by the other party.   **1.226**

Secondly, an agreement between spouses living together[916] which regulated their rights in the event of their future separation was at one time invalid on the ground that it was thought to have a tendency to break up the marriage.[917] A more relaxed approach is taken today to both   **1.227**

---

[904] *Benyon v Nettlefield* (1850) 3 Mac & G 94; cf *Coral Leisure Group Ltd v Barnett* [1981] ICR 503, 508 (where the allegation failed on the facts); *The Siben* [1996] 1 Lloyd's Rep 35, 62.

[905] *Pearce v Brooks* (1866) LR 1 Ex 213.

[906] *Barclays Bank plc v O'Brien* [1994] 1 AC 180, 198.

[907] eg *Tanner v Tanner* [1975] 1 WLR 1346; *Paul v Constance* [1977] 1 WLR 527; *Ghaidan v Mendoza* [2004] UKHL 30, [2004] 2 AC 557.

[908] See 1.69.

[909] *Baker v White* (1690) 2 Vern 215.

[910] cf *Gibson v Dickie* (1815) 3 M & S 463; *Thomas v Thomas* (1842) 2 QB 851.

[911] *Hermann v Charlesworth* [1905] 2 KB 123.

[912] *Spiers v Hunt* [1908] 1 KB 720: for an exception, see *Fender v St John Mildmay* [1938] AC 1 (promise made after decree nisi of divorce).

[913] Law Reform (Miscellaneous Provisions) Act 1970, s 1. Agreements to enter into civil partnerships likewise have no contractual force: Civil Partnership Act 2004, s 73.

[914] Law Reform (Miscellaneous Provisions) Act 1970, s 2. Similar provisions apply where a civil partnership is terminated: Civil Partnership Act 2004, s 74.

[915] *Shaw v Fitzgerald* [1992] 1 FLR 357.

[916] Not if they are already separated: *Wilson v Wilson* (1848) 1 HLC 538.

[917] See *Brodie v Brodie* [1917] P 271 (agreement made *before* the marriage).

ante-nuptial and post-nuptial agreements. Although the parties to a marriage cannot oust the jurisdiction of the courts to make financial orders should the parties separate or divorce, a court will generally have regard to and give effect to a post-nuptial agreement.[918] Similarly, while it was once contrary to public policy for a couple about to get married to make an arrangement that provided for the contingency that they might separate, the courts today adopt a similar approach to that applicable to post-nuptial agreements and will have regard to and generally give effect to such agreements provided that (i) the parties have entered into it freely with a full appreciation of its implications and (ii) it would not be unfair to hold the parties to their agreement.[919]

1.228 Thirdly, agreements tending to facilitate divorce, eg by specifying a wife's right to mainte-nance, were formerly viewed with suspicion;[920] but such agreements are now (collusion being no longer a bar to divorce) positively encouraged by the law.[921] They would now be invalid only if they were corrupt bargains intended to deceive the court.[922]

(iv) Parental responsibility

1.229 Parental responsibility for a child cannot be surrendered or transferred[923] but may (in effect) be shared between the parents where (because they were not married when the child was born) it was originally in the mother.[924]

(v) Excluding jurisdiction of the courts

1.230 A contract purporting to exclude the jurisdiction of the courts is invalid at common law since its enforceability could enable parties to evade peremptory rules of law.[925] Accordingly, the rules of an association cannot validly give its committee exclusive power to construe its rules.[926] Similarly, a wife cannot in a separation agreement bind herself, in return for her husband's promise to pay her an allowance, not to apply to the court for maintenance;[927] though, by statute, she can enforce the husband's written promise to make the payment.[928]

1.231 Arbitration agreements are valid to the extent that they merely require parties to resort to arbitration before going to court.[929] Such an agreement can,[930] and in some cases must,[931] be enforced, normally[932] by staying an action brought in breach of it. At common law, an arbitration agreement was, however, invalid if it deprived parties of their right to go to court on a completed cause of action or if it excluded (or made nugatory) the court's power to con-trol arbitrators' decisions on points of law.[933] By statute, parties are 'free to agree how their disputes are to be resolved';[934] but this principle is 'subject to such safeguards as are necessary

---

[918] *MacLeod v MacLeod* [2008] UKPC 64, [2010] 1 AC 298.
[919] *Granatino v Radmacher* [2010] UKSC 42, [2011] 1 AC 534, at [75].
[920] *Churchward v Churchward* [1895] P 7.
[921] Matrimonial Causes Act 1973, s 33A.
[922] See *Sutton v Sutton* [1984] Ch 184, 194.
[923] Children Act 1989, s 2(9); cf at common law *Vansittart v Vansittart* (1858) D & J 249, 259.
[924] Children Act 1989, ss 2(1), 4(1)(b) and (3).
[925] See *Anctil v Manufacturers' Life Insurance Co* [1899] AC 604.
[926] *Lee v Showmen's Guild of Great Britain* [1952] 2 QB 329.
[927] *Hyman v Hyman* [1929] AC 601; and see EPL 2.144.
[928] Matrimonial Causes Act 1973, s 34.
[929] *Scott v Avery* (1855) 5 HLC 811.
[930] *Channel Tunnel Group Ltd v Balfour Beatty Construction Ltd* [1993] AC 334; Arbitration Act 1996, s 86(2).
[931] Arbitration Act 1996, s 9(4).
[932] For an exception, see Arbitration Act 1996, s 91 (consumer arbitration agreements).
[933] *Czarnikow v Roth Schmidt & Co* [1922] 2 KB 478; *Home and Overseas Insurance Co Ltd v Mentor Insurance Co (UK) Ltd* [1989] 1 Lloyd's Rep 473, 485.
[934] Arbitration Act 1996, s 1(b).

in the public interest'[935] and enforcement or recognition of arbitral awards may be refused on grounds of public policy.[936] An appeal also lies from such awards to the court on a point of law,[937] but parties to a written arbitration agreement can, by agreement, exclude such judicial control.[938] An appeal is available only if the parties so agree or with the leave of the court.[939] Such leave is to be given only where the point of law substantially affects the rights of one or more of the parties *and* the decision of the arbitrator is *either* obviously wrong *or* raises a point of 'general public importance' and is 'open to serious doubt'; it must also be 'just and proper' for the court to determine the point.[940]

(vi) Perverting the course of justice

An agreement to compromise a criminal charge may itself amount to an offence[941] and be **1.232** illegal on that ground; but even where this is not the case such an agreement is generally [942] illegal since the public has an interest in the enforcement of the criminal law.[943] On a similar principle, corrupt bargains relating to non-criminal proceedings in the outcome of which the public has an interest (such as bankruptcy proceedings)[944] are illegal.

(vii) Deceiving public authorities

A contract is illegal if its object is to deceive the Revenue or other public authorities in their **1.233** function as tax-gathering bodies.[945]

(viii) Corrupting the public service

Contracts for the sale of public offices, commissions in the armed forces or honours are **1.234** illegal.[946] The same is sometimes, but not necessarily, true of contracts which involve 'lobbying' for government contracts.[947]

(ix) Trading with an enemy

It is a statutory offence to trade with an 'enemy' of war;[948] and a contract involving such **1.235** trading is illegal at common law.[949]

(x) Foreign relations

A contract is illegal if its object is to do an act in a friendly foreign country which is illegal **1.236** by its law.[950]

---

[935] Arbitration Act 1996, s 1(b).

[936] Arbitration Act 1996, s 81(1)(c).

[937] Arbitration Act 1996, s 69.

[938] Arbitration Act 1996, ss 5(1), 45(1), 69(1); for a restriction see s 87(1).

[939] Arbitration Act 1996, ss 45(2), 69(2).

[940] Arbitration Act 1996, s 69(2) and (3).

[941] Criminal Law Act 1967, ss 1, 5(1) (concealing arrestable offence).

[942] For an exception, see *Fisher & Co v Apollinaris Co* (1875) LR 10 Ch App 297.

[943] eg *R v Panayiotou* [1973] 3 All ER 112.

[944] *Elliott v Richardson* (1870) LR 5 CP 744; cf *Kearly v Thomson* (1890) 24 QBD 742.

[945] *Alexander v Rayson* [1936] 1 KB 169; *Miller v Karlinski* (1945) 62 TLR 85; contrast *21st Century Logistics Solutions v Madysen Ltd* [2004] EWHC 231 (QB), [2004] 2 Lloyd's Rep 92, where a seller's intention to defraud the Revenue of VAT was said to be 'too remote' from the contract to render it 'unenforceable on the ground of illegality' (at [19]).

[946] *Garforth v Fearon* (1787) 1 H B1 327; *Morris v McCullock* (1763) Amb 432; *Parkinson v College of Ambulance Ltd* [1925] 2 KB 1 (and see Honours (Prevention of Abuses) Act 1925).

[947] Contrast *Lemenda Trading Co Ltd v African Middle East Petroleum Co Ltd* [1988] QB 448 with *Tekron Resources Ltd v Guinea Investments Co* [2003] EWHC 2577 (Comm), [2004] 2 Lloyd's Rep 26, at [101].

[948] Trading with the Enemy Act 1939.

[949] *Sovfracht (V/O) v Van Udens etc* [1943] AC 203.

[950] eg *Foster v Driscoll* [1929] 1 KB 470.

(xi) *Undue restraints on personal liberty*

1.237   A contract may, in extreme cases, be illegal because it unduly restricts the personal liberty of a party: eg if a contract of loan imposes such restrictions on the borrower as to reduce him to a quasi-servile condition.[951]

(c) Restraint of trade

1.238   At common law, contract terms in restraint of trade are prima facie void because of their tendency to cause hardship to the party restrained and injury to the public;[952] but they are valid if reasonable and not contrary to the public interest. They can be divided into the following categories; some of them are also prohibited by legislation governing competition law.[953]

(i) *Sale of a business and employment*

1.239   The validity of a covenant by the seller of a business not to compete with his buyer and of one by a former employee not to compete with his ex-employer depends on the following three factors:

1.240   **A 'proprietary interest'.**   The buyer of a business pays for, amongst other things, the goodwill of that business; and his interest in that goodwill is 'proprietary' in the sense of being to some extent protected even in the absence of a covenant.[954] This interest does not extend to other businesses already carried on by him at the time of the contract; or to businesses which he proposes to carry on thereafter.[955] An employer's 'proprietary interest' is more narrowly defined. It does not arise merely because he would suffer from the employee's competitive use of skills acquired during employment.[956] The employer must normally [957] show *either* that the employee has come into contact with his customers or clients so as to acquire influence over them *or* that the employee has learned his 'trade secrets' (such as secret processes) or certain kinds of highly confidential information.[958] Where the relationship of the parties is neither that of vendor and purchaser nor that of employer and employee, the relative bargaining power of the parties is taken into account in defining the interest. Thus the vendor-purchaser test has been applied to agreements between professional partners,[959] and the employer-employee test to one between a comparatively unknown song-writer and his publisher.[960]

1.241   **Reasonableness.**   Reasonableness depends primarily on the relation between the restraint and the 'interest' meriting protection, so that the reasonableness of the *area* of the restraint depends on the area in which the business to be protected was carried on;[961] and its reasonableness in point of *time* depends on the period for which that business was likely to keep its clientele.[962] In employment cases, the courts are more likely to uphold 'solicitation covenants' (against soliciting the employer's customers) than 'area covenants' (against working in

---

[951] *Horwood v Millar's Timber and Trading Co Ltd* [1917] 1 KB 305.

[952] *Mitchell v Reynolds* (1711) P Wms 181, 190.

[953] See 1.248.

[954] *Trego v Hunt* [1896] AC 7.

[955] See *Nordenfelt v Maxim Nordenfelt Guns & Ammunitions Co* [1894] AC 535.

[956] *Herbert Morris Ltd v Saxelby* [1916] 1 AC 688.

[957] For other possible (non-'proprietary') interests, see *Eastham v Newcastle United Football Club Ltd* [1964] Ch 413.

[958] *Faccenda Chicken Ltd v Fowler* [1987] Ch 117; these interests are 'proprietary' in the sense that they are to some extent protected even in the absence of a covenant: cf at n 954.

[959] See *Kerr v Morris* [1987] Ch 90.

[960] *Schroeder Music Publishing Co Ltd v Macaulay* [1974] 1 WLR 1308.

[961] Contrast the *Nordenfelt* case, n 955 with *Mason v Provident Clothing & Supply Co Ltd* [1913] AC 724.

[962] See *M & S Draper Ltd v Reynolds* [1957] 1 WLR 9.

a designated area).[963] A lifelong area covenant[964] is now unlikely to be enforced[965] but the same is not true of a lifelong restraint on the disclosure of confidential information[966] since this does not prevent the ex-employee from working for others. Exceptionally, the doctrine of restraint of trade may apply to certain rights, such as those relating to the exploitation of image rights, which operate during the currency of the contract.[967]

In determining the issue of reasonableness, the court also has regard to the adequacy of the **1.242** consideration given for the restraint and to its fairness to the weaker party where there is inequality of bargaining power.[968] These requirements must be satisfied in addition to those stated in 1.240.

Public interest. A restraint which satisfies the requirement of reasonableness is nevertheless **1.243** invalid if it is contrary to the interests of the public.[969] The two requirements are not easy to separate; but where the party restrained possessed some skill for which there was an unsatisfied public need[970] the restraint might be contrary to the public interest even though it was 'reasonable'.

(ii) Restrictive trading agreements

At common law, such agreements restricting competition between suppliers of goods and **1.244** services are subject to the restraint of trade doctrine[971] but differ from agreements of the kind discussed above in that the interest meriting protection may be a purely 'commercial', as opposed to a 'proprietary' one.[972] Such agreements were, moreover, not often struck down for unreasonableness,[973] the courts being generally content to give effect to agreements made between parties bargaining on equal terms.[974] This approach did little to protect third parties who might be prejudiced by the operation of the agreement. Occasionally such prejudice was taken into account and the agreement struck down at the suit of a party to it as contrary to the public interest;[975] and to a limited extent the common law was able to give relief to third parties prejudiced by its operation.[976]

(iii) Exclusive dealing

Exclusive dealing agreements (such as agreements not to buy or sell goods of a certain descrip- **1.245** tion except from or to a specified person, or 'sole agency' agreements) were only rarely subjected to the restraint of trade doctrine. This approach was, however, challenged in a line of cases relating to 'solus' agreements by which garage owners undertook, usually in return for financial help in developing their premises, to buy petrol only from the oil company providing this help, and to accept various other restrictions. Such agreements were held to be within the restraint

---

[963] See *SW Strange Ltd v Mann* [1965] 1 WLR 629; *Gledhow Autoparts Ltd v Delaney* [1965] 1 WLR 1366; *T Lucas & Co Ltd v Mitchell* [1974] Ch 129; contrast *Hollis & Co v Stocks* [2000] IRLR 712 (one year covenant operating within 10-mile radius enforced).
[964] As in *Fitch v Dewes* [1921] 2 AC 158; contrast *Bridge v Deacons* [1984] AC 705 (fixed term solicitation covenant).
[965] See *Fellowes & Son v Fisher* [1976] QB 122.
[966] *A-G v Barker* [1990] 3 All ER 257; *A-G v Blake* [2001] 1 AC 268.
[967] *Proactive Sports Management Ltd v Rooney* [2011] EWCA Civ 1444, [2012] All ER 2 (Comm) 815.
[968] *Nordenfelt* case, n 955, at 565; *A Schroeder Music Publishing Co Ltd v Macaulay* [1974] 1 WLR 1308.
[969] *Wyatt v Kreglinger & Fernau* [1933] 1 KB 793; *Bull v Pitney-Bowes Ltd* [1967] 1 WLR 273.
[970] eg *Dranez Anstalt v Hayek* [2002] EWCA Civ 1729, [2003] 1 BCLC 278, at [25].
[971] *McEllistrim v Ballymacelligott Cooperative Agricultural & Dairy Society Ltd* [1919] AC 548.
[972] See *McEllistrim* case, n 971, at 564.
[973] *McEllistrim* case, n 971, at 564.
[974] *English Hop Growers v Dering* [1928] 2 KB 174.
[975] *Kores Manufacturing Co Ltd v Kolok Manufacturing Co Ltd* [1959] Ch 108.
[976] *Eastham v Newcastle United Football Club Ltd* [1964] Ch 413; *Nagle v Feilden* [1966] 2 QB 633; *R v Jockey Club, ex p RAM Racecourses Ltd* [1993] 2 All ER 225; *R v Disciplinary Committee of the Jockey Club, ex p Aga Khan* [1993] 1 WLR 909.

of trade doctrine,[977] though that doctrine would still not apply to agreements which 'merely regulate the normal commercial relation between the parties',[978] such as most sole agency (or distributorship) agreements. Where an exclusive dealing agreement is within the doctrine, the normal requirements for its validity must be satisfied: ie, there must be an 'interest' meriting protection (though a 'commercial' interest suffices);[979] the agreement must be 'reasonable' (a requirement that may lead to an enquiry into its fairness)[980] and it must not be contrary to the public interest.[981]

(iv) Restrictions on land use

1.246 Land may be sold subject to restriction on its use, such as prohibitions against building or trading there. These are not normally subject to the restraint of trade doctrine; and one reason for this position is that the purchaser had 'no previous right to be there' and so he gives up 'no right or freedom which he previously had'.[982] This reasoning, however, ignores the possibility that a restriction imposed on a purchaser may be contrary to the public interest; and legislation makes it possible for such a restriction to be discharged (on payment of compensation) if it 'would impede some reasonable user of the land for public or private purposes'.[983]

(v) Other agreements

1.247 The categories of restraint of trade are not closed[984] and restrictive trading agreements not within any of the groups described above may be invalid by statute[985] or be subject at common law to the restraint of trade doctrine if they have the effect of 'fettering a person's freedom in the future to carry on his trade, business or profession'.[986] Such agreements are not necessarily invalid at common law, but they do require justification under the restraint of trade doctrine.

(vi) Competition law

1.248 Certain agreements affecting trade are prohibited and void under European Union (EU) legislation and the Competition Act 1998.[987] These prohibitions can apply to some agreements which are subject to the restraint of trade doctrine at common law but they apply only to agreements if their effect on competition is an 'appreciable' as opposed to an 'insignificant' one in percentage terms.[988] They are concerned with the adverse effects of agreements on the economy as a whole, while the common law is at least equally concerned with their effects on the party restrained. An agreement which fails to satisfy the common law tests of validity but satisfies those imposed by EU law cannot be struck down in England for failure to comply with the common law rules.[989]

---

[977] *Esso Petroleum Co Ltd v Harper's Garage (Stourport) Ltd* [1968] AC 269; undertakings given by major oil companies now regulate such agreements.
[978] *Esso* case, n 977, at 327, 328.
[979] *Esso* case, n 977, at 327, 328.
[980] *A Schroeder Music Publishing Co Ltd v Macaulay* [1974] 1 WLR 1308; *Watson v Prager* [1991] 1 WLR 726.
[981] *Esso* case, n 977, at 321, 324, 341.
[982] *Esso* case, n 977, at 298.
[983] Law of Property Act 1925, s 84.
[984] *Esso* case, n 977, at 337.
[985] Auction (Bidding Agreements) Act 1927.
[986] *Shearson Lehman Hutton Inc v MacLaine Watson & Co Ltd* [1989] 2 Lloyd's Rep 570, 615.
[987] Article 101 Treaty on the Functioning of the European Union; Competition Act 1998, Chapter I; ss 47A and 47B of the Act provide for the payment of compensation to persons who suffer loss or damage as a result of an infringement of its provisions.
[988] *Völk v Ets Vervaeke* [1969] CMLR 273; cf *Passmore v Morland plc* [1999] 3 All ER 1005.
[989] *Days Medical Aids Ltd v Pihsiang Machinery Manufacturing Co Ltd* [2004] EWHC 44 (Comm); [2004] 1 All ER (Comm) 991, at [254]–[265].

(3) Effects of Illegality

(a) Enforcement

Illegality may prevent the enforcement of a contract (or where, as in the restraint of trade **1.249**
cases, illegality affects only one term of it, the enforcement of that term). A court will never
order a party to do the act which is illegal but it may sometimes award damages for failure
to do it or enforce the other party's counter-promise. The law in this area is in a state of
some uncertainty. In some cases the courts have emphasized that the withholding of judicial
remedies is a rule of law which is based on public policy and not on the perceived balance of
merits between the parties to any particular dispute.[989a] But in other cases greater emphasis
has been placed on the need for a more proportionate response which takes into account the
significance of the illegality and the injustice of denying a claim on account of it.[989b] The
resolution of this tension in the law awaits its definitive resolution.[989c]

(i) Position of guilty party

A guilty party cannot enforce the contract,[990] even though the other party is equally guilty **1.250**
and so gets the windfall of receiving the former's performance for nothing. The rule has been
justified on the ground that 'the courts will not lend their aid to such [ie a guilty] plaintiff',[991]
but it can operate harshly[992] where the claimant is morally innocent because the offence in
question is one of strict liability or he is acting under a mistake of law. Its severity is mitigated
in various ways: eg by holding that a person is not a 'guilty' party for this purpose merely
because the contemplated[993] or even the actual[994] method of performance is unlawful; by
allowing him to sue the other party for a tort independent of the contract;[995] and occasionally by legislation.[996]

(ii) Position of innocent party

An illegal contract cannot be enforced by a person who is innocent merely in the sense of **1.251**
being ignorant of or mistaken about the rule of law giving rise to the illegality.[997] When
a party is innocent because of his ignorance of relevant facts, some cases have allowed,[998]
while others have rejected,[999] his claim. The two groups of cases can perhaps be reconciled
on the ground that in the former (but not in the latter) the purpose of the rule of law
infringed was merely to impose penalties on the offender, and not to invalidate contracts.
An alternative distinction between the two groups may be that the court is more likely to
put the innocent party into the position in which he would have been if the contract had

---

[989a] *Les Laboratoires Servier v Apotex Inc* [2014] UKSC 55, [2015] AC 430, at [13]–[22].

[989b] *Hounga v Allen (Anti-Slavery International intervening)* [2014] UKSC 47, [2014] 1 WLR 2889.

[989c] *Bilta (UK) Ltd v Nazir* [2015] UKSC 23, [2015] 2 WLR 1168, at [13]–[17], [34], [174].

[990] eg *Pearce v Brooks* (1866) LR 1 Ex 213; *Cowan v Milburn* (1867) LR 2 Ex 230.

[991] *Holman v Johnson* (1775) 1 Cowp 341, 343; and see *Tinsley v Milligan* [1994] 1 AC 340, 358–361, 363–364.

[992] The rule is, however, not affected by Human Rights Act 1998, Sch 1 Pt II: *Shanshal v Al Kishtaini* [2001] EWCA Civ 264, [2001] 2 All ER (Comm) 601.

[993] *Waugh v Morris* (1873) LR 8 QB 202.

[994] *St John Shipping Corp v Joseph Rank Ltd* [1957] 1 QB 267. But the claim would have been barred if the claimant had 'knowingly participated' in the illegal method of performance: *Hall v Woolston Hall Leisure Ltd* [2001] 1 WLR 225, 234. However, there are signs of a more flexible approach in recent cases, where regard is had to matters such as proportionality: *Parkingeye Ltd v Somerfield Stores Ltd* [2012] EWCA Civ 1338, [2013] 2 WLR 939.

[995] *Saunders v Edwards* [1987] 1 WLR 1116.

[996] eg Road Traffic Act 1988, ss 65(4), 75(7).

[997] *Nash v Stevenson Transport Ltd* [1936] 2 KB 128.

[998] *Bloxsome v Williams* (1824) 3 B & C 232; *Archbolds (Freightage) Ltd v Spanglett Ltd* [1961] 1 QB 374.

[999] *Re Mahmoud and Ispahani* [1921] 2 KB 716.

not been made[1000] than into that in which he would have been if it had been *performed*.[1001] Where the illegality arises from legislation for the protection of a class its purpose is not promoted by denying a remedy to an innocent member of that class; and in some such cases such a person is by statute given the right to enforce the contract.[1002]

1.252   An innocent party may be entitled to restitution in respect of benefits conferred on the other under the illegal contract[1003] or to damages in tort where he has been induced to enter into contract by a misrepresentation as to its legality.[1004] These remedies differ from enforcement of the contract in that they will not compensate the claimant for loss of his expectation interest.[1005] The innocent party may also be entitled to damages for breach of a 'collateral warranty' that the main contract was lawful.[1006] These damages are equal to the amount that he could have recovered under the main contract, had it not been illegal. It is not easy to see why, if the public interest bars such recovery, the same amount should be recoverable under the 'collateral warranty'; and, if there is no such public interest bar, it would be better to allow a claim on the main contract.

(b) Severance

(i) Severance of promises

1.253   Where one party's promises are only partly illegal, that part can be severed, and the lawful part enforced, if three conditions are satisfied. First, the illegal promise must not be so seriously illegal as to contaminate the whole contract: eg it must not be one for the deliberate commission of a crime.[1007] Secondly, under the so-called 'blue pencil' test, it must be possible to sever the illegal part by merely deleting words: the promise cannot be in some other way redrafted so as to make it lawful.[1008] Thirdly, severance must not change the nature of the contract so as to turn it into a transaction wholly different from that intended by the parties.[1009] Even where parts of an illegal promise cannot be severed, other unrelated parts of the contract may remain enforceable: eg, an employee who has made a wholly void promise in restraint of trade can be restrained from breach of his duty of fidelity.[1010] The contract as a whole will be invalid only if its main object was to secure the illegal restraint.[1011]

(ii) Severance of consideration

1.254   A partly illegal promise may constitute the consideration for a counter-promise, usually to pay for the former promise or its performance. On a claim to enforce the counter-promise, the question then arises whether the illegal part of the consideration for it can be severed. This cannot be done if that part constituted the whole or a substantial part of the consideration for the counter-promise;[1012] but if the main part of the consideration was lawful, then that promise can be enforced even though there was also some subsidiary illegal

---

[1000]   This was the nature of the claim in the cases cited in n 998.
[1001]   This was the nature of the claim in the case cited in n 999.
[1002]   Financial Services and Markets Act 2000, ss 26, 27, 28, 30.
[1003]   See 1.256 et seq.
[1004]   *Shelley v Paddock* [1980] QB 348.
[1005]   See 1.04.
[1006]   *Strongman (1945) Ltd v Sincock* [1955] 2 QB 525.
[1007]   See *Bennett v Bennett* [1952] 1 KB 249, 252.
[1008]   *Mason v Provident Clothing & Supply Co Ltd* [1913] AC 724.
[1009]   *Attwood v Lamont* [1920] 3 KB 571.
[1010]   *Commercial Plastics Ltd v Vincent* [1965] 1 QB 623.
[1011]   *Amoco Australia Pty v Rocca Bros Motor Engineering Pty Ltd* [1975] AC 561; contrast *Alec Lobb (Garages) Ltd v Total Oil (Great Britain) Ltd* [1985] 1 WLR 173.
[1012]   *Lound v Grimwade* (1888) 39 Ch D 605.

consideration for it[1013] (unless that part involved the deliberate commission of a criminal or immoral act).[1014] The subsidiary part is not strictly severed (but simply disregarded) since the counter-promise is enforced in full: eg where an employee who has entered into too wide a covenant in restraint of trade recovers his wages.[1015]

(c) Collateral transactions

The illegality of one contract may infect another (itself lawful) contract if the latter helps in the performance of the former, or if its enforcement would amount to indirect enforcement of the illegal one: thus a loan of money is illegal if it is made to enable the borrower to make or to perform an illegal contract.[1016] But a contract is not illegal merely because one of the parties to it is also a party to a second illegal contract remotely connected with the first.[1017] **1.255**

(d) Restitution

(i) General rule: no recovery of money or property

A party who cannot enforce an illegal contract cannot as a general rule recover back money paid or property transferred by him under it.[1018] The rule is meant to deter the making of illegal contracts, but where the claimant is innocent, it scarcely achieves this result; and where the defendant runs an illegal business, deterrence is more likely to be promoted by allowing than by dismissing restitution claims against him. The rule is therefore subject to many exceptions. **1.256**

(ii) Exceptions

Class-protecting statutes. Statutes passed for the protection of a class of persons (such as tenants) sometimes expressly provide that members of that class can recover back payments made by them in breach of the statute.[1019] Such a right of recovery also exists at common law, even in the absence of such express statutory provisions.[1020] **1.257**

Illegal contract made under pressure. Recovery of money paid or property transferred is sometimes allowed on the ground that the claimant was 'forced' to enter into the contract, either by the other party[1021] or by pressure of extraneous circumstances.[1022] The pressure must be such as to make it in the court's view excusable for the claimant to enter into the illegal contract.[1023] **1.258**

Fraud or mistake inducing the illegal contract. Money paid or property transferred can be reclaimed by a person who was induced to enter into the contract by a fraudulent misrepresentation as to its legality.[1024] This right does not extend to cases in which the misrepresentation was innocent,[1025] though if the claimant is entitled to, and does, rescind the **1.259**

[1013] See *Goodinson v Goodinson* [1954] 2 QB 118 (actual decision obsolete since Matrimonial Causes Act 1973, s 34).
[1014] *Bennett v Bennett*, n 1007, at 254.
[1015] *Carney v Herbert* [1985] AC 301, 311.
[1016] *De Begnis v Armistead* (1833) 10 Bing 107; *Spector v Ageda* [1973] Ch 30.
[1017] *Euro-Diam Ltd v Bathurst* [1990] QB 1; contrast *Re Trepca Mines Ltd* [1963] Ch 199 (on the illegality of such a contract now, see 1.212).
[1018] eg *Scott v Brown* [1892] 2 QB 724.
[1019] Rent Act 1977, ss 57, 95, 125; *Gray v Southouse* [1949] 2 All ER 1019.
[1020] *Kiriri Cotton Ltd v Dewani* [1960] AC 192.
[1021] *Atkinson v Denby* (1862) 7 H & N 934.
[1022] *Kiriri Cotton* case, n 1020, at 205; *Liebman v Rosenthal* 57 NYS 2d 875 (1945).
[1023] *Bigos v Bousted* [1951] 1 All ER 92 (where this requirement was not satisfied).
[1024] *Hughes v Liverpool Victoria Legal Friendly Society* [1916] 2 KB 482.
[1025] *Harse v Pearl Life Assurance Co* [1904] 1 KB 558.

contract for misrepresentation,[1026] he can then recover back the money or property on that ground. This course would not normally be open to him where one of the bars to rescission had arisen;[1027] but these seem not to apply where the restitution claim is based, not on misrepresentation, but on illegality.[1028]

1.260 A payment is recoverable by a person who made it under a mistake (shared by both parties) as to the circumstances affecting the legality of the contract.[1029]

1.261 'Repentance'. The law seeks to encourage a party to give up the 'illegal purpose' by allowing him to recover money or property if he 'repent[s] before it is too late'.[1030] To bring this rule into operation it is first necessary for the claimant to 'repent': it is not enough for the illegal purpose to be simply frustrated by the defendant's failure or refusal to perform.[1031] Secondly, the repentance must come 'before it is too late'; and it will be too late if it comes after the illegal purpose or a substantial part of it has been carried out.[1032] But the mere fact that acts have been done in preparation for achieving the illegal purpose is not a bar to the restitution claim.[1033]

1.262 **No reliance on the contract or its illegality.** Money paid or property transferred under an illegal contract can be recovered back if the claimant can establish his right or title to it without relying on the contract or on its illegality.[1034] If, eg, a thing is pledged or let out under an illegal contract, that contract can transfer a special property to the bailee notwithstanding its illegality; and so long as that special property endures, the owner cannot recover back the thing.[1035] But once the special property has come to an end the owner can recover back the thing by simply relying on his title: eg when the term of hire has expired or where the hirer's right to retain the thing has come to an automatic end in consequence of the hirer's breach.[1036] Where, by contrast, goods are *sold* under an illegal contract, the *entire* property in them can pass to the buyer notwithstanding the illegality.[1037] The seller then has no title left on which to rely (eg in the event of the buyer's failure to pay in accordance with agreed credit terms). A payment of money likewise normally vests the entire property in the payee so that the payor cannot recover it back by relying on his title except where the money is not paid out but only deposited with a stakeholder.[1038]

1.263 Where the claim is made by a transferee, he will have to rely on the contract but may nevertheless succeed if he does not have to rely on its illegality. For example, a buyer of goods to whom property has passed under an illegal contract but to whom the goods have not been delivered can recover them from a third party (to whom they have been delivered),[1039] or from a person who takes them away from him,[1040] on the strength of his title.

[1026] See 1.175.
[1027] See 1.180–1.187.
[1028] In the fraud cases described at n 1024.
[1029] *Oom v Bruce* (1810) 12 East 225; for the view that mistake of one suffices, see *Edler v Auerbach* [1950] 1 KB 359, 374 (*sed quaere*).
[1030] *Harry Parker Ltd v Mason* [1940] 2 KB 590, 609.
[1031] *Bigos v Bousted* [1951] 1 All ER 92. However the courts may be willing to permit recovery in cases where there has been no performance under the contract and the purpose has been frustrated by the actions of third parties or by actions beyond the claimant's control: *Patel v Mirza* [2014] EWCA Civ 1047, [2015] 2 WLR 405.
[1032] *Kearly v Thomson* (1890) 24 QBD 742.
[1033] *Taylor v Bowers* (1876) 1 QBD 291; *Tribe v Tribe* [1996] Ch 107.
[1034] *Bowmakers Ltd v Barnet Instruments Ltd* [1945] KB 65, 71.
[1035] *Taylor v Chester* (1869) LR 4 QB 309.
[1036] *Bowmakers* case, n 1034.
[1037] *Singh v Ali* [1960] AC 167.
[1038] *O'Sullivan v Thomas* [1895] 1 QB 698 (money deposited under a contract then void).
[1039] *Belvoir Finance Co Ltd v Stapleton* [1971] 1 QB 210.
[1040] *Singh v Ali* [1960] AC 167.

The principles stated in 1.261 and 1.262 also apply where the title acquired is an equitable one and can be established without relying on the illegality;[1041] though whether it can be so established sometimes depends on highly technical distinctions which determine whether property acquired by (or with means provided by) A in B's name is presumed to be held by B on trust for A or intended as a gift to B.[1042] Such distinctions have little relevance to the policy of the rule of law, the violation of which makes the contract illegal. Even where, under them, there is no right of recovery, there may be one under another of the grounds discussed above: eg on the ground of 'repentance'.[1043]

1.264

The principle of recovery without reliance on the contract or its illegality may not apply where the thing is such that it is unlawful to deal with it at all.[1044]

1.265

(iii) Scope of general rule

The general rule stated in 1.255 has been held not to apply to marriage brokage contracts,[1045] perhaps reflecting an earlier equitable view[1046] which rejected that rule, and giving rise to the possibility of reviving this view where to do so would promote the policy of the invalidating rule.

1.266

I. Lack of Capacity

This section deals with the contractual capacity of natural persons; corporate contractual capacity is discussed in EPL chapter 3.

1.267

(1) Minors

Minors are persons below the age of 18. The law limits their contractual capacity so as to protect them against bargains which are unfair or improvident; at the same time, it seeks to avoid unnecessary injustice to adults who deal fairly with minors. The practical importance of the subject has been reduced by the lowering of the age of majority[1047] (formerly 21) and by changing social conditions;[1048] but it is far from negligible in relation to (eg) employment contracts and the activities of under-age entertainers or athletes.

1.268

(a) Valid contracts

(i) Necessaries

A minor is bound by contracts for necessaries; his liability was said to arise for his own good,[1049] on the (not altogether convincing) theory that the supplier would not give credit

1.269

[1041] *Tinsley v Milligan* [1994] 1 AC 340.

[1042] Contrast *Tinsley v Milligan*, n 1041 with *Chettiar v Chettiar* [1962] AC 294. In *Tinsley v Milligan* the first of the presumptions referred to in the text was applied when a house occupied by an unmarried cohabiting couple had been conveyed into the names of *one* of them. In *Stack v Dowden* [2007] UKHL 17, [2007] 2 AC 432 the majority of the House of Lords regarded the presumption as no longer dispositive of the rights of such a couple where the house had been conveyed into the joint names of *both* of them.

[1043] *Tribe v Tribe* [1996] Ch 107.

[1044] *Bowmakers'* case, n 1034, at 72 (obscene book); see also *The Siben (No 2)* [1996] 1 Lloyd's Rep 35, 62 (consideration for such subject matter; *sed quaere*).

[1045] *Hermann v Charlesworth* [1905] 2 KB 123.

[1046] *Morris v McCullock* (1763) Amb 432.

[1047] Family Law Reform Act 1969, ss 1, 9.

[1048] See *Allen v Bloomsbury Health Authority* [1993] 1 All ER 651, 661.

[1049] *Ryder v Wombwell* (1868) LR 4 Ex 32, 38.

unless he could enforce liability. Necessaries include goods[1050] and services (such as education and medical or legal services)[1051] supplied to the minor. They are not confined to necessities but extend to goods or services suitable to maintain the minor in 'the state, station and degree...in which he is';[1052] but 'mere luxuries'[1053] cannot be necessaries. The supplier must show that the goods or services are not only capable of being, but that they actually are, necessaries at the time at which they are, or are to be,[1054] supplied.[1055] The minor is liable for no more than a reasonable price[1056] where this is less than the contract price. If an adult pays the supplier, the minor must reimburse the payor[1057] (to the extent that the charge was reasonable); and if an adult lends money to the minor to enable him to pay for necessaries the lender can sue on the loan to the extent that it is so used.[1058] Legislation relating to the maintenance of children by absent parents[1059] does not directly affect a minor's liability for necessaries but may indirectly do so if it results in his being adequately supplied with the goods and services in question.

(ii) Employment and analogous contracts

1.270 A minor is bound by a contract of employment if it is on the whole for his benefit.[1060] So long as this requirement is satisfied, he is bound even though some terms of the contract are disadvantageous to him,[1061] so long as they are not harsh and oppressive.[1062] These principles apply also where the minor is not strictly an employee but enters into a contract by which he makes a living as (eg) an athlete, author or entertainer.[1063] But he is not liable under 'trading contracts': eg where goods are sold by,[1064] or supplied to,[1065] him in the course of his business.

(b) Voidable contracts

1.271 For reasons which are not altogether clear, a minor is in some cases bound by a contract unless he repudiates it. This rule applies where he agrees to buy or sell land[1066] or to take or grant a lease of land;[1067] where he incurs liability for calls on shares in a company;[1068] where he enters into a contract of partnership;[1069] and where he enters into a marriage settlement.[1070] He must repudiate during minority or within a reasonable time of his majority.[1071]

[1050] Sale of Goods Act 1979, s 3(2).

[1051] *Helps v Clayton* (1864) 17 CBNS 553; *Roberts v Gray* [1913] 1 KB 250; *Sherdley v Sherdley* [1988] AC 213, 225.

[1052] *Peters v Flemming* (1840) 6 M & W 42, 46.

[1053] *Chapple v Cooper* (1844) 13 M & W 252, 258.

[1054] See *Roberts v Gray*, n 1051; *Nash v Inman* [1908] 2 KB 1, 12.

[1055] *Nash v Inman*, n 1054.

[1056] Sale of Goods Act 1979, s 3(2), as to which see n 1050.

[1057] *Earle v Peale* (1712) 10 Mod 67.

[1058] *Marlow v Pitfeild* (1719) 1 P Wms 558.

[1059] Child Support Act 1991, s 1(1); see also Children Act 1989, s 15 and Sch 5, discussed in EPL ch 2.

[1060] *Clements v London & North Western Rly* [1894] 2 QB 482; *Mills v IRC* [1975] AC 38, 53; for statutory regulation, see, eg, Employment of Children Act 1973.

[1061] As in the *Clements* case, n 1060.

[1062] *De Francesco v Barnum* (1889) 43 Ch D 165; cf *Goodwin v Uzoigwee* [1993] Fam Law 65.

[1063] *Doyle v White City Stadium Ltd* [1935] KB 110; *Chaplin v Leslie Frewin (Publishers) Ltd* [1966] Ch 71.

[1064] *Cowern v Nield* [1912] 2 KB 419.

[1065] *Mercantile Union Guarantee Corp Ltd v Bell* [1937] 2 KB 498.

[1066] *Whittingham v Murdy* (1889) 60 LT 956; *Orakpo v Manson Investments Ltd* [1978] AC 95, 106.

[1067] *Davies v Beynon-Harris* (1931) 47 TLR 424.

[1068] *North-Western Rly v M'Michael* (1850) 5 Ex 114.

[1069] See *Lovell & Christmas v Beauchamp* [1894] AC 607. The Limited Liability Partnerships Act 2000 does not refer to minors.

[1070] *Edwards v Carter* [1893] AC 360.

[1071] *Edwards v Carter* [1893] AC 360.

Repudiation relieves him from future liabilities[1072] but does not entitle him to recover money paid or property transferred by him under the contract[1073] unless the effect of the repudiation is to bring about a 'total failure of consideration'.

(c) Other contracts

A contract outside the categories discussed in 1.268 to 1.270 does not bind the minor unless **1.272** he ratifies it after reaching full age;[1074] but it does bind the other party.[1075] Money paid or property transferred by the minor under such a contract cannot be recovered back by him merely on the ground that the contract did not bind him;[1076] while conversely property in goods which are its subject matter can pass to the minor by delivery in pursuance of the contract.[1077] Property can similarly pass *from* him under such a contract.[1078]

(d) Liability in tort

A minor's contractual incapacity cannot be circumvented by suing him in tort merely because **1.273** the act constituting a breach of an invalid contract amounts also to a tort.[1079] He is liable in tort only for doing something wholly outside the scope of the acts envisaged by the parties when they made the contract.[1080]

(e) Liability in unjust enrichment

A minor can sometimes be ordered to make restitution in respect of benefits obtained by him **1.274** under a contract which cannot be enforced against him because of his minority.

(i) Minors' Contracts Act 1987, section 3(1)

In the situation just described, this subsection gives the court a discretion 'if it is just and equit- **1.275** able to do so' to 'require [the minor] to transfer to the [other party] any property[1081] acquired by the [minor] under the contract, or any property representing it'. Thus if non-necessary goods have been delivered to the minor and not paid for, he can be ordered to restore them; if he has resold them, he can be ordered to restore the money or an object bought with it. But no such order can be made once he has dissipated the thing obtained or its proceeds since in that case there is no longer any 'property obtained' or 'property representing it' on which the order can operate. The order must be one to *restore* property, not to *pay* for it out of the minor's other assets. Where proceeds have been paid into the minor's bank account, the distinction between these two concepts may be hard to draw; and the court will in such cases make the order only if to do so will not amount to indirect enforcement of the invalid contract.

(ii) Effects of minor's fraud

A minor is not liable on a contract merely because he had procured it by a fraudulent mis- **1.276** representation (typically as to his age);[1082] nor does the misrepresentation make him liable in

---

[1072] There are conflicting views on the question whether repudiation also has retrospective effects: see *North-Western Rly v M'Michael*, n 1068, at 125; *Steinberg v Scala (Leeds) Ltd* [1923] 2 Ch 452, 463.

[1073] *Steinberg v Scala (Leeds) Ltd*, n 1072.

[1074] See *Williams v Moor* (1843) 11 M & W 256.

[1075] *Bruce v Warwick* (1815) 6 Taunt 118; but *specific* performance is not available to the minor: *Flight v Bolland* (1828) 4 Russ 298.

[1076] *Wilson v Kearse* (1800) Peake Add Cas 196; *Corpe v Overton* (1833) 10 Bing 252, 259.

[1077] *Stocks v Wilson* [1913] 2 KB 235, 246.

[1078] *Chaplin v Leslie Frewin (Publishers) Ltd* [1966] Ch 71.

[1079] *Fawcett v Smethurst* (1914) 84 LJKB 473.

[1080] *Burnard v Haggis* (1863) 14 CBNS 45; *Ballet v Mingay* [1943] KB 281.

[1081] 'Property' here includes money: see *Law of Contract, Minors' Contracts* (Law Com No 134, 1984) para 4.21.

[1082] *Bartlett v Wells* (1862) 1 B & S 836.

tort[1083] for the value of what he had obtained.[1084] In equity, such fraud gives rise to liability to restore what has been obtained;[1085] but there is no need to resort to this jurisdiction now that such restitution is available, without proof of fraud, under the Minors' Contracts Act 1987.[1086] The interest of the equity cases lies in their insistence on the nature of the liability as being (like that under the Act) one to *restore* (not to *pay* for) benefits obtained. Hence to the extent that those benefits have been dissipated there is no liability to restore in equity.[1087]

(iii) Restitution at common law

1.277 A minor may be liable to make restitution in respect of a benefit obtained by him under an invalid contract: eg where he has been paid for goods sold by him under a trading contract but not delivered. According to one case,[1088] he is so liable only where he is guilty of fraud; but it would be more appropriate to restrict the remedy to cases where the benefit so obtained, or its proceeds, remained in his hands so that, where the benefit had been dissipated, the liability could not be enforced against his other assets.[1089] In the absence of fraud, the adult could seek restitution under the 1987 Act;[1090] but that remedy is discretionary while the common law remedy, which is preserved by section 3(2) of the Act, lies (where available) as of right.

(2) Mental Patients

(a) General

1.278 A contract with a mental patient[1091] is valid[1092] except in two situations. First, if the other party knows that the patient's disability prevented him from understanding the transaction,[1093] the contract can be avoided by the patient.[1094] Secondly, if the patient's disorder is so serious that his property is subject to the control of the court, then he is not[1095] (though the other party is)[1096] bound by the contract if it purports to dispose of the property or (perhaps) otherwise interferes with the court's control over it. A contract which does not initially bind the patient becomes binding on him by his ratification of it after he is cured.[1097]

(b) Necessaries

1.279 Under the rules stated in 1.277, a mental patient may be bound by a contract for necessaries; but where he is not so bound he must nevertheless pay a reasonable price for them.[1098] There is no such liability where medical treatment is supplied under the National Health Service,[1099] though such cases can give rise to the question whether the treatment is lawful in spite of the patient's lack of capacity to consent to it.[1100]

[1083] See 1.273.

[1084] *R Leslie Ltd v Sheill* [1914] 3 KB 607.

[1085] *Clarke v Cobley* (1789) 2 Cox 173.

[1086] See 1.275.

[1087] *R Leslie Ltd v Sheill*, n 1084, at 619, doubting this aspect of *Stocks v Wilson* [1913] 2 KB 235, 247.

[1088] *Cowern v Nield* [1912] 2 KB 419.

[1089] cf 1.275 and 1.276.

[1090] See 1.275.

[1091] A convenient expression to refer to a 'person who lacks capacity because of an impairment of, or a disturbance in the functioning of, the mind or brain' within the Mental Capacity Act 2005, s 2.

[1092] *Hart v O'Connor* [1985] AC 1000.

[1093] See *Re K* [1988] Ch 310.

[1094] *Imperial Loan Co v Stone* [1892] 1 QB 599.

[1095] *Re Walker* [1905] 1 Ch 160.

[1096] cf *Baldwyn v Smith* [1900] 1 Ch 588.

[1097] *Manches v Trimborn* (1946) 115 LJ KB 305.

[1098] Mental Capacity Act 2005, s 7.

[1099] *Re F* [1990] 2 AC 1, 74.

[1100] *Re F* [1990] 2 AC 1, 74; *Re C* [1994] 1 WLR 290; Mental Capacity Act 2005, ss 24–26.

(3) Drink or Drugs

A person cannot escape from liability on a contract merely because, when he made it, his **1.280** commercial judgment was impaired by drink;[1101] but he can avoid the contract if he was then so drunk that he could not understand the nature of the transaction and the other party knew this.[1102] The right of avoidance is lost by ratification after the effects of drink have worn off.[1103] These rules could, perhaps, be applied by analogy to persons whose judgment was impaired by drugs.[1104] By statute, a drunkard is liable for necessaries supplied to him while suffering from temporary incapacity to contract.[1105]

J. Plurality of Parties

Normally, each side of a contract consists of only one party. Our concern here, however, is **1.281** with contractual promises made by or to two or more persons, so that there is either more than one debtor, or more than one creditor.

(1) Promises by More than One Person

(a) Definitions

If A and B each *separately* promise to pay C £100, there are two independent contracts under **1.282** which C is entitled to £100 from A and to a further £100 from B.[1106] But if in the same contract they *together* make the promise, C is entitled to no more than £100 in all and the further effects of the promise depend on whether it is *joint* or *joint and several*. It is joint if it consists of a single promise by both A and B; and joint and several if it consists of such a single promise coupled with a separate promise by each. A promise by two or more persons is deemed to be joint unless it provides the contrary:[1107] eg by saying 'we and each of us promise'.

(b) Similarities

Each promisor is (whether the promise is joint or joint and several) liable in full but if he **1.283** pays more than his share he is, unless the contract otherwise provides,[1108] entitled to contribution assessed by dividing the debt by the number of debtors who were solvent when the right to contribution arose.[1109]

If the creditor releases one of the co-debtors, the others are also released[1110] unless the release **1.284** on its true construction reserves the creditor's rights against them.[1111]

A defence available to one debtor is not available to the others if it was personal to him (eg that he **1.285** was a minor)[1112] but is so available if it goes to the root of the claim (eg if it is that the creditor has

---

[1101] But *specific* enforcement against him may be refused: *Malins v Freeman* (1836) 2 Keen 25, 34.

[1102] *Gore v Gibson* (1845) 13 M & W 623.

[1103] *Matthews v Baxter* (1873) LR 8 Ex 132.

[1104] *Irvani v Irvani* [2000] 1 Lloyd's Rep 412, 425.

[1105] Sale of Goods Act 1979, s 3(2).

[1106] *Mikeover Ltd v Brady* [1989] 3 All ER 618; cf *Heaton v Axa Equity and Law Life Assurance Society* [2002] UKHL 15, [2002] 2 AC 329.

[1107] *Levy v Sale* (1877) 37 LT 709.

[1108] As in contracts in which the relationship of the two promisors is that of principal debtor and surety.

[1109] *Hitchman v Stewart* (1855) 3 Drew 271.

[1110] *Nicholson v Revill* (1836) 4 A & E 675 (joint liability); *Jenkins v Jenkins* [1928] 2 KB 501 (joint and several liability); cf *Jameson v CEGB* [1999] 1 All ER 193 (concurrent tort liability).

[1111] *Johnson v Davies* [1999] Ch 117, 127–128. A similar question of construction can arise where the debtors' liability arises under two entirely separate contracts: see the *Heaton* case, n 1106.

[1112] *Lovell & Christmas v Beauchamp* [1894] AC 607; Minors' Contracts Act 1987, s 2.

not performed his part of the contract).[1113] A guarantor (who usually undertakes joint and several liability with the principal debtor) is similarly not liable if the principal contract is illegal.[1114]

(c) Differences

1.286 At common law the liability of a joint debtor passed on his death to the others;[1115] but this rule was not followed in equity, at least in partnership cases, so that the liability of the deceased was enforceable against his estate.[1116] This rule now probably prevails[1117] and also applies where the liability was joint and several.[1118]

1.287 An action on a joint promise must as a general rule be brought against all the debtors;[1119] but there are many qualifications of this rule.[1120] If under one of these, or because one joint debtor does not plead non-joinder of the other, judgment is given against one alone (but not satisfied) the creditor can, by statute, sue the others.[1121] An unsatisfied judgment against one of a number of joint and several debtors does not bar the creditor's right to sue the others.[1122]

(2) Promises to More than One Person

(a) Definitions

1.288 If A makes separate promises to pay £100 each to X and Y he is cumulatively liable for £200; but he may also make a single promise to them both to pay them £100 and no more. Such a promise is *joint* if X and Y are together entitled to the whole of the promised payment (eg if they are the lessors of premises leased to A)[1123] but *several* if each of X and Y is entitled only to a proportionate part (eg if each is owner of part of a cargo insured by A). By statute, certain covenants in deeds made with two or more persons jointly are to be 'construed as being also made with each of them',[1124] so that they are both joint and several.[1125]

(b) Effects of the distinctions

1.289 On the death of a *joint* creditor his rights pass to the others by survivorship,[1126] but this doctrine does not apply between *several* creditors,[1127] and in equity its effect was mitigated by presuming that a contract for the repayment of money to a number of lenders created a several right in each lender.[1128]

1.290 In an action on a *joint* promise all the creditors must (if living) be joined to the action,[1129] but there is no such requirement where the promise is *several*.[1130]

[1113] *Pirie v Richardson* [1927] 1 KB 448.
[1114] *Swan v Bank of Scotland* (1836) 10 Bli NS 627.
[1115] *Cabell v Vaughan* (1669) 1 Wms Saund 291 n 4(f).
[1116] *Kendall v Hamilton* (1879) 4 App Cas 504, 517; *Thorpe v Jackson* (1837) 2 Y & C Ex 553.
[1117] By virtue of the Senior Courts Act 1981, s 49(1).
[1118] *Read v Price* [1909] 1 KB 577.
[1119] *Cabell v Vaughan*, n 1115.
[1120] eg *Wilson, Sons & Co Ltd v Balcarres Brook Steamship Co Ltd* [1893] 1 QB 422; Insolvency Act 1986, s 345(4).
[1121] Civil Liability (Contribution) Act 1978, s 3.
[1122] *Blyth v Fladgate* [1891] 1 Ch 337.
[1123] As in *Bradburne v Botfield* (1845) 14 M & W 559.
[1124] Law of Property Act 1925, s 81.
[1125] For recognition of this concept at common law, see *Palmer v Mallet* (1887) 36 Ch D 411, 421.
[1126] *Anderson v Martindale* (1801) 1 East 497.
[1127] *Withers v Bircham* (1824) 3 B & C 254.
[1128] See *Steeds v Steeds* (1889) 22 QBD 537.
[1129] *Sorsbie v Park* (1843) 12 M & W 146; *Thompson v Hakewill* (1865) 19 CB NS 713.
[1130] *Palmer v Mallet* (1887) 36 Ch D 411.

Payment to or a release granted by one of a number of *joint* creditors prima facie discharges **1.291**
the debt;[1131] but this rule does not apply where the whole is paid to or a release is granted by
one of a number of *several* creditors since each is separately entitled to his share.[1132] Similarly,
a defence available against one of a number of *joint* creditors is generally[1133] available against
the others;[1134] but this rule does not apply where the creditors have *several* rights.[1135]

A promise made to two persons *jointly* can be enforced by all (or the survivor) even though **1.292**
consideration for it was provided by only one; and where the promise is 'joint and several'
a surviving co-promisee can enforce the promise even though the whole consideration was
provided by his deceased co-promisee.[1136] Where the promise is *several* consideration must,
it seems, be provided by any promisee claiming to enforce it.

K. Third Parties

(1) Benefiting Third Parties

The situation here to be discussed is that in which A contracts with B to confer a benefit on **1.293**
C. This situation must be distinguished from that in which C is mentioned in the contract
between A and B only as a person to whom A can pay or deliver what is due to B so as to
obtain a good discharge;[1137] and from that in which A enters, in relation to the same subject
matter, into both the main contract with B and also into a second collateral contract with
C.[1138] In the former case, C is not an intended beneficiary while in the latter he is a party to
a separate contract with A.

(a) Privity of contract at common law

The general common law rule is that rights arising under a contract can be enforced or relied **1.294**
upon only by the parties to the contract.[1139] If, eg, A promised B to pay a sum of money
to C, then at common law C could not enforce the promise.[1140] This rule is subject to
many exceptions, the most important of which is now contained in the Contracts (Rights
of Third Parties) Act 1999[1141] ('the 1999 Act'). This Act subjects the common law rule to
a 'wide-ranging exception' but leaves it 'intact for cases not covered by'[1142] the exception
because they either fall outside its scope[1143] or are specifically excepted from the Act.[1144]
Other exceptions to the common law rule remain in force[1145] and are not subject to the

---

[1131] *Powell v Broadhurst* [1901] 2 Ch 160, 164; *Wallace v Kelsall* (1840) 7 M & W 264, 274.
[1132] *Steeds v Steeds*, n 1128.
[1133] Unless it is personal to one of the creditors.
[1134] *P Samuel & Co v Dumas* [1924] AC 431, 445.
[1135] *Hagedorn v Bazett* (1813) 2 M & S 100.
[1136] *McEvoy v Belfast Banking Co* [1935] AC 24 (bank deposit in names of two persons).
[1137] See *Coulls v Bagot's Executor and Trustee Co Ltd* [1967] ALR 385; contrast *Thavorn v Bank of Credit & Commerce International SA* [1985] 1 Lloyd's Rep 259.
[1138] eg *Shanklin Pier Ltd v Detel Products Ltd* [1951] 2 KB 854; *Charnock v Liverpool Corporation* [1968] 1 WLR 1498; *Re Charge Card Services* [1987] Ch 150, aff'd [1989] Ch 497.
[1139] *Dunlop Pneumatic Tyre Co Ltd v Selfridge & Co Ltd* [1915] AC 847, 853.
[1140] *Tweddle v Atkinson* (1861) 1 B & S 393; *Beswick v Beswick* [1968] AC 58, 72, 81, 83, 92–93, 95.
[1141] See 1.304–1.312.
[1142] Law Commission, *Privity of Contract: Contracts for the Benefit of Third Parties* (Law Com No 242, 1996) (hereinafter 'Report') paras 5.16, 13.2. The 1999 Act is based on this Report.
[1143] eg because the third party is not 'expressly identified' in the contract, as s 1(3) of the 1999 Act requires: 1.304.
[1144] 1999 Act, s 6 (1.309).
[1145] 1999 Act, s 7(1) (1.310).

provisions of the 1999 Act. The operation and scope of the rule and the other exceptions to it therefore still call for discussion.

(i) Operation of the contract

1.295 Although a contract between A and B for the benefit of C cannot generally be enforced by C, it remains binding between A and B; but such a contract does give rise to special problems with regard to B's remedies against A.

1.296 **Promisee's remedies.** Where the contract is specifically enforceable in equity,[1146] B can so enforce it against A and C will then obtain the intended benefit.[1147] But where A promises B to pay a sum of money to C and fails to do so, B cannot generally claim that sum for himself;[1148] and though B could claim restitution of his own performance where this remedy was otherwise available,[1149] such a remedy could be wholly inadequate.[1150] Where A's breach has caused loss to B, B can recover damages in respect of that loss from A: eg, where B has contracted with C for the performance to be rendered by A, or (perhaps) where, on A's breach, B has incurred expense in securing an equivalent benefit for C.[1151] But, as damages in a contractual action are meant to compensate a claimant for his own loss,[1152] B cannot in general recover substantial damages where the only loss resulting from A's breach is suffered by C. This position is, however, 'most unsatisfactory':[1153] as it could give rise to a 'legal black hole'[1154] in allowing A to escape all substantial liability for an established breach. It is therefore subject to exceptions: eg, damages can be recovered by an agent in respect of loss suffered by his undisclosed principal;[1155] by a local authority in respect of a loss suffered ultimately by its inhabitants;[1156] and by a shipper of goods in respect of loss suffered by a consignee to whom the goods have been transferred and who has not acquired any contractual rights of his own against the carrier in respect of the latter's breach.[1157] B can likewise recover damages from A where A's breach of a building contract adversely affects C to whom the site is later transferred[1158] or who already owned it when the contract was made.[1159] The 'narrower ground'[1160] for this conclusion is that it amounts simply to an extension of the earlier carriage cases. The building cases have also been explained on the 'broader ground'[1161] that in

---

[1146] A promise by A to B to render personal services to C would not be so enforceable.

[1147] *Beswick v Beswick* [1968] AC 58; for enforcement of promises *not to sue* C (by staying such an action), see *Gore v Van der Lann* [1967] 2 QB 31; *Snelling v John G Snelling Ltd* [1973] 1 QB 87.

[1148] See the *Coulls* case, n 1137, at 409–411; for an exception, see *Cleaver v Mutual Reserve Fund Life Association* [1892] 1 QB 147, where C had been convicted of murdering B. The sum could also be claimed by B for himself where A's promise to B was to pay it to C *or as B might direct*: see *The Spiros C* [2001] 2 Lloyd's Rep 319, 331. The same reasoning can apply where A promises to render some performance other than to pay money: see *Mitchell v Ede* (1840) 1 Ad & El 888.

[1149] Part performance by A (as in *Beswick v Beswick*, n 1147) may bar this remedy.

[1150] eg where a life insurance policy matures soon after its commencement as a result of the death of the person insured.

[1151] See after n 1161.

[1152] *The Albazero* [1977] AC 774, 846.

[1153] *Woodar Investment Development Ltd v Wimpey Construction Co Ltd* [1980] 1 WLR 277, 291.

[1154] *Darlington BC v Wiltshier (Northern) Ltd* [1995] 1 WLR 68, 79.

[1155] *Siu Yin Kwan v Eastern Insurance Co Ltd* [1994] 2 AC 199, 207; *Boyter v Thompson* [1995] 2 AC 629, 632.

[1156] *St Albans City and District Council v International Computers Ltd* [1996] 4 All ER 481.

[1157] *Dunlop v Lambert* (1839) 6 Cl & F 600, 627 as explained and limited in *The Albazero*, n 1152.

[1158] *Linden Gardens Trust Ltd v Lenesta Sludge Disposals Ltd* [1994] 1 AC 85.

[1159] *Darlington BC v Wiltshier Northern Ltd* [1995] 1 WLR 68, approved in *Alfred McAlpine Construction Ltd v Panatown Ltd* [2001] 1 AC 518, 531, 566 ('the *Panatown* case').

[1160] The *Panatown* case, n 1159, at 575.

[1161] *Linden Gardens* case, n 1158, at 96–97 (at least if 'the repairs have been or are likely to be carried out': *Linden Gardens* case, n 1158, and see the *Panatown* case, see n 1159).

them B recovers damages in respect of his *own* loss, ie the cost to B of providing the benefit to C that A should have, but has failed to, provide. On neither view, however, is A liable to B for substantial damages where C has an independent right against A in respect of the loss under a separate contract between A and C.[1162] Any damages recoverable by B under the above exceptions in respect of C's (but not damages in respect of B's own)[1163] loss must be held by B for C.[1164] The need to extend the exceptions further is reduced where C can enforce a term in the contract between A and B against A under the 1999 Act;[1165] but B's rights against A are preserved by the Act[1166] and continue to be significant: eg, where under the Act A has a defence against C which is not available against B.[1167]

Position between promisee and third party. Where A promises B to make a payment to C **1.297** and performs this promise, B is not entitled to recover that payment from C[1168] unless it was made to C as B's nominee. Before performance by A, the contract can be varied by agreement between A and B so as to provide for payment to B, but normally B has no unilateral right to demand payment to himself;[1169] the point is important where it is a matter of concern to A that provision should be made for C.[1170] Where A fails to perform, C cannot normally compel B to bring against A any of the actions described in 1.295.

(ii) Scope of the doctrine

Under the common law doctrine of privity, C cannot obtain rights *arising under* a contract **1.298** between A and B. But he may benefit from it indirectly[1171] and it may also give rise to the possibility of A's being liable to C in tort.

Liability in negligence. A contract between A and B may give rise to a relationship **1.299** between A and C in which A owes a duty of care to C: eg, that of carrier and passenger or cargo-owner.[1172] Similarly, where A contracts with B to provide professional services, A may be liable to C for negligence in the performance of the contract.[1173] All such tort liability differs from liability on the contract in that it depends on negligence, while contract liability is often strict;[1174] and in that it does not normally[1175] arise if A simply repudiates the contract with B or takes no steps in its performance. Nor (except in cases of misrepresentation or negligence in providing professional services) is A generally liable in tort to C for purely economic loss.[1176] Nor, even where the damage is physical, is A liable for it to C where it results simply from a defect in the very thing supplied by A (causing it to disintegrate)[1177] or where C has neither the legal ownership of nor a possessory title to the thing damaged.[1178] Moreover, in a tort action the claimant cannot normally recover

---

[1162] *Panatown* case, n 1159, at 571; since there is no 'legal black hole' (n 1154) in such a case, there is no need to extend the present exception to it.

[1163] See after n 1161.

[1164] *The Albazero*, n 1152, at 845; *Linden Gardens* case, n 1158.

[1165] See 1.304.

[1166] 1999 Act, s 4.

[1167] See 1999 Act, s 3(4).

[1168] See *Beswick v Beswick* [1968] AC 58 (where A had to be compelled to make the payment).

[1169] See 1.296, n 1148.

[1170] As in *Re Stapleton-Bretherton* [1941] Ch 482.

[1171] eg *Hirachand Punamchand v Temple* [1911] 2 KB 330 (1.59).

[1172] *Austin v Great Western Rly Co* (1867) LR 2 QB 442; *The Antonis P Lemos* [1985] AC 711.

[1173] eg *White v Jones* [1995] 2 AC 207; *Henderson v Merrett Syndicates Ltd* [1995] 2 AC 145.

[1174] See 1.414.

[1175] For an exception, see *White v Jones*, n 1173.

[1176] *Simaan General Contracting Co v Pilkington Glass Ltd (No 2)* [1988] QB 758; *Customs & Excise Commissioners v Barclays Bank plc* [2006] UKHL 28, [2007] 1 AC 181.

[1177] *Aswan Engineering Establishment Co v Lupdine Ltd* [1987] 1 WLR 1.

[1178] *The Aliakmon* [1986] AC 785; *The Starsin* [2003] UKHL 12, [2004] 1 AC 715.

damages in respect of his expectation interest[1179] so that where, eg, A's defective performance of a building contract with B causes loss to C, C cannot in a tort action recover from A the cost of making the defects good.[1180]

1.300 Such building contract cases must be distinguished from cases in which A, a solicitor, is engaged by B to draw up a will leaving property to C and A either does nothing to carry out the instructions[1181] or carries them out negligently,[1182] so that C does not get the intended benefit. In some such cases[1183] C has recovered the value of that benefit from A. One ground for upholding such claims has been that, if they were rejected, A would be under no substantial liability for an admitted breach, B's estate having suffered no loss; but they have been upheld even where A's negligent breach did cause loss to B's estate.[1184] The disappointed beneficiary cases can be explained on the ground that in them the benefit intended for C is (unlike that in the building contract cases)[1185] not the product of A's work but existed independently of it and before the conclusion of the contract between A and B. They have been described as 'unusual'[1186] but their principle has nevertheless been extended to closely analogous situations: eg, where, as a result of A's negligence in performing a contract with B, C was deprived of benefits under a pension scheme or a trust.[1187]

1.301 **Intimidation.** The tort of intimidation may be committed when A, by threatening to break his contract with B, induces B to act to C's detriment[1188] (eg to stop doing business with C). C's claim against A in such a case is not one to enforce the contract between A and B[1189] but one for compensation for loss suffered by C as a result of A's unlawful threats against B.

(b) Exceptions to the doctrine

(i) Judge-made exceptions

1.302 **Agency, assignment and land law.** A number of originally judge-made exceptions to the doctrine of privity arise under the rules relating to agency, assignment and covenants affecting land. These are discussed elsewhere in this book.[1190]

1.303 **Trusts of promises.** In equity, a promise by A to B in favour of C can be enforced against A by C,[1191] joining B as a party to the action,[1192] if B can be regarded as trustee for C of A's promise. B can be so regarded if three conditions are satisfied: he must have intended to take the promise for C's benefit (rather than for his own);[1193] his intention to benefit C must be final and

---

[1179] See 1.04.

[1180] *D & F Estates Ltd v Church Commissioners for England* [1989] AC 177.

[1181] *White v Jones*, n 1173.

[1182] *Ross v Caunters* [1980] Ch 287; *Hill v van Erp* (1997) 142 ALR 687.

[1183] eg those cited in nn 1181 and 1182; contrast *Hemmens v Wilson Browne* [1995] Ch 223; *Walker v Geo H Medlicott & Son* [1999] 1 WLR 727.

[1184] *Carr-Glynn v Frearsons* [1999] Ch 326.

[1185] At n 1180.

[1186] *Goodwill v Pregnancy Advisory Service* [1996] 1 WLR 1397, 1403.

[1187] *Gorham v British Telecommunications plc* [2000] 1 WLR 2129; *Richards v Hughes* [2004] EWCA Civ 266, [2004] PNLR 35.

[1188] *Rookes v Barnard* [1964] AC 1129. Intimidation has been described as 'only one variant of a broader tort usually called…"causing loss by unlawful means"': *OBG Ltd v Allan; Douglas v Hello! Ltd; Mainstream Properties Ltd v Young* [2007] UKHL 21, [2008] 1 AC 1, at [7].

[1189] *Rookes v Barnard*, n 1188.

[1190] See EPL ch 9 and EPL 4.98–4.101.

[1191] *Les Affréteurs Réunis SA v Leopold Walford (London) Ltd* [1919] AC 801.

[1192] *The Panaghia P* [1983] 2 Lloyd's Rep 653, 655.

[1193] See *West v Houghton* (1879) 4 CPD 197; *Vandepitte v Preferred Accident Insurance Corporation* [1933] AC 70.

irrevocable;[1194] and it must be coupled with an intention to *create a trust* to C's favour. This last requirement is hard to define and is mainly responsible for the restricted scope of the exception. The courts have become reluctant (where the words 'trust' or 'trustee' are not used) to infer the existence of a trust, since such an inference will deprive A and B of their right to rescind or vary the contract by agreement.[1195] The inference is most likely to be drawn where B obtained A's promise so as to secure the performance of an antecedent legal obligation owed by B to C.[1196] The trust device probably applies only to promises to pay money or transfer property.[1197]

(ii) *Contracts (Rights of Third Parties) Act 1999*

Third party's right of enforcement. The main purpose of the 1999 Act is to enable a third **1.304** party to acquire rights under a contract if and to the extent that the parties to the contract so intend. Section 1 accordingly provides that a person (C) who is not a party to a contract can in his own right enforce a term in a contract between A (the promisor) and B (the promisee) if (a) the contract expressly provides that he may; or (b) the term purports to confer a benefit on C[1198] unless (in this latter case) it appears on a proper construction of the contract that A and B did not intend the term to be enforceable by C.[1199] It is also necessary for C to be expressly identified in the contract by name, as a member of a class or as answering a particular description (but not for C to have been in existence when the contract was made);[1200] and C will not have a right to enforce a term otherwise than subject to and in accordance with any other relevant terms of the contract[1201] (such as one expressly excluding C's right or specifying time limits for claims under the contract). Where a term 'excludes or limits' liability, references to C's 'enforcing' it are to be 'construed as references to his availing himself of the exclusion or limitation'.[1202] There is no need for C to provide consideration for A's promise.[1203] Under these provisions C would, in many cases previously governed by the doctrine of privity, now have a contractual right against A.[1204] But this would not be true in all such cases: eg in the 'disappointed beneficiary' cases[1205] C would still have no *contractual* rights against the solicitor.

The 1999 Act does not in general use the fiction of C's having become a party to the con- **1.305** tract[1206] but it does provide that for the purpose of enforcing his right C is to have any remedy that would have been available to him if he had been a party to the contract.[1207] He

---

1194 *Re Sinclair's Life Policy* [1938] Ch 799.
1195 *Re Schebsman* [1944] Ch 83, 104; contrast *Re Flavell* (1883) 25 Ch D 89.
1196 See *Re Independent Air Travel Ltd The Times*, 20 May 1961.
1197 *Southern Water Authority v Carey* [1985] 2 All ER 1077, 1083.
1198 1999 Act, s 1(1). A contract term does not 'purport to confer a benefit' on a third party simply because the position of the third party will be improved if the contract is performed. In order for a term to 'purport to confer a benefit', one of the purposes of the parties' bargain (rather than one of its incidental benefits if performed) must have been to benefit the third party (*Dolphin Maritime & Aviation Services Ltd v Sveriges Angfartygs Assurans Forening* [2009] EWHC 716 (Comm), [2009] 2 Lloyd's Rep 123).
1199 1999 Act, s 1(2). The burden under s 1(2) of proving that A and B did not intend the term to be enforceable by C rests on A: *Nisshin Shipping Co Ltd v Cleaves & Co Ltd* [2003] EWHC 2602 (Comm), [2004] 1 Lloyd's Rep 38; *The Laemthong Glory* [2005] EWCA Civ 519, [2005] 1 Lloyd's Rep 632; *Prudential Assurance Co Ltd v Ayres* [2007] EWHC 775 (Ch), [2007] 3 All ER 946; *Great Eastern Shipping Co Ltd v Far East Chartering Ltd (The Jag Ravi)* [2012] EWCA 180, [2012] 1 Lloyd's Rep 637.
1200 1999 Act, s 1(3): *Avraamides v Colwill* [2006] EWCA Civ 1533.
1201 1999 Act, s 1(4).
1202 1999 Act, s 1(6).
1203 Report, n 1142, para 6.8 fn 8.
1204 eg probably in a case such as *Beswick v Beswick* [1968] AC 58, (unless the facts fell within s 1(2)).
1205 See 1.300.
1206 cf 1999 Act, s 7(4). For an exception see 1999 Act, s 3(6) (1.308, n 1214).
1207 1999 Act, s 1(5).

can therefore recover damages in respect of expectation loss,[1208] subject to the usual tests of remoteness, and mitigation, though these might lead to different results where the action was brought by C from those which would follow if it were brought by B.[1209]

1.306 **Right to rescind or vary the contract.**   Where C has a right under section 1 to enforce a term of a contract, the right of A and B to rescind or vary the contract by agreement without C's consent is limited but not altogether removed. The general principle, laid down in section 2(1), is that A and B lose this right if C has communicated his assent to the term to A; or if A knows that C has relied on the term; or if A can reasonably foresee that C would rely on the term and C has relied on it. But these conditions may be modified by the terms of the contract;[1210] and the court can in specified circumstances dispense with C's consent: eg where it cannot be obtained because his whereabouts cannot reasonably be ascertained.[1211]

1.307   The restrictions described in 1.305 do not normally apply where A promises B to perform in favour of C *or as B shall direct*.[1212] If B later directs A to perform in favour of D, the contract is not *varied* but will be performed in accordance with its original terms by A's performing in favour of D.

1.308 **Promisor's defences against third party.**   Section 3 deals with the situation in which A seeks, in an action by C to enforce a term of the contract, to rely by way of defence or set-off on matters which would have been available to A if proceedings to enforce the contract had been brought by B. The general principle is that A can so rely on such a matter against C if it 'arises from or in connection with the contract [between A and B] and is relevant to the term' sought to be enforced by C.[1213] A could, eg, rely against C on a valid exemption clause in the contract between A and B or on B's repudiatory breach. Where C's enforcement takes the form of reliance by him on an exemption or limitation clause in the contract between A and B, C likewise cannot rely on it if he could not have done so, had he been a party to the contract:[1214] eg if, on that supposition, it would have been ineffective under the Unfair Contract Terms Act 1977.[1215] The general principle stated above can be modified by agreement between A and B.[1216] The 1999 Act also provides for A to be able to rely against C on defences and counterclaims which would not have been available to A against B but would have been available to A against C if C had been a party to the contract.[1217]

1.309 **Exceptions to third party's entitlement.**   Section 6 lists cases to which C's right of enforcement under section 1 does not extend. In some of these excepted cases, the common law rules as to contracts for the benefit of third parties continue to apply, so that C will generally acquire no rights: eg, C cannot enforce 'any term of a contract of employment against an employee'.[1218] In others, C has, or can acquire, rights against A under other rules of law: eg where he is the transferee of a bill of lading issued by A to B, his rights are governed by other legislation[1219] to the exclusion of the 1999 Act.[1220]

[1208] See 1.04.
[1209] eg the test of remoteness would be foreseeability of C's (not B's) loss.
[1210] 1999 Act, s 2(3).
[1211] 1999 Act, s 2(4).
[1212] cf 1.296, n 1148
[1213] 1999 Act, s 3(2)(a).
[1214] 1999 Act, s 3(6).
[1215] See 1.112.
[1216] 1999 Act, s 3(5).
[1217] 1999 Act, s 3(4).
[1218] 1999 Act, s 6(3)(a).
[1219] Carriage of Goods by Sea Act 1992.
[1220] 1999 Act, s 6(5).

Third party's other rights.   C is not deprived by the 1999 Act of any rights which he may   **1.310**
have apart from its provisions:[1221] eg under other exceptions to the doctrine of privity; in
cases which fall outside its scope; or under a direct collateral contract between A and C. The
point is important not only where C has no right under the 1999 Act and does have one
under other rules,[1222] but also where he has rights both under the 1999 Act and apart from
it.[1223] By making his claim apart from the 1999 Act, C can avoid the restriction which it
imposes on claims made under it.

Relation to other legislation.   Section 7(4) provides that C is not to be treated as a party to   **1.311**
the contract between A and B for the purpose of other legislation. If, eg, that contract were on
A's standard terms of business, the requirement of reasonableness under the Unfair Contract
Terms Act 1977[1224] would not apply in favour of C (but only in favour of B). By way of
exception or quasi-exception to this principle, where a claim under the 1999 Act is made on
behalf of or by C in respect of C's death or personal injury, A cannot rely on an exemption
clause in his contract with B which is void under the 1977 Act[1225] because it seeks to exclude
or limit liability in respect of death or personal injury resulting from negligence.[1226]

Promisee's rights.   The fact that C has acquired rights under the contract 'does not affect   **1.312**
any right of the promisee [B] to enforce any term of the contract'.[1227] To avoid the risk of A's
being made liable in respect of the same loss to both B and C, the 1999 Act directs the court
to reduce any award to C to such extent as it thinks appropriate to take account of the sum
recovered by B.[1228]

(iii) Other statutory exceptions

Insurance.   The doctrine of privity can be particularly inconvenient in relation to contracts   **1.313**
of insurance;[1229] and in this field it is, in addition to being modified by the trust device and by
agency, subject to statutory exceptions. These apply where a person insures his or her life for
the benefit of his or her spouse, civil partner or children;[1230] where a motor insurance policy
covers a person driving a car with the consent of the insured;[1231] where a person who insures
property has only a limited interest in it (so as to enable him to insure for the full value, paying
over any amount in excess of his own interest which he may recover to other persons interested
in the property);[1232] and where a house which is insured is destroyed by fire (so as to entitle
'any person...interested' to require insurance moneys to be laid out towards reinstating the
house).[1233] The scheme established under statute between the Law Society and insurers for
the compulsory insurance of solicitors against liability for professional negligence[1234] also
gives rise 'by virtue of public law' to rights and duties between solicitors and the insurers.[1235]

[1221] 1999 Act, s 7(1).

[1222] eg in the 'disappointed beneficiary' cases: see n 1181.

[1223] As in *Nisshin Shipping Co Ltd v Cleaves & Co Ltd* [2003] EWHC 2602, [2004] 1 All ER (Comm) 481.

[1224] See 1.113.

[1225] 1977 Act, s 2(1) (1.112).

[1226] 1999 Act, s 7(2) disapplies s 2(2), but not s 2(1), of the 1977 Act.

[1227] 1999 Act, s 4; a restitution claim by B, though not one to 'enforce' the contract, seems likewise to be unaffected by the 1999 Act.

[1228] 1999 Act, s 5.

[1229] In Australia there is some support for not applying the doctrine to such contracts: *Trident General Insurance Co Ltd v McNiece Bros Pty Ltd* (1988) 65 CLR 107; cf, in Canada, *Fraser River Pile and Dredge Ltd v Can-Dive Services Ltd* [2000] 1 Lloyd's Rep 199.

[1230] Married Women's Property Act 1882, s 11; Civil Partnership Act 2004, s 70.

[1231] Road Traffic Act 1988, s 148(7).

[1232] Marine Insurance Act 1906, s 14(2).

[1233] Fire Prevention (Metropolis) Act 1774, s 83.

[1234] Under Solicitors Act 1974, s 37.

[1235] *Swain v Law Society* [1983] AC 598, 611.

1.314 Insurance against liability to third parties does not strictly confer any contractual rights on third parties but by statute such third parties have in certain cases the right to enforce the rights of the insured under the policy directly against the insurer.[1236] Where the third party is the victim of a motor accident he has a right against the Motor Insurers' Bureau even though the driver was not insured or cannot be traced.[1237]

1.315 **Law of Property Act 1925, section 56(1).** This subsection provides that 'A person may take ... the benefit of any ... covenant or agreement over or respecting land or other property, although he may not be named as a party to the conveyance or other instrument'. In the 1925 Act 'property' (unless the context indicates the contrary) includes 'any thing in action';[1238] and since a contractual promise falls within these words, it was at one time argued that any written promise by A to B to pay money to C was enforceable by C under section 56(1).[1239] The prevailing view, however, is that the subsection applies only in favour of a person to whom the instrument purports to make a grant or with whom it purports to make a covenant:[1240] in other words, only where C is a party in all but in name.

(2) Binding Third Parties

(a) Third party generally not bound

1.316 A contract between A and B cannot impose a positive obligation on C (such as one to pay £100 to B) and this aspect of the doctrine of privity is not affected by the Contracts (Rights of Third Parties) Act 1999[1241] or by the other exceptions to the doctrine which have been discussed in this section. Under exceptions discussed elsewhere in this book,[1242] C may sometimes be so bound: eg under the law of agency or under the law governing covenants relating to land. He may also sometimes be bound by an exemption clause in a contract to which he was not a party.[1243]

(b) Scope of the rule

1.317 C may be adversely affected by a contract between A and B in ways which fall short of requiring him actually to perform terms of that contract. Two possibilities call for discussion.

(i) Contract creating proprietary or possessory rights

1.318 If a contract between A and B creates such rights in favour of B, and C later acquires an interest in the subject matter (eg by buying goods hired out by A to B and in B's possession),[1244] then C must respect those antecedent rights.[1245]

(ii) Inducing breach of contract

1.319 The principle stated in 1.317 does not apply where B has no proprietary or possessory right in the subject matter, but only a contractual right relating to it: eg where B is the voyage or

---

[1236] Third Parties (Rights Against Insurers) Act 1930, s 1 (which will be repealed when the Third Parties (Rights Against Insurers) Act 2010 is brought into effect); Road Traffic Act 1988, ss 151–153.

[1237] See *Gardner v Moore* [1984] AC 548, 556; *White v White* [2001] UKHL 29, [2001] 1 WLR 481.

[1238] Law of Property Act 1925, s 205 (1)(xx).

[1239] *Beswick v Beswick* [1966] Ch 538 *per* Lord Denning MR and Danckwerts LJ.

[1240] *Beswick v Beswick* [1968] AC 58, 94, 106; *Amsprop Trading Ltd v Harris Distribution Ltd* [1997] 1 WLR 1025.

[1241] Report, n 1142, paras 10.32, 7.6.

[1242] See EPL ch 9 and EPL 4.98–4.101.

[1243] See 1.323–1.327.

[1244] See further at n 1254.

[1245] See *Port Line Ltd v Ben Line Steamers Ltd* [1958] QB 146, 166, where B's claim failed as he had *no* 'proprietary or possessory interest' and for the reason given in n 1253.

time charterer of A's ship.[1246] But if, while the charterparty is in force, A sells the ship to C, the question arises whether B can in any way enforce his rights under the charterparty against C.[1247] Clearly, B cannot require C to *perform* A's obligation to render services under the charter, but an injunction may sometimes be available to restrain C from conduct[1248] inducing a breach of the contract between A and B. One view was that this remedy was based on B's having, by virtue of his contract with A, acquired an equitable interest in the ship.[1249] But this reasoning would have the undesirable result[1250] of applying the doctrine of constructive notice to commercial dealings in chattels; and the preferable view is that C's liability, if any, is based on (or on the analogy of) the tort of inducing A to break his contract with B.[1251] Such liability depends on C's intending to induce the breach,[1252] and hence on his having actual knowledge (and not merely constructive notice) of, not only the contract, but also the term alleged to have been broken.[1253] The same requirement probably has to be satisfied where B's right is one, not *of* actual, but *to* the future, possession of a chattel: eg, under a contract of hire, the period of which had not yet begun when C acquired the thing from A.[1254]

(3) Exemption Clauses and Third Parties

(a) Benefiting third parties

(i) Privity and exceptions

Under the doctrine of privity, C could not, in general, take the benefit of an exemption **1.320** clause[1255] in a contract between A and B. He could do so only if one of the exceptions to the doctrine (such as B's having acted as his or A's agent) operated in his favour;[1256] or where the clause was incorporated into a direct contract between A and C, implied from dealings between them;[1257] or where such dealings gave rise to a bailment relationship between A and C which by implication incorporated the clause.[1258] It followed that such an exemption clause did not protect C merely because he was an employee or agent engaged by B for the purpose of performing B's contract with A.[1259] The 1999 Act now entitles C to 'enforce' an

---

[1246] Such a charter gives B no more than a contractual right to require A to render services by use of the ship: see *The Scaptrade* [1983] AC 694, 702.

[1247] This question is distinct from that whether B can enforce the charterparty *against A* by restraining A from dealing with C in a manner inconsistent with it: see *Lauritzencool Ltd v Lady Navigation Inc* [2005] EWCA Civ 579, [2005] 1 WLR 3686, at [16].

[1248] Not from mere inaction: *Law Debenture Trust Corp v Ural Caspian Oil Corp Ltd* [1993] 1 WLR 138, 146; for a successful appeal on another point, see [1995] Ch 152.

[1249] *Lord Strathcona Steamship Co v Dominion Coal Co* [1926] AC 108.

[1250] *Manchester Trust Ltd v Furness Withy* [1895] 2 QB 539, 545.

[1251] *Lumley v Gye* (1853) 2 El & Bl 216.

[1252] *OBG Ltd v Allan; Douglas v Hello! Ltd; Mainstream Properties Ltd v Young* [2007] UKHL 21, [2008] 1 AC 1, at [8], [62]; and see n 1250. The requisite intention can be negatived by mistake of law: at [202]; *Meretz Investments NV v ACP Ltd* [2006] EWHC 74 (Ch), [2007] Ch 197, at [370], [372].

[1253] The tort claim failed for want of such knowledge in the *Port Line* case, n 1245 and in the *Mainstream* case, n 1252, at [69], [200], [202]; and see also at [40], [191], [192], [200]. Deliberately shutting one's eyes would be equivalent to knowledge: *Mainstream* case, n 1252, at [41] and [192]. A fortiori, there is no liability for this tort where no breach is induced: see the *OBG* case, n 1252, at [86] and the *Douglas* case, n 1252, at [129], [248] (where the defendants were held liable on other grounds).

[1254] As in *The Stena Nautica (No 2)* [1982] 2 Lloyd's Rep 336 (where the present point did not strictly arise).

[1255] Including a limitation of liability clause.

[1256] eg *Hall v North-Eastern Rly* (1875) LR 10 QB 437.

[1257] *Elder Dempster & Co v Paterson Zochonis & Co* [1924] AC 522, as explained in *Adler v Dickson* [1955] 1 QB 158, 189.

[1258] *Elder Dempster & Co v Paterson Zochonis & Co* [1924] AC 522, as explained in *The Pioneer Container* [1994] 2 AC 324, 339–340.

[1259] *Scruttons Ltd v Midland Silicones Ltd* [1962] AC 446.

exemption clause in a contract between A and B,[1260] but only if the requirements of the Act are satisfied; and in some pre-1999 cases they were plainly not satisfied: eg, because C was not 'expressly identified'[1261] in the contract.[1262]

(ii) Himalaya clauses

1.321 The position described in 1.319 was regarded as inconvenient and avoided by so-called 'Himalaya clauses'[1263] in the contract between A and B. The effect of these elaborate clauses is that, once A begins performance of his contract with B, a separate contract arises between A and C,[1264] giving C the benefit of specified provisions[1265] in the contract between A and B to the extent to which they were valid[1266] in that contract and covered the acts of C giving rise to the loss.[1267] Himalaya clauses were generally upheld by the courts.[1268] Under the 1999 Act, less elaborate clauses will protect C,[1269] but only subject to the provisions of that Act and on a different ground: ie, not because there is a contract between A and C, but because C is entitled to enforce a term in a contract between A and B.[1270]

(iii) Clauses defining duties

1.322 A term in the contract between A and B may be relevant as limiting the duty of care owed by C (eg as building subcontractor) to A and so give C a defence to an action in tort by A.[1271]

(b) Binding third parties

(i) General rule

1.323 The general rule is that C is not bound by an exemption clause in a contract between A and B. Hence if A's breach of that contract amounts to a tort against C, then C will not be adversely affected by such a clause.[1272]

(ii) Exceptions

1.324 C may be bound by an exemption clause in a contract between A and B if B acted as C's or A's agent, if only for the limited purpose of restricting C's rights against A by the clause;[1273] or if an implied contract to this effect between A and C could be inferred from their conduct in pursuance of the contract between A and B.[1274] In both these situations C is bound by

---

[1260] Section 1(6) (see 1.304). An exclusive jurisdiction clause would not be covered by s 1(6); cf n 1265.

[1261] See s 1(3) of the Act.

[1262] See eg the *Midland Silicones* case, n 1259.

[1263] So named after the ship in *Adler v Dickson*, n 1257.

[1264] *The Eurymedon* [1975] AC 154.

[1265] See *The Mahkutai* [1996] AC 650 (exclusive jurisdiction clause not covered).

[1266] See *The Starsin* [2003] UKHL 12, [2004] 1 AC 715, where this requirement was not satisfied.

[1267] See *Raymond Burke Motors Ltd v Mersey Docks & Harbour Co* [1986] 1 Lloyd's Rep 155 (acts done by C before beginning of performance of main contract not covered).

[1268] *The Eurymedon*, n 1264; *The New York Star* [1981] 1 WLR 138; contrast *The Suleyman Stalskiy* [1976] 2 Lloyd's Rep 609.

[1269] By virtue of s 1(6).

[1270] cf, in the United States, *Norfolk Southern Railway v James N Kirby Ltd* 125 S Ct 395, 399 (2000).

[1271] *Junior Books Ltd v Veitchi Co Ltd* [1983] 1 AC 520, 546; the dictum was doubted in *The Aliakmon* [1986] AC 785, 817 (where the question was whether C was *bound* by the clause) and in *Linklaters Business Services v Sir Robert McAlpine Ltd* [2010] EWHC 1145 (TCC), [2010] BLR 537 Akenhead J stated (at [27]) that it was now 'in practice inconceivable' that a duty of care would be found to exist on the facts of *Junior Books*.

[1272] *The Aliakmon*, n 1271.

[1273] *The Kite* [1933] P 164, 181; *Norfolk Southern Railway* case, n 1270.

[1274] *Pyrene Co Ltd v Scindia Navigation Co Ltd* [1954] 2 QB 402, as explained in the *Midland Silicones* case, n 1259.

the clause because there is a contract between him and A; but in the situations described in 1.324 to 1.326 C is so bound even though there is no such contract.

Bailment on terms.   C may entrust goods to B under a bailment (eg for carriage or for   **1.325** cleaning) and authorize B to employ a subcontractor (A). C will then be bound by any terms of the sub-bailment to A to which C has consented,[1275] even though there is no contract between A and C.[1276] This rule has been applied *only* where the relationship between C and A was that of bailor and sub-bailee.[1277] It seems to be based on the fact that the sub-bailment is the sole source of A's duty to C;[1278] and therefore not to apply where C does not need to rely on the bailment to establish A's duty of care to him.[1279]

Clauses defining duties.   The terms of A's contract with B may be relevant to the scope   **1.326** of any duty of care owed by A to C: eg, where the term defines work to be done by A as a subcontractor employed by B for the purpose of the performance of a main contract between B and C.[1280]

Derivative rights.   A contract between A and B may contain (1) a promise by A to B to render   **1.327** some performance to C and (2) an exemption clause in favour of A. If C sues A to enforce the first of these promises under the 1999 Act, A can rely on the second[1281] since C's right, being derived from B's, is subject to the restrictions which govern B's rights.[1282] This reasoning does not apply where C's claim is not one to enforce a term of the contract between A and B but arises in tort and apart from the 1999 Act: such a claim is not affected by its provisions.[1283]

L. Transfer of Contractual Rights

A contractual right, such as a debt owed by A to B, can be transferred by B to C by a pro-   **1.328** cess called assignment. This is a transaction between B (the creditor or assignor) and C (the assignee).[1284] A (the debtor) is not a party to it and his consent to it is not required.[1285]

(1) Law and Equity

(a) Substantive difference

Originally, the common law did not generally[1286] give effect to the assignment of a 'chose   **1.329** in action' (ie, of a right such as a contract debt which could be asserted only by bringing an

---

[1275] *Morris v CW Martin & Sons Ltd* [1966] 1 QB 716, 729; *The Pioneer Container* [1994] 2 AC 324; *East West Corp v DKBS 1912 AF A/S* [2003] EWCA Civ 83; [2003] QB 1509, at [24], [69].

[1276] *Targe Towing Ltd v Marine Blast Ltd* [2004] EWCA Civ 346; [2004] 1 Lloyd's Rep 721, at [28]; alternatively, C's consent to the terms of the bailment may bind C by virtue of an implied contract of the kind described in 1.324: *Sandeman Coprimar SA v Transitos y Transportes Integrales SL* [2003] EWCA Civ 113, [2003] QB 1270, at [63]–[65].

[1277] See *Scruttons Ltd v Midland Silicones Ltd* [1962] AC 446 where the defendants were not bailees. There is perhaps some support in the speech of Lord Goff in *Henderson v Merrett Syndicates Ltd* [1995] AC 145, 196 for the view that C may be bound by the clause even where there is no bailment between C and A.

[1278] *The Pioneer Container*, n 1275, at 336.

[1279] *The Kapetan Markos NL (No 2)* [1987] 2 Lloyd's Rep 321, 340.

[1280] *Junior Books* case, n 1271, at 534.

[1281] 1999 Act, s 3(2).

[1282] See Report, n 1142, para 10.24.

[1283] 1999 Act, s 7(1).

[1284] Only voluntary assignment of this kind is discussed here. For assignment by operation of law on death, bankruptcy or insolvency of a creditor, see EPL chs 7 and 19.

[1285] *Mulkerrins v PricewaterhouseCoopers* [2003] UKHL 41; [2003] 1 WLR 1937, at [15].

[1286] The most significant exception to the general rule related to negotiable instruments such as bills of exchange and promissory notes: see EPL ch 14.

action) since it feared that to do so might lead to maintenance or champerty by encouraging officious intermeddling by C in litigation between A and B. Equity did not share this fear[1287] and gave effect to such assignments[1288] unless they in fact produced such undesirable consequences.[1289] The common law did recognize other methods, such as a tripartite contract known as novation[1290] and acknowledgement by A to C,[1291] by which C could become entitled to enforce B's claim against A, but only (unlike assignment) with A's consent.

(b) Procedure

1.330 In enforcing assignments, equity distinguished between legal choses (such as contract debts, enforceable in common law courts) and equitable choses (rights enforceable only in courts of equity). Assignments of the latter were enforced by allowing the assignee to sue the debtor in the Court of Chancery. But this could not be done where the chose was legal since that court did not enforce such rights. Effect to an assignment of a legal chose was given by allowing the assignee to sue the debtor in the name of the assignor, who could be compelled by a court of equity to allow his name to be so used in a common law action.[1292]

(2) *Statutory Assignment*

1.331 The Judicature Act 1873 provided for the administration of common law and equity in one unified court system. It thus removed the need for the assignee of a legal chose to sue in the name of the assignor and recognized this state of affairs by making the provision for statutory assignments which is now contained in section 136(1) of the Law of Property Act 1925.[1293] This section provides that the legal right to a 'debt or other legal thing in action' is transferred to the assignee if the assignment is 'absolute' and in writing and if written notice of it has been given to the debtor. An assignment which does not comply with these requirements can remain effective as an equitable one;[1294] but while a statutory assignee can sue the debtor *alone* an equitable assignee must *join the assignor* as a party to the action,[1295] so as to avoid the prejudice which the debtor might suffer if one of these parties were not before the court.[1296]

(a) 'Absolute' assignment

1.332 In accordance with the principle just stated, assignments are not 'absolute' within section 136(1) (and so take effect in equity only) where it is desirable to have the assignor before the court. For example A may be B's tenant and B may assign the accruing rent to C as security for a loan from C to B until the loan is repaid. B's presence before the court is then desirable in an action by C against A since without it the question whether anything remained due from B to C could not be determined so as to bind B. The assignment is therefore not absolute[1297] and B must be joined to the action by C. The assignment would, however, be absolute if it provided for *reassignment* of the debt to B when he had repaid the loan[1298] for in such a case A can safely go on paying C until he gets notice of the reassignment and is not concerned with the state of

---

[1287] *Wright v Wright* (1750) 1 Ves Sen 409, 411.
[1288] *Crouch v Martin* (1707) 2 Vern 595; *Ryall v Rowles* (1750) 1 Ves Sen 348.
[1289] See 1.347.
[1290] See *Rasbora Ltd v JCL Marine Ltd* [1977] 1 Lloyd's Rep 645.
[1291] *Shamia v Joory* [1958] 1 QB 448.
[1292] See *Re Westerton* [1919] 2 Ch 104, 111.
[1293] Re-enacting Judicature Act 1873, s 25(6).
[1294] *German v Yates* (1915) 32 TLR 52.
[1295] See *The Aiolos* [1983] 2 Lloyd's Rep 25, 33; *Weddell v JA Pearce & Major* [1988] Ch 26, 40.
[1296] Where there is no such practical need for joinder of the assignor, the courts no longer insist on such joinder: *The Mount I* [2001] EWCA Civ 68; [2001] 1 Lloyd's Rep 597, at [60].
[1297] *Durham Bros v Robertson* [1898] QB 765.
[1298] *Tancred v Delagoa Bay, etc, Rly Co* (1889) 23 QBD 239.

accounts between B and C. An assignment of part of a debt is likewise not absolute:[1299] here the potential prejudice to A arises if he denies the existence of the debt; for he could have to make this denial good many times over if each assignee could sue him alone.[1300]

(b) 'Debt or other legal thing in action'

A 'debt' in section 136(1) is a sum certain due under contract or otherwise.[1301] 'Other legal thing in action' includes an equitable chose.[1302] Provision for the transfer of certain things in action is governed by special statutory provisions which sometimes must be used instead of section 136(1)[1303] and sometimes provide an alternative mechanism (to that provided by that subsection) for making the transfer.[1304] **1.333**

(3) Assignment and Authority to Pay

An assignment can take the form either of an agreement between assignor and assignee, or of a direction to the debtor telling him that the debt has been made over to the assignee[1305] (to whom, in such a case, notice of the assignment must be given).[1306] A direction which merely authorizes the debtor to pay a third party is not an assignment.[1307] Where, eg, a person draws a cheque on his bank, payable to a third party, he does not assign part of his balance to the payee.[1308] **1.334**

(4) Formalities

An assignment can take effect as a statutory one only if it is in writing, but there is, in general, no such or other formal requirement for an equitable assignment. Writing is, however, necessary for the validity of a 'disposition of an equitable interest';[1309] and also where the contract creating the debt imposes such a requirement. For the protection of creditors, certain assignments must be registered.[1310] **1.335**

(5) Notice to the Debtor

An equitable assignment is valid even without notice to the debtor, but there are three reasons for giving it. First, if written it may turn the assignment into a statutory one.[1311] Secondly, notice (even if oral) perfects the assignee's title against the debtor[1312] who, if he disregards it and pays the assignor, must make a second payment to the assignee.[1313] Thirdly, successive **1.336**

[1299] *Re Steel Wing Co Ltd* [1921] 1 Ch 349.
[1300] For the same reason, the creditor must in such a case be joined to an action by an assignee: *Walter and Sullivan Ltd v J Murphy & Son Ltd* [1955] 2 QB 584.
[1301] eg under statute: *Dawson v Great Northern & City Rly Co* [1905] 1 KB 260.
[1302] *Re Pain* [1919] 1 Ch 38, 44.
[1303] eg Companies Act 2006, s 544 (shares in companies).
[1304] eg Marine Insurance Act 1906, s 50: *The Mount I* [2001] EWCA Civ 68; [2001] 1 Lloyd's Rep 597, at [74] (marine policies); Carriage of Goods by Sea Act 1992, s 2(1)(a) (bills of lading).
[1305] *William Brandt's Sons & Co v Dunlop Rubber Co* [1905] AC 454, 462.
[1306] *Re Hamilton* (1921) 124 LT 737.
[1307] *Timpson's Exors v Yerbury* [1936] 1 KB 645.
[1308] Bills of Exchange Act 1882, s 53(1); *Deposit Protection Board v Dalia* [1994] 2 AC 367, 400.
[1309] Law of Property Act 1925, s 53(1)(c), re-enacting Statute of Frauds 1677, s 9.
[1310] eg Companies Act 2006, s 860, esp subs (7)(f); Insolvency Act 1986, s 344.
[1311] See 1.331.
[1312] *Warner Bros Records Inc v Rollgreen Ltd* [1976] QB 430.
[1313] *Jones v Farrell* (1857) 1 De G & J 208; so far as *contra*, dicta in the *Warner Bros* case, n 1312, are with respect open to question in view of the developments described in 1.330: cf *Three Rivers DC v Bank of England* [1996] QB 292, 315.

assignees rank in the order in which they give notice to the debtor,[1314] provided that, where the chose assigned is equitable, the notice is in writing.[1315]

(6) Consideration

1.337 The question whether an assignment needs to be supported by consideration arises where the assignor (or his estate) disputes the validity of the assignment.[1316] The overriding principle is that consideration is not necessary where the assignment is a completed gift; whether it has this character depends on the following factors.

(a) Assignment and promise to assign

1.338 A mere promise to assign (as opposed to an actual assignment) is not a completed gift and is binding only if it is supported by consideration so as to have contractual force. An attempt to assign a future right (eg the benefit of a contract not yet made) can operate only as a promise to assign;[1317] but this is not true of an assignment of a right to become due under an existing contract[1318] (eg of future rent under an existing lease).

(b) Further acts to be done by assignor

1.339 A gift is incomplete if the donor fails to make it in the way (if any) prescribed for its subject matter: ie: if something more has to be done by him to transfer the subject matter to the donee.[1319] The donor can be required to do that 'something more' only if he has promised to do so and if the donee has provided consideration for that promise.[1320]

(i) Statutory assignment

1.340 It follows from the reasoning in 1.338 that a statutory assignment need not be supported by consideration, there being nothing more that the assignor need do to transfer the subject matter.[1321]

(ii) Equitable assignment

1.341 The mere fact that a gratuitous assignment is not statutory (and so can take effect only in equity) does not make it an imperfect gift. It will most obviously not make the gift imperfect where the assignment is not statutory for want only of written notice[1322] since such notice can be given by the assignee himself. Where the assignment is not statutory because it is not in writing, the execution of the writing is 'something more' which *could* have been done by the assignor. But as there was no requirement of writing in equity for the assignment of a legal chose,[1323] the assignment can be a completed gift where the intention that it should take effect as such is clear.[1324] Where the assignment is not statutory because it is not absolute it will often be intended to take effect as a contract: eg where it is made as security for a loan

---

[1314] *Dearle v Hall* (1828) 3 Russ 1.

[1315] Law of Property Act 1925, s 137(3).

[1316] For procedure in such a case, see Law of Property Act 1925, s 136(1). The point is of no concern to the debtor: *Walker v Bradford Old Bank Ltd* (1884) 12 QBD 511.

[1317] *Glegg v Bromley* [1912] 3 KB 474.

[1318] eg *Hughes v Pump House Hotel Co Ltd* [1902] 2 KB 190.

[1319] *Milroy v Lord* (1862) DF & J 264. For mitigations of the rigour of this rule, see *T Choithram International v Pagarani* [2001] 1 WLR 1 and *Pennington v Waine* [2002] EWCA Civ 227, [2002] 1 WLR 2075.

[1320] In the present context a deed or nominal consideration does not suffice: *Kekewich v Manning* (1851) 1 DM & G 176; *Dillon v Coppin* (1839) 4 My & Cr 647.

[1321] *Harding v Harding* (1886) 17 QBD 442.

[1322] *Holt v Heatherfield Trust Ltd* [1942] 2 KB 1.

[1323] See 1.335.

[1324] *German v Yates* (1915) 32 TLR 52; *Olsson v Dyson* (1969) 120 CLR 365 *contra* seems to be based on the questionable assumption that s 136(1) (1.331) *requires* (and does not merely *permit*) the gift to be made by way of statutory assignment.

(though the assignee's forbearance to sue on the loan will then usually satisfy the requirement of consideration).[1325] If the assignment is not absolute because it is subject to some other condition, the gift will be imperfect if satisfaction of the condition requires some further act of the assignor, such as his approval of work done by the assignee.[1326]

(7) 'Subject to Equities'

The object of the rule that an assignee takes 'subject to...equities'[1327] is to protect the debtor **1.342** against the risk of being made liable to the assignee for more than he would, if there had been no assignment, have liable to the assignor.[1328] Hence if nothing is due to the assignor because he has not performed his part of the contract, then the assignee takes nothing.[1329] If the assignor's performance was defective, any damages to which the debtor was entitled in respect of that breach can be set off so as to reduce his liability to the assignee;[1330] though a payment, once made to the assignee, cannot be recovered back *from him* on account of a later breach by the assignor making *the latter* liable to restore it.[1331] If the contract has been induced by the assignor's fraud, the debtor can, by rescinding it, avoid liability to the assignee; and in cases of fraud he should be able to do this even where he can no longer return the subject matter of the contract.[1332]

A claim which the debtor has against the assignor under some transaction *other* than the **1.343** contract assigned can be set up against the assignee only if it arose before the debtor received notice of the assignment.[1333]

The rule that an assignee takes subject to equities does not apply against a holder in due **1.344** course of a negotiable instrument, such as a bill of exchange.[1334]

(8) Rights which are Not Assignable

Rights cannot be assigned if the contract giving rise to them expressly prohibits assign- **1.345** ment;[1335] though a purported assignment of such rights may make the assignor liable to the assignee.[1336] Assignability is further restricted in the following situations.

(a) Personal contracts

B cannot assign the benefit of his contract with A if the contract is of such a kind that it **1.346** would be unreasonable to expect A to perform in favour of anyone except B. This may be so because the contract was one of personal confidence (so that at common law an

---

[1325] See 1.44.
[1326] *Re McArdle* [1951] Ch 669.
[1327] *Mangles v Dixon* (1852) 3 HLC 702, 732.
[1328] *Dawson v Great Northern & City Rly Co* [1905] 1 KB 260; *Offer Hoar v Larkstone Ltd* [2006] EWCA Civ 1079; [2006] 1 WLR 2926.
[1329] cf *Tooth v Hallett* (1869) LR 4 Ch App 242.
[1330] cf *Government of Newfoundland v Newfoundland Rly* (1888) 13 App Cas 199.
[1331] *The Trident Beauty* [1994] 1 WLR 161.
[1332] *Stoddart v Union Trust Ltd* [1912] 1 KB 181, so far as *contra*, overlooks the rule governing rescission for fraud stated in 1.179 and is viewed with scepticism in *Banco Santander SA v Bayfern Ltd* [2001] 1 All ER (Comm) 776, 778–779.
[1333] *Stephens v Venables* (1862) 30 Beav 625; cf *The Raven* [1977] 1 WLR 578 (claim against intermediate assignee).
[1334] Bills of Exchange Act 1882, s 38(2).
[1335] *Linden Gardens Trust Ltd v Lenesta Sludge Disposals Ltd* [1994] 1 AC 85.
[1336] *Re Turcan* (1888) 40 Ch D 5; cf *Don King Productions Inc v Warren* [2000] Ch 291.

employer cannot assign the benefit of his employee's obligation to serve);[1337] or because requiring A to perform in favour of C would subject him to duties more onerous than those undertaken, or deprive him of benefits bargained for, under his original contract with B.[1338]

(b) Mere rights of action

1.347 An assignment is invalid if it in fact savours of the wrongs of maintenance or champerty.[1339] For this reason, a right of action in tort cannot generally[1340] be assigned. A liquidated contract claim can be assigned even though the debtor denies liability.[1341] The same is true of a contested contract claim for unliquidated damages if it does not in fact tend to lead to maintenance or champerty; eg where the assignee has a proprietary interest,[1342] or even a 'genuine commercial interest',[1343] in the subject matter. But an assignment of such a claim was held invalid where the assignee took it with a view to reselling it and sharing with his buyer the considerable profits expected from its enforcement.[1344]

(c) Public policy

1.348 On grounds of public policy, a wife cannot assign rights to maintenance and similar payments awarded to her in matrimonial proceedings;[1345] and a public officer (other than one paid out of local funds)[1346] cannot assign his salary.[1347] Other statutory restrictions on assignment are based on similar grounds of public policy.[1348]

(9) Assignment Distinguished from Transfer of Liabilities

1.349 Assignment is the transfer of a right without the consent of the debtor. There is at common law no converse process by which a liability can be transferred without the consent of the creditor[1349] so as to deprive him of his rights against the original debtor. He can be so deprived only with his agreement by a novation extinguishing the original debtor's liability and substituting for it that of a new debtor.[1350] There are, however, situations in which C becomes liable to A for a performance originally undertaken by B; and others in which A cannot object to performance by C of such an obligation.

[1337] *Nokes v Doncaster Amalgamated Collieries* [1940] AC 1014, 1026; for legislation affecting some such cases, see 1.351.

[1338] *Kemp v Baerselman* [1906] 2 KB 604; contrast *Tolhurst v Associated Portland Cement Co* [1903] AC 414, where there was no such prejudice to A.

[1339] See 1.329.

[1340] Exceptionally such rights can be assigned to an insurer who has compensated the victim of the tort who will also on making such compensation be subrogated to the victim's rights: *King v Victoria Insurance Co* [1896] AC 250; *Hobbs v Marlowe* [1978] AC 16, 37.

[1341] *County Hotel & Wine Co Ltd v London & North-Western Rly Co* [1918] 2 KB 251, 258; it makes no difference that the assignment is taken with an oblique motive (such as that of making the debtor bankrupt: *Fitzroy v Cave* [1905] 2 KB 364).

[1342] *Defries v Milne* [1913] 1 Ch 98; *Ellis v Torrington* [1920] 1 KB 399.

[1343] *Trendtex Trading Ltd v Crédit Suisse* [1982] AC 679, 703. A case in which there was held to be no such interest is *Simpson v Norfolk NHS Trust* [2011] EWCA Civ 1149, [2012] 1 All ER 1423.

[1344] *Trendtex Trading Ltd v Crédit Suisse* [1982] AC 679, 703.

[1345] *Watkins v Watkins* [1896] P 222.

[1346] *Re Mirams* [1891] 1 QB 594.

[1347] *Methwold v Walbank* (1750) 2 Ves Sen 238; *Liverpool Corp v Wright* (1859) 28 LJ Ch 868.

[1348] eg Social Security Administration Act 1992, s 187; Pensions Act 1995, s 91.

[1349] *Linden Gardens Trust Ltd v Lenesta Sludge Disposals Ltd* [1994] 1 AC 85, 103.

[1350] eg *Miller's case* (1876) 3 Ch D 391; *Customs & Excise Commissioners v Diners Club Ltd* [1989] 1 WLR 1196.

(a) Benefit and burden

The principle of 'benefit and burden' applies where a benefit transferred by B to C is conditional on the discharge by C of an obligation owed by B to A.[1351] This principle has occasionally been extended to cases where discharge of the burden is *not* made a condition of the enjoyment of the benefit; but, to avoid conflict with the general rule that an assignee incurs no liability under the contract assigned,[1352] this extension (known as the 'pure principle of benefit and burden')[1353] is restricted in two ways. First, the burden must be 'relevant to the exercise of the right'[1354] so that the principle did not apply where the right was to occupy one house and the burden to keep the roof of another in repair.[1355] Secondly, B and C must intend to subject C to B's contractual obligation to A; and such an intention will not be inferred merely from the fact that the relationship of B and C is that of assignor and assignee.[1356] Even if C is liable to A, B remains so liable until C performs.

1.350

(b) Legislation

The benefit and burden of a contract of employment may be transferred as a result of the transfer of the employer's undertaking;[1357] but the employee's 'fundamental right...to choose his employer' is preserved in the sense that it is open to him to choose not to enter the employment of the transferee.[1358] A transferee who acquires contractual rights under a bill of lading contract may also incur contractual liabilities under it[1359] but the original shipper remains liable.[1360]

1.351

(10) Vicarious Performance

A's obligation to B may be discharged if C performs it with A's authority,[1361] with B's consent and with the intention of discharging it.[1362] The same result generally follows even where B is unwilling to accept performance from C instead of from A;[1363] but in two situations B can insist on personal performance from A. He can do so first where the contract expressly or impliedly provides that the obligation in question will be performed by A and by no one else;[1364] and secondly where the contract is 'personal' in the sense that it is unreasonable to require B to accept performance from anyone except A (typically because B relied, when making the contract, on A's skill and judgment).[1365]

1.352

Where vicarious performance is permitted, the principle that there can be no 'assignment of liabilities'[1366] is not infringed. No liability is *transferred*, so that A remains liable to B for

1.353

[1351] eg *Astley v Seddon (No 2)* (1876) 1 Ex D 496.

[1352] *Young v Kitchin* (1878) 3 Ex D 127.

[1353] *Tito v Waddell (No 2)* [1977] Ch 106, 302.

[1354] *Rhone v Stephens* [1994] 2 AC 310, 322.

[1355] *Rhone v Stephens* [1994] 2 AC 310, 322.

[1356] *Tito v Waddell (No 2)* [1977] Ch 106, 302.

[1357] Transfer of Undertakings (Protection of Employment) Regulations 2006, SI 2006/246: *Newns v British Airways plc* [1992] IRLR 575, 576.

[1358] *North Wales Training and Enterprise Council v Astley* [2006] UKHL 29; [2006] 1 WLR 2420 at [55].

[1359] Carriage of Goods by Sea Act 1992, s 3(1).

[1360] Carriage of Goods by Sea Act 1992, s 3(3).

[1361] See *Crantrave Ltd v Lloyd's Bank plc* [2000] QB 914, where a bank (C) paid a debt of one of its customers (A) without A's authority.

[1362] See *Re Rowe* [1904] 2 KB 483, where there was no such intention.

[1363] *British Waggon Co v Lea & Co* (1880) 5 QBD 149.

[1364] *Davies v Collins* [1945] 1 All ER 247.

[1365] eg *Edwards v Newland* [1950] 2 KB 534; *John McCann & Co v Pow* [1974] 1 WLR 1643, 1647.

[1366] See 1.349.

C's defective performance[1367] (unless A's only undertaking is not to render the performance but to arrange for it to be rendered by C)[1368] and C incurs no liability under the contract between A and B; though C may be liable to B for defective performance in tort[1369] and even for non-performance if B is a third party beneficiary to a sub-contract between A and C.[1370]

M. Performance

1.354   Due performance of a contractual duty discharges the duty and prima facie entitles the party performing it to enforce the other party's undertakings; while failure in performance may give the victim the right to terminate the contract.

(1) Method of Performance

(a) When performance is due

1.355   Performance is due without demand[1371] unless the contract or legislation otherwise provides[1372] or unless the party required to perform cannot without demand reasonably be expected to know that performance is due.[1373] Where performance is due on a specified day, there is no default until the end of that day.[1374]

(b) Tender

1.356   Tender must be at a reasonable hour.[1375] Tender of money requires actual production of (as opposed to a mere offer to produce)[1376] the amount due.[1377] Where a bad tender is rejected and followed within the time fixed for performance by another, good, tender, the latter must generally[1378] be accepted.[1379]

(c) Payment by cheque or credit card

1.357   Payment by cheque is (rebuttably)[1380] presumed to be conditional on the cheque's being honoured.[1381] By contrast, payment for goods or services by credit card discharges the customer; if the issuer of the card fails to pay, the supplier's remedy is against the issuer and not against the customer.[1382]

[1367]   *Stewart v Reavell's Garage* [1952] 2 QB 545; *Wong Mee Wan v Kwan Kim Travel Services Ltd* [1996] 1 WLR 38.

[1368]   *Wong Mee Wan*, n 1367, at 41–42 (where the contract was not of this kind).

[1369]   cf *British Telecommunications plc v James Thomson & Sons (Engineers) Ltd* [1999] 2 All ER 241.

[1370]   Contracts (Rights of Third Parties) Act 1999, s 1; 1.304.

[1371]   *Walton v Mascall* (1844) 13 M & W 452.

[1372]   *Esso Petroleum Co Ltd v Alstonbridge Properties Ltd* [1975] 1 WLR 1474; Commonhold and Leasehold Reform Act 2002, s 166.

[1373]   *British Telecommunications plc v Sun Life Assurance Society plc* [1996] Ch 69, 74.

[1374]   *The Lutetian* [1982] 2 Lloyd's Rep 140; *The Afovos* [1983] 1 WLR 195.

[1375]   Sale of Goods Act 1979, s 29(5).

[1376]   *Farquharson v Pearl Assurance Co Ltd* [1937] 3 All ER 124; cf *Finch v Brook* (1834) 1 Bing NC 253.

[1377]   *Betterbee v Davis* (1811) 3 Camp 70.

[1378]   ie, unless the first tender is a repudiation or the creditor has acted to his detriment in reliance on it.

[1379]   *Tetley v Shand* (1871) 25 LT 658; cf *Borrowman Phillips & Co v Free & Hollis* (1878) 4 QBD 500.

[1380]   *Sard v Rhodes* (1836) 1 M & W 153.

[1381]   *Sayer v Wagstaff* (1844) 14 LJ Ch 116; *Re Romer & Haslam* [1893] 2 QB 286 treats the condition as precedent; *Jameson v Central Electricity Generating Board* [2000] 1 AC 455, 478 treats it as subsequent. Cf *Esso Petroleum Ltd v Milton* [1997] 1 WLR 938 (payment by direct debit).

[1382]   *Re Charge Card Services Ltd* [1989] Ch 497.

(d) Alternatives

A contract may call for alternative methods of performance without specifying which party **1.358** has the right to choose between them. The law then has to settle the point: eg where a loan is 'for six or nine months' its period is at the option of the borrower.[1383]

(2) *Termination for Failure to Perform*

(a) Introduction

(i) *Nature of the remedy*

Failure to perform in accordance with the contract is often a breach, giving the injured party **1.359** remedies (such as damages) for the *enforcement* of the contract.[1384] It may also (even where it is not a breach) give rise to the remedies here to be discussed, by which a party seeks to *undo* the contract by refusing to perform his part or to accept further performance or by returning the defective performance with a view to reclaiming his own. Where the failure is due to a supervening event which occurs without default of either party and fundamentally disrupts performance, the contract is automatically discharged under the doctrine of frustration.[1385] Our concern here is with cases in which the failure is not of this kind.

(ii) *Practical considerations*

The injured party may prefer termination to damages since termination is available even **1.360** where the failure is not a breach; since mere refusal to perform does not require legal proceedings; and since termination may enable him to escape from what, for him, is or has become a bad bargain. The other party, by contrast, may wish to resist termination where he has partly performed or otherwise incurred expenses for the purpose of performance; or where on a falling market the financial prejudice to him of being deprived of the benefit of his bargain exceeds that which the victim would suffer by reason of the defect in performance. The complexity of the subject is due to the need to strike a balance between these conflicting interests.

(b) The order of performance

(i) *Conditions precedent, concurrent conditions and independent promises*

A party is entitled to refuse to perform where, under the rules relating to the order of performance, his performance is not yet due. Under these rules, performance by A may be a promissory[1386] *condition precedent* to the liability of B: eg, where A agrees to work for B at a monthly salary payable in arrear, payment from B is not due until A has done a month's work.[1387] The two performances are *concurrent conditions* where A and B undertake to perform simultaneously: eg in a contract for the sale of goods prima facie the seller cannot claim payment unless he is ready and willing to deliver, nor the buyer delivery unless he is ready and willing to pay.[1388] Where promises are *independent* A can enforce B's promise even though he has not performed his own.[1389]

The courts will, where possible, classify performances as concurrent conditions and so reduce **1.362** the risk of requiring A to perform without any security for B's performance.[1390] But where

---

[1383] *Reed v Kilburn Co-operative Society* (1875) LR 10 QB 264.
[1384] See ch 4.
[1385] See section O.
[1386] For the distinction between promissory and contingent conditions, see 1.29.
[1387] *Morton v Lamb* (1797) 7 TR 125; *Miles v Wakefield MDC* [1987] AC 539, 561, 574; cf *Trans Trust SPRL v Danubian Trading Co* [1952] 2 QB 297.
[1388] Sale of Goods Act 1979, s 28.
[1389] *Pordage v Cole* (1669) 1 Wms Saund 619; *Taylor v Webb* [1937] 2 KB 283, 290.
[1390] See *Kingston v Preston* (1773) 2 Doug 689.

simultaneous performance is not possible (as in contracts for work to be done over time and paid for on completion) performance by one party is necessarily a condition precedent of the other's liability.[1391] Even where simultaneous performance is possible, a promise may be classified as independent because it is of only trivial importance,[1392] because such was the intention of the parties[1393] or because the commercial setting makes such a classification appropriate.[1394]

(ii) Effects of the distinction

1.363 It follows from the nature of an independent promise[1395] that failure to perform such a promise does not justify termination. Failure by A to perform a condition precedent or concurrent condition justifies B's refusal to perform for so long as the refusal continues.[1396] But it does not of itself justify outright termination in the sense of B's refusal ever to perform (or to accept performance from A).[1397] It has this effect only where A's failure is (in accordance with the principles to be discussed below)[1398] of such a kind as to justify termination.

(iii) Wrongful refusal to accept performance

1.364 The rule that B is under no liability if A has failed to perform a condition precedent or concurrent condition may be displaced if, before A's performance was due, B has, by indicating that he would refuse to accept it, repudiated the contract. A is then entitled to accept the repudiation by terminating the contract, and if he does terminate he is liberated from his duty to perform, so that he can recover damages without showing that he could, but for B's repudiation, have performed that duty.[1399] This is so not only where B's repudiation induces A's failure[1400] (by causing him to abandon efforts to perform) but also where A could not have performed, even if B had not repudiated.[1401] The purpose of applying the rule to such cases appears to be to discourage premature repudiation. If A does *not* accept B's repudiation, A is not liberated from his own duty so that his failure to perform will make him liable in damages and, if repudiatory, justify rescission by B.[1402]

(c) General requirement of substantial failure

1.365 Performance may be in the *order* required by the rules just stated but be deficient in quantity or quality or be late. The general rule (to which there are important exceptions)[1403] is that the right to terminate then arises only if the defect in performance deprives the injured party of 'substantially the whole benefit'[1404] which he was to obtain. It is hard to give precise meaning to such a vague phrase, but a number of practical factors can be identified as relevant in this context.

[1391] See at n 1387.

[1392] *Huntoon Co v Kolynos (Inc)* [1930] Ch 528.

[1393] *The Odenfeld* [1978] 2 Lloyd's Rep 357.

[1394] *Gill & Duffus SA v Berger & Co Inc* [1984] AC 382.

[1395] See 1.361.

[1396] *Wiluszynski v Tower Hamlets LBC* [1989] ICR 493.

[1397] So that an employee's failure to work does not justify dismissal merely because it justifies withholding of pay.

[1398] In 1.365 et seq.

[1399] *British and Beningtons v North-Western Cachar Tea Co* [1923] AC 48; cf *Braithwaite v Foreign Hardwood Co* [1905] 2 KB 543, as explained in *The Simona* [1989] AC 788, 805.

[1400] eg *Bulk Oil (Zug) AG v Sun International Ltd* [1984] 1 Lloyd's Rep 531, 546.

[1401] As in the *British & Beningtons* case, n 1399.

[1402] *The Simona*, n 1399.

[1403] See 1.367–1.386.

[1404] *Photo Production Ltd v Securicor Transport Ltd* [1980] AC 827, 849.

One such factor is the desire to avoid the unjust enrichment which can follow from allow- **1.366**
ing the injured party to keep the other's defective performance without paying for it.[1405]
Another is the reluctance to allow termination where the less drastic remedy of damages will
provide adequate compensation,[1406] particularly where the prejudice that termination would
cause to the party in breach would be wholly out of proportion to the loss suffered by the
injured party as a result of the breach. The courts have regard also to the reasonableness of
requiring the injured party to accept further performance: this factor will favour termination
where the failure in performance gives rise to uncertainty as to future performance[1407] or
where the ratio of the failure is high in relation to the performance promised.[1408] Ulterior
motives may also be taken into account, so that a failure is not readily classified as substantial
where the injured party's real reason for terminating is not to avoid any prejudice resulting from the failure but to escape from a bad bargain.[1409] The list of relevant factors is by
no means exhaustive;[1410] but it can help in predicting the operation of the requirement of
substantial failure.

(d) Exception to the requirement of substantial failure

Notwithstanding the identification of the factors described in 1.365, the requirement of **1.367**
substantial failure is a source of uncertainty. This is mitigated by a number of exceptions to
the requirement, but these have in turn attracted criticism because the certainty which they
promote is sometimes achieved only at the expense of justice.

(i) Express provisions

In the interests of certainty, literal effect is as a general rule given to express provisions **1.368**
entitling one party (A) to terminate on the other's (B's) failure to perform exactly in accordance with the contract.[1411] The possible hardship to B where the failure is only trivial is mitigated in various ways. The provision will be strictly construed;[1412] and A must act exactly in
accordance with it, so that he is not justified in terminating *before* B's failure in performance
even though that failure is at the time of termination certain to occur.[1413] B may also be
entitled to 'relief against forfeiture'[1414] (ie extra time to perform)[1415] where, but only where,
termination would deprive him of a proprietary or possessory right.[1416] Under the Consumer
Rights Act 2015, a cancellation clause in a contract between a trader and a consumer may be

---

[1405] See, eg *Boone v Eyre* (1779) 1 Hy Bl 273 n; 2 W Bl 1312.

[1406] *Decro-Wall International SA v Practitioners in Marketing Ltd* [1971] 1 WLR 361.

[1407] *Bradford v Williams* (1872) LR 7 Ex 259; *Poussard v Spiers* (1876) 1 QBD 410; contrast *Bettini v Gye*
(1876) 1 QBD 183 and *Hong Kong Fir Shipping Co Ltd v Kawasaki Kisen Kaisha Ltd* [1962] 2 QB 26.

[1408] *Warinco AG v Samor SpA* [1979] 1 Lloyd's Rep 450; *Maple Flock Co Ltd v Universal Furniture Products
(Wembley) Ltd* [1934] 1 KB 148.

[1409] *Dakin v Oxley* (1864) 15 CBNS 647, 667–668; *The Hansa Nord* [1976] QB 44, 71. On the other
hand, the law does not in general require a party to give the correct reason for his decision to terminate at
the time of termination. The focus of the law is upon whether he has the right to terminate, not whether he
was aware of that right and asserted it at the time of termination: *The Mihalis Angelos* [1971] 1 QB 164, 195,
200, 204.

[1410] *Aerial Advertising Co v Batchelor's Peas Ltd* [1938] 2 All ER 788 (where termination was allowed) does
not fit readily within any of the factors listed here.

[1411] eg *The Laconia* [1977] AC 850; *Union Eagle Ltd v Golden Achievement Ltd* [1997] AC 514.

[1412] *Rice v Great Yarmouth BC* [2001] LGLR 4.

[1413] *The Mihalis Angelos* [1971] 1 QB 164.

[1414] Law of Property Act 1925, s 146; Consumer Credit Act 1974, ss 88, 89. A landlord's right to forfeit
certain leases is further restricted by Commonhold and Leasehold Reform Act 2002, ss 167–170.

[1415] *Nutting v Baldwin* [1995] 1 WLR 201, 208.

[1416] Not where the right is merely contractual: *The Scaptrade* [1983] 2 AC 694 (time charter); *Sport
International Bussum BV v Inter-Footwear Ltd* [1984] 1 WLR 776; contrast *BICC plc v Burndy Corp* [1985]
Ch 232.

struck down as unfair;[1417] and if the clause is oppressive it may be open to challenge at common law.[1418] A clause entitling A to refuse to pay in default of exact performance by B may also be invalid as a penalty.[1419]

(ii) Entire and severable obligations

1.369 **Entire obligations.**   An obligation is 'entire' if complete performance of it by B is required before A's counter performance becomes due.[1420] Where, eg, a contract for the carriage of goods by sea provides for payment of freight at the agreed destination, it imposes an entire obligation on the carrier (B) to get the goods there;[1421] and where a building contract provides for payment on completion, it imposes an entire obligation on the builder (B) to complete the work.[1422] A is not liable to make the agreed payment even though B gets the goods nearly to the destination or nearly finishes the work.

1.370 **Severable obligations.**   A contract imposes severable obligations if payment from A falls due on performance of specified parts by B: eg where a contract for the carriage of goods by sea provides for payment of freight of so much *per ton*; or where a building contract provides for part payments as specified stages of the work are completed. If B carries only part of the cargo, or performs only some of the stages of the building contract, he is entitled to corresponding part payments[1423] (though liable in damages for his failure to perform the rest of the contract).[1424]

1.371 **Contract imposing both entire and severable obligations.**   The same contract may impose both entire and severable obligations: eg a contract of carriage may impose an entire obligation to get the cargo to the agreed destination but entitle the carrier to the full freight even where as a result of his breach of another term of the contract the goods arrive damaged.[1425] Similarly, a building contract may impose an entire obligation as to the *amount* of work to be done but not as to its quality. Slight defects in the work will then not deprive the builder of his right to be paid.[1426] It is sometimes said that in such cases there has been substantial performance of an entire contract;[1427] but where one of the *obligations* under the contract is entire, this *means* that it must be completely performed, so that there is no scope for the view that anything less can suffice.

(iii) Conditions, warranties and intermediate terms

1.372 **Statement of the distinction between conditions and warranties.**   'Condition' is here used in its promissory sense[1428] to refer to a contractual term any breach of which gives the injured party the right to terminate. This usage makes a point, not about the *order* of performance,[1429] but about the *conformity* of the performance rendered with that promised. A seller who tenders goods on the buyer's tender of the price thereby performs a 'concurrent

---

[1417] See 1.119 et seq; and see Sch 2 Part 1 para 8 of the Act.
[1418] *Timeload Ltd v British Telecommunications plc* [1995] Entertainment and Media LR 459, 467.
[1419] *Gilbert-Ash (Northern) Ltd v Modern Engineering (Bristol) Ltd* [1974] AC 689.
[1420] *Cutter v Powell* (1795) 6 TR 320.
[1421] *St Enoch Shipping Co Ltd v Phosphate Mining Co* [1916] 2 KB 624; contrast *The Dominique* [1989] AC 1056 (freight *earned* on loading though not *payable* till discharge).
[1422] *Sumpter v Hedges* [1893] 1 QB 673.
[1423] *Ritchie v Atkinson* (1808) 10 East 295.
[1424] *Atkinson v Ritchie* (1808) 10 East 530.
[1425] *Dakin v Oxley* (1864) 15 CB NS 646; *The Brede* [1974] QB 233.
[1426] *Hoenig v Isaacs* [1952] 2 All ER 176; though the express terms of the contract can impose an entire obligation as to quality: *Eshelby v Federated European Bank* [1932] 1 KB 423.
[1427] *Geipel v Smith* (1872) LR 7 QB 404, 411; *Dakin v Lee* [1916] 1 KB 566, 598.
[1428] See 1.29.
[1429] See 1.361.

condition'[1430] but will be in breach of condition (in the present sense) if the goods are not up to sample.[1431] Failure to perform a condition in the former sense results *ipso facto* in the buyer's performance not becoming due,[1432] while breach of condition in the latter sense gives the buyer an option to terminate.[1433] A warranty (in modern legal usage)[1434] is a term the breach of which gives the injured party a right to damages but not (at least generally)[1435] a right to terminate.[1436]

Bases of the distinction.   One ground for classifying a term as a condition is that the par-   **1.373**
ties intended it to take effect as such.[1437] Their use of the word 'condition' with reference to the term will generally produce this effect;[1438] but it is not decisive and may, particularly where the term can be broken in a way which will cause only trifling loss, be construed simply to refer to a term of the contract.[1439]

Where the intention of the parties is not discoverable from the terms of the contract, the   **1.374**
courts have relied on the requirement of substantial failure so as to classify terms as conditions if their breach caused or was likely to cause serious prejudice to the injured party.[1440] But terms have also been classified by judicial decision or by legislation[1441] as conditions even though their breach may not cause such prejudice;[1442] and, once so classified, they will, in the interests of commercial certainty, give rise to a right to terminate 'without regard to the magnitude of the breach'.[1443]

Intermediate terms.   Some applications of the rule just stated have been criticized as 'exces-   **1.375**
sively technical';[1444] for the rule enables a party to terminate even where the breach has not caused him any loss and even where his motive is to escape from a bad bargain. The requirements of certainty here conflict with those of justice; and the latter are promoted by recognition of the category of intermediate terms.[1445] These differ from conditions in that their breach gives rise to a right to terminate only[1446] if it amounts, or gives rise, to a substantial failure;[1447] and from warranties in that there is no prima facie rule that the only remedy for breach is in damages.

Where a term has not been classified as a condition by either express agreement or previous   **1.376**
judicial decision or legislation, the judicial tendency is (in the interests of justice) to 'lean in

---

[1430] See 1.361.
[1431] Sale of Goods Act 1979, s 15.
[1432] *The Good Luck* [1992] 1 AC 233, 262.
[1433] See 1.420.
[1434] 'Warranty' was formerly used to refer to terms now described as conditions: eg *Behn v Burness* (1863) 3 B & S 751, 755. For survival of a similar usage, see 1.422.
[1435] See 1.381.
[1436] Sale of Goods Act 1979, s 61(1) (definition of 'warranty').
[1437] *Glaholm v Hays* (1841) 2 Man & G 257, 266; Sale of Goods Act 1979, s 11(3).
[1438] *Dawsons Ltd v Bonin* [1922] 2 AC 413.
[1439] *Wickman Ltd v Schuler AG* [1974] AC 235. Although *Wickman* has subsequently been described as the 'high-water mark' of the courts' reluctance to classify a term as a condition: *Heritage Oil and Gas Ltd v Tullow Uganda Ltd* [2014] EWCA Civ 1048, at [33].
[1440] *Glaholm v Hays*, n 1437, at 268; *Bentsen v Taylor* [1893] 2 QB 274, 281; *Couchman v Hill* [1947] KB 554, 559.
[1441] See Sale of Goods Act 1979, ss 12–15.
[1442] *Bunge Corp v Tradax Export SA* [1981] 1 WLR 711, 724.
[1443] *Lombard North Central plc v Butterworth* [1987] QB 527, 535.
[1444] *Reardon Smith Line Ltd v Hansen Tangen* [1976] 1 WLR 989, 998.
[1445] *Hong Kong Fir* case, n 1407, at 70; *The Hansa Nord* [1976] QB 44.
[1446] See the *Hong Kong Fir* case, n 1407.
[1447] As in *Federal Commerce & Navigation v Molena Alpha* [1979] AC 757. The test 'sets the bar high' (*Telford Homes (Creekside) Ltd v Ampurius Nu Homes Holdings Ltd* [2013] EWCA Civ 577, [2013] 4 All ER 377, at [48]) when deciding whether the consequences of the breach are sufficiently serious to justify termination.

favour'[1448] of classifying it as an intermediate term, so that only a serious breach of it will justify termination. The interests of certainty, however, give rise to a countervailing tendency to classify clauses in commercial contracts as conditions if they lay down a precise time[1449] by, or interval within, which acts of performance have to be done or notices given.[1450] The reason for this trend is that breaches of such terms are easy to establish and that strict compliance with them is in general of vital commercial importance. It follows that a time clause which is clearly *not* of such importance[1451] is unlikely to be classified as a condition. Conversely, a previously unclassified term other than one specifying a precise time will take effect as a condition if its exact performance is regarded by the parties as vital[1452] or if there is other evidence of their intention to give it this effect.[1453]

1.377 **Restrictions on the right to terminate for breach of condition.** The right to terminate a contract for the sale of goods for breach of certain statutorily implied terms contained in the Sale of Goods Act 1979 cannot, unless the parties otherwise agree, be exercised by a buyer where the breach is 'so slight that it would be unreasonable'[1454] for the injured party to reject the goods. This restriction is intended to prevent abuses of the right to reject (such as its exercise for oblique motives) but it is a regrettable source of uncertainty. It is also one-sided, being inapplicable to the converse case of a breach of condition by a buyer.[1455] A breach which is not 'slight' is not necessarily of the degree of seriousness which would justify termination for breach of an intermediate term.

1.378 A consumer who is party to a contract with a trader for the supply of services is given a rather different set of rights from those applicable to contracts of sale governed by the Sale of Goods Act 1979. In the case where the goods do not conform to the contract, the consumer buyer is given a broader range of rights, which include[1455a] the short-time right to reject,[1455b] the right to repair or replacement[1455c] and the right to a price reduction or the final right to reject.[1455d] Where the buyer asks for repair or replacement, he must not reject the goods until the seller has had a reasonable time to comply with the request (unless giving the trader that time would cause significant inconvenience to the consumer).[1455e]

1.379 The right to terminate for breach of condition can be excluded by an express contractual term such as a non-cancellation or non-rejection clause, subject to the rules which determine the validity and construction of exemption clauses.[1463]

[1448] *Tradax Internacional SA v Goldschmidt SA* [1977] 2 Lloyd's Rep 604, 612; *Bunge Corp v Tradax Export SA* [1981] 1 WLR 711, 715, 727 (where the term in question was classified as a condition).

[1449] If the time is not precise, the term is likely to be classified as intermediate: see the respective treatment of clauses 21 and 22 in *Bremer Handelsgesellschaft mbH v Vanden Avenne-Izegem PVBA* [1978] 2 Lloyd's Rep 109.

[1450] *Bunge Corp v Tradax Export SA*, n 1448; *Toepfer v Lenersan-Poortman NV* [1980] 1 Lloyd's Rep 143.

[1451] *State Trading Corporation of India Ltd v M Golodetz Ltd* [1989] 2 Lloyd's Rep 277.

[1452] *The Post Chaser* [1981] 2 Lloyd's Rep 695, 700.

[1453] eg *Tradax Export SA v European Grain & Shipping Co* [1983] 2 Lloyd's Rep 100.

[1454] Sale of Goods Act 1979, s 15A. Similar restrictions apply where goods are supplied to a person under a contract other than one of sale: see Supply of Goods (Implied Terms) Act 1973, s 11A; Supply of Goods and Services Act 1982, s 5A. cf also Sale of Goods Act 1979, s 30(2A) (delivery of wrong quantity).

[1455] As in *Bunge Corp v Tradax Export SA* [1981] 1 WLR 714.

[1455a] The rights set out in ss 20–24 of the Consumer Rights Act 2015 are not exhaustive: see Consumer Rights Act 2015, s 19(9)–(11).

[1455b] Consumer Rights Act 2015, s 22.

[1455c] Consumer Rights Act 2015, s 23.

[1455d] Consumer Rights Act 2015, s 24.

[1455e] Consumer Rights Act 2015, s 23(6) and (7).

[Footnotes 1456–1462 have been deleted in the paperback edition.]

[1463] See section D.

Where a non-fraudulent misrepresentation inducing a contract is incorporated in it as a **1.380** condition,[1464] the right to rescind for misrepresentation is subject to the discretion of the court,[1465] but this discretion probably does not extend to the right to terminate for breach.[1466]

Termination for breach of warranty.   Where a representation inducing a contract is incor- **1.381** porated in it as a warranty, the right to rescind for misrepresentation survives such incorporation,[1467] subject to the discretion of the court referred to in 1.380.

Where a breach of warranty leads or amounts to a substantial failure in performance, there may **1.382** be a right to terminate on this ground in spite of the classification of the term as a warranty.[1468]

A consumer who is party to a contract with a trader for the supply of goods is given a right **1.383** to reject the performance by the trader and this right to reject may take the form of either a short-term right to reject or a final right to reject.

(iv) Breach of fundamental term

Breach of a fundamental term[1473] will usually have serious effects; but where a carrier com- **1.384** mits such a breach by deviating, the cargo-owner can terminate even though the deviation is 'for practical purposes irrelevant'.[1474]

(v) Deliberate breach

Termination is not justified merely because the breach is deliberate, for such a breach may **1.385** be trivial[1475] or reflect an honest attempt to overcome temporary difficulties in performance. The deliberate nature of the breach will, however, justify termination in two situations: where it amounts to fraud[1476] and where it is evidence of an 'intention no longer to be bound by the contract'.[1477] The fact that a party declares that he will perform only in a manner inconsistent with his obligations under the contract may be evidence of such an intention.[1478] But it will not have this effect merely because a party in good faith asserts a view of his duties under the contract which the court later holds to have been mistaken.[1479] The central question which is to be asked in cases of this type is whether, looking at all the circumstances objectively, ie, from the perspective of a reasonable man in the position of the innocent party, the contract breaker has clearly shown an intention to abandon and altogether refuse to perform the contract.[1480] The answer given by a court to that question will depend very heavily on the facts of the individual case.[1481] Where the breach can be cured, refusal to cure it can also be

---

[1464] See Misrepresentation Act 1967, s 1(a).

[1465] Misrepresentation Act 1967, s 2(2).

[1466] See 1.178.

[1467] Misrepresentation Act 1967, s 1(a).

[1468] *The Hansa Nord* [1976] QB 44, 83. The point is not, however, clearly established by authority. The more traditional view is that a breach of a warranty only gives rise to a claim for damages.

[Footnotes 1469–1472 have been deleted in the paperback edition.]

[1473] For this concept, see 1.100.

[1474] *Suisse Atlantique* case [1967] 1 AC 361, 423.

[1475] *Suisse Atlantique* case [1967] 1 AC 361, 435; *De Montfort Fine Art Ltd v Acre 1127 Ltd (in liquidation)* [2011] EWCA Civ 87.

[1476] *Flight v Booth* (1834) 1 Bing NC 370, 376.

[1477] *Freeth v Burr* (1874) LR 9 CP 208, 213; *Bradley v H Newsom Sons & Co* [1919] AC 16, 52.

[1478] *Withers v Reynolds* (1831) 2 B & Ad 882; *Total Oil Great Britain Ltd v Thompson Garages (Biggin Hill) Ltd* [1972] QB 318, 322.

[1479] *Woodar Investment Development Ltd v Wimpey Construction Ltd* [1980] 1 WLR 277.

[1480] *Eminence Property Developments Ltd v Heaney* [2010] EWCA Civ 1168, [2011] 2 All ER (Comm) 223.

[1481] As a consequence, the cases are not at all easy to reconcile: contrast, eg, *Federal Commerce & Navigation Co Ltd v Molena Alpha Inc* [1979] AC 757 and *Woodar Investment Development Ltd v Wimpey Construction UK Ltd* [1980] 1 WLR 277.

evidence of an 'intention not to be bound' so that its deliberate nature can justify termination where the breach, apart from this factor, would not have done so.[1482]

(vi) Unilateral contracts and options

1.386   Where A promises B £100 if B walks to York, and B makes no counter-promise, his accomplishing the walk is a contingent condition[1483] of A's liability to pay the £100, which does not accrue till B has completed the walk.[1484] Even in a bilateral contract, a stipulation (eg as to giving a specified notice) may amount, not to a promise, but to a condition of the other party's liability[1485] which will then not accrue until the stipulation is precisely performed. Contractual provisions which, on their true construction, specify the circumstances in which an option (eg to purchase) becomes exercisable are likewise conditions which must be precisely performed[1486] unless the contract, on its true construction, otherwise provides.[1487]

(e) Limitations on the right to terminate

1.387   The right to terminate may be prevented from arising by contractual provisions such as non-cancellation clauses.[1488] Our concern here, however, is with cases in which the right, having once arisen, is later lost or limited.

(i) Waiver or election

1.388   **Concepts.**   Two processes must be distinguished. The first ('waiver in the sense of election') is that by which a party who is entitled to terminate a contract indicates that he will nevertheless perform it: eg if a charterer declares that he will load a cargo in spite of the shipowner's breach of condition.[1489] This election to affirm the contract deprives him of the right to terminate for that breach, though not of his right to damages.[1490] The second ('total waiver') is that by which a party purports *wholly* to give up some or all of his rights in respect of the breach: ie not merely his right to terminate but also his right to performance (or damages).[1491] Our concern here is with the first process, the requirements of which in one respect resemble, and in another differ from, those of the second.

1.389   **Requirement of representation.**   The requirement of a 'clear and unequivocal' representation in cases of total waiver is discussed in 1.53. An 'unequivocal act or statement' is also required for waiver in the sense of election:[1492] there is, eg, no such waiver where the injured party continues to perform or to accept performance while calling for the other's failure to be cured[1493] or reserving his position if this is not done.[1494] Mere failure to terminate is not of itself an election to affirm[1495] but such an election may be inferred from unreasonable delay in terminating where it is commercially reasonable to expect prompt action.[1496]

[1482] *Hong Kong Fir* case, n 1407, at 54, 64.
[1483] See 1.29.
[1484] See 1.16.
[1485] See *Shires v Brock* (1977) 247 EG 127; *United Dominions Trust Ltd v Eagle Aircraft Ltd* [1968] 1 WLR 74.
[1486] *West Country Cleaners (Falmouth) Ltd v Saly* [1966] 1 WLR 1485.
[1487] *Little v Courage Ltd* (1995) 70 P & CR 469.
[1488] See 1.379.
[1489] *Bentsen v Taylor* [1893] 2 QB 274; cf *The Kanchenjunga* [1990] 1 Lloyd's Rep 391; *The Happy Day* [2002] EWCA Civ 1068, [2002] 2 Lloyd's Rep 487, at [64], [65], [68].
[1490] The right to damages may be barred by another term of the contract, as in *The Kanchenjunga*, n 1489.
[1491] See 1.52 et seq.
[1492] *The Mihalios Xilas* [1979] 1 WLR 1018, 1024.
[1493] *Cobec Brazilian Trading & Warehousing Corp v Alfred C Toepfer* [1983] 2 Lloyd's Rep 386.
[1494] *Bremer Handelsgesellschaft mbH v Deutsche Conti Handelsgesellschaft mbH* [1983] 2 Lloyd's Rep 45.
[1495] *Bremer Handelsgesellschaft mbH v Deutsche Conti Handelsgesellschaft mbH* [1983] 2 Lloyd's Rep 45; *Allen v Robles* [1969] 1 WLR 1193.
[1496] *The Laconia* [1977] AC 850, 872; *The Balder London* [1980] 2 Lloyd's Rep 489, 491–493.

No requirement of action in reliance. Total waiver requires the party invoking it to have **1.390**
relied on the representation giving rise to the waiver;[1497] but there is no such requirement for
waiver in the sense of election.[1498] This distinction between the two processes is sometimes
obscured by the unqualified use of 'waiver' to refer to both of them[1499] and by the fact that
some cases raise issues relating to both types of waiver.[1500]

Knowledge. Waiver in the sense of election (being based on affirmation of the con- **1.391**
tract)[1501] requires knowledge, not only of the facts giving rise to the right to terminate,
but of the existence of the right itself.[1502] If, however, A so conducts himself as to give B
reasonable grounds for believing that A has (after B's breach) affirmed the contract, then
A may be estopped by his implied representation from denying that he has affirmed.[1503]
For this purpose, there is no requirement of A's knowledge of the breach; but the estoppel
(unlike actual waiver in the sense of election)[1504] operates only if B has acted in reliance on
A's implied representation.

(ii) Voluntary acceptance of a benefit

Partial performance no bar to termination. The mere fact that one party has by part **1.392**
performance conferred a benefit on the other does not bar the latter's right to terminate. The
courts may, indeed, take this factor into account in determining whether there has been a
serious failure in performance;[1505] but they cannot take this course in cases falling within
exceptions to that requirement. If, eg, there is a failure to complete performance of an entire
obligation by a builder's doing only part of the agreed work,[1506] or by a carrier's carrying
goods only part of the way to the agreed destination,[1507] then the injured party need not pay
the agreed remuneration. It makes no difference that the failure causes no loss to the injured
party[1508] or that his loss is less than the benefit to him of the partial performance. Unjust
enrichment of the victim, as well as hardship to the party in breach, can result from these
rules; these defects are mitigated in ways to be discussed below.

Requirement of 'new contract'. An injured party who, under the rules just stated, is **1.393**
not liable for the agreed remuneration may be liable for a reasonable sum. There is such
liability if his acceptance of the partial performance is 'voluntary' so as to give rise to the
inference of a new contract to pay such a sum: eg if the owner of goods which cannot be
carried to the agreed destination asks for their delivery elsewhere;[1509] or if the owner of the
site of an incomplete building makes use of loose materials left on the site by the default-
ing builder.[1510] No such new contract can, however, be inferred from the owner's merely
retaking his own property: he must, in general, have a real 'option whether he will take the
benefit'.[1511]

[1497] See 1.55.
[1498] See eg *The Athos* [1981] 2 Lloyd's Rep 74, 87–88 (aff'd on this point [1983] 1 Lloyd's Rep 127);
The Kanchenjunga [1990] 1 Lloyd's Rep 391, 399; *Oliver Ashworth Holdings v Ballard (Kent) Ltd* [2000]
Ch 12, 27.
[1499] eg *The Eurometal* [1981] 1 Lloyd's Rep 337, 341.
[1500] eg *Bremer Handelsgesellschaft mbH v C Mackprang Jr* [1979] 1 Lloyd's Rep 221.
[1501] *Kwei Tek Chao v British Traders & Shippers Ltd* [1954] 2 QB 459, 477.
[1502] *Peyman v Lanjani* [1985] Ch 457.
[1503] *Peyman v Lanjani* [1985] Ch 457, 501.
[1504] See 1.390.
[1505] See 1.366, n 1405.
[1506] *Sumpter v Hedges* [1898] 1 QB 673; *Bolton v Mahadeva* [1972] 1 WLR 1009.
[1507] *Metcalfe v Britannia Ironworks Co* (1877) 2 QBD 423.
[1508] As in *Hopper v Burness* (1876) 1 CPD 137.
[1509] *Christy v Row* (1808) 1 Taunt 300.
[1510] As in *Sumpter v Hedges* [1898] 1 QB 673.
[1511] *Sumpter v Hedges* [1898] 1 QB 673, 676.

1.394 **Exceptions to requirement of 'new contract'.** A person may be liable to pay a reasonable sum although his acceptance of the benefit was not truly 'voluntary': eg where a cargo-owner simply retakes possession of his own goods after the carrier's unjustified deviation;[1512] and perhaps where an employee commits a repudiatory breach by 'working to rule' and the employer 'of necessity'[1513] accepts the services so rendered.[1514]

1.395 The right to reject goods for breach of a condition is barred by 'acceptance';[1515] and although this will not normally take place unless the buyer has had an opportunity of examination,[1516] it need not be truly 'voluntary' as there is no requirement for the buyer to have become aware of the breach. However, where the buyer has the right to reject all the goods, he does not by accepting some lose the right to reject the rest.[1517] Even after acceptance, he may[1518] also be allowed to rescind where a misrepresentation inducing the contract was later incorporated in it as a condition.[1519] The rule that the right to reject for breach of condition is barred by 'acceptance' may not apply where as a result of the breach the performance rendered is 'totally different from that which the contract contemplates':[1520] eg where peas are delivered under a contract for the sale of beans.

1.396 A buyer who 'accepts' delivery of the wrong quantity of goods must pay for that quantity at the contract rate[1521] even though the 'acceptance' is (for the reason stated in 1.394) not truly 'voluntary.'

1.397 **Part payment.** Failure to complete payments due under a contract may justify termination.[1522] The question whether the payee must restore the payments received by him is discussed in chapter 3.[1523]

(iii) Wrongful prevention of performance

1.398 Where A is prevented by B's wrongful repudiation from completing performance of an entire obligation, A can recover a reasonable remuneration for the work that he has done.[1524] A's right in such a case does not depend on the receipt of any benefit by B.

(iv) Both parties in breach

1.399 It has been suggested that where A's breach consists in failing to avoid the consequences of B's, then neither party can terminate.[1525] But there is little point in holding parties to a contract which each of them has repudiated and the normal rule is that where both parties have simultaneously committed repudiatory breaches each can terminate.[1526]

(v) Apportionment Act 1870

1.400 Under this Act, certain 'periodical payments in the nature of income' (such as rents and salaries) are, unless the contract otherwise provides, 'to be considered as accruing from day to day

---

[1512] *Hain Steamship Co Ltd v Tate & Lyle Ltd* (1936) 41 Commercial Cases 350, 358, 367.
[1513] *Miles v Wakefield MDC* [1987] AC 539, 553.
[1514] *Miles v Wakefield MDC* [1987] AC 539, 553, 561; the point is left open at 552 and 576.
[1515] Sale of Goods Act 1979, s 11(4).
[1516] Sale of Goods Act 1979, s 35.
[1517] Sale of Goods Act 1979, s 35A.
[1518] Subject to Misrepresentation Act 1967, s 2(2) (1.172).
[1519] Misrepresentation Act 1967, s 1(a).
[1520] *Suisse Atlantique* case [1967] 1 AC 361, 393.
[1521] Sale of Goods Act 1979, s 30(1).
[1522] See *The Blankenstein* [1985] 1 WLR 435, 446.
[1523] See 3.76–3.104.
[1524] *Planché v Colburn* (1831) 8 Bing 14.
[1525] *Bremer Vulkan Schiffbau und Maschinenfabrik v South India Shipping Corp* [1981] AC 909, 947; *The Hannah Blumenthal* [1983] 1 AC 854.
[1526] *State Trading Corporation of India v M Golodetz Ltd* [1989] 2 Lloyd's Rep 277, 286.

and shall be apportionable in respect of time accordingly'. These words literally apply even in favour of a party in breach: eg an employee who left in breach of contract or was justifiably dismissed during a payment period specified in the contract. Judicial opinion tends, though not conclusively, to support the view that, in such a case, the guilty party can, under the Act, recover a proportionate payment.[1527]

(3) Stipulations as to Time

1.401 Failure to perform a stipulation as to time does not differ intrinsically from any other failure to perform; but the subject calls for separate discussion because it has acquired its own terminology and because special rules apply to such stipulations in contracts for the sale of land.

(a) Classification

1.402 Stipulations as to the time of performance are divided into those which are, and those which are not, 'of the essence' of the contract. Where the stipulation is of the essence, any failure (however trivial) to comply with it justifies termination; where the stipulation is not of the essence, failure to comply with it justifies termination only if the delay amounts to a serious failure in performance. Time is most obviously of the essence if the contract expressly says so,[1528] or if it says that failure to perform on time is to be a ground for termination[1529] or that the stipulation is a 'condition'.[1530] In the absence of such express words, some stipulations as to time are prima facie classified by law: eg, in a charterparty a stipulation as to the time of sailing is of the essence,[1531] while one as to the time of loading is not.[1532] The possibly harsh consequences of classifying time stipulations as of the essence may incline the court to reject this classification in cases of first impression,[1533] while the requirements of certainty may, especially in 'mercantile contracts'[1534] favour such a classification.

(b) Sale of land

(i) Whether time of essence

1.403 At common law, stipulations as to the time of performance in contracts for the sale of land were of the essence;[1535] but this view was rejected in equity,[1536] which now prevails.[1537] As a general rule, therefore, time is not of the essence in such contracts so that a delay not amounting to a serious breach will not of itself justify termination.[1538] The general rule, however, does not apply where the contract expressly provides that time is to be of the essence;[1539] where the subject matter is such as to be likely to fall or to rise rapidly in value[1540] or in

---

[1527] There is a conflict of opinion on the point in *Moriarty v Regent's Garage* [1921] 1 KB 432, 434, 448–449 (actual decision reversed on another ground [1921] 2 KB 766); in *Item Software (UK) Ltd v Fassih* [2004] EWCA Civ 1244; [2005] ICR 450 one member of the court at [94], [116]–[121] favoured the view stated in the text above, while the other two did not find it necessary to decide the point.
[1528] See 1.403.
[1529] See *Union Eagle Ltd v Golden Achievement Ltd* [1997] AC 514.
[1530] In the sense discussed in 1.372; *The Scaptrade* [1983] 2 AC 694, 703.
[1531] *Glaholm v Hays* (1841) 2 Man & G 257.
[1532] *Universal Cargo Carriers Corp v Citati* [1957] 2 QB 401.
[1533] *United Scientific Holdings Ltd v Burnley BC* [1978] AC 904, 940 ('prima facie not of the essence').
[1534] *Bunge Corp v Tradax Export SA* [1981] 1 WLR 711, 716.
[1535] *Parkin v Thorold* (1852) 16 Beav 59, 65.
[1536] *Parkin v Thorold*, n 1535.
[1537] Law of Property Act 1925, s 141 (1.406).
[1538] *United Scientific* case, n 1533, at 942.
[1539] *Union Eagle* case, n 1529.
[1540] *Hudson v Temple* (1860) 29 Beav 536; *Newman v Rogers* (1793) 4 Bro CC 391.

relation to the obligation to pay the deposit by a particular time.[1541] It has also been said not to apply where the sale is of a 'commercial' nature;[1542] though now that land and houses fluctuate rapidly in value the continuing validity of the distinction between those contracts for the sale of land which are, and those which are not, 'commercial' has rightly been questioned.[1543] A stipulation is also of the essence if it provides for the time of performance of an act by one party which is a condition precedent to the very existence of the contract or to the liability of the other party.[1544]

(ii) Waiver

1.404 A party may waive a stipulation which is of the essence by granting the other an extension of time; performance within the extended time is then of the essence.[1545]

(iii) Notice

1.405 Where time is not of the essence of a contract for the sale of land under the rules stated in 1.403, the injured party can issue a notice to the other party, as soon as the latter is in default,[1546] purporting to make time of the essence by calling on him to complete within the time specified in the notice. This must be the time specified for this purpose in the contract, or, if no time is so specified, a reasonable time.[1547] If *either* party then fails to perform within the time specified in the notice, the other may be entitled to terminate.[1548] However, the serving of such a notice cannot impose an additional obligation on the recipient.[1549] So, in the case where the default which has led to the issue of the notice is a breach of a warranty or of an innominate term, a failure to comply with the notice will not, of itself, amount to a repudiatory breach, although it may provide evidence from which a court may be able to infer that the non-performing party has evinced an intention no longer to be bound by the contract. The reason that a failure to comply in such a case is not necessarily repudiatory is that a unilateral notice cannot have the effect of turning a warranty or an innominate term into a condition.[1550]

(iv) Law of Property Act 1925, section 141

1.406 This section provides that stipulations as to time which are not of the essence of a contract under the rules of equity 'are also construed and have effect at law in accordance with the same rules'. It follows that delay is no longer a ground of termination merely because it would formerly have been one at common law;[1551] that a party who terminates when he could not have done so in equity is liable in damages for wrongful repudiation;[1552] and that the party guilty of the delay is in breach and liable in damages for loss resulting from the delay.[1553]

[1541] *Samarenko v Dawn Hill House Ltd* [2011] EWCA Civ 1445, [2012] 2 All ER 476.
[1542] eg, *Bernard v Williams* (1928) 44 TLR 437; *Lock v Bell* [1931] 1 Ch 35.
[1543] *United Scientific* case, n 1533, at 924; *Union Eagle* case, n 1529, at 519.
[1544] *Re Sandwell Park Colliery Co* [1929] 1 Ch 277; cf *Hare v Nicholl* [1966] 2 QB 130.
[1545] *Barclay v Messenger* (1874) 43 LJ Ch 449.
[1546] *Behzadi v Shaftsbury Hotels Ltd* [1992] Ch 1.
[1547] *Behzadi v Shaftsbury Hotels Ltd* [1992] Ch 1.
[1548] *Finkielkraut v Monohan* [1949] 2 All ER 234; *Quadrangle Development and Construction Co Ltd v Jenner* [1974] 1 WLR 68.
[1549] *Samarenko v Dawn Hill House Ltd* [2011] EWCA Civ 1445, [2013] Ch 36.
[1550] *Samarenko v Dawn Hill House Ltd* [2011] EWCA Civ 1445, [2013] Ch 36 *Urban I (Blonk Street) Ltd v Ayres* [2013] EWCA Civ 816, [2014] 1 WLR 756, at [44].
[1551] *Raineri v Miles* [1981] AC 1050, 1082–1083.
[1552] *Stickney v Keeble* [1915] AC 386, 404; *Rightside Properties Ltd v Gray* [1975] Ch 72.
[1553] *Raineri v Miles*, n 1551.

N. Breach

(1) What Amounts to Breach?

A breach of contract is committed when a party, after performance from him has become **1.407**
due,[1554] fails or refuses to render it or incapacitates himself from rendering it.

(a) Types of breach

(i) Failure or refusal to perform

Failure or refusal to perform a contractual stipulation is a breach only where an obligation to **1.408**
perform has been undertaken. No such obligation is undertaken by the promisee under a unilateral contract,[1555] who therefore commits no breach by failing to do the stipulated act. Similarly,
an apparently bilateral contract may be in the nature of a tender by one party, not binding the
other unless and to the extent that he accepts it.[1556] Difficulty can also arise in determining
the extent of the obligation of a promisor: eg, whether an employer promises merely to pay his
employee[1557] or to provide him with work.[1558] The answer to this question is likely to depend
on whether the employee needs to work to acquire or retain a skill or reputation.[1559]

(ii) Defective performance

Very seriously defective performance can be regarded as non-performance: eg where peas are **1.409**
delivered instead of beans. But a breach is also committed where performance is of the same
kind as that promised and differs from it in point of time, quantity or quality.

(iii) Incapacitating oneself

A person may break a contract by incapacitating himself from performing it: eg where, hav- **1.410**
ing chartered his ship to X, he then sells and delivers her to Y.[1560] The disablement must render the breach inevitable.[1560a] Mere insolvency does not incapacitate a person who is under
an obligation to pay money:[1561] it has this effect only if no assets are set aside out of his estate
for performance of the contract.[1562]

(b) Without lawful excuse

(i) Concept

After a contractual duty has arisen,[1563] an event may occur excusing performance. The event **1.411**
may so seriously affect performance as to discharge both parties by frustration.[1564] But even
where it is less drastic it may excuse one party from performing: eg an employee is not in breach
if he is prevented from working by temporary illness.[1565] A party may also have an excuse for
non-performance if his decision to terminate is justified by the other's failure to perform.[1566]

[1554] For refusal *before* performance has become due, see 1.431–1.438.
[1555] See 1.07.
[1556] *Churchward v R* (1865) LR 1 QB 173; cf *Firstpost Homes Ltd v Johnson* [1995] 1 WLR 1567.
[1557] *Turner v Sawdon* [1901] 2 KB 653; *Delaney v Staples* [1992] 1 AC 687, 692 ('garden leave').
[1558] *Langston v AUEW* [1974] 1 WLR 185.
[1559] *Herbert Clayton & Jack Waller Ltd v Oliver* [1930] AC 209.
[1560] *Omnium d'Entreprises v Sutherland* [1919] 1 KB 618.
[1560a] *Geden Operations Ltd v Dry Bulk Handy Holdings Inc (M/V 'Bulk Uruquay')* [2014] EWHC 885 (Comm).
[1561] *Re Agra Bank* (1867) LR 5 Eq 160.
[1562] *Ex p Chalmers* (1873) LR 8 Ch App 289.
[1563] See 1.361–1.363.
[1564] See section O.
[1565] See *Poussard v Spiers* (1876) 1 QBD 410, 414.
[1566] See 1.359 et seq.

1.412 Excuses may also be provided by the contract itself: eg by 'exceptions' for delays caused by strikes or weather. Such 'exceptions' are not exemption clauses;[1567] their purpose is not to exclude liabilities but to define duties.

(ii) Whether excuse must be stated

1.413 The party relying on the excuse must show that it existed at the time of his refusal[1568] but need not, in general,[1569] then state the excuse or even have known of its existence.[1570] A buyer can, eg, justify rejection on account of a breach of condition of which he did not know (but which existed) at the time of rejection.[1571] But this rule would not apply where failure to specify the breach deprived the seller of the chance of curing it[1572] by making a fresh, good tender within the time allowed for performance.[1573] Even where there is no longer any such chance of curing the unstated breach, the injured party can also lose his right to rely on it where his purported rejection was preceded by 'acceptance' of the defective performance.[1574]

(c) Standard of duty

(i) Strict liability

1.414 Many contractual duties are strict.[1575] Lack of fault is, eg, no excuse for inability to pay money brought about by failure of a bank or by exchange control;[1576] or for inability to deliver generic goods due to difficulties of supply or transport.[1577] A seller of goods is likewise strictly liable for defects of quality.[1578] The same is true of a repairer or builder in respect of components supplied by him.[1579]

(ii) Liability based on fault

1.415 Liability for breach of a contract to provide services is often based on fault (ie on negligence):[1580] this is generally[1581] true of contracts to provide professional services.[1582] In a contract to provide services and components, liability for the service aspect is based on fault.[1583]

[1567] *The Angelia* [1973] 1 WLR 210 (disapproved on another point in *The Nema* [1982] AC 724).

[1568] *British & Benington v North-Western Cachar Tea Co* [1923] AC 48.

[1569] See n 1572 for an exception.

[1570] *Ridgway v Hungerford Market Co* (1835) 3 A & E 171; *Taylor v Oakes, Roncoroni & Co* (1922) 38 TLR 349, 351 (aff'd *Taylor* (1922) 38 TLR 349, 517).

[1571] *Arcos Ltd v EA Ronaasen & Sons* [1933] AC 470.

[1572] *Heisler v Anglo-Dal Ltd* [1954] 1 WLR 1273, 1278.

[1573] See 1.356.

[1574] *Panchaud Frères SA v Etablissement General Grain Co* [1970] 1 Lloyd's Rep 53, as explained in *BP Exploration Co (Libya) Ltd v Hunt* [1979] 1 WLR 783, 810–811.

[1575] *Raineri v Miles* [1981] AC 1050, 1086.

[1576] *Universal Corp v Five Ways Properties Ltd* [1979] 1 All ER 552; *Congimex SARL (Lisbon) v Continental Grain Export Corp (New York)* [1979] 2 Lloyd's Rep 346.

[1577] *Barnett v Javeri & Co* [1916] 2 KB 390; *Lewis Emanuel & Son Ltd v Sammut* [1959] 2 Lloyd's Rep 629.

[1578] *Frost v Aylesbury Dairy Co Ltd* [1905] 1 KB 608; *Daniels & Daniels v White & Sons Ltd & Tarbard* [1938] 4 All ER 258. Lack of fault can, however, be a defence to a seller's liability to a consumer in respect of certain public statements relating to goods: Consumer Rights Act 2015, s 9(5).

[1579] *GH Myers & Co v Brent Cross Service Co* [1934] 1 KB 46; *Young & Marten Ltd v McManus Childs Ltd* [1969] 1 AC 454.

[1580] Supply of Goods and Services Act 1982, s 16(3)(a). Consumer Rights Act 2015, s 49(i).

[1581] An architect is strictly liable for errors of design: *Greaves & Co (Contractors) Ltd v Baynham Meikle & Partners* [1975] 1 WLR 1095, 1101; *IBA v EMI (Electronics) Ltd* (1980) 14 Building LR 1, 47–48.

[1582] eg *Clark v Kirby-Smith* [1964] Ch 506; *Bagot v Stevens Scanlan & Co Ltd* [1966] 1 QB 197; *Henderson v Merrett Syndicates Ltd* [1995] 2 AC 145.

[1583] *Young v Marten* case, n 1579.

(iii) Modification of standards

It is generally possible to vary the standards of liability described above by the contract **1.416**
itself;[1584] and they may also be varied by legislation.[1585]

(iv) Fault and excuses for non-performance

A party cannot rely on a supervening event which is due to his fault as a ground of frus- **1.417**
tration[1586] or (generally)[1587] as an excuse for non-performance of the kind described in
1.411.

(v) Fault and contingent conditions

A party cannot rely on the non-occurrence of a contingent condition precedent if he has **1.418**
deliberately prevented the occurrence of the event or if he has failed to perform a duty
(imposed by the contract) to bring it about.[1588]

(d) Breach and lawful termination

Where a contract provides for termination by notice, a declaration by the party entitled so to **1.419**
terminate it that he will no longer perform may, if not intended as an exercise of the power to
terminate by notice, amount to a breach:[1589] eg where an employee goes on strike after notice
no shorter than that required to terminate the contract.[1590]

(2) Effects of Breach

(a) The option to terminate or affirm

(i) No automatic termination

A breach which justifies termination[1591] gives the victim the option to terminate or to **1.420**
affirm.[1592] It does not (in general)[1593] automatically discharge the contract (even if this says
that it is to become 'void' on breach);[1594] for if it did have this effect the party in breach
would be able to rely on his own wrong to improve his position under the contract[1595] or to
deprive the victim of benefits under it.[1596]

(ii) Employment contracts

At one time there was authority to support the view that the rule stated in 1.420 did not **1.421**
apply to employment contracts, so that these were automatically terminated when the
employee was wrongfully dismissed or left in breach of contract.[1597] That view has now

---

[1584] eg by a 'force majeure' clause excusing a seller in the event of difficulty of supply arising from specified causes.

[1585] eg Carriage of Goods by Sea Act 1971, s 3, reducing the common law strict liability of a carrier for unseaworthiness (*Steel v State Line Steamship Co* (1877) 3 App Cas 77, 86) to one of due diligence.

[1586] See 1.470.

[1587] Except perhaps where illness prevents performance of personal services: cf 1.472.

[1588] See 1.30.

[1589] *Bridge v Campbell Discount Co Ltd* [1962] AC 600 (hire-purchase).

[1590] *Simmons v Hoover Ltd* [1977] QB 284; *Miles v Wakefield MDC* [1987] AC 539, 562.

[1591] On the grounds discussed in section M of this chapter.

[1592] *Howard v Pickford Tool Co* [1951] 1 KB 417, 421; *Heyman v Darwins Ltd* [1942] AC 356, 361, HL; *The Simona* [1989] AC 788, 800.

[1593] For a quasi-exception, see 1.423.

[1594] *New Zealand Shipping Co v Société des Ateliers etc* [1919] AC 1; *Alghussein Establishment v Eton College* [1988] 1 WLR 587.

[1595] *Alghussein* case, n 1594; *Boston Deep Sea Fishing & Ice Co v Ansell* (1888) 39 Ch D 339, 364.

[1596] See *Decro-Wall International v Practitioners in Marketing Ltd* [1971] 1 WLR 361; *Lusograin, etc v Bunge AG* [1986] 2 Lloyd's Rep 654.

[1597] eg *Sanders v Ernest A Neale Ltd* [1974] ICR 565.

been discarded by the Supreme Court who affirmed that the elective theory also applies to contracts of employment so that a repudiation of the contract of employment terminates the contract only if and when the other party elects to accept the repudiation.[1598] Further, the requirement that the repudiation be accepted requires a real acceptance, namely 'a conscious intention to bring the contract to an end, or the doing of something that is inconsistent with its continuation'.[1599]

(iii) Insurance contracts

1.422 Breach by the insured of a 'warranty' (such as a promise not to run specified risks) discharges the insurer from the date of the breach without any election on his part.[1600] In this context, there is no risk of the wrongdoer's benefiting from his wrong by the victim's discharge.[1601]

(iv) Qualifications

1.423 The general rule giving the victim the option to terminate or to affirm is subject to the practical limitation that damages may be reduced if he fails to take reasonable steps to mitigate his loss. Such steps may put it out of his power to perform the original contract and he will then be taken to have terminated that contract: eg, where a wrongfully dismissed employee takes another job.[1602] Conversely, the mitigation requirement may put pressure on the victim, not exactly to affirm the contract, but to accept performance not strictly in accordance with it: eg, they may require a buyer to accept late delivery on a rising market.[1603]

(v) Exercising the option

1.424 The option to terminate is commonly exercised by giving notice of termination to the party in breach; but any other unequivocal indication of intention to terminate suffices.[1604] The option can be exercised in an appropriate case by 'inactivity': eg, by the injured party's failing to take steps which he would have been expected to take, if he had regarded the contract as still in force.[1605] Temporary refusal to perform until the breach is cured or performance resumed does not amount to exercise of the option to terminate.[1606] There is no inconsistency between terminating for breach and claiming damages for the same breach.[1607]

(b) Effects of termination

(i) On the obligations of the victim

1.425 The victim is released by termination from obligations to perform which had not yet accrued at the time of termination.[1608] He is not released from obligations which had already accrued at that time; and an obligation may have accrued before, though it was not to be performed until after, termination.[1609] He is also not released from certain 'ancillary' obligations.[1610]

[1598] *Geys v Société Générale, London Branch* [2012] UKSC 63, [2013] 1 AC 513.

[1599] *Geys v Société Générale, London Branch* [2012] UKSC 63, [2013] 1 AC 513, at [17].

[1600] Marine Insurance Act 1906, s 33(3); *The Good Luck* [1992] 1 AC 233.

[1601] In *The Good Luck*, n 1600, a *third party* so benefited, but under a separate contract between that party and the victim.

[1602] *Gunton v Richmond-upon-Thames LBC* [1981] Ch 448, 468; *Dietman v LB of Brent* [1987] ICR 737 (aff'd [1988] ICR 842).

[1603] *The Solholt* [1983] 1 Lloyd's Rep 605.

[1604] *Gunton's* case, n 1602, at 468.

[1605] *Vitol SA v Norelf Ltd* [1996] AC 800.

[1606] *Wiluszynski v Tower Hamlets LBC* [1989] ICR 493.

[1607] *General Bill Posting Co Ltd v Atkinson* [1909] AC 118.

[1608] *Photo Production Ltd v Securicor Transport Ltd* [1980] AC 827, 849.

[1609] *The Dominique* [1989] AC 1056; cf *Hurst v Bryk* [2002] 1 AC 185.

[1610] See n 1619.

On termination, the victim may be entitled to the return of payments made before termin- **1.426** ation (eg to the price of rejected goods). Where he has failed to make a payment (due before termination) to the return of which he would have been so entitled on termination, he should be relieved from liability to make it, since it makes no sense to hold him liable in one action for what he could recover back in another.[1611]

(ii) On the obligations of the party in breach

The effects of the injured party's election to terminate on the obligations of the guilty party **1.427** depend on a distinction between the latter's primary obligations to perform (eg to make payments specified in the contract) and his secondary obligation to pay damages for the breach.[1612] The general rule is that the election to terminate releases the guilty party from primary obligations not yet due at the time of termination;[1613] but that it does not release him from primary obligations already then due[1614] (except to the extent that a payment then due could, if it had been duly made, have been recovered back by him)[1615] or from his secondary obligation in damages.[1616] This can extend to loss suffered by reason of the premature termination of the contract: eg where, after termination of a contract on account of the guilty party's failure to make payments under the contract, the injured party disposes of the subject matter for less than the amount due to him under the original contract, had it run its full course.[1617]

(iii) Contrary indications

The above rules as to the effects of termination can be displaced by contrary agreements **1.428** or other indications of contrary intention.[1618] For example, termination does not release a party from an 'ancillary' obligation, such as one to submit disputes under the contract to arbitration.[1619]

(c) Effects of failure to terminate

If the injured party affirms or simply fails to terminate, the primary obligations of both par- **1.429** ties remain in force;[1620] though under the rules relating to the order of performance[1621] the injured party's primary obligation will not have accrued where the breach amounted to a failure to perform a promissory condition precedent.

(d) Change of course

Election to terminate precludes subsequent affirmation since it releases the guilty party **1.430** from his primary obligations.[1622] Affirmation, whether in the form of a simple demand for performance or of proceedings for specific performance,[1623] does not of itself preclude

---

[1611] cf (for the position of the guilty party in such a situation) n 1615.

[1612] *Photo Production* case, n 1608, at 849.

[1613] *Photo Production* case, n 1608, at 849. For exceptions, see 1.428. There is also no such release where the injured party is (exceptionally) discharged without election: *The Good Luck* [1992] AC 233, 263 (insurance: see 1.422).

[1614] *Brooks v Beirnstein* [1909] 1 KB 98.

[1615] See *McDonald v Denys Lascelles Ltd* (1933) 48 CLR 457, approved in *Johnson v Agnew* [1980] AC 367, 396.

[1616] *Lep Air Services Ltd v Rolloswin Investments Ltd* [1973] AC 331, 350; *The Blankenstein* [1985] 1 WLR 435.

[1617] *Overstone Ltd v Shipway* [1962] 1 WLR 117.

[1618] *Yasuda Fire & Marine Insurance Co of Europe v Orion Marine Insurance Underwriting Agency Ltd* [1995] QB 174.

[1619] *Heyman v Darwins Ltd* [1942] AC 356; cf Arbitration Act 1996, s 7.

[1620] *The Simona* [1989] AC 788.

[1621] See 1.361.

[1622] *Johnson v Agnew* [1980] AC 367, 393.

[1623] As in *Johnson v Agnew*, n 1622.

termination for a continuing failure to perform.[1624] It precludes rescission only if it is accompanied by other circumstances from which a waiver of the right to terminate can be inferred.

(3) Repudiation Before Performance is Due

(a) Concept of anticipatory breach

1.431 A party commits an anticipatory breach if, before his performance is due, he either renounces the contract or disables himself by his 'own act or default'[1625] from performing it. Disablement can result not only from an act but also from an omission such as failing to make an effective supply contract with a third party, but a party who *has* made such a contract will not be in anticipatory breach merely by reason of that third party's default.[1626]

1.432 The victim can either 'accept' the anticipatory breach or continue to press for performance. Acceptance can be by taking legal proceedings, by notice, by conduct and even by omission unequivocally indicating intention to accept.[1627]

(b) Effects of acceptance

(i) Damages

1.433 Acceptance of an anticipatory breach entitles the victim to damages at once, before the time fixed for performance[1628] and even though his right under the contract is still subject to a contingent condition precedent (eg that of surviving the promisor[1629] or a third party).[1630] Where a person repudiates liability to make future payments, the objection that he will thus have to pay damages before the debt was due is (at least in part) met by allowing 'a discount for accelerated payment'.[1631]

(ii) Termination

1.434 Termination for anticipatory breach is available where the likely effects of the breach satisfy the requirement of 'substantial' failure[1632] and (probably) where one of the exceptions to that requirement[1633] (other than the exception arising from express provisions for termination)[1634] applies.

1.435 The question whether the prospective failure justifies termination depends in cases of *renunciation* on whether the victim at the time of termination *reasonably believed* that the guilty party did not intend to perform.[1635] But in cases of *disablement* it has been said that it must at the time of termination be *already certain* that the prospective failure would turn out to be sufficiently serious to justify termination.[1636] A's reasonable belief that B would not be able to

---

[1624] *Johnson v Agnew*, n 1622; cf *Tilcon Ltd v Land and Real Estate Investments Ltd* [1987] 1 All ER 615; *Stocznia Gdanska SA v Latvian Shipping Co* [2002] EWCA Civ 889, [2002] 2 All ER (Comm) 786, at [100].

[1625] *Universal Cargo Carriers Corp v Citati* [1957] 2 QB 401, 441.

[1626] The *Citati* case, n 1625, gives rise to difficulty in this context: see *FC Shepherd & Co Ltd v Jerrom* [1987] QB 301, 323.

[1627] *Vitol SA v Norelf Ltd* [1996] AC 800.

[1628] *Hochster v De la Tour* (1853) 2 E & B 678.

[1629] *Synge v Synge* [1894] 1 QB 466.

[1630] *Frost v Knight* (1872) LR 7 Ex 111 (actual decision obsolete since Law Reform (Miscellaneous Provisions) Act 1970, s 1).

[1631] *Lep Air Services Ltd v Rolloswin Investments Ltd* [1973] AC 331, 356.

[1632] See 1.365.

[1633] eg breach of condition, as is assumed in the *Citati* case, n 1625.

[1634] As in *The Afovos* [1983] 1 WLR 195 (where a dictum at 203 restricting the right to rescind for anticipatory breaches to those that are 'fundamental' is therefore unnecessary and, it is submitted, too restrictive). And see 1.368, n 1413.

[1635] *The Hermosa* [1982] 1 Lloyd's Rep 570, 580.

[1636] *Citati* case, n 1625, at 449–450.

perform should not be (and is not) a ground for holding B liable in damages;[1637] but it would be more convenient to allow such a belief to justify A's termination,[1638] as it does where B's breach is in part actual and gives rise to uncertainty as to his future ability to perform.[1639]

Termination releases the victim from his duty to perform and entitles him to damages without having to show that he could (but for the anticipatory breach) have performed that duty.[1640] **1.436**

(c) Effects of not accepting the breach

If the victim affirms the contract (or simply does not accept the breach) both parties remain bound by the contract and damages cannot be claimed before the time fixed for performance.[1641] The right to damages may, before then, be lost: eg if the guilty party withdraws his repudiation[1642] or lawfully puts an end to the contract under a cancelling clause[1643] or if the contract is frustrated.[1644] **1.437**

Affirmation should not bar termination in the face of a continuing anticipatory breach;[1645] certainly a mere call for performance in response to the breach does not have this effect since it does not of itself amount to affirmation.[1646] **1.438**

O. Frustration

(1) Introduction

Under the doctrine of frustration, a contract may be discharged by supervening events which make its performance impossible or illegal or frustrate its purpose. The doctrine was developed in cases of supervening destruction of the subject matter,[1647] originally as a modification of an earlier view[1648] (traces of which remain)[1649] that contractual duties were generally[1650] not discharged by supervening impossibility.[1651] Its purpose is to allocate or divide the loss resulting from the supervening event by discharging the party who was to render the now impossible performance from his duty to render it and the party who was to receive it from his duty to pay for it.[1652] On the other hand, it should not discharge a party merely because an 'uncontemplated turn of events' has turned the contract, for him, into a bad bargain.[1653] **1.439**

[1637] This was the actual point decided in the *Citati* case, n 1625.

[1638] cf the rule in cases of frustration: stated in 1.458.

[1639] *Hong Kong Fir* case, n 1407, at 57; *Snia v Suzuki & Co* (1924) 29 Commercial Cases 284.

[1640] *British & Beningtons v North-Western Cachar Tea Co Ltd* [1923] AC 48; 1.364.

[1641] Except perhaps where they are claimed in lieu of specific performance.

[1642] *Harrison v Northwest Holt Group Administration Ltd* [1985] ICR 668.

[1643] *The Simona* [1989] AC 788.

[1644] *Avery v Bowden* (1855) 5 E & B 714.

[1645] For conflicting views on the point, contrast *Stocznia Gdanska SA v Latvian Shipping Co* [1997] 2 Lloyd's Rep 228, 235 (set aside [1998] 1 WLR 574, 594) with *Stocznia Gdanska SA v Latvian Shipping Co (No 3)* [2001] 1 Lloyd's Rep 537 and (on appeal) [2002] EWCA Civ 889, [2002] 2 Lloyd's Rep 436, at [97]–[100], inclining to the view stated in the text above. For the same view in cases of actual breach, see 1.430.

[1646] *Yukong Line Ltd of Korea v Rendsburg Investments Corp of Liberia* [1996] 2 Lloyd's Rep 604.

[1647] Starting with *Taylor v Caldwell* (1863) 3 B & S 826.

[1648] *Paradine v Jane* (1647) Aleyn 26.

[1649] eg *Ashmore & Son v Cox & Co* [1899] 1 QB 436; *Lewis Emanuel & Son Ltd v Sammut* [1959] 2 Lloyd's Rep 629, 642.

[1650] There were exceptions, eg contracts of personal service: see *Taylor v Caldwell*, n 1647, at 836.

[1651] For discharge by supervening *illegality* see, eg *Atkinson v Ritchie* (1809) 10 East 530, 534–535.

[1652] *Taylor v Caldwell*, n 1647, at 840 ('*both* parties are excused').

[1653] *British Movietonenews Ltd v London and District Cinemas* [1952] AC 166, 185.

Partly for this reason and partly because parties commonly make express provisions for supervening events, the courts have imposed strict limits on the scope of the doctrine,[1654] particularly where the prevention of performance is only partial or temporary,[1655] and where there is no actual impossibility or illegality.[1656] When deciding in a particular case whether or not a contract has been frustrated, the courts adopt what has been termed a 'multi-factorial' approach.[1657] Factors which the courts take into account when deciding whether or not a contract has been frustrated include: 'the terms of the contract itself, its matrix or context, the parties' knowledge, expectations, assumptions and contemplations, in particular as to risk, as at the time of contract, at any rate so far as these can be ascribed mutually and objectively and then the nature of the supervening event, and the parties' reasonable and objectively ascertainable calculations as to the possibilities of future performance in the new circumstances.'[1658]

(2) Applications

(a) Impossibility

1.440 Supervening impossibility of performance is not of itself a ground of discharge. It will not, eg, have this effect where a party's contractual duty is strict,[1659] so that he can be said to have *undertaken* that its performance will be possible. Discharge can occur only where there is no such undertaking but merely an *assumption* by the parties about the continued possibility of performance.

(i) Destruction of a particular thing

1.441 A contract may be discharged by the destruction of its subject matter: eg of a music-hall to be made available under the contract for a series of concerts.[1660] For this purpose, a thing which is so seriously damaged as to have become 'for business purposes something else'[1661] is taken to have been destroyed; and destruction of part of the subject matter suffices if it is so serious as to defeat the main purpose of the contract.[1662] Destruction of something which is not the subject matter of the contract but is essential for its performance can suffice: eg of the factory in which machinery is to be installed.[1663]

1.442 In certain types of contracts, destruction of the subject matter is governed by rules relating to the passing of risk, and these can displace the principle of discharge. For example, where goods are sold and destroyed after the risk has passed to the buyer,[1664] he is not discharged from his duty to pay, while the seller, though discharged from his duty to deliver, is not discharged from certain other duties.[1665]

[1654] eg *The Nema* [1982] AC 724, 752; *CTI Group Inc v Transclear SA* [2008] EWCA Civ 856, [2008] 2 Lloyd's Rep 526.

[1655] See 1.441 and 1.445; cf the 'Suez' cases (1.450).

[1656] See 1.451.

[1657] *The Sea Angel* [2007] EWCA Civ 547, [2007] 2 Lloyd's Rep 517, at [111].

[1658] *The Sea Angel* [2007] EWCA Civ 547, [2007] 2 Lloyd's Rep 517, at [111].

[1659] See 1.414; cf also 1.442.

[1660] *Taylor v Caldwell*, n 1647; cf Sale of Goods Act 1979, s 7.

[1661] *Asfar & Co v Blundell* [1896] 1 QB 123, 128 (dates contaminated by sewage).

[1662] As in *Taylor v Caldwell*, n 1647.

[1663] *Appleby v Myers* (1867) LR 2 CP 651.

[1664] See Sale of Goods Act 1979, s 20(1).

[1665] eg duties to tender documents giving the buyer rights against the carrier or insurer: see *Manbré Saccharine Co Ltd v Corn Products Co Ltd* [1919] 1 KB 198.

(ii) Death or disability of a particular person

Contracts of employment or agency are discharged by the death of either party;[1666] other **1.443**
contracts involving the exercise by one party of personal skill are discharged by the death
of that party. The same is true where a party is physically disabled from performing or
receiving performance;[1667] and where continued performance would seriously endanger his
health.[1668]

(iii) Unavailability

In general. A contract may be frustrated if its subject matter, though not ceasing to exist, **1.444**
becomes unavailable: eg through requisition[1669] or detention.[1670] A contract for personal
services may similarly be frustrated through the conscription[1671] or illness[1672] of the person
who was to render them.

Temporary unavailability. Unavailability at the time fixed for performance will frustrate **1.445**
a contract if that time is of the essence:[1673] eg where the contract is one to play in a concert
on a specified day.[1674] Even if time is not of the essence, frustration can result where the
delay is so long that performance after its end would no longer serve the originally contemplated purpose of the person who was to have received it;[1675] or if such performance
would impose substantially different obligations from those originally undertaken on the
party who was to render it. This could be the position because, by the end of the delay,
economic conditions had so changed as either substantially to increase the costs of that
party[1676] or to bring the originally agreed remuneration out of line with that then payable
for the services.[1677]

Where the amount of performance due is measured by the time taken to render it, a claim **1.446**
made after the end of the delay may be merely for any balance then due (eg for the unexpired
term of a time charter). Such a claim will fail if the delay lasts or is likely to last for so long
that no, or only a relatively insignificant, part of the originally agreed performance then
remains possible;[1678] but it will succeed if the part then remaining possible is substantial.[1679]
An employee's temporary illness will similarly frustrate the contract of employment only if it
is so serious as to put an end 'in a business sense'[1680] to the possibility of further performance.

(iv) Failure of source of supply

Whether contract frustrated. A contract which expressly provides for goods to be taken **1.447**
from a specified source may be discharged by failure of that source[1681] (eg where a specified
crop fails or a seller is cut off from a specified foreign source by war or natural disaster). The

---

[1666] *Campanari v Woodburn* (1854) 15 CB 400; *Whincup v Hughes* (1871) LR 6 CP 78 (apprenticeship).
[1667] *Jackson v Union Marine Insurance Co Ltd* (1874) LR 10 CP 125, 145.
[1668] *Condor v The Barron Knights Ltd* [1966] 1 WLR 87.
[1669] *Re Shipton Anderson & Co* [1915] 3 KB 676; *Bank Line Ltd v Arthur Capel & Co* [1919] AC 435.
[1670] eg *The Evia (No 2)* [1983] 1 AC 736.
[1671] *Morgan v Manser* [1948] 1 KB 184.
[1672] eg *Hart v AR Marshall & Sons (Bulwell) Ltd* [1977] 1 WLR 1067.
[1673] See 1.402.
[1674] *Robinson v Davison* (1871) LR 6 Ex 269.
[1675] *Jackson v Union Marine Insurance Co* (1874) LR 10 CP 125.
[1676] eg *Metropolitan Water Board v Dick, Kerr & Co* [1918] AC 119.
[1677] This seems to be the reason why the contract was frustrated in *Bank Line Ltd v Arthur Capel & Co*
[1919] AC 435.
[1678] *Countess of Warwick Steamship Co v Le Nickel SA* [1918] 1 KB 372; *The Nema* [1982] AC 724.
[1679] *Tamplin Steamship Co Ltd v Anglo-Mexican Petroleum Co* [1916] 2 AC 397.
[1680] *Jackson's* case, n 1675, at 145; *Hart's* case, and see n 1672.
[1681] *Howell v Coupland* (1876) 1 QBD 258.

contract will not be frustrated if it contains no reference to a source intended by only one party.[1682] If the unspecified source is contemplated by both parties, the contract will be frustrated by supervening illegality if in time of war that source becomes an enemy source.[1683] The physical failure of a mutually contemplated source may also frustrate the contract[1684] where it would not be reasonable to expect the parties to provide in the contract for such failure.

1.448 **Partial failure.**   Where total failure of a source would frustrate a contract,[1685] its partial failure excuses the seller to the extent of the deficiency.[1686] He must deliver[1687] (though the buyer need not accept)[1688] the quantity actually produced.

1.449 Where a seller has made more than one contract specifying the source, its partial failure may prevent him from fulfilling them all but not from fulfilling one or more. Such a partial failure of supply will not generally suffice to frustrate any of the supply contracts. The reason given for this is that none of the contracts can be frustrated because the supplier's choice as to which contracts to fulfil amounts to an 'election', excluding the doctrine.[1689] This conclusion seems harsh given that there is no true election where partial failure makes it impossible to fulfil all the contracts.[1690] A supplier who wishes to protect its position in a case of this type must insert an express term into the contract (eg, a force majeure clause) which entitles it to allocate the remaining supplies on a *pro rata* or some other basis among the various purchasers.[1691]

(v) Method of performance impossible

1.450 A contract can be frustrated if it provides that it is to be performed *only* by a method that becomes impossible.[1692] Impossibility of a stipulated method that is not intended to be exclusive does not frustrate a contract if performance by another method which remains possible would not be fundamentally different from that specified;[1693] the same is a fortiori true if the method which becomes impossible was merely contemplated by both parties.[1694] No such fundamental difference was held to have arisen when closure of the Suez Canal imposed on one of the parties the extra expense of a longer voyage.[1695]

(b) Impracticability

(i) General rule

1.451 The concept of 'impossibility' is itself a relative one, depending on the current state of technology and on the amount of trouble that one is prepared to take to overcome obstacles. Nevertheless, 'impracticability' goes beyond 'impossibility', covering cases in which performance remains possible but becomes severely more burdensome to the party required to

---

[1682] *Blackburn Bobbin Co Ltd v TW Allen & Sons Ltd* [1918] 2 KB 467; cf *Congimex SARL (Lisbon) v Continental Grain Export Corp (New York)* [1979] 2 Lloyd's Rep 346, 353 (source of payment).
[1683] *Re Badische Co* [1921] 2 Ch 331.
[1684] This was conceded in *Lipton Ltd v Ford* [1917] 2 KB 647.
[1685] See 1.447.
[1686] This was the actual result in *Howell v Coupland*, n 1681.
[1687] *HR & S Sainsbury Ltd v Street* [1972] 1 WLR 834.
[1688] Sale of Goods Act 1979, s 30(1) (subject to Sale of Goods Act 1979, s 30(2A)).
[1689] cf *The Super Servant Two* [1990] 1 Lloyd's Rep 1.
[1690] See 1.473.
[1691] See *Tennants (Lancashire) Ltd v CS Wilson & Co Ltd* [1917] AC 495, 511–512; *Bremer Handelsgesellschaft mbH v Vanden Avenne-Izegem PVBA* [1978] 2 Lloyd's Rep 109, 115, 128.
[1692] *Nickoll & Knight v Ashton Edridge & Co* [1901] 2 KB 126.
[1693] eg *The Captain George K* [1970] 2 Lloyd's Rep 21.
[1694] *Tsakiroglou & Co Ltd v Noblee Thorl GmbH* [1962] AC 93.
[1695] As in the cases cited in nn 1693 and 1694.

render it. While there are some judicial statements to the effect that impracticability (or 'commercial impossibility') can be a ground of discharge,[1696] no actual decision supports this view, while others seem to contradict it.[1697] The prevailing view is that impracticability is not, in general, a ground of frustration.[1698]

(ii) Exceptional situations

Increased cost of performance may be a ground of discharge where the supervening event **1.452** delays performance[1699] or where the cost is incurred to avoid supervening illegality.[1700] In such cases, however, discharge results not from 'pure' impracticability, but from impracticability combined with temporary impossibility or prospective illegality. Express provisions for discharge may also sometimes[1701] be brought into operation by severe increases in cost;[1702] but since the main purpose of such provisions is to *extend* the scope of discharge to situations *not* covered by the common law doctrine, such cases give no support to the view that such increases would discharge the contract under that doctrine. In a contract of indefinite duration, there is often[1703] a power to terminate by giving reasonable notice and one motive for so terminating may be that performance has become more onerous for the party giving the notice.[1704] But there is no such power to terminate a fixed term contract[1705] so that these cases, too, do not support any general principle of discharge for impracticability at common law; indeed if there were such a principle, discharge would be automatic[1706] and not by notice.

(iii) Inflation and currency fluctuations

Inflation and currency fluctuation are not grounds of discharge at common law.[1707] The pos- **1.453** sibility that extreme inflation might be so regarded cannot be ruled out, though legislative regulation is the more likely reaction to such a development.

(c) Frustration of purpose

Frustration of purpose occurs where the effect of a supervening event is to make one party's **1.454** performance useless to the other: eg where rooms were hired for the days fixed for King Edward VII's coronation processions for the purpose of enabling the hirer to watch the processions, which because of the illness of the King failed to take place on those days.[1708] The principle applies only if no part of purpose intended by *both* parties can be achieved:[1709]

[1696] eg *Horlock v Beal* [1916] AC 486, 492; *The Furness Bridge* [1977] 2 Lloyd's Rep 367, 377.

[1697] eg *Davis Contractors Ltd v Fareham UDC* [1956] AC 696; and see the 'Suez cases' (1.449); cf *The Mercedes Envoy* [1995] 2 Lloyd's Rep 559, 563.

[1698] eg *Tennants* case, n 1691, at 510; *British Movietonenews Ltd v London & District Cinemas* [1952] AC 166, 185; *Thames Valley Power Ltd v Total Gas Power Ltd* [2005] EWHC 2208 (Comm), [2006]1 Lloyd's Rep 441, at [50].

[1699] See 1.445, n 1676.

[1700] *Cory (Wm) & Son v London Corporation* [1951] 1 KB 8 (aff'd [1951] 2 KB 476); special considerations of public interest apply in cases of supervening illegality; see 1.455.

[1701] Though not generally: see, eg, *Brauer & Co (Great Britain) Ltd v James Clark (Brush Materials) Ltd* [1952] 2 All ER 497; *B & S Contracts and Designs Ltd v Victor Green Publications Ltd* [1984] ICR 419; and the *Thames Valley* case, n 1698.

[1702] *Tradax Export SA v André & Cie SA* [1976] 1 Lloyd's Rep 416, 423.

[1703] Not always: see *Watford BC v Watford RDC* (1988) 86 LGR 524.

[1704] As in *Staffordshire Area Health Authority v South Staffordshire Waterworks Co* [1978] 1 WLR 1387.

[1705] See *Kirklees MBC v Yorkshire Woollen District Transport Co Ltd* (1978) 77 LGR 448.

[1706] See 1.475.

[1707] *British Movietonenews* case, n 1698, at 185; *Wates Ltd v GLC* (1983) 25 Building LR 1, 34.

[1708] *Krell v Henry* [1903] 2 KB 740; the principle was applied in another context in *Denny, Mott & Dickson v James B Fraser & Co Ltd* [1944] AC 265 but its scope will be not be extended (*North Shore Ventures Ltd v Anstead Holdings Inc* [2010] EWHC 1485 (Ch), at [310]).

[1709] *Leiston Gas Co v Leiston-cum-Sizewell UDC* [1916] 2 KB 428, esp 433.

thus where premises were bought, the buyer intending to redevelop them, there was no discharge merely because 'listing' of the building made the redevelopment more difficult or even impossible.[1710] Such restrictions are necessary to avert the danger that the principle might be invoked simply to get out of a very bad bargain.

(d) Illegality

(i) Types of illegality

1.455 The rule that supervening illegality discharges a contract is based not so much on the need to allocate loss between the parties as on the public interest in ensuring compliance with the law.[1711] This public interest is particularly strong where in time of war the contract would involve trading with the enemy: the contract is discharged even though its performance might not be impossible.[1712] Other prohibitions can similarly discharge a contract: eg a contract which provides for goods to be exported[1713] can be frustrated by prohibition of export.

(ii) Antecedent and supervening prohibitions

1.456 Our present concern is with supervening prohibitions, as opposed to antecedent ones (which may make a contract void *ab initio*).[1714] This distinction is however blurred where at the time of contracting a law is in force prohibiting performance without the consent of some public body which then refuses to give it. If the refusal is due to a change of government policy with regard to giving such consent, that change can be regarded as a supervening event, leading to frustration.[1715]

(iii) Partial or temporary illegality

1.457 Supervening partial or temporary illegality frustrates a contract only if it defeats the main object of the contract.[1716] If the contract is not frustrated, such illegality nevertheless excuses a party from rendering that part of the performance which has become illegal.[1717]

(e) Prospective frustration

1.458 At the time of the supervening event, it may not be certain, but only highly likely, that its effects on performance will be such as to frustrate the contract. To prevent rights from being left indefinitely in suspense, the contract can then be frustrated at once, even though a later event unexpectedly restores the possibility of performance.[1718] However, where an event such as a strike causes delays which might be slight or serious, frustration occurs only when the delay has continued for so long as to cause a reasonable person to believe that it would interfere fundamentally with performance.[1719]

[1710] *Amalgamated Investment & Property Co Ltd v John Walker & Son Ltd* [1977] 1 WLR 164.

[1711] *Islamic Republic of Iran Shipping Lines v Steamship Mutual Underwriting Association (Bermuda) Ltd* [2010] EWHC 2661 (Comm), [2011] 1 Lloyd's Rep 195, at [100].

[1712] eg *Fibrosa Spolka Ackcyjna v Fairbairn Lawson Combe Barbour Ltd* [1943] AC 32.

[1713] Not one in which this is merely the intention of one party: see *D McMaster & Co v Cox McEwen & Co* 1921 SC (HL) 1; *Congimex, etc, v Tradax Export SA* [1983] 1 Lloyd's Rep 250.

[1714] See section H.

[1715] This was assumed in *Maritime National Fish Ltd v Ocean Trawlers Ltd* [1935] AC 524, where the plea of frustration failed on grounds stated in 1.473.

[1716] As in the *Denny Mott* case, n 1708.

[1717] See *Cricklewood Property & Investment Trust Ltd v Leighton's Investment Trust Ltd* [1945] AC 221, 233, 244; *Sturcke v SW Edwards Ltd* (1971) 23 P & CR 185, 190.

[1718] *Embiricos v Sydney Reid & Co* [1914] 3 KB 45.

[1719] *The Nema* [1982] AC 724, 753.

(f) Alternatives

1.459 A contract imposes an alternative obligation if it requires a person to do X or Y so that at the time of contracting it is impossible to tell which is due.[1720] Such a contract is not discharged by supervening impossibility or illegality of only one of the specified performances; the other must then normally[1721] be rendered.[1722] The position is different where a contract requires a person to do X with a liberty to substitute Y. Here X is due until Y is substituted and if, before then, X becomes impossible or illegal the contract is discharged.[1723]

(g) Leases of land

1.460 A lease of land can be frustrated.[1724] But supervening events will only rarely have this effect[1725] since in a long lease each party takes the risk that circumstances may change during its currency; since the ratio of the interruption of the intended use of the premises to the length of the lease is likely to be small;[1726] and since the effect on the lease of some potentially frustrating events is likely to be dealt with by its express terms (such as covenants to repair). It has accordingly been held that leases were not frustrated where the premises were destroyed by enemy action[1727] or requisitioned[1728] or where the intended use of the premises was prohibited by wartime legislation.[1729] Even where the lease is not frustrated, supervening events may provide an excuse for non-performance of individual obligations under it.[1730]

(h) Sale of land

1.461 A contract for the sale of land can be frustrated;[1731] but such a contract is not frustrated by the destruction of buildings on the land for the sake of which it was bought. At common law, this followed from the rule that risk passed to the purchaser on contract;[1732] and although this rule is now commonly excluded by agreement,[1733] the contract is likely to contain further express provisions dealing with destruction of or damage to buildings, and such provisions will in turn exclude frustration.

1.462 A contract for the sale of land with buildings to be erected on it can be frustrated, not by destruction of the partly completed buildings, but by delay caused by the supervening event.[1734]

1.463 A contract for the sale of land is not frustrated by the making of a compulsory purchase order relating to the land.[1735] But where actual requisition prevents the vendor from performing

---

[1720] In the interests of clarity, such a contract should specify which party is entitled to choose whether X or Y is to be performed: *Mora Shipping Inc v Axa Corporate Solutions Assurance SA* [2005] EWCA Civ 1069; [2005] 2 Lloyd's Rep 769, at [56].

[1721] ie unless the contract otherwise provides: *Sociedad Iberica de Molturacion SA v Tradax Export SA* [1978] 2 Lloyd's Rep 545.

[1722] *The Furness Bridge* [1977] 2 Lloyd's Rep 367.

[1723] See *The Badagry* [1985] 1 Lloyd's Rep 395; cf *Reardon Smith Line Ltd v Ministry of Agriculture, Fisheries and Food* [1963] AC 691.

[1724] *National Carriers Ltd v Panalpina (Northern) Ltd* [1981] AC 675.

[1725] *National Carriers Ltd v Panalpina (Northern) Ltd* [1981] AC 675, 692, 697.

[1726] cf 1.446.

[1727] *Redmond v Dainton* [1920] 2 KB 256.

[1728] *Matthey v Curling* [1922] 2 AC 180 (where the tenant received compensation for the requisition).

[1729] *Cricklewood* case, n 1717.

[1730] *Cricklewood* case, n 1717, at 233; *Baily v De Crespigny* (1869) LR 4 QB 180.

[1731] This is assumed in *Amalgamated Investment & Property Co Ltd v John Walker & Son Ltd* [1977] 1 WLR 164.

[1732] *Paine v Meller* (1801) 6 Ves 349.

[1733] But the rule appears not to be excluded in Law Society's Standard Conditions of Sale (5th edn).

[1734] *Wong Lai Ying v Chinachem Investment Co Ltd* (1979) 13 Building LR 81.

[1735] *Hillingdon Estates Co v Stonefield Estate Co* [1952] Ch 627.

his obligation to transfer vacant possession, specific performance is not available to him[1736] and the purchaser is entitled to the return of his deposit.[1737]

(3) Limitations

(a) Contractual provisions for the event

1.464 Contracting parties can expressly provide that the risk of specified supervening events is to be borne by one of them[1738] or that on the occurrence of such events their obligations are to be modified[1739] in some way not available under the common law doctrine. This is typically done by inserting into the contract a force majeure clause or a hardship clause. A risk-allocating provision may also be implied from the nature of the transaction.[1740] In general, all such provisions exclude frustration.[1741]

1.465 On grounds of public policy, the parties cannot exclude discharge by supervening illegality where continued performance would involve trading with an enemy in time of war.[1742]

1.466 An express provision may literally appear to cover the allegedly frustrating event but be held on its true construction to cover only a less serious interference with performance. The provision will then not exclude frustration.[1743] Similarly, a clause may fail to make *complete* provision for the event: eg it may provide an excuse for non-performance for, or give a right to cancel to, one party without excluding frustration.[1744]

1.467 Parties commonly provide for modification or discharge of their obligations on the occurrence of specified events even though these might not frustrate the contract at common law. Where obligations are thus discharged, this result follows by virtue of the express provisions and not under the common law doctrine.[1745]

(b) Foreseeability

1.468 Where a supervening event is or can be foreseen by the parties, the prima facie inference is that they have allocated the risk of its occurrence by the contract, so that an event which 'was or might have been anticipated'[1746] is not a ground of discharge.[1747] The question whether such an inference is actually to be drawn depends, however, on the degree and extent of foreseeability. Frustration is not excluded merely because the parties could as a remote contingency have foreseen the event.[1748] The event must have been readily foreseeable: ie be one which persons of ordinary intelligence would regard as likely to occur. The event and its consequences must also have been foreseeable in some detail: to exclude frustration, it is not, eg, enough that *some* interference with performance was or could have been foreseen if the interference which actually occurs is wholly different in extent from the foreseen or foreseeable one.[1749]

[1736] *Cook v Taylor* [1942] Ch 349.

[1737] *James Macara Ltd v Barclay* [1945] KB 148.

[1738] *Budgett v Binnington & Co* [1891] 1 QB 35, 41.

[1739] eg by provisions for postponed performance: see *Victorian Seats Agency v Paget* (1902) 19 TLR 16 or for flexible pricing: see *Wates v GLC* (1983) 25 Building LR 1.

[1740] *Larrinaga & Co Ltd v Societe Franco-Americaine des Phosphates de Medulla* (1923) 92 LJ KB 455.

[1741] *Joseph Constantine Steamship Line v Imperial Smelting Co* [1942] AC 154, 163.

[1742] *Ertel Bieber & Co v Rio Tinto Co Ltd* [1918] AC 260.

[1743] *Metropolitan Water Board v Dick, Kerr & Co* [1918] AC 119.

[1744] *Bank Line Ltd v Arthur Capel & Co* [1919] AC 435.

[1745] So that the Law Reform (Frustrated Contracts) Act 1943 does not apply to such discharge.

[1746] *Krell v Henry* [1903] 2 KB 740, 752.

[1747] *Walton Harvey Ltd v Walker & Homfrays Ltd* [1931] 1 Ch 274.

[1748] *The Sea Angel* [2007] EWCA Civ 547, [2007] 2 Lloyd's Rep 517, at [127].

[1749] As in *WJ Tatem Ltd v Gamboa* [1939] 1 KB 132 and *The Eugenia* [1964] 2 QB 226; dicta in these cases on discharge by foreseeable events go further than necessary.

The inference that the risk of foreseen or readily foreseeable events is allocated by the con- **1.469** tract may be displaced: eg by evidence that the parties intended, if the event occurred, 'to leave the lawyers to sort it out';[1750] or by the fact that a provision which they made for it is incomplete.[1751] On grounds of public policy a foreseen event can also frustrate a contract if its performance after the event would involve trading with an enemy.[1752]

(c) Self-induced frustration

(i) Discharge generally excluded

A party cannot rely on 'self-induced frustration',[1753] ie, on an obstacle to performance **1.470** wholly or partly brought about by his voluntary conduct or by that of those for whom he is responsible. Thus he cannot rely on his own breach of the contract as a ground of frustration,[1754] even where it takes the form of an omission (such as failing to make a ship seaworthy)[1755] and even where the other party's breach also contributes to an allegedly frustrating delay.[1756]

A party cannot rely as a ground of frustration on his own deliberate act (or its consequences) **1.471** even where the act is not a breach of the contract;[1757] but the other party may be able to do so. Thus where an employee is prevented from working because he has been imprisoned on conviction for an offence unconnected with his employment, he cannot, but his employer can, rely on the imprisonment as a ground of frustration.[1758]

(ii) Negligence

A party cannot generally rely as a ground of frustration on an event brought about by his **1.472** negligence; but there may be an exception to this rule where the negligence takes the form of his failing to take care of his health.[1759]

(iii) Choosing between contracts

A person may enter into several contracts with different parties and a supervening event may **1.473** then reduce his capacity to perform, so that he can no longer perform all, but can still per- form some, of those contracts. In such a case, if he then devotes his now limited capacity to the performance of some of those contracts, he cannot rely on frustration as discharging him from the others as his inability to perform these is due to his 'election' to perform the former ones.[1760] Such reasoning is, however, rather harsh given that, where the reduction in his capacity to perform is due to an event for which he was not responsible, his only choice (to which of the contracts he will devote that reduced capacity) is not a truly voluntary one.[1761]

(iv) Burden of proof

The burden of proving that frustration is self-induced is on the party who so alleges.[1762] **1.474**

[1750] *The Eugenia*, n 1749, at 234.
[1751] As in the *Bank Line* case, n 1744.
[1752] cf 1.465.
[1753] *Bank Line* case, n 1744, at 234.
[1754] eg *The Eugenia*, n 1749.
[1755] *Monarch Steamship Co v A/B Karlshamns Oljefabriker* [1949] AC 196.
[1756] *The Hannah Blumenthal* [1983] 1 AC 854.
[1757] *Denmark Production Ltd v Boscobel Productions Ltd* [1969] 1 QB 699.
[1758] *FC Shepherd & Co Ltd v Jerrom* [1987] QB 301.
[1759] *Joseph Constantine Steamship Line v Imperial Smelting Co* [1942] AC 154, 166–167.
[1760] *Maritime National Fish Ltd v Ocean Trawlers Ltd* [1935] AC 524; *The Super Servant Two* [1990] 1 Lloyd's Rep 1.
[1761] cf 1.449.
[1762] *Joseph Constantine* case, n 1759.

(4) Legal Effects of Frustration

(a) In general

1.475 Frustration terminates the contract with effect from the time of the frustrating event.[1763] It operates automatically (without the need for any election) so that it can usually[1764] be invoked by either party and not only by the party likely to be prejudiced by the frustrating event. It may thus be invoked by the other party with a view to profiting from the event: eg by a shipowner who claims that requisition has frustrated a time charter where the government compensation for requisition exceeds the charterparty hire.[1765] The courts can prevent such misuse of the doctrine only by holding that the interference with performance has not been sufficiently serious to frustrate the contract.[1766]

(b) Problems of adjustment

1.476 Problems of adjustment arise where one party has or should have performed wholly or in part before the frustrating event while the other's counterperformance was not to be rendered until after that event. The common law rules on this subject have been largely superseded by the Law Reform (Frustrated Contracts) Act 1943 ('the 1943 Act') but continue to apply to cases excepted from its provisions.[1767]

(i) Money paid or payable in advance

1.477 **Common law.** At common law, money paid before frustration can (unless the contract otherwise provides)[1768] be recovered back by the payor only[1769] if the frustrating event brings about a 'total failure of consideration': eg, where it prevents delivery of any of the goods for which an advance payment had been made.[1770] If in such a case money should have been but was not so paid, liability to pay it must be discharged since there is no point in requiring a party to pay money to the return of which he would then immediately be entitled.[1771]

1.478 **Statute.** By section 1(2) of the 1943 Act, money paid before discharge is repayable (without any requirement of 'total failure of consideration') and money which should have been but was not so paid ceases to be payable. But the court has a discretion to allow the party to whom money is so paid (or payable) to retain (or recover) the whole or any part of the sum so paid (or payable) if he has incurred expenses in or for the purpose of the performance of the contract. In exercising this 'broad discretion',[1772] the court can take account of the fact that the payor has also incurred expenses which are wasted as a result of the frustrating event.[1773]

[1763] *Hirji Mulji v Cheong Yue Steamship Co Ltd* [1926] AC 497, 505.

[1764] For an exception, see 1.471.

[1765] eg *The Isle of Mull* 278 F 131 (1921).

[1766] eg in the *Tamplin* case [1916] 2 AC 397 (see 1.445); cf also the *Tsakiroglou* case [1962] AC 93 (see 1.449).

[1767] See 1.483 and 1.484.

[1768] *Fibrosa* case [1943] AC 32, 43, 77; and see n 1779.

[1769] *Whincup v Hughes* (1871) LR 6 CP 78.

[1770] *Fibrosa* case, n 1768.

[1771] *Fibrosa* case, n 1768, at 53–54. cf 1.426, n 1611; and 1.427, n 1615.

[1772] *Gamerco SA v ICM/Fair Warning (Agency) Ltd* [1995] 1 WLR 1226, 1236; insurance moneys received by the claimant must generally be disregarded: 1943 Act, s 1(5).

[1773] *Gamerco* case, n 1772.

(ii) Other benefits

Common law. At common law, a party who has conferred benefits other than money can- **1.479**
not recover anything if the contract is frustrated before the other's performance became due:
eg, under a contract by which a builder agreed to do work on a customer's house for payment
due on completion, the builder cannot recover anything in respect of part of the work done
before frustration.[1774]

Statute. Section 1(3) of the 1943 Act provides that if one party (A) has, before the time **1.480**
of discharge, obtained a 'valuable benefit' by reason of anything done by the other (B) in or
for the purpose of the performance of the contract, then the court can allow B to recover
such sum (not exceeding the value of the benefit) as it 'considers just'. In identifying the
'valuable benefit', the court has regard, not to the cost to B of his performance, but to the
'end product'[1775] received by A, at least where the nature of the contract is such that its full
performance would have left some such 'product' in A's hands.

In deciding how much to award, the court must (under section 1(3)(b)) take account of the **1.481**
effect of the frustrating event in relation to the benefit: thus in the building contract example
given in 1.478, the 'just sum' might vary according to whether frustration resulted from
supervening illegality or the destruction of the house. In the latter case, the court may not
be able to make any award under the Act, given that the value of the benefit acts as a ceiling
upon the 'just sum',[1776] although this conclusion has not been without its critics. Expenses
incurred by A can also be taken into account in assessing the 'just sum'.[1777]

(iii) Severability

Section 2(4) of the 1943 Act provides for severable parts of the contract to be treated, for **1.482**
the purposes of the Act, as separate contracts. If, eg, a contract for personal services provided
for quarterly payments,[1778] the provisions of the 1943 Act discussed above would apply in
respect of the quarter in which the contract was frustrated.

(iv) Contrary agreement

The provisions of section 1 of the 1943 Act can be excluded by agreement so that it is **1.483**
open to the parties to make their provision for the consequences of the frustration of their
contract: eg, to the effect that an advance payment should be retained by the payee in any
event.[1779]

(v) Excluded contracts

The 1943 Act does not apply to contracts for the carriage of goods by sea, to insurance **1.484**
contracts, or to contracts for the sale of specific goods where the cause of frustration is the
perishing of the goods.[1780] These exceptions are intended to preserve a number of previously
established rules, ie the rules that freight payable on delivery could not be claimed,[1781] and
that freight paid in advance could not be recovered back,[1782] if frustration prevented the
carrier from reaching the agreed destination; the rule that there could be no apportionment

---

[1774] *Appleby v Myers* (1867) LR 2 CP 651.
[1775] *BP (Exploration) Libya Ltd v Hunt* [1979] 1 WLR 783; aff'd [1981] 1 WLR 232, [1983] 2 AC 352.
[1776] *BP (Exploration) Libya Ltd v Hunt* [1979] 1 WLR 783, 801.
[1777] 1943 Act, s 1(3)(a).
[1778] As in *Stubbs v Holywell Rly* (1867) LR 2 Ex 311.
[1779] 1943 Act, s 2(3).
[1780] 1943 Act, s 2(5)(a), (b) and (c).
[1781] See 1.369.
[1782] *Byrne v Schiller* (1871) LR 6 Ex 319.

of insurance premiums once the risk had begun to run;[1783] and the rules laid down by the Sale of Goods Act 1979 with respect to discharge by the destruction of specific goods.[1784] The 1943 Act does, however, apply to contracts for the sale of goods which are *not* specific, and where contracts for the sale of specific goods are frustrated for some reason *other* than the destruction of the goods. It is hard to find any satisfactory reasons for these distinctions.

(c) Effects of frustration contrasted with those of mistake

1.485 Events of the kind that can frustrate a contract are sometimes compared with circumstances about the existence of which parties are mistaken at the time of contracting, so that their consent is nullified.[1785] Mistake and frustration are, however, 'different juristic concepts',[1786] the former requiring parties affirmatively to believe in the existence of circumstances which do not in fact exist while the latter requires no affirmative belief that the allegedly frustrating event will not occur. Since it is easier to discover existing facts than to foresee the future, the test of mistake is also stricter than that of frustration.[1787] Moreover, while mistake makes a contract void *ab initio*, frustration discharges it only with effect from the frustrating event;[1788] and the 1943 Act does not apply to cases of invalidity for mistake as to antecedent events.[1789]

[1783] *Tyrie v Fletcher* (1777) 2 Cowp 666, 668.

[1784] Sale of Goods Act 1979, s 7.

[1785] See, eg, the citation of frustration cases in the mistake case of *The Great Peace* [2002] EWCA Civ 1407, [2003] QB 679, at [61]–[76] (1.133, n 563); and see nn 1786 and 1789.

[1786] *Joseph Constantine* case [1942] AC 154, 186; cf *Fibrosa* case [1943] AC 32, 77; cf *The Great Peace*, n 1785, at [83] (tests of frustration 'may not be adequate in the context of mistake').

[1787] See examples given in *The Epaphus* [1987] 2 Lloyd's Rep 215, 218, 220.

[1788] See 1.136 and 1.475.

[1789] *The Great Peace*, n 1785, at [161].

2

TORTS AND EQUITABLE WRONGS

A. Introduction

The French word 'torts' is used by English law to denote many of its civil wrongs. Scots law **2.01** uses 'delict'.[1] However, for historical reasons, the law of torts is only a subset of the law of civil wrongs. A tort is defined in formal terms as a civil wrong which gives rise to an action for damages, other than one which is exclusively a breach of contract or breach of trust or other equitable obligation. In the words of Sir Percy Winfield:

> Tortious liability arises from the breach of a duty primarily fixed by the law: such duty is towards persons generally and its breach is redressible by an action for unliquidated damages.[2]

---

[1] Many of the leading cases in tort happen to be Scottish: *Donoghue v Stevenson* [1932] AC 562, HL; *Bourhill v Young* [1943] AC 92, HL; *Hughes v Lord Advocate* [1963] AC 837, HL; *Junior Books Ltd v Veitchi Co Ltd* [1983] 1 AC 520, HL.

[2] PH Winfield, *The Province of the Law of Tort* (1931) 32.

2.02   This definition is not adequate.[3] The requirement that the primary duty be fixed by law and good against persons generally excludes tortious liability based upon a responsibility which is genuinely and voluntarily assumed.[4] Even less defensible to modern eyes is the specific exclusion which Winfield made of those breaches of duties which were originally recognized by the courts of Chancery rather than the courts of common law.[5] Historically, the consequence has been the exclusion of equitable wrongs from consideration alongside torts even when the equitable wrongs are materially identical to torts, such as deceit and negligence. Other casualties are breach of trust and fiduciary duty, dishonest assistance in a breach of trust or fiduciary duty, and breach of confidence. The last mentioned of these has been heavily influential in pushing open the door.[6] Especially with the multiplication of litigation based on breach of fiduciary duties, the traditional definition creates an evident danger of needlessly developing two parallel, and overlapping, laws of civil wrongs; a law of torts at common law and a law of meta-torts in equity. Some judges have resisted this tendency.[7] One of the leading texts, *Clerk and Lindsell on Torts*, now includes extended treatment of the equitable wrongs of breach of confidence and breach of fiduciary duty although it has not opened the door to other equitable wrongs.[8] A rational account of the law of civil wrongs cannot confine itself to torts.[9]

2.03   In order to present a more coherent picture here of the operation of civil wrongs we therefore consider, alongside torts, those equitable wrongs that are motivated by identical concerns (such as deceit and negligence) as well as other breaches of duty in equity, namely breach of trust and fiduciary duty, dishonest assistance in a breach of trust or fiduciary duty, and breach of confidence. In order to appreciate the operation of these civil wrongs, it is necessary to look to the structure and then to the scope of wrongdoing at both common law and equity together, although the emphasis will inevitably be on torts, which are the main corpus of English civil wrongs.

2.04   There is no simple answer to the question of whether the availability of damages under the Human Rights Act 1998 makes a public authority's violation of a person's rights under the European Convention on Human Rights a 'tort'.[10] The Law Commission took the view that the Act did create a new cause of action (in effect a form of action for breach of statutory duty)[11] but Lord Bingham denied that the 1998 Act was 'a tort statute',[12] and his view is

---

[3] WVH Rogers, *Winfield and Jolowicz on Tort* (18th edn, 2010) 1–4; M Jones and A Dugdale (eds), *Clerk and Lindsell on Torts* (21st edn. 2014) 1-03.

[4] See 2.168–2.174.

[5] Winfield, *Province*, n 2, at 113–115.

[6] P North, 'Breach of Confidence: Is There a New Tort?' (1972) 12 J Society of Public Teachers of Law 149. In *Campbell v Mirror Group Newspapers Ltd* [2004] UKHL 22, [2004] 2 AC 457, 465, at [14], Lord Nicholls described breach of confidence as a tort and said that 'the essence of the tort is better encapsulated now as misuse of private information'.

[7] For instance, Millett LJ in *Bristol and West Building Society v Mothew* [1998] Ch 1, CA and in *Paragon Finance plc v DB Thakerar & Co* [1999] 1 All ER 400, CA (approved by Lord Walker in *Hilton v Barker Booth & Eastwood* [2005] UKHL 8, [2005] 1 WLR 567). See also Lord Browne-Wilkinson in *Henderson v Merrett Syndicates Ltd* [1995] 2 AC 145, 205, HL; discussion in S Elliott, 'Fiduciary Liability for Client Mortgage Frauds' (1999) 13 Trust Law International 74, esp 81. Arguing for a single law of civil wrongs: P Birks, 'Civil Wrongs: A New World' *Butterworth Lectures 1990–91* (1992) 55; J Edelman, *Gain-based Damages* (2002) ch 2.

[8] M Jones and A Dugdale (eds), *Clerk and Lindsell on Torts* (21st edn. 2014) ch 27 (breach of confidence and privacy) 10-18ff (breach of fiduciary duty).

[9] A Burrows, 'We Do This At Common Law But That in Equity' (2002) 22 OJLS 1, 9.

[10] What is said in this paragraph is referring to what has been termed the 'vertical effect' of the 1998 Act: for its 'horizontal effect' see D Feldman (ed), *English Public Law* (2nd edn, 2009) 19.53–19.60.

[11] Law Commission, *Damages Under the Human Rights Act 1998* (Law Com No 266, 2000) para 4.20.

[12] *R (on the application of Greenfield) v Secretary of State for the Home Department* [2005] UKHL 14, [2005] 1 WLR 673, at [19].

supported by the fact that while in tort cases full compensatory damages are generally available as of right, the award of damages under the Act is discretionary, and must be shown to be necessary to achieve 'just satisfaction'.[13] In any case, since such claims lie only against public authorities, they are considered in the companion volume dealing with public law,[14] although mention is made of them in this chapter where they overlap with private law wrongs such as negligence and private nuisance.[15]

(1) Structure

(a) The legacy of history

At common law, the law of torts grew up without a unified structure.[16] The development of the law of torts from the writ of trespass and the originally supplementary actions on the case created a list of wrongs. The list, alphabetic since no other classification was available, survived into the nineteenth century and continues to have a ghost life long after the abolition of the forms of action.[17] The forms of action, essentially set forms of winning propositions, were replaced by causes of action, essentially configurations of facts disclosing a right realizable in court. However, the names of the old forms of action continued to be used to describe the causes of action.

2.05

The English law of torts still appears to consist of a list of over 70 wrongs, distinct though sometimes overlapping, each with its own name and conditions of liability.[18] The persistence of named torts is to some extent a matter of habit and convenience rather than substance. As Diplock LJ said in *Letang v Cooper*, 'when, since 1873, the name of a form of action is used to identify a cause of action, it is used as a convenient and succinct description of a particular category of factual situation which entitles one person to obtain from the court a remedy from another person'.[19]

2.06

Recent decisions of the House of Lords have discussed the limits of liability for torts in terms of the historical origins of particular torts and the appropriateness of using one tort rather than another.[20] In this sense, it is still true to say that at common law we have a law of torts rather than a law of tort.

2.07

In the years following the abolition of the forms of action, debate raged about the structure of the law of torts. Two prominent views emerged in the United States in the late nineteenth century. One view was that the law of torts should be structured around the invasion of particular rights such as rights to personal security (assault, battery, false imprisonment) or to real property (trespass to land and waste).[21] In contrast, a completely different approach was that the structure of the law of torts ought to be more general and focus upon the fault of the defendant. On this view, torts should be divided according to whether they are based on intentional

2.08

---

[13] Human Rights Act 1998, s 8(3).

[14] D Feldman (ed), *English Public Law* (2nd edn, 2009) 19.39–19.44.

[15] See 2.108 and 2.251.

[16] JH Baker, *An Introduction to English Legal History* (4th edn, 2002) 401–465; D Ibbetson, *A Historical Introduction to the Law of Obligations* (1999) 39–70, 97–125, 153–187.

[17] The abolition of the forms of action was a three-stage process, in which the second stage, the Common Law Procedure Act 1852, was decisive. Baker, n 16, at 53–70, esp 67–69.

[18] BA Rudden, 'Torticles' (1991–92) 6/7 Tulane Civil Law Forum 105.

[19] [1965] 1 QB 232, 243, CA.

[20] *Hunter v Canary Wharf Ltd* [1997] AC 655, HL; *Cambridge Water Co Ltd v Eastern Counties Leather plc* [1994] 2 AC 264, HL; *Spring v Guardian Assurance plc* [1995] 2 AC 296, HL; *Gregory v Portsmouth City Council* [2000] 1 AC 419, HL.

[21] T Cooley, *A Treatise on the Law of Torts or the Wrongs which Arise Independent of Contract* (1880) chs 6, 10.

acts, negligent acts or acts without any requirement of fault (strict liability).[22] The same debate occurred later in England with one group of leading torts scholars adopting the traditional, Blackstonian, view that the law of torts should be structured around the particular rights protected[23] and another arguing for a general principle of liability for fault.[24] Underlying these two theories were deep questions about the nature of liability for civil wrongs. As we will see, English common law did not exclusively adopt either position but adopted a bi-focal structure with one group in which the torts focused upon the particular right which is infringed and another group in which the torts focused generally upon the fault of the defendant.[25] As we will also see, concurrently with this common law development of the law of torts, the courts of Chancery independently developed the same structure for equitable wrongs.

(b) The place of negligence in the law of torts

2.09   The traditional Blackstonian structure of the law of torts was a common law picture of liability as based on a list of distinct nominate torts, reflecting infringements of particular rights. But that conceals the structure of modern tort law and especially the relationship between the tort of negligence and most of the other torts. Negligence, although correctly described as a tort, is 'innominate'. It does not, even obliquely, identify any particular right, or protected interest, because negligence describes a standard of liability. A secondary right to compensation arises where damage has been caused by the fault of the defendant. The same is true of deceit and other torts which focus on fraudulent intention of the defendant.[26] The focus of negligence and deceit is on the blameworthy conduct of the defendant in causing harm. In other torts, the focus is on the particular right protected. Indeed most nominate torts are identified precisely as protecting a particular right, and the degree of desired protection thus dictates the rules of liability within the particular tort.

2.10   Defamation protects reputation. Conversion protects property rights in goods. Trespass to land and private nuisance protect property rights in land. In effect, therefore, the list of torts is a mixed list, with some wrongs defined in terms of protected rights and torts such as negligence or deceit potentially cutting across all protected nominate rights and belonging in a series in which the liability focuses upon fault rather than particular rights.

2.11   All the nominate rights-based torts resist generalization. Negligence, by contrast, is capable of generalization and was the chief engine of the huge expansion of tort liability throughout most of the twentieth century. Negligence became the most wide-ranging of all forms of tort liability.[27] But the growth of negligence liability did more than expand the scope of

---

[22] Anon, 'The Theory of Torts' (1872) 7 Am L Rev 652. Although the article is not signed, as Vandevelde has observed much of the language in the article appears in OW Holmes, *The Common Law* (1889): K Vandevelde, 'A History of the Prima Facie Tort: The Origins of a General Theory of Intentional Tort, (1990) 19 Hoftstra L Rev 447.

[23] W Blackstone, *Commentaries on the Laws of England* (1765) Book III. See J Salmond, *Torts* (2nd edn, 1910) 8–9; A Goodhart, 'The Foundations of Tortious Liability' (1938) 2 MLR 1.

[24] F Pollock, *The Law of Torts* (1887); P Winfield, *The Province of the Law of Tort* (1931) 32–39. One initial review of Pollock complained that 'the full extent of the fundamental [scientific] principle that a man is liable for all the consequences of his acts which as a reasonable man he ought to have foreseen...has not yet been thoroughly worked out by the courts': Anon (1886–1887) 12 Law Mag & L Rev 5th Ser 270, 275, 277.

[25] Although one commentator has issued a cry for a return to a structure based solely on particular or nominate rights. See R Stevens, *Torts and Rights* (2007).

[26] See 2.354–2.355.

[27] T Weir, 'The Staggering March of Negligence' in P Cane and J Stapleton (eds), *The Law of Obligations: Essays in Celebration of John Fleming* (1998) 97. A claim in negligence has become an almost invariable long stop behind other claims: 'Since *Anns v Merton London Borough Council* [1978] AC 728 put the floodgates on the jar, a fashionable plaintiff alleges negligence': *CBS Songs Ltd v Amstrad Consumer Electronics plc* [1988] AC 1013, 1059, HL, *per* Lord Templeman.

that tort; it also had important effects on the rest of the law of torts, and indirectly on the law of contract. In some instances negligence has replaced older forms of liability: *Donoghue v Stevenson*[28] made the older category of chattels dangerous *per se* redundant.[29] More commonly, nominate torts were infiltrated by aspects of negligence. The *Wagon Mound*[30] test of remoteness of damage propounded as particularly appropriate for negligence is now also applied to nominate torts.[31] Nuisance, though not absorbed by negligence, overlaps with it, and is increasingly influenced by the idea of fault-based liability which underpins it.[32]

English law's tolerance of concurrent liability increases the difficulty of coherent classification.[33] A negligent defamatory statement in a reference causing economic loss may now be actionable as negligence or defamation;[34] a malicious defamatory statement may be actionable as defamation or malicious falsehood;[35] and an intentional deprivation of liberty may be actionable as false imprisonment or misfeasance in public office.[36] There may be very strong reasons why an action based on negligence might be preferred to one based upon a particular nominate right. In *Spring v Guardian Assurance plc*[37] an employer had written a reference which negligently proceeded on incorrect facts, thus prejudicing the employee's employment prospects. Within the tort of defamation this reference was clearly the subject of qualified privilege. Hence the employer could not be liable in the absence of proof of malice.[38] However, the House of Lords held that this was a case in which, in the tort of negligence, the employer could be liable for the claimant's pure economic loss. **2.12**

The overlap between liability for the infringement of particular protected rights and liability for negligence has been extremely controversial. For instance, there is a dictum of Lord Phillips in the Court of Appeal in *D v East Berkshire NHS Trust*[39] which is flatly against what was allowed in *Spring v Guardian Assurance*. He said that there is no question of sidestepping the defence of qualified privilege by advancing a claim for defamation in the guise of a claim in negligence.[40] Concurrent liability in tort and contract, accepted and largely unproblematic in cases of negligence causing physical injury, has provoked controversy about the proper function of the law of torts where the loss is economic.[41] In these cases the extension of negligence appears to achieve results which the law of contract could not reach. In some **2.13**

---

[28] [1932] AC 562, HL.

[29] *Griffiths v Arch Engineering Ltd* [1968] 3 All ER 217, Newport Assizes.

[30] *Overseas Tankship (UK) Ltd v Morts Dock and Engineering Co Ltd (The Wagon Mound)* [1961] AC 388, PC.

[31] *Overseas Tankship (UK) Ltd v Miller Steamship Co Pty Ltd (The Wagon Mound) (No 2)* [1967] 1 AC 617, PC; *Cambridge Water Co Ltd v Eastern Counties Leather plc* [1994] 2 AC 264, HL.

[32] *Leakey v National Trust* [1980] QB 485, CA; *Overseas Tankship (UK) Ltd v Miller Steamship Co Pty Ltd (The Wagon Mound) (No 2)* [1967] 1 AC 617, PC.

[33] *Henderson v Merrett Syndicates Ltd* [1985] 2 AC 145, HL, discussed in AS Burrows, *Understanding the Law of Obligations* (1998) 16–34.

[34] *Spring v Guardian Assurance* [1995] 2 AC 296, HL.

[35] *Joyce v Sengupta* [1993] 1 WLR 337, CA, but see also *Lonrho v Fayed (No 5)* [1993] 1 WLR 1489, CA.

[36] *Karagozlu v Commissioner of Police of the Metropolis* [2006] EWCA Civ 1691, [2007] 2 All ER 1055.

[37] [1995] 2 AC 296, HL.

[38] [1995] 2 AC 296, 346, HL.

[39] [2003] EWCA Civ 1151, [2004] QB 558, 594, at [102]. There was no comment on this point on appeal to the House of Lords: *JD v East Berkshire Community Health NHS Trust* [2005] UKHL 23, [2005] 2 AC 373.

[40] The claims in *D v East Berkshire NHS Trust* were for psychiatric harm resulting from false accusations of child abuse which, as Lord Phillips remarked, have the elements of defamation. Perhaps the extreme sensitivity of investigations into child abuse suffices to distinguish this case from the commercial world of the *Spring* case.

[41] *Henderson v Merrett Syndicates* [1995] 2 AC 145, HL; *Junior Books v Veitchi Co Ltd* [1983] 1 AC 520, HL; *White v Jones* [1995] 2 AC 207, HL.

views 'could not reach' means 'ought not to be reached', so that the new position in the law of tort directly negatives a considered position. There are, all in all, very few aspects of the law of obligations which have remained wholly unaffected by the principles of negligence, and not infrequently the cross-cutting intrusion of the tort of negligence has proved disruptive.

(2) Scope

(a) The scope of each group of civil wrongs

2.14 As Professor Lawson explained in 1951, and as we have seen, civil wrongs in England historically divide into two groups. One group of civil wrongs consists of liability for harm caused by fault and another focuses upon infringements of particular rights.[42] In this respect English law is bifocal, like German law.[43] The largest, and most dominant, member of the first group of civil wrongs is the tort of negligence, although we have already seen that other prominent members are torts involving fraudulent intention, like deceit. The potentially broad scope of the tort of negligence is constrained by a concept described as 'duty of care'.[44] Although negligence was also historically actionable in courts of Chancery, these duty of care rules were developed in more detail at common law.

2.15 The second group of wrongs, namely those concerned with particular rights, are a collection of causes of action, each made up of three main components: a particular right protected by the law, conduct affecting that right which the law sanctions, and a remedy by which the right is protected and the conduct sanctioned.[45] It is necessary to ask both whether a particular recognized right has been infringed, and also against what forms of infringing conduct protection is given. This second group of civil wrongs is therefore constrained by the need for a protected right and the required conduct which will suffice to amount to an infringement of the particular recognized right.

(b) Acts and omissions

2.16 In either group of cases, whether liability is based upon fault causing harm or upon the infringement of a particular right, the wrongful conduct may be either an act, a statement, or a failure to act. Liability for acts which cause damage to others is more general than liability for failure to take steps to prevent harm to others. Liability for failure to act is imposed only in particular circumstances or where there is a special relationship between the parties: 'There must be some special justification for imposing an obligation of this character. Compulsory altruism needs more justification than an obligation not to create dangers to others when acting for one's own purposes.'[46] Special considerations also limit liability for words, both in the general tort of negligence and in the torts of defamation, deceit, and malicious falsehood.

(c) Nominate rights

2.17 The list of nominate rights is not closed, but some interests are only given partial protection and others are not protected at all. English law has been criticized, eg, for its reluctance to recognize the invasion of privacy as an independent tort.[47] At the centre of the law of torts is the

---

[42] FH Lawson, *The Rational Strength of English Law* (1951) 122–123.

[43] §823 of the *Bürgerliches Gesetzbuch* provides for delictual liability consequent upon infringement of protected interests whereas §826 focuses upon acts *contra bonos mores*.

[44] *Dorset Yacht Co Ltd v Home Office* [1969] 2 QB 412, 426, CA, *per* Lord Denning MR.

[45] P Cane, *The Anatomy of Tort Law* (1998) 1. The author examines each of the three components in chs 2, 3, and 4, although he speaks of 'interests' rather than rights.

[46] *Stovin v Wise* [1996] AC 923, 930, HL, *per* Lord Nicholls.

[47] BS Markesinis, 'Subtle Ways of Legal Borrowing: Some Reflections on the Report of the Calcutt Committee "On Privacy and Related Matters"' in B Pfister and MR Will (eds), *Festschrift für Werner Lorenz*

protection of persons from physical injury and, to a limited extent, from psychological harm, but other interests, such as freedom of movement and reputation, are also protected. Torts are also the main source of civil remedies for physical damage to property and infringements of rights to possess or enjoy land or goods. Other rights, such as the right to confidential information, are protected by equity.

Both torts and equitable wrongs have a part in the protection of intellectual property and other commercial rights. Thus, a party to a contract has rights which are protected, not only in the law of contract, but also by the tort of inducing breach of contract.[48]   **2.18**

(d) Conduct amounting to infringement of nominate rights

Liability in modern English law for infringement of particular nominate rights can be based on fault but in some cases the liability for the infringement of a particular right is strict. Although there is usually reference to a requirement of 'intention', if the tort is protecting rights to the person, to property, liberty or reputation, 'intention' usually means no more than that the act is willed; trespass to goods, to land and to the person, defamation, conversion and detinue are all examples of strict liability torts where fault is irrelevant.[49] In equity, liability for breach of fiduciary duty is also strict. Vicarious liability, the liability of an employer for torts committed by his employees in the course of their employment, is a form of strict liability but the dominant view is that it is not a type of wrongdoing, for the employer is not conceived to have been in any breach of duty.   **2.19**

On the other hand, other particular rights such as the right to confidential information in equity are only infringed when the defendant is at fault. Fault may be negligence or unreasonableness, which nowadays are both essentially the failure to observe community standards of behaviour, or it may arise from a culpable state of mind. Negligence is the general standard of fault liability in tort, corresponding to the French *faute* or Roman *culpa*.   **2.20**

(e) Remedies[50]

The routine consequence of a tort is that the victim acquires a right to a money award, which is in general called damages and is usually a right to compensation.[51] However, a further aim of torts is to prevent, or to prevent repetition of, a wrong. In some torts therefore, damages take second place to the remedy of an injunction, if damages are sought at all. Torts can also be used to determine title to, or to obtain restitution of, chattels or land.[52] Other remedies of a self-help kind are available in some torts but not encouraged.   **2.21**

---

zum Siebzigsten Geburtstag (1991) 717–737, and 'Our Patchy Law of Privacy: Time To Do Something About It' (1990) 53 MLR 802. See further at 2.344–2.348.

[48] Running back to *Lumley v Gye* (1853) 2 El & Bl 216, 118 ER 749.

[49] See 2.337 for discussion of 'intention'. Civilians on the whole prefer to avoid the term 'wrong' or any equivalent in order to admit the possibility of strict liability: C von Bar, *The Common European Law of Torts* (1998) 3. English law has had no difficulty in treating as a wrong any conduct which takes its consequences by virtue of its characterization as a breach of duty, even when that duty is so designed as to be broken even without fault: P Birks, 'The Concept of a Civil Wrong' in D Owen (ed), *Philosophical Foundations of Tort Law* (1997) 31; T Honoré, 'The Morality of Tort Law' in D Owen (ed), *Philosophical Foundations of Tort Law* (1997) 73, 88–94.

[50] For a full account of remedies see ch 4.

[51] It is not usual to refer to gain-based awards in equity as 'damages' (*Watson v Holliday* (1882) 20 Ch D 780, aff'd (1883) 52 LJ Ch 543, CA), although the phrase 'gain-based damages' is sometimes used to describe these awards, particularly when they are made at common law: see J Edelman, *Gain-based Damages* (2002).

[52] See 2.303–2.305.

2.22 The principal remedy for torts is an award of damages. Some torts are actionable only if harm is caused, others are actionable without proof of damage (*per se*).[53] The distinction is an accident of history but can be rationalized. Torts actionable without proof of damage are either torts where damage can be presumed, or they are torts whose function is to protect particular rights from any invasion, whether or not damage has resulted. Nominal damages may be given to signify that a right has been invaded although no harm has been done.

2.23 The main measure and purpose of damages is to compensate for harm. However, the American, and indeed the Roman, experience shows that a purely compensatory law of civil wrongs is not a jurisprudential necessity but simply a choice made by particular systems at particular times. For its part, English law has never unequivocally embraced the dogma that the law of civil wrongs must concern itself solely with compensation for losses.[54] And while common law damages to punish and deter wrongdoing are currently exceptional, the right to compensation for equitable wrongdoing—which is rarely called damages although it amounts to the same thing[55]—has historically been regarded as more exceptional than gain-based awards such as an account of profits.

B. Negligence: Basic Concepts

2.24 In an analysis of states of mind, negligence contrasts with intention. Negligence means blameworthy inadvertence. At common law and in equity, however, negligence is usually a description of conduct rather than of a mental state. It is conduct which fails to conform to a required standard of care. However, not all negligent conduct gives rise to liability, nor is liability for negligence, where it exists, unlimited. The common law tort of negligence has been subject to considerably more development and scrutiny than its equitable counterpart. For this reason, the focus on negligence in this chapter is upon the tort of negligence, although we will see that negligence can also be actionable in equity.[56]

2.25 The boundaries of liability for the tort of negligence are drawn by the three principal elements of the tort, a duty of care, breach of that duty, and damage caused by that breach. The defences to actions for negligence then impose further limits. Negligence is tortious, and liability will follow, if it is a breach of a duty of care owed to the claimant which has caused damage of an actionable kind, subject to defences. This reasonably straightforward sentence provides the programme for the exposition which follows.

---

[53] The interplay between 'damage', which is harm done, and 'damages', which is the award made, is inescapable.

[54] It is undeniable that gain-based awards are regularly made for wrongs: see J Edelman, *Gain-based Damages* (2002), and 4.145–4.162. However, the House of Lords has twice endeavoured to commit the law to the proposition that all measures of recovery other than compensation for loss are anomalous: *Rookes v Barnard* [1964] AC 1129, HL; *Cassell & Co v Broome* [1972] AC 1027, HL. But the speech of Lord Wilberforce in the latter case rightly shows that English law has been more pragmatic. See also Law Commission, *Aggravated, Exemplary and Restitutionary Damages* (Law Com No 247, 1997).

[55] *Bartlett v Barclays Bank Trust Co Ltd (No 2)* [1980] Ch 515, 545, *per* Brightman LJ ('not readily distinguishable from damages except with the aid of a powerful legal microscope'). See also P Birks, 'Civil Wrongs: A New World' *Butterworth Lectures 1990–91* (1992); J Edelman, 'Gain-Based Damages and Compensation' in A Burrows and A Rodger (eds), *Mapping the Law: Essays in Honour of Peter Birks* (2006).

[56] *Henderson v Merrett Syndicates Ltd* [1995] 2 AC 145, 205, HL, *per* Lord Browne-Wilkinson; *Bristol and West Building Society v Mothew* [1998] Ch 1, 16–18, CA, *per* Millett LJ; *Hilton v Barker Booth Eastwood* [2005] UKHL 8, at [29], *per* Lord Walker.

(1) Duty of Care

The duty of care is the main conceptual device for expressing the limits on liability for neg-   **2.26**
ligence. The inquiry into the duty of care operates at two levels. First, it answers the general
question whether there can in principle be a right not to be subjected to damage by carelessness in the kind of situation to which the particular facts belong. Secondly, it addresses the
question whether on the particular facts the defendant did indeed owe a duty to the claimant.
If he did, the first element of liability slots immediately into place. The existence of a duty
of care is a question of law. Much of the historical importance of the duty concept lies in its
use to control the growth of the tort and determine its frontiers at a time when issues of fact
were tried by juries.[57]

By way of example, a question can be formulated whether there is any duty of care in respect   **2.27**
of words spoken or written (a) if the words cause physical damage (as by causing the person
addressed to fall over a cliff) and (b) if they cause the person addressed to lose some money
(as by investing badly). That question is probing the frontiers of the tort of negligence. We
might instead ask, very bluntly, 'Can a person be liable for negligent statements?' The way in
which an inquiry of that kind is put in the law of negligence is always to ask whether there is,
in the given circumstances, a duty of care.

(a) The neighbour principle

The modern approach to the duty of care has roots running back to the seventeenth cen-   **2.28**
tury,[58] but nowadays it may for all practical purposes be regarded as founded on Lord
Atkin's formulation of the neighbour principle in *Donoghue v Stevenson*.[59] The question
in that case was whether, if a person became ill through consuming contaminated food
(here ginger beer contaminated by the remains of a snail), an action in negligence could lie
against the manufacturer. By a majority the House of Lords held that it could. Lord Atkin's
approach was to assemble the fragments of the nineteenth century law of negligence under
one principle:

> [I]n English law there must be, and is, some general conception of relations giving rise to a
> duty of care, of which the particular cases found in the books are but instances. The liability
> for negligence, whether you style it such or treat it as in other systems as a species of 'culpa',
> is no doubt based upon a general public sentiment of moral wrongdoing for which the
> offender must pay. But acts or omissions which any moral code would censure cannot in a
> practical world be treated so as to give a right to every person injured by them to demand
> relief. In this way rules of law arise which limit the range of complainants and the extent of
> their remedy. The rule that you are to love your neighbour becomes in law, you must not
> injure your neighbour; and the lawyer's question, Who is my neighbour? receives a restricted
> reply. You must take reasonable care to avoid acts or omissions which you can reasonably
> foresee would be likely to injure your neighbour. Who, then, in law is my neighbour? The
> answer seems to be—persons who are so closely and directly affected by my act that I ought

---

[57] D Ibbetson, *A Historical Introduction to the Law of Obligations* (1999) 170–174.

[58] JH Baker, *Introduction to English Legal History* (4th edn, 2002) 410–411; D Ibbetson, *A Historical
Introduction to the Law of Obligations* (1999) 164–174, 178–181, 188–193. Of particular interest and importance: (1) Buller's *Nisi Prius* (1767/1772) 36; (2) Sir William Jones, *Essay on the Law of Bailments* (1781) esp
6–8, 42–44, 66–68; (3) Chancery formulations of the duty of trustees from *Charitable Corporation v Sutton*
(1742) 2 Atk 400, 406; 26 ER 642, 645, *per* Lord Hardwicke LC, to *Clough v Bond* (1838) 3 M & C 490,
496; 40 ER 1016, 1018, *per* Lord Cottenham LC; (4) Brett MR in *Heaven v Pender* (1883) 11 QBD 503,
509, CA.

[59] [1932] AC 562, HL. For the background, see A Rodger, 'Mrs Donoghue and Alfenus Varus' (1988) 41
CLP 1, and 'Lord Macmillan's Speech in *Donoghue v Stevenson*' (1992) 108 LQR 236.

reasonably to have them in contemplation as being so affected when I am directing my mind to the acts or omissions which are called in question.[60]

2.29 It is as well to say at once, though we shall have to return to the matter in greater detail below, that Lord Atkin knew very well that foreseeability could not itself be the single key to finding a duty of care. The whole structure of his speech shows that he regarded the passage quoted above as an open-textured principle formulated to hold together all the known islands of liability, and, further, that he never intended the general principle to be more than a guide to the interpretation and development of the specific rules of liability instantiated in the decided cases.[61] Lord Atkin would certainly have agreed with Professor Baker when he says:

> The definition in advance of all the situations in which a duty of care is owed to one's neigh-bour is impossible; and despite attempts to formulate a general rule, a policy decision has to be made whenever new cases arise. Indeed, over the course of time very different outer limits have been set to the notion of actionable wrong in the context of negligence. Although the 'neighbour' principle was voiced three centuries ago in words which might still be accepted today, in practice far fewer kinds of injury were then under its ambit.[62]

2.30 In this passage Baker encapsulates the notion, still essential to the understanding of the law of negligence, that a general principle can have a constant validity and utility even though, under varying social circumstances, it is likely to be realized in different ranges of liability. It is easy to suppose that, under the open-textured principle, the frontiers of liability constantly expand, but they can also contract.

(b) The onset of caution

2.31 Expansionist resort to the neighbour principle reached its apogee in the 1970s, at which time a lay observer might have been forgiven for thinking that the general principle had become an immediate rule of liability. In *Anns v Merton London BC*[63] Lord Wilberforce allowed himself to say:

> The position has now been reached that in order to establish that a duty of care arises in a particular situation, it is not necessary to bring the facts of that situation within those of previous situations in which a duty of care has been held to exist. Rather the question has to be approached in two stages. First one has to ask whether, as between the alleged wrongdoer and the person who has suffered damage there is a sufficient relationship of proximity or neighbourhood such that, in the reasonable contemplation of the former, carelessness on his part may be likely to cause damage to the latter—in which case a prima facie duty of care arises. Secondly, if the first question is answered affirmatively, it is necessary to consider whether there are any considerations which ought to negative, or to reduce or limit the scope of the duty or the class of person to whom it is owed or the damages to which a breach of it may give rise.[64]

---

[60] [1932] AC 562, 580, HL. The Biblical background will be apparent. In the Book of Leviticus it is laid down that we should love our neighbour as ourselves, and 'neighbour' is explicitly extended to 'alien': Lev 19.18, 33. Compare in the New Testament: Mt 22.38, 39; Mt 19.19; Rom 13.9; Gal 5.14; Jas 2.8. Lord Atkin's immediate reference is to the lawyer's question at Lk 10.29 and the answering parable of the Good Samaritan, Lk 10.30–10.37.

[61] Lord Atkin's understanding of the interpretative relationship between the general and the particular, essential to common law method, is brilliantly explained by Lord Devlin in *Hedley Byrne & Co Ltd v Heller & Partners Ltd* [1964] AC 465, 524, HL.

[62] JH Baker, *Introduction to English Legal History* (4th edn, 2002) 415.

[63] [1978] AC 728, HL.

[64] [1978] AC 728, 751–752, HL.

That was the position to which earlier cases seemed to have arrived.[65] Nor could Lord **2.32** Wilberforce's statement be faulted, since the second stage of his inquiry made evident room for eliminating any overkill implicit in the first. However, the prima facie liability established by the first inquiry seemed to give the law a dynamic in favour of constantly expanding the frontiers of liability. In consequence, a reaction set in, which favours something approaching a return to the traditional approach in which the one tort of negligence is seen, less as a federation united by the neighbour principle, and more as a confederation of islands of liability, each with its own semi-independent regime.[66] This shift of emphasis was achieved in *Caparo Industries plc v Dickman*[67] and by a seven-judge decision of the House of Lords in *Murphy v Brentwood District Council*.[68] In the latter the *Anns* case was formally overruled, and the approach which it had adopted was repudiated.

Experience shows that the effect of this change of emphasis should not be exaggerated. It **2.33** bears chiefly on the special areas which are discussed below,[69] and it chiefly means that the court is supposed to start on the other foot, assuming that there is no duty of care until a careful three-pronged inquiry has been made. The second and third of these inquiries are linguistically less than satisfactory since they do little more than encode, and obscure, the policy decision referred to by Professor Baker in the passage quoted above.[70]

(c) The three-pronged inquiry

The questions which the cases now ask are, first, whether the defendant should have foreseen **2.34** harm to the claimant; secondly, whether there was a relationship of proximity between the claimant and the defendant; and, thirdly, whether it is fair, just, and reasonable that the defendant should owe a duty of care to the claimant.[71]

(i) Foreseeability

The first condition for the existence of a duty of care remains that the defendant should be **2.35** able to foresee that his conduct may cause injury, in the widest sense of that word, to the claimant. If no injury of any kind should be anticipated to the claimant, then no duty is owed to him. It is irrelevant that the defendant should have foreseen injury to a person other than the claimant. No one can found a claim on a duty of care owed to another person.[72]

Although a duty of care can arise towards a particular person by virtue of an assumption **2.36** of responsibility for the interests of that person, in general there is no requirement that the defendant must have foreseen injury to the claimant as an individual person. Many duties of care arise in standard relationships, in which the beneficiaries of the duty form a class and the class happens to include the claimant. So, all users of the highway owe a duty of care to all other users, and all employers owe a duty of care to their employees. Where duties are owed

---

[65] Especially *Dorset Yacht Co v Home Office* [1970] AC 1004, 1027, HL, *per* Lord Reid.

[66] For the position in other Commonwealth countries, see WVH Rogers (ed), *Winfield and Jolowicz on Tort* (18th edn, 2010) 5–24.

[67] [1990] 2 AC 605, HL.

[68] [1991] 1 AC 398, HL; *Junior Books Co Ltd v Veitchi Co Ltd* [1983] 1 AC 520, HL, decided almost exactly fifty years after *Donoghue v Stevenson* [1932] AC 562, HL is widely thought to mark the limit of expansionism and to have been the trigger for the new caution.

[69] 2.86–2.187.

[70] 2.29.

[71] *Caparo Industries plc v Dickman* [1990] 2 AC 605, 617–618, HL, *per* Lord Bridge.

[72] *Palsgraf v Long Island Railroad Co* 162 NE 99 (NY, 1928): a passenger tried to board a train as it was leaving the station, railwaymen assisting him caused him to drop a packet, which happened to contain fireworks. The fireworks exploded and caused a weighing machine to fall on P, who had innocently been waiting for her train to pull in on the next platform. It was not foreseeable to the railwaymen that what they were doing could injure P and they owed no duty to her. See also *Bourhill v Young* [1943] AC 92, HL.

to a certain class, there is no assumption that every member is a stereotypical representative of the community. So eg duties are owed to disabled people in situations in which it is likely that disabled people may be present.[73]

2.37   In situations in which negligent conduct is likely to cause physical injury or damage to persons or property, foreseeability is almost invariably conclusive as to the existence of a duty of care. It should not be overlooked that in practice that one sentence covers the majority of cases that arise. The complexities which so trouble the courts arise on the periphery of that large area in which there is no doubt as to the existence of the duty of care.

2.38   This is why Roman law never needed the concept of a duty of care: its delict of wrongful loss (*damnum iniuria datum*) contemplated liability only for loss arising from physical damage. It is also, in part, the reason why, writing shortly after *Donoghue v Stevenson*, the great Romanist, WW Buckland, could describe the English requirement of a duty of care as 'the fifth wheel on the coach'.[74] In fact, however, it turns out that, even in the case of physical injuries, there are some cases in which foreseeability is not conclusive of duty.[75] The most obvious case is that in general there is, as it is always said, no duty to intervene to rescue a child drowning in one foot of water.[76]

(ii) Proximity

2.39   Lord Atkin himself said, in *Donoghue v Stevenson*, that liability for foreseeable injury was limited by the requirement of proximity.[77] Proximity was a requirement superadded to neighbourhood and, like neighbourhood, it was to be understood abstractly or metaphysically, not simply in terms of geographical propinquity. There must be some close connection between the parties. However, the impalpable nature of closeness when it is not confined to physical facts means that this requirement has become a perfect tool for hiding policy decisions in situations in which there is reason to be apprehensive about escalating and perhaps uninsurable liabilities. Physical damage, physically caused, sets its own limits. Once the law contemplates allowing liability to extend to loss which does not arise from physical injury or damage, these fears become real, and artificial restrictions are then understandably invoked.

2.40   It is not surprising, therefore, to find that judges can themselves be puzzled by the requirement of proximity and are occasionally willing to admit that it is indeed code for the pragmatic restriction of a worrying liability. In *Caparo Industries plc v Dickman*, Lord Bridge said that 'proximity' was one of those terms which:

> are not susceptible of any such precise definition as would be necessary to give them utility as practical tests, but amount in effect to little more than convenient labels to attach to the features of different specific situations which, on a detailed examination of all the circumstances, the law recognizes pragmatically as giving rise to a duty of care of a given scope.[78]

2.41   Psychiatric injury lies on the boundary of the physical. If we count it as falling just inside that boundary, it is a species of physical injury which already awakens the kinds of anxiety associated with liability for non-physical losses. It is all too foreseeable that every crash will bring with it a wave of psychiatric harm. However, the policy of the common law is generally

---

[73] *Haley v London Electricity Board* [1965] AC 778, HL.

[74] WW Buckland, 'The Duty to Take Care' (1935) 51 LQR 637, 639.

[75] 2.109 (psychiatric injury) and 2.44 (wrongful life).

[76] *Stovin v Wise* [1996] AC 923, 930–931, HL, *per* Lord Nicholls.

[77] [1932] AC 562, 580–582, HL.

[78] [1990] 2 AC 605, 618, HL. For defences of proximity see A Kramer, 'Proximity as Principles: Directness, Community Norms and the Tort of Negligence' (2003) 11 Tort L Rev 70; C Witting, 'Duty of Care: An Analytical Approach' (2005) 25 OJLS 33.

opposed to granting remedies to third parties for the effects of injuries to other people.[79] Television illustrates the possibility of the breadth of liability that would otherwise result. Millions may be traumatized by witnessing disaster. Hence, in such 'secondary victim' cases reliance is placed on the restrictive potential of the requirement of proximity, and only those present at the scene of the accident or its immediate aftermath and bound by ties of love and affection to the primary victim can recover for psychiatric injury.[80]

Again, where loss is suffered through reliance on statements which turn out to be untrue, there **2.42** is the same danger of an escalating and disproportionate liability. Here the requirement of proximity is again invoked. Usually this is only satisfied where there is a voluntary assumption of responsibility to the party relying upon the statement.[81] There will be no proximity when the defendant has no direct control over a situation.[82] Nor is the relationship between the police and the class of all potential victims of a murderer or rapist proximate, with the effect that those who suffer at his hands cannot complain of his not having been caught earlier.[83]

(iii) Fair, just and reasonable

Given the all-embracing and manipulable nature of 'proximity', there seems little room for **2.43** any further requirement, and some judges have clearly regarded the third inquiry as superfluous.[84] There are, however, cases in which even foreseeability and proximity would not suffice to impose a duty of care. Such cases have usually concerned arguments for limiting the duties of public authorities,[85] but they can turn on commercial considerations[86] or, again, on considerations of distributive justice.[87]

The law relating to wrongful life is also probably best explained under this sub-head. At **2.44** common law, there is a recognized duty to the child *in utero* to take care not to harm it.[88] However, the child can bring no action for failure to terminate the pregnancy—ie, no action

---

[79] *JD v East Berkshire Community Health NHS Trust* [2005] UKHL 23, [2005] 2 AC 373, at [100]–[105], *per* Lord Rodger.

[80] See 2.109ff.

[81] A requirement first recognized in *Hedley Byrne & Co Ltd v Heller & Partners Ltd* [1964] AC 465, HL. See further 2.164–2.174.

[82] *Sutradhar v Natural Environment Research Council* [2006] UKHL 33, [2006] 4 All ER 490, at [38]. See also 2.149.

[83] *Hill v Chief Constable of West Yorkshire* [1989] AC 53, HL; *Brooks v Commissioner of Police for the Metropolis* [2005] UKHL 24, [2005] 1 WLR 1495.

[84] *Caparo Industries plc v Dickman* [1990] 2 AC 605, 633, HL, *per* Lord Oliver; *Stovin v Wise* [1996] AC 923, 931–933, HL, *per* Lord Nicholls.

[85] *X (Minors) v Bedfordshire CC* [1995] 2 AC 633, HL. Loose use of 'fair, just and reasonable' to deny any duty of care towards parents and children on the part of child protection authorities has had to be revised in the aftermath of *Osman v UK* (1998) 5 BHRC 293, ECHR and in the light of the incorporation of the European Convention by the Human Rights Act 1998, so that it is now accepted that a common law duty of care is owed to the children. However, one reason why it is not owed to the parents, whose lives stand in equal danger of being ruined when such interventions go wrong, is that it would create a conflict of interest incompatible with the paramountcy of the interests of the children: *JD v East Berkshire Community Health NHS Trust* [2005] UKHL 23, [2005] 2 AC 373. See 2.107. See also *B v Attorney General of New Zealand* [2003] UKPC 61, [2003] 4 All ER 833.

[86] *Marc Rich & Co AG v Bishop Rock Marine Co Ltd (The Nicholas H)* [1996] 1 AC 211, HL.

[87] *Frost v Chief Constable of South Yorkshire* [1999] 2 AC 455, HL. The immunity of advocates from suits in professional negligence provided another example of the exclusion of a duty of care on the grounds of public policy. A duty of care was thought to be inimical to the public interest in eliminating impediments to the smooth and reliable running of the process of litigation and adjudication. However, the House of Lords held that in modern conditions the exclusion of a duty of care can no longer be justified: *Arthur JS Hall & Co v Simons* [2002] 1 AC 615, HL.

[88] *Burton v Islington Health Authority* [1993] QB 204, CA.

for wrongful life.[89] The duty is not negatived for want of foreseeability or proximity but first, difficult quantification problems aside, because to allow the action would be inconsistent with the sanctity of life and, secondly, because it was beyond the power of reason to conceive of a duty owed to a person to terminate that person's existence, so that the duty of care could not include a duty to terminate. To these reasons must be added the intolerable burden upon doctors and others in giving abortion advice under the threat of civil liability.[90] These reasons operated at common law, but the Congenital Disabilities (Civil Liability) Act 1976 comes to the same conclusion:[91] the Act requires the court to assume that the child would have been born healthy, not that it would not have been born at all.[92] Similar considerations of fairness, justice and reasonableness also explain why, although a duty to terminate can be owed to a parent,[93] no such duty is imposed on doctors, who undertake the sterilization of adults, in respect of the expenses involved in the subsequent arrival of a healthy child.[94] A doctor's liability for a failed sterilization is limited to an award for the pain and suffering of the birth as well as a fixed conventional award of £15,000 to reflect the injury to the autonomy of the parents.[95]

(iv) Summary

2.45 Most cases involve straightforward physical injury to persons or damage to property caused by the defendant's activity. In such cases the neighbour principle applies and a duty of care results. On the periphery of that core, where there is physical harm but not of a straightforward kind or where the harm consists in pure economic loss without physical injury or damage, the second and third phases of the inquiry become prominent. And, in addition, some weight is given to the desire not to extend the law beyond the liabilities recognized in the past. There is not and there cannot be a single test for the existence of a duty of care. Professor Stapleton has identified a menu of duty factors.[96] In broad terms it can be said that, in the awkward periphery, the existence and the scope of a duty require consideration of the parties by whom and to whom the duty may be owed, the conduct in respect of which the duty is to be owed, and the kind of harm in respect of which it is to be owed. But this is hardly more helpful than saying that all relevant matters and arguments must be considered. The function of the three-pronged test is to provide a framework for the discussion and thus to group the arguments which may be deployed.

---

[89] *McKay v Essex Area Health Authority* [1982] QB 1166, CA: the court held that a duty to terminate could not be owed to a child deformed because its mother had rubella. See also *Harriton v Stephens* [2006] HCA 15, (2006) 226 CLR 52.

[90] Law Commission, *Injuries to Unborn Children* (Law Com No 60, 1974) para 89.

[91] A disabled child may rely on this Act to sue the person responsible, though not the mother unless the cause arose from her driving a motor vehicle—an exception created to give the child the benefit of the compulsory motor insurance regime. It has been recommended that a general rule be applied to both parents restricting claims against them to those in respect of which there is compulsory insurance: *Royal Commission on Civil Liability and Compensation for Personal Injury* (1978) Cmnd 7054–1 vol 1, paras 1471, 1472.

[92] Congenital Disabilities (Civil Liability) Act 1976, s 1(1), (2).

[93] *Rance v Mid-Downs Health Authority* [1991] QB 587.

[94] *McFarlane v Tayside Health Board* [2000] 2 AC 59, HL. This exclusion of a duty of care extends to lost earnings on the part of the mother (*Greenfield v Irwin* [2001] EWCA Civ 113, [2001] 1 WLR 1279). The exclusion does not extend to the expense of caring for a disabled child attributable to the disability (*Parkinson v St James and Seacroft University Darlington Memorial Hospital NHS Trust* [2001] EWCA Civ 530, [2002] QB 266, the correctness of which was doubted by Lords Bingham and Scott but affirmed by Lords Nicholls, Hope and Hutton in *Rees v Darlington Memorial Hospital NHS Trust* [2003] UKHL 52, [2004] 1 AC 309, at [9], [147], [35], [57], [91]).

[95] *Rees v Darlington Memorial Hospital NHS Trust* [2003] UKHL 52, [2004] 1 AC 309. The High Court of Australia, by a majority of 4:3 took the opposite view that the parents could recover the whole cost of the upbringing of the unwanted child (*Cattanach v Melchior* (2003) 215 CLR 1), although most Australian states passed legislation shortly thereafter to reverse this decision.

[96] J Stapleton, 'Duty of Care Factors: A Selection from the Judicial Menus' in P Cane and J Stapleton (eds), *The Law of Obligations: Essays in Celebration of John Fleming* (1999) 59.

(2) Breach

(a) The traditional standard at common law

The standard by which negligence is judged at common law has traditionally been regarded as **2.46** an objective one. It was negligent to fail to take the care expected by the community for the activity in question. The personification of community standards was simply the reasonable man, the man on the Clapham omnibus, more recently the commuter in the underground.[97]

What a reasonable person would do in the circumstances was, to some extent, a question of **2.47** fact on which evidence could be given. Expert evidence, evidence of trade or professional practice, and regulations such as the highway code, could all give factual content to the standard of care, but in the last resort it was the court that decided what was reasonable in the circumstances.

Nettleship v Weston demonstrates the traditional approach.[98] The court there held that a **2.48** learner driver on her third lesson was negligent if she failed to display the competence of an experienced driver. The whole court agreed that this was the standard required with regard to other highway users. Lord Denning's view was that the application of the objective standard to learners was simply an allocation of risk in an activity covered by compulsory insurance. Megaw LJ preferred to say that varying standards would make the law too complicated.

The reasonable person was intended to represent the average citizen but, since he was the judi- **2.49** cial idea of the average citizen, there was undoubtedly a tendency to think that the reasonable person has rather high standards of care. Moreover, the more the law of tort moved towards becoming an insurance-based compensation system, the more prudent and far-sighted the reasonable person became.

(b) Tailoring the standard to the circumstances of the defendant

The reasonable person at common law was not always entirely divorced from the circum- **2.50** stances of the defendant. Consideration of the defendant's circumstances was permitted in cases of those who, from mental illness or other incapacity, had no understanding of what they were doing,[99] and for children, from whom it was required only that such care be taken as could reasonably be expected of a child of that age.[100] But these exceptions were traditionally narrow. In most cases it was thought that a defendant could not hope to plead his personal failings of knowledge or skill to avoid paying compensation for damage he had caused. It was no defence that he was doing his incompetent best. The defendant was measured against the external standard of the reasonable person and no account was taken of the fact that he might be incapable of reaching it. The conflict between a standard of care focusing purely on the reasonable person and a standard focused on the reasonable person with the attributes of the defendant, was first recognized by the Romans who labelled the first *culpa levis in abstracto* and the second *culpa levis in concreto*. The contrast is not between different levels of duty. The concrete duty might be higher or lower than the abstract one depending upon the ability of the defendant. Rather, the contrast is between different ways of proving fault.

---

[97] *McFarlane v Tayside Health Board* [2000] 2 AC 59, 82, HL, *per* Lord Steyn. An early formulation of negligence as guided by the conduct of the reasonable man is *Blyth v Birmingham Waterworks Co* (1856) 11 Ex 781, 784, 156 ER 1047, 1049, *per* Alderson B.

[98] [1971] 2 QB 691, CA.

[99] *Morriss v Marsden* [1952] 1 All ER 925, a claim for battery, but Stable J took the rule to be of general application. See also *Mansfield v Weetabix Ltd* [1998] 1 WLR 1263, CA.

[100] *Mullin v Richards* [1998] 1 WLR 1304, CA.

2.51 In the case of equitable wrongs there were more significant departures from the abstract standard than the traditional position at common law. A company director was expected by courts of equity to exercise the standard of care of a reasonable person with his or her level of skill and experience.[101] On the other hand, trustees were expected to live up to the standard that an ordinary person would exercise in making an investment for a person for whom he felt morally obliged to provide. No provision was made for the trustee who had a lower level of experience or skill than was ordinary.[102]

2.52 More recently common law cases have also begun to depart from the purely abstract notion of the reasonable man. In *Wilsher v Essex Area Health Authority*[103] a junior doctor was held not to be negligent for mistakenly inserting an umbilical catheter into a baby's vein, although a senior doctor was negligent for failing to notice this error. Only Glidewell LJ thought that the junior doctor should be judged by a purely objective standard for the profession.[104] In contrast, Mustill LJ considered that the duty of care should be confined to the post assumed by the doctor. Browne-Wilkinson V-C posed a test which was tailored most closely to the circumstances of the defendant. His Lordship said that a court should consider the experience and knowledge of the particular doctor, explaining that doctors at the beginning of a post have less experience than those at the end; they cannot be held at fault for failing to meet a standard attainable only by experience. There was no suggestion by either Browne-Wilkinson V-C or Mustill LJ, or any factual basis to conclude, that the junior doctor had held himself out to the baby's parents as having only limited medical experience.[105]

2.53 There are signs that the more concrete approach of Browne-Wilkinson VC will prevail. In a recent decision of the House of Lords, concerning whether an advocate was negligent, two Law Lords (with whom another two agreed) held that advice given by the advocate was 'within the range of that to be expected of reasonably competent counsel of the appellant's seniority and purported experience.'[106] There could be no justification for a different approach to the standard of care expected of a plumber or a builder. Indeed, in some omissions cases the courts have gone even further and considered not merely the reasonable person with the defendant's skill and experience but even the financial means of the defendant. In *Goldman v Hargrave*, the defendant occupier was liable for failure to protect his neighbour from a natural disaster emanating from his land, although the physical and material resources of the defendant were relevant to a finding of negligence, since 'the law must take account of the fact that the occupier on whom the duty is cast has, ex hypothesi, had this hazard thrust

---

[101] *Lagunas Nitrate Co v Lagunas Syndicate* [1899] 2 Ch 392, 435, CA, *per* Lindley MR; *Re City Equitable Fire Insurance Co* [1925] 1 Ch 407, 428–429; an appeal to the Court of Appeal was dismissed and this point was not addressed: [1925] 1 Ch 501, CA. In *Re D'Jan of London Ltd* [1993] BCC 646, CA, Hoffmann LJ held that the standard should mirror that in the Insolvency Act 1986, s 214(4) and should require satisfaction of both the concrete and abstract standards therein.

[102] *Speight v Gaunt* (1883) LR 9 App Cas 1, 4, *per* Selborne LC, 19, *per* Lord Blackburn, 33, *per* Lord Fitzgerald, HL; *Re Whiteley* (1886) 33 ChD 347, CA; *Nestle v National Westminster Bank plc* [1993] 1 WLR 1260, 1267, CA. It is unlikely that the duty enshrined in the Trustee Act 2000, s 1(1), namely 'such care and skill as is reasonable in the circumstances' has changed this position since the circumstances include 'special knowledge or experience that it is reasonable to expect of a person acting in the course of that kind of business' (s 1(1)(b)).

[103] [1987] QB 730, CA. Reversed on other grounds [1988] AC 1074, HL.

[104] Even this abstract approach could involve very difficult questions. What is the standard of care for the practitioner of traditional Chinese medicine? *Shakoor v Situ* [2001] 1 WLR 410.

[105] cf *Herrington v British Railways Board* [1972] AC 877, 899, HL.

[106] *Moy v Pettmann Smith (a firm)* [2005] UKHL 7, [2005] 1 WLR 581, at [62], *per* Lord Carswell. See also at [22], *per* Lord Hope; *contra* Baroness Hale at [25]. See also *Vowles v Evans* [2003] EWCA Civ 318, [2003] 1 WLR 1607, at [28] (volunteer referee taken from the crowd cannot reasonably be expected to show the same level of skill as one who holds himself out as a referee).

upon him through no seeking or fault of his own.'[107] The Court of Appeal took the same view in another natural disaster case:

> The criteria of reasonableness include, in respect of a duty of this nature, the factor of what the particular man—not the average man—can be expected to do, having regard, amongst other things, where a serious expenditure of money is required to eliminate or reduce the danger, to his means.[108]

There is also further indication that the defendant's resources should be considered in other situations where the law imposes a duty to take positive action to protect others.[109] **2.54**

(c) A higher standard where special skills are professed

If the defendant professes to have particular skills, at both common law and equity he is judged by the standard which would have been exercised by a reasonable person with the knowledge and skills professed, regardless of his actual expertise or experience.[110] There is much detailed law on these matters to be found in the relevant specialist work, be it medical law or construction law. There may be an initial question as to which trade or professional standard is the one professed. A prison hospital, for instance, is a subsidiary part of an institution with other functions, and cannot be expected to have the same resources as a hospital whose specialized function is the treatment of mental illness.[111] Similarly, a difficult question not considered in *Wilsher* is whether an inexperienced defendant who remains silent about his inexperience holds himself out as having the level of skill of the ordinary person in that profession or trade. **2.55**

An exclusionary test which demonstrates attainment of the standard of care required of the medical profession, or any other person professing some skill or competence, is the *Bolam* test.[112] In the *Bolam* case McNair J laid down that a doctor: **2.56**

> is not guilty of negligence if he has acted in accordance with a practice accepted as proper by a responsible body of medical men skilled in that particular art...merely because there is a body of opinion who would take a contrary view.[113]

Recent reformulations have emphasized that the body of professional opinion must be respectable and reasonable as well as responsible.[114] The court must be satisfied that the body of opinion relied on has a logical basis and that, in forming their views, the experts have weighed the comparative risks and benefits and reached a defensible conclusion on the matter. Legal professional opinions can also be held to be wrong although judges must be careful not to decide the case on the basis of what they would have done.[115] **2.57**

Particularly in medical cases, the state of knowledge at the time may be important. The question is whether the defendant acted reasonably in the light of what was known then, not what **2.58**

---

[107] [1967] 1 AC 645, 663–664, PC, *per* Lord Wilberforce.

[108] *Leakey v National Trust* [1980] 1 QB 485, 526, CA, *per* Megaw LJ.

[109] *Smith v Littlewoods Organisation Ltd* [1987] AC 241, 269, HL, *per* Lord McKay; *Stovin v Wise* [1996] AC 923, 933, HL, *per* Lord Nicholls.

[110] The classic statement in equity is that of Brightman J in *Bartlett v Barclays Bank Trust Co Ltd (No 1)* [1980] Ch 515, 534. See now Trustee Act 2000, s 1(1). At common law see *Chaudhry v Prabhakar* [1989] 1 WLR 29, CA.

[111] *Knight v Home Office* [1990] 3 All ER 237.

[112] *Bolam v Friern Hospital Management Committee* [1957] 1 WLR 582, 587.

[113] *Bolam v Friern Hospital Management Committee* [1957] 1 WLR 582, 587.

[114] *Bolitho v City & Hackney Health Authority* [1998] AC 232, 241–242, HL.

[115] *Edward Wong Finance Co Ltd v Johnson, Stokes and Master* [1984] AC 296, PC. For the warning about judges deciding cases see *Moy v Pettmann Smith (a firm)* [2005] UKHL 7, [2005] 1 WLR 581, at [19], *per* Lord Hope.

is known now.[116] A doctor's duties include warning the patient of the inevitable risks of treatment. In England the extent of the duty to warn is also a matter of professional judgment, subject to the overall control of the court.[117]

(d) Costs and risks

2.59 What reasonable care requires in a given situation is often to be ascertained by weighing in the balance four considerations: the likelihood that the activity in question will cause damage, the likely severity of the damage if it occurs, the difficulty and expense of averting the danger and, in appropriate cases, the value to society of the activity undertaken.[118] If, therefore, damage although foreseeable is very unlikely to happen, it may well not be negligent to fail to take steps to avoid it.[119] But if even an unlikely risk can be eliminated without difficulty or expense, and particularly if the damage is likely to be severe if it does occur, the reasonable man would take the necessary steps.[120]

2.60 When considering the severity of the likely damage, it is relevant that the defendant knows or ought to know that the damage will be particularly severe to a particular person; eg, to an employee known to have only one eye.[121] The reasonable man also takes into account the likely presence of persons with reasonably common disabilities.[122] The importance of the object to be attained may be an important factor. Highly dangerous conduct is justified if it is the only chance of saving life,[123] provided that other lives are not unreasonably imperilled.[124]

(e) Proof of negligence

2.61 As in all civil cases, the burden of proving negligence, and of proving that the negligence caused or contributed to damage, lies on the claimant. The standard of proof required in civil cases is the balance of probabilities. The claimant has to show that it is more probable than not that the defendant was negligent and caused or contributed to the damage.

2.62 The general rules of evidence in civil cases apply. Two aspects of the law of evidence particularly concern the law of tort. The first is the Civil Evidence Act 1968, section 11, which permits evidence of a criminal conviction to be admitted in civil proceedings to show that the person committed the wrong, unless the contrary is proved. The section, therefore, creates only a presumption which can be rebutted by, eg, new evidence which shows that the conviction was wrong.

2.63 The second presumption is a presumption of negligence arising from the circumstances: *res ipsa loquitur* (the matter speaks for itself). If the accident which injured the claimant is one which does not usually happen unless someone has been negligent, and the claimant can show that the event causing damage was under the control of the defendant or his employees, then, in the absence of an explanation, the court may presume that the defendant was negligent. Both the leading authorities concerned claimants who were injured while walking

---

[116] *Roe v Minister of Health* [1954] 2 QB 66, CA.

[117] *Sidaway v Royal Bethlem Hospital* [1985] AC 871, HL. Contrast the position in Australia: *Rogers v Whittaker* (1992) 175 CLR 479, HCA.

[118] The first three considerations constitute the 'Learned Hand formula'. Justice Learned Hand said that a breach of duty would occur when 'B<PL', ie where the Burden of taking care was less than the Probability multiplied by the gravity of the Loss: *US v Carroll Towing Co* 159 F 2d 169, 173 (2d Cir, 1947).

[119] *Bolton v Stone* [1951] AC 850, HL.

[120] *Wagon Mound (No 2)* [1967] 1 AC 617, PC.

[121] *Paris v Stepney BC* [1951] AC 367, HL.

[122] *Haley v London Electricity Board* [1965] AC 778, HL.

[123] *Baker v TE Hopkins & Sons Ltd* [1959] 1 WLR 966, CA. See also Compensation Act 2006, s 1.

[124] *Ward v LCC* [1938] 2 All ER 341.

in Victorian London by objects falling from premises occupied by the defendant.[125] The presumption arises only where the cause of the accident is not known. Whether the accident is one which does not normally happen without negligence is a matter for the judge.

There has been controversy about the level of explanation by the defendant required to rebut **2.64** the presumption. It is obviously sufficient for the defendant to prove how the accident happened or, if that is unknown, to prove that he was not negligent. If the defendant cannot prove either the cause or the absence of negligence, there is some suggestion that the claimant should win; ie, that the presumption operates to shift the burden of proof. But that would put claimants with no evidence in a better position than those with some evidence. The orthodox view is that it is sufficient for the defendant to produce a reasonable alternative explanation of the accident: that the accident could have happened without his negligence. This is probably the current position.[126]

It is in the nature of the presumption that it applies only in commonplace situations where **2.65** evidence of negligence is hardly required. It might therefore be said to be no presumption at all, evidence of facts being in itself evidence of the negligence. The Supreme Court of Canada has indeed decided that the presumption serves no useful purpose in modern law.[127] It was, however, applied by the Privy Council in *George v Eagle Air Services Ltd*.[128]

(3) Damage

Once it is established that a defendant was under a duty of care and was in breach of that duty, **2.66** it remains for the claimant to establish that he has suffered relevant damage. Relevant damage is damage caused by the breach of duty. However, since there is no end to the causes of causes, there has to be some cut-off. Hence, damage which is caused by the breach may yet be too remote. Causation and remoteness are therefore the principal matters to be considered under this head.

(a) Causation

Negligence is only actionable if it causes damage. Duties of care are duties to avoid causing **2.67** damage. Sometimes the duty is cut down, so as to be a duty to avoid causing only a particular kind of damage. It is for the claimant to prove that the defendant's breach of duty caused the damage of which he complains. It is not necessary to show that the defendant was the sole, or even the major, cause so long as he proves that but for the defendant's negligence the damage would not have happened. Difficult problems arise where there are multiple possible causes.

(i) The 'but for' test

The general test of causation is the 'but for' test. If the injury to the claimant would not have **2.68** occurred but for the negligence of the defendant, that negligence is an operative cause.[129] The 'but for' rule is adequate for simple cases. More difficult causation problems require more elaborate solutions. For instance, recovery will be denied although the 'but for' test is apparently satisfied, in cases where the injury arises by coincidence. Examples include a taxi that

---

[125] *Byrne v Boadle* (1863) 2 H & C 722, 159 ER 299; *Scott v London & St Katherine Docks Co* (1865) 3 H & C 596, 159 ER 665.
[126] *Ng Chun Pui v Lee Chuen Tat* [1988] RTR 298, PC.
[127] *Fontaine v Loewen Estate* [1998] 1 SCR 424, SCC, on which see M McInnes, 'The Death of *Res Ipsa Loquitur* in Canada' (1998) 114 LQR 547.
[128] [2009] UKPC 21, [2009] 1 WLR 2133.
[129] *Barnett v Chelsea and Kensington Hospital Management Committee* [1969] 1 QB 428; *Performance Cars Ltd v Abraham* [1962] 1 QB 33, CA. Reforming causation to recognize that 'but for' is simply one way of proving the test for causation, namely where the breach of duty is 'historically involved' as a factor in the damage suffered, is powerfully advocated by Professor Stapleton: J Stapleton, 'Cause-in-Fact and the Scope of Liability for Consequences' (2003) 119 LQR 388.

is hit by a falling tree injuring the passenger which would not have occurred if the taxi had not been speeding,[130] or allegedly careless advice that leads a claimant to take over a business which collapses years later.[131] The line separating coincidental events from applicable 'but for' causes can be a fine one. In *Chester v Afshar*[132] the claimant agreed to a back operation but the doctor had negligently failed to advise her of an unavoidable 1–2 per cent risk of permanent injury. When the unwarned injury resulted she claimed that but for the doctor's negligence she would not have had the operation on that day, but would have deferred it. A bare majority of the House of Lords concluded that even though the same risk would exist whenever the operation took place, the injury suffered on that day was not simply a coincidence and causation was satisfied because the claimant's right to choose had been violated. The paragraphs which follow identify four situations which are generally thought to cause difficulties for a straightforward application of the 'but for' test.

(ii) Increased risk of damage which results

2.69 The traditional rule is that it is not sufficient to show that the defendant's negligence increased the risk of injury. Evidence is required to show that out of several possible causes the defendant's negligence was a 'but for' cause on the balance of probabilities. In *Wilsher v Essex AHA*[133] a premature baby became blind. Expert evidence adduced five possible causes of this outcome. One of these was that the health authority, through the doctors, had negligently administered too much oxygen. But there was no evidence to justify the conclusion that on the balance of probabilities that cause had operated. Hence the claim failed. This rule has the potential to produce harsh results in cases where medical knowledge is not able to establish but-for causation on a balance of probabilities. A claimant who can show a 51 per cent degree of probability that the defendant's negligence injured him gets full compensation. Another claimant, who can show only a 49 per cent degree of probability, gets nothing.

2.70 An apparent erosion of this rule occurred in *Fairchild v Glenhaven Funeral Services Ltd.*[134] A number of workers who had contracted mesothelioma after multiple exposures to asbestos arising from the negligence of successive employers sought to recover damages from the employers. Medical evidence showed that a single fibre of asbestos was just as likely to cause mesothelioma as multiple exposures so it was impossible on the current state of scientific knowledge to prove on the balance of probabilities which employer caused the mesothelioma. The House of Lords held that it was in the interests of justice that the claimant could recover. It was enough that an employer had materially increased the likelihood of the claimant's injury. An attempt to extend this principle to the whole of medical negligence was narrowly rejected by the House of Lords in *Gregg v Scott.*[135] In that case, negligent medical advice caused a nine-month delay in the treatment of the claimant's cancer, reducing his chance of survival from 42 per cent to 25 per cent. A majority of the House of Lords refused to award damages for the reduction in his chance of survival, seeing *Wilsher* as an impermeable obstacle.[136]

2.71 After *Gregg*, it might have been thought that *Fairchild* represented only a very narrow exception to the traditional rule. But just one year later the House of Lords squarely confronted the

---

[130] The example given by Lord Walker in *Chester v Afshar* [2004] UKHL 41, [2005] 1 AC 134, at [94].
[131] *Galoo Ltd v Bright Grahame Murray* [1994] 1 WLR 1360, CA.
[132] [2004] UKHL 41, [2005] 1 AC 134, HL.
[133] [1988] AC 1074, HL; cf *Pickford v Imperial Chemical Industries plc* [1998] 1 WLR 1189, HL.
[134] [2002] UKHL 22, [2003] 1 AC 32.
[135] [2005] UKHL 2, [2005] 2 AC 176.
[136] Contrast cases where the chance lost is a *financial* chance: *Allied Maples Group Ltd v Simmons & Simmons* [1995] 1 WLR 1602, CA; *Kitchen v Royal Air Force Association* [1958] 1 WLR 563, CA and the contract case of *Chaplin v Hicks* [1911] 2 KB 786, CA.

limits of *Fairchild* and confined *Wilsher* and *Gregg*. In *Barker v Corus plc*[137] the House heard three joint appeals involving claimants who suffered mesothelioma after successive periods of exposure to asbestos by different employers including, in one case, a period of self-employment. A majority of the House of Lords held that the *Fairchild* principle applied whenever a defendant materially increased the risk that the claimant would suffer damage even if the defendant could not be proved to have caused the damage because it was impossible to show, on a balance of probability, that it was not caused by some other exposure to the same risk.[138] The principle applied irrespective of whether the other possible causes were tortious or non-tortious. Lord Hoffmann argued that since liability in these cases was based upon the negligent increase in a risk of the injury which the claimant suffered, it followed that the damage was the creation of that risk, and that therefore the cases were not anomalous at all: but for the defendant's negligence the risk would not have been increased.[139] It followed that an employer should only be liable for the proportion of damages corresponding to the extent to which it increased the risk,[140] with the result that the employee therefore bore the risk of under-compensation if one or more employers became insolvent. Although this proportionate liability approach strains the language of the Fatal Accidents Act 1976,[141] and has been reversed by Parliament in mesothelioma cases,[142] it now applies to all other cases apart from mesothelioma.

Two qualifications to this principle were introduced in *Barker*. The first qualification was that **2.72** there must be a single 'causative agent'. All the possible causal agents must operate in the same way. *Wilsher* was therefore distinguished because the five possible causes of blindness were all different. This introduces a very fine distinction between causal agents which operate in the same way and those which do not. A second qualification introduced by Lord Hoffmann in *Barker v Corus* was that actual damage must still be suffered: a person cannot claim for a risk unless it has materialized.[143] The denial of liability in *Gregg v Scott* was re-explained as based on the fact that the claimant had not died.[144] One is left to wonder what the result would be if a future claimant like Mr Gregg were to die the night before judgment. Finally,

---

[137] [2006] UKHL 20, [2006] 2 AC 572, noted A Kramer (2006) 122 LQR 547.

[138] [2006] UKHL 20, [2006] 2 AC 572, at [17], Lord Hoffmann (Lords Walker and Scott and Baroness Hale agreeing).

[139] Lord Rodger, in a strong dissent on this issue, considered that the damage was the injury that resulted and that *Barker*, like the cases before it, was an exception to the but-for test: [2006] UKHL 20, [2006] 2 AC 572, at [72], [90]. Lord Rodger's view as to the nature of the damage was subsequently endorsed by two members of the Supreme Court in an appeal concerning the interpretation of employers' liability insurance policies: see *Durham v BAI (Run Off) Ltd (in scheme of arrangement)* [2012] UKSC 14, [2012] 1 WLR 867, at [52], [64]–[65], *per* Lord Mance SCJ, [77], *per* Lord Clarke SCJ.

[140] [2006] UKHL 20, [2006] 2 AC 572, at [35], [43]. Not yet fully resolved are cases where the defendant's negligence is proved to have materially contributed to the disease rather than just increased the risk, although not necessarily amounting to a but-for cause: *Bonnington Castings Ltd v Wardlaw* [1956] AC 613, HL is probably now best understood as requiring liability only for the extent of the material contribution. Compare *Holtby v Brigham & Cowan (Hull) Ltd* [2000] 3 All ER 421, CA with *Mountford v Newlands School* [2007] EWCA Civ 21, at [18]–[20], where liability was imposed for the full extent of the injury. See further, SH Bailey, 'Causation in Negligence: What is a Material Contribution?' (2010) 30 LS 167.

[141] Section 1 of the Fatal Accidents Act 1976, which was the basis of the claim in *Barker*, provides for liability to dependants where 'death is caused by any wrongful act, neglect or default', not where there is a material increase in the risk of the death which results. On the approach in *Barker* it appears that s 1 would be satisfied even where the predominant 'cause' of death was non-tortious despite the literal wording of the Act.

[142] Compensation Act 2006, s 3. This provision affects only the consequences of tort liability being imposed in a mesothelioma case, and not the circumstances in which such liability arises in the first place (which remains a matter for the courts): *Sienkiewicz v Greif (UK) Ltd* [2011] UKSC 10, [2011] 2 AC 229.

[143] A simple, fictitious example was given by Latham LJ in *Gregg v Scott* [2002] EWCA Civ 1471, at [39] of persons exposed to asbestos dust near a factory who suffer no injuries save the statistical possibility of future harm.

[144] [2006] UKHL 20, [2006] 2 AC 572, at [48]; cf at [38].

in *Sienkiewicz v Greif (UK) Ltd*,[145] the Supreme Court held that the claimant had to establish only that the defendant had materially increased the risk, and that there was no scope for a rival approach based on the doubling of the background risk. The Court also rejected a second argument to the effect that materially increasing the risk meant at least doubling the risk associated with environmental exposure. According to Lord Rodger, a risk was material for these purposes if it was more than de minimis.[146]

(iii) Successive unrelated events

2.73 Suppose that C's leg is injured due to the negligence of D and that, on the balance of probabilities, it is in an irremediable condition: he will never be able to use the leg again. In that condition he is attacked by robbers and, having been shot, suffers an amputation of his already injured leg. It is clear that the second wrongdoer's liability will be reduced by the disablement which happened before they shot C, for the quality of life and earning capacity of the victim are already seriously impaired,[147] but the question arises whether D's liability for the injured leg is affected by the amputation, on the ground that this eliminated the long-term impact of the initial disablement. In *Baker v Willoughby*, the House of Lords held it was not.[148]

2.74 The same result would seem at first sight to follow when, after the first injury, C contracts an illness which, as effectively as a second tort, deprives him of his earning capacity. In fact the opposite result is reached. In *Jobling v Associated Dairies Ltd* an employee was wrongfully injured and later found to be seriously and irremediably ill.[149] His damages for loss of earnings were reduced. The distinction drawn by Lords Keith and Russell was that the tortious event in *Baker* involved a subsequent injury which could not be characterized as a vicissitude of life which should be taken into account as a possibility at the time of the initial injury. In another decision, faced with successive torts—albeit where the first tort (an eye injury from an attack) was a cause of the second (negligent treatment)—the Court of Appeal saw no inconsistency between the *Baker* and *Jobling* and followed the former, making no reduction in the award.[150]

(iv) Aggravations by the claimant's own conduct

2.75 If C's own careless conduct increases the damage caused by D, that will usually operate as contributory negligence, leading to a reduction in C's damages.[151] The court may, however, regard C's conduct as so unreasonable as to break the causal chain of responsibility. In *McKew v Holland Hannen & Cubitts (Scotland) Ltd*[152] the claimant was injured by the defendant and later broke his ankle. He argued that the second injury was a simple sequel to the first, caused by the tort. But the House of Lords held that he had brought it entirely on himself by rashly insisting on descending stairs in his injured condition without assistance. An easier explanation of this result, as we will see with aggravations caused by the conduct of a third party, may be to say that it is not a qualification of the but for test but an application of principles

---

[145] [2011] UKSC 10, [2011] 2 AC 229. See S Steel and D Ibbetson, 'More Grief on Uncertain Causation in Tort' [2011] CLJ 451.

[146] [2011] UKSC 10, [2011] 2 AC 229, at [161]. The result is that in mesothelioma cases covered by s 3 of the Compensation Act 2006, a defendant responsible for an increased risk of, say, 10% may be held liable for the totality of the claimant's injury.

[147] *Murrell v Healy* [2001] EWCA Civ 486, [2001] 4 All ER 345.

[148] [1970] AC 467, HL.

[149] [1982] AC 794, HL.

[150] *Rahman v Arearose Ltd* [2001] QB 351, CA.

[151] 2.189–2.202.

[152] [1969] 3 All ER 1621, HL. Contrast *Wieland v Cyril Lord Carpets Ltd* [1969] 3 All ER 1006. It seems that contributory negligence was not pleaded in *McKew's* case: see *Spencer v Wincanton Holdings Ltd* [2009] EWCA Civ 1404, [2010] PIQR P8, at [22].

of legal causation or remoteness of damage. It is then easy to see why unreasonable actions of the claimant himself, but which the defendant had a duty to prevent, such as suicide whilst in police custody, will not prevent the imposition of liability.[153]

(v) Aggravations by the conduct of a third party

If by negligent behaviour D knocks C unconscious, thus giving X a chance to steal C's wallet **2.76** from him, there are two ways in which it might be said that D is not liable for the theft by X. The intervention by X might be said to break the chain of causation, so that D did not cause the loss of C's wallet. Alternatively, it might be said that D did cause that loss but that the loss is nevertheless too remote to be recoverable. On the whole the latter is the more easily intelligible technique which, as we have seen, explains why liability will still be imposed in a case in which it is found that D was under a duty to prevent any X from doing the very thing that happened. So, if a decorator who is working for a householder goes out to buy some new supplies and leaves the door open, so that a thief can enter and steal, the decorator will be held to have been under a duty to keep the house safe and will be liable for the loss caused by the theft.[154]

The general rule is that D is not liable for damage caused by an independent third party solely **2.77** by virtue of the fact that his negligence facilitated the tort. Thus in *Lamb v Camden London BC*[155] the local authority negligently damaged a water main. The escaping water undermined the claimant's house. The house had to be vacated because of subsidence. Squatters then moved in and did a good deal of damage. It could have been held that the squatters were an entirely new event, breaking the chain of causation: the negligent authority did not cause the damage which the squatters caused. Such a strained analysis used to be called *novus actus interveniens*, the intervention of a new act, restarting the chain of causation. In fact the court negatived the liability of the authority for the squatter damage by using the language of remoteness. It was clearly easier to take it that the negligent digging did cause the loss arising at the end of the chain of causes, while invoking the cut-off principle in order to deny recovery of that particular loss.

(b) Remoteness

Despite proving that the defendant caused or substantially contributed to the damage, the **2.78** claimant may not recover all the loss so caused. The consequences of the tort (or some of them) may be so unusual or extreme that they cannot fairly be attributed to the defendant.[156] We have noted that some items may be excluded as not having been caused by the defendant. Leaving those aside, a loss which was caused by the defendant may be excluded on the ground that he owed no duty in respect of loss of that kind. A number of modern negligence cases have used the duty argument rather than remoteness to limit the extent of liability for economic loss.[157] However, exclusions are usually put down to remoteness: although the defendant did owe a relevant duty of care and its breach caused loss, some of that loss was too remote. The ever-enlarging cone of causation simply has to be cut off at some point.

---

[153] *Reeves v Commissioner of Police of the Metropolis* [2000] 1 AC 360, HL; *Corr v IBC Vehicles Ltd* [2008] UKHL 13, [2008] AC 884.
[154] *Stansbie v Troman* [1948] 2 KB 48, CA. cf 2.95–2.97.
[155] [1981] QB 625, CA.
[156] J Cartwright, 'Remoteness of Damage in Contract and Tort: A Reconsideration' [1996] CLJ 488.
[157] *Banque Bruxelles Lambert SA v Eagle Star Insurance Co Ltd* [1997] AC 191, HL. Public policy is as much an issue in remoteness of damage questions as it is in the duty of care: *Pritchard v JH Cobden Ltd* [1988] Fam 22, CA; *Meah v McCreamer (No 2)* [1986] 1 All ER 943. In so far as modern formulations of duty are often expressed as duties to take care in respect of particular kinds of damage, duty and remoteness issues become more difficult to distinguish.

(i) Direct consequences

2.79   There have been two lines of authority on the test for remoteness. The first was that the risk of unforeseeable consequences should be borne by the person whose negligence caused them. On this view, represented by *Re Polemis and Furness, Withy & Co Ltd*,[158] the defendant was liable for all direct consequences of his negligence. Foreseeability was considered to go to culpability, not to compensation. To determine culpability, you needed to know that a defendant had failed to take precautions against foreseeable harm. Once he was culpable, he must compensate for all the direct consequences.[159] 'Directness' of causation was on this view the arbiter of recoverability.

2.80   In the *Polemis* case itself the defendant stevedores negligently dropped a plank into the hold of a ship. Some damage was foreseeable from such an event. A falling plank is likely to do damage on impact. In fact, however, the ship was utterly destroyed. There was petrol vapour in the hold, and the fall caused a spark, and thence an explosion and a fire. The extreme consequence was directly caused but not foreseeable. The defendants were held liable.

(ii) Foreseeable consequences

2.81   The other view, introduced by the first of the celebrated *Wagon Mound* cases[160] and now dominant,[161] is that the defendant should only be liable for foreseeable damage. In that case a ship negligently spilled oil into the waters of Sydney Harbour and sailed off. Three days later and some hundreds of yards away the oil ignited and burned down a wharf. The fire was caused because a spark from welding operations fell on a piece of rag, which caught fire and in turn set off the floating oil. On the expert evidence in that case, although pollution damage was certainly foreseeable, nobody thought it possible for the oil to ignite, and so the damage was too remote.[162]

(iii) Narrowing the distance between the two views

2.82   The seeming difference between the two tests of remoteness is much reduced by the fact that, even under the foreseeability test of the *Wagon Mound* case a distinction is taken between the foreseeability of the general kind of damage and foreseeability of the damage which actually happened. It is not necessary that the defendant ought to have foreseen the damage which actually happened, so long as he should have foreseen damage of that general kind. Hence actual damage which counts as foreseeable may not have been foreseeable at all, in the sense that it may be a hundred times worse than what could be foreseen.

2.83   Thus in *Hughes v Lord Advocate*[163] a hole in the road was lit by paraffin lamps during roadworks. It was foreseeable that young boys might play with the lamps, might fall in the hole and might get burned. But when boys started messing with the lamps what actually happened was once again a major explosion. Yet such an escalation is taken to be within the foreseeable risk, because it was of the same generic type as what could be foreseen. Even the

---

[158] [1921] 3 KB 560, CA.

[159] [1921] 3 KB 560, 570–72, CA, *per* Bankes LJ.

[160] *Overseas Tankship (UK) Ltd v Morts Dock and Engineering Co Ltd (The Wagon Mound)* [1961] AC 388, PC.

[161] J Cartwright, 'Remoteness of Damage in Contract and Tort: A Reconsideration' [1996] CLJ 488, 513. The foreseeability test of remoteness has been extended to other torts: see, eg, *The Wagon Mound (No 2)* [1967] 1 AC 617, PC (public and private nuisance); *Cambridge Water Co v Eastern Counties Leather plc* [1994] 2 AC 264, 306, HL (*Rylands v Fletcher*). But there are exceptions: a defendant in the tort of deceit cannot plead that the losses caused were unforeseeable: *Smith New Court Securities Ltd v Scrimgeour Vickers (Asset Management) Ltd* [1997] AC 254, 265–267, HL.

[162] Different expert evidence led to a different factual conclusion in *The Wagon Mound (No 2)* [1967] 1 AC 617, PC.

[163] [1963] AC 837, HL.

fire in the *Polemis* case itself might at a stretch be said to be foreseeable on this basis. In contrast with the decision in *Hughes*, in *Doughty v Turner Manufacturing Ltd*[164] burns from an explosion of molten metal were held to be different from foreseeable burns from a splash of the same molten metal. Although *Doughty* has now been doubted by the Privy Council,[165] the decisions as to whether damage is within the foreseeable type remain erratic.[166]

(iv) The 'eggshell skull' rule

This is another manifestation of the same phenomenon. The rule that the tortfeasor must **2.84** take his victim as he finds him has remained constant during varying formulations of the remoteness test. Provided the initial injury was foreseeable, a tortfeasor cannot complain if the consequences of that injury turn out to be unexpectedly serious because of some pre-existing susceptibility of the claimant.[167] This 'eggshell skull' rule is particularly significant in personal injury cases.

For many years this rule did not carry over to claims for economic loss. In *Liesbosch (Dredger)* **2.85** *v SS Edison*[168] the House of Lords had to decide whether defendants who had sunk the claimants' dredger had to make good the extortionately high costs incurred by the claimants in hiring another to finish their contract. This outlay was disallowed because it was attributable to the fact that the claimants could not buy a replacement owing to their own impecuniosity. In *Lagden v O'Connor*[169] the House of Lords confronted this apparent contradiction. Mr Lagden's car was damaged as a result of Ms O'Connor's negligence. He could not afford to hire a replacement while his car was being repaired without the extension of credit from a credit hire company. The House of Lords unanimously departed from *Liesbosch* and accepted that impecuniosity is an economic characteristic of a victim that must be taken as it is found in the same way as his physical characteristics.[170]

C. Negligence: Particular Cases

This section gathers together four troublesome applications of the tort of negligence, the **2.86** two most common of which—psychiatric injury and economic loss—are concerned with the special regimes necessitated by the type of harm suffered by the claimant, in particular with the restricted recognition of any duty of care in respect of those kinds of loss. However, the section begins with a restriction which arises, not from the type of harm, but from the distinction between doing and not doing.

---

[164] [1964] 1 QB 518, CA.

[165] *Attorney General for the British Virgin Islands v Hartwell* [2004] UKPC 12, [2004] 1 WLR 1273, at [27]–[30], PC.

[166] In *Bradford v Robinson Rentals Ltd* [1967] 1 WLR 337 frostbite was the same kind of damage as a cold, but in *Tremain v Pike* [1969] 1 WLR 1556 Weill's disease, carried in rat urine, was different from other rat contaminations and infections; physical injury and psychological harm are the same kind of damage: *Page v Smith* [1996] AC 155, HL. In *Jolley v Sutton LBC* [1998] 1 WLR 1546, CA the court thought foreseeable injuries to 13-year-olds from playing with a boat were not the same as injuries which happened trying to repair it, but the House of Lords disagreed: [2000] 1 WLR 1082, HL, restoring the first instance finding and observing that these are decisions of fact, not reducible to propositions of law, so that comparing one outcome with another was 'a sterile exercise': [2000] 1 WLR 1082, 1089, HL, *per* Lord Steyn.

[167] *Smith v Leech Brain & Co Ltd* [1962] 2 QB 405: small burn became fatal through cancer, because of undetected pre-cancerous condition.

[168] [1933] AC 449, HL.

[169] [2003] UKHL 64, [2004] 1 AC 1067.

[170] [2003] UKHL 64, [2004] 1 AC 1067, at [6] (Lord Nicholls), [61] (Lord Hope) approving B Coote, 'The Liesbosch and Impecuniosity' (2001) 60 CLJ 511. The House divided only on the issue of whether the full hire charges could be recovered without deduction for additional benefits received by Mr Lagden.

(1) Omissions

2.87 Lord Atkin's neighbour principle began by pointing out that there are limits to the law's enforcement of morals: 'The rule that you are to love your neighbour becomes in law, you must not injure your neighbour, and the lawyer's question, Who is my neighbour? receives a restricted reply.'[171] One important element in this gap between law and morals concerns omissions to act. It is often readily foreseeable that, if we do not take action, another will suffer harm, but the law has difficulty in imposing liability for omissions, for harm which the defendant has not actively done but has allowed to come about.

(a) The general nature of the problem

2.88 Every legal system has to face this problem. The main arguments for not in general requiring positive action were elegantly summarized by Lord Hoffmann in *Stovin v Wise*.[172] He distinguished three strands, political, moral, and economic:

> In political terms it is less of an invasion of an individual's freedom for the law to require him to consider the safety of others in his actions than to impose upon him a duty to rescue or protect. A moral version of this point may be called the 'why pick on me?' argument. A duty to prevent harm to others or to render assistance to a person in danger or distress may apply to a large and indeterminate class of people who happen to be able to do something. Why should one be held liable rather than another? In economic terms, the efficient allocation of resources usually requires an activity should bear its own costs. If it benefits from being able to impose some of its costs on other people...the market is distorted because the activity appears cheaper than it really is.[173]

2.89 The distinction between acts and omissions might sometimes seem to be only a matter of verbal formulation. Omitting to give a signal is negligent driving. Almost every negligent act entails the omission of precautions. However, the broad distinction between causing harm and failing to prevent it is usually clear. An omission is a failure to intervene to prevent the consequences of acts other than one's own or of events not of one's own creation. In such cases of failure to intervene, in the absence of a duty to take action there is arguably no causal link between the inert defendant and the harm which occurs.

2.90 The legal duty cannot but be restricted. Even when the damage in question is physical, foreseeability that it will occur unless the intervention is made will not itself establish a legal duty to act. Hence the law must, rather cautiously, identify the factors which put a person under a responsibility to take action in the interest of another. There is no exhaustive list and no generally applicable test.

(b) Responsibility for other persons

2.91 One basis for a positive duty to act is a relationship such that one person is responsible for the welfare of the other or responsible for preventing the other from doing harm to third parties. The routine example supposes a child drowning in shallow water and affirms that there is no obligation on a nearby adult to rescue it.[174] That will certainly not be true in cases in which the defendant genuinely assumes responsibility for another or undertakes to look after the other person. A callous adult *in loco parentis* will not escape liability for a child left to drown

---

[171] 2.28.

[172] [1996] AC 923, HL.

[173] [1996] AC 923, 943–944, HL. Further discussion: E Weinrib, 'The Case for a Duty to Rescue' (1980)90 Yale LJ 247; RW Wright, 'Standards of Care in Negligence Law' in DG Owen (ed), *Philosophical Foundations of Tort Law* (1997) 272–274; I England, 'The Duty to Control Conduct of Other Persons: The Prevention of Crime', ch 13 in his *The Philosophy of Tort Law* (1993).

[174] 2.38 and 2.87–2.107.

in shallow water. Schools, for instance, may be under an obligation to prevent injury to their young pupils, and to prevent them getting out and causing accidents.[175] But the burden is not unlimited; it depends on the nature of the undertaking. It is reasonable to expect a school to take responsibility for training its pupils in sports and for supervising them, but the duty does not extend to insuring them against sporting accidents.[176] In contrast, in *Watson v British Boxing Board of Control*[177] the Boxing Board was held liable for negligence when Watson, a boxer, suffered serious brain damage from a cerebral haemorrhage and could not be treated expeditiously at the ringside. The Board had not organized the fight but controlled the sport, the object of which was physical injury, and assumed responsibility for keeping the degree of that injury within reasonable bounds. Further, the boxing community was not so large as to open up the prospect of indeterminate liability and comprised individuals whose character and disposition rendered protection from excesses especially necessary. The Board's counter-argument that it should be spared liability because it operated on a not-for-profit basis was rejected.

These common law positive duties to act so as to protect another may arise in a number of relationships recognized in tort law as well as by contract. The commonest is the employer's duty to provide employees with a safe system of work. That duty arises in both tort and contract.[178] Again a host may in some circumstances be responsible for the welfare of his guests, under a duty to protect them from violence[179] or to attempt to rescue them from danger.[180] However, the host's duty will rarely extend to third parties as, for instance, where a drunken guest leaves the host's party and injures a third party by negligent driving.[181] Similarly, one who engages in a rescue attempt may be under a duty to carry it through carefully to the extent that his resources permit.[182] A bookmaker, on the other hand, is not generally responsible for protecting his clients from the consequences of an addiction to gambling.[183] **2.92**

There are some relationships in which an even higher positive duty is imposed. These relationships involve persons such as trustees, directors or solicitors, commonly called 'fiduciaries'. They are required to act positively to protect the interests of their beneficiaries with reasonable care, but are also expected to show loyalty. Unless authorized, they must abstain from any interest of their own which might tempt them to sacrifice the beneficiaries' interests.[184] **2.93**

(c) Responsibility for dangers on property

The liability of an occupier of premises for the safety of his visitors is a positive duty to take steps to see that the visitors are reasonably safe.[185] The occupation of land and buildings also imposes duties to protect neighbours' property from damage arising from the occupier's property.[186] However, if the danger arises from the natural condition of **2.94**

---

[175] *Camarthenshire CC v Lewis* [1955] AC 549, HL.
[176] *Van Oppen v Clerk to the Bedford Charity Trustees* [1990] 1 WLR 235, CA; cf *Reid v Rush & Tompkins Group plc* [1990] 1 WLR 212, CA—no duty on employer to insure employee working overseas.
[177] [2001] QB 1134, CA.
[178] *Johnstone v Bloomsbury HA* [1992] QB 333, CA. Professional duties may include the duty to protect people from financial loss: *Henderson v Merrett Syndicates Ltd* [1995] 2 AC 145, HL; *White v Jones* [1995] 2 AC 207, HL.
[179] *Everett v Comojo (UK) Ltd* [2011] EWCA Civ 13, [2012] 1 WLR 150 (management of bar).
[180] *Horsley v MacLaren (The Ogopogo)* [1971] 2 Lloyd's Rep 410, SCC (private host of boat party).
[181] *Childs v Desormeaux* [2006] SCC 18, [2006] 1 SCR 643, SCC.
[182] *Horsley v MacLaren (The Ogopogo)* [1971] 2 Lloyd's Rep 410.
[183] *Calvert v William Hill Credit Ltd* [2008] EWCA Civ 1427, [2009] Ch 330.
[184] See 2.332–2.336.
[185] Occupiers' Liability Act 1957, see 2.176–2.182.
[186] *Goldman v Hargrave* [1967] 1 AC 645, PC; *Leakey v National Trust* [1980] QB 485, CA.

the land, the personal resources of the occupier may be taken into account in determining precisely what it is reasonable for the occupier to do for the protection of his neighbour.[187]

(d) Responsibility for the torts of others

2.95 Duties to prevent wrongful conduct by others are exceptional. If the miscreant is in the custody of the police or some other public authority, the authority may be under a such a duty. Prison authorities for instance are under a duty to prevent prisoners from attacking other inmates, and they may exceptionally be liable to persons whose property is damaged by prisoners in the course of an escape.[188] However, special considerations apply to public authorities. These are considered immediately below.

2.96 A leading authority on the possible liability of private citizens for the acts of others is *Smith v Littlewoods Organization Ltd.*[189] There the claimants sought to make the owners of a mothballed building liable for not preventing vandals from getting into it and setting it on fire, to the ultimate damage of the claimants' neighbouring property. It was conclusive against the owners having been under any duty that they did not know and had not been informed that strangers were obtaining entry. There was a marked difference of emphasis as to the approach their Lordships would have taken had the defendants had that knowledge. Lord Mackay thought that if the knowledge made the dangerous acts of the intruding vandals foreseeable and probable, then there would have been a duty to intervene to keep them out. Lord Goff thought it would require something more exceptional. There might be a duty in such circumstances if there were some known source of danger in the building and it was known that intruding trespassers might spark it off. Lord Goff's speech emphasizes that it is only very rarely that one person can incur a personal liability for the wrongful conduct of another.[190]

2.97 Lord Goff's approach to the issue of third party liability was preferred to that of Lord Mackay in the later House of Lords decision in *Mitchell v Glasgow City Council.*[191] According to Lord Brown, generally speaking people were not liable for the crimes of others: 'A is not ordinarily liable to victim B for injuries (or damage) deliberately inflicted by third party C'.[192] Building on Lord Goff's analysis in the earlier case, Lord Hope identified three situations in which such liability could exceptionally arise: (1) where the defendant created the source of danger;[193] (2) where the third party was under the supervision or control of the defendant;[194] and (3) where the defendant had assumed a responsibility to the claimant which lay within the scope of the duty that was alleged.[195] A very similar threefold categorization was adopted by Lord Brown.[196]

---

[187] *Goldman v Hargrave* [1967] 1 AC 645, PC; *Leakey v National Trust* [1980] QB 485, CA. See also 2.177.

[188] *Dorset Yacht Co v Home Office* [1970] AC 1004, HL.

[189] [1987] AC 241, HL, discussed in BS Markesinis, 'Negligence, Nuisance, and Affirmative Duties of Action' (1989) 105 LQR 104.

[190] See also 2.385–2.387, distinguishing such personal liability from vicarious liability.

[191] [2009] UKHL 11, [2009] 1 AC 874.

[192] [2009] UKHL 11, [2009] 1 AC 874, at [80].

[193] See, eg, *Haynes v Harwood* [1935] 1 KB 146, CA.

[194] See, eg, *Home Office v Dorset Yacht Co Ltd* [1970] AC 1004, HL.

[195] See, eg, *Stansbie v Troman* [1948] 2 KB 48, CA.

[196] [2009] UKHL 11, [2009] 1 AC 874, at [82].

(e) Liability of public bodies for failure to prevent damage

This is an important and controversial area of the law about which a great deal has been **2.98** written.[197] Only a brief outline can be given here. The necessary background is that, in English law, a public authority has no immunity from actions in tort, unless and so far as the body is able to invoke the defence of statutory authority for the acts in question. In principle, therefore, a public authority can be liable for breach of statutory duty to prevent damage, if the statute is construed as so intending. The difficult questions arise when it merely has a power to prevent harm. It was for a long time clear that there was no duty to exercise a power to prevent harm. Hence an authority could not be made liable in negligence in its chosen exercise of the power unless it made things worse than they would have been if it had done nothing at all. For doing nothing at all it would incur no liability.[198]

(i) The Anns case

That assumption was thrown into doubt by the decision of the House of Lords in *Anns* **2.99** *v Merton London BC*.[199] In that case it was accepted that a local authority with power to inspect the foundations of new buildings before the building went ahead could be liable in negligence for the manner in which it exercised that power, notwithstanding the fact that bad inspection could not make matters worse than no inspection at all. Thirteen years later the *Anns* case was overruled in *Murphy v Brentford DC*.[200]

(ii) Return to the pre-Anns position?

There is no doubt of the effect of *Murphy v Brentwood DC* on the law as to the inspection **2.100** by local authorities of foundations, but the wider question, whether statutory powers can be the basis for a common law duty of care, remains, after extensive litigation, controversial. Revisiting the matter in *Stovin v Wise*,[201] the House of Lords showed itself divided.

Lord Nicholls and Lord Slynn, dissenting, thought that the *Anns* decision had liberated the **2.101** law from the 'unacceptable yoke' of immunity from liability from negligence in the exercise of statutory powers, but Lord Hoffmann, speaking for the majority, was prepared to go no further than to leave open the question whether there could be any exceptions at all to the negative in *East Suffolk Rivers Catchment Board v Kent*.

On the facts of *Stovin v Wise* itself there was no liability. An accident had occurred on a **2.102** stretch of road which the local council knew to be dangerous because visibility was impaired by a bank of earth on neighbouring British Rail land. The council had been in dilatory negotiation with British Rail for months, until the matter had gone cold. The council had not availed itself of its statutory power to order British Rail to remove the obstruction. Nevertheless it was for the council to order its priorities. Mere foreseeability of injury did not put it under any duty to put roads and, in particular, this black spot at the top of its list. Lord Hoffmann thought that, if there were to be any exceptions, it could only be where it would be irrational not to exercise the power and, even then, there would have to be a discoverable policy in the relevant statute in favour of compensating those who suffered from failure to do so.

---

[197] R Bagshaw, 'The Duties of Care of Emergency Service Providers' [1999] LMCLQ 71; C Booth and D Squires, *The Negligence Liability of Public Authorities* (2006); D Nolan, 'The Liability of Public Authorities for Failing to Confer Benefits' (2011) 127 LQR 260.
[198] *East Suffolk Rivers Catchment Board v Kent* [1941] AC 74, HL.
[199] [1978] AC 728, HL.
[200] [1991] 1 AC 398, HL.
[201] [1996] AC 923, HL.

2.103 In *Gorringe v Calderdale MBC*[202] the claimant skidded and collided with a bus on a sharp bend in the road. The question for the House of Lords was whether the highway authority should be liable for failing to maintain a sign on the roadway which warned motorists to slow down. Lord Hoffmann's general approach was applied and the authority was held not to be liable for its pure omission. Lord Hoffmann described as 'ill advised' speculation his earlier comments on irrationality and said that he could not imagine a case in which a common law duty could be founded simply upon the failure (however irrational) to provide some benefit which a public authority has power to provide.[203]

2.104 The line between a failure to act and a careless act can sometimes be very fine. An example is the decision of the Court of Appeal in *Kane v New Forest DC*.[204] There the claimant was seriously injured as he emerged from a New Forest footpath on to a road. The defendant planning authority had required the construction of the path as part of a development to which it had consented. It had been warned more than once that the path could not safely give on to the inside of a bend, but it had not ensured that plans to open up the blind spot were carried through. The claimant's action was summarily dismissed on the basis of *Stovin v Wise*, but the Court of Appeal allowed it to proceed, distinguishing *Stovin v Wise* on the basis that the instant case was not a pure omission because the danger had been created by the defendant's act in requiring the construction of the footpath and its knowledge that it had been constructed in a dangerous way. It is a fine line between this decision and the later decision in *Gorringe*, where it was the earlier roadworks of the highway authority that had removed the 'slow' sign.

2.105 In *Stovin v Wise*, Lord Hoffmann also considered an alternative argument in favour of liability, based on general reliance by the public on measures being taken against a given harm. Mason J suggested in *Sutherland Shire Council v Heyman* that a duty of care would attach in a case in which powers were designed to prevent or minimize a risk of personal injury of such magnitude or complexity that individuals could not or probably would not take adequate steps to protect themselves.[205] Lord Hoffmann did not reject this approach but thought that it would require careful and difficult analysis in practice. For instance did it apply to the public's relationship with the fire brigades? Did the public rely on the brigades or on their insurance?

2.106 The answer to this question was given in the conjoined appeals in *Capital and Counties plc v Hampshire County Council*.[206] The Court of Appeal held that the traditional rule applied: fire brigades could only be sued if their intervention actually made things worse: 'If therefore they fail to turn up or fail to turn up in time because they have carelessly misunderstood the message, got lost on the way or run into a tree, they are not liable.'[207] Here the Court of Appeal showed no enthusiasm for any exceptions. It rejected any liability based on a specific assumption of responsibility to put out a particular fire arising from the acceptance of a call; liability was imposed only in the two cases where the intervention of the fire brigade made matters

---

[202] [2004] UKHL 15, [2004] 1 WLR 1057.
[203] [2004] UKHL 15, [2004] 1 WLR 1057, at [32] (Lord Hoffmann). See also at [4]–[5] (Lord Steyn).
[204] [2001] EWCA Civ 878, [2002] 1 WLR 312.
[205] [1985] 157 CLR 424, 464, HCA. A possible example of this approach in England is *Perrett v Collins* [1998] 2 Lloyd's Rep 255, CA, where the relevant defendant was the Popular Flying Association, exercising statutory powers under the Civil Aviation Act 1992 in relation to the airworthiness of small planes. See D Brodie, 'The Negligence of Public Authorities: A Traditional Solution' [1999] LMCLQ 16.
[206] [1997] QB 1004, CA. The opposite result was reached in the High Court of Australia in *Pyrenees Shire Council v Day* (1998) 192 CLR 330, HCA.
[207] [1997] QB 1004, 1030, CA, *per* Stuart Smith LJ. See also *OLL Ltd v Secretary of State for Transport* [1997] 3 All ER 897, where May J held that the coastguard could not be liable for misdirecting other rescue services; and *Michael v CC South Wales Police* [2015] UKSC 2, [2015] 2 All ER 635, where it was held that the police had owed no duty of care to a woman who made an emergency call reporting a threat by her former partner to kill her, and who was murdered by him before the police arrived at her house.

worse by turning off the sprinkler system. The general principle must reflect the court's view that fire brigades have difficult decisions to make between the conflicting interests of different property owners. In *Kent v Griffiths* where there was no such conflict, the Court of Appeal held that an ambulance service did incur a duty of care to attend once it accepted a call and undertook promptly to attend.[208]

(iii) Conflict of interest arguments

The competing interests of parties may affect the incidence of duties owed by public author-   **2.107**
ities. In *Jain v Trent Strategic Health Authority*, it was held there was no duty by a regulatory authority to the owners of a nursing home because such a duty might conflict with the authority's primary responsibility to the residents of the home.[209] According to Lord Scott:

> [W]here action is taken by a state authority under statutory powers designed for the benefit or protection of a particular class of persons, a tortious duty of care will not be held to be owed by the state authority to others whose interests may be adversely affected by an exercise of the statutory power.[210]

Other examples of the operation of this 'conflict of interest' principle are *JD v East Berkshire Community Health NHS Trust*,[211] where it was held that those carrying out duties under child protection legislation owed no duty to the parents of a child they suspected of being abused, and *Harris v Evans*,[212] where it was held that a proprietor of bungee-jumping facilities had no claim in negligence for economic loss he suffered after being served with local authority prohibition notices issued on the faulty advice of safety inspectors.

(iv) Claims for damages under the Human Rights Act 1998

Claims for damages can also now be brought against public authorities under the Human Rights   **2.108**
Act 1998, on the grounds that the authority has violated the rights of the claimant under the European Convention on Human Rights.[213] Such actions are sometimes brought concurrently with claims in negligence, but the Human Rights Act may give protection in circumstances where the common law of negligence does not, as where, eg, the complaint concerns an omission on the authority's part, as opposed to positive conduct causing harm,[214] or where the claimant has not suffered a form of harm which amounts to 'damage' for negligence purposes.[215]

(2) Psychiatric Injury

Mental suffering in the form of pain, fear, emotional distress or shock is clearly actionable   **2.109**
so far as it is an aspect of physical injury. Most personal injury actions will include claims for pain and suffering and loss of the amenities of life. Emotional and psychiatric damage which is not an aspect of the claimant's own physical injury is treated as a special case.[216] It is subjected to restrictive rules which, precisely because restriction of liability is their function, can seem arbitrary and unjust. One reason for this special treatment is that knowledge

---

[208] [2000] 2 WLR 1158, CA.
[209] [2009] UKHL 4, [2009] 1 AC 853.
[210] [2009] UKHL 4, [2009] 1 AC 853, at [28].
[211] [2005] UKHL 23, [2005] 2 AC 373.
[212] [1998] 1 WLR 1285, CA.
[213] Human Rights Act 1998, s 7.
[214] See, eg, *Van Colle v Chief Constable of Hertfordshire* [2008] UKHL 50, [2009] 1 AC 225. Lord Bingham, dissenting, regretted the disparity between the two regimes, but the majority were unconcerned.
[215] See, eg, *Keenan v United Kingdom* (2001) 33 EHRR 38, ECtHR (solitary confinement of a mentally ill prisoner could amount to inhuman and degrading treatment for the purposes of Art 3 of the Convention even if no tangible injury resulted).
[216] It is comprehensively treated in PR Handford, *Mullany and Handford's Tort Liability for Psychiatric Damage* (2nd edn, 2006).

of psychiatric illness is relatively recent and has been regarded as presenting difficulties of proof. Another is certainly a fear of an excessive number of claims, of opening the floodgates of litigation and raising insurance premiums to unacceptable levels.

2.110　In modern times this fear has been fuelled by the relatively few occasions on which horrific events, such as the Hillsborough stadium disaster, have been caught on television, witnessed by millions of people, all of them potentially traumatized. We are still some way from understanding the true scale of the possible escalation of liability. Whether the fear is justified or not, it has caused claims for psychiatric damage to be surrounded by increasingly complicated restrictions on recovery.

(a) The earliest instances of liability

2.111　The law on recovery for psychiatric damage developed slowly. Liability for intentional conduct causing shock and illness was imposed in *Wilkinson v Downton* in 1897.[217] The first successful action for negligently causing shock resulting in a miscarriage was *Dulieu v White & Sons* in 1901, where the defendant negligently drove his van into the public house where the claimant was serving behind the bar.[218] Kennedy J emphasized, however, that she recovered because she was in fear for her own personal safety.

2.112　Psychiatric damage caused by fear for others was not admitted until *Hambrook v Stokes Bros* in 1925, where a mother suffered shock through fear that her children had been run over by a runaway lorry which she saw gathering speed downhill towards the place where she had just left them.[219] The Court of Appeal could not accept that only those who feared for themselves could sue: a mother whose first thought was for her children must be allowed to recover.

2.113　*Hambrook v Stokes* set the pattern in which the law would develop for the rest of the century. It opened the door to relational or 'secondary' victims who had suffered shock. But it also introduced a limiting requirement, that the shock must result from what the mother had heard or seen with her own unaided senses, not from what she had been told by a third party. Both aspects of the innovation have been productive of much litigation. The only one of the early cases to reach the House of Lords was *Bourhill v Young*.[220] The pursuer had been an immediate witness of a highway collision in Edinburgh. The shock caused her to miscarry. However, the crash was between strangers. It did not involve anyone near and dear to herself, and she herself was not at risk of any physical impact. The House held that the motorcyclist responsible for the accident owed no duty of care to her because he could not reasonably have foreseen that she would be affected by his negligence.

2.114　It is probably now unnecessary to go back to the older decisions. The extensive litigation of the last 20 years, in particular the four leading decisions of the House of Lords since 1982, has given detailed consideration to the modern law.

(b) Four leading cases in outline

2.115　Two of the four major decisions are closely connected. They both arose from the Hillsborough football stadium disaster. Due to police mismanagement, a large number of people were crowded into one part of the ground. In the resulting crush 95 people were killed and over 400 were injured. *Alcock v Chief Constable of South Yorkshire* was an action brought by

---

[217] [1897] 2 QB 57; PR Glazebrook, '*Wilkinson v Downton*: A Centenary Postscript' (1997) 32 Irish Jurist (NS) 46. See 2.340–2.343. Liability in modern law for words or conduct intended to cause physical or psychiatric damage without justification or excuse is considered in *James Rhodes v OPO* [2015] UKSC 32.
[218] [1901] 2 KB 669.
[219] [1925] 1 KB 141, CA.
[220] [1943] AC 92, HL.

relatives and friends of the victims for compensation for the psychiatric damage caused by the event.[221] All their claims failed. *Frost v Chief Constable of South Yorkshire* was an action brought by the police officers on duty at Hillsborough for the psychiatric damage they had suffered.[222] Their actions also failed.

The other two decisions arose from highway accidents. In *McLoughlin v O'Brian* a mother   **2.116** suffered serious illness in the immediate aftermath of a catastrophic road accident which injured her husband and two of her children and caused the death of her third child.[223] She was told of the accident some two hours after it happened and, driven to the hospital, saw the injuries and heard of the death. Her claim succeeded. In *Page v Smith* the claimant himself was involved in a motor accident of a relatively minor kind, in that nobody suffered physical injury.[224] He almost immediately suffered a relapse into chronic fatigue syndrome, from which he had previously suffered. He was held to have a good claim.

It is notable that in the mass disaster cases the House of Lords insists on the need to main-   **2.117** tain, and even to raise, the barriers against excessive liability. In both the highway cases, a more relaxed view was taken. In *McLoughlin v O'Brian* Lord Bridge went so far as to say that knowledge of psychiatric problems had advanced to the stage where it was no longer necessary to have special rules. Lord Wilberforce was more cautious, preferring to mark out special rules for sufficient proximity, and in the *Alcock* case a unanimous House of Lords preferred Lord Wilberforce's three-pronged test of sufficient proximity.

The present law on psychiatric damage can only be stated in terms of special rules. To start   **2.118** with there is a general exclusion of recovery for mere misery, as distinct from illness arising from shock. Thereafter it is necessary to distinguish between primary and secondary victims.

(c) The requirement of psychiatric illness

Leaving aside the suffering which is an aspect of physical injury, compensation is given only   **2.119** for a recognized psychiatric illness, hence not for such ordinary human emotions as grief or anxiety, however foreseeable.[225] The line may be hard to draw, since grief may in extreme cases develop into a psychiatric disorder, which is then actionable.[226] There is one statutory exception to the exclusion of damages for grief: a fixed award for bereavement is payable to the spouse or civil partner of a person or the parents of an unmarried minor tortiously killed under section 1A of the Fatal Accidents Act 1976.[227]

The name used in the early cases, which at first required shock producing physical conse-   **2.120** quences, is nervous shock. Some judges have criticized the term as pre-scientific.[228] With the advance of science the unprovable requirement of physical lesion has mutated to psychiatric illness, but one of the most significant aspects of the first Hillsborough case, *Alcock v Chief Constable of South Yorkshire Police*, is that it emphasized the requirement of shock. The psychiatric illness must have been brought on by a shock. Lord Keith said that the illness

---

[221] [1992] 1 AC 310, HL.
[222] [1999] 2 AC 455, HL.
[223] [1983] 1 AC 410, HL.
[224] [1996] AC 155, HL.
[225] *Reilly v Merseyside HA* (1995) 6 Med LR 246, CA; *Rothwell v Chemical and Insulating Co Ltd* [2007] UKHL 39, [2008] 1 AC 281.
[226] *Vernon v Bosley (No 1)* [1997] 1 All ER 577, CA: a father witnessed unsuccessful attempts to save his children from a car in a river, and later suffered pathological grief syndrome, for which damages were awarded. Note, however, *Vernon v Bosley (No 2)* [1999] QB 18, CA.
[227] See 4.131.
[228] *McLoughlin v O'Brian* [1983] 1 AC 410, 432, HL, *per* Lord Bridge; *Attia v British Gas plc* [1988] QB 304, 317, CA, *per* Bingham LJ.

must be caused by 'a sudden assault on the nervous system'[229] or, in Lord Ackner's words, 'the sudden appreciation by sight or sound of a horrifying event which violently agitates the mind'.[230] It is not argued that psychiatric illness is more likely, or more likely to be serious, if produced by a single, sudden event, so it is hard to see the rule as anything other than an arbitrary device for limiting the number of claimants. The rule has produced harsh decisions, in which parents who have watched a child's lingering death in hospital have been denied compensation because their psychiatric illness was not the result of a single sudden event.[231] However, recent decisions have shown flexibility as to what counts as a single 'event'. In *North Glamorgan NHS Trust v Walters*,[232] eg, a period of 36 hours during which a mother saw her baby die was held to be a single, horrifying event. It is not completely clear whether this restrictive requirement also applies to primary, as opposed to secondary, victims.[233]

(d) Primary victims

2.121　The distinction between primary and secondary victims is central to the modern law. A primary victim is one who is, or reasonably believes himself to be, within the area of physical danger.[234] A secondary victim is one who is not in the danger area but suffers shock because of a relationship with the primary victim.

2.122　A primary victim can recover for psychiatric illness on the foundation of the duty of care owed by the defendant not to cause physical injury. If there is a danger of physical injury, the claimant can recover for psychiatric injury whether or not physical injury occurs, and whether or not psychiatric injury was foreseeable. In *Page v Smith* a man recovered for the recurrence of his chronic fatigue syndrome when involved in a minor collision between two cars which would not have been likely to cause shock to the average person, on the grounds that he was in the area of physical danger. Prior to this case, it had been settled law that foreseeability of shock was an essential element in all shock cases. However, the House of Lords held in *Page* that for foreseeability purposes no distinction should be drawn between physical and psychiatric harm, so that a primary victim physically endangered by the defendant's negligence need not establish that psychiatric injury had been foreseeable as well. By contrast, Lord Lloyd explained, secondary victims were required to prove the foreseeability of psychiatric harm because, not being in the area of physical danger, psychiatric harm was the only form of personal injury a secondary victim could sustain.[235]

2.123　This sharp distinction between the rules applicable to primary and secondary victims has proved controversial.[236] Lord Lloyd's justification for drawing it was that the restrictions on recovery by secondary victims, being control mechanisms imposed for reasons of policy, were not necessary in claims by primary victims. A similar point was made by Lord Oliver in the *Alcock* case,[237] but he drew the line in a different place. Lord Oliver's distinction was between those directly involved in an accident as participants and those who merely witness injury to others. As his

---

[229] [1992] 1 AC 310, 398, HL.

[230] [1992] 1 AC 310, 401, HL.

[231] *Sion v Hampstead Health Authority* [1994] 5 Med LR 170. The Law Commission has recommended the abolition of the shock requirement: Law Commission, *Liability for Psychiatric Illness* (Law Com No 249, 1998) para 5.33.

[232] [2003] EWCA Civ 1792, [2003] PIQR P16.

[233] 2.125.

[234] *Page v Smith* [1996] AC 155, HL; *McFarlane v EE Caledonia Ltd* [1994] 2 All ER 1, CA.

[235] [1996] AC 155, 187, HL, *per* Lord Lloyd of Berwick.

[236] For criticism, see the speech of Lord Goff in *Frost v Chief Constable of South Yorkshire* [1999] 2 AC 455, HL; and S Bailey and D Nolan, 'The *Page* v Smith Saga: A Tale of Inauspicious Origins and Unintended Consequences' [2010] CLJ 495. cf Law Commission, *Liability for Psychiatric Illness* (Law Com No 249, 1998) paras 5.45–5.54.

[237] [1992] 1 AC 310, 407–408, HL.

examples showed, not all participants were persons in physical danger. Direct participation seemed to be a more flexible and appropriate test of proximity than physical danger.

Subsequent litigation has followed the *Page v Smith* classification but a later decision of the **2.124** House of Lords suggests that some flexibility remains. In *W v Essex CC*[238] the House of Lords refused to strike out an action by parents who had not witnessed the sexual abuse of their children and had been in no danger themselves, but felt responsible for unwittingly allowing the child abuser into their home. On the other hand, in *Rothwell v Chemical and Insulating Co Ltd*[239] the House of Lords held that a claimant who had developed clinical depression when he realized that he had been negligently exposed to asbestos dust by an employer, with the result that he was at a higher risk of asbestos-related disease, was not a primary victim. According to Lord Rodger, in order for a claimant to qualify as a primary victim, the psychiatric injury must have been triggered by 'the immediate effects of a past traumatic event'.[240]

The distinction between primary and secondary victims, derived from the model of traumatic **2.125** catastrophes, does not comfortably cover situations in which there is no single traumatic event. In *Barber v Somerset County Council*[241] employees, including school teachers, had suffered breakdowns and continuing psychiatric injury because of years of overwork, exacerbated by innovations and efficiency gains such as are now commonplace. Such claimants count as primary victims. There are no artificial inhibitions of their right to recover damages from their employer, as there are for secondary victims, and an employee suffering psychiatric injury at work is now treated no differently in principle from an employee suffering physical injury.[242]

However, in such cases, an instrument of restraint is old-fashioned insistence on the standard **2.126** of the reasonable person in the employer's position, endowed with neither special prescience nor limitless resources. The early signs of mental illness are often not visible and, if they are picked up, there is often not much that can be done. It is rarely reasonable to sack someone for his own good. However, if a victim has asked for assistance, or has been treated in an exploitative and unsympathetic manner, psychiatric harm may be reasonably foreseeable.[243] Further, psychiatric injury may also be reasonably foreseeable if the employer knows that particular stresses carry with them the risk of psychiatric injury, even if the vulnerability of the particular employee is not known.[244]

(e) Secondary victims

The conditions governing the recovery of compensation by secondary victims received their **2.127** present form in *Alcock v Chief Constable of Yorkshire*,[245] in which the House of Lords unanimously adopted the triple test of proximity proposed by Lord Wilberforce in *McLoughlin v O'Brian*.[246] It was necessary to show proximity of relationship, proximity in time and space,

---

[238] [2001] 2 AC 592, HL; *Dooley v Cammell Laird & Co Ltd* [1951] 1 Lloyd's Rep 271.

[239] [2007] UKHL 39, [2008] 1 AC 281.

[240] [2007] UKHL 39, [2008] 1 AC 281, at [95].

[241] [2002] EWCA Civ 76, [2002] 2 All ER 1, CA. The principles were affirmed by the House of Lords: [2004] UKHL 13, [2004] 1 WLR 1089, HL.

[242] *Hartman v South Essex Mental Health and Community Care NHS Trust* [2005] EWCA Civ 6, [2005] ICR 782.

[243] This was the case of Mrs Jones in the conjoined appeals in the Court of Appeal [2002] EWCA Civ 76, [2002] 2 All ER 1. No appeal was brought to the House of Lords by the employer in her case. 'Close to the borderline', but allowing recovery, was Mr Barker's case where the only known information was that the employee had taken three weeks' leave for reasons explained by his doctor as stress-related: *Barber v Somerset County Council* [2004] UKHL 13, [2004] 1 WLR 1089.

[244] *Melville v Home Office* [2005] EWCA Civ 6, [2005] ICR 782.

[245] [1992] 1 AC 310, HL.

[246] [1983] 1 AC 410, HL.

and hearing or seeing the event or its immediate aftermath with one's own unaided senses, rather than being told by a third party. Lord Wilberforce had speculated on the answer to be given to a claimant who had watched a traumatic event on television.

2.128   In *Alcock*, these criteria were applied to the claims of various relatives and friends of the primary victims, who had been affected by the disaster in different ways: being present in another part of the stadium, watching the disaster on live television or identifying bodies some hours later. There was a high degree of agreement both as to result and as to reasoning. None of the claims succeeded, since none satisfied every element in Lord Wilberforce's profile of close proximity.

(i) Proximity of relationship

2.129   Recovery is not limited to parents and spouses, or indeed to any specific relationship. Proximity of relationship requires a close tie of love and affection, which is a question of fact to be established by evidence. In some relationships, such as parents or spouses, the closeness of the tie can be presumed, unless there is evidence to the contrary. No firm guidance was given as to which relationships benefited from the presumption of affection. Lord Keith was willing to include fiancées but not grandchildren, Lord Ackner was not willing to include brothers, much less brothers-in-law.

(ii) Proximity in time and space

2.130   It was not enough to have witnessed the disaster on live television, because pictures of the suffering of identifiable individuals were not shown and, since such pictures would be contrary to the broadcasting code of ethics, it was not foreseeable that they would be. Nor was it enough to have witnessed the accident from another part of the stadium, since individual relatives were not identifiable; nor to have identified the body nine hours later. That was not part of the immediate aftermath.[247]

(iii) Hearing and seeing

2.131   Watching live television was not sufficient proximity in the circumstances of the code of ethics. If pictures of individuals had been shown, the fact that they should not have been shown would justify a conclusion that the chain of causation had been broken. There was, however, some support for the idea that an unexpected disaster on television, such as an exploding balloon, might cause actionable psychiatric damage to the relatives of those known to be aboard. It has since been held that if the accident is not actually seen at any stage, there can be no recovery for 'survivor's guilt' by one who thinks himself unwittingly responsible for it.[248]

2.132   Suppose that the traumatized person has witnessed the event but that it was brought about by the primary victim himself, negligently or deliberately seeking to injure himself. Can the primary victim be sued in the same way as rescuers have succeeded in recovering for physical injury from those who negligently put themselves in danger?[249] It has been held in *Greatorex v Greatorex*,[250] following dicta in a number of cases,[251] that in such a case the witness has no action. A father who as a fireman was a rescuer of his own son from a car crash caused by the son's drunken and careless driving could not claim to be a primary victim, not

---

[247]   Compare the time gap of around two hours in *McLoughlin v O'Brian* [1983] 1 AC 410, HL. Recovery was also allowed in *Galli-Atkinson v Seghal* [2003] EWCA Civ 697, where the interval between the accident and the claimant seeing the victim's body in the mortuary was two hours and the purpose of the visit to the mortuary was not merely formal identification.

[248]   *Hunter v British Coal Corporation* [1999] QB 140, CA.

[249]   *Harrison v British Railways Board* [1981] 3 All ER 679.

[250]   [2000] 1 WLR 1970.

[251]   *Alcock v Chief Constable of South Yorkshire* [1992] 1 AC 310, 418, HL, citing the judgment of Deane J in *Jaensch v Coffey* (1984) 155 CLR 549, HCA.

having faced any physical danger himself. On the other hand he did satisfy the restrictive conditions which normally allow secondary victims to recover—relationship of affection, direct perception, immediate aftermath. However, he could not recover in respect of his post-traumatic stress disorder because on the facts it was not appropriate to recognize a duty of care. One reason given was that such actions would be potentially productive of family strife. Perhaps more convincing was the argument that liability would curtail an individual's right of self-determination. There are issues of individual autonomy here which, in the Law Commission's view, should be dealt with in legislation.[252]

(iv) Other possible cases

2.133 From the whole class of those who suffer foreseeable psychiatric injury, the *Alcock* guidelines, with their combination of the distinction between primary and secondary victims and the profile of special proximity, effectively eliminated the majority of potential claimants. There nevertheless remained some doubtful cases.

2.134 **The unrelated spectator.** Both Lord Ackner and Lord Keith thought that there might be accidents so dreadful that psychiatric illness would be foreseeable even to unrelated bystanders. However, as the Law Commission commented, if Hillsborough were not such a disaster, it was difficult to imagine what would be, and the possibility of such a claim by unrelated bystanders appears to have been ruled out in the subsequent Court of Appeal decision of *MacFarlane v EE Caledonia Ltd*.[253]

2.135 **The rescuer.** It was argued in *Frost v Chief Constable of South Yorkshire*[254] that the common law's policy of encouraging rescuers should entitle them to recover as participants in, or primary victims of, an accident.[255] However, the House of Lords held that, while the status of rescuer precluded the defences of *volenti non fit injuria* (no wrong to one who consents) or *novus actus interveniens* (new event interrupts the chain of causation),[256] a rescuer could only recover for psychiatric injury on the same basis as other claimants, as a primary victim in the area of physical danger, or as a secondary victim related to the primary victim and otherwise within the required profile of close proximity.

2.136 **The employee.** It was also argued in the *Frost* case that, as part of the duty to provide a safe system of work, an employer owed a duty to employees to take reasonable care not to expose them to psychiatric injury. The answer was again negative: the duty owed to employees did not exempt them from satisfying the other conditions of recovery for psychiatric injury.[257] However, the situation is different where the psychiatric injury results not from a traumatic event but from the stress of the employee's work. It is clear in modern employment law that an employer's responsibilities can extend further than physical safety.[258] In *Walker v Northumberland CC*, without reference to the psychiatric injury cases, it was held that the defendants were liable for subjecting one of their employees to excessive stress in dealing, without proper support, with child abuse cases.[259] There was one special feature in the *Walker* case. Walker had been persuaded to return to work after a first breakdown by a promise to provide additional support. In the House of Lords in *Barber v Somerset County Council*,[260] Lord Rodger observed that the corollary to this was that the contract of employment should

---

252 Law Com No 249, paras 5.43 and 6.49.
253 [1994] 2 All ER 1, CA.
254 [1999] 2 AC 455, HL.
255 *Chadwick v British Railway Board* [1967] 1 WLR 912.
256 Paras 2.203 and 2.68.
257 [1999] 2 AC 455, 464 (Lord Griffiths), 497–498 (Lord Steyn), 506–507 (Lord Hoffmann), HL.
258 *Johnstone v Bloomsbury HA* [1992] QB 333, CA; *Malik v BCCI* [1998] AC 20, HL.
259 [1995] 1 All ER 737.
260 [2004] UKHL 13, [2004] 1 WLR 1089, at [31]–[35].

be scrutinized carefully to see whether such an undertaking is contractually limited in any way. The undertaking or assumption of particular responsibility also explains the decision of the Court of Appeal in *Butchart v Home Office*[261] to wave aside the restrictions in *Frost* in a case in which a psychologically vulnerable prisoner suffered psychological harm after being left with an at-risk prisoner who committed suicide.

2.137 **Shooting the messenger.** It is unclear whether an action lies against one who negligently communicates distressing information which causes psychiatric injury. The only modern authority, *AB v Tameside and Glossop HA*, decided that the authority had not in fact been negligent but did not decide the issue of principle.[262] It could be argued that a distinction should be made between true and false information in the interests of free speech.[263] In *Leach v Chief Constable of Gloucestershire*[264] the court refused to strike out a claim for compensation for failure to provide counselling for the task of listening to distressing information.

2.138 **The immediate aftermath.** The immediate aftermath rule is still largely undefined. In the *Alcock* case, Lord Keith, following the High Court of Australia,[265] thought that the aftermath remains 'immediate' as long as the victim is in the distressing untreated condition produced by the traumatic incident.[266] Lord Ackner and Lord Jauncey emphasized the relevance of lapse of time. However, in *W v Essex County Council*[267] Lord Slynn did not strike out the action of parents who only discovered that their children had been sexually abused after several weeks.

2.139 **Damage to property.** In *Attia v British Gas* the Court of Appeal refused to strike out a claim for psychiatric damage caused by the claimant's witnessing the destruction of her house by fire.[268] The case may be explained as turning on remoteness of damage consequent on an admitted breach of duty.

(f) Reform

2.140 It goes almost without saying that this accretion of rules is not capable of logical or scientific explanation. Nor has the House of Lords sought to provide one. Lord Oliver thought that they represented the current judicial view of what was acceptable, and that the whole matter would ultimately be better dealt with by legislation.[269]

2.141 The shape of the problem is clear. First, the complexity of the present law is not redeemed by clarity in the resolution of individual cases. There is no clearer evidence of this than the need for repeated appeals to the House of Lords. Secondly, there is the evident arbitrariness of the distinctions made, which are little more than elaborations of the lines which were drawn on an ad hoc basis in the decisions of the first half of the twentieth century. Thirdly, there are persistent uncertainties, particularly about the borderlines between the rules It is not so clear how these problems might be solved. Indeed the state of the law reflects the difficulty of coming up with solutions which are principled and practical.

---

[261] [2006] EWCA Civ 239, [2006] 1 WLR 1155.

[262] (1997) 8 Med LR 91, CA: communicating HIV exposure. The health authority made concessions which eliminated the point of principle.

[263] Law Com No 249, paras 7.32–7.33.

[264] [1999] 1 WLR 1421, CA.

[265] [1992] 1 AC 310, 397–398, HL following *Jaensch v Coffey* (1984) 155 CLR 549, HCA.

[266] eg *McLoughlin v O'Brian* [1983] 1 AC 410, HL: visit to hospital where injured members of the family were being treated, one having died.

[267] [2000] 2 WLR 601, HL.

[268] [1988] QB 304, CA.

[269] *Alcock v Chief Constable of South Yorkshire* [1992] 1 AC 310, 418–19, HL. This opinion was echoed in *Frost v Chief Constable of South Yorkshire* [1999] 2 AC 455, 500, HL, *per* Lord Goff.

There are two radical solutions, and several compromises. The choice between them will depend **2.142** on how well, on reflection, each meets the criticisms of the present state of the law and the anomalies which it creates, while retaining public confidence. There can be no question of the anomalies. As Lord Goff said in the *Frost* case, if two rescuers enter a train after a crash and are equally affected by the horrors of the spectacle before them, both suffering long-term psychiatric consequences, their right to recover will depend on whether the carriage they happened to be working in was liable to collapse, since the (unrealized) threat of physical injury will lead to classification as a primary victim and hence to damages for psychiatric injury.[270]

The *Frost* case itself reflects the necessity of public acceptability. Lord Hoffmann frankly **2.143** acknowledged that the reason for his decision was that it would not be publicly acceptable for police officers at Hillsborough to be compensated when the relatives of the victims were not.[271] Again, applicability speaks for itself. Repeated judgments of the House of Lords have failed to clarify the criteria upon which cases should be settled.

The first radical solution is powerfully argued by the leading authority on liability for psy- **2.144** chiatric illness, Professor Handford.[272] His solution is to stop treating psychiatric illness as a special category of tortious liability and to apply instead the general rules and tests for establishing liability for physical harm. However attractive this strategy might appear to be—it received the support of Lord Bridge in *McLoughlin v O'Brian*[273]—it is unlikely that is open to the English courts in the absence of legislation. It assumes that the floodgates anxieties are unreal and the fear of hugely increased insurance premiums correspondingly illusory. Moreover, in the absence of jury trial such a solution might merely transfer the problem from the appellate courts to the courts of first instance. It is not clear that anomalies which emerge from the finding of the facts will ever be more acceptable to the public than the anomalies which currently lie open in the statement of the law.

The alternative radical solution is proposed by Professor Stapleton. She would be prepared to **2.145** abolish all claims for psychiatric injury not consequential on physical harm.[274] This solution is equally unavailable to English courts in the absence of legislation. In other respects, it may have much to commend it in discouraging show trials designed to pinpoint blame rather than to compensate for loss. But perhaps for this very reason it is unlikely to be publicly acceptable.

The Law Commission's investigation of this area has not resulted in support for either of the **2.146** radical solutions, certainly not for any hasty repudiation of the floodgates argument.[275] The Commission's judgment is that some improvements could be achieved and that legislation is desirable to that end. It proposes no more than modification of the regime worked out in the cases, tending towards a slight expansion of liability. The proposals would remove the requirement of shock[276] and, for close relationships, the requirement of witnessing the event or its aftermath.[277] It would also introduce a statutory list of the relationships in which a close tie is deemed to exist,[278] though without restraining judicial development of protection for unrelated bystanders.[279]

---

[270] [1999] 2 AC 455, 487, HL.
[271] [1999] 2 AC 455, 510, HL.
[272] PR Handford, *Mullany and Handford's Tort Liability for Psychiatric Damage* (2nd edn, 2006) ch 15.
[273] [1983] 1 AC 410, HL.
[274] J Stapleton, 'In Restraint of Tort' in P Birks (ed), *The Frontiers of Liability* (1994) vol 2, 95–96.
[275] Law Commission, *Liability for Psychiatric Illness* (Law Com No 249, 1998) paras 6.8–6.10.
[276] Law Commission, *Liability for Psychiatric Illness*, para 5.33.
[277] Law Commission, *Liability for Psychiatric Illness*, para 6.16.
[278] Law Commission, *Liability for Psychiatric Illness*, para 6.26.
[279] Law Commission, *Liability for Psychiatric Illness*, para 7.15.

(3) Economic Loss

2.147 In a loose sense the great majority of actions in tort are concerned to make good economic loss. However, serious problems are encountered wherever the loss in question has arisen independently of physical damage. Separate nominate torts provide for the recovery of such pure economic loss in certain situations in which it is intentionally caused.[280] In actions for negligence, economic loss can be recovered if it is the direct result of physical damage to the claimant's person or property. Thus an action for damages for personal injuries will usually include a claim for loss of earnings caused by the injury and for medical expenses incurred. But the general rule is that there is otherwise no duty of care in respect of economic loss. There has been constant pressure to break down this barrier.

(a) The exclusion of liability for foreseeable pure economic loss

2.148 The difficult area is 'pure' economic loss, financial losses suffered other than as a result of physical damage to the claimant's person or property. There is on some facts a fine line between economic loss arising from physical damage and pure economic loss,[281] but, once the loss is classified as 'pure' economic loss, the general rule is that it is not recoverable in an action for negligence. A number of reasons are commonly put forward for this position.

2.149 The exclusion of liability is most frequently justified by the floodgates argument, the fear that claims for pure economic loss would lead to indeterminate, unmanageable liability. Convincing examples of the danger are easily found. Releasing the foot-and-mouth disease virus will entail physical damage to some but may bring financial disaster to a whole interdependent agricultural community.[282] Carelessly cutting a power cable in an industrial area may cause a wholly unpredictable amount of financial loss to an unpredictable number of businesses dependent on it, and these financial losses may spread in an ever-widening circle.[283] In such cases the floodgates danger is a real one. In others it is less convincing.

2.150 There are other arguments to justify the denial of any duty of care to protect people from pure economic loss. Such further objections can include the undesirability of the interference of tort law with market principles of competition and distortion of market principles of risk (against which it is often said that an efficient activity should bear its own costs). It is said to be easier, and more efficient, to insure against one's own losses than the losses of others and that protection of financial and commercial rights is properly a matter for the law of contract. A secondary argument allied to the floodgates argument is that the indeterminacy of these claims undermines commercial certainty. Finally, in the public law context, there are often implications for the resources and budgets of local authorities.[284]

(b) Economic loss arising from damage to another's person or property

2.151 The longest and most consistently negative line of English authority is the succession of cases which have rejected claims for economic loss resulting from damage to someone else's person or property. The traditional position of the common law is clear: only the person injured in a personal injury case, or a person with a possessory or proprietary right to property which

---

[280] 2.356–2.362.
[281] Hence the dissenting judgment of Edmund Davies LJ in *Spartan Steel and Alloys Ltd v Martin & Co Ltd* [1973] QB 27, arguing that, provided economic loss was foreseeable and direct, the occurrence of physical damage was irrelevant.
[282] *Weller & Co v Foot & Mouth Disease Research Institute* [1969] 1 QB 569.
[283] *Spartan Steel and Alloys Ltd v Martin & Co Ltd* [1973] QB 27, 38–39, CA, *per* Lord Denning MR.
[284] *Yuen Kun Yeu v AG of Hong Kong* [1988] AC 175, PC; *Murphy v Brentwood DC* [1991] 1 AC 398, HL.

is damaged can sue for resulting economic loss.[285] In personal injury cases this position has been modified to some degree by statute, as by the Fatal Accidents Acts, and also by some still imperfectly understood developments in the law of damages.[286] These developments are confined to family relationships and others very similar.

The exclusion of liability is rigorously maintained in other contexts. Thus in *Spartan Steel* **2.152** *and Alloys Ltd v Martin & Co Ltd*[287] the defendants' negligence damaged a cable belonging to the electricity board, causing a power failure. The claimants, whose factory was brought to a standstill, obtained damages for the physical damage to metal in their furnaces at the time of the failure and for the financial loss resulting from that physical damage, but not for the general financial loss of business incurred during the period before power was restored. A majority of the Court of Appeal held that the last item was pure economic loss and irrecoverable. It not infrequently happens that such an interruption of the power supply forces shops and offices to close. There is no liability in negligence for the lost business.

Since the principal argument used to deny recovery in these cases is the floodgates argument, **2.153** a question arises whether an exception to the general rule should be admitted on facts in which the floodgates danger does not exist, because the class of persons likely to be affected is known to be limited. In Australia this exception has been made.[288] Thus in *Caltex Oil* *(Australia) Ltd v The Dredge Willemstad*,[289] the defendants had damaged an undersea oil pipeline and put the claimants to the expense of transporting oil by different means. The High Court allowed recovery of this economic loss because the claimants belonged to a limited class of identifiable persons who would suffer from such negligence.

In England, however, the exclusionary rule has been strictly adhered to even where the danger **2.154** of indeterminate liability is remote. In *Candlewood Navigation Corporation Ltd v Mitsui OSK Lines (The Mineral Transporter)*,[290] a time charterer of a damaged ship was refused recovery in tort for want of the relevant proprietary right to the ship. There the Privy Council expressly rejected the High Court of Australia's *Willemstad* exception. The main reason given was that the rule against recovery of relational loss was clear, well-known and internationally accepted. Admitting exceptions would detract from the clarity and certainty of the rule.

In *Leigh and Sillivan Ltd v Aliakmon Shipping Co Ltd (The Aliakmon)*,[291] buyers of steel coils **2.155** shipped to them from Korea sued the carriers in tort for negligently damaging them en route. They lost. Even though risk had passed to them, so that they still had to pay the seller under the contract of sale, at the relevant time the property had not yet passed so they had no proprietary right to the damaged goods.[292] In the Court of Appeal Robert Goff LJ argued for an

---

[285] *Cattle v Stockton Waterworks* (1875) LR 10 QB 453.

[286] *Hunt v Severs* [1994] 2 AC 350, HL. The underlying proposition is that damages representing the reasonable value of gratuitous care provided to a disabled victim will be awarded to the victim to be held on trust for the carer. To the contrary: *Kars v Kars* (1996) 187 CLR 354, HCA. See further, P Matthews and M Lunney, 'A Tortfeasor's Lot is not a Happy One' (1995) 58 MLR 395; S Degeling, 'Trusts of Damages' (1999) 13 Trust Law International 1.

[287] [1973] QB 27, CA.

[288] *Caltex Oil (Australia) Ltd v The Dredge Willemstad* (1976) 136 CLR 529, HCA; *Perre v Apand Pty Ltd* (1999) 198 CLR 180, HCA. The *Perre v Apand Pty* argument for recovery of economic loss caused by the immobilization of property was rejected in *D Pride & Partners (a firm) v Institute for Animal Health* [2009] EWHC 685 (QB).

[289] (1976) 136 CLR 529, HCA.

[290] [1986] AC 1, PC.

[291] [1986] AC 785, HL. But see now the Carriage of Goods by Sea Act 1992 which changed the law applicable to this case without altering the general rule.

[292] The proprietary interest necessary to found a claim in tort can however be an equitable one: *Shell UK Ltd v Total UK Ltd* [2010] EWCA Civ 180, [2011] QB 86.

exception to be made in such a case of 'transferred loss',[293] but this was robustly rejected in the House of Lords. For the moment, therefore, no breach has been made in this restrictive rule.[294]

(c) Disappointingly defective goods and houses

2.156 If I buy a disappointingly defective thing, my first hope of redress will be the contract. The seller may be in breach of an express or implied term as to its quality. If he is, he will have to make good my economic loss, the difference between the value of what he was contractually liable to supply and what he did supply. The question is whether there can also be a liability in tort.

(i) The starting point

2.157 The starting point is that there will be no liability outside contract in the absence of physical damage. If the defect is such as to make me ill or inflict some other kind of actual damage, I may turn to tort. One advantage of doing so will be that tortious redress will not be confined by privity of contract. In tort, but not in contract, a manufacturer who sold to my seller or a sub-contractor who worked for my seller can be reached. However, *Donoghue v Stevenson*,[295] which established the liability of manufacturers to consumers for defective goods in negligence, did not go beyond negligent defects which caused physical injury or damage; it offered no redress for the economic loss inherent in having paid for a useless thing. And statutory reform of the law, strengthening the position of consumers in relation to liability for defective goods in tort, has continued to be confined to claims for personal injury or damage to property.[296]

2.158 In the case of defective buildings, the law's starting point is the same. However, larger sums are at stake (and, often, more distress too) and the *caveat emptor* principle generally rules out redress against the seller in contract. As a consequence there has been stronger pressure on the law of tort to provide redress for the loss suffered by the purchaser of a badly built house.

2.159 A statutory solution has been enacted, but for a number of reasons, some of which are no longer operative, it appears not to meet the need. The Defective Premises Act 1972 works within a limitation period of six years which runs from the completion of the dwelling. Many defects take longer to emerge. The Act would be more useful if it had run the period from 'discoverability' as does the Latent Damage Act 1986.[297] Subject to this fatal shortcoming, the Defective Premises Act 1972 imposes on those who take on work for the provision of a dwelling a duty to ensure that it is constructed in a workmanlike manner so that the dwelling is fit for habitation. And this duty extends beyond contract to all who acquire an interest in the building.[298] At common law, the courts eventually yielded to the pressure for redress outside contract, but, at least in England, they later recanted. The complexities of such cases ramify, reaching into, inter alia, the identity of the defendants, the limitation of actions, and

---

[293] [1985] QB 350, 399, CA.

[294] There is one apparently exceptional case, in which a majority of the House of Lords allowed a cargo owner, required to contribute to the cost of a collision at sea, to recover his contributions from the negligent defendant although his cargo was undamaged: *Morrison Steamship Co Ltd v Steamship Greystoke Castle* [1947] AC 265, HL. It is usually explained as a peculiarity of maritime law relating to general average contribution and has not been followed in other contexts: *Candlewood Navigation Corporation Ltd v Mitsui OSK Lines (The Mineral Transporter)* [1986] AC 1, 24, PC; *Leigh and Sillivan Ltd v Aliakmon Shipping Co Ltd* [1986] AC 785, HL.

[295] [1932] AC 562, HL.

[296] Consumer Protection Act 1987 Part 1; 2.267–2.273.

[297] Inserting ss 14A and 14B into the Limitation Act 1980. This regime allows three years after discoverability, subject to a 15-year long stop.

[298] Defective Premises Act 1972, s 1(1) and s 3.

the nature of the damage. Our primary concern at this point is with the nature of the damage, though that issue cannot be entirely separated from the other questions.

(ii) Two expansionist cases

Two cases seemed to accept the possibility of suing in negligence for this kind of purely **2.160** economic disappointment. Fifty years after the decision in *Donoghue v Stevenson* another Scottish case allowed recovery for defects in a building which had not caused physical damage and was not alleged to be dangerous. *Junior Books Co Ltd v Veitchi Co Ltd*[299] was the high point of builders' liability. A subcontractor had constructed the floor of a factory. The floor's surface developed many small cracks but it caused no damage to anything else, nor any injury to any person. It was simply a disappointingly defective floor, bad value for money. The customer leap-frogged the contractor and was able to recover in negligence against the subcontractor. It is a curious fact that, in the retrenchment described immediately below, the *Junior Books* case has never been overruled. It stands in precarious isolation, not condemned but never followed.[300] It has to be regarded as turning on its own particular facts,[301] but it is not clear quite what the peculiarity of those facts should be said to be.[302]

The other expansionist case was the ill-fated decision of the House of Lords in *Anns v* **2.161** *Merton London BC*, which had been decided five years earlier.[303] It had several aspects. First, so far as there had been any doubt, it made clear that *Donoghue v Stevenson* did apply to buildings: those responsible for constructing a building which causes physical damage to persons or other property are liable on ordinary negligence principles. Secondly, it held that local authorities were liable in tort if they negligently exercised their statutory powers to control house construction. Thirdly, it expanded the definition of physical damage to include defects in the thing itself. Physical damage was to include the costs of repairing dangerous defects in the structure, even though the building had not yet caused injury to persons or other property.[304] The seductive argument was that no distinction could be taken between physical damage which was actually brought about and the cost of preventing it coming about. How, eg, could the law distinguish between the costs of an accident caused by a lorry with defective brakes and the cost of putting the brakes right before the accident happened?

(iii) Retrenchment

The second and third of these propositions have been swept away The former, for a time of **2.162** great importance, was rejected in *Murphy v Brentwood DC*.[305] As for the crucial extension of the notion of physical damage, this transgression of the line between contract and tort

---

[299] [1983] 1 AC 520, HL.

[300] It has been said that in practice it is now 'inconceivable' that the circumstances in *Junior Books* would give rise to an effective cause of action in negligence for the cost of replacing or repairing the defective floor: *Linklaters Business Services v Sir Robert McAlpine Ltd* [2010] EWHC 1145 (TCC), at [27], *per* Akenhead J.

[301] '[It] cannot be regarded as laying down any principle of general application in the law of tort or delict': *D & F Estates Ltd v Church Commissioners* [1989] AC 177, 202, HL, *per* Lord Bridge.

[302] *Tate & Lyle Industries v GLC* [1983] 2 AC 509, HL; *Simaan General Contracting Co v Pilkington Glass Ltd (No 2)* [1988] QB 758, CA; *Greater Nottingham Co-operative Society Ltd v Cementation & Piling & Foundations Ltd* [1989] QB 71, CA. In Scotland *Junior Books* is applied but only where pursuer and defender are connected by a chain of contracts: JM Thomson, 'A Prophet not Rejected in its own Land' (1994) 110 LQR 361.

[303] [1978] AC 728, HL.

[304] *Anns v Merton London BC* [1978] AC 728, 759–760, HL, approving *Dutton v Bognor Regis UDC* [1972] 1 QB 373, CA and Laskin J (dissenting) in *Rivtow Marine Ltd v Washington Ironworks* [1974] SCR 1189,1223, SCC.

[305] [1991] 1 AC 398, HL.

was questioned in *D & F Estates v Church Commissioners for England & Wales*,[306] and then also rejected in *Murphy*, a case very similar on its facts to *Anns*.[307] The facts of *Murphy* were that the house which the claimant had bought from a developer had been constructed over a filled-in site and supposedly stabilized by means of a huge concrete raft which was put in beneath the foundations. A decade later the house began to crack as subsidence set in. The cause proved to be the inadequacy of the concrete raft. The claimant had to take a £35,000 reduction in the selling price. To have done the necessary repairs would have cost somewhat more. An action to recover the reduction in value was brought against the local authority for negligently inspecting the foundations, relying on the *Anns* decision, but it was thrown out and with it the law as developed in that case.

2.163 An unfortunate side effect of *Murphy v Brentwood* is its impact on duties of manufacturers to warn consumers of defects in their products which come to the manufacturers' knowledge after the product has been in circulation. It has been held that the exclusion of liability for potentially dangerous products causing only economic disappointment relieves manufacturers of any general duty to warn consumers of such defects discovered in their products. Hence such a duty will now only be found where there is a special relationship between the parties.[308] This can only encourage manufacturers to keep quiet about defects in their products.

(d) The *Hedley Byrne* principle

2.164 So far we have established that in England there is almost no possibility of recovering pure economic loss in any action in negligence. There is one exceptional line of cases. Expressed at a very general level, pure economic loss is recoverable in negligence if there is a special relationship between the parties which raises a duty of care specifically in relation to that particular kind of loss.

2.165 In *Hedley Byrne & Co Ltd v Heller & Partners Ltd*[309] a bank's credit reference was alleged to have caused financial loss to a firm that relied on it by giving credit to a client who turned out to be uncreditworthy. The reference had been given 'without responsibility' and this disclaimer was held to be effective to protect the defendants, but the House of Lords went on to consider the question of liability in principle. It was held, reversing *Candler v Crane Christmas & Co*,[310] that, if there was a special relationship between the parties, there could be liability for negligent misstatements causing economic loss. The *Hedley Byrne* principle is the major exception to the general rule that pure economic loss is not recoverable in negligence. It has been greatly expanded and its scope is still at some points uncertain.

(i) *Words, acts, omissions*

2.166 The speeches in *Hedley Byrne* were mainly concerned with the need to place restrictions on liability for words which, it was argued, carry particular danger of indeterminate liability. Very little attention was given in the case itself to the fact that the loss was economic loss. Lord Devlin thought the distinction irrelevant. It has since become clear that the nature of the loss is the heart of the problem: relatively little difficulty has been experienced with cases

---

[306] [1989] AC 177, HL. In *Robinson v PE Jones (Contractors) Ltd* [2011] EWCA Civ 9, [2012] QB 44, the Court of Appeal, following *D & F Estates*, held that building contractors do not owe a concurrent duty in tort to protect house purchasers from economic loss.

[307] [1991] 1 AC 398, 471, 475, 489, HL. Lord Bridge would have allowed the cost of repairing a defective building so near the boundary of the land as to constitute a danger to neighbouring property or the highway (at 475), an exception later applied in *Morse v Barratt (Leeds) Ltd* (1992) 9 Const LJ 158.

[308] *Hamble Fisheries Ltd v Gardner & Sons Ltd* [1999] 2 Lloyd's Rep 1, CA.

[309] [1964] AC 465, HL.

[310] [1951] 2 KB 164, CA.

of negligent misstatements causing physical damage.[311] But it was argued and for a long time accepted that the *Hedley Byrne* principle was limited to negligent misstatements causing economic loss.[312]

The line between negligent statements and negligent acts proved hard to draw, however, **2.167** particularly with respect to professional services which are often a combination of the two, a survey, examination or service resulting in a certificate or advice. The distinction also served to conceal, and sometimes to create, anomalies between the liability of different persons involved in the manufacture and distribution of products.[313] The decision of the House of Lords in *Henderson v Merrett Syndicates*[314] extended the *Hedley Byrne* principle to include negligence in the provision of services, within a special relationship. The category of negligent misrepresentations will continue to be significant because of its links with contract rules concerning remedies for misrepresentation, but it no longer marks the limits of *Hedley Byrne* liability. That depends on the relationship between the parties.

(ii) Special relationships, assumption of responsibility and reliance

The speeches in *Hedley Byrne & Co Ltd v Heller & Partners Ltd* did require a special relation- **2.168** ship between the parties, but the nature of the special relationship required for liability was discussed only in general terms. Statements made informally in the course of a social relationship were excluded.[315] Their Lordships emphasized as pointing to a duty: the possession of special knowledge or special skill, a voluntary assumption of responsibility, reasonable reliance on the maker of the statement, and the relationship's resemblance to contract. A general business relationship, such as that of banker and customer, would suffice, but a special relationship arising out of a particular transaction was not excluded.

The principal importance of the *Hedley Byrne* decision was in extending the non-contractual **2.169** liability of professional advisers, particularly in financial services. The leading decisions concern such professional liability, but an early attempt to limit the operation of the principle to persons in the business of giving advice, or claiming the skill of a professional adviser, has not been followed in England.[316] Most cases have required a special relationship equivalent to contract, in which there has been an assumption of responsibility by one party and reasonable reliance by the other. It is said that an assumption of responsibility and reasonable reliance on it establish proximity and make it fair, just, and reasonable to impose liability for financial loss.[317]

The assumption of responsibility test has been criticized for its ambiguity.[318] The test has been **2.170** described judicially as being neither helpful nor realistic.[319] It is capable of both a broad and a narrow interpretation. The narrow interpretation emphasizes the contractual analogy, first drawn

---

[311] See, eg, *Clay v AJ Crump & Sons Ltd* [1964] 1 QB 533, CA.

[312] PS Atiyah, 'Negligence and Economic Loss' (1967) 83 LQR 248.

[313] J Stapleton, 'Duty of Care and Economic Loss: A Wider Agenda' (1991) 107 LQR 249.

[314] [1995] 2 AC 145, HL.

[315] *Chaudhry v Prabhakar* [1989] 1 WLR 29, CA is a borderline case. The decision may depend on an unwise concession in the court below.

[316] *Mutual Life and Citizens Assurance Co Ltd v Evatt* [1971] AC 793, PC; *Esso Petroleum Ltd v Mardon* [1976] QB 801, CA.

[317] *Henderson v Merrett Syndicates* [1995] 2 AC 145, HL; *Williams v Natural Life Health Foods* [1998] 1 WLR 830, HL.

[318] Stapleton condemns the assumption of responsibility concept as a restatement of the problem masquerading as a solution: J Stapleton, 'Duty of Care Factors: A Selection from the Judicial Menus' in P Cane and J Stapleton, *The Law of Obligations: Essays in Celebration of John Fleming* (1998) 59, 64–65. See also S Whittaker, 'The Application of the Broad Principle of *Hedley Byrne*' (1997) 17 LS 169 and K Barker, 'Wielding Occam's Razor: Pruning Strategies for Economic Loss' (2006) 26 OJLS 29.

[319] *Smith v Eric S Bush* [1990] 1 AC 831, 862, HL, *per* Lord Griffiths.

by Lord Devlin in the *Hedley Byrne* case.[320] The tacit premise is that, since a person can by contract make himself responsible for pure economic loss, the only problem is the technical one that under English law there is no parol contract, properly so called, in the absence of consideration. The 'relationship equivalent to contract' approach thus requires that the *Hedley Byrne* principle be confined to bilateral relationships, of which the essence is mutuality.[321] It also explains why liability may depend upon whether the parties arranged their relationship, perhaps through intermediaries, in a manner designed to avoid an assumption of contractual liability.[322]

2.171 This narrow approach, which relies on the contractual analogy, runs into difficulty with the decision of the House of Lords in *White v Jones*.[323] There a majority of the House of Lords held that a solicitor could be liable to disappointed beneficiaries for negligently drawing up or failing to draw up a will. In the particular case, the intended beneficiaries knew of the testator's intentions, but the whole House agreed that this was not a significant factor. There was no assumption of responsibility, in any natural sense, to the potential beneficiaries. *White v Jones* was subsequently extended beyond the legal profession.[324]

2.172 In *Customs and Excise Commissioners v Barclays Bank Plc*[325] the House of Lords accepted that the contractual analogy cannot strictly be insisted upon in pure economic loss cases. In that case, the Commissioners sought to hold Barclays Bank liable for loss suffered when the bank carelessly released money from frozen accounts. The Commissioners argued that Barclays Bank had assumed a responsibility to ensure that there were no payments from the accounts which had been frozen after a legal order obtained by the Commissioners had been served on the bank. The House of Lords unanimously held that the bank owed no duty of care to the Commissioners. Responsibility had not been voluntarily assumed: it had been thrust upon the bank.[326] All their Lordships observed that the further the concept of assumption of responsibility departs from the contractual analogy and the less it focuses on the actual actions and manifested intentions of the defendant, the less useful it becomes.[327] The way forward signalled by the House of Lords is to regard genuine assumption of responsibility as sufficient for liability but not necessary.[328] Other cases may fall within the usual threefold test of duty, developed incrementally.

---

[320] [1964] AC 465, 528–529, HL. See eg *Commissioner of Police of the Metropolis v Lennon* [2004] EWCA Civ 130, [2004] 1 WLR 2594.

[321] Hence Lord Mustill's dissent in *White v Jones* [1995] 2 AC 207, HL. cf *Williams v Natural Life Health Foods* [1998] 1 WLR 830, 834–838, HL, *per* Lord Steyn.

[322] A recent decision has insisted that a second stage of analysis must be whether the recognition of a duty of care would interfere with any contractual structure or regime chosen by the parties: *Riyad Bank v Ahli United Bank (UK) plc* [2006] EWCA Civ 780. See also *West Bromwich Albion Football Club Ltd v El Safty* [2006] EWCA Civ 1299.

[323] [1995] 2 AC 207, HL.

[324] *Gorham v British Telecommunications plc* [2000] 1 WLR 2129, CA, holding an insurance company liable for negligent pensions advice and applying the principle to recognize a duty of care towards the dependants of a man who made it clear that his aim was to benefit his family.

[325] [2006] UKHL 28, [2007] 1 AC 181.

[326] The line between this decision and *Spring v Guardian Assurance plc* [1995] 2 AC 296, HL is a fine one. In *Spring*, an investment company was held to have voluntarily assumed responsibility for an ex-employee's reference, even though the regulatory body required the employer to supply a reference. However, it might be said that the company assumed this responsibility by voluntarily entering into the employment contract with the employee.

[327] *Spring v Guardian Assurance plc* [1995] 2 AC 296, HL, at [5] (Lord Bingham), [38] (Lord Hoffmann), [52] (Lord Rodger), [73] (Lord Walker), [93] (Lord Mance). See also *Martin v Commissioners of Her Majesty's Revenue and Customs* [2006] EWHC 2425 (Ch).

[328] *Spring v Guardian Assurance plc* [1995] 2 AC 296, HL, at [4], *per* Lord Bingham, [52], *per* Lord Rodger, [33], *per* Lord Mance. See also *Ministry of Housing and Local Government v Sharp* [1970] 2 QB 223, CA, which was approved by the House of Lords in *Customs and Excise Commissioners*, and in which Lord Denning had emphasized (at 268) that the recovery of pure economic loss in that case could not be based on a voluntary assumption of responsibility by a clerk performing his statutory duty.

However, conflicts immediately emerge when the threefold test is used as a general approach   **2.173**
for cases of pure economic loss. In *Smith v Eric S Bush* a purchaser was allowed to recover
from the mortgagee's negligent surveyor whom the purchaser had relied upon.[329] The contrast
with *Caparo Industries plc v Dickman* is striking.[330] In that case an action was brought against
accountants for alleged negligence in auditing the accounts of a company. The claimants had
not themselves commissioned the accountants but had relied on them first in buying shares
in the company and then in taking it over. The House of Lords held that the defendants owed
no duty of care to the claimants, either as prospective investors or as shareholders who had
taken over the company because there was no special relationship between them. The general
principle of proximity seems to be that commercial parties can usually be expected to rely on
their own advisers[331] but if it can be shown that a statement, though nominally addressed
to others was actually intended to influence the claimant, that may be enough to establish
responsibility.[332]

This approach to proximity was restated in similar terms in *Sutradhar v Natural Environment*   **2.174**
Research Council.[333] The absence of a reference to possible arsenic contamination in a geologi-
cal report in Bangladesh induced the health authorities to take no action to prevent arsenic
contamination, but no duty was owed because there was no proximity in the sense of a measure
of control over and responsibility for the potentially dangerous situation.

(4) Statutory Negligence

This section discusses two areas where statutes have replaced the common law of negligence.[334]   **2.175**
Statutory negligence in this sense should not be confused with two quite different relationships between statute and the common law. The first, the circumstances in which there may
be liability for common law negligence in the exercise of a statutory power or duty, has already
been discussed.[335] The power or duty is statutory, but the liability is for breach of a common
law duty. The second possible source of confusion is the separate tort of breach of statutory duty.
Statutes not directed to the law of tort but imposing duties or regulating standards, for breach of
which a criminal penalty is usually imposed, sometimes specify whether breach of the statute is
also to give rise to civil liability. Many do not. If they do not, the approach of English courts to
these statutes has been to ask whether Parliament intended to confer a private right of action.[336]
Discerning an unexpressed intention is a task of some difficulty; Lord Denning described it as a
'game of chance'.[337] Where this intention is found, however, the action for breach of statutory
duty is regarded as a distinct tort, which can and often does operate concurrently with negligence liability. The standard of liability in an action for breach of statutory duty depends on the
wording of the statute in question. Liability is generally stricter than negligence, but there are
instances where the common law duty of care is more demanding than the statutory duty.[338]

---

[329] [1990] 1 AC 831, HL (undeterred by a disclaimer of responsibility by the surveyor, which was also
held to be unreasonable and therefore ineffective against the purchaser under the Unfair Contract Terms Act
1977, for houses at this lower end of the market).

[330] *Caparo Industries plc v Dickman* [1990] 2 AC 605, HL.

[331] *James McNaughton Paper Group Ltd v Hicks, Anderson & Co* [1991] 2 QB 113, CA.

[332] *Morgan Crucible Co Ltd v Hill Samuel Bank Ltd* [1991] Ch 295, CA.

[333] [2006] UKHL 33, [2006] 4 All ER 490, HL.

[334] On statutes in the law of tort generally see K Stanton et al, *Statutory Torts* (2003).

[335] 2.98–2.106.

[336] K Stanton, *Breach of Statutory Duty in Tort* (1986); R Buckley, 'Liability in Tort for Breach of Statutory
Duty' (1984) 100 LQR 204; G Williams, 'The Effect of Penal Legislation in the Law of Tort' (1960) 23 MLR 233.

[337] *Ex p Island Records* [1978] 1 Ch 122, 135, CA.

[338] *Bux v Slough Metals Ltd* [1973] 1 WLR 1358, CA.

Many actions for breach of statutory duty previously related to safety in employment, but a recent legislative change means that the tort's role in this context is now much reduced.[338a]

(a) The Occupiers' Liability Acts 1957 and 1984

2.176 Replacing excessively complicated common law, these Acts are a code governing the liability of an occupier of premises to persons injured there.[339] The 1957 Act provides for an occupier's duty to his visitors and the 1984 Act provides for people other than visitors. The test of occupation is based on control, but there can be more than one occupier, and it is not necessary that an occupier have entire or exclusive control of the premises.[340]

(i) The duty to visitors

2.177 Section 2(2) of the 1957 Act says that an occupier owes to his visitors the duty 'to take such care as in all the circumstances of the case is reasonable to see that the visitor will be reasonably safe in using the premises for the purposes for which he is invited or permitted to be there'. The duty imposed on the occupier is a duty of positive action, to see that visitors are reasonably safe. Under section 1(1) the duty is in respect of dangers arising from the state of the premises or from things done or omitted to be done on them. By section 1(3)(a) premises include any fixed or moveable structure, vessel, vehicle or aircraft. Visitors are persons who enter with the occupier's express or implied invitation or permission: 'persons who would at common law be treated as his invitees or licensees' (section 1(2)).[341] Most of the provisions of the 1957 Act express general principles of the modern law of negligence. Children must be expected to be less careful than adults (section 2(3)(a)). A person on the premises in the exercise of his calling can be expected to appreciate and guard against any special risks of his calling (section 2(3)(b)).[342] An occupier is not responsible for risks which the visitor has willingly accepted as his (section 2(5)). Warning a visitor of a danger may not be enough, unless the warning enables the visitor to be reasonably safe (section 2(4)(a)). Under section 2(4)(b) an occupier is not without more to be liable for a danger created by an independent contractor provided the occupier himself was not negligent. That is, the occupier's liability is not in such a case a simple vicarious liability.

(ii) Excluding liability

2.178 The exclusion of liability has caused difficulty. The section 2(2) duty is subject to section 2(1), which allows the occupier to vary the duty 'so far as he is free to and does extend, restrict, modify or exclude his duty to any visitor or visitors by agreement or otherwise'. The phrase 'by agreement or otherwise' has been held by the majority of a divided Court of Appeal to enable an occupier to exclude liability for negligence by unilateral declaration.[343] This decision must now be read subject to the Unfair Contract Terms Act 1977 (as amended by the Occupiers' Liability Act 1984, section 2), which limits the power to exclude liability for breach of duties arising from the occupation of premises used for the business purposes of the occupier.[344] Liability for negligence causing death or personal injury on such premises cannot be excluded, liability for other loss or damage only if the exclusion is reasonable.

[338a] Enterprise and Regulatory Reform Act 2013, s 69 (amending the Health and Safety at Work etc Act 1974, s 47(2)).

[339] *Maguire v Sefton MBC* [2006] EWCA Civ 316, [2006] 1 WLR 2550.

[340] *Wheat v E Lacon & Co Ltd* [1966] AC 552, HL.

[341] *Dunster v Abbott* [1954] 1 WLR 58, CA.

[342] *Roles v Nathan* [1963] 1 WLR 1117, CA.

[343] *White v Blackmore* [1972] 2 QB 651, CA.

[344] Unfair Contract Terms Act 1977, s 1(3); Occupiers' Liability Act 1984, s 2.

(iii) Trespassers and other uninvited entrants

The Occupiers' Liability Act 1984 replaces the common law on an occupier's responsibilities **2.179**
to persons who are not his visitors, either because they have entered as of right, or because
they are trespassers. Until 1972, the law with regard to trespassers was harsh: an occupier was
liable only for intentionally or recklessly harming a trespasser.[345] The rule became increasingly difficult to defend, particularly in the case of trespassing children, and was displaced by
the House of Lords in *Herrington v British Railways Board*.[346]

The 1984 Act to a great extent adopts the *Herrington* decision. According to section 1(3), an **2.180**
occupier owes a duty to persons other than visitors if he is aware or has reasonable grounds to
believe that the premises are dangerous, if he also knows or has reasonable grounds to believe
that someone is or might be in the vicinity of the danger and if the risk is one against which
in the circumstances he can reasonably be expected to offer that person some protection. But
there will not be a duty unless there is an inherent danger in the premises themselves. An
abandoned building will not be dangerous merely because it is alluring for children who may
climb, and fall from, the walls or fire escapes.[347] Furthermore, the occupier must have actual
knowledge of the danger to persons on the premises or of facts pointing to the danger; it is not
enough that he ought to have known.[348] Where these conditions are satisfied, and a duty is
owed under the 1984 Act, the duty is to take such care as is reasonable in all the circumstances
of the case to see that the uninvited entrant does not suffer death or personal injury.[349]

The 1984 Act contains provisions similar to the 1957 Act on warnings and assumption of **2.181**
risk, but says nothing about the effect of notices excluding liability. It can be argued that the
duty to uninvited persons is a minimum standard which cannot be excluded. The Act does
not cover property damage and does not apply to persons using the highway, whose position
is therefore governed by the common law.[350]

The decision in *Tomlinson v Congleton BC*[351] was decided under the 1984 Act but shows that, **2.182**
like the 1957 Act, the 1984 Act also expresses general principles of the law of negligence.
The local authority had converted an old gravel pit and the surrounding land into a lake and
park which attracted many visitors. Families went there to picnic and paddle, but swimming
was known to be dangerous. The local authority put up notices prohibiting it but knew that
teenagers and others often ignored them. Tomlinson, intending to swim, walked into the
water and then, standing knee-deep took a disastrous dive which broke his neck on a sand-
bank. Once he decided to swim he became a trespasser. His claim under the 1984 Act failed.
The central reason, which would have been an answer to any action in negligence, was that,
in the terms of section 1(3) of the 1984 Act, it was not reasonable to expect the council to
protect him from dangers manifestly inherent in his chosen activity. Even if there had been
no notices the council would not have been liable. It was all the more unreasonable to expect
protection given that effective measures to prevent swimming would have carried a high
social cost, in that they would have reduced access and amenity for the thousands of visitors
who used the site for the leisure activities for which it had been intended.[352]

---

[345] *Robert Addie and Sons (Collieries) Ltd v Dumbreck* [1929] AC 358, HL.
[346] [1972] AC 877, HL.
[347] *Keown v Coventry Healthcare NHS Trust* [2006] EWCA Civ 39, [2006] 1 WLR 953.
[348] *Herrington v British Railways Board* [1972] AC 877, 941, HL, *per* Lord Diplock; *Swain v Natui Ram Puri* [1996] PIQR P442, CA.
[349] Occupiers' Liability Act 1984, s 1(4).
[350] *McGeown v Northern Ireland Housing Executive* [1995] 1 AC 233, HL.
[351] [2003] UKHL 47, [2004] 1 AC 46.
[352] A similar tragedy in *Donoghue v Folkestone Properties Ltd* [2003] EWCA Civ 231, [2003] QB 1008 was dealt with under s 1(3)(b) of the 1984 Act. The claimant broke his neck when he hit a concealed pile in the defendant's harbour but he was diving at midnight in the middle of winter and, pursuant to that section,

(b) The Congenital Disabilities (Civil Liability) Act 1976

2.183 At the time the Congenital Disabilities (Civil Liability) Act 1976 was passed, there was no English authority on whether a child could sue the person responsible for causing him to be born disabled. It was widely thought that the courts would, following decisions in other jurisdictions, allow such an action at common law, and this view was subsequently confirmed by an action brought by children born before 1976.[353] Nevertheless the Law Commission recommended a statute to deal with the difficult policy issues involved.[354] The Act replaces the common law for claims by children born after the commencement date.

2.184 Under section 1 a right of action is given to any child born disabled as a result of an occurrence which affected the ability of his parents to have a normal child, or affected the mother during pregnancy or her or the child during birth. The child can sue the person responsible for the occurrence. If the person responsible was the child's mother, however, the child cannot sue her unless she caused the disability by driving a motor vehicle at a time when she knew or ought to have known that she was pregnant. The exception is obviously dictated by insurance considerations. It is not so easy to defend the discrimination between mothers and fathers. It has been recommended that the child should be able to sue either parent for activities for which insurance is compulsory, but neither parent otherwise.[355]

2.185 The Act was extended by the Human Fertilisation and Embryology Act 1990 to cover cases in which the child is born disabled because of negligence in infertility treatments, whether in implantation or in the storage of eggs or sperm. This right of action is subject to a most unusual limitation, namely that the child's right of action is conditional on there being a concurrent right of action by the parent: the defendant can only be liable if he was or would have been liable to the parent if the parent had suffered an injury and sued in due time.[356]

2.186 The special considerations raised by a claim of this kind are shown in the defences to such an action. Although in theory the action is the child's, the child's claim may be affected by the contributory negligence of its parents, by a contract made by the parents or, in the case of an injury to the parents preceding the conception of the child, by the parents' knowledge of the risk of the child being born disabled, unless it was only the father who knew of the risk.[357]

2.187 The Act has, apparently, not produced litigation, no doubt partly because of the difficulty of proving a connection between antenatal negligence and a congenital disability. Actions by parents for losses suffered by themselves due to the birth of a disabled or unwanted child are not affected by the Act, but are limited by other policy considerations.[358]

D. Negligence: Defences

2.188 The principal defences to a negligence action are contributory negligence and assumption of risk (traditionally embodied in a Latin tag: *volenti non fit injuria*, which means 'no wrong

---

the claim was dismissed because there was no reason to anticipate swimmers at that time. See also *Harvey v Plymouth City Council* [2010] EWCA Civ 860, [2010] PIQR 1018.

[353] *Burton v Islington HA* [1993] QB 204, CA. See P Cane, 'Injuries to Unborn Children' (1977) 51 ALJ 704.

[354] Law Commission, *Injuries to Unborn Children* (Law Com No 60, 1974).

[355] *Report of the Royal Commission on Civil Liability and Compensation for Personal Injury* (Cmnd 7054, 1978) vol 1, paras 1471–1472.

[356] Section 1A(2).

[357] Section 1(4), (6), (7).

[358] *McFarlane v Tayside Health Board* [2000] 2 AC 59, HL; *Rees v Darlington Memorial Hospital NHS Trust* [2003] UKHL 52, [2004] 1 AC 309. See discussion in 2.44.

is done to one who consents'). A third defence, that the claimant should be barred from recovery because of his participation in illegal conduct, is sometimes accepted. Again reliance has in the past been placed on a Latin maxim: *ex turpi causa non oritur actio*, which means 'no action arises from a disgraceful cause'. This defence is controversial and its basis remains obscure.

(1) Contributory Negligence

At common law, the contributory negligence of the claimant was a complete defence. **2.189** Someone whose carelessness as to his own safety contributed to the damage otherwise caused by the defendant, was barred from recovery.[359] The manifest injustice of this rule, which took no account of the relative fault of the parties, was partly mitigated by the doctrine of last opportunity: that the party who had the last opportunity to avoid the accident and negligently failed to take it was treated as being solely responsible. Thus, where the claimant's donkey was killed when the defendant drove his cart into it, it was held that, despite the fact that the claimant had negligently allowed the animal to graze on the road, the defendant was liable because, but for his negligent driving, he could have avoided it.[360] In order further to mitigate the common law's basic position, the last opportunity doctrine was stretched to include cases in which the defendant did not in fact have the last opportunity to avoid the disaster but would have had if he had exercised due care.[361]

Both versions of the doctrine of last opportunity, actual and constructive, were unsatisfac- **2.190** tory. The common law rule was swept away by the Law Reform (Contributory Negligence) Act 1945. Following the precedent set by the Maritime Conventions Act 1911,[362] it was replaced by a regime which gave the courts a power to apportion responsibility for the damage between the parties. Section 1(1) of the 1945 Act provides:

> Where any person suffers damage as the result partly of his own fault and partly of the fault of any other person or persons, a claim in respect of that damage shall not be defeated by reason of the fault of the person suffering the damage, but the damages recoverable in respect thereof shall be reduced to such extent as the court thinks just and equitable having regard to the claimant's share in the responsibility for the damage.

Since the abrogation of the common law rule, there has been no need for the last opportunity **2.191** rule. Attempts to revive it as an aspect of the independent issue of causation were robustly resisted.[363] The operation of the 1945 Act can be discussed in terms of its constituent elements: fault, contribution, damage, and apportionment.

(a) Fault

The 1945 Act applies where a person suffers damage as the result partly of his own fault and **2.192** partly of the fault of any other person or persons. 'Fault' is defined in section 4 to mean 'negligence, breach of statutory duty or other act or omission which gives rise to a liability in tort or would, apart from this Act, give rise to the defence of contributory negligence'. The

---

[359] The foundational study remains G Williams, *Joint Torts and Contributory Negligence* (1951).
[360] *Davies v Mann* (1842) 10 M & W 546, 152 ER 588.
[361] *British Columbia Electric Railway v Loach* [1916] 1 AC 719, PC. Analysis in G Williams, *Joint Torts and Contributory Negligence* (1951) 244–245.
[362] Itself 'to some extent declaratory of the Admiralty rule in this respect': *Admiralty Commissioners v SS Volute* [1922] 1 AC 129, 144, HL, *per* Viscount Birkenhead.
[363] *Davies v Swan Motor Co* [1949] 2 KB 291, 318 (Evershed LJ), 321 (Denning LJ), CA; cf *Jones v Livox Quarries Ltd* [1952] 2 QB 608, CA.

first part of the definition clearly refers to the fault of the defendant.[364] It is not necessary to prove that the claimant's contributory fault was a tort; all that is necessary is that the claimant's damage was partly his own fault. It need not be shown that the claimant owed a duty to the defendant.[365]

2.193 'Fault' can include a deliberate act of self-injury by the claimant, since it would be absurd if damages were reduced for mere carelessness but not for intentional self-injury.[366] Contributory negligence is a description of the claimant's conduct, not his state of mind.

2.194 The criterion of contributory fault, or negligence, is an objective one. Children, however, are only expected to show the degree of care that could reasonably be expected of a child of that age.[367] It is probable that a similar test is applied to disabled persons, such as the blind.[368] There may be other relaxations of a strictly objective standard. Since it is part of an employer's duty to protect employees from the consequences of their own inattention, it is said that courts will be reluctant to find contributory negligence by the employee if the employer is in breach of a statutory duty to his employees. Similarly, courts are reluctant to reduce the damages of someone injured in the act of rescue, but may do so if a professionally trained rescuer is careless as to his own safety.[369] If the defendant creates a dangerous emergency in which the claimant is forced to make an instant choice between 'alternative dangers', the claimant is not penalized for choosing the wrong one.[370]

(b) Contribution

2.195 Contributory negligence requires proof of causative effect. Just as the claimant must show that the defendant's negligence caused damage, so a defendant relying on contributory negligence must show that it was a partial cause of the claimant's damage. Hence, although it is negligent for a passenger in a car not to wear a seat belt, there will be no reduction of his damages for an accident caused by the driver unless there is evidence that wearing a seat belt would have reduced or prevented his injuries.

2.196 It is a question of fact whether the negligence was causally relevant, but it is often more a matter of speculation than proof. In *Stapley v Gypsum Mines Ltd*,[371] Stapley and Dale, miners of equal status, were instructed not to work under an unsafe roof until they had repaired it. Finding that the repair would be difficult, by a joint decision they abandoned the task and went back to work. The roof collapsed and Stapley was killed. Stapley's negligence was clearly partly a cause of his death. The question which divided the House of Lords was whether Dale's agreement to abandon the repair had also contributed to the accident. The majority thought that, without Dale's agreement, Stapley would probably not have gone back to work. The minority pointed out that there was no evidence how far, if at all, Dale had influenced Stapley's decision. Furthermore, even if the fault of the claimant was one of a sequence of events which resulted in the injury, no deduction will be made for contributory negligence if it was 'too remote . . . to be properly regarded as a cause of the injury',[372] as where the claimant's alleged

---

[364] Williams, n 359, at 318.

[365] *Davies v Swan Motor Co Ltd* [1949] 2 KB 291, CA.

[366] *Reeves v Commissioner of Police of the Metropolis* [2000] 1 AC 360, HL.

[367] *Yachuk v Oliver Blais Co Ltd* [1949] AC 386, PC; *Mullin v Richards* [1998] 1 WLR 1304, CA.

[368] *Haley v London Electricity Board* [1965] AC 778, HL.

[369] *Harrison v British Railways Board* [1981] 3 All ER 679.

[370] *Jones v Boyce* (1816) 1 Stark 493, 171 ER 540 (passenger leaped from coach in danger and broke his leg, though with hindsight it was clear that, had he not leaped, he would not have been injured).

[371] [1953] AC 663, HL.

[372] *St George v Home Office* [2008] EWCA Civ 1068, [2009] 1 WLR 1670, at [51], *per* Dyson LJ.

fault in falling into a lifestyle of drink and drug addiction as a teenager contributed to his falling from a top bunk in prison during a withdrawal seizure at the age of 29.[373]

(c) Damage

The defence applies when the claimant's fault was partly the cause of his damage. In a typical **2.197** case, negligence by both parties may have contributed to the accident, but this is not the test. Carelessness by the claimant in not wearing a crash helmet or a seat belt does not make an accident more likely, but may well make the injuries more serious if there is an accident, and thus contribute to the damage suffered by the claimant.[374] It is not clear how wide this category of contributory negligence, the failure to take safety measures at some time before commencing an activity, is. Seat belts and crash helmets are closely related to the activity which causes the injury. It is not obvious that a careless failure to take a prescribed drug on the morning of the accident, which has the effect of making the injuries sustained more serious, should be treated the same way.

(d) Apportionment

The Act provides that the claimant's damages 'shall be reduced to such extent as the court **2.198** thinks just and equitable having regard to the claimant's share in the responsibility for the damage'.[375] It is not clear whether responsibility is to be assessed in terms of comparative blameworthiness or comparative causative significance. In so far as the question is discussed at all, it appears that the courts treat both issues as relevant.[376] In any event a wide discretion is conferred to do whatever the court thinks is 'just and equitable'. Most apportionments are a matter of general impression, and not susceptible to much argument.

There is disagreement in Court of Appeal decisions on the question whether a finding of 100 **2.199** per cent contributory negligence is permissible,[377] but the possibility was not ruled out by the House of Lords in *Reeves v Commissioner of Police of the Metropolis*. In that case the police had failed in their duty to take care to prevent a person in custody from committing suicide. It was decided in the end that the suicide was 50 per cent responsible for his own death.[378]

In *Froom v Butcher*[379] the Court of Appeal, in order to avoid expensive enquiries in individ- **2.200** ual seat belt cases, said that, if the damage would have been prevented altogether by wearing a seat belt, the reduction for contributory negligence should be 25 per cent, but if the effect of a seat belt would have been to make the injuries less severe, the reduction should be 15 per cent. Although the wording of the Act suggests that the apportionment should be a matter for the judge in each case, Lord Denning, in giving this guidance, said that he thought that this tariff would be just and equitable in the great majority of cases.[380]

---

[373] *St George v Home Office* [2008] EWCA Civ 1068, [2009] 1 WLR 1670, at [51], *per* Dyson LJ. On the relationship between addiction and contributory negligence, see also *Calvert v William Hill Credit Ltd* [2008] EWCA Civ 1427, [2009] Ch 330, at [61]–[72], *per* Sir Anthony May P.

[374] *O'Connell v Jackson* [1972] 1 QB 270, CA; *Froom v Butcher* [1976] QB 286, CA.

[375] Section 1(1).

[376] *Stapley v Gypsum Mines* [1953] AC 663, 682, HL, *per* Lord Reid. See also *Jackson v Murray* [2015] UKSC 5, [2015] 2 All ER 805, at [50], *per* Lord Hodge.

[377] *Pitts v Hunt* [1991] 1 QB 24, 48, CA, *per* Beldam LJ. Compare Buxton LJ and contrast Morritt LJ in *Reeves v Commissioner of Police of the Metropolis* [1998] 2 All ER 381, CA.

[378] [2000] 1 AC 360, HL. Compare *Corr v IBC Vehicles Ltd* [2008] UKHL 13, [2008] 1 AC 884 (no deduction where employee who developed severe depression after a workplace accident subsequently committed suicide).

[379] [1976] QB 286, CA.

[380] In *Gregory v Kelly* [1978] RTR 426 there was an aggravating factor, in that the driver who left his seat belt undone also knew the car was defective, so that 40% was deducted. In *Capps v Miller* [1989] 1 WLR 839, CA, a motorcyclist who was wearing a crash helmet but had not fastened the chin-strap suffered a deduction of 10%.

2.201 In cases where the claimant is suing more than one defendant and is answered by a plea of contributory negligence, it is important to keep distinct the exercises of apportioning responsibility under the 1945 Act and contribution proceedings between the defendants under the Civil Liability (Contribution) Act 1978. The question whether the claimant's damages are to be reduced for contributory negligence is decided as between the claimant on the one hand and the defendants jointly on the other, while contribution concerns only the defendants.[381]

(e) Contributory negligence and other torts

2.202 The Law Reform (Contributory Negligence) Act 1945, section 4 expressly makes contributory negligence available as a defence to an action for breach of statutory duty. It is not a defence to an action for deceit,[382] or for assault and battery.[383] The position where the defendant's liability is strict is less clear. The Animals Act 1971, section 10 and the Consumer Protection Act 1987, section 6(4) provide that contributory negligence is to be a defence. The Torts (Interference with Goods) Act 1977, section 11 excludes the defence in proceedings founded on conversion or intentional trespass to goods. The New Zealand Court of Appeal has held that contributory negligence can be a defence to a claim based on breach of fiduciary duty,[384] but this ruling can be criticized on the grounds that it is of the essence of a fiduciary relationship that the beneficiary is relieved of the need to watch over his own affairs and monitor the fiduciary.[385]

(2) Consent, Assumption of Risk

2.203 The Latin tag *volenti non fit injuria* (no wrong is done to one who consents) embraces both the defence of consent to an act which would otherwise be a tort and the defence that the claimant agreed to assume the risk of injury. Consent is the appropriate formulation for intentional acts, while assumption of risk better describes the operation of the *volenti* defence in a negligence action.

(a) The operation of the defence

2.204 *Volenti non fit injuria*, whether in the form of consent to intentional acts or in the form of assumption of the risk of negligence, is an absolute defence. A person who has consented has not suffered a wrong and is not entitled to any compensation. There is no apportionment. Consequently, although there may be a considerable overlap on the facts of a case between the defences of contributory negligence and *volenti*, the effect of the defences became markedly different in 1945.

2.205 Unsurprisingly, cases since 1945 have shown a reluctance to accept the *volenti* defence where apportionment for contributory negligence is available as an alternative. Although they may often overlap, there is an essential difference between the two defences: contributory negligence implies, however objectively, fault; consent and assumption of risk may not. It is not necessarily blameworthy to take risks; taking risks may be the object of the exercise. The desire to limit the scope of the defence has nevertheless led to fine distinctions in the cases and a substantial measure of statutory control.

---

[381] *Fitzgerald v Lane* [1989] AC 328, HL.

[382] *Alliance and Leicester BS v Edgestop* [1993] 1 WLR 1462; *Standard Chartered Bank v Pakistan National Shipping Corp (No 2)* [2002] UKHL 43, [2003] 1 AC 959.

[383] *Pritchard v Co-operative Group Ltd* [2011] EWCA Civ 329, [2012] QB 320.

[384] *Day v Mead* [1987] 2 NZLR 443.

[385] JA Handley, writing extra-judicially, in PD Finn (ed), *Essays on Damages* (1992) 126–127.

(b) Acceptance of the risk

The requirements are that there must be both knowledge of the risk and free acceptance of **2.206**
it. The latter requirement has been particularly important in actions brought by employees
against employers. The courts take the view that economic pressure to do dangerous work
prevents the defence being used against an employee in all but the most exceptional cases.[386]
The defence is always displaced where there is evidence of pressures, whether social, economic
or merely force of habit.[387] Where, however, two workers combined together deliberately to
short-circuit mandatory safety procedures, the House of Lords accepted, emphasizing the
extreme nature of the facts, that each had accepted the risks inherent in the negligence of the
other.[388]

The cases further distinguish between acceptance of the ordinary risks of an enterprise and **2.207**
acceptance of the risk that the enterprise will be carried out negligently; the former does
not imply the latter.[389] Similarly in some cases a distinction is drawn between acceptance
of the physical risk that one may be injured, and acceptance of the legal risk of not being
compensated for the injury. A claimant who gratuitously agreed to teach a neighbour to drive
but made specific enquiries about insurance cover was making it clear that he expected to
be compensated for injuries, so that the knowledge that injury might ensue did not amount
to a relevant acceptance of the risk.[390] Indeed, there is some authority for the view that the
defence only applies where the facts show an agreement to waive any claim for negligence. In
the driving instructor case, *Nettleship v Weston*, Lord Denning MR went so far as to suggest
that nothing short of such agreement would be sufficient.[391]

The defence will not succeed where the voluntary act of the claimant is precisely the one **2.208**
which the defendant is under a duty to prevent.[392] The defence was therefore held inapplicable where a prisoner found to be of sound mind hanged himself, since to have allowed the
defence would have rendered nugatory the duty on the police to take care to prevent suicide
by persons in custody. Duties to prevent others deliberately injuring themselves are rare, but
this is one of them.

It is generally accepted that assumption of risk cannot be pleaded against someone injured **2.209**
whilst attempting to rescue a person in danger, whether the danger was created by a third party
or by the very person in danger.[393] This encouragement of rescue attempts is also extended to
members of public rescue services. A member of a fire brigade injured in the course of fight-
ing a fire can therefore sue the householder whose negligence started the fire.[394] Similarly, it is
accepted that the intervention of a rescuer is always to be regarded as reasonably foreseeable.

(c) Consent

Acceptance of risk is the appropriate language to cover cases of unintentional conduct, but where **2.210**
the conduct is intentional the better substatement of the defence is in terms of consent. The
simplest example is participation in a contact sport. Voluntary participation in rugby precludes

---

[386] *Smith v Baker & Sons* [1891] AC 325, HL.
[387] *ICI v Shatwell* [1965] AC 656, 687–688, HL, *per* Lord Pearce.
[388] *ICI v Shatwell* [1965] AC 656, HL.
[389] *Slater v Clay Cross Co Ltd* [1956] 2 QB 264, CA.
[390] *Nettleship v Weston* [1971] 2 QB 691, CA.
[391] *Nettleship v Weston* [1971] 2 QB 691, 701, CA. This position is approved by A Jaffey, 'Volenti Non Fit
Iniuria' [1985] CLJ 87.
[392] *Reeves v Commissioner of Police of the Metropolis* [2000] 1 AC 360, HL.
[393] *Baker v TE Hopkins & Son Ltd* [1959] 1 WLR 966, CA; *Chadwick v British Railways Board* [1967] 1
WLR 912; *Harrison v British Railways Board* [1981] 3 All ER 679.
[394] *Ogwo v Taylor* [1988] AC 431, HL.

an action for battery.[395] It is different where the incident is completely outside the rules of the game, as where one player commits a serious and dangerous foul on another.[396] Normal physical contact in everyday life, jostling in a street or on a crowded bus, has been regarded as protected by implied consent to such contact, but it may be that there is simply a general exception from liability for all contact which is generally acceptable in the ordinary course of everyday life.[397]

2.211 The most difficult questions about the operation of the defence of consent are those concerning consent to medical treatment.[398] A medical procedure involving physical contact is a battery if performed without the consent of the patient, except in special circumstances. An adult has an unquestioned right to refuse medical treatment, however irrationally, provided he understands the consequences of his decision.[399]

2.212 The first major difficulty is where the patient is unable to consent because, temporarily or permanently, he lacks capacity to do so. If an emergency arises during the course of an operation while the patient is unconscious, steps taken to deal with it may be justified by the argument of necessity, provided that no more is done than is reasonably required. If the patient is a child, parents may consent on his behalf or the child may be made a ward of court. If, due to mental disability, the incapacity is permanent, patients may be treated if it is in their best interests, to save life or to improve or prevent deterioration in their physical or mental health. Even the sterilization of an adult patient with a very serious mental disability can be justified under this head.[400]

2.213 The position of children is more complicated. A minor over the age of 16 can consent to any medical treatment without parental consent.[401] And in *Gillick v West Norfolk & Wisbech AHA*,[402] the House of Lords held that a child under 16 can also give a valid consent provided he is mature enough to understand the nature of the treatment.

2.214 It does not follow that children also have the right to refuse treatment. Under the Children Act 1989, a child of sufficient understanding can refuse consent to medical and psychiatric investigations,[403] but outwith these statutory provisions, it has been held that a child's refusal can be overridden by the consent of someone with parental responsibility.[404] If parents refuse their consent to medical treatment, the paramount consideration in deciding whether to override that refusal is the welfare of the child, but the reality may be that the welfare of the child is dependent on the co-operation of the parent.[405]

2.215 Consent must be freely given. Thus courts must be aware that apparent consent to medical treatment by persons in prison may not be true consent. The reality of consent is a question of fact to be determined in the individual case.[406] If the patient is not told the nature and purpose of the operation, the consent will be ineffective and the operation a battery.[407] The doctor or surgeon has a duty of care to warn the patient of the risks of treatment. The extent of this obligation is

---

[395] *Simms v Leigh RFC* [1969] 2 All ER 923.

[396] *Condon v Basi* [1985] 1 WLR 866, CA.

[397] *Re F (A Mental Patient: Sterilization)* [1990] 2 AC 1, 72–73, HL, *per* Lord Goff.

[398] Comprehensive discussion in A Grubb, J Laing and J McHale (eds), *Principles of Medical Law* (3rd edn, 2010) chs 8–10.

[399] *Re T (Adult: Refusal of Treatment)* [1993] Fam 95, CA; *Re B (Adult: Refusal of Treatment)* [2002] EWHC 429, [2002] 2 All ER 449.

[400] *Re F (A Mental Patient: Sterilization)* [1990] 2 AC 1, HL.

[401] Family Law Reform Act 1969, s 8.

[402] [1986] AC 112, HL.

[403] See ss 38(6), 43(8), and 44(7).

[404] *Re R (Wardship: Consent to Treatment)* [1992] Fam 11, CA; *Re W (A Minor) (Medical Treatment)* [1993] Fam 64, CA.

[405] *Re T (A Minor) (Wardship: Medical Treatment)* [1997] 1 WLR 906, CA.

[406] *Freeman v Home Office (No 2)* [1984] QB 524, CA.

[407] *Chatterton v Gerson* [1981] QB 432.

controversial. Until recently, the leading English case was *Sidaway v Royal Bethlem Hospital*,[408] where the majority held that it was to be determined in the same way as other claims of medical negligence, by asking whether the doctor followed a practice in warning of risks which would be accepted as proper by a competent body of professional opinion, subject to the overriding jurisdiction of the court to decide that disclosure of a particular risk was obviously necessary.

In the *Sidaway* case only Lord Scarman advocated the test, which has been adopted elsewhere, **2.216** of asking whether the risk was one which a prudent patient would wish to know, rather than one which doctors are accustomed to reveal.[409] However, in *Montgomery v Lanarkshire Health Board* [409a] the Supreme Court disapproved *Sidaway* and held that a doctor has a duty to take reasonable care to ensure that a patient is aware of any risk which a reasonable patient would be likely to consider significant, or which the doctor knows or should know this particular patient is likely to consider significant. In most cases there will not be a very big difference between the two approaches: most doctors will advise their patients of risks which a reasonable patient would consider significant. But a doctor may still withhold information which he reasonably considers would be seriously detrimental to the patient's health.

(d) Statutory invalidation of some consents

It frequently happens that protection from liability is sought through notices or contractual terms **2.217** which purport to secure the other's consent to acting at his own risk. A number of statutes have intervened to render some such consents or purported consents ineffective. Typical is section 7 of the Consumer Protection Act 1987 which prevents the limitation or exclusion of the liability for defective products imposed by the Act by any contract term, notice or other provision.

The Road Traffic Act 1988, section 149, re-enacting earlier legislation, makes ineffective any **2.218** antecedent agreement or understanding between the user of a vehicle and his passenger which purports to negative or restrict the user's liability to persons required by the Act to be covered by an insurance policy. Section 149(3) provides: 'The fact that a person so carried has willingly accepted as his the risk of negligence on the part of the user shall not be treated as negativing any such liability of the user.' After some initial hesitation, it is now settled that section 149(3) covers implied assumption of risk as well as express agreements. So in *Pitts v Hunt*, it was held that the plea could not be raised even against a pillion passenger who had incited and encouraged a motor cyclist to drive dangerously while drunk, thus causing the accident in which the passenger was injured and the motor cyclist killed.[410] The passenger was, however, then barred from recovery by the defence of illegality, which will be discussed immediately below.

In situations where the Road Traffic Act 1988 does not apply, the courts unhesitatingly apply **2.219** the defence of *volenti* to participants in drunken joyriding. *Morris v Murray* was an extreme case involving a flight in a light aircraft which ended in disaster.[411] The plane crashed, the claimant was injured, and the pilot was killed. The evidence was that the claimant and the pilot had been drinking heavily all afternoon. Nevertheless the claimant agreed to go flying with the pilot and helped him get the plane ready. The Court of Appeal held that the deceased's estate could not be liable because the claimant had accepted the risk.

---

[408] [1985] AC 871, HL.
[409] [1985] AC 871, 886, HL. See also *Canterbury v Spence* 464 F 2d 772 (DC Cir, 1972); *Rogers v Whittaker* (1992) 175 CLR 479, HCA.
[409a] [2015] UKSC 11, [2015] 2 All ER 1031.
[410] *Pitts v Hunt* [1991] 1 QB 24, CA.
[411] [1991] 2 QB 6, CA.

2.220 The Unfair Contract Terms Act 1977 contains a general control of business liability. It restricts the effectiveness of attempts to restrict or exclude obligations arising in the course of a business or from the occupation of premises used for business purposes of the occupier.[412] Section 2 provides that in such contexts:

> A person cannot by reference to any contract term or to a notice given to persons generally or to particular persons exclude or restrict his liability for death or personal injury resulting from negligence.

2.221 In the case of other loss or damage, section 2(2) provides that a person cannot so exclude or restrict his liability for negligence except in so far as the term or notice satisfies the requirement of reasonableness. Further, under section 2(3) where a contract term or notice purports to exclude or restrict liability for negligence a person's agreement to or awareness of it is not of itself to be taken as indicating his voluntary acceptance of any risk.

2.222 The proper interpretation of section 2(3) is not certain. It may be that the distinction is between knowledge of or agreement to the term or notice, which of itself is not sufficient, and knowledge of and agreement to run the risk, which is. The requirement of full knowledge of and full consent to a risk should not be watered down by the blanket terms of a contract or notice.

(3) Illegality, Public Policy

2.223 The third general defence to a negligence action is the most obscure in both scope and rationale. It is clear that in a number of cases a claimant's action may be defeated by his involvement in illegal or immoral conduct, either independently or in a joint illegal enterprise with the defendant. One burglar cannot hope to sue another for failing to take reasonable care in blowing open a safe. In *Clunis v Camden and Islington Health Authority*[413] the claimant was a mental patient who had been released from hospital. After his release he attacked and killed a man. He was convicted of manslaughter. He sued the health authority, alleging that its negligent care had brought his troubles upon him. The Court of Appeal threw the case out saying that he could not build a claim on homicide. Though all might agree on that proposition, the principle has proved difficult to enunciate.

(a) Theoretical and technical difficulties

2.224 If the claimant has committed a crime, he should pay the criminal penalty appointed. To deprive him also of compensation for personal injuries is to use the law of tort to impose an extra punishment which may well be out of all proportion to the seriousness of the crime. Arguably, to bar the civil claim is to confuse the functions of the civil and the criminal law. Behind that theoretical problem there is the more technical one of drawing a line between the cases in which the criminality will and those in which it will not bring about a civil forfeiture.[414]

---

[412] Under s 14 'business' includes a profession and the activities of government departments and local and public authorities. On 'occupation of premises used for business purposes of the occupier', see also s 1(3)(b), as amended by the Occupiers' Liability Act 1984, s 2. For amendments to s 2, see Consumer Rights Act 2015, sch 4.

[413] [1998] QB 978, CA.

[414] The same difficulty confronts the law of restitution of unjust enrichment: 3.204–3.215.

(b) Practical difficulties

The practical difficulties raised by the defence are serious ones. It is accepted that not all **2.225** illegal conduct will bar an action. Many parties in actions for personal injuries suffered in road traffic accidents were committing a highway offence at the time of the accident, but their right to compensation is not questioned in any but the most extreme cases (such as *Pitts v Hunt*, which is revisited immediately below). In actions for breach of statutory duty arising out of an injury at work, it has long been settled that the claimant worker's own breach of a safety regulation will not bar the action, because the purpose of the regulation is to protect the worker.[415] The defence has been said to preclude only claims founded on criminal or 'quasi-criminal' acts contrary to the public law of the state and which engage the public interest. [415a]

Furthermore, the relationship between the illegality defence and the other defences has not **2.226** been clarified. In *Pitts v Hunt*, it was held that although the defence of assumption of risk was barred by the Road Traffic Act 1988, section 149(3), the defence of illegality was nonetheless available.[416] But in *National Coal Board v England*, it was held that the inclusion of breach of statutory duty in the definition of 'fault' in the Law Reform (Contributory Negligence) Act 1945 made it clear that contributory negligence was the appropriate defence where the claimant himself was in breach.[417]

(c) Justifications

A number of justifications have been put forward for the illegality defence. One possible **2.227** argument is that the need to deter criminal conduct justifies the use of tort to reinforce the criminal law. In formal terms this is unsatisfactory. Since in many cases both sides have been involved in the illegal conduct, the effect of the bar is that, while one side may be deterred, the other partner in the same criminal conduct is relieved of liability. The substance, of course, is likely to be that it is the defendant's insurance company which is relieved of liability, while the claimant's losses are met by social security and the National Health Service.

A second justification might be that the defence prevents the criminal claimant from profit- **2.228** ing from his illegality. This is an accepted proposition in other areas of law and can sometimes be effective in a tort case. A professional burglar bringing an action for personal injuries would be unlikely to succeed in a claim for loss of future earnings.[418]

Another argument is that the defence of illegality, though not generally appropriate in tort **2.229** cases, is held in reserve for cases where it is necessary to uphold the dignity or integrity of the law. This was the position of the Supreme Court of Canada in *Hall v Hebert*. McLachlin J, delivering the majority judgment, said that the illegality bar should be used only in very lim- ited circumstances. It is, she said, a weapon designed to preserve the 'the integrity of the legal system', and exercisable only where this concern is in issue, namely 'where a damage award in a civil suit would, in effect, allow a person to profit from illegal or wrongful conduct, or would permit an evasion or rebate of a penalty prescribed by the criminal law'.[419]

---

[415] *National Coal Board v England* [1954] AC 403, HL. See also *Progress & Properties v Craft* (1976) 135 CLR 651, HCA.
[415a] *Les Laboratoires Servier v Apotex Inc* [2014] UKSC 55, [2014] 3 WLR 1257.
[416] 2.218 and 2.231.
[417] [1954] AC 403, HL.
[418] *Burns v Edman* [1970] 2 QB 541.
[419] *Hall v Hebert* [1993] 2 SCR 159, 169, SCC. See also *Hounga v Allen* [2014] UKSC 47, [2014] 1 WLR 2889, where it was said that the illegality defence was based on the public interest in preserving the integrity of the legal system (but where the limit placed on its operation by McLachlin J was not accepted).

2.230 Another justification for the defence, endorsed by the High Court of Australia in a succession of cases,[420] is that illegality should bar an action where the illegal conduct was such as to make it inappropriate or impossible to formulate an appropriate standard of care. The Court reasoned that if a reasonable person would not engage in the activity in question, then no standard of reasonableness could be set, and that if it was impossible to formulate a standard of care, then it followed that there could be no duty of care in the first place. However, while this approach may explain why one burglar cannot sue another for negligence in blowing up a safe, it is less satisfactory when it comes to activities, such as driving, in which there is a generally accepted standard of care but the question is whether that standard is to be applied to criminally engaged parties. Nor can it explain the *Clunis* case discussed above, where it would not have been difficult to set a standard of health authority care of mental patients in the community.

(d) The English authorities

2.231 The English courts have taken a variety of approaches to the illegality defence in tort cases. In *Pitts v Hunt*,[421] it was held that the fact that the claimant had incited the defendant to heavy drinking and dangerous driving on the highway barred his action for personal injuries which he suffered when the motorcycle they were riding on crashed. A majority of the Court of Appeal apparently endorsed the Australian approach, holding that in the circumstances of the case it was impossible to set a standard of care. By contrast, Beldam LJ, while agreeing with the result, argued that the defence applied because the seriousness of the illegality was such that compensating the claimant would shock the public conscience. This 'public conscience' approach was, however, later disapproved by the House of Lords in *Tinsley v Milligan* in the context of the assertion of property rights,[422] and in *Clunis*[423] the Court of Appeal held that a test based on shocking the public conscience was also inappropriate to distinguish between criminal activity which would bar recovery in tort and activity which would not.

2.232 The currently dominant approach derives from the decision of the House of Lords in *Gray v Thames Trains Ltd*.[424] The claimant suffered depression and post-traumatic stress disorder following his involvement in a railway disaster caused by the defendant's negligence, and as a result he stabbed a man to death, was convicted of manslaughter and imprisoned. He sought damages for loss of earnings and general damages for his detention, his feelings of guilt and his damaged reputation. Lord Hoffmann said that the defence of illegality contained a narrow and a wider rule. The narrow rule was that a claimant could not recover for damage which was the consequence of a sentence imposed upon him for a criminal act. And the wider rule was that a claimant could not recover for damage which was the consequence of his own criminal act. On the facts, the claim for loss of earnings was caught by the narrow rule, and the other claims were caught by the wider rule.

2.233 There is little to object to in the narrower version of the rule, which is consistent with the concern for the integrity of the law emphasized in *Hall v Hebert*, and which offers a straightforward explanation for the decision in *Clunis*. More difficulty arises out of the wider version of the rule, where an apparently straightforward causation test conceals the making of a difficult value judgment. In the *Gray* case, Lord Hoffmann distinguished between cases where,

---

[420] *Smith v Jenkins* (1970) 119 CLR 397, HCA; *Jackson v Harrison* (1978) 138 CLR 438, HCA; *Gala v Preston* (1991) 172 CLR 243, HCA. cf *Miller v Miller* [2011] HCA 9, 242 CLR 446 .
[421] [1991] QB 24, CA.
[422] [1994] 1 AC 340, HL. See also *Stone & Rolls Ltd (in liquidation) v Moore Stephens (a firm)* [2009] UKHL 39, [2009] 1 AC 1391, at [97], *per* Lord Scott.
[423] [1998] QB 978.
[424] [2009] UKHL 33, [2009] AC 1339.

although the damage would not have happened but for the tortious conduct of the defendant, it was caused by the criminal act of the claimant; and cases where, although the damage would not have happened without the criminal act of the claimant, it was caused by the tortious act of the defendant. A case in the former category was *Vellino v Chief Constable of the Greater Manchester Police*, where a criminal injured while seeking to evade arrest by jumping out of a second-floor window failed in his claim for damages from the police for not anticipating and guarding against his attempted escape.[425] By contrast, *Revill v Newbery*, where a burglar recovered damages from an occupier who inadvertently shot him while he was trying to break into the occupier's garden shed, fell into the latter category.[426] However, whether causation is really a sound basis on which to differentiate between these two scenarios is open to doubt and in *Hounga v Allen*[426a] the Supreme Court signalled a shift away from this approach towards a focus on whether the illegal conduct and alleged tort were 'inextricably linked'.

It is equally difficult to reconcile the Court of Appeal's decisions on physical assault. In *Lane v Holloway*,[427] where gratuitous provocation provoked a disproportionate counterattack, Lord Denning took the view that illegal conduct by the claimant, though relevant to a claim for exemplary damages, should not affect his claim for compensatory damages. On the other hand, in *Murphy v Culhane*, an assault in the course of a fight raised the defences of illegality, *volenti non fit injuria* and 100 per cent contributory negligence, and the Court of Appeal seemed to think that the defence of illegality was available.[428] **2.234**

E. Wrongs Actionable Concurrently with Negligence

English law has no objection to concurrent liability, whether between torts or equitable wrongs and some other category of cause of action such as contract[429] or between one wrong and another. We have already drawn attention to the fact that negligence cuts across nominate torts which derive their identity from the nature of the particular right which is infringed by their commission.[430] With every step the growth of negligence in the twentieth century increased the frequency of this kind of concurrence.[431] The process still continues.[432] This section will look briefly at the principal torts with which negligence liability may co-exist.[433] In some cases the co-existence is peaceful; in others an infiltration of older rules by negligence is in progress. **2.235**

The difference between co-existence and infiltration matters. Since the rights-based torts are not now protected by rules of priority and subsidiarity such as marked the early battles between established actions and the action on the case,[434] they can only survive insofar as **2.236**

---

[425] [2001] EWCA Civ 1249, [2002] 1 WLR 218. See also *Joyce v O'Brien* [2013] EWCA Civ 546, [2014] 1 WLR 70, where the illegality defence defeated a claim by a thief who fell from a speeding van carrying a stolen ladder against the van's driver.

[426] [1996] QB 567, CA. See also *Delaney v Pickett* [2011] EWCA Civ 1532, [2012] RTR 187 (no defence of illegality where a passenger in a car being used to transport a large quantity of cannabis was injured after the driver lost control of the vehicle).

[426a] [2014] UKSC 47, [2014] 1 WLR 2889.

[427] [1968] 1 QB 379, CA.

[428] [1977] QB 94, CA.

[429] *Henderson v Merrett Syndicates Ltd* [1995] 2 AC 145, HL.

[430] 2.09–2.13.

[431] T Weir, 'The Staggering March of Negligence' in P Cane and J Stapleton (eds), *The Law of Obligations: Essays in Celebration of John Fleming* (1998) 97, esp 102–118.

[432] See, eg, *Spring v Guardian Assurance plc* [1995] 2 AC 296, HL (negligence cuts across defamation).

[433] For breach of statutory duty, see 2.175.

[434] J Baker, *Introduction to English Legal History* (4th edn, 2002) 67, with 341, 394, 406, and 424.

they continue to offer advantages over the innominate action for negligence. The advantage which most of them offer is that the claimant is relieved of the burden of proving fault. It follows that if the advance of negligence takes the form of infiltration—ie, the insertion in the nominate tort of a new requirement that negligence be proved—that infiltrated nominate tort must almost certainly sicken and die. For it thus loses the advantage which was the *raison d'être* of its survival. Weir thus says, of the relation between negligence and trespass to the person:

> The most obvious take-over of one tort by another took place in 1959 when Diplock LJ decided at first instance that it no longer stated a cause of action to plead 'You shot me'—a classic allegation of trespass to the person—but that, in order to get into court one must add 'intentionally or negligently'.[435]

(1) Trespass

2.237 Trespass *vi et armis* (with force and arms) was once the dominant tort or family of torts. The requirement of 'force and arms' was satisfied by any contact with the claimant's body or goods and land in his possession. The claimant pleaded an attack dressed up as done with force and arms but only had to show that the defendant did the interfering act.[436] It is easy to understand the liability as having historically been strict, and it has frequently been so understood, but that is at best a formal truth. The reality was that a defendant would generally plead the general issue, affirming that he was not guilty of the trespass alleged. The real facts would come out before the jury, and the jury would not find for the claimant if the defendant had not been at fault. Nor was this the exercise of an illegitimate discretion for the law, when the old procedures allowed the judges to state it, held that there was no liability if the act happened 'utterly without the defendant's fault'.[437]

2.238 There was a significant departure from the substance of the earlier law when it was decided in relatively recent times that a claimant must allege and be prepared to prove either negligence or, in trespass, intention.[438] The important point is that proof of intention is understood simply as meaning proof that the interfering act was willed even if none of the consequences was desired. A person who digs on his land and strikes a cable which is hidden under the land is not liable for trespass because the 'act of interference' was not intended.[439] Liability is imposed, subject to defences, for the willed interfering act, however impossible it was for the defendant to discover, or avoid, the consequences. It seems that this must be the law for all kinds of trespass now.[440]

(a) Trespass to the person: battery

2.239 In cases of negligent contact leading to injury and damage there are now almost no advantages in suing in trespass instead of negligence, except perhaps its being actionable *per se* without proof of damage. In cases of intentional conduct actionability *per se* used to support, in an appropriately outrageous case, an award of exemplary damages.[441]

---

[435] Weir, n 431, at 108.

[436] Baker, n 434, at 456–459.

[437] *Weaver v Ward* (1616), *Gibbons v Pepper* (1695). Both of these are now only to be read in J Baker and S Milsom, *Sources of English Legal History: Private Law to 1750* (1986) 331–337, since the authors there use sources superior to the laconic printed reports. See also D Ibbetson, *A Historical Introduction to the Law of Obligations* (1999) 156–158.

[438] *Fowler v Lanning* [1959] 1 QB 426; *Letang v Cooper* (1965) 1 QB 232, CA.

[439] *National Coal Board v JE Evans & Co (Cardiff) Ltd* [1951] 2 KB 861, CA.

[440] Even incursions into land: *League Against Cruel Sports v Scott* [1986] QB 240.

[441] *Prince Albert v Strange* (1849) 2 De G & Sm 652, 690; 64 ER 293, 310, *per* Knight Bruce VC.

Of more general importance are cases of non-negligent contact. It remains the law that **2.240** liability for an intentional trespass starts from an assumption of the prima facie unlawfulness of intentional contact, which the defendant has then to excuse or justify. This has enormous significance in relation to medical treatment. Every treatment involving direct contact with a patient's body, and necessarily, therefore, all surgery, is prima facie a battery—ie, a trespass with force and arms against the person.[442] Much of the law relating to medical practice thus turns on the definition of defences to that prima facie liability. Hence the case law focuses on the limits of consent and the extent to which necessity can be invoked in place of it.[443]

(b) Trespass to the person: false imprisonment

False imprisonment is no more than a subform of trespass to the person. 'Imprisonment' is a **2.241** misnomer. False confinement would be nearer the mark. If, even for a short time, a person is confined on all sides, whether in a building or out of doors, the person who has brought about his confinement, or has instigated or induced it,[444] will have committed this tort. He will be liable unless he can point to a legal justification. It is not necessary for the claimant to have known at the time of his confinement that he was confined.[445] This form of trespass is an important bulwark in the defence of liberty, especially against agents of the state and courts which exceed their jurisdiction.[446] It shares this role with the tort of malicious prosecution.[447] A prisoner lawfully held in prison has no 'residual liberty' as against the prison governor or anyone acting on his behalf such as would ground a false imprisonment action,[448] but it seems likely that such an action would lie where the liberty they ought to have within the prison system is curtailed by someone acting without the governor's authority, such as rioting fellow prisoners or a prison officer acting in bad faith,[449] as eg where a prisoner is held hostage by others during a prison riot. As a strict liability tort, the action exists even where a prison governor acts in good faith and in accordance with current case law which is subsequently overruled.[450]

False imprisonment is actionable *per se*, and negligence is not. However, an action in false **2.242** imprisonment lies only where the defendant intended to imprison the claimant,[451] and so in

---

[442] The heterodox view expressed in *Wilson v Pringle* [1987] QB 237, CA that there must be a hostile contact was repudiated in *Re F (Mental Patient: Sterilization)* [1990] 2 AC 1, HL. In that case a woman with a serious mental disability was sterilized, and it was held that in the circumstances her best interests served the turn of consent.

[443] *Re F (Mental Patient: Sterilization)* [1990] 2 AC 173, HL is now the leading case. See also *Gillick v Wisbech and Norfolk AHA* [1986] AC 112, HL (children, consent of parents); *Marshall v Curry* [1933] 3 DLR 260, Nova Scotia SC (diseased testicle removed during hernia operation); *Murray v McMurchy* [1949] 2 DLR 442, British Columbia SC (sterilization during Caesarian).

[444] *Davidson v Chief Constable of North Wales* [1994] 2 All ER 597, CA. The case ultimately shows that merely to give information which leads to arrest and confinement does not amount to instigating and procuring the imprisonment. See also *Iqbal v Prison Officers Association* [2009] EWCA Civ 1312, [2010] QB 732.

[445] *Murray v Ministry of Defence* [1988] 1 WLR 692, HL.

[446] *Houlden v Smith* (1850) 14 QB 841, 117 ER 323; *O'Connor v Isaacs* [1956] 2 QB 288, CA.

[447] 2.349.

[448] *R v Deputy Governor of Parkhurst Prison, ex p Hague* [1992] 1 AC 58, HL.

[449] *R v Deputy Governor of Parkhurst Prison, ex p Hague* [1992] 1 AC 58, 164, HL, *per* Lord Bridge. A prisoner's loss of residual liberty in these circumstances may amount to 'damage' for the purposes of the tort of misfeasance in public office: *Karagozlu v Metropolitan Police Commissioner* [2006] EWCA Civ 1691, [2007] 1 WLR 1881. See also *Iqbal v Prison Officers Association* [2009] EWCA Civ 1312, [2010] QB 732, at [37], *per* Lord Neuberger, [63]–[65], *per* Smith LJ.

[450] *R v Governor of Brockhill Prison, ex p Evans (No 2)* [2001] AC 19, HL. However, if a court makes a mistake and issues a judgment for a sentence longer than was intended, the error has to be corrected by due process of law. If it is not corrected and the prisoner serves longer than he should have done, there is no false imprisonment on the part of the Governor: *Quinland v Governor of Swaleside Prison* [2002] EWCA Civ 174, [2003] QB 306.

[451] *Iqbal v Prison Officers Association* [2009] EWCA Civ 1312, [2010] QB 732, at [72], *per* Smith LJ.

cases of unintentional but negligent confinement (as where a security guard carelessly locks an employee inside a deserted office building for the night) the claim must be bought in negligence, and damage shown. Whether the imprisonment itself counts as damage for these purposes remains unclear.[452]

(c) Trespass to land or goods

2.243 Trespass to land is committed by direct physical interference with another's possession of land without legal justification. The typical trespass is entering land without the consent (express or implied) of the possessor but other direct interferences with the possessor's rights are also trespasses. A visitor can become a trespasser if he exceeds the limits of his licence to enter, eg by disobeying a 'No Swimming' notice.[453] Since possession of land includes possession of such airspace as is necessary for ordinary use and enjoyment, an advertising sign projecting over land can be a trespass,[454] but an aeroplane flying several hundred feet overhead is not.[455] Conversely, the possessor of the surface of land is entitled to the substrata, to the depth at which they are exploitable.[456] The intrusion must be a voluntary act but it is no defence that the trespasser did not intend to trespass or thought the land belonged to him. There are, however, a number of recognized justifications, ranging from police powers to enter to legislation widening public access to the countryside.[457] Trespass to goods, direct interference with another's possession of goods, has been largely overshadowed in modern law by the tort of conversion, but is occasionally useful.[458]

(2) Nuisance

2.244 The tort of nuisance is divided into two strands, public nuisance and private nuisance.[459] Both private and public nuisance are frequently joined with claims in negligence.[460]

(a) Public nuisance

2.245 The word 'nuisance', which, like 'annoy', is connected with the Latin *nocumentum* (harm), is not inherently specialized. It can refer to any obnoxious conduct. Public nuisance is always stated with corresponding breadth as any interference with the rights of the public as such.[461] In practice the only recurrent case is obstructing or endangering the highway.[462] Public nuisance is a crime. It only becomes a tort when someone suffers 'special damage'—ie, when some individual is harmed to a degree quite different from the widespread annoyance to the general public. Unlike in private nuisance, in tort actions for public nuisance damages can be recovered for personal injury.[463]

---

[452] See D Nolan, 'New Forms of Damage in Negligence' (2007) 70 MLR 59, 60–70.
[453] *Tomlinson v Congleton BC* [2003] UKHL 47, [2004] 1 AC 46.
[454] *Kelsen v Imperial Tobacco Co* [1957] 2 QB 554.
[455] *Bernstein v Skyviews & General Ltd* [1978] QB 479, and Civil Aviation Act 1949.
[456] *Bocardo SA v Star Energy UK Onshore Ltd* [2010] UKSC 35, [2011] 1 AC 380 (drilling for oil at up to 2,800 feet below neighbouring land a trespass).
[457] Countryside and Rights of Way Act 2000.
[458] *Penfolds Wines Pty Ltd v Elliott* (1946) 74 CLR 204, HCA. See also 2.317 and 2.322.
[459] See J Murphy, *The Law of Nuisance* (2010); C Gearty, 'The Place of Private Nuisance in a Modern Law of Torts' [1989] CLJ 214; D Nolan, '"A Tort Against Land": Private Nuisance as a Property Tort' in D Nolan and A Robertson (eds), *Rights and Private Law* (2012).
[460] *Overseas Tankship (UK) Ltd v Miller Steamship Co Pty Ltd (The Wagon Mound) (No 2)* [1967] 1 AC 617, PC; *Bolton v Stone* [1951] AC 850, HL; *Goldman v Hargrave* [1967] 1 AC 645, HL. On the relation between nuisance and negligence, see 2.252–2.253.
[461] *A-G v PYA Quarries Ltd* [1957] 2 QB 169, 190–191, CA, *per* Denning LJ.
[462] Including navigable waterways: *Tate and Lyle Industries Ltd v GLC* [1983] 2 AC 509, HL.
[463] *Corby Group Litigation v Corby BC* [2008] EWCA Civ 463, [2009] QB 335.

(b) Private nuisance

Private nuisance is by contrast only a tort. It has become specialized as the arbiter between **2.246** competing uses of land. It is concerned with the relations between neighbours. The wider social interest in the control of land use falls mostly to public law, especially to the law relating to planning, public health, and the protection of the environment.

(i) The role of private nuisance

Private nuisance protects land and the enjoyment of land from interference arising from unrea- **2.247** sonable user of other land.[464] One neighbour's rights have to be balanced against another's. In *Bamford v Turnley*,[465] Pollock CB spoke of the 'compromises that belong to social life' and went on to observe that actionability must always turn on a somewhat vague standard of reasonableness in the circumstances. He emphasized the need for the law to be sensitive to context:[466]

> That may be a nuisance in Grosvenor Square which would be none in Smithfield Market, that may be a nuisance at midday which would not be so at midnight, that may be a nuisance which is permanent and continual which would be no nuisance if temporary or occasional.

The protected right is the use and enjoyment of private land or, more accurately, the value **2.248** of the use and enjoyment of private land.[467] Common examples of actionable nuisance are pollution from insistent noise, smells, smoke, and other fumes. Certain kinds of interference with the use and enjoyment of private land are, however, never actionable in nuisance. In *Hunter v Canary Wharf Ltd*,[468] eg, where a recently built skyscraper blocked the television reception in neighbouring properties, the House of Lords held that no action could lie for interference caused by a *building* on nearby property, while not ruling out the possibility that *activities* which interfered with television reception could constitute a nuisance.

(ii) Unreasonable user

According to Lord Lloyd in the *Hunter* case: **2.249**

> Private nuisances are of three kinds. (1) nuisance by encroachment on a neighbour's land; (2) nuisance by direct physical injury to a neighbour's land; and (3) nuisance by interference with a neighbour's quiet enjoyment of his land.[469]

The third of these forms is in practice dominant, and it is in relation to it, and not the first two, that the need arises for a balance to be struck, taking into account all the circumstances of time, place, level of activity, frequency, and so on. So, while, even as long ago as 1938, neighbours had to tolerate building operations in a busy London street such as Oxford Street, the weighing and balancing concluded that they did not have to put up with an insufferable quantity of dust and night shift working.[470] The nature of the locality will often be an important element in the balancing exercise.[471] A reasonable user in an industrial estate may well be quite unreasonable in a residential area.

---

[464] The defendant must be the creator of the nuisance, the occupier of the land from which it emanates, or the landlord. See further *Lippiatt v South Gloucester CC* [1999] 4 All ER 149, CA (occupiers); *Hussain v Lancaster CC* [1999] 4 All ER 125, 144, CA; *Coventry v Lawrence (No 2)* [2014] UKSC 46, [2014] 3 WLR 555 (landlords).
[465] (1860) 3 B & S 62, 122 ER 25.
[466] (1860) 3 B & S 62, 79; 122 ER 25, 31.
[467] *Hunter v Canary Wharf Ltd* [1997] AC 655, 688 (Lord Goff), 704–706 (Lord Hoffmann), HL.
[468] [1997] AC 655, HL.
[469] [1997] AC 655, 695, HL, *per* Lord Lloyd.
[470] *Andreae v Selfridge & Co* [1938] Ch 1, CA.
[471] *Halsey v Esso Petroleum Co Ltd* [1961] 1 WLR 683.

2.250 The striking of this balance is essentially a question of fact. There are a number of guidelines. Thus, there is no protection for especially sensitive uses to which a claimant may have put his land.[472] And no ordinary everyday user of one's own property can ever amount to a nuisance.[473] It is no defence that the claimant came to the nuisance,[474] but the fact that the defendant and his activity were there first may affect the remedy;[475] nor is it a defence that the activity was carried on for the public benefit, although public interest may affect whether a claimant is awarded damages rather than an injunction;[476] statutory authority may also legitimate what would otherwise be an actionable nuisance, either expressly[477] or by implication.[478] The fact that a development has planning permission does not in itself give any immunity,[479] but planning permission may be relevant in determining whether an injunction should be awarded.[480] Finally, malice is relevant in determining the nature of a user of land as being unreasonable, for nobody should have to put up with malicious activities by neighbours. Hence a malicious interference with amenity will nearly always be unreasonable.[481]

(iii) Delimiting the sphere of nuisance

2.251 In *Hunter v Canary Wharf Ltd*[482] the House of Lords drew clearer lines around the tort of nuisance, insisting on its role as protecting the use and enjoyment of land. The clarification had two aspects. The first was a return to the strict rule that a claimant must be a person entitled to exclusive possession of the land. To allow a licensee or a family member to sue, as had happened,[483] was to overstep the boundary between protecting land and protecting personal interests.[484] Secondly, even a claimant entitled to exclusive possession must not under this head seek to recover for personal injury, though the presence of such injury may evidence interference with the amenity of the land.[485] The decision in *Hunter* may however be outflanked by the Human Rights Act 1998, since Article 8 of the European Convention on Human Rights protects the homes and private lives of all citizens, not just those with exclusive possession. In *Dobson v Thames Water Utilities Ltd*,[486] one of the households affected by an alleged nuisance included a child claimant, whose parents, the property owners, were also claimants. It was held that if in such a case the child were to have a claim under the 1998 Act, and the parents in nuisance, then whether a separate award of damages

---

[472] *Bridlington Relay Ltd v Yorkshire Electricity Board* [1965] Ch 436.

[473] *Southwark LBC v Mills* [2001] 1 AC 1, HL (municipal flats with no soundproofing; sounds of all everyday activities, however annoying and inconvenient, could not amount to an actionable nuisance).

[474] *Sturges v Bridgman* (1879) 11 Ch D 852, CA. Cf *Coventry v Lawrence* [2014] UKSC 13, [2014] AC 822, at [53]–[58], *per* Lord Neuberger P.

[475] *Miller v Jackson* [1977] QB 966, CA; *Kennaway v Thompson* [1981] QB 88, CA.

[476] *Miller v Jackson* [1977] QB 966, CA; *Dennis v Ministry of Defence* [2003] EWHC 793 (QB), [2003] Env LR 34 (public interest in training pilots for the Ministry of Defence a factor in awarding damages in lieu of an injunction). However, damages in lieu of an injunction are the exception, not the rule: *Watson v Croft Promosport Ltd* [2009] EWCA Civ 15, [2009] 3 All ER 249.

[477] *Allen v Gulf Oil Refining Ltd* [1981] AC 1001, HL (statutory authority to construct an oil refinery provided a defence in respect of such smells and fumes as were a necessary incident of refining oil). cf *Tate and Lyle Industries Ltd v GLC* [1983] 2 AC 509, HL.

[478] *Marcic v Thames Water Utilities Ltd* [2003] UKHL 66, [2004] 2 AC 42. The House of Lords held that liability for common law nuisance would be inconsistent with the procedures for controlling the water industry under the Water Industry Act 1991.

[479] *Wheeler v JJ Saunders Ltd* [1996] Ch 19, CA; *Coventry v Lawrence* [2014] UKSC 13, [2014] AC 822.

[480] *Coventry v Lawrence* [2014] UKSC 13, [2014] AC 822.

[481] *Hollywood Silver Fox Farm v Emmett* [1936] 2 KB 468.

[482] [1997] AC 655, HL.

[483] *Khorasandjian v Bush* [1993] QB 727, CA.

[484] *Hunter v Canary Wharf Ltd* [1997] AC 655, 691–693, HL, *per* Lord Goff.

[485] *Hunter v Canary Wharf Ltd* [1997] AC 655, 696, HL (Lord Lloyd), 706 (Lord Hoffmann).

[486] [2009] EWCA Civ 28, [2009] 3 All ER 319.

to the child was appropriate would depend on the facts.[487] Claims in respect of physical damage to the land itself, which have always been within the tort of nuisance, may later be expelled. Professor Gearty has argued that interference with amenity, and in particular the availability of an injunction to bring that interference to an end, should be recognized as the only proper business of nuisance.[488] The House of Lords was not unsympathetic to that analysis.[489]

(iv) The relationship between nuisance and negligence

Liability in nuisance is not based on negligence. Nor is it right to say that it is a strict liability. **2.252** The truth is more complex. Both negligence and nuisance employ the concept of reasonableness, though each with a different focus. The negligence inquiry is whether the defendant has taken reasonable care. In nuisance the question is whether the claimant has suffered an unreasonable interference with his use and enjoyment of his property. But an affirmative answer to the latter question may suggest unreasonableness on the part of the defendant and may indeed be influenced by carelessness or malice on his part. It is also clear that in some cases the defendant will not be liable unless he has been negligent in the full sense. Thus, when the defendant is the occupier of the offending land and is being sued for a natural nuisance or for a nuisance created by some third party for whom he is not immediately responsible, he will only be liable if he has either made use of the state of affairs that causes the nuisance or negligently allowed the nuisance to continue.[490] For instance, in *Delaware Mansions Ltd v Westminster City Council*[491] the House of Lords held that reasonable remedial expenditure could be recovered in respect of damage done by a continuing natural nuisance of which the defendant knew or ought to have known. It was essential that the defendant had notice of the damage and a reasonable opportunity for abatement. Lord Cooke explained that the choice of label, nuisance or negligence, had no significance in this context.[492]

Even in other cases in which negligence is not necessary, there is much to be said for Lord **2.253** Reid's view that nuisance always involves 'fault of some kind'.[493] This is not contradicted by the proposition that if the defendant is the creator of the nuisance, proof that he took reasonable care to prevent his activities causing a nuisance will not exonerate him if the interference is in fact unreasonable.[494] Although it may, therefore, be right to say that fault of a kind is always present in an actionable nuisance, this is not a case in which a requirement of negligence has simply been implanted. Nuisance has not become a context-specific application of the tort of negligence.

(3) The Liability in Rylands v Fletcher

When a liability is named by reference only to a leading case, it is a sure sign of uncer- **2.254** tainty as to its nature and provenance. In *Rylands v Fletcher*[495] the defendants employed a contractor to construct a reservoir on his land. While excavating the reservoir bed, the

---

[487] See further on the relationship between private nuisance and the Human Rights Act 1998, D Nolan, 'Nuisance' in D Hoffman (ed), *The Impact of the UK Human Rights Act on Private Law* (2011).
[488] C Gearty, 'The Place of Private Nuisance in a Modern Law of Torts' [1989] CLJ 214.
[489] *Hunter v Canary Wharf Ltd* [1997] AC 655, 692, HL, *per* Lord Goff.
[490] *Sedleigh-Denfield v O'Callaghan* [1940] AC 880, HL; *Goldman v Hargrave* [1967] 1 AC 645, HL; *Leakey v National Trust* [1980] QB 485, CA.
[491] [2001] UKHL 55, [2002] 1 AC 321.
[492] [2001] UKHL 55, [2002] 1 AC 321, at [31].
[493] *The Wagon Mound (No 2)* [1967] 1 AC 617, 639, PC.
[494] *Cambridge Water Co v Eastern Counties Leather plc* [1994] 2 AC 264, 300, HL, *per* Lord Goff.
[495] (1868) LR 3 HL 330. A Simpson, 'Bursting Reservoirs and Victorian Tort Law' in his *Leading Cases in the Common Law* (1995); GT Schwartz, '*Rylands v Fletcher*, Negligence and Strict Liability' in P Cane and J Stapleton (eds), *The Law of Obligations: Essays in Celebration of John Fleming* (1998) 209; D Nolan, 'The Distinctiveness of *Rylands v Fletcher*' (2005) 121 LQR 421.

contractors discovered some old shafts, which had been filled in with soil. Neither the defendants nor the contractors knew that these shafts led to old mine workings, which were in turn connected, by means of other underground workings, to the claimant's colliery. A few days after the reservoir was filled with water, one of the shafts burst downwards and the water passed through the old workings and flooded the claimant's mine. The defendants were held liable without regard to fault. In the Court of Exchequer Chamber, Blackburn J said:[496]

> We think the true rule of law is that the person who, for his own purposes, brings on his land and collects and keeps there anything likely to do mischief if it escapes, must keep it at his peril, and, if he does not do so, he is prima facie answerable for all the damage which is the natural consequence of its escape.

2.255　This formulation was approved on appeal, though in the House of Lords Lord Cairns LC added one restrictive requirement, that the dangerous activity must be a non-natural use of the land.[497] This was later interpreted instrumentally to narrow the strict liability. However, as we shall see immediately below, the House of Lords has now said that that kind of exaggerated artificiality should be abandoned.

(a) A general strict liability for dangerous things?

2.256　There was a question whether the prima facie strict liability was in respect of highly dangerous things generally or only in respect of highly dangerous escapes from land. *Read v Lyons*[498] settled that question in favour of the narrower view. The claimant was a munitions inspector injured by an exploding shell while working in the defendant's factory. The House of Lords held that since the claimant was on the defendant's premises when the explosion occurred, the strict liability rule did not apply.

(b) Reintegration into the general law

2.257　Cut down in this way, and in addition made subject to a number of defences, this strict liability barely justifies its independent existence. In Australia the High Court decided that it should be absorbed into negligence.[499] In England the approach was also to integrate *Rylands v Fletcher*, though back towards nuisance rather than negligence.

2.258　In *Cambridge Water Co v Eastern Counties Leather plc*[500] the defendants used a potent chemical in their tanning factory which, unknown to them and unforeseeably, slowly leaked into the claimant water company's borehole. The toxicity was such that the borehole had to be abandoned and a new one made in another place. Claims were made in negligence, nuisance, and *Rylands v Fletcher*. In relation to the last of these, the House of Lords held that there could be no liability for an unforeseeable harm, for the rules of remoteness of damage should be the same as for nuisance. It was also said that the restrictive interpretation of the requirement of 'non-natural user' had become unnecessarily artificial and could be dispensed with in favour of a more generous understanding. Thus, the storage of large quantities of chemicals on industrial premises would count as a non-natural user and there would be a strict liability for foreseeable harm in the event of an escape.[501]

---

[496] (1866) LR 1 Ex 265, 279.
[497] (1868) LR 3 HL 330, 339.
[498] [1947] AC 156, HL.
[499] *Burnie Port Authority v General Jones Pty Ltd* (1994) 179 CLR 520, HCA.
[500] [1994] 2 AC 264, HL.
[501] *Cambridge Water Co v Eastern Counties Leather plc* [1994] 2 AC 264, 309, HL, *per* Lord Goff.

In *Transco plc v Stockport Metropolitan Borough Council*,[502] an action was brought to recover the **2.259** costs of measures taken to protect a gas main following an escape of water from a pipe supplying a residential tower block. The House of Lords was invited to consider following the example of the High Court of Australia in absorbing *Rylands v Fletcher* into negligence. This invitation was declined. Their Lordships decided, with varying degrees of enthusiasm, that strict liability still had a part to play, limited though it was by judicial interpretation and statutory regimes, and by Lord Bingham and Lord Hoffmann's emphasis on the need for an exceptionally high risk of danger and mischief for the principle to come into play.[503] Their Lordships also endorsed the *Cambridge Water* analysis of *Rylands v Fletcher* as a species of nuisance, from which analysis it followed that claimants in actions under the rule would need a proprietary interest in the affected land,[504] and that claims for personal injury would not be countenanced.[505]

(4) Liability for Animals

The law on liability for animals is multi-layered. It is possible to apply the general law of neg- **2.260** ligence or nuisance. Thus, the smell of pigs can be an actionable nuisance,[506] and there can be liability in negligence for personal injuries caused by dogs on the run.[507] The applicability of these ordinary principles was formerly inhibited to some extent by the holding in *Searle v Wallbank*[508] that there was no duty of care to keep animals from straying on to the highway. Behind the general law, there is now a statutory regime derived directly from ancient common law.

(a) The common law

The common law early developed a special regime of strict liability for animals,[509] resting in **2.261** part on cattle trespass and in part on what was loosely known as the *scienter* rule. The word *scienter* (knowingly) comes from the old pleadings which alleged that the defendant had 'knowingly kept' (*scienter retinuit*) the dangerous animal.

For the purposes of the *scienter* liability, animals were divided into two categories, those wild **2.262** by nature (*ferae naturae*) and those tame by nature (*mansuetae naturae*). In relation to tame species the owner would only be liable if the damage was due to a vicious abnormal propensity of which he actually knew. In relation to wild species people were taken to know of their savage propensities. So, for wild animals, liability was doubly strict. The distinction between the two categories had nothing to do with the individual animal. It was a classification of species. 'If a person wakes up in the middle of the night and finds an escaping tiger on top of his bed and suffers a heart attack, it would be nothing to the point that the intentions of the tiger were quite amiable.'[510]

(b) Statutory reform

In 1953 the Goddard Committee proposed that, with the exception of strict liability for cat- **2.263** tle trespass, which was thought to be conveniently clear for farmers, the old law should be

---

[502] [2003] UKHL 61, [2004] 2 AC 1.
[503] [2003] UKHL 61, [2004] 2 AC 1, at [10], *per* Lord Bingham, [49], *per* Lord Hoffmann.
[504] As held in *McKenna v British Aluminium Ltd* [2002] Env LR 30, a case predating *Transco*.
[505] [2003] UKHL 61, [2004] 2 AC 1, at [9], *per* Lord Bingham, [35], *per* Lord Hoffmann, [52], *per* Lord Hobhouse. See also *Read v Lyons* [1947] AC 156, 170–171, HL, *per* Lord Macmillan.
[506] *Wheeler v JJ Saunders Ltd* [1996] Ch 19, CA.
[507] *Draper v Hodder* [1972] 2 QB 556, CA.
[508] [1947] AC 341, HL.
[509] P North, *Civil Liability for Animals* (2012). For the old law, see G Williams, *Liability for Animals* (1939).
[510] *Behrens v Bertram Mills Circus Ltd* [1957] 2 QB 1, 17–18, *per* Devlin J.

replaced by the general principles of negligence.[511] This simplification was rejected by the Law Commission in 1967.[512] The Commission's central argument was that this area was very suitable for strict liability, which gave a clear signal of the need to insure. The Commission's own proposal was an updating of the old common law categories. This was enacted as the Animals Act 1971.

2.264 An important change was the abolition, by section 8, of the *Searle v Wallbank* immunity in respect of animals straying on to the highway. Other sections amended but left more or less intact the common law categories.

2.265 Rather than wild and tame, the Act categorizes species as dangerous or non-dangerous and creates special provisions for dogs and trespassing livestock. A dangerous species is one which is not usually domesticated in the British Isles and which, when fully grown, is likely to cause severe damage. Liability for damage caused by such animals rests on the keeper or the head of the household of a keeper who is under 16.[513] Liability is strict, subject to defences. A similar liability attaches, under section 2(2) of the Act, to damage caused by a non-dangerous animal where the keeper knows of an abnormality which renders it likely to be dangerous and the damage is attributable to that known abnormality. Abnormality is used here as shorthand for the convoluted words of the section which refer to 'characteristics of the animal which are not normally found in animals of the same species or are not normally so found except at particular times or in particular circumstances'. In *Mirvahedy v Henley*[514] the House of Lords decided that the owners of a horse which had panicked, escaped from its field and collided with a car were liable to the injured driver. With great difficulty the majority concluded that a horse which was frightened was a horse in particular circumstances and that to bolt uncontrollably was a normal response in those circumstances. The minority disagreed, interpreting 'particular circumstances' to mean 'special circumstances', as where a cow has a young calf with her.

2.266 The scheme of the Act is straightforward, but the drafting has caused trouble, particularly in relation to liability for non-dangerous species. 'The language of section 2(2) is both oracular and opaque. Judges and jurists have spent the last forty years seeking to elucidate its meaning.'[515]

(5) Product Liability

2.267 *Donoghue v Stevenson*[516] provided the basis for the modern law of liability in negligence for defective products. Lord Atkin stated the principle that a manufacturer owes a duty of care to the ultimate consumer.[517]

2.268 This principle has been construed broadly. Manufacturers include repairers.[518] And Lord Atkin's 'consumer' can be any foreseeable victim of physical injury, as for instance a pedestrian run over by a defective vehicle. Also, the pre-1932 category of things dangerous in themselves

---

[511] *Report of the Committee on the Law of Civil Liability for Damage Done by Animals* (Cmnd 8746, 1953).
[512] Law Commission, *Civil Liability for Animals* (Law Com No 13, 1967).
[513] An animal may have more than one keeper. In such a case there is no reason why one keeper may not sue another: *Flack v Hudson* [2001] QB 698, CA.
[514] [2003] UKHL 16, [2003] 2 AC 491.
[515] *Goldsmith v Pratchett* [2012] EWCA Civ 183, [2012] PIQR P11, at [31], *per* Jackson LJ. See also *Cummings v Grainger* [1977] QB 397, CA; *Curtis v Betts* [1990] 1 WLR 459, CA; *Wallace v Newton* [1982] 1 WLR 375; *Turnbull v Warrener* [2012] EWCA Civ 412, [2012] PIQR P16.
[516] [1932] AC 562, HL.
[517] [1932] AC 562, 599, HL.
[518] *Haseldine v CA Daw & Son Ltd* [1941] 2 KB 343, CA.

has become redundant, since the negligence standard can apply flexibly to all degrees of danger.[519] It is, however, still true that the manufacturer is not liable in tort for pure economic loss suffered as the result of acquiring a defective product.[520] Nor is there any liability for failure to warn of a dangerous defect if in the event only economic loss materializes.[521]

Liability in negligence and liability in contract are supplemented by a strict liability regime **2.269** for defective products. This was enacted in Part 1 of the Consumer Protection Act 1987 to comply with European Community law in Directive (EEC) 85/374. By section 2(6) liability under the Act is cumulative with other remedies, and by section 7 it may not be excluded or limited. The same limitation periods apply as for personal injury cases but there is a long-stop of ten years from the date when the product was put into circulation, after which no action can be brought.[522] Difficult and unresolved questions can arise as to when a product is put into circulation, eg if this runs from the time it is provided to a subsidiary distributor.[523]

The aim of the Act was to impose strict liability for defective products which cause death or **2.270** personal injury or damage to property which is intended for private use, occupation, or consumption, and so used.[524] A product is defective if its safety is not such as persons generally are entitled to expect.[525] The standard of safety that persons are generally entitled to expect has been discussed in several cases. In *A v National Blood Authority*,[526] where it was conceded that blood was a product for the purposes of the Act, it was held that legitimate expectations were not limited by what was scientifically possible at the time, at least unless the public was warned as to dangers not discoverable. Thus the public was entitled to rely on blood being uninfected, even though there was no available test for Hepatitis C at that time.[527] In *Tesco Stores Ltd v Pollard*[528] the Court of Appeal held that what persons are generally entitled to expect need not be the same as a design standard, of which few people would be aware. In that case, a child resistant cap on dishwashing powder was harder to open than a screw top and as safe as persons were entitled to expect even though it did not conform to the British safety standard.

Those liable for damage caused by a defective product are the producer, including producers **2.271** of component parts, a person who puts a brand name or trade name on a product, a person who imports the product into an EU member state from outside the member states, and a supplier who fails, on request, to identify one of those to whom primary liability attaches, or failing that the person who supplied the product to him.[529]

The defences to this strict liability are set out in section 4. The most controversial is the **2.272** 'development risks' defence: 'that the state of scientific and technical knowledge at the relevant time was not such that a producer of products of the same description as the product

---

[519] *Griffiths v Arch Engineering Ltd* [1968] 3 All ER 217.

[520] *Murphy v Brentwood* [1991] 1 AC 398, HL; *Muirhead v Industrial Tank Specialities* [1986] QB 507, CA; *Hamble Fisheries Ltd v Gardner and Sons Ltd (The Rebecca Elaine)* [1999] 2 Lloyd's Rep 1, CA. See 2.156–2.163.

[521] *Hamble Fisheries Ltd v Gardner and Sons Ltd (The Rebecca Elaine)* [1999] 2 Lloyd's Rep 1, CA.

[522] Limitation Act 1980, s 11A. The standard periods are three years from the damage, an alternative period from the date of the claimant's knowledge and a power to override the limitation period, subject to the long-stop.

[523] *O'Byrne v Sanofi Pasteur MSD Ltd* [2006] 1 WLR 1606, ECJ.

[524] Consumer Protection Act 1987, s 5.

[525] Consumer Protection Act 1987, s 3.

[526] [2001] 3 All ER 289.

[527] cf *Richardson v LRC Products Ltd* [2000] Lloyd's Rep Med 280 (public awareness of unreliability of condoms) and *Abouzaid v Mothercare (UK) Ltd, The Times*, 20 February 2001, CA, criticized (2001) 151 NLJ 424 (eye lost through defective elastic strap, irrelevant that producer unaware of danger).

[528] [2006] EWCA Civ 393, CA.

[529] Consumer Protection Act 1987, s 2.

in question might be expected to have discovered the defect if it has existed in his products while they were under his control'.[530] The defence is directed only to where there was actual or accessible knowledge of the risk, but whether it was possible to avoid the risk by taking reasonable care is irrelevant.[531] The effect of this defence is to put the risk of harm from unsuspected side effects on the consumer rather than the producer. Criticisms have been made of the formulation of the defence in the 1987 Act, which appears more generous to producers than the equivalent provision in the Directive, but a challenge to the formulation of the defence in the Act on these grounds was rejected by the European Court of Justice.[532]

2.273 Much was expected of the introduction of strict liability for defective products but in the event it has produced very little litigation. The Act does not specify the damages awards available; it simply refers to liability 'for the damage'.[533] In 1993 it was held that exemplary damages were not available for this statutory wrong because of a purported principle that they were not available for any tort recognized after 1964.[534] That principle has since been overturned, leaving open the possibility of exemplary damages under the Act.[535] However, exemplary damages are very unlikely to become prolific given the restraint exercised in their award in English law. Without the routine availability of exemplary damages there is little chance that strict product liability will be as important in Europe as it has been in the United States.

(6) Defamation

2.274 Until relatively recently defamation would not have been said to be a tort which overlapped with negligence and would have been treated in the section which is concerned with rights protected by strict liability.[536] However, the House of Lords has now allowed one incursion by negligence.[537] Although that incursion may yet be contained or even repulsed, it is on that basis that defamation is treated on this side of the line.

2.275 Defamation is notoriously the most technical of torts. Some degree of technicality is to be expected, not only because it protects a right which is immaterial, so that infringements are not delimited by physical facts, but also because its protection of the right to reputation, and, to a degree,[538] self-esteem, is in constant conflict with the wider interest in freedom of speech. Artificiality is therefore inescapable.

2.276 Another factor militates in the same direction. Because of the importance of the interests at stake, and the difficulty not only of achieving the right balance but also of putting any conclusion for the claimant into money, defamation has been an outpost of the civil jury.[539] This means that there has been much detailed regulation of the respective functions of the judge and the jury, as well as many niceties of pleading.

2.277 These factors explain but do not entirely justify the state of the law. Defamation has undoubtedly been a tort of great and often arbitrary complexity which for many years seemed highly

---

[530] Consumer Protection Act 1987, s 4(1)(e).
[531] *A v National Blood Authority* [2001] 3 All ER 289.
[532] Case C-300/95 *EC Commission v UK* [1997] ECR 1–2649.
[533] Consumer Protection Act 1987, s 2.
[534] *AB v South West Water Services Ltd* [1993] QB 507, CA.
[535] *Kuddus v Chief Constable of Leicestershire Constabulary* [2001] UKHL 29, [2002] 2 AC 122.
[536] See P Mitchell, *The Making of the Modern Law of Defamation* (2005).
[537] 2.12–2.13. See E Descheemaeker, 'Protecting Reputation: Defamation and Negligence' (2009) 29 OJLS 605.
[538] Through the award of 'aggravated damages': *Cassell & Co Ltd v Broome* [1972] AC 1027, HL. See 2.340–2.343.
[539] The Defamation Act 1996, ss 8–10, already provides for summary disposal of claims on certain conditions. Jury trial is now unusual, though: Defamation Act 2013, s 11.

resistant to reform. A number of important changes have now been made, and more are to be expected. The Defamation 2013 Act provides that a statement is not defamatory unless its publication has caused or is likely to cause serious harm to the reputation of the claimant (section 1). It enacts statutory defences of truth (section 2), honest opinion (section 3) and publication on a matter of public interest (section 4) which replace their common law equivalents. It introduces a single publication rule to prevent repeated claims based on the same material (section 8) and provides that trial shall be without a jury unless the court orders otherwise (section 11). Other sections deal with the procedure to be followed in establishing a defence in actions brought against the operators of websites and amend the rules applicable to reports protected by privilege.

(a) The defamatory statement

According to the traditional definitions, a defamatory statement is one which tends to bring **2.278** the claimant into 'hatred, ridicule or contempt', or which tends to make right-thinking people 'shun or avoid him'. These traditional formulae are clearly too narrow for modern law, which interprets defamation increasingly broadly. Pluralism makes for additional difficulties, since it connotes the acceptance of the existence of communities with different notions of 'right-thinking'. And times change. In 1934 the Court of Appeal held that it was defamatory to say of a Russian princess that she had been raped by the 'mad monk' Rasputin.[540] By 1996 it could be held actionable to say of an actor that he was 'hideously ugly'.[541] Such a case can clearly only be explained by a double evaluation, first of the subcommunity in which the statement is likely to take effect and then of the values of that community as themselves acceptable or unacceptable.[542]

A statement which is not defamatory on its face may nevertheless be defamatory by virtue **2.279** of an innuendo. In such a case the claimant is generally obliged to plead and prove special facts which support the innuendo. A simple case involved the publication of a picture of 'X and his fiancée'. This was defamatory by innuendo because, to those who knew X's wife, the suggestion was that she cohabited with him without being married.[543]

(b) Libel and slander

The statement may be published in written or permanent form, in which case it will be a libel.[544] **2.280** Otherwise, it will amount only to slander. Libel is at common law actionable *per se*, without proof of actual damage but a statement is now only defamatory if it has caused or is likely to cause serious harm to the claimant's reputation.[545] Modern methods of communication have rendered the distinction between libel and slander highly tenuous.[546]

(c) Publication

The claimant must show that the defamatory statement was published to a third party. The first **2.281** condition is that a third party must have received it. That is not sufficient in itself. It must at least

---

[540] *Youssoupoff v Metro-Goldwyn-Mayer Pictures Ltd* [1934] 50 TLR 581, CA.

[541] *Berkoff v Burchill* [1996] 4 All ER 1008, CA.

[542] Failing at the second stage: *Sim v Stretch* [1936] 2 All ER 1237, HL; *Byrne v Deane* [1937] 1 KB 818, CA; cf *Blennerhasset v Novelty Sales Services Ltd* (1933) 175 Law Times Journal 393.

[543] *Cassidy v Daily Mirror Newspapers Ltd* [1929] 2 KB 331, CA. This kind of imputation could barely be regarded as defamatory these days.

[544] *Monson v Tussauds Ltd* [1894] 1 QB 671, CA (waxwork representation could be a libel).

[545] Defamation Act 2013, s 1. For a body trading for profit, harm to reputation is not serious unless it has caused or is likely to cause serious financial loss.

[546] Broadcasting Act 1990, s 166; Theatres Act 1968, ss 4, 7. Its abolition was recommended as long ago as 1975: *Report of the Committee on Defamation* (Cmnd 5909, 1975).

have been foreseeable that the third party would receive it. For example, a defamatory statement in a letter to the claimant but sent to a business address, will be taken to have been published to his staff unless marked 'Private and Confidential', since the ordinary practice is for most letters to be opened other than by the addressee.[547] In *Hough v London Express Newspaper Ltd*[548] it was held that the publication of a defamatory statement need not be proved to have been made to a third party who did take the words to be defamatory, provided only that some people might have done. In that case the newspaper had described the claimant's wife in words which did not match her character and might have led people to believe that she was not in fact married to him. There was, however, no evidence that any person had actually taken the words in that sense.

(d) Strict liability

2.282 Though somewhat moderated by defences, liability is strict. The old allegation that the statement was published 'maliciously' has been emptied of meaning. This process has recently been documented anew, attention being drawn to the increasing tension with the protection of free speech.[549] It is not necessary to show that the defendant intended to injure the claimant, nor that the statement was intended to refer to the claimant, nor even, at common law, that the defendant could have known that it might be taken to be defamatory of the claimant. A fictional story of a character given the rare name 'Artemus Jones' was held to have defamed a barrister of that very name.[550] Moreover, it is not for the claimant to show that the statement was untrue.

2.283 Every repetition of a defamatory statement is a new publication and gives the claimant a separate action against each successive publisher, although statute now protects many of those who become unwittingly involved.[551] The person who made the original publication will himself also be answerable for the republications if republication was foreseeable.[552]

(e) Defences

2.284 It will be evident therefore that protection of free speech falls largely to the defences, although in one important area the courts have taken a more positive stand and have eliminated the very possibility of actions for defamation.[553]

2.285 There are four common law defences, to some extent amended by statute, and a number of statutory defences. The common law defences are justification (or truth), fair comment, absolute privilege, and qualified privilege. The defences of fair comment and qualified privilege are destroyed by proof of malice, which in this context has a substantive meaning, namely the abuse of free speech for an improper motive.

---

[547] *Huth v Huth* [1915] 3 KB 32, CA.

[548] [1940] 2 KB 507, CA, not easily reconciled with *Sadgrove v Hole* [1901] 2 KB 1, CA.

[549] P Mitchell, 'Malice in Defamation' (1998) 114 LQR 639, rightly concluding that tensions were brought to the surface by the ruling in *Derbyshire CC v Times Newspapers Ltd* [1993] AC 534, HL that Art 10 of the European Convention on Human Rights, guaranteeing free speech, merely expresses the common law on the same matter. Without ruling out strict liability altogether, the Court of Appeal in *Kerry O'Shea v MGN* [2001] EMLR 40 held that it would be a breach of Art 10 of the Convention to impose it where a pornographic photograph caused some people to think that the claimant was the woman depicted.

[550] *E Hulton & Co v Jones* [1910] AC 20, HL. See further, P Mitchell, 'Artemus Jones and the Press Club' (1999) 20 Jo Legal History 64.

[551] Defamation Act 1996, s 1; Defamation Act 2013, s 10.

[552] *Slipper v BBC* [1991] 1 QB 283, CA (newspaper reviews of a television programme); *McManus v Beckham* [2002] EWCA Civ 939, [2002] 1 WLR 2982.

[553] 2.295.

(i) Justification

Justification is an absolute defence.[554] Telling the truth can never be actionable in defamation, **2.286**
however unworthy the motive. The only exception relates to the provisions concerning reviving
spent offences under the Rehabilitation of Offenders Act 1974. There is not yet a tort of protection of privacy in England but developments in the law relating to breach of confidence have
now made it possible to say that the revelation of true but private facts can be actionable.[555]

(ii) Absolute privilege

In the same way, absolute privilege is absolute: malice makes no difference. Statements **2.287**
absolutely privileged are those made in Parliament or in reports published by order of
Parliament,[556] and those made in judicial proceedings and in accurate contemporaneous
reports of judicial proceedings.[557] There are other narrow categories of absolute privilege, the
precise limits of which are not perfectly clear, as for instance communications between high
officials and their advisors and between lawyers and their clients.

(iii) Qualified privilege

Qualified privilege is a defence in the absence of malice. The defence rests on both common **2.288**
law and statute, the statutory defence being additional to the common law.[558] The statutory
defence applies to reports of notices and proceedings of public and semi-public bodies and
general meetings of public companies. There is qualified privilege at common law wherever
there is a duty to communicate information and an interest in receiving it. For the press the
defence stops some way short of covering everything that the public might have some interest in hearing. It extends only to matters in respect of which there can be said to be a duty
to report. A more private example is the writing of references, as for instance when a person
applies for a new job. It is precisely at this point that the law of negligence has invaded the
law of defamation, undermining the law which formerly seemed clear, that a referee could
not be liable in the absence of malice proved by the claimant.[559]

It is clear that the law in this area is not in a satisfactory condition, not only because of this inva- **2.289**
sion, but because the concepts of duty and corresponding interest are inherently uncertain.[560] A
particularly difficult question is whether there should be a general defence of qualified privilege
in relation to all political information. The English answer has been that there should not. That
is considered immediately below.[561] Another area of confusion has arisen because of the privilege deriving from *Reynolds v Times Newspapers Ltd*,[562] also considered below. In *Loutchansky
v Times Newspapers (No 2)*[563] the newspaper had sought to expose a Russian businessman as a
gangster and money launderer. It made no attempt to justify this allegation, preferring to plead
qualified privilege. The Court of Appeal's judgment, delivered by Lord Phillips MR, held that
the trial judge had been wrong to ask whether the newspaper had been under a duty to publish
in the sense of being open to legitimate criticism if it had not done so. There certainly had to
be cases in which publication would be privileged even though a decision not to publish would

---

[554] See now Defamation Act 2013, s 2.
[555] See 2.344–2.348.
[556] Parliamentary Papers Act 1840 (subject to waiver by the defendant: Defamation Act 1996, s 13).
[557] Defamation Act 1996, s 15. The absolute privilege of witnesses has been extended to those who make
a complaint to the police: *Westcott v Westcott* [2008] EWCA Civ 818, [2009] QB 407.
[558] Defamation Act 1996, s 15, Sch 1. See now Defamation Act 2013, s 7.
[559] 2.12–2.13; *Spring v Guardian Assurance plc* [1995] 2 AC 296, HL.
[560] The evolution of the defence is examined in P Mitchell, 'Duties, Interests, and Motives: Privileged
Occasions in Defamation' (1998) 18 OJLS 381.
[561] 2.296.
[562] [2001] 2 AC 127, HL.
[563] [2001] EWCA Civ 1805, [2002] QB 783.

not have been open to criticism. The Court of Appeal sent this issue back for the judge to ask, bearing in mind the tensions between private and public interests, whether responsible journalists would have thought it right to publish. This test could not but pre-empt the issue of malice, in that responsible journalists would not publish on that motivation.

(iv) Honest opinion

2.290   Honest opinion is the statutory defence which replaces the common law defence of fair comment on a matter of public interest, recognized in *Reynolds v Times Newspapers Ltd*[564] as a bulwark of freedom of the press. The common law defence has been abolished.[565] The honest opinion defence is not confined to matters of public interest. The defendant must show that the statement complained of was a statement of opinion and that an honest person could have held the opinion at the time.[566] The defence is defeated if the claimant shows that the defendant did not hold the opinion.[567]

2.291   Honest opinion, like its predecessor fair comment, extends only to expressions of opinion, not to statements of fact, but the statement must indicate, whether in general or specific terms, the basis of the opinion.[568]

(v) Publication on matter of public interest

2.292   In *Reynolds v Times Newspapers Ltd*,[569] the House of Lords, and particularly Lord Nicholls, considered that a defence (which was inaccurately described as a privilege) should arise where a defendant could show that in the particular circumstances of an individual case there should be a defence for the publication of material which was in the public interest. The importance of the media, as watchdog and bloodhound, was fully recognized, and the courts were enjoined to incline in favour of free speech. This defence was applied in *Jameel v Wall Street Journal Europe Sprl*.[570] The Wall Street Journal published an article which suggested that there were reasonable grounds to suspect the involvement of the appellants in the witting or unwitting channelling of funds to terrorist organizations. A majority of the House of Lords held that the circumstances of publication met the conditions for this defence. The test to be applied is threefold. First, it must be in the public interest that the subject matter of the material be published. Second, making allowance for editorial judgement, the inclusion of the defamatory statement in the report must be justifiable; the more serious the allegation, the more important it is that it should make a real contribution to the public interest element in the article. Third, the steps taken to gather and publish the information must be responsible and fair. In *Jameel* the first two requirements of this test were easily satisfied: the public interest in relation to financing of terrorist activities was plain and the inclusion of the names of large and respectable Saudi businesses was an important part of the story. The third element was satisfied having regard to the circumstances, including the steps taken to verify the story, the opportunity given to the Jameel group to comment and the propriety of publication in the light of US diplomatic policy at the time. Although intended for (and usually invoked by) journalists and media organizations, this defence is also available to other defendants

---

[564] [2001] 2 AC 127, HL.
[565] Defamation Act 2013, s 3(8).
[566] Defamation Act 2013, s 3.
[567] Defamation Act 2013, s 3(5).
[568] Defamation Act 2013, s 3(3).
[569] [2001] 2 AC 127, HL.
[570] [2006] UKHL 44, [2007] 1 AC 359. See also *Flood v Times Newspapers Ltd* [2012] UKSC 11, [2012] 2 AC 273, where the Supreme Court rejected an argument that it could never be in the public interest for the detailed allegations underlying a criminal investigation to be published before the investigation was complete or any charges brought.

provided the three conditions are satisfied.[571] The common law *Reynolds* defence was abolished and replaced by the Defamation Act 2013, s 4. Section 4 makes it a defence to an action for defamation that the statement in question was on a matter of public interest and that the defendant reasonably believed that publishing the statement was in the public interest. In deciding whether the defence has been established, the court must have regard to all the circumstances and make such allowance for editorial judgement as it considers appropriate.

A special form of the *Reynolds* defence applies in cases of 'reportage', where the thrust of a repetition of a defamatory allegation is not the truth of the allegation, but the fact that it has been made.[572] Reportage of this kind is protected by the defence even if steps are not taken to ensure the accuracy of the information, as long as it was in the public interest to report the fact of the allegation having been made, and those reporting the allegation acted responsibly, and did so in a 'fair, disinterested and neutral way', without adopting the allegation as their own.[573] Cases of this kind have been described by Lord Phillips P as 'an example of circumstances in which the public interest justifies publication of facts that carry defamatory inferences without imposing on the journalist any obligation to attempt to verify the truth of those inferences'.[574] **2.293**

(vi) Offer of amends

The most important statutory defence is the offer of amends. Under sections 2–4 of the Defamation Act 1996 an offer to publish a correction and an apology and to pay such compensation as may be agreed may bar any subsequent action for defamation, provided the defamer neither knew nor had reason to know that the statement was defamatory of the person in question.[575] **2.294**

(f) Political speech and political institutions

Two decisions of the House of Lords have enlarged the freedom to comment on political matters. In *Derbyshire CC v Times Newspapers Ltd*,[576] *The Times* had published articles casting doubt on the propriety of the claimant council's management of its pension funds. The House of Lords held that it would be directly contrary to the public interest if institutions of central or local government were to have the right to sue for defamation, since this would impede the discovery of malpractices which ought to be revealed. This principle has since been extended to political parties.[577] Individual politicians are not thereby deprived of the right to sue. **2.295**

In *Reynolds v Times Newspapers Ltd*,[578] *The Times* newspaper was sued by the former Prime Minister of Ireland for articles alleging that he had misled the Irish Parliament, the Dáil. The newspaper argued that political information fell within the defence of qualified privilege as being invariably information which it was the duty of the media to publish and the interest of the public to know. The public for its part had a legitimate interest in demanding such information. This is a position taken in some major Commonwealth jurisdictions.[579] However, the House of Lords thought that a generic political defence of that kind would make an unnecessary sacrifice of the protection of reputation. It would be better to build up a case law profile of the circumstances in which a defence would arise **2.296**

---

[571] *Seaga v Harper* [2008] UKPC 9, [2009] 1 AC 1.
[572] *Roberts v Gable* [2007] EWCA Civ 721, [2008] QB 502.
[573] *Roberts v Gable* [2007] EWCA Civ 721, [2008] QB 502, at [61], *per* Ward LJ.
[574] *Flood v Times Newspapers Ltd* [2012] UKSC 11, [2012] 2 AC 273, at [35].
[575] *Milne v Express Newspapers* [2004] EWCA Civ 664, [2005] 1 WLR 772.
[576] [1993] AC 534, HL.
[577] *Goldsmith v Bhoyrul* [1998] QB 459.
[578] [2001] 2 AC 127, HL.
[579] See further, F Trindade, 'Defamatory Statements and Political Discussion' (2000) 116 LQR 185.

for publication of political information. The defence of publication on a matter of public interest (Defamation Act 2013, section 4) will require the court to have regard to all the circumstances of the case.

(g) Damages

2.297 Exemplary and aggravated damages are discussed below.[580] Defamation not infrequently gives rise to the latter and in one case to the former, namely where it is necessary to show that tort does not pay. It is only necessary to say here that there was previously great concern about the inflated levels of awards, seemingly out of all proportion to the sums recovered for personal injury. This concern resulted in a determination to exercise some control over the jury's freedom, and hence the passage of section 8 of the Courts and Legal Services Act 1990, which allows the Court of Appeal to reduce excessive awards to a reasonable level.[581]

(h) Defamation and other torts

2.298 We have already seen the overlap between the tort of defamation, which protects the nominate right to reputation, and the general tort of negligence, which is concerned with a general right not to suffer damage by the carelessness of another. We saw that the infiltration of negligence allows a claimant to prevent defences such as qualified privilege being raised.[582] Defamation also overlaps with another general tort which focuses upon the fault of the defendant rather than a particular right of the claimant, namely malicious falsehood. Defamation requires the publication of a defamatory statement. Malicious falsehood is designed to cover the case in which a lie told about someone does damage to his financial interests, without being defamatory. The original case was 'slander of title': it is not defamatory to say that a person has a bad title to his land, but it is a potent means of inflicting loss. Again, it is not defamatory to say that a person is no longer trading from such and such premises, but it can cost him business.[583]

2.299 The overlap arises because a false statement does not cease to be a malicious falsehood merely because it is also defamatory. To say that a person is a thief is defamatory, but to say it maliciously and so to harm his financial prospects is also malicious falsehood.[584]

2.300 Faced with a choice between the two torts the claimant will generally choose defamation. In the absence of privilege there is then no requirement to prove malice; the onus is on the defendant to prove that the allegations were true; and conditional fee arrangements are possible. On the other hand there is no legal aid for defamation cases, but for malicious falsehood there is. Such tactical choices are not frowned upon.[585]

---

[580] 4.163–4.165 and 4.92.

[581] Invoked in *Rantzen v Mirror Group Newspapers Ltd* [1994] QB 670, CA. See also *John v Mirror Group Newspapers Ltd* [1997] QB 586, CA; In *Tolstoy Miloslavsky v UK* (1995) Series A no 316 (1995) 20 EHRR 442 (award of £1.5m defamation damages against Count Tolstoy breached his right to freedom of expression under Art 10 of the European Convention) the European Court of Human Rights condemned the level of an award of £1.5m made against Count Tolstoy as in breach of Article 10 of the European Convention on Human Rights.

[582] *Spring v Guardian Assurance plc* [1995] 2 AC 296, HL.

[583] *Joyce v Motor Surveys Ltd* [1948] Ch 252.

[584] *Joyce v Sengupta* [1993] 1 WLR 337, CA. On the basis that some instrument is better than none, claimants whose real problem was harassment or invasion of privacy have chosen now defamation (*Tolley v JS Fry & Sons Ltd* [1931] AC 333, HL), now malicious falsehood (*Kaye v Robertson* [1991] 1 FSR 62, CA).

[585] But an ingenious attempt to switch from defamation to conspiracy in order to sidestep the defence of justification met with no sympathy in *Lonrho plc v Fayed (No 5)* [1993] 1 WLR 1489, CA.

F. Strict Liability: Interference with Property Rights

The law's protection of property rights has two aspects. There is first the protection of the **2.301** claimant's right to the physical integrity of his assets. Here the law lays down what it will do about damage. Then there is the protection of the right to control the asset, where the law says what it will do when another person assumes control without consent, as for instance by finding, or taking, or buying from a non-owner.

When a chattel or land is damaged, redress is usually sought through the tort of negligence, **2.302** although it may also be sought in trespass, which was formerly the dominant wrong. Unlike negligence, trespass liability is strict although the act must be willed. This has already been considered.[586] The primary tort in relation to interference with chattels is now conversion, which focuses upon interferences with control. The first two subsections are concerned only with corporeal property. The third section deals briefly with incorporeals.

(1) Common Law

(a) No *vindicatio* at common law

In classical Roman law a claimant could go to court and make a direct assertion of his own- **2.303** ership of the asset in question: 'That cow, Buttercup, is mine!' That assertion was called the *vindicatio*.[587] Such a claim has nothing to do with the law of torts or civil wrongs. It is a pure proprietary claim, in that it is nothing other than the assertion of the proprietary right. There is probably no system in which such a pure proprietary claim does all the work of protecting this right. But in some it stands in the front line.

In English law, on the common law side, if it comes to litigation, there is no *vindicatio*. **2.304** Outside the court there is nothing to prevent the claimant saying, 'That cow, Buttercup, is mine!' The person in possession may concede and surrender Buttercup. Within imperfectly defined limits, the claimant can also have recourse to self-help to take back his asset.[588] However the common law simply does not recognize a demand in court which consists in the direct assertion of ownership. There is, in this sense, no pure proprietary remedy, no *vindicatio*.

The one exception to this might be said to be the action to recover land, formerly the action **2.305** of ejectment. In the early days of the common law the writ of right and the writs of entry might have been said to be pure proprietary claims, with the additional and exceptional feature, unknown to the classical *vindicatio*, that judgment would be for the surrender of possession of the thing itself.[589] However, the real actions gave way to a special action of trespass with force and arms which was in turn in due course equipped with that characteristic which gave the real actions their name, the order to surrender the thing itself.[590] Statutory reforms, first as part of the abolition of the forms of action and then aimed to speed up the recovery

---

[586] 2.235–2.248, and 2.243.

[587] WW Buckland, *A Textbook of Roman Law from Augustus to Justinian* (P Stein ed, 3rd edn, 1963) 675; F Schulz, *Classical Roman Law* (1951) 368–372.

[588] Reasonable force, short of violence, may be used if no trespass to land is involved, and even some degree of trespass to land appears to be permitted, again without violence: S Gleeson, *Personal Property Law* (1997) 304; FH Lawson, *Remedies of English Law* (2nd edn, 1980) chs 1 and 2. Under the Consumer Credit Act 1974, owners within s 92 may not enter premises without a court order. Violent entry is a criminal offence under the Criminal Law Act 1977, s 6.

[589] This is the root of 'real property'—property in respect of which a claim would yield the *res* (thing) itself. See EPL 4.14–4.16.

[590] AWB Simpson, *A History of the Land Law* (2nd edn, 1986) 144–149.

of possession against squatters, have broken every meaningful link with the tort of trespass. The modern action to recover land is essentially a *vindicatio* which gives specific recovery. The claimant does not prove absolute entitlement but merely a better right to possession than the defendant.

(b) Parasitic protection at common law

2.306 Although lacking direct protection through the simple assertion of property rights, the common law recognized two forms of claim in the law of obligations, one in the law of wrongs and the other in the law of unjust enrichment. The former says: 'You ought to pay me money because you have committed a wrong in that you have interfered with such and such a thing to which I had a better possessory right than you.' The latter says, 'You ought to pay me the value of such and such a thing to which I had a better right than you, by the receipt of which you have been enriched at my expense.' The law of unjust enrichment having been fragmented and concealed, the latter claim has rather rarely come out into the open. No more will be said of it here save to say that enrichment is concerned with an abstract measure of value and indirectly protects all assets, whilst a majority of the House of Lords has recently insisted that the torts involving interferences with property rights are confined to tangible things in which the claimant has a possessory right good against all the world.[591]

(i) *Two wrongs under one statutory umbrella*

2.307 The Torts (Interference with Goods) Act 1977 'abolished' the old action of detinue and created a loosely unified regime for all interferences with goods, including damage actionable in negligence.[592] For the protection of rights to possession and control of goods the Act left intact two wrongs. One was trespass with force and arms, in the form which used to be known as *de bonis asportatis* (concerning goods carried away). This tort of trespass to goods requires a direct and intentional interference with the claimant's possessory right to the chattel. The other wrong was conversion, which began life as one species of the originally supplementary actions called trespass on the case, or simply case. Conversion is indisputably dominant, and frequently overlaps with trespass to goods, so that eg a thief who drives off with your car commits both torts. The overlap is not complete, however, and conversion does not completely cover the field of trespass to goods. Clamping a car may constitute a trespass, eg,[593] but is unlikely to amount to the assertion of control required for a conversion.

(ii) *Conversion*

2.308 The heart of the tort of conversion is an act of assertion of control, but it is an act denatured by the deletion of all traces of dishonesty or lesser degrees of fault. It is enough that the assertion of control is intended and without the consent of the defendant, who has the superior right to possession. In outline, the old action on the case for conversion used to recite, first, that the claimant was possessed of such and such a silver cup as of his own proper goods; secondly, that he casually lost the same and the defendant found it;[594] and thirdly that the

---

[591] *OBG Ltd v Allan* [2007] UKHL 21, [2008] 1 AC 1. Lord Nicholls and Baroness Hale dissented on the basis that the distinction between tangibles and intangibles lacks any rhyme or reason although, oddly, both required proof of fault in an action for unlawful interference with (intangible) trade rights. Further discussion of unjust enrichment at 3.46–3.55.

[592] Torts (Interference with Goods) Act 1977, ss 1, 2.

[593] See, eg, *Arthur v Anker* [1997] QB 564, CA, where however the clamper could rely on the defence of *volenti non fit injuria*.

[594] Because of this allegation of finding the action was often called 'trover' (cf the modern French '*trouver*'). The allegation of loss and finding was no more than a standard formal explanation of the arrival of the thing in the defendant's hands. The formal allegation could not be traversed. The real story would come out before the jury.

defendant fraudulently converted the cup to his own use, to the claimant's damage.[595] At the heart of this heavily fictitious pleading was a notion of misappropriation. Conversion expanded from this action for misappropriation to a central idea of control, covering much of the ground of detinue.[596] In 2002, Lord Nicholls said that it included any voluntary act, inconsistent with the rights of the owner, which excludes him from the use and enjoyment of the chattel.[597]

Strict liability. Part of the reason why conversion expanded as a tort of strict liability might **2.309** have been in order to allow it to do the work of the missing *vindicatio*. However, the tort of conversion went well beyond the Roman vindicatio, at least in its classical form, since the action was commonly brought even when the defendant no longer had possession.[598] The development of conversion was achieved in the manner characteristic of the law's development under the forms of action, by holding that the allegations of fraud could not be traversed, so that they became merely decorative: in its original scope involving misappropriations, the liability was established by the objective fact of the misappropriation, however innocent. Thus a cycle shop which sells my bicycle commits the tort, even if it has no reason whatever to think that the bicycle is not its own. And if one person grinds another's corn into flour without the other's consent, that too is a conversion.[599] As Cleasby B said in *Fowler v Hollins*, 'Persons deal with the property in chattels or exercise acts of ownership over them at their peril.'[600] Both conversion and, in this function, trespass, are the same in this respect.

Assertion of control. Not only is liability strict but the expansion of conversion from misap- **2.310** propriation to an assertion of control means that the tort now includes any voluntary exercise of control over a thing which is inconsistent with the claimant's superior right to possession of it. Thus a carrier or warehouseman commits conversion if he delivers to the wrong person;[601] an auctioneer converts when he sells for another;[602] one who refuses to deliver up a thing to another with a better title is nowadays treated as converting the thing,[603] although such a refusal was formerly no more than evidence from which to infer a conversion;[604] one who consumes or intentionally destroys a thing converts it, though mere damage is not a conversion;[605] and successive possessors who each act inconsistently with the claimant's right to possession can all be liable for conversion.[606] Storage is not in itself a conversion, since to store on the orders of the wrong person is not to deny the true owner's right to possession.[607] A careless act resulting in loss or destruction cannot be a conversion, for, even on an objective analysis, without a voluntary act there can be no assertion of rights inconsistent with those of the claimant.[608]

---

[595] Examples in JH Baker and SFC Milsom, *Sources of English Legal History: Private Law to 1750* (1986) 531–539.
[596] *Baldwin v Cole* (1705) 6 Mod 212, 212; 90 ER 1290, 1290, *per* Holt CJ.
[597] *Kuwait Airways Corp v Iraqi Airways Co (Nos 4 and 5)* [2002] UKHL 19, [2002] 2 AC 883, at [39].
[598] Ultimately the justification for the development of strict liability can only be as a 'salutary rule for the protection of property': *Fowler v Hollins* (1872) LR 7 QB 616, 639, Exch Ch, *per* Cleasy B.
[599] *Hollins v Fowler* (1875) LR 7 HL 757, 768, *per* Blackburn J.
[600] (1872) LR 7 QB 616, 639, Exch Ch.
[601] *Hiort v Bott* (1874) LR 9 Ex 86.
[602] *RH Willis & Son v British Car Auctions Ltd* [1978] 1 WLR 438, CA.
[603] *Howard E Perry & Co Ltd v British Railways Board* [1980] 1 WLR 1375.
[604] *Isaack v Clark* (1615) 2 Buls 306, 80 ER 1143; 1 Rolle 127, 81 ER 377.
[605] *Simmons v Lillystone* (1853) 8 Exch 431, 255 ER 1417.
[606] *Kuwait Airways Corp v Iraqi Airways Co (Nos 4 and 5)* [2002] UKHL 19, [2002] 2 AC 883.
[607] *Hollins v Fowler* (1875) LR 7 HL 757, 767, *per* Blackburn J. Applied in *Marcq v Christie, Manson & Woods Ltd* [2003] EWCA Civ 731, [2004] QB 286 (returning an unsold painting to the purported owner who had instructed the sale was not conversion although it would have been different if the painting had been delivered to a new purchaser).
[608] *The Arpad* [1934] P 189, 232, CA, *per* Maugham LJ.

2.311 **Claimant with a better right to possession.** The proper claimant is a person with a better right to possession than the defendant, and this in turn means that the thing in question must be susceptible of possession,[609] which pure incorporeals are not. A finder can sue,[610] since he has the general property in the goods, albeit by a very short possessory title. His very possession gives him a right to possess. Similarly, a bailee in possession, whatever form that bailment takes, has a right to possess although the bailment gives him only a special property in the thing. The bailee who sues for conversion is under a duty to his bailor to account for that portion of the recovered damages which exceed his own loss.[611] Even a thief can sue. That there is almost no exception based on illegality on the part of the possessor is affirmed in a fine judgment of the Court of Appeal in *Costello v Chief Constable of Derbyshire Constabulary*.[612] Under section 19 of the Police and Criminal Evidence Act 1984 the police had seized from Costello a Ford Escort car. The temporary purpose of that seizure having been exhausted, they refused to return it on the ground that it had been stolen and Costello knew that. Although they were held to be correct in those beliefs they were compelled to return the car to him. The wrongful possessor had a right to possession which could only be defeated by statute. Statute apart, the only exception was that the court would not order the delivery up of something to a person if it would be unlawful for him to receive it, as for instance prohibited drugs or a gun for which he held no licence.[613]

2.312 The importance of relative title was formerly emphasized by the rule that a defendant could not plead a *jus tertii*—ie, he could not adduce evidence that a third party had a better title than the claimant—except in the case in which the claimant was relying solely on his own possession. This has been changed by section 8 of the Torts (Interference with Goods) Act 1977. In the *Costello* case the police were not in a position to resist Costello's claim by invoking this section because they could not identify the third party nor join him as a party to the action as the section requires.

2.313 **Money orders.** The tort of conversion gives rise to both loss-based and gain-based rights.[614] This follows from the House of Lords' analysis of the meaning of the old language of 'waiver of tort' in *United Australia Ltd v Barclays Bank Ltd*.[615] Instead of the usual action for compensatory damages, an action for 'money had and received' could be brought for money obtained through the commission of a tort.[616] 'Waiver of tort' usually described that practice. The House of Lords held that, so far as concerned the tort of conversion, the proper analysis of that practice in a world no longer dominated by forms of action was that the tort gave rise to two secondary rights. The one cause of action gave the claimant a choice between a compensatory and a gain-based claim. It was not a case of switching from a cause of action in tort to a cause of action in unjust enrichment and certainly did not connote any ratification or forgiveness of the tort.

2.314 Under section 3 of the Torts (Interference with Goods) Act 1977 the claimant's right to a money order is expressed as a right to damages. In view of the fact that the claimant has

---

[609] Also, if it adds anything, the thing must be capable of possession as property, so that conversion cannot be brought in respect of a part of a human body, unless it has been transformed into a laboratory specimen: *Dobson v North Tyneside HA* [1997] 1 WLR 596, CA.

[610] *Armory v Delamirie* (1722) 1 Strange 505, 93 ER 664; see EPL 4.422– 4.423.

[611] *The Winkfield* [1902] P 42, CA.

[612] [2001] EWCA Civ 381, [2001] 1 WLR 1437, following and further explaining *Webb v Chief Constable of Merseyside Police* [2000] 2 QB 427, CA.

[613] [2001] EWCA Civ 381, [2001] 1 WLR 1437, at [34].

[614] 4.149–4.152.

[615] [1943] AC 1, HL.

[616] *Lamine v Dorrell* (1705) 2 Ld Raym 1216, 92 ER 303.

a choice between two measures of recovery, it has to be assumed that the word 'damages' includes both compensatory (loss-based) awards and gain-based awards.[617]

So far as compensatory damages are concerned, the Act allows recovery of the value of the **2.315** chattel together with any consequential loss. There are three areas of difficulty. The first is the date for valuing the chattel. This will be important where the chattel has either depreciated or appreciated in value in the intervening period. So far as fluctuations of the market are concerned, the pre-1977 position seems to have been that in actions for conversion the relevant date was the date of the conversion, whereas in actions of detinue, the relevant date was that of the judgment. Although detinue is said to have been abolished, it is probably still necessary to identify in a claim whether, before 1977, the claim would have arisen in detinue or in conversion.[618] The second area of difficulty is in cases in which the value of the chattel is greater than the loss that has been suffered. There are cases pulling in both directions but the prevailing authority suggests that the award will not exceed the amount of the loss.[619] The third area of difficulty is causation of loss. Where there have been successive tortfeasors, such as successive converters, the application of the 'but for' test of causation leads to the conclusion than none but the first possessor is liable. We saw that the same difficulty arose in relation to successive events after a negligent act which are sufficient to cause the same loss. In *Kuwait Airways Corp v Iraqi Airways Co (Nos 4 and 5)*[620] during the invasion of Kuwait, the Iraqi Air Force took possession of several of the claimant's aircraft and flew them to Iraq. A law was passed incorporating the aircraft into the defendant's fleet and the defendants took possession and asserted control over the aircraft. The difficulty the claimants faced was showing that their loss had been caused by the defendants, since but for the defendants' possession, the Iraqi Air Force would still have deprived the claimants of their aircraft. In the leading speech in the House of Lords, Lord Nicholls explained that although it could not be said, by application of the but for test for causation, that each successive converter might not have caused an owner loss, the test for causation should focus only on whether the claimant would have suffered the loss in question had he retained the goods and not been deprived of them by the particular defendant.[621] The focus of the tort is the effect of the actions of the defendant on the claimant's property rights; acts of third parties are irrelevant.[622]

When damages are assessed so as to compensate the claimant for the whole value of a claim- **2.316** ant's right to goods, the payment of those damages extinguishes the claimant's right. The same applies to payments made on the same basis under settlements. The precise conditions under which this happens are spelled out in section 5 of the 1977 Act.

Specific delivery. Conversion formerly gave only a money award. The Act changed that. In any **2.317** action for interference with goods the claimant may choose instead to ask for an order for delivery up of the thing in question 'giving the defendant the alternative of paying damages by reference to the value of the goods, together in either alternative with payment of any consequential

---

[617] It is certain that the Act elsewhere uses 'damages' to include gain-based awards, even when the cause of action is unjust enrichment rather than a wrong: see the example give in s 6(2)(b). See also J Edelman, *Gain-Based Damages* (2002) 118.

[618] *BBMB Finance (Hong Kong) Ltd v Eda Holdings Ltd* [1990] 1 WLR 409, PC (date of conversion); *IBL Ltd v Coussens* [1991] 2 All ER 133, CA (date of judgment).

[619] [2002] UKHL 19, [2002] 2 AC 883, at [63], Lord Nicholls approving cases including *Hiort v London and North Western Railway Co* (1879) 4 Ex D 188, where no recovery was allowed when the claimant's goods were misdelivered but the claimant would equally have received no payment for his goods if, instead of misdelivering the goods, the railway company had delivered them in accordance with his instructions. See also *Borders (UK) Ltd v Commissioner of Police of the Metropolis* [2005] EWCA Civ 197.

[620] [2002] UKHL 19, [2002] 2 AC 883.

[621] [2002] UKHL 19, [2002] 2 AC 883, at [78]–[86].

[622] See, eg, *Hiort v London and North Western Railway Co* (1879) 4 Ex D 188.

damages'.[623] In addition the court itself is entitled, in its discretion, to make an order for delivery up and payment of consequential damages without the option for payment of the value.[624]

2.318 **Limitation.** The operation of time limits here plays an important part in the law's compromise between the sanctity of ownership and the security of transactions. Under the Limitation Act 1980 the basic time limit for actions of conversion is six years, and, exceptionally, the expiry of the period of limitation extinguishes the claimant's title.[625] Time does not however run against a thief.[626] A purchaser from the thief will also convert the goods. In respect of that conversion, time will begin to run if the purchase is made in good faith, and after six years from that good faith conversion the title of the victim of the theft will be extinguished.[627] Note, however, that even in this case the action against the thief himself is preserved.[628]

(2) Equity

(a) Exclusion from common law protections

2.319 An equitable owner has no access to the common law means discussed above. *In MCC Proceeds Inc v Lehman Bros International (Europe)*,[629] American shares were held in trust for MCC Proceeds. The trustee, in breach of trust, mortgaged the shares as security for a loan. MCC's claim in equity encountered the objection that the defendants were bona fide purchasers for value without notice of the equitable right. In this case MCC tried to sue the defendant in conversion, to which there is in general no bona fide purchase defence. The claim failed on more than one ground, above all because MCC could not bring conversion, which is a common law action based on a right to immediate possession. Further, the common law does not recognize the equitable title of the beneficiary of a trust.[630]

2.320 There are just two qualifications. First, if a beneficiary under a trust is in possession he can bring an action for conversion, not *qua* equitable owner, but just in the same way as anyone who has a possessory title.[631] Secondly, a trustee almost always has the legal right and the legal means of protecting it. Unless the trustee has transferred that right himself,[632] or it has exceptionally passed against his will,[633] he can and must bring his common law action on the trust's behalf, and if he will not, he can be joined as co-defendant.

(b) The equitable *vindicatio*

2.321 By '*vindicatio*' is meant the direct assertion of a proprietary right. Unlike the common law, equity does know such a claim. A claimant can say, 'That Rolls Royce is mine!' What he actually asks for is a declaration that the defendant holds the Rolls Royce on trust for him. In *Macmillan Inc v Bishopsgate Investment Trust plc (No 3)*,[634] Macmillan's plea was

---

[623] Torts (Interference with Goods) Act 1977, s 3(2)(b), (3). Specific delivery orders are not available in the case of money: s 14(1).

[624] Torts (Interference with Goods) Act 1977, s 3(2)(a), (3). See *Pendragon plc v Walon Ltd* [2005] EWHC 1082 (QB).

[625] Limitation Act 1980, ss 2 and 3.

[626] Limitation Act 1980, s 4(1).

[627] Limitation Act 1980, s 4(2).

[628] Limitation Act 1980, s 4(1).

[629] [1998] 4 All ER 675, CA.

[630] *MCC Proceeds Inv v Lehmann Bros International (Europe)* [1998] 4 All ER 675, CA.

[631] *Healey v Healey* [1915] 1 KB 938. The extension of this case to an equitable owner with no possessory title in *International Factors Ltd v Rodriguez* [1979] QB 351, CA was illegitimate.

[632] As in *Re Montagu's Settlement Trusts* [1987] Ch 264.

[633] See, eg, *Lipkin Gorman v Karpnale Ltd* [1991] 2 AC 548, HL.

[634] [1996] 1 WLR 387, CA.

essentially 'Please say that all the financial institutions to which our trustee gave our Berlitz shares now hold those shares on trust for us, and please order them to hand them over.'

The *vindicatio* is abstract. 'That is mine!' is the assertion of a conclusion from facts. Facts **2.322** have to be adduced which in law substantiate the proposition. In the *Macmillan* case the relevant facts were all in place but encountered a defence. The disgraced tycoon, Maxwell, had procured a gratuitous transfer of Macmillan's shares in circumstances which made the transferee a resulting trustee, and then, very soon afterwards, he had caused the transferee to make an express declaration of trust in favour of Macmillan. Maxwell then transferred his shares to lending institutions as security for huge loans. Macmillan's difficulty was that its equitable ownership was vulnerable to destruction by bona fide purchase of the legal title.

(c) Parasitic protection in equity

There is further parasitic protection in equity through the obligation arising from the know- **2.323** ing receipt of assets dissipated in breach of trust. This liability has a requirement of fault, variously put as dishonesty,[635] carelessness in the form of failing to make the inquiries which a reasonable person would have made in the circumstances,[636] and, more recently, an amorphous test of unconscionability.[637]

In many cases in which trust property gets into the wrong hands someone who has assisted **2.324** in the misdirection will incur a liability for 'dishonest assistance' and will have to make good the beneficiaries' loss, whether or not he received the property himself. 'Dishonest assistance' unequivocally requires proof of dishonesty on the part of the alleged accessory to the misdirection.[638]

(3) Incorporeal Assets

Conversion and trespass focus on possession. And the Torts (Interference with Goods) Act **2.325** 1977 not only makes no change in that but underlines the fact that its regime does not apply to incorporeal assets when in section 14(1) it defines goods as 'all chattels personal other than things in action and money'. For present purposes a 'thing in action', which contrasts with 'thing in possession' may be regarded as any valuable right which, failing voluntary compliance, depends for its realization on an action brought in court.

Documentary intangibles, such as cheques,[639] are in a special position. The paper, almost **2.326** valueless in itself, is a corporeal chattel like any other, but in addition the document is treated as representing the underlying obligation 'Into this category fall bills of lading, negotiable bills of exchange and a range of other negotiable instruments'.[640] In England this list does not include shares, unless they are bearer shares, which are nowadays rarely found.[641]

Among the most important incorporeal assets are intellectual property rights[642] and also **2.327** confidential information, although confidential information is not protected solely as wealth

---

[635] *Re Montagu's Settlement Trusts* [1987] Ch 264.
[636] *Belmont Finance Corporation Ltd v Williams Furniture Ltd (No 2)* [1980] 1 All ER 393, CA.
[637] *Bank of Credit and Commerce International (Overseas) Ltd v Akindele* [2001] Ch 437, CA.
[638] See 2.363–2.366.
[639] *United Australia Ltd v Barclays Bank Ltd* [1941] AC 1, HL.
[640] E McKendrick, *Goode on Commercial Law* (4th edn, 2010) 53.
[641] Contrast the American shares involved in *MCC Proceeds Inc v Lehman Bros International (Europe)* [1998] 4 All ER 675, CA.
[642] See EPL ch 6 (intellectual property). For the torts of passing off and injurious falsehood, see EPL 6.99–6.107.

but sometimes as a particular emanation of privacy. Of the intellectual property rights, only copyright is indirectly protected by the tort of conversion because the tort of conversion is concerned only with tangible things.[643] The ownership of reproduced copyrighted material vests in the holder of the copyright with the consequence that he can sue for conversion.[644] It is, however, broadly true that the regimes for redressing infringements of such rights operate in much the same way as does the tort of conversion in relation to corporeal chattels. That is to say, the available remedial rights are commonly compensatory or disgorgement awards: they either make good the claimant's loss or strip out the infringer's profit. And these remedial rights are backed by injunctions to compel discontinuance of the infringement. Furthermore liability is strict, as it is in conversion. However, a difference has crept in, in that fault has sometimes been invoked both at common law and in statutes as relevant to the measure of compensation. This has not been approached in a principled manner, however, with the consequence that the presence and absence of fault has different consequences in relation to different infringements. These variations are considered below.[645]

G. Strict Liability: Breach of Fiduciary Duty

(1) Difficulty in Definition of a Fiduciary

2.328 Equity's wrong of strict liability is breach of fiduciary duty. Fiduciary is anglicized Latin which conveys notions of honour, honesty, trust and faithfulness. The archetypal fiduciary is the trustee but there are other fiduciary relationships, such as a company director/company,[646] agent/principal[647] and solicitor/client,[648] which are characterized by these same notions of honour, honesty, trust and faith.[649] A fiduciary relationship will arise where 'one party is reasonably entitled to repose and does repose trust and confidence in the other, either generally or in the particular transaction'.[650] However, despite the etymology and constant reference to trust in fiduciary relationships, the concept is neither sufficient nor necessary for a fiduciary relationship. It is not sufficient because some relationships of trust have not traditionally been regarded as fiduciary: parent/child, teacher/student or doctor/patient.[651] It is also not sufficient because the presence of actual trust in a relationship does not create a fiduciary relationship; a purchaser and a vendor are not in a fiduciary relationship if the purchaser places actual trust and confidence in the vendor. On the other hand, the presence of actual trust is not a necessary condition because a bare trustee is still a fiduciary even though he has very little power to affect the interests of the beneficiary and even if the beneficiary has never met the trustee and has never placed any actual trust or confidence in him.

---

[643] *OBG Ltd v Allan* [2007] UKHL 21, [2008] 1 AC 1. See 2.306.
[644] *Caxton Publishing Co Ltd v Sutherland Publishing Co Ltd* [1939] AC 178, HL.
[645] From 4.153–4.154.
[646] *Regal (Hastings) Ltd v Gulliver* [1967] 2 AC 134, HL; *Ultraframe (UK) Ltd v Fielding* [2005] EWHC 1638 (Ch).
[647] *Boston Deep Sea Fishing and Ice Co v Ansell* (1888) 39 Ch D 389, CA.
[648] *Hilton v Barker Booth Eastwood* [2005] UKHL 8, [2005] 1 WLR 567.
[649] P Birks, 'The Content of Fiduciary Obligation' (2002) 16 Trust Law Int 34, 36.
[650] *Estate Realties Ltd v Wignall* [1991] 3 NZLR 482, 492, per Tipping J, NZCA.
[651] In *Sidaway v Bethlem Royal Hospital* [1985] AC 871, 884, HL, Lord Scarman insisted that the doctor/patient relationship was not fiduciary. Canadian law insists that it is: *Norberg v Wynrib* (1992) 92 DLR (4th) 449; *McInerney v MacDonald* [1992] 2 SCR 138, SCC. Compare also *Hedley Byrne & Co Ltd v Heller & Partners Ltd* [1964] AC 465, 509, HL, per Lord Hodson (parent/child an accepted category of fiduciary relation).

Another attempt at definition is the famous statement of Mason J in the High Court of **2.329** Australia in *Hospital Products Ltd v United States Surgical Corporation*.[652] After referring to the concepts of trust and confidence, Mason J placed emphasis on a different characteristic:

> the fiduciary undertakes or agrees to act for or on behalf of or in the interests of another person in the exercise of a power or discretion which will affect the interests of that other person in a legal or practical sense.

Similarly, many cases refer to a hallmark of the fiduciary relation as 'vulnerability', in the sense of a high level of power that a fiduciary has to affect the interests of a beneficiary.[653] However, these concepts of power, discretion and vulnerability are too broad because many commercial relationships will involve one party with significant power to affect the interests of the other. Such commercial relationships are rarely fiduciary. A related definition of a fiduciary relationship focuses upon the requirement to serve exclusively the interests of a person or group of persons.[654] But this is circular: it defines the fiduciary relationship by reference to the duties which are imposed once a person is characterized as a fiduciary.

A third approach suggests that courts should reason by analogy from the core fiduciary case of a **2.330** trustee to other similar trustee-like relationships of trust and confidence.[655] But this process of reasoning by analogy is fraught with difficulty: how can degrees of trust and confidence be measured? Where should a line be drawn? Can it really be said that analogies can be drawn between, eg, custodial trustees and non-custodial directors?[656] For the moment, it seems that the only safe course is to list those relationships which the courts have accepted to be fiduciary: trustee/beneficiary, director/company, solicitor/client, partner/partner and so on, whilst also remembering that a relationship may be fiduciary in relation to some of its incidents but not others.[657]

(2) Duties of Care Owed by Fiduciaries

We saw earlier in this chapter that in limited situations the common law regards as wrongful **2.331** the failure to act reasonably to protect the interests of another; a failure to take positive and reasonable action to protect another from harm.[658] Apart from contractual duties, situations of assumption of responsibility are the most obvious examples of situations in which such positive duties arise. Trustees and other fiduciaries are one class of persons who are subject to this duty of positive action. Their duty to protect the beneficiary from harm, such as by taking care in investment of trust assets, is nothing but a requirement of positive action connoting a duty of care, with the consequence that the wrong committed by breach of that duty is not distinct from the tort of negligence.[659] But, in the case of fiduciaries, there is a further,

---

[652] (1984) 156 CLR 41, 68, HCA.

[653] *Hospital Products Ltd v United States Surgical Corporation* (1984) 156 CLR 41, 142, HCA, *per* Dawson J; *Frame v Smith* (1987) 42 DLR (4th) 81, 99, SCC, *per* Wilson J.

[654] P Finn, 'The Fiduciary Principle' in T Youdan (ed), *Equity, Fiduciaries and Trusts* (1989) 31.

[655] P Birks, 'The Content of Fiduciary Obligation' (2002) 16 Trust Law Int 34.

[656] A point made in J Getzler, 'Rumford Market and the Genesis of Fiduciary Obligations' in A Burrows and A Rodger (eds), *Mapping the Law: Essays in Honour of Peter Birks* (2006).

[657] For the argument that the focus in fiduciary cases should shift from discussion of which types of relationship are fiduciary to whether particular fiduciary duties are expressed or implied in particular relationships, see J Edelman, 'When do Fiduciary Duties Arise?' (2010) 126 LQR 302.

[658] See 2.91–2.97.

[659] *Henderson v Merrett Syndicates Ltd* [1995] 2 AC 145, 205, HL, *per* Lord Browne-Wilkinson; *Bristol and West Building Society v Mothew* [1998] Ch 1, 16–18, CA, *per* Millett LJ; *Hilton v Barker Booth Eastwood* [2005] UKHL 8, [2005] 1 WLR 567, at [29], *per* Lord Walker; P Birks, 'The Content of Fiduciary Obligation' (2002) 16 Trust Law Int 34. This view is rejected by JD Heydon, 'Are the Duties of Company Directors to Exercise Care and Skill Fiduciary?' and J Getzler, 'Am I my Beneficiary's Keeper? Fusion and Loss-Based Fiduciary Remedies' in S Degeling and J Edelman (eds), *Equity in Commercial Law* (2005).

higher, duty owed by the principal, who is also bound to abstain from any interest of his own which might tempt him to sacrifice the beneficiary's interests. This higher duty, to act in a disinterested way unless authorized otherwise, is the characteristic fiduciary obligation.

(3) The Fiduciary Duties of Loyalty[660]

2.332 The fiduciary duty to act in a disinterested way unless authorized otherwise has historically been expressed as two particular duties. The first is a duty on the fiduciary not to pursue, without authority, an interest which conflicts, or might conflict, with his duty to take positive and reasonable action to protect the interests of the principal. Second, he is under a duty not to profit from his fiduciary position without authorization. The two duties are closely related. Indeed, the first duty almost completely swallows the second because there will be few situations in which a fiduciary makes an unauthorized profit that does not arise from a conflict between his interests and the positive duty owed to his principal. But the second 'no-profit' duty still serves the important purpose of focusing upon situations in which there is a heightened degree of risk that the fiduciary will favour his own interests.[661] It provides an easier evidential route for the protection of the interests of the beneficiary or principal than positive proof of the first no-conflict rule; this role of easing the proof of the claimant's case is consistent with the origins of the no-profit duty as an offshoot of the no-conflict duty.[662]

2.333 The most common remedy for a breach of a fiduciary duty is not compensation but either disgorgement of profits or an order that any asset acquired in breach of fiduciary duty is held on trust for the principal. The leading case is *Keech v Sanford*.[663] A lease of the profits of the Rumford Market had been devised to the defendant trustee to hold on trust for an infant. Towards the expiry of the term, the trustee asked to renew the lease for the infant but the lessor refused because he would not be able to protect his interest against an infant beneficiary. The trustee then renewed the lease for himself. King LC held that the trustee had breached his duty in taking the benefit of the lease: 'though I do not say that there is a fraud in this case, yet he should rather have let it run out, than to have had the lease to himself... the trustee is the only person of all mankind who might not have the lease'.[664] The lease was ordered to be assigned to the infant and the trustee was ordered to account for all the profit he had derived from the lease.

2.334 As we have seen, the trustee is the archetypal fiduciary but not the only one. A famous example of an order for disgorgement of unauthorized fiduciary profits in other relationships of trust and confidence is *Boardman v Phipps*.[665] The appellants were a solicitor to a trust and a beneficiary under the trust. They acquired information in the course of representing the trust which allowed them to make a considerable profit from the purchase of shares in a company

---

[660] M Conaglen, *Fiduciary Loyalty* (2010).

[661] M Conaglen, 'The Nature and Function of Fiduciary Loyalty' (2005) 121 LQR 452, 467. The rule is 'based on the consideration that human nature being what it is, there is danger, in such circumstances, of the person holding a fiduciary position being swayed by interest rather than duty': *Bray v Ford* [1896] AC 44, 51–52, HL, *per* Lord Herschell. For a contrary view that the concern of these duties is with the motives, or deemed motives, of the principal see L Smith, 'The Motive not the Deed' in J Getzler (ed), *Rationalizing Property, Equity and Trusts: Essays in Honour of Edward Burn* (2003).

[662] A McLean, 'The Theoretical Basis of the Trustee's Duty of Loyalty' (1969) 7 Alberta L Rev 218, 219–227.

[663] (1726) Select Cas Temp King 61; 25 ER 223. Discussed in J Getzler, 'Rumford Market and the Genesis of Fiduciary Obligations' in A Burrows and A Rodger (eds), *Mapping the Law: Essays in Honour of Peter Birks* (2006).

[664] (1726) Select Cas Temp King 61, 62; 25 ER 223, 223.

[665] [1967] 2 AC 46, HL. See also *Regal (Hastings) Ltd v Gulliver* [1967] 2 AC 134, HL (liability of directors to disgorge profits made in breach of fiduciary duty).

in which the trust also owned shares. Although the trust could not have purchased the shares, and although the trust benefitted by the increased share price, the appellants were required to disgorge their profits to the beneficiaries. They were entitled to a deduction from the account of a liberal allowance for their work and skill, but despite their good faith were not excused from the breach of their fiduciary duty because they had not obtained fully informed consent for their actions from all the beneficiaries of the trust. One difficulty with the decision of the majority is their treatment of the beneficiary as owing fiduciary duties to the other beneficiaries in the same way as did the solicitor to the trust. But unlike the solicitor/client relation, the beneficiary/beneficiary relation does not share any of the usual attributes of a fiduciary relationship.[666] However, in the majority, Lord Cohen was content to observe that this point had not been taken in the courts below and, he thought, rightly so since it would have been a strange result if the solicitor were required to disgorge profits but the beneficiary, with whom he acted jointly, was not.[667]

It will be apparent from the discussion above that fiduciary duties, and the high level of loyalty that they require, are qualitatively different duties from the more standard duties of fiduciary and non-fiduciary alike including the ordinary duty to take care, as well as other duties which focus upon fault such as the fiduciary's duty not to act in bad faith.[668] However, the higher level duties of loyalty imposed on a fiduciary are closely related to these standard duties. As Birks has observed, the fiduciary duty cannot exist without the lower level duty of care because the fiduciary duty exists for the prophylactic purpose of ensuring that the fiduciary takes care in carrying out his duties.[669] Lord Nicholls has made a similar point, explaining that the most common remedy for breach of fiduciary duty—disgorgement of profits—has the function of reinforcing 'the duty of fidelity owed by a trustee or fiduciary by requiring him to account for any profits he derives from his office or position', thereby ensuring that 'trustees and fiduciaries are financially disinterested in carrying out their duties'.[670] **2.335**

A very difficult question is whether this degree of prophylactic protection is still required today. Over the last century there have been cries that the fiduciary obligation is too strict.[671] The great American trusts scholar John Langbein has now taken up this case, arguing that there are now many procedures by which a fiduciary can be monitored and that the no-conflict and no-profit duties can work to prevent a fiduciary acting in the best interests of the principal.[672] **2.336**

---

[666] *Featherstonhaugh v Fenwick* (1810) 17 Ves 298; *Kennedy v De Trafford* [1897] AC 180, 186–90, HL; *Re Biss* [1903] 2 Ch 40, CA.

[667] [1967] 2 AC 46, 104.

[668] *Klug v Klug* [1918] 2 Ch 67; *Tempest v Lord Camoys* (1882) 21 ChD 571. The duty upon a trustee not to act on the basis of irrelevant or inadequate considerations is better understood as a fiduciary *power* to avoid transactions rather than a duty. The exercise of the trustee's power effects restitution of an unjust enrichment obtained where the consent of the trustee is vitiated, usually by mistake: *Re Hastings Bass* [1975] Ch 75; *Sieff v Fox* [2005] EWHC 1312 (Ch), [2005] 3 All ER 693.

[669] P Birks, 'The Content of Fiduciary Obligation' (2002) 16 Trust Law Int 34.

[670] *Attorney General v Blake* [2001] 1 AC 268, 280, HL.

[671] WG Hart, 'The Development of the Rule in *Keech v Sandford*' (1905) 21 LQR 258; S Cretney, 'The Rationale of *Keech v Sandford*' (1969) 33 Conv (NS) 161.

[672] JH Langbein, 'Questioning the Trust Law Duty of Loyalty: Sole Interest or Best Interest?' (2005) 114 Yale LJ 929; JH Langbein, 'Mandatory Rules in the Law of Trusts' (2004) 98 NWU L Rev 1105. cf J Getzler, 'Rumford Market and the Genesis of Fiduciary Obligations' in A Burrows and A Rodger (eds), *Mapping the Law: Essays in Honour of Peter Birks* (2006) 597–598, arguing that the weight of legal history and recent frauds in the United States suggest this call for reform is premature.

H. Intentional Wrongs

2.337 Every civil wrong can be committed intentionally, but hitherto there has been no discussion of situations in which intent has to be proved in order to engender liability. 'Intention' is a slippery term used in the law of wrongs in different ways.[673] It is used in relation to the wrongs in this section to signify a desired harmful consequence. In contrast, we have seen that torts such as trespass, assault and battery are only intentional in the sense that the act of interference was willed. However, the definition of intention in relation to the wrongs in this section, as a desired harmful consequence, is not without difficulty. It is not enough that the defendant knows that his actions will cause the harmful consequence if they are not desired as an end or means to an end. Nor is it enough that consequences are likely. Many of these cases involving intentional wrongs struggle with the question of the proof of this intention. An attractive solution was proposed by Lord Millett. In his dissent in a decision concerning the tort of misfeasance in public office Lord Millett argued that intention could be proved either by evidence or by inference. Knowledge that conduct will harm the claimant is one way of establishing an inference.[674] The more uncertain the likelihood the more difficult it will be to draw the inference.

2.338 A difficulty with the bi-focal structure of the English law of civil wrongs is that it is unclear which intentional wrongs fall within the first group of wrongs, namely those concerned with infringement of rights, and which fall within the second group, namely those concerned with fault causing loss. In the first group, intentional wrongs are concerned with rights which are protected but only if the right is infringed intentionally. Strong examples are the non-economic rights which German law draws together under the word '*Persönlichkeit*' which is better translated by the non-existent 'personhood' rather than by the more obvious but misleading 'personality'. The quality of being a person, personhood, demands respect—respect for autonomy, privacy, and equal dignity. Infringements of these rights will be an important concern in the future, and not only because of the incorporation of the European Convention on Human Rights. Yet English law has barely begun to realize the extent to which it is equipped to deal with them.

2.339 In the second group, intentional wrongs are concerned with the fault of the defendant causing loss to the claimant. The intention, namely the desire for an illegitimate harmful consequence, is the required degree of fault. Although there is no general tort of intentionally causing loss to another, the tort of misfeasance in public office and the tort of simple conspiracy are strong candidates for classification in this group. In particular, the latter does not require a claimant to show any right which has been infringed (there usually will be no right because the harmful conduct is otherwise lawful); it is enough that the defendant intended the harmful consequences. Just as negligence overlaps with torts that protect particular rights, the tort of misfeasance in public office also overlaps with other torts which protect particular rights (such as the right to liberty).[675]

---

[673] J Finnis, 'Intention in Tort Law' in D Owen (ed), *Philosophical Foundations of Tort Law* (1995). See also *OBG Ltd v Allan* [2007] UKHL 21; [2008] 1 AC 1, at [42]–[43], *per* Lord Hoffmann.

[674] *Three Rivers District Council v Governor and Company of the Bank of England (No 3)* [2003] 2 AC 1, 235, HL.

[675] *Karagozlu v Commissioner of Police of the Metropolis* [2006] EWCA Civ 1691, [2007] 1 WLR 1881.

(1) Humiliation and Distress

It is well settled that mental injury is only actionable in the tort of negligence if it takes the form of a recognized psychiatric illness. It has however been argued that if the harm is caused intentionally, the scope of recovery should be wider, extending to anxiety, humiliation and distress.[676] **2.340**

The recognition of a separate tort of intentionally causing emotional distress, while not excluded by the House of Lords, now seems unlikely. In *Wainwright v Home Office*,[677] Mrs Wainwright, on a visit to her son in prison, was subjected to an invasive strip search by prison officers looking for drugs. The search did not conform to established procedures. She suffered emotional distress but not psychiatric illness. One of her arguments was that the Home Office should be liable for this emotional distress. The argument failed because the prison officers had not intended to cause distress, but Lord Hoffmann reserved his position on whether intentionally causing distress actually is a tort, or whether it was desirable that it should be: 'in institutions and workplaces all over the country, people constantly do and say things with the intention of causing distress and humiliation to others. This shows lack of consideration and appalling manners but I am not sure that the right way to deal with it is always by litigation.'[678] Later decisions have refused recovery even where distress is intentionally inflicted by unlawful means.[679] **2.341**

Where, however, a recognized tort has been committed intentionally, English law has always been willing to enhance the award of damages where the behaviour of the tortfeasor was outrageous, such as to indicate contempt for the victim, as a person of no account.[680] Such awards have in the past been described as 'aggravated damages', but are now more openly recognized as compensation for injury to feelings, including the indignity, mental suffering, humiliation or distress suffered by the victim.[681] The award makes good the infringement of the right to respect for persons as persons. **2.342**

Some protection is also given by statutory remedies, civil and criminal, created by the Protection from Harassment Act 1997 for a course of conduct likely to cause harassment. The Act was designed to cover stalking and other forms of pestering[682] but the statutory language is broad,[683] and it is capable of applying to unjustified gas bills accompanied by threatening letters[684] and to the behaviour of an aggressive and intimidating neighbour.[685] Further development is likely to be under the aegis of the Human Rights Act 1998 or through development of a tort of infringement of privacy.[686] When the *Wainwright* case went to the European Court of Human Rights, the Court held that the way in which the search was conducted was an infringement of the European Convention. Strict compliance with search procedures was required to 'protect the dignity of those being searched from being assailed any further than is necessary'.[687] **2.343**

---

[676] P Glazebrook, '*Wilkinson v Downton*: A Centenary Postscript' (1997) 32 Irish Jurist 46, 48. But if the words or conduct intended only to cause distress actually result in physical or psychiatric illness, the defendant is liable: *James Rhodes v OPO* [2015] UKSC 32, at [87], *per* Lady Hale and Lord Toulson.

[677] [2003] UKHL 53, [2004] 2 AC 406.

[678] [2003] UKHL 53, [2004] 2 AC 406, at [46].

[679] *Mbasogo v Logo Ltd* [2006] EWCA Civ 1370, [2007] QB 846.

[680] *Prince Albert v Strange* (1849) 2 De G & Sm 652, 690; 64 ER 293, 310, *per* Knight Bruce VC.

[681] *Richardson v Howie* [2004] EWCA Civ 1127.

[682] cf *Khorasandjian v Bush* [1993] QB 727, CA; *Burris v Azadani* [1995] 1 WLR 1372, CA. The Act protects individuals not corporate persons: *Daiichi UK Ltd v Stop Huntingdon Animal Cruelty* [2003] TLR 570.

[683] *Majrowski v Guy's and St Thomas's NHS Trust* [2006] UKHL 34, [2007] 1 AC 224.

[684] *Ferguson v British Gas Trading Ltd* [2009] EWCA Civ 46, [2010] 1 WLR 785.

[685] *Jones v Ruth* [2011] EWCA Civ 804, [2012] 1 WLR 1495.

[686] See 2.344–2.348.

[687] *Wainwright v United Kingdom* [2006] ECHR 807, at [48].

(2) Breach of Confidence and Infringement of Privacy[688]

2.344   The wrong of breach of confidence is another excellent example that shows torts to be but a sub-category of the law of wrongdoing, which includes equitable wrongs. Breach of confidence historically arose at common law, it was nurtured and developed in the courts of equity and, with its modern expansion to cover the territory of privacy, has now been described by Lord Nicholls as a tort.[689]

2.345   Traditionally, the action for breach of confidence required the infringement of a claimant's right to the confidentiality of information where the claimant was in a relationship with the defendant. This restrictive requirement of a prior relationship was doomed after the decision of the House of Lords in 1990 in *Attorney General v Guardian Newspapers (No 2)*.[690] The House of Lords held that a duty of confidence owed to the Crown was broken by *The Sunday Times* when it serialized parts of Peter Wright's book, *Spycatcher*, which it knew to contain confidential state information, although strictly there was no relationship between the newspaper and the Crown. It was also suggested in that case that the duty would arise even where the defendant accidentally came across an obviously confidential document.[691] In 2001, Sedley LJ took a further step and suggested that the wrong of breach of confidence had now given birth to a tort of infringement of privacy. In that case, *Douglas v Hello!*,[692] film stars were trying to stop unauthorized publication of their wedding pictures and Sedley LJ said that they had a 'right to privacy' which was 'grounded in the equitable doctrine of breach of confidence, which accords recognition to the fact that the law has to protect not only those whose trust has been abused but also those who find themselves subject to an unwanted intrusion into their personal lives'.[693] However, only two years later cold water was poured on this development by the House of Lords in *Wainwright v Home Office*, with the House denying that there was a tort of infringement of privacy, primarily because of difficulties of definition.[694]

2.346   Despite the assertion that no general right to privacy exists in English law, *Wainwright* did not halt the movement towards the common law protection of some aspects of private life. Avoiding the vague language of invasion of privacy, judges began to bring precision to identifying the content of the right being protected. In *Campbell v MGN Ltd*[695] the defendant newspaper published an article about the attendance at Narcotics Anonymous of the supermodel, Naomi Campbell. The article was accompanied by an unflattering photo of her leaving the premises. A majority of the House of Lords held that this infringed her right to confidentiality of personal medical information.[696]

2.347   The decision of the House of Lords in *Campbell* was significantly affected by the Human Rights Act 1998 incorporating, in particular, Article 8 of the European Convention on Human Rights, which states that 'Everyone has the right to respect for his private and family life, his home and his correspondence', and Article 10, protecting the right to freedom of

---

[688] The definitive study of this area is R Toulson and C Phipps, *Confidentiality* (2nd edn, 2006) esp ch 7 'Confidentiality and Privacy'. See also EPL 6.44– 6.50.

[689] *Campbell v MGN Ltd* [2004] UKHL 22, [2004] 2 AC 457, at [14].

[690] [1990] AC 109, HL.

[691] [1990] AC 109, 281, HL. See also *Saltman Engineering Co Ltd v Campbell Engineering Co Ltd* [1948] 65 RPC 203, 215, CA.

[692] [2001] QB 967, CA.

[693] [2001] QB 967, 1001, CA.

[694] [2003] UKHL 53, [2004] 2 AC 406.

[695] [2004] UKHL 22, [2004] 2 AC 457.

[696] *Campbell v MGN Ltd* [2004] UKHL 22, [2004] 2 AC 457, at [17], although Lord Nicholls dissented in the result, finding that the information was not private.

expression Lord Nicholls said that 'the time has come to recognize that the values enshrined in articles 8 and 10 are now part of the cause of action for breach of confidence'.[697] In *Von Hannover v Germany*,[698] the European Court of Human Rights held that press photographs taken in public places of Princess Caroline of Hannover infringed her privacy and that the German courts had infringed her Article 8 right to respect for her private and family life by denying her a remedy. According to the Court, Article 8 required 'the adoption of measures designed to secure respect for private life even in the sphere of the relations of individuals between themselves'.[699]

After *Campbell*, the central issue in actions for breach of a claimant's right to confidential-   **2.348**
ity of personal information will be determining what counts as personal information. The broad approach to this issue taken by the courts is consistent with the Convention. A public figure, like Naomi Campbell, was entitled to protection of personal information. The Prince of Wales had a right to the confidentiality of matters about which he wrote in his private journal, even when they related to issues upon which he spoke in public.[700] And in *Douglas v Hello! (No 3)*,[701] the Court of Appeal held that *Hello!* magazine infringed the claimant film stars' right to personal information by publishing photographs of their gala wedding despite the fact that there had been considerable pre-event publicity in the tabloid press and despite the bride and groom's exclusive agreement giving a rival magazine rights to attend, take photographs and publish details about the wedding. In a separate appeal by *OK!*, a bare majority of the House of Lords held that this right to keep information private encompassed even *OK!*'s commercial rights to the confidentiality of the information prior to publication.[702]

(3) Harassment by Legal Process

There are well-established torts which deal specifically with the use of the courts to har-   **2.349**
ass another. Malicious prosecution is the most important. It is an important protection for the individual but one which is narrowly construed, for the obvious reason that it would otherwise unacceptably deter the bringing of prosecutions. The tort is committed when legal proceedings, nearly always criminal proceedings, fail, and the claimant, formerly defendant, can show that they were brought without reasonable cause and maliciously. These last words embody two requirements, which inevitably run together. Absence of reasonable and probable cause means absence of belief in the guilt or liability of the accused person or an honest belief in guilt such that no ordinarily prudent person would have entertained on the basis of the facts as they were believed to be.[703] Malice means the presence of an ulterior motive beyond the desire to see the accused convicted, as for instance to continue a long-running dispute.[704] When, as often happens, a servant of the state is the defendant, this is a tort where exemplary damages are available.[705]

On a somewhat lower plane, the tort of abuse of legal process is committed when litigation   **2.350**
is instituted in pursuit of an ulterior motive. The exact shape of this tort remains uncertain,

---

[697] *Campbell v MGN Ltd* [2004] UKHL 22, [2004] 2 AC 457, at [17].

[698] (2004) 40 EHRR 1, ECHR.

[699] (2004) 40 EHRR 1, at [57], ECHR.

[700] *Associated Newspapers Ltd v Prince of Wales* [2006] EWCA Civ 1776. Private sexual activity is similarly protected: *Mosley v News Group Newspapers Ltd* [2008] EWHC 1777 (QB).

[701] [2005] EWCA Civ 595, [2006] QB 125.

[702] Appeal conjoined in *OBG Ltd v Allan* [2007] UKHL 21, [2008] 1 AC 1.

[703] *Glinski v McIver* [1962] AC 726, HL; cf *Gibbs v Rea* [1998] AC 786, PC.

[704] *Martin v Watson* [1996] 1 AC 74, HL.

[705] 4.163–4.165. Public servants may also be liable for the tort of misfeasance in a public office: see 2.355.

and even its existence has been viewed with scepticism.[706] Nevertheless its existence is warranted by *Grainger v Hill*,[707] where the defendant was made liable for using arrest for debt as a means to force the claimant to give up the registration documents of his vessel, without which he could not sail.

(4) Intentionally Causing Economic Loss

2.351 The duty of care not to inflict pure economic loss negligently is closely restricted.[708] The same is true where economic loss is deliberately inflicted. There is no simple proposition to the effect that, if the claimant can prove intent to cause such loss, all those restrictions simply fade away. There usually has to be an additional element of wrongfulness. Subject to that qualification it is nevertheless true that the law does give more robust redress for intentionally inflicted economic loss.

2.352 In a competitive world individuals and corporations are constantly trying to do each other down. The leading case which underlines the obstacles to the simple proposition in the previous paragraph is *Allen v Flood*.[709] A trade union official told an employer that his men would not work alongside the claimants. In this way he brought it about that the employer got rid of the claimants, who then sued the official. The crucial fact was that all the workers in question were employed on a day-to-day basis. It followed that the official had not threatened a breach of contract, nor had he insisted that the employer break his contract with the claimants. The House of Lords held that a malicious motive could not render unlawful conduct which was in itself entirely lawful.

2.353 This decision has been regretted by some judges, Lord Devlin being one of them.[710] It nevertheless remains the foundation of the English law of intentionally inflicted pure economic loss. It means in effect that the element of unlawfulness which cannot usually be supplied by malice alone has to be satisfied by the recognition of a series of economic torts.

(a) Deceit, fraud and misfeasance in public office

2.354 Deceit is the most ancient of the economic torts. It is an obvious exception to any requirement of independent unlawfulness. Deceit is another wrong concurrently actionable both at common law and in equity.[711] In its modern incarnation it requires a false representation made by the defendant, intending that the claimant should act upon it. It is, however, still open to question whether deceit (which requires a representation) is not simply a species of the *genera* of acts done with fraudulent intention (described as *dolus* in Roman law). Other species of such a genus would include fraudulent acts such as bribery even though there is no representation made to the principal,[712] and the tort of misfeasance in public office, which

---

[706] *Metall und Rohstoff AG v Donaldson, Lufkin, Jenrette Inc* [1990] 1 QB 391, CA.
[707] (1838) 4 Bing NC 212, 132 ER 769, applied in *Parton v Hill* (1864) 10 LT 415. The case is, however, susceptible of analysis in other ways, as for instance as an example of the tort of intimidation.
[708] See 2.147ff.
[709] [1898] AC 1, HL.
[710] *Rookes v Barnard* [1964] AC 1129, 1216, HL; P Devlin, *Samples of Law-Making* (1962) 10–13.
[711] *Peek v Gurney* (1873) LR 6 HL 377, 393, HL, *per* Lord Chelmsford speaking of the action in equity: 'It is precisely analogous to the common law action for deceit. There can be no doubt that Equity exercises a concurrent jurisdiction in cases of this description, and the same principles applicable to them both must prevail both at Law and in Equity.'
[712] *Mahesan S/O Thambiah v Malaysian Government Officers Co-operative Housing Society* [1979] AC 374, 376, PC. cf *Armitage v Nurse* [1998] Ch 241, 250, CA, *per* Millett LJ ('the common law knows no generalised tort of fraud').

involves a deliberate abuse of power by a public official causing loss to the defendant.[713] Like negligence, however, the general right not to suffer loss as a result of these fraudulent acts is restricted. In *Magill v Magill*,[714] a husband brought a claim for losses as a result of fraudulent misrepresentations by his former wife that he was not the father of their children. The High Court of Australia unanimously held that his former wife was not liable. Four judges explained that policy reasons required that the action for deceit stop outside the door of the family home.[715] Although, a first instance judge in England has reached the opposite conclusion,[716] the reasoning of the High Court of Australia is compelling.

In cases of misfeasance by a public official which causes loss, the requisite element of intention is satisfied if the public official knows his act is illegal or is recklessly indifferent to its legality.[717] The same is true of deceit. The element of fraudulent intention requires that it be shown that the defendant knew that his statement was untrue, or had no belief in its truth, or was reckless as to whether it was true or false. This was the effect of the House of Lords' decision in *Derry v Peek*.[718] Mere negligence is not deceit. In the period after *Derry v Peek* it was thought that there was no liability in damages for negligent misstatements causing economic loss.[719] That changed in 1964 with *Hedley Byrne & Co Ltd v Heller & Partners Ltd*.[720] The two liabilities remain very different. In deceit, in order to mark the law's disapproval of fraud, the defendant is liable for all losses flowing directly from the tort, whether they were foreseeable or not.[721] Further, the defence of contributory negligence is not available.[722]

2.355

(b) The economic torts

This label is used to describe a group of torts which are linked together by their subject matter, causing economic loss by interfering with the trade of others, and by their political history.[723] Many have been developed in cases involving trade union action, and they serve as a crucial element of the legal background to labour disputes. The economic torts also have a relationship with torts protecting intellectual property,[724] and with the legal rules directed at ensuring fair competition, some of which are enforceable by private action and so form a parallel regime operating alongside the common law actions under consideration here.[725] None of these wider implications can be explored in this outline. They are, however, the cause of much of the difficulty and uncertainty of the law in this area.

2.356

---

[713] The tort of misfeasance in public office: *Watkins v Secretary of State for the Home Office* [2006] UKHL 17, [2006] 2 AC 395.

[714] [2006] HCA 51, 231 ALR 277.

[715] [2006] HCA 51, 231 ALR 277, at [42] (Gleeson CJ), [88] (Gummow, Kirby and Crennan JJ), [140] (Hayne J); cf [207] (Heydon J).

[716] *P v B (Paternity: Damages for Deceit)* [2001] 1 FLR 1041.

[717] *Three Rivers District Council v Governor and Company of the Bank of England (No 3)* [2001] UKHL 16, [2003] 2 AC 1.

[718] (1889) 14 App Cas 337, HL.

[719] *Candler v Crane Christmas & Co* [1951] 2 KB 164, CA. The equitable evasion in *Nocton v Ashburton* [1914] AC 932, HL remained discreetly in the shadows.

[720] [1964] AC 465, HL. See 2.164ff.

[721] *Doyle v Olby (Ironmongers) Ltd* [1969] 2 QB 158, CA; *Smith New Court Securities Ltd v Scrimgeour Vickers (Asset Management) Ltd* [1997] AC 254, HL. See also *Clef Aquitaine SARL v Laporte Materials (Barrow) Ltd* [2000] 3 All ER 493, CA.

[722] *Alliance and Leicester BS v Edgestop Ltd* [1993] 1 WLR 1462; *Standard Chartered Bank v Pakistan National Shipping Co (No 2)* [2002] UKHL 43, [2003] 1 AC 959.

[723] T Weir, *Economic Torts* (1997); P Cane, *Tort Law and Economic Interests* (2nd edn, 1996); H Carty, *An Analysis of the Economic Torts* (2001).

[724] See EPL ch 6.

[725] See R Whish and D Bailey, *Competition Law* (7th edn, 2012) ch 8.

(i) Procuring breach of contract

2.357 The most straightforward of the economic torts is also one of the oldest. In *Lumley v Gye*[726] the claimant had a contract with an opera singer to sing in a series of concerts. The defendant, knowing of this contract, persuaded her to break it by offering her more money to sing at his theatre. The Court of Queen's Bench found for the claimant and the decision was subsequently approved in the House of Lords in *Allen v Flood*.[727] The tort can only be committed intentionally and the defendant must know, or at least be reckless as to,[728] the terms of the contract. There is a defence of justification in a few, not well-defined, circumstances.[729]

2.358 For a time the *Lumley v Gye* tort was extended from direct inducement of a breach of contract to include indirect inducement,[730] and, much more controversially, to interference with the performance of a contract, even though no breach was caused.[731] However, the House of Lords has now affirmed that the distinction between direct and indirect inducement is unhelpful and that the tort is one of accessory liability, so that a breach of contract is required for interference with the performance of a contract to amount to the tort of inducing breach of contract.[732]

(ii) Intimidation

2.359 If it is tortious to persuade someone to break a contract, it may also be tortious to threaten to break one. In *Rookes v Barnard*[733] the facts were very similar to those of *Allen v Flood*.[734] The one crucial difference was that the union had contracted not to engage in strike action. Hence the threat to withdraw labour was a threat of a breach of contract. The House of Lords held that this amounted to the wrong of intimidation, which can be regarded as a form of the wider tort of causing loss by unlawful means. In *Rookes v Barnard* the union's threat was that it would induce its members, a third party, to break their contracts with the claimant. It remains an open question whether the tort can be committed by a defendant threatening to break his own contract with the claimant.[735]

(iii) Causing loss by unlawful means

2.360 In *Merkur Island Shipping Corporation v Laughton*[736] Lord Diplock gave the blessing of the House of Lords to this tort as the 'genus' tort of which he suggested that inducing breach of contract was a species. It might have been neat if this single unifying tort could have held together all these economic torts. However, there were at least two problems with Lord Diplock's reasoning. The first, identified by Lord Hoffmann in the leading speech in the House of Lords in *OBG Ltd v Allan*,[737] is that the tort of inducing breach of contract is a tort of accessory liability, whereas the tort of causing loss by unlawful means is concerned with primary liability. He defined the latter as 'acts intended to cause loss to the claimant by interfering with the freedom of a third party in a way which is unlawful as against that third

---

[726] (1852) 2 El & Bl 216, 118 ER 749. See further, S Waddams, 'Johanna Wagner and the Rival Opera Houses' (2001) 117 LQR 431.

[727] [1898] AC 1, HL; 2.352.

[728] *Emerald Construction Co v Lowthian* [1966] 1 WLR 691, CA.

[729] *Brimelow v Casson* [1924] 1 Ch 302; *Edwin Hill and Partners v First National Finance Corporation plc* [1989] 1 WLR 225.

[730] *DC Thomson Ltd v Deakin* [1952] Ch 646, CA.

[731] *Torquay Hotel Ltd v Cousins* [1969] 2 Ch 106, CA; cf T Weir, *Economic Torts* (1997) 37.

[732] *OBG Ltd v Allan* [2007] UKHL 21; [2008] 1 AC 1, [44].

[733] [1964] AC 1129, HL.

[734] [1898] AC 1, HL.

[735] Described by Lord Hoffmann as raising 'different issues': *OBG Ltd v Allan* [2007] UKHL 21, [2008] 1 AC 1, at [61].

[736] [1983] 2 AC 570, HL.

[737] *OBG Ltd v Allan* [2007] UKHL 21, [2008] 1 AC 1, at [44].

party and which is intended to cause loss to the claimant'.[738] A further obstacle exists to the genus tort in the form of the tort called conspiracy to injure.

(iv) Conspiracy   Unlawful means conspiracy is a separate tort, with a wider concept of unlaw- **2.361** fulness than that employed in the tort of causing loss by unlawful means.[739] This tort can take two forms, depending on whether unlawful means are used. Unlawful means conspiracy is a relatively uncomplicated tort, the separate existence of which was confirmed by the House of Lords in *Lonrho plc v Fayed*.[740] By contrast, conspiracy to injure, which consists in a combination of two or more persons acting with the intention of harming the claimant, but not using unlawful means, is an anomaly. It is difficult now to explain why mere numbers should make unlawful what would otherwise be lawful. In *Lonrho plc v Shell Petroleum Ltd (No 2)*,[741] Lord Diplock regretted the anomaly but thought it too well established to be discarded.[742] The tort is of little practical importance, because acts done with the predominant purpose of advancing the conspirators' own interests are justifiable.[743] Only a combination whose purpose is to harm the claimant is actionable. But a tort in which liability does depend on an unlawful purpose, rather than unlawful means, adds to the incoherence of this area of law.

The economic torts are full of difficulties. Almost every aspect of the rules which govern them **2.362** has given rise to complicated litigation. What sort of intention is required?[744] What counts as an interference with trade?[745] What amounts to unlawful means?[746] Even after two recent House of Lords decisions which sought to bring clarification,[747] intractable problems still plague this area of the law.[748]

(5) Dishonest Assistance in a Breach of Fiduciary Duty

Rarely, if ever, in discussion of wrongs that involve claims for economic loss do academics **2.363** or judges include the equivalent equitable wrongs. We have seen that the torts of deceit and negligence were historically actionable as wrongs in equity as well as at common law. An equitable wrong that lays fair claim to be treated alongside the economic torts, particularly the tort of inducing a breach of contract, is dishonest assistance in a breach of fiduciary duty. Lord Hoffmann has recently confirmed that this equitable wrong includes dishonest assistance in the breach of any fiduciary duty, not merely in a breach of trust.[749] The most difficult question considered by the courts so far is the meaning of 'dishonest'. A future issue that may arise is the meaning of breach of fiduciary duty in this context or whether dishonest assistance in a breach of any equitable duty should be sufficient. We have seen that a consensus is emerging that negligence by a fiduciary is not a breach of fiduciary duty. To adopt that approach here would reach the same conclusion as the

---

[738] *OBG Ltd v Allan* [2007] UKHL 21, [2008] 1 AC 1, at [51].

[739] *Revenue and Customs Commissioners v Total Network SL* [2008] UKHL 19, [2008] 1 AC 1174.

[740] [1992] 1 AC 448, HL.

[741] [1982] AC 173, HL.

[742] [1982] AC 173, 189, HL.

[743] *Crofter Hand-Woven Harris Tweed Co Ltd v Veitch* [1942] AC 435, HL.

[744] *Lonrho plc v Fayed* [1992] 1 AC 448, HL.

[745] *RCA Corporation v Pollard* [1983] Ch 135, CA.

[746] *Lonrho Ltd v Shell Petroleum Co Ltd (No 2)* [1982] AC 173, HL; *Michaels v Taylor Woodrow Developments Ltd* [2001] Ch 493.

[747] *OBG Ltd v Allan* [2007] UKHL 21, [2008] 1 AC 1; *Revenue and Customs Commissioners v Total Network SL* [2008] UKHL 19, [2008] 1 AC 1174.

[748] H Carty, 'The Economic Torts in the 21st Century' (2008) 124 LQR 641.

[749] *Barlow Clowes International Ltd v Eurotrust International Ltd* [2005] UKPC 37, [2006] 1 WLR 1476, at [28]. See also Lord Nicholls, 'Knowing Receipt: The Need for a New Landmark' in W Cornish et al (eds), *Restitution: Past, Present and Future* (1998) 244.

common law does in refusing to recognize a 'free-standing' general tort of dishonest assistance in any tort.[750]

2.364 In 1995, Lord Nicholls gave the advice of the Privy Council in *Royal Brunei Airlines v Tan*,[751] where the defendant managing director had misapplied money paid to it which was paid on trust for the airline. The managing director paid it into the company current account instead of the trust account into which he knew it was supposed to be paid. The Privy Council held that the test was one of dishonesty and that in a commercial setting that simply meant conduct which was commercially unacceptable. The managing director had acted dishonestly.

2.365 Subsequently, in the leading speech in the House of Lords in *Twinsectra Ltd v Yardley*,[752] Lord Hutton said that dishonesty is 'a standard which combines an objective test and a subjective test... it must be established that the defendant's conduct was dishonest by ordinary standards of reasonable and honest people and that he himself realised that by those standards his conduct was dishonest'.[753] Lord Hoffmann also said that dishonesty 'requires a dishonest state of mind, that is to say, consciousness that one is transgressing ordinary standards of honest behaviour'.[754] This seemed to be a combined objective/subjective test. It was heavily criticized both academically[755] and judicially.[756]

2.366 Matters were clarified by Privy Council in *Barlow Clowes International Ltd v Eurotrust International Ltd*.[757] The case involved an enormous fraud by high-flying 1980s entrepreneurs who promised high returns from investment in gilt-edged securities to unsuspecting investors. A central question for the Privy Council was whether one of the directors of an off-shore company who had acted as intermediaries had dishonestly assisted in the scheme to misappropriate the investors' funds. The director had suspected that the funds received might have been derived from a fraud on the public but decided not to make inquiries because of his subjective view that the client's instructions are all important. Lord Hoffmann argued that both his speech and Lord Hutton's speech in *Twinsectra* had been misunderstood. Neither he nor Lord Hutton meant to suggest that there was any subjective element to the test: the defendant need not have reflected at all on what were ordinary standards of honest behaviour and the decision in *Twinsectra* had not departed from the Privy Council's objective approach in *Tan*.[758] It was dishonest to act as intermediary whilst entertaining a clear suspicion that the money was held on trust or was being misappropriated by the directors.[759] The dust now appears to have settled in favour of this

---

[750] *Credit Lyonnais Bank Nederland NV v Export Credits Guarantee Department* [2000] 1 AC 486, HL, where, at the least, it was held that the ECGD could not be vicariously liable for an employee where only the acts of assistance, not the tort assisted, were within the course of the employee's employment. However, the case shows that we are some distance from understanding 'assistance' at common law.

[751] [1995] 2 AC 378, PC.

[752] [2002] 2 AC 164, HL.

[753] [2002] 2 AC 164, HL, at [27].

[754] [2002] 2 AC 164, HL, at [20].

[755] A Pedain, 'Dishonest Assistance: Guilty Conduct or a Guilty Mind?' [2002] CLJ 524 at 525–526; C Rickett, 'Quistclose Trusts and Dishonest Assistance' [2002] RLR 112; Lord Walker, 'Dishonesty and Unconscionable Conduct in Commercial Life: Some Reflections on Accessory Liability and Knowing Receipt' (2005) 27 Sydney L Rev 187, 197.

[756] *US International Marketing Ltd v National Bank of New Zealand Ltd* [2004] 1 NZLR 589, NZCA.

[757] [2005] UKPC 37, [2006] 1 WLR 1476.

[758] [2005] UKPC 37, [2006] 1 WLR 1476, at [15]–[16], [18].

[759] Difficult second-order questions still remain about how the line should be drawn between objective honesty and dishonesty: see J Edelman, 'The Expansion of Dishonest Assistance in the Privy Council' (2006) 1 Journal of Equity 22.

reinterpretation of *Twinsectra* and an objective test of dishonesty,[760] although a surprising later decision of the Court of Appeal held that a bank is not dishonest if it suspects a class of transaction as involving money laundering but does not suspect the particular transaction in question.[761]

I. Vicarious Liability

(1) Personal Liability and Vicarious Liability Distinguished

There are a number of situations in which one person is liable for the acts of another but in which the reason is that the person liable is himself contemplated as being in breach of duty. The claimant's cause of action is then the defendant's own wrong, and the defendant is personally, not vicariously, liable. Vicarious liability as understood in English law is liability imposed upon a person even though he has committed no wrong and simply because of his relationship to the person who has committed the wrong.[762] Vicarious liability therefore involves the attribution of the liability of the wrongdoer to the defendant, not attribution of the wrongdoer's act.[763] Provided the relationship of the defendant satisfies the requirements of vicarious liability, it does not matter if the wrong is a common law tort, equitable wrong or statutory wrong: 'the policy reasons underlying the common law principle are as much applicable to equitable wrongs and breaches of statutory obligations as they are to common law torts'.[764]   **2.367**

(a) Personal liability exemplified

There are a number of different ways in which one may incur a personal liability for the acts of another. It helps to keep them completely separate from vicarious liability.   **2.368**

(i) Personal duty of care

A corporation is personally liable for the authorized acts of its directors and employees because the corporation cannot act otherwise than by its directors and servants.[765] So too, a principal is personally liable for an agent acting with his authority: *qui facit per alium facit per se*. We have also seen that exceptional circumstances may be such as to put the defendant under a common law duty of care in protecting the claimant from the acts of a third party.[766] In equity, too, a trustee is liable for negligent management, and negligent management includes negligent supervision of others more directly engaged in the trust affairs. A duty of care may also be broken by careless selection of an agent or other contractor (*culpa in eligendo*).[767]   **2.369**

---

[760] *Fresh 'N' Clean (Wales) Ltd v Miah* [2006] EWHC 903 (Ch).

[761] *AbouRahmah v Abacha* [2006] EWCA Civ 1492.

[762] All of the acts comprising the wrongdoing must, however, be closely connected with the relationship between the wrongdoer(s) and the principal: *Credit Lyonnais Bank Nederland NV v ECGD* [2000] 1 AC 486, HL.

[763] *X (Minors) v Bedfordshire CC* [1995] 2 AC 633, 739–740, HL; *Majrowski v Guy's and St Thomas's NHS Trust* [2006] UKHL 34, [2007] 1 AC 224. Against the powerful tide of modern authority, the 'Master's Tort' theory—which sees 'vicarious liability' as based upon attribution of a servant's acts and therefore indistinguishable from personal liability—is favoured by R Stevens, 'Vicarious Liability and Vicarious Action' (2007) 123 LQR 30. See further, G Williams, 'Vicarious Liability: Tort of the Master or of the Servant?' (1956) 72 LQR 522.

[764] *Majrowski v Guy's and St Thomas's NHS Trust* [2006] UKHL 34, [2007] 1 AC 224, HL, at [10].

[765] *Williams v Natural Life Health Foods Ltd* [1998] 1 WLR 830, HL.

[766] *Stansbie v Troman* [1948] 2 KB 48, CA; *Home Office v Dorset Yacht Co* [1970] AC 1004, HL; 2.76.

[767] *Aiken v Stewart Wrightson Members Agency Ltd* [1995] 1 WLR 1281. The liability for an agent imposed in *Gran Gelato v Richcliff (Group) Ltd* [1992] Ch 560 is, however, hard to explain.

(ii) Strict liability for careful provision

2.370 In isolated pockets there is the more extreme possibility that the defendant may be found to have been under a duty to ensure that care was taken of the claimant. That is to say, he may be under a strict liability in respect of the care provided through others. This is often somewhat confusingly referred to as a 'non-delegable duty of care'.

2.371 This terminology indicates that the person in question is deemed to be under a personal duty of care which, in the following sense, cannot be delegated, namely that, when he seeks to discharge it through others, the acts of those others are still his acts and their carelessness is his carelessness. This seems to be an unnecessarily complicated way of saying that such a person is strictly liable to ensure that care is exercised by others. The incidence of such a duty is of special importance wherever independent contractors are used, since in principle there is no vicarious liability for an independent contractor.

2.372 Although this strict duty is sometimes not sufficiently differentiated from a duty of care in provision, supervision, and management,[768] there seems little doubt that Denning LJ intended to introduce it as a quite distinct basis for the liability of hospitals and health authorities.[769] However, in that field the exact status of this strict duty to ensure adequate care is still in doubt.[770] The increasing use of independently contracted staff, rather than employees, will bring the matter to a head. There are a number of other more or less secure examples, including highway authorities and others employing contractors to work on the highways, although the courts have tended to narrow the ambit of their strict duty;[771] and employers in relation to their employees, who are entitled to safe systems of work and equipment[772] and competent co-workers.[773] In *Woodland v Essex CC*,[773a] Lord Sumption identified two broad categories of case where such a strict duty would arise: those where the defendant employed a contractor to undertake an inherently dangerous task; and those where the defendant had assumed a responsibility towards the claimant. The facts of *Woodland*, where a local education authority was held liable for the negligence of employees of a contractor hired to provide swimming lessons, fell into the latter category.

(iii) Inducing or assisting

2.373 The third possibility is that in circumstances in which the criminal law would speak of accessory liability or liability in the second degree, a defendant may make himself liable for inducing, procuring or assisting the commission of a wrong. In the common law such a person is said to commit the tort in which he participates and may in some cases commit the tort of conspiracy;[774] we have also seen that in equity there is a distinct wrong of 'dishonest assistance in a breach of fiduciary duty'.[775]

---

[768] See, eg, *Bull v Devon AHA* [1993] 4 Med LR 117, CA.

[769] *Cassidy v Ministry of Health* [1951] 2 KB 343, CA; *Roe v Minister of Health* [1954] 2 QB 66, CA.

[770] I Kennedy and A Grubb, *Principles of Medical Law* (2nd edn, 2004) 409–411. It has been held, eg, that it does not extend to sending samples for testing by an independent company: *Farraj v King's Healthcare NHS Trust* [2009] EWCA Civ 1203.

[771] *Salsbury v Woodland* [1970] 1 QB 324, CA; *Rowe v Herman* [1997] 1 WLR 1390, CA. See also *Leichhardt Municipal Council v Montgomery* [2007] HCA 6, 233 ALR 200.

[772] Employers' Liability (Defective Equipment) Act 1969; *Coltman v Bibby Tankers* [1988] AC 276, HL.

[773] *McDermid v Nash Dredging and Reclamation Co Ltd* [1987] AC 906, HL. Some confusion has been introduced by *Square D Ltd v Cook* [1992] ICR 262, CA, which appears to have undermined the strictness of the duty.

[773a] [2013] UKSC 66, [2014] AC 537.

[774] P Sales, 'The Tort of Conspiracy and Civil Secondary Liability' [1990] CLJ 491, esp 504.

[775] See 2.363–2.366.

(b) Vicarious liability properly so-called

Vicarious liability is a form of strict liability imposed without any suggestion that the person **2.374** in question has been guilty of any breach of duty. The exposure to this kind of liability inheres in the position occupied by the person made liable and the relation which that position bears to that of the actual wrongdoer. As we shall see, the case of greatest importance is that of the employer. The employer is liable for the torts of his employee committed in the course of the employee's employment.

The vicariously liable employer is a joint tortfeasor with the employee. The victim can sue **2.375** either or both, and in principle the employer's vicarious liability is secondary, so that, having paid the damages, the person liable, and by subrogation his insurer, has a right of recourse against the primary wrongdoer,[776] much as a surety has a right to reimbursement from the principal debtor.[777] In practice this right of recourse is little used; it lives in a limbo created by the likelihood that, if it were, it would be abolished by Act of Parliament.[778]

(2) Rationalia of Vicarious Liability

It is certain that, if there were no vicarious liability, there would be constant pressure on the **2.376** edges of personal liability, as indeed there already is where vicarious liability is not available, for almost without exception tort victims prefer to sue the employer rather than the employee. The employer will have the longer purse and, even more importantly, is more likely to carry insurance. After all the employer can spread the risk by taking out insurance and treating the premiums as a cost of the business. The alternative would require individual employees to take out insurance themselves, but that would lead to all sorts of difficulties with uninsurable individuals. Avoiding those difficulties would almost certainly involve transferring the insurance burden back to employers.

Whether this practical reality discloses any thoroughly convincing case for the necessity of **2.377** vicarious liability is open to question.[779] It must certainly be true that vicarious liability tends to encourage employers to take steps to ensure that their employees are properly trained to be aware of risks and so far as possible to avoid them. Economists have embroidered this simple fact so as to present vicarious liability as an engine of economic efficiency, tending to raise the costs of businesses which are inefficient.[780] Lord Nicholls has argued that the rationale for vicarious liability is a combination of all these matters.[781]

(3) Categories of Vicarious Liability

There is only one significant category of person subject to vicarious liability, namely employ- **2.378** ers. Their vicarious liability is then confined to the torts of employees committed in the

---

[776] *Lister v Romford Ice and Cold Storage Co* [1957] AC 555, HL; *Morris v Ford Motor Co* [1973] QB 792, CA.

[777] 3.106–3.118, 3.278–3.282.

[778] La Forest J of the Supreme Court of Canada argued in a minority judgment that the courts should hold that the employer's liability now displaced the liability of the employee altogether: *London Drugs Ltd v Kuehne & Nagel* [1992] 3 SCR 299, SCC. One way or another La Forest J's arguments are likely to prevail sooner or later. Meanwhile see *Merrett v Babb* [2001] QB 1174, CA (employee sued personally, employer having gone into liquidation).

[779] Full discussion in PS Atiyah, *Vicarious Liability* (1967) ch 2.

[780] This 'enterprise liability' rationale is presented in Canada as an argument that the party that gets the benefit should bear the burden: *Bazley v Curry* [1999] 2 SCR 534, SCC and *Jacobi v Griffiths* [1999] 2 SCR 470, SCC.

[781] *Majrowski v Guy's and St Thomas's NHS Trust* [2006] UKHL 34, [2007] 1 AC 224, at [9].

course of their employment. The simplicity of this picture is disrupted in two ways. First, from time to time there have been attempts to extend the range of vicarious liability to other relationships loosely analogous to employment by reason of the control of one person over another. Secondly, there is great and increasing difficulty in distinguishing employment from other similar relationships.

(a) Other relationships

2.379   Statute aside (eg the Partnership Act 1890), enlargement of vicarious liability has not gone far. Where it has been attempted it has been driven by the desire to give victims the benefit of insurance carried by the vicarious defendant. In *Launchbury v Morgans*,[782] the defendant's car had been used by her husband to go out on the town with his friends. After a while, when drink had rendered him incompetent, one of his friends had taken over the driving and had crashed the car. The injured passengers sued the defendant on the basis that she was vicariously liable for the negligent driving of her car. This argument, having succeeded in the Court of Appeal, was heavily pruned in the House of Lords. But the House left intact the proposition that the vicarious liability would subsist in a case in which the car was being driven at the owner's request and for the owner's purposes.

2.380   This extension has had little or no impact, evidently because of changes in the law and practice of car insurance. However, it stands as an invitation to extend the range of vicarious liability. In *JGE v Trustees of the Portsmouth Roman Catholic Diocesan Trust*,[783] vicarious liability was imposed on a Roman Catholic diocese for sexual abuse of the claimant by a priest in the diocese, even though the priest was not an employee. A majority of the Court of Appeal followed Canadian authority[784] in holding that the law of vicarious liability had moved beyond the confines of a contract of employment, and that the relationship between a bishop and a priest was so close in character to that of employer and employee that it was just and fair to hold the diocese vicariously liable. This approach has now been approved by the Supreme Court on similar facts.[785]

2.381   An example of the limits of enlargement of vicarious liability is a trustee who is not vicariously liable for his co-trustee or for those whom he appoints as his agents in the management of the trust. If the trustee is to be liable for things that he has done, it will be because of his own breach of duty: 'The conduct of the [trustee] is to be judged by the standard applied in *Speight v Gaunt*,[786] namely, that a trustee is only bound to conduct the business of the trust in such a way as an ordinary prudent man would conduct a business of his own.'[787] In this way the trustee may incur a liability for having failed in supervising the agent or for having allowed unbusinesslike steps to be taken, but he will never be vicariously liable. That is to say, he will not be liable merely because of his position in relation to the actual delinquent.

(b) Employees

2.382   If the term 'employee' is used loosely it covers a variety of relationships. An employer is only liable for those who come within the now outmoded term 'servant'. The Romans

---

[782] [1973] AC 127, HL. See also *Moynihan v Moynihan* [1975] IR 192, Sup Ct of Ireland, on vicarious liability within the family (negligence in serving tea).
[783] [2012] EWCA Civ 938.
[784] *John Doe v Bennett* [2004] 1 SCR 436, SCC.
[785] *The Catholic Child Welfare Society v The Institute of the Brothers of the Christian Schools* [2012] UKSC 56.
[786] (1883) 9 App Cas 1, HL.
[787] *Re Lucking's Will Trusts* [1968] 1 WLR 866, 874, *per* Cross J, discussing the Trustee Act 1925, ss 23 and 30(1).

distinguished between hire of services (*locatio conductio operarum*) and hiring out jobs to be done (*locatio conductio operis faciendi*). The servant of English law falls within the former: one whose service is hired, while the latter, one who takes on a job to be done, is an independent contractor. There is no vicarious liability for independent contractors. If an independent contractor commits a tort, the only way of reaching his 'employer' is to establish a personal liability, as discussed above.[788]

The line between employees and independent contractors has become increasingly diffi-   **2.383**
cult to draw, partly because of changing employment practices and partly because the word 'employee' (used in the sense of 'servant') has come under pressure by reason of its importance in many different contexts. Vicarious liability is one, but very different considerations creep in when the question is entitlement to benefits, compensation for employment protection legislation, or, the selection of the appropriate tax regime.

It used to be thought that the key was control. If the worker was subject to close control in the   **2.384**
manner in which he performed his task, he would be a servant but not if he enjoyed a measure of autonomy in achieving a given end. But the control test is controversial. The Court of Appeal recently held, in *Viasystems (Tyneside) Ltd v Thermal Transfer (Northern) Ltd*[789] that a fitter and his mate, provided by their employer, the third defendants, on a 'labour only' basis to the second defendant subcontractor were employed by both the second and third defendants. May LJ reasoned that both parties were employers because of the degree of control they both exerted over the fitter and fitter's mate, but Rix LJ argued that both parties were employers because of the integration of the fitter and fitter's mate into each organization. An influential article by Richard Kidner argues that the law will not be intelligible until it abandons hope of a single test of employment in all contexts and focuses in the present context on the function of vicarious liability as making businesses bear the risks inherent in their activity. He proposes a test based on a basket of factors weighed in the light of that overall goal.[790] A development along these lines seems inevitable. Meanwhile, the possibility (first accepted in *Viasystems*) that two different defendants could each be vicariously liable for the single tortious act of another has now received the imprimatur of the Supreme Court.[791]

Some brief examples will further illustrate the difficulties. In *Ready-Mixed Concrete v Minister*   **2.385**
of Pensions[792] McKenna J held that for National Insurance purposes a lorry driver was not an employee, but an independent contractor. The company had gone over to a new system using owner-drivers. The driver in question had switched to the new scheme, buying his own lorry on hire purchase. The driver's pattern of life did not change. His lorry was painted in the same livery, he wore the same uniform, and he took the same orders. On the other hand he was now paid piece rates, not a wage, and he had to meet the running expenses of his lorry. Furthermore—though this is not decisive[793]—his contract described him as an independent contractor. In the judgment of McKenna J the balance tipped against his being an employee. He was running his own business as a carrier.

---

[788] E McKendrick, 'Vicarious Liability and Independent Contractors—A Re-examination' (1990) 53 MLR 770 argues for extension of that primary liability.
[789] [2005] EWCA Civ 1151, [2006] QB 510. Distinguished on similar facts in *Hawley v Luminar Leisure* [2006] EWCA Civ 30.
[790] R Kidner, 'Vicarious Liability: For Whom Should the Employer be Liable?' (1995) 15 LS 47.
[791] *The Catholic Child Welfare Society v The Institute of the Brothers of the Christian Schools* [2012] UKSC 56, at [20]–[21], *per* Lord Phillips.
[792] [1968] 2 QB 497.
[793] *Ferguson v John Dawson & Partners Ltd* [1976] 1 WLR 1213, CA; on the other side of the line is *Massey v Crown Life Insurance Co* [1978] 1 WLR 676, CA.

2.386 In *O'Kelly v Trust House Forte plc*[794] casual waiters worked on a regular basis for private functions, as needed. They were held not to be employees and therefore not entitled to compensation for unfair dismissal. There was no mutuality of obligation. That is, they were not bound to respond to the summons on any day. Similarly, in *Hall v Lorimer*[795] a 'vision mixer' working for a number of television companies and described as 'freelance' was held not to be an employee. There the issue was tax. By contrast, in *Lee Ting Sang v Chung Chi-Keung*[796] a skilled stonemason working as the need arose for different employers and remunerated on piece rates was held to be an employee in multiple employments and therefore entitled to compensation for personal injury as an employee.

2.387 As we have seen, the rationalia of vicarious liability are slippery. If one once accepts its practical necessity in the modern world, that same necessity cannot easily be confined within the elusive technicalities of the 'master-servant' relationship.

(4) The 'Course of Employment'

2.388 Difficult as it is to draw a clean line between employees *stricto sensu* and independent contractors, it is barely less awkward to find the boundary around those torts of an employee for which the employer is vicariously liable and those for which he is not. The rule is that to attract vicarious liability the tort must be committed by the employee in the course of his employment. However, this formula has proven easier to utter than to apply.

(a) Misperformance of the employment contract

2.389 In one sense a tort can hardly ever be within the course of the employment. Unless authorized or ratified by the employer, every tort is at best a deviation from proper performance of the employment contract. Hence the line lies between misperformance of the contract and wrongs which can be said to have nothing relevantly to do with the contract. In *Century Insurance Co Ltd v Northern Ireland Road Transport Board*[797] a tanker driver delivering petrol to a garage began to smoke and thus caused an explosion. This has become the classic example of a misperformance in the course of employment. For a century the classic formulation was that of Sir John Salmond, who said that a wrongful act was deemed to be done by a 'servant' in the course of his employment if it was 'either (a) a wrongful act authorised by the master, or (b) a wrongful and unauthorised *mode* of doing some act authorised by the master'.[798]

2.390 But this test was notoriously difficult to apply. An example is *LCC v Cattermoles (Garages) Ltd*[799] in which a worker in a garage drove a vehicle out on to the highway and did damage. He had no driving licence and had been expressly forbidden to drive. Nevertheless, the Court of Appeal held the garage to be vicariously liable. It was admitted to be a borderline case. In *Rose v Plenty*[800] the Court of Appeal held employers liable where a milkman, in the teeth of contrary orders, had taken a 13-year-old helper on his rounds with him and had caused the boy an injury through bad driving. And in *Kay v ITW Ltd*[801] the Court of Appeal came to the same conclusion where the defendant's driver did damage when driving another firm's

---

[794] [1984] QB 90, CA.
[795] [1992] 1 WLR 939.
[796] [1990] 2 AC 374, PC.
[797] [1942] AC 509, HL.
[798] J Salmond, *Law of Torts* (1907) 83.
[799] [1953] 1 WLR 997, CA.
[800] [1976] 1 WLR 141, CA. Contrast *Twine v Bean's Express Ltd* (1946) 175 LT 131, CA; *Conway v George Wimpey & Co Ltd* [1951] 2 KB 266, CA.
[801] [1968] 1 QB 140, CA.

lorry. Here the negligence was in the course of his employment only because he drove the other lorry in order to move it, so that his own truck could then get in.

Road accidents while driving to and from work were not in the course of employment, but **2.391** where a job required driving a road accident would generally be within the course of that employment. In *Smith v Stages* [802] the employees had been sent out on an emergency repair mission a long drive from their usual place of work. Having worked non-stop for 24 hours, they rushed home without taking a break. Negligent driving caused an accident. This was within the course of their employment. Similarly a coach driver who, contrary to express instructions, allowed himself to be persuaded to take a long detour when bringing boys home from camp, was still within his course of employment when he crashed. [803]

(b) Wilful wrongs: fraud and violence

It used to be thought that an employer would never be liable for wilful wrongs committed **2.392** for the employee's own purposes. That seems to be the implication of Sir John Salmond's test. But there were a number of cases where the employer was nevertheless held vicariously liable. When a bus conductor first grew abusive and then turned to violence against a passenger, it was held that this conduct, though on his bus, was outside the course of his employment. [804] On the other hand a dangerous prank involving deliberately pushing a motorized truck into a fellow employee was not outside the course of the driver's employment. His employers were therefore liable when the prank misfired and its victim was injured in earnest. [805]

(c) Reconciliation

Clarity in the definition of 'course of employment' has perhaps been enhanced since the deci- **2.393** sion of the House of Lords to abolish the Salmond formulation in *Lister v Hesley Hall Ltd.* [806] The defendant in that case was a children's home which was held to be vicariously liable for the warden's sexual abuse of two teenage boys. The warden's conduct was in the course of his employment because his acts were sufficiently closely connected with the employment. The 'close connection' test has since been applied in a number of other cases involving wilful tortious wrongdoing [807] and equitable wrongdoing [808] and there is little doubt that it will be applied in other cases of misperformance of an employment contract. Although legal clarity is enhanced, there remains the difficult factual question of when the wrong will be sufficiently 'closely connected' with the employment. All that can be said is that the question is an 'evaluative judgment'. [809]

---

[802] [1989] AC 928, HL.

[803] *Hemphill Ltd v Williams* [1966] 2 Lloyd's Rep 101, HL.

[804] *Keppel Bus Co Ltd v Ahmad* [1974] 1 WLR 1082, PC.

[805] *Harrison v Michelin Tyre Co Ltd* [1985] 1 All ER 918.

[806] [2001] UKHL 22, [2002] 1 AC 215, following the Canadian approach in *Bazley v Curry* [1999] 2 SCR 534, SCC and *Jacobi v Griffiths* [1999] 2 SCR 470, SCC. The Australian courts have rejected this approach: *New South Wales v Lepore* [2003] HCA 4, 212 CLR 511; *Sweeney v Boylan Nominees Pty Ltd* [2006] HCA 19, 226 CLR 161.

[807] *Mattis v Pollock* [2003] EWCA Civ 887, [2003] 1 WLR 2158; *Bernard v Attorney General of Jamaica* [2004] UKPC 47. In sexual abuse cases, it has recently been said that vicarious liability will be imposed 'where a defendant, whose relationship with the abuser put it in a position to use the abuser to carry on its business or to further its own interests, has done so in a manner which has created or significantly enhanced the risk that the victim or victims would suffer the relevant abuse': *The Catholic Child Welfare Society v The Institute of the Brothers of the Christian Schools* [2012] UKSC 56, at [86], *per* Lord Phillips.

[808] *Dubai Aluminium Co Ltd v Salaam* [2002] UKHL 48, [2003] 2 AC 366.

[809] *Dubai Aluminium Co Ltd v Salaam* [2002] UKHL 48, [2003] 2 AC 366, at [25]–[26], *per* Lord Nicholls.

3

UNJUST ENRICHMENT

A. Introduction*

(1) Unjust Enrichment and Restitution

The modern English law of unjust enrichment developed as the law of restitution. That name **3.01** was determined by Robert Goff and Gareth Jones' decision to publish their seminal book on the subject with the title *The Law of Restitution*.[1] At the time the subject was virtually unknown in England. Since then the highest appellate courts have come to affirm that unjust enrichment is a discrete source of rights and obligations in English private law.[2] To reflect

---

* *Author's note*. I am grateful to Andrew Burrows and Frederick Wilmot-Smith for their insightful comments on a draft of this chapter.

[1] R Goff and G Jones, *The Law of Restitution* (1966), following the American Law Institute, *Restatement of the Law, Restitution* (1937). cf the hybrid title of the American Law Institute, *Restatement of the Law, Third: Restitution and Unjust Enrichment* (2011).

[2] *Lipkin Gorman (a firm) v Karpnale Ltd* [1991] 2 AC 548, 559–560, 572 and 578, HL; *Woolwich Equitable Building Society v IRC* [1993] AC 70, 154 and 196–197, HL; *Westdeutsche Landesbank Girozentrale*

this, Goff and Jones' book has been retitled *The Law of Unjust Enrichment*;[3] the title of this chapter was chosen for the same reason.

3.02   The difference between unjust enrichment and restitution is the difference between event and response.[4] Unjust enrichment at a claimant's expense is an event to which the law responds by giving the claimant different rights according to circumstances. A right to restitution is one possible response to the event of unjust enrichment. When a defendant is unjustly enriched at his expense, a claimant may acquire a restitutionary right that the enrichment be reversed.

3.03   Responses to unjust enrichment other than restitution are also possible, eg a prophylactic right to shift responsibility for enriching a defendant onto a third party.[5] Furthermore, a right to restitution may arise from events other than unjust enrichment. For example, restitution is a possible response to wrongdoing. Suppose that a defendant trespasses on a claimant's land. Founding on the tort, the claimant can claim compensation for loss or restitution of the defendant's gain.[6] His restitutionary right arises from the wrong, not from unjust enrichment.[7]

(2) Unjust Enrichment as a Legal Concept

3.04   By comparison with civil law systems, English law was slow to recognize unjust enrichment as a source of rights and obligations. The rules discussed in this chapter were formerly thought to make up the law of 'quasi-contract', shakily conceptualized as part of the law of contract, or else were treated as isolated incidents of equitable doctrine.[8] The theory that 'quasi-contractual' claims rested on implied contract was memorably articulated in *Sinclair v Brougham*,[9] but was decisively rejected in the *Westdeutsche* case,[10] and is now 'a ghost of

---

v Islington LBC [1996] AC 669, 710, HL; *Banque Financière de la Cité v Parc (Battersea) Ltd* [1999] 1 AC 221 ('*BFC*'), 227 and 234, HL; *Dubai Aluminium Co Ltd v Salaam* [2002] UKHL 48, [2003] 2 AC 366, at [76]; *Criterion Properties plc v Stratford UK Properties LLC* [2004] UKHL 28, [2004] 1 WLR 1846, at [4]; *Deutsche Morgan Grenfell Group plc v IRC* [2006] UKHL 49, [2007] 1 AC 558 ('*DMG*'), at [21]; *Sempra Metals Ltd v IRC* [2007] UKHL 34, [2008] 1 AC 561, at [27]; *Cobbe v Yeoman's Row Management Ltd* [2008] UKHL 55, [2008] 1 WLR 1752, at [40]; *R (Child Poverty Action Group) v Secretary of State for Work and Pensions* [2010] UKSC 54, [2011] 2 AC 15 ('*CPAG*'), at [21]; *Test Claimants in the FII Group Litigation v HMRC* [2012] UKSC 19, [2012] 2 AC 337 ('*FII* (SC)'), at [58] and [81]. All prefigured by *Fibrosa Spolka Akcyjna v Fairbairn Lawson Combe Barbour Ltd* [1943] AC 32, 61, HL.

[3]   C Mitchell, P Mitchell and S Watterson (eds), *Goff & Jones: The Law of Unjust Enrichment* (8th edn, 2011). cf A Burrows, *A Restatement of the English Law of Unjust Enrichment* (2012).

[4]   P Birks, 'Misnomer' in W R Cornish et al (eds), *Restitution: Past, Present and Future* (1998).

[5]   eg exonerative relief for sureties: C Mitchell, *The Law of Contribution and Reimbursement* (2003) paras 14.38–14.45; insurers' subrogation rights: C Mitchell and S Watterson, *Subrogation: Law and Practice* (2007) paras 10.05–10.06 and 10.30–10.39.

[6]   *Ministry of Defence v Ashman* (1993) 66 P & CR 195, CA; *Severn Trent Water Ltd v Barnes* [2004] EWCA Civ 570, [2004] 2 EGLR 95. The fact that these remedies are different does not mean that they are necessarily inconsistent and the question whether a claimant can have *both* remedies should depend on their underlying purposes and the extent to which these overlap: P Birks, 'Inconsistency Between Compensation and Restitution' (1996) 112 LQR 375; L Bently and C Mitchell, 'Combining Money Awards for Patent Infringement' [2003] RLR 79; S Watterson, 'An Account of Profits or Damages? The History of Orthodoxy' (2004) 24 OJLS 471.

[7]   *Sempra*, n 2, at [231], endorsing P Birks, *Unjust Enrichment* (2nd edn, 2005) 11–16. It is disputed whether the term 'restitution' should describe the disgorgement of third-party receipts as well as the return of benefits received from a claimant: *Devenish Nutrition Ltd v Sanofi-Aventis SA* [2008] EWCA Civ 1086, [2009] Ch 390, at [144]. Restitution for wrongs is discussed at 4.145–4.162.

[8]   D Ibbetson, *A Historical Introduction to the Law of Obligations* (1999) 276–93.

[9]   [1914] AC 398, HL.

[10]   *Westdeutsche* (HL), n 2, at 710, followed in *Haugesund Kommune v Depfa ACS Bank* [2010] EWCA Civ 579, [2012] Bus LR 1, at [87]. See too *Sempra*, n 2, at [112]–[113]; *Benedetti v Sawiris* [2010] EWCA Civ 1427 ('*Benedetti* (CA)'), at [141].

the past'.[11] Nor is it 'appropriate...to draw a distinction between law and equity' by dividing claims in unjust enrichment into different categories governed by different principles according to their jurisdictional origin,[12] and in appropriate cases extending equity's auxiliary jurisdiction to make good the inadequacy of common law remedies is a 'permissible step in the progress which [has been] made towards developing...a coherent law of restitution.'[13]

It has been said that unjust enrichment is a high-level principle of justice lacking substantive **3.05** doctrinal content.[14] However, unjust enrichment is not an abstract moral principle, but a 'unifying legal concept, which explains why the law recognises, in a variety of distinct categories of case, an obligation on the part of the defendant to make fair and just restitution for a benefit derived at the expense of a plaintiff and which assists in the determination, by the ordinary processes of legal reasoning, of the question whether the law should, in justice, recognise such an obligation in a new or developing category of case'.[15] Thus the 'unjust' element in 'unjust enrichment' is a 'generalisation of all the factors which the law recognises as calling for restitution'.[16] These vary from one set of cases to another. In this way the law of unjust enrichment more closely resembles the law of torts (recognizing various reasons why harm must be compensated) than it does the law of contract (embodying a single principle that expectations engendered by binding promises must be fulfilled).[17]

(3) Actions in Unjust Enrichment

A claimant must show three things to make out a claim in unjust enrichment: that the **3.06** defendant was enriched, that his enrichment was gained at the claimant's expense, and that his enrichment at the claimant's expense was unjust.[18] If these requirements are satisfied, then the questions arise, whether there is any defence to the claim or any legal ground for the defendant's enrichment. If not, then it must be asked what remedy should be awarded. Some preliminary comments will be made about each of these matters.

(a) Enrichment

In the past English law gave claimants different types of action to recover the value of differ- **3.07** ent types of benefit. Money fell to the action for money had and received. Actions for *quantum meruit* and *quantum valebat* awards dealt with services and goods. Actions for money paid to the defendant's use lay where the defendant was benefited through the claimant's payment to a third party, eg to discharge the defendant's liability to a creditor.[19]

---

[11] *Cleveland Bridge UK Ltd v Multiplex Constructions (UK) Ltd* [2010] EWCA Civ 139, at [121]. On the distinction between claims in contract and unjust enrichment, see also *BFC*, n 2, at 232–233.

[12] *Nelson v Larholt* [1948] 1 KB 339, 343.

[13] *Sempra*, n 2, at [185].

[14] *Baylis v Bishop of London* [1913] 1 Ch 127, 140, CA; *Holt v Markham* [1923] 1 KB 504, 513, CA.

[15] *Pavey and Matthews Pty Ltd v Paul* (1987) 162 CLR 221, 256–257. See too *David Securities Pty Ltd v Commonwealth Bank of Australia* (1992) 275 CLR 353, 379; *Equuscorp Pty Ltd v Haxton* [2012] HCA 7, (2012) 246 CLR 498, at [29]–[30].

[16] K Mason, J Carter and G Tolhurst, *Restitution Law in Australia* (2nd edn, 2008) [166]; approved in *Barnes v Eastenders Cash & Carry plc* [2014] UKSC 16, [2015] AC 1 ('*Barnes*'), at [102].

[17] S Smith, 'Unjust Enrichment: Nearer to Tort than Contract' in R Chambers, C Mitchell and J Penner (eds), *Philosophical Foundations of the Law of Unjust Enrichment* (2009) 202–206.

[18] *BFC*, n 2, at 227; *Cressman v Coys of Kensington (Sales) Ltd* [2004] EWCA Civ 47, [2004] 1 WLR 2775, at [22]; *Chief Constable of Greater Manchester v Wigan Athletic AFC Ltd* [2008] EWCA Civ 1449, [2009] 1 WLR 1580, at [38], [54] and [62]; *Benedetti v Sawiris* [2013] UKSC 50, [2014] AC 938 ('*Benedetti* (SC)'), at [10]; *Investment Trust Companies (in liq) v HMRC* [2015] EWCA Civ 82 ('*ITC* (CA)'), at [26].

[19] The latter counts all required the plaintiff to recite that the benefit was conferred at the defendant's request. Where an actual request was made and the benefit conferred, the claim was contractual. But the law would infer the making of a request in some circumstances that would now be regarded as giving rise to liability in unjust enrichment: eg an action for money paid to the defendant's use would lie where the plaintiff

3.08   Over 150 years have elapsed since the abolition of the forms of action, and the law of unjust enrichment now rests on a single set of principles. The key issue is no longer whether particular types of benefit have been transferred, but whether the defendant has been enriched by receiving value.[20] A single set of rules determines the identification and quantification of enrichment,[21] and there is no need for the courts to protect defendants by requiring different claims to be brought to recover different types of benefit, and or by debarring claims in respect of some types of benefit.[22]

(b)   At the claimant's expense

3.09   This term signifies that the claimant suffered a loss that was sufficiently closely linked with the defendant's gain for the law to hold that there was a transfer of value between them. This rule reflects the principle that the law of unjust enrichment is not concerned with the disgorgement of gains by defendants, nor with compensation for losses sustained by claimants, but with the reversal of transfers between claimants and defendants.[23] Whether a transfer has taken place is a question of combined fact and law: it turns on the application of legal tests to the facts of the case. Unfortunately, though, it is uncertain what these tests are, and this area of the law needs rationalization and restatement.

(c)   Unjust factors

3.10   The law must say when an enrichment at another's expense is an unjust enrichment. Civil law systems commonly approach this issue by asking if there is a legal ground for the transfer between the parties; if there is not, the defendant's enrichment is unjustified and restitution will follow. English law approaches the issue differently, by asking if there is a positive reason for restitution, or 'unjust factor', ie a legally recognized factor making the defendant's enrichment unjust.[24] The claimant must show that the facts disclose a ground of recovery established by authority, or justifiable by principled analogical reasoning from authority: the courts have no 'discretionary power to order repayment whenever it seems . . . just and equitable to do so'.[25] However, 'the categories of unjust enrichment are not closed',[26] and the courts have the power to recognize new grounds of recovery.[27]

---

was compelled to pay the defendant's debt as 'the compulsion [was] evidence of the request': *Osborne v Rogers* (1669) 1 Wms Saund 264, 265n; 85 ER 318, 320. See too *Exall v Partridge* (1799) 8 TR 308, 101 ER 1405; *Moule v Garrett* (1872) LR 7 Ex 101, 104.

[20]   It has been argued that receipt of value is not the only way in which defendants can be enriched, and that they can also be enriched by the receipt of legal rights: R Chambers, 'Two Kinds of Enrichment' in Chambers et al, n 17; A Lodder, *Enrichment in the Law of Unjust Enrichment and Restitution* (2012) chs 3–5. If correct, this argument could have significant consequences for the way in which the courts decide when claimants should be entitled to proprietary restitutionary remedies (as to which see 3.234ff).

[21]   Not everyone agrees that there should be one law for all enrichment received, in whatever form: P Watts, 'Restitution: A Property Principle and a Services Principle' [1995] RLR 30; B McFarlane, 'Unjust Enrichment, Rights and Value' in D Nolan and A Robertson (eds), *Rights and Private Law* (2011).

[22]   eg claims to recover mistaken improvements to land, on which see Tang Hang Wu, 'An Unjust Enrichment Claim for the Mistaken Improver of Land' [2011] Conv 8.

[23]   *Roxborough v Rothmans of Pall Mall Australia Ltd* (2001) 208 CLR 516, at [26]; *Kingstreet Investments Ltd v New Brunswick (Department of Finance)* [2007] SCC 1, [2007] 1 SCR 3, at [32]; *TFL Management Services Ltd v Lloyds TSB Bank plc* [2013] EWCA Civ 1415, [2014] 1 WLR 2006 ('*TFL*'), at [51]; *Menelaou v Bank of Cyprus plc* [2013] EWCA Civ 1960, [2014] 1 WLR 854 ('*Menelaou*'), at [29].

[24]   *BFC*, n 2, at 227; *Kleinwort Benson Ltd v Lincoln CC* [1999] 2 AC 349, 363, 386, 395, and 409, HL; *FII* (SC), n 2, at [81].

[25]   *Kleinwort Benson Ltd v Birmingham CC* [1997] QB 380, 387, CA.

[26]   *CTN Cash & Carry Ltd v Gallaher Ltd* [1994] 4 All ER 714, 720, CA.

[27]   As demonstrated by *Woolwich*, n 2, which is discussed at 3.127ff. For discussion of the courts' power to develop the law, see *Gibb v Maidstone and Tunbridge Wells NHS Trust* [2010] EWCA Civ 678, [2010] IRLR 786, at [26]–[27].

Some scholars have argued that English law would do better to adopt the civilian 'absence of **3.11** basis' model, among other reasons because it achieves a tighter conceptual unity by grounding recovery on a single juristic principle.[28] Peter Birks also took the view that as a matter of authority English law was committed to the civilian approach by certain cases concerned with the recovery of payments under void but fully executed interest rate swap contracts.[29]

It is implausible that English law would work more efficiently, or more fairly, if it adopted **3.12** the 'absence of basis' approach. On the contrary, it seems likely that such a change would produce confusion and uncertainty,[30] especially if the courts were to adopt Birks' 'limited reconciliation' of the two approaches by treating unjust factors as reasons why, higher up, there is no legal ground for the defendant's acquisition.[31] The courts often fare badly when asked to operate several tests at once, particularly when the content of these tests and the relationship between them is imperfectly understood.

Nor has English law switched to 'absence of basis' reasoning. In making this claim, Birks **3.13** was too quick to reject other explanations of the closed swap cases.[32] He also ignored the *Woolwich* case, where Lord Goff expressly declined to award restitution on the footing that there had been no legal ground for the defendant's enrichment. Lord Goff said that English law 'might have developed so as to recognise a *condictio indebiti*—an action for the recovery of money on the ground that it was not due. But it did not do so'.[33] These dicta were subsequently endorsed in *Deutsche Morgan Grenfell Group plc v IRC*[34] and in *Test Claimants in the FII Group Litigation v HMRC*, where Lord Sumption held that it is still 'necessary, as the law presently stands, to bring the facts within one of the categories of case in which the law recognises that the recipient's retention of the money would be unjust'.[35]

The following grounds for recovery can be identified in the cases: lack of consent and want **3.14** of authority; mistake; duress; undue influence; failure of basis; secondary liability; necessity; undue payments to public bodies; ultra vires payments by public bodies; illegality; reversal of judgments; and insolvency policies. The first four concern situations where the claimant's intention to benefit the defendant is deficient; the next concerns the situation where the basis on which the defendant is enriched fails to materialize; the last seven concern situations where restitution is awarded to accomplish various policy objectives that do not turn on the parties' intentions.

---

[28] eg S Meier, 'Unjust Factors and Legal Grounds' in D Johnston and R Zimmermann (eds), *Unjustified Enrichment: Key Issues in Comparative Perspective* (2002); Birks (2005), n 7, at ch 5.

[29] Birks (2005), n 7, at 108–113, citing *Kleinwort Benson Ltd v Sandwell BC*, reported with *Westdeutsche Landesbank Girozentrale v Islington LBC* [1994] 4 All ER 890; and *Guinness Mahon plc v Kensington & Chelsea RLBC* [1999] QB 215, CA. These were 'closed swap' cases: the parties had both fully performed their obligations under a contract which was then discovered to have been void.

[30] The differences between English law and German law, which takes an 'absence of basis' approach, are emphasized in T Krebs, *Restitution at the Crossroads: A Comparative Study* (2001) and A Sanders, 'Absence of Problems? A Critical German Perspective on an Absence of Basis Analysis' in S Elliott, B Häcker and C Mitchell (eds), *Restitution of Overpaid Tax* (2013). These differences are played down in S Meier, 'No Basis: A Comparative View' and G Dannemann, 'Unjust Enrichment as Absence of Basis: Can English Law Cope?', both in A Burrows and Lord Rodger (eds), *Mapping the Law* (2006).

[31] Birks (2005), n 7, at 116, developed in T Baloch, 'The Unjust Enrichment Pyramid' (2007) 123 LQR 636.

[32] Failure of basis was identified as the ground of recovery in *Guinness Mahon*, n 29, for reasons that are considered at 3.87. Recovery could also have been awarded on the ground of mistake of law in line with *Lincoln*, n 24.

[33] *Woolwich*, n 2, at 172.

[34] *DMG*, n 2, at [21].

[35] *FII* (SC), n 2, at [162]. But note the discussion at 3.130.

3.15 No rule prevents a claimant from relying on one ground of recovery at common law in preference to another.[36] However, a claimant with a statutory right to restitution may be prevented from relying on a common law right.[37]

(d) Defences and presence of legal grounds

3.16 A defendant can make two types of argument in reply to a claim in unjust enrichment: he can deny that the claimant has established an element of his action, or admit that the claimant has established a prima facie right to restitution, but argue that restitution should be reduced or withheld for another reason.[38] Distinguishing between 'denials' and 'defences' can make it easier to understand the substance of a defendant's arguments. It can also matter because the burden of proving the elements of a claim lies on the claimant, while defences must generally be pleaded and proved by the defendant.[39]

3.17 The courts do not always draw a clear distinction between denials and defences. A case in point is the argument that a defendant should escape liability because there is a legal ground for his enrichment, such as a contract or statute. Under civilian systems that impose liability for unjustified enrichment where there is no legal ground for the defendant's enrichment, this argument operates as a denial: because there is a legal ground for his enrichment, this is not unjustified. Under English law, it is less clear what kind of argument is being made. On one view, the presence of a legal ground is a defence: the claimant can establish all the elements of a claim in unjust enrichment, but there is another reason why he is not entitled to restitution.[40] On another view, the presence of a legal ground prevents the claimant from establishing an unjust factor: because there was a contract between the parties, eg, the defendant cannot show that he made a mistake of a kind that entitles him to restitution.[41]

3.18 Eight other arguments can also be made by defendants in reply to claims in unjust enrichment. Each can plausibly be characterized as a defence, but some may be better understood as denials. These are: change of position; ministerial receipt; bona fide purchase; estoppel; counter-restitution impossible; passing on; limitation; and illegality.

(e) Remedies

3.19 Some remedies for unjust enrichment prevent a defendant from being unjustly enriched at a claimant's expense.[42] Remedies of this kind are rare because a claimant who knows that a defendant will be unjustly enriched at his expense can usually avoid this outcome without needing to obtain a court order, simply by choosing not to transfer a benefit to him.

---

[36] cf *Lincoln*, n 24, at 387 (no rule forcing a claimant to rely on mistake rather than failure of basis or vice versa); *DMG*, n 2 , followed in *Littlewoods Retail Ltd v HMRC* [2015] EWCA Civ 515, at [119] and [142] (no rule forcing a claimant to rely on the rule in *Woolwich*, n 2, rather than mistake of law).

[37] See 3.221–3.222.

[38] J Goudkamp and C Mitchell, 'Denials and Defences in the Law of Unjust Enrichment' in C Mitchell and W Swadling (eds), *The Restatement Third, Restitution and Unjust Enrichment: Critical and Comparative Essays* (2013).

[39] *David Securities*, n 15, at 379 and 384. cf *Birmingham*, n 25, at 399–400; *Bank of Credit and Commerce International (Overseas) Ltd v Akindele* [2001] Ch 437, 456, CA; *Getronics Holdings Emea BV v Logistic & Transport Consulting Co* [2004] EWHC 808 (QB), at [22]–[24]. Exceptionally, once a defendant has pleaded a limitation defence, the burden of proof is placed on the claimant to show that his claim was brought in time: Law Commission *Limitation of Actions* (LCCP No 151, 1998) paras 9.23–9.25; Law Commission, *Limitation of Actions* (Law Com No 270, 2001) para 5.29.

[40] eg *Investment Trust Companies (in liq) v HMRC* [2012] EWHC 458 (Ch), [2012] STC 1150 ('*ITC* (Ch)'), at [88], where Henderson J held it to be a 'defence' that claims to recover money paid as VAT that is not due can only be brought under the VAT Act 1994, s 80, and that HMRC can therefore keep such money if it is received from a payor to whom the statute gives no claim. On appeal the CA disagreed with the judge's interpretation of the statute, but not with his characterization of the issue: *ITC* (CA), n 18, at [70]–[82].

[41] eg *Lincoln*, n 24, at 407–408.

[42] See n 5.

Most remedies for unjust enrichment are restitutionary. There is a potential terminological **3.20** confusion here that needs to be avoided. Compensatory remedies for wrongdoing are sometimes described as 'restitutionary', meaning that they restore the claimant to the position that he would have occupied had the wrong not been committed.[43] In the context of claims for unjust enrichment, the term is used differently, to denote remedies that reverse an enrichment gained by the defendant at the claimant's expense.[44]

Claimants in unjust enrichment are most frequently awarded a personal restitutionary remedy, ie an order that the defendant should pay a sum representing the value of the enrichment he received at the claimant's expense. Less often claimants are entitled to a proprietary restitutionary remedy, ie an order declaring that the claimant has a new ownership or security interest in property held by the defendant, usually accompanied by consequential orders such as an order that the property should be conveyed to the claimant, or an order that it should be sold and a share of the proceeds remitted to the claimant. Although they are necessarily directed to a defendant, such orders are also exigible against third parties.[45] **3.21**

B. Enrichment

(1) Date of Enrichment

The questions whether a defendant has been enriched, and if so, to what extent, are tested at **3.22** the date of receipt. Consistently with this, a cause of action to recover the value of a mistaken payment accrues at the date of receipt.[46] So do a cause of action to recover the value of money paid on a basis that immediately fails[47] and a cause of action to recover the value of money paid as tax which was not due.[48] Likewise, a cause of action to recover the value of a debt discharged by a claimant who was only secondarily liable to the creditor accrues at the date of payment.[49] Even where a cause of action does not accrue until later, eg because it is founded on a failure of basis that post-dates receipt of the benefit,[50] the extent of the defendant's enrichment is still tested at the date of receipt. Thus an Australian judge has held that 'the obligation of a purchaser who accepts and retains goods under an incomplete or unenforceable contract, to make payment of a reasonable price for the benefit so obtained is based on the principles of unjust enrichment and requires the payment of the value of the benefit . . . as it was at the time that the benefit was taken.'[51] The same rule applies to services claims: the cause of action accrues when the services are rendered,[52] and the services are valued as at the same date.[53]

---

[43] At common law: *British Transport Commission v Gourley* [1956] AC 185, 208, HL; *Heil v Rankin* [2001] QB 272, 292, CA; *HMRC v Holland* [2010] UKSC 51, [2011] Bus LR 111, at [48]. In equity: *Nocton v Lord Ashburton* [1914] AC 932, 952, HL; *Target Holdings Ltd v Redferns (a firm)* [1996] AC 421, 434, HL.
[44] *Sempra*, n 2, at [28]; *AXA Insurance UK plc v Thermonex Ltd* [2012] EWHC B10 (Mercantile), [2013] TCLR 3, at [66].
[45] cf *Re Flint (a bankrupt)* [1993] Ch 319; *Mountney v Treharne* [2002] EWCA Civ 1174, [2003] Ch 135.
[46] *Baker v Courage & Co* [1910] 1 KB 56; *Lincoln*, n 24, at 386 and 409; *Fea v Roberts* [2005] EWHC 2186 (Ch), (2005) 8 ITELR 231, at [61].
[47] *Kleinwort Benson Ltd v South Tyneside MBC* [1994] 4 All ER 972, 978.
[48] *Woolwich*, n 2, at 171.
[49] *Davies v Humphreys* (1840) 6 M & W 153, 168–169; 151 ER 361, 367–368; *Wolmershausen v Gullick* [1893] 2 Ch 514; Merchant Shipping Act 1995, s 190; Limitation Act 1980, s 10.
[50] *David Securities*, n 15, at 389.
[51] *Dowell v Custombuilt Homes Pty Ltd* [2004] WASCA 171 [98]. See too *BP Exploration Co (Libya) Ltd v Hunt (No 2)* [1979] 1 WLR 783, 836.
[52] *Sydney CC v Woodward* [2000] NSWCA 201, at [94]; *Coshott v Lenin* [2007] NSWCA 153, at [17].
[53] *Benedetti* (SC), n 18, at [14], adding that where services are performed over an extended period the relevant date is when they are completed, which on the facts of the case was when there was 'no possibility of, or need for' further services.

(2) Money

3.23 Money is the very measure of enrichment. It is impossible to deny that a receipt of money is enriching.[53a] There is a question, however, as to how the use value of money should be handled. Where a claimant pays money to a defendant who is thereby saved the expense of borrowing an equivalent sum at compound interest, the benefit gained by the defendant includes the use value as well as the face value of the money. This is the value of the opportunity to use the money, which is measured by reference to the defendant's saved borrowing costs.[53b]

3.24 Nevertheless, in *Westdeutsche Landesbank Girozentrale v Islington LBC*,[54] the majority of the court held that in these circumstances compound interest is not payable unless the case falls within the scope of a special equitable jurisdiction; otherwise the courts' power to award pre-judgment interest derives exclusively from their jurisdiction to award simple interest under section 35A of the Senior Courts Act 1981. As Lord Goff and Lord Woolf said in their dissenting speeches, this was unsatisfactory as it left the courts unable to order restitution of the full benefit received by the defendant.[55]

3.25 In *Sempra Metals Ltd v IRC*,[56] the House of Lords revisited this issue and came to a different conclusion. The claimants mistakenly paid tax sooner than was legally required and claimed the use value of the money during the period of prematurity, asserting that the measure of this benefit equated to a compound interest award. Their claims succeeded, according to Lord Hope and Lord Nicholls because they had claims in unjust enrichment at common law to recover the use value of the money,[57] and according to Lord Walker because the court should exercise an equitable discretion in the claimants' favour to award an equivalent sum.[58]

3.26 The amount awarded in *Sempra* represented a rate of interest that was lower than commercial rates to reflect the fact that the Government can borrow money more cheaply than commercial borrowers, eg by issuing Treasury Bills. It appears from Lord Nicholls' speech that he conceived this result to reflect the principle, discussed immediately below, that defendants can rely on evidence of their personal characteristics to argue that benefits in kind are worth less to them than they are to other people.[59] In *Benedetti v Sawiris*, however, it was suggested that the result in *Sempra* can be explained on the different basis that the defendant's enrichment was valued objectively, by reference to the individuated market rate for Government borrowing, which is lower than the market rate for commercial borrowing because the Government is a better credit risk than commercial borrowers.[59a]

(3) Benefits in Kind

3.27 When benefits are received in kind the central problem is easy to understand. It turns on the subjectivity of value. While money is the very measure of enrichment, benefits in kind have

---

[53a] *Test Claimants in the FII Group Litigation v HMRC (No 2)* ('*FII (No 2)*') [2014] EWHC 4302 (Ch), [2015] BTC 3, at [420].

[53b] *Sempra*, n 2, at [32]–[33] and [117], emphasizing the difference between the defendant's opportunity to use the money and whatever secondary gains the defendant might make from his actual use of the money.

[54] *Westdeutsche* (HL), n 2.

[55] *Westdeutsche* (HL), n 2, at 691 and 719–720.

[56] *Sempra*, n 2. It was assumed that the claimants had made a mistake of law, following *Lincoln*, n 24.

[57] *Sempra*, n 2, at [26], [36] and [112].

[58] *Sempra*, n 2, at [184]–[187].

[59] *Sempra*, n 2, at [118]–[119] and [128].

[59a] *Benedetti* (SC), n 18, at [22], [107], [126]–[127] and [186]. See too *Littlewoods* (CA), n 36, at [153]. cf *Kowalishin v Roberts* [2015] EWHC 1333 (Ch): the individuated market rate for a defendant may also be higher than the general market rate for commercial borrowers if he is an unusually poor credit risk, and in this case the objective value of his saved borrowing costs is correspondingly higher than the general market rate.

different values to different people. The objective value of a benefit may be discovered by reference to the general market, or to the parties' dealings if they have had any.[60] However, a defendant may consider that a benefit is not worth its objective value, eg because he would have preferred to spend his money on something else if he had had a free choice. As Lord Nicholls observed in *Sempra*, 'it may be unjust to treat the defendant [in such a case] as having received a benefit possessing the value it has to others.'[61]

To avoid this injustice, the court may assess the value of the benefit by reference to the **3.28** defendant's personal value system rather than the market. This is sometimes described as 'subjective devaluation'.[62] In *Sempra*, and again in *Benedetti*, the majority also held that once a claimant has established that the defendant has received a benefit with an objective value, the burden of proof lies on the defendant to show that it was worth less to him.[63] This suggests that the 'subjective devaluation' argument may be a defence rather than a denial that the claimant has established the 'enrichment' element of his claim.[64]

There is sometimes no danger that a defendant's freedom to make his own spending choices will **3.29** be compromised if he is ordered to repay the objective value of a benefit. There is no such danger where he has received a benefit that is as unequivocally enriching as the receipt of money. Examples are benefits in kind that are subsequently realized in money[65] or otherwise turned to profitable account,[66] and the saving of inevitable expense resulting from the discharge of a liability owed to the claimant[67] or a third party,[68] or from the receipt of necessary services.[69]

Nor can a defendant complain of interference with his freedom of choice where he has actually **3.30** exercised a choice to accept a benefit which he knows has not been offered gratuitously, or at less than its objective value. The best example is where the defendant has expressly requested

---

[60] *Scarisbrick v Parkinson* (1869) 20 LT 175; *Way v Latilla* [1937] 3 All ER 759, HL; *BP*, n 51, at 805–806; *Guinness Mahon*, n 29, at 240; *Humber Oil Terminals Trustee Ltd v Associated British Ports* [2012] EWHC 1336 (Ch), [2012] L & TR 28, at [155]. See too *Benedetti* (SC), n 18, at [56], [168] and [182]: where the parties agree a price for services for which there is no general market, their agreed price may be the only evidence of what the services are worth.

[61] *Sempra*, n 2, at [119]. See too *Regional Municipality of Peel v Ontario* [1992] 3 SCR 762, at [25].

[62] eg *Cressman* n 18, at [28]; *Sempra*, n 2, at [119]. *Benedetti* (SC), n 18, at [18]. cf Lord Reed's discussion in *Benedetti* (SC), n 18 at [110]–[119], where he accepted that defendants should be allowed to make the argument from freedom of choice, but preferred not to express this argument in the language of enrichment, which he believed should always be assessed objectively. For this view, see also J Edelman, 'The Meaning of Loss and Enrichment' in Chambers et al, n 17, at 235–239; Lodder, n 20, at ch 6.

[63] *Sempra*, n 2, at [48], [116]–[117], and [186]; *Benedetti* (SC), n 18, at [21]. *Sempra* was a claim for the use value of money, meaning the value of the opportunity to use money, paid by the claimant to the defendant. At [118], Lord Nicholls said that in such cases a defendant who makes no actual use of the money might rely on that fact to prove that he would not have been willing to pay the market rate for the opportunity to use it because he did not need or want this benefit. As noted by Henderson J in *Littlewoods Retail Ltd v HMRC (No 2)* [2014] EWHC 868 (Ch), [2014] STC 1761, at [369]–[373], the significance of this was that the court might then limit recovery to the value subjectively ascribed by the defendant to the opportunity, because forcing him to pay its objective value would unfairly deprive him of his freedom to choose whether to buy it and, if so, how much to pay for it. In *Littlewoods* (CA), n 36, at [148]–[199] the court went further, and held that if a defendant's actual use of money yields a benefit that is worth less than the market value of the opportunity to use the money then this opportunity can never have been worth more to the defendant than the lower amount.

[64] See 3.16–3.17 for the distinction between 'denials' and 'defences'.

[65] *Greenwood v Bennett* [1973] QB 195, CA.

[66] *Salna v Awad* [2011] ABCA 20, (2011) 330 DLR (4th) 214, at [34]–[35].

[67] *Gibb*, n 27. cf *Test Claimants in the FII Litigation v HMRC* [2010] EWCA Civ 103, [2010] STC 1251 ('*FII* (CA)') [178]–[184], discussed at 3.219; *Clark v In Focus Asset Management & Tax Solutions Ltd* [2012] EWHC 3669 (QB), [2013] PNLR 14, at [37]–[41].

[68] *Exall*, n 19; *Johnson v Royal Mail Steam Packet Co* (1867) LR 3 CP 38.

[69] *Craven-Ellis v Canons Ltd* [1936] 2 KB 403, CA; *R (Rowe) v Vale of White Horse DC* [2003] EWHC 388 (Admin), [2003] 1 Lloyd's Rep 418.

a benefit. In such cases the parties usually have a contract, in which case the contract will govern their relationship, and the claimant will not be allowed to claim in unjust enrichment if this would subvert their contractual arrangements.[70] But a claim in unjust enrichment may lie where the parties had a contract which has been abandoned or terminated for breach, or where their agreement has been frustrated or was legally unenforceable, or where they were negotiating towards a contract but never settled the terms prior to the claimant's performance.[71]

3.31 Where the parties had a contract that was terminated following a repudiatory breach, it is a controversial question, to which the cases do not give a consistent answer,[72] whether the defendant's enrichment should be valued by reference to the market price or the contract price. The arguments favouring the use of a contractual valuation are, first, that it respects the defendant's freedom of choice as it requires him to pay no more than the amount which he agreed; and, secondly, that where the defendant is the party in breach, and the market price is higher than the contract price, he should not be permitted to reduce his liability by invoking the contract while refusing to abide by its terms. Arguments favouring the use of a market valuation are, first, that it takes account of the fact that the claimant may not have bargained solely for price-related benefits, but may also have expected to receive other benefits that will not materialize once the contract has gone off, eg marketplace reputation, or the opportunity to bargain for further work down the line. Secondly, where the claimant is the party in breach, and the contract price is higher than the market price, he should not be allowed to increase his right by relying on the terms of the contract while refusing to abide by its terms.

3.32 It is also controversial whether an objective market valuation should be imposed on a defendant who forgoes a reasonable opportunity to reject a benefit that has obviously not been offered at less than market value. On one view, such 'free acceptance' of the benefit is unconscientious conduct that precludes him from making the argument based on respect for freedom of choice.[73] On another, imposition of market value is unfair because his behaviour may simply reflect indifference to the benefit being rendered. On the latter view, it would be preferable to impose market value only where the defendant's conduct shows that he wanted the benefit, but was unwilling to pay for it.[74] In *Cressman v Coys of Kensington (Sales) Ltd*[75] both tests were satisfied and so the court did not have to choose between them: the defendant registered a car with a personalized number plate in his name, knowing that the opportunity to do so had come to him through the claimant's mistake, and intending not to pay for the benefit he thereby acquired.

3.33 The question whether free acceptance should affect the valuation of benefits received by a defendant is distinct from the question whether free acceptance makes it unjust for the defendant to be enriched at his expense. Recent dicta suggest that the courts are moving towards the recognition of free acceptance as an unjust factor, without much consideration of the policy arguments for and against such a development, and without clearly distinguishing the enrichment question from the unjust factor question.[76] However, they have not yet

---

[70] See 3.226.

[71] Examples are *Benedetti* (SC), n 18; *William Lacey (Hounslow) Ltd v Davis* [1957] 1 WLR 932; *Pavey*, n 15; *Vedatech Corp v Crystal Decisions Ltd* [2002] EWHC 818 (Ch).

[72] *Lodder v Slowey* [1904] AC 442, PC, affirming (1901) 20 NZLR 321, NZCA; *Pavey*, n 15, at 257; *Rover International Ltd v Cannon Film Sales Ltd* [1989] 1 WLR 912, 927–928, CA; *Renard Constructions (ME) Pty Ltd v Minister for Public Works* (1992) 26 NSWLR 234, 276–278, NSWCA; *Stephen Donald Architects Ltd v King* [2003] EWHC 1867 (TCC), at [75]–[76]; *Taylor v Motability Finance Ltd* [2004] EWHC 2619 (Comm); *Sopov v Kane Constructions Pty Ltd (No 2)* [2009] VSCA 141, (2009) 257 ALR 182.

[73] P Birks, 'In Defence of Free Acceptance' in A Burrows (ed), *Essays on the Law of Restitution* (1991).

[74] A Burrows, 'Free Acceptance and the Law of Restitution' (1988) 104 LQR 576.

[75] *Cressman*, n 18, at [26]–[32]. See too *Harrison v Madejski* [2014] EWCA Civ 361, at [59].

[76] Discussions in *Becerra v Close Brothers* QBD, 25 June 1999; *Rowe v Vale of White Horse DC* [2003] EWHC 388 (Admin), [2003] 1 Lloyd's Rep 418, at [12]–[14]; *Wigan*, n 18, at [38]–[45], reviewing [2007]

awarded restitution on this ground, as no claim resting on free acceptance has succeeded on the facts.[77]

In *Chief Constable of Greater Manchester v Wigan Athletic AFC Ltd*[78] and in *Benedetti v Sawiris* **3.34** before the Court of Appeal,[79] the question arose whether there is free acceptance where a defendant takes an unwanted benefit which has been bundled together with a wanted benefit and offered on the basis that he can either take (and pay for) both benefits or take neither. On each occasion the court held that there is no free acceptance because the defendant has no free choice whether to take the unwanted benefit. This was incorrect: the defendant is free to reject the unwanted benefit as he can choose to take neither benefit. The fact that he would prefer to take the wanted benefit and reject the unwanted benefit makes no difference.

What happens if there is evidence of a general market price for a benefit and also evidence **3.35** that the parties agreed a different price? In *Benedetti*, Lord Reed distinguished two reasons why this might occur. First, one party may command a better price for his goods or services in the market than other sellers owing to their superior quality; or one party may be able to procure benefits more cheaply than other buyers, eg owing to his superior creditworthiness, as in *Sempra*. In such cases, there is no variance between the parties' agreed value and the individuated market value, and this is therefore the objective value of the benefit. Secondly, however, the parties may have agreed a different price from the general market price because one is a better negotiator than the other, and in this case the parties' dealings will be ignored when determining the objective value of the benefit, because 'in the absence of a contract neither party's intentions or expectations is determinative of their mutual rights and obligations'.[79a]

What happens if a defendant subjectively overvalues a benefit? Does it follow from the fact **3.36** that the law takes a defendant's subjective preferences into account to attribute a lower value to a benefit than the objective value where he would not have been willing to pay so much that it should also take his subjective preferences into account to attribute a higher value to a benefit than the objective value where he would have been willing to pay more? In *Benedetti*, the Supreme Court held that this does not follow, and that in the latter case the defendant will be liable for no more than the objective value of the benefit. The law excuses a defendant from paying more than he would have been willing to pay in order to protect his freedom of choice. That freedom would not be protected by requiring him to pay more than he would have needed to pay. Even if he would have been willing to pay more if this had been necessary, he would not have chosen to pay more if this had been unnecessary.[79b]

EWHC 3095 (Ch) esp [126]; *Benedetti* (CA), n 10, at [119]–[120], reviewing [2009] EWHC 1330 (Ch), at [574]); *Dry Bulk Handy Holding Inc v Fayette International Holdings Ltd* [2012] EWHC 2107 (Comm), [2012] 2 Lloyd's Rep 594, at [81]. Ordering restitution on the ground of free acceptance may be inconsistent with the law's general aversion to imposing liability for omissions—although it may be that omissions-based liabilities for gain are easier to justify than such liabilities for loss, because less restrictive of personal liberty: K Barker, 'Coping with Failure? Re-Appraising Pre-Contractual Remuneration' (2003) 19 JCL 105.

[77] cf *Brenner v First Artists' Management Pty Ltd* [1993] 2 VR 221, 260, Vic Sup Ct; *Angelopoulos v Sabatino* [1995] SASC 5536, (1995) 65 SASR 1, at [35]; *Andrew Shelton & Co Pty Ltd v Alpha Healthcare Ltd* [2002] VSC 248, (2002) 5 VR 577, at [109]. These all treat *Pavey*, n 15, as a case of the same kind, although the HCA did not identify 'free acceptance' as the ground of recovery in the case. The same analysis can also be found in *W Cook Builders Pty Ltd (in liq) v Lumbers* [2007] SASC 20, (2007) 96 SASR 406, 423. This decision was overturned in *Lumbers v W Cook Builders Pty Ltd (in liq)* [2008] HCA 27, (2008) 232 CLR 635, where the majority doubted that free acceptance is a coherent concept, but the main ground for their decision was that allowing recovery would stultify the parties' contractual arrangements.

[78] *Wigan*, n 18. The case concerned the provision of policing services at football matches.

[79] *Benedetti* (CA), n 10. The case concerned the provision of advisory services in connection with a take-over bid. There was no appeal to the SC from the CA's disposal of the point discussed in the text.

[79a] *Benedetti* (SC), n 18, at [99]. See too Lord Clarke's comments at [31].

[79b] *Benedetti* (SC), n 18, at [27]–[33], [120]–[121] and [193]–[200].

[Footnotes 80–83 have been deleted in the paperback edition.]

C. At the Claimant's Expense

3.37   The requirement that a defendant's enrichment must have been received 'at the claimant's expense' has hardly been discussed in two-party cases, probably because it seems to be obvious that the requirement must have been satisfied on any sensible view of what it means.[84] However, in *Test Claimants in the FII Group Litigation v HMRC*,[85] the Court of Appeal held that a 'but for' causal test should be used, subject to a remoteness cap governed by a 'directness' test. There has also been some discussion of the rule in more complex multi-party cases, where the courts have recognized that it is unhelpful to address the problems that arise using 'loose and generalised...language and concepts which are not appropriate to a legal analysis of the situation'.[86] Two of these problems are worthy of particular note.

(1) Corresponding Loss and Gain

3.38   The first arises where the defendant gains a benefit and the claimant suffers a loss, but one is larger than the other. Can the claimant recover any greater sum than the highest amount common to the parties' loss and gain? The courts have always insisted that the law of unjust enrichment is not concerned with compensation for loss, and have refused to award restitution in cases where the claimant has suffered a loss but the defendant has gained nothing.[87] And in cases where the defendant has been enriched, but his gain is less than the claimant's loss, the claimant's right of recovery has always been capped at the amount of the defendant's gain.[88]

3.39   Cases where the defendant's gain is greater than the claimant's loss are more controversial. As long ago as 1776, in *Hambly v Trott*,[89] Lord Mansfield said that in such a case a claim for the entire value of the defendant's gain would lie, suggesting that there is no need for a claimant to show a corresponding loss, and that it suffices to show that the defendant's gain has come 'from' the claimant in a looser causal sense. More recent cases are also consistent with this approach. In *Kleinwort Benson Ltd v Birmingham CC*,[90] restitution was awarded although the claimant had eliminated its initial loss by passing it on to a third party. One reason given was that loss is irrelevant to claims in unjust enrichment, although other considerations also led to the court's decision.[91] Again, in *Trustee of the Property of FC Jones & Son (a firm) v Jones*[92] the defendant used the claimant's money to speculate on the potato futures market and multiplied the amount received fivefold; she had committed no wrong, but was ordered to pay over her entire gain.

3.40   Against these authorities must be set *BP Exploration Co (Libya) Ltd v Hunt (No 2)*.[93] This concerned a claim under the Law Reform (Frustrated Contracts) Act 1943. Under a joint venture with Hunt, BP undertook prospecting work in the Libyan desert which increased

---

[84]   See eg *Cressman*, n 18, at [24]; *Cobbe*, n 2, at [40].

[85]   *FII* (CA), n 67, at [182]; not considered on appeal: *FII* (SC), n 2. The court's application of this test to the facts was unconvincing because it misidentified the enrichment which was the subject-matter of the claim: see 3.219. It also seems unlikely that a 'directness' test for remoteness is capable of generating predictable outcomes.

[86]   *Uren v First National Home Finance Ltd* [2005] EWHC 2529 (Ch), at [22].

[87]   As in eg *Sorrell v Finch* [1977] AC 728, HL; *Peel*, n 61; *Regalian plc v London Docklands Development Corp* [1995] 1 WLR 212.

[88]   As in eg *Sempra*, n 2.

[89]   (1776) 1 Cowp 371, 375, 98 ER 1136, 1138. cf *Sympson v Juxon* (1624) Cro Jac 699, 79 ER 607.

[90]   *Birmingham*, n 25. See too *Mason v NSW* (1959) 102 CLR 108, 146.

[91]   See 3.194.

[92]   [1997] Ch 159, CA.

[93]   *BP*, n 51, aff'd [1981] 1 WLR 232, CA; [1983] 2 AC 352, HL.

the value of Hunt's share of an oil concession. The joint venture was frustrated when the concession was expropriated, and BP claimed that it was entitled to be paid a 'just sum' under section 1(3). Robert Goff J, who considered that the statute embodies principles of the law of unjust enrichment, held that the enhancement of Hunt's share was worth some $85 million. However he ordered Hunt to pay BP less than a quarter of this, a result that must be explained on the basis that this was the cost to BP of conferring the benefit. This suggests that English law resembles Canadian law, which insists that there must be not only a plus to the defendant but a corresponding minus to the claimant.[94] So does Lord Scarman's statement in Parliament when introducing the bill that became the Civil Liability (Contribution) Act 1978,[95] that a claimant who settles with a creditor and then looks to a defendant for a contribution cannot 'recover a higher amount . . . than that which he has agreed to pay.'[96]

Should the English courts take the wide or the narrow view? There are two reasons for think- **3.41** ing that the narrow view is preferable.[97] One is that there is no normative justification for ordering a defendant to hand over a gain which does not correspond to a claimant's loss, in the absence of consent or wrongdoing. The law of unjust enrichment is concerned with reversing defective transfers, and in such a case there is no transfer between the parties. The second (connected) reason is that it wastes scarce judicial resources to use the court system as a mechanism for reallocating a benefit between two parties when neither party positively deserves it.[98]

(2) Remote Recipients

A second issue that awaits definitive resolution is when claims in unjust enrichment should be **3.42** permitted against remote recipients, ie those who are 'remotely' enriched because they receive benefits which ultimately emanate from the claimant but which have passed through the hands of one or more intermediate parties. The courts have only recently begun to consider the question of when such claims should be permitted, and academic opinion is divided: some scholars argue that the law should operate a restrictive 'directness' rule that would disallow restitution, subject to exceptions;[99] others favour a wider causal test subject to limitations.[100]

Participants in this debate agree that there are good reasons why many 'indirect' transfers **3.43** should not be reversed. Various bad effects can flow from this,[101] including contradiction

---

[94] *Pettkus v Becker* [1980] 2 SCR 834, 848; *Pacific National Investments Ltd v City of Victoria* [2004] SCC 75, [2004] 3 SCR 575, at [14] and [20]–[21].

[95] 'The 1978 Act is an application of the principle that there should be restitutionary remedies for unjust enrichment': *Dubai* (HL), n 2, at [76].

[96] *Hansard*, HL (series 5) vol 395, col 251 (18 July 1978). See too *Gnitrow Ltd v Cape plc* [2000] 1 WLR 2327, 2331, CA.

[97] M McInnes, 'At the Plaintiff's Expense: Quantifying Restitutionary Relief' [1998] CLJ 472, 476–477. Further discussion: RB Grantham and CEF Rickett, 'Disgorgement for Unjust Enrichment' [2003] CLJ 159; Birks (2005), n 7, at 78–82; M Rush, *The Defence of Passing On* (2006) chs 5–7.

[98] *Roxborough*, n 23, at [118]. Where a claimant has passed on a loss to a third party who can himself recover from the claimant, it may still be desirable to let the claimant recover from the defendant, provided that he is legally bound to pass the benefit back up the line to the third party; see 3.190–3.191.

[99] eg G Virgo, *The Principles of the Law of Restitution* (2nd edn, 2006) 105–112; B McFarlane, 'Unjust Enrichment, Property Rights and Indirect Recipients' [2009] RLR 37, esp 56–59; A Burrows, *The Law of Restitution* (3rd edn, 2011) 69–85.

[100] eg Birks (2005), n 7, at 86–98; C Mitchell, 'Liability Chains' in J Edelman and S Degeling (eds), *Unjust Enrichment in Commercial Law* (2008); S Watterson, '"Direct Transfers" in the Law of Unjust Enrichment' (2011) 64 CLP 435.

[101] It has also been said that claims against remote recipients should be forbidden because where a benefit has been provided indirectly via a third party 'the defendant will have been enriched at the third party's expense': *Armstrong DLW GmbH v Winnington Networks Ltd* [2012] EWHC 10 (Ch), [2013] Ch 156, at [97]. This incorrectly assumes that where an enrichment passes from a claimant to a third party to a defendant, the defendant cannot have been enriched at the expense of the claimant *and* the third party.

of the contractual arrangements entered by the parties,[102] contradiction of the pari passu principle of insolvency law,[103] increased risks of double recovery and double liability,[104] and the practical difficulties of managing litigation between multiple interconnected parties.[105] Many of these problems could be solved by the application of separate rules, however, and there is a consensus that forbidding all claims against remote recipients would be undesirable, as this would deny restitution to meritorious claimants. The dispute between the two sides therefore boils down to a question of strategy: would the law be clearer and fairer if it adopted a narrow test subject to exceptions, or a wide test subject to limitations?

3.44 It has been said that the law would need to be 'reformulated' if a wide test were to be adopted, and that 'framing the general rule in acceptable terms' is difficult 'if it is not confined to direct recipients'.[106] It has also been said that the case law to date discloses too few examples of recovery against remote recipients for the courts to formulate a principled statement of the wide test.[106a] However, it overstates matters to say that a narrow 'direct enrichment' rule represents the current 'formulation' of the law: judicial dicta on the point are sparse and generally unreasoned because the question has only recently been presented to the courts in a way that enables them to identify and explore the policy issues in play.[107] It is true that framing a wide test subject to limitations is difficult, but so too is framing a narrower test subject to exceptions, and there is no consensus among those who favour the latter approach as to which types of transfer should count as 'direct' transfers,[108] nor is there a consensus as to which situations are sufficiently exceptional for recovery to be justified.[109]

3.45 Whichever approach is preferable, it is clear that 'remote' enrichments have been recovered in various situations: where the claimant pays a third party to whom the defendant owes a debt and the debt is thereby discharged;[110] where the claimant's agent performs services for the defendant;[111] where the claimant's agent pays money to the defendant;[112] and where

---

[102] cf *MacDonald Dickens & Macklin (a firm) v Costello* [2011] EWCA Civ 930, [2012] QB 244, at [23].

[103] cf *Yew Sang Hong Ltd v Hong Kong Housing Authority* [2008] HKCA 109, at [13] and [30]–[32].

[104] cf *Trustor AB v Smallbone* CA, 9 May 2000, at [63] (double recovery); *Greatworth v Sun Fook Kong Construction Ltd* [2006] HKCFI 356, at [52] (double liability).

[105] cf *SmithKline Beecham plc v Apotex Europe Ltd* [2006] EWCA Civ 658, [2007] Ch 71, at [41]–[42].

[106] *ITC* (Ch), n 40, at [67], relying on *Birmingham*, n 25, at 393, 395 and 400, in preference to several subrogation cases: *Bannatyne v D & C MacIver* [1906] 1 KB 103, CA; *Butler v Rice* [1910] 2 Ch 277; *B Liggett (Liverpool) Ltd v Barclays Bank Ltd* [1928] 1 KB 48, as explained in *Re Cleadon Trust Ltd* [1939] Ch 286, CA; and *Filby v Mortgage Express (No 2) Ltd* [2004] EWCA Civ 759.

[106a] *ITC* (CA), n 18, at [68], warning against 'the dangers of moving to a general principle prematurely'.

[107] Henderson J's own judgment in the *ITC* case is unusual to the extent that he identifies and discusses these issues the first in which the issues were clearly identified and discussed: *ITC* (Ch), n 40, at [68]. Subsequent cases in point are *Menelaou*, n 23, at [29]–[42]; *TFL*, n 23, at [51]–[65]; *Relfo Ltd (in liq) v Varsani* [2014] EWCA Civ 360, [2015] 1 BCLC 14 ('*Relfo* (CA)'); *ITC* (CA), n 18, at [41]–[69].

[108] It is salutary to compare the factual findings made in relation to this point in *Menelaou v Bank of Cyprus plc* [2012] EWHC 1991 (Ch), at [22] and *Relfo Ltd (in liq) v Varsani* [2012] EWHC 2168 (Ch) ('*Relfo* (Ch)'), at [86]–[87].

[109] Watterson, n 100, at 442.

[110] Where the claimant and defendant owe a common liability, a contribution or reimbursement claim may follow: see 3.106ff.

[111] eg *Wigan*, n 18, at [49], affirming [2007] EWHC 3095 (Ch), at [126]. In such cases, the courts may wish to prevent the third party from bringing a claim because this would subvert the contractual arrangements between the parties: eg *Brown & Davis Ltd v Galbraith* [1972] 1 WLR 997, CA; *Lumbers* (HCA), n 77; *Costello*, n 102. It is tempting for courts to produce this result by denying that the defendant is enriched at the third party's expense, but more rational and more transparent for them to accept that his enrichment is at the third party's expense (as well as at the employer's expense), but to hold that there are other reasons why his claim must fail.

[112] eg *Stevenson v Mortimer* (1778) 2 Cowp 805, 806; 98 ER 1372, 1373; *Holt v Ely* (1853) 1 El & Bl 795, 118 ER 634; *Niru Battery Manufacturing Co v Milestone Trading Ltd (No 1)* [2002] EWHC 1425 (Comm), [2002] 2 All ER (Comm) 705 ('*Niru (No 1)* (Comm)'), at [145].

the claimant can use the rules of following and tracing to show that the defendant received an asset from a third party, which originally came from the claimant, or an asset which represents the traceable proceeds of such an asset.[113] They have also been recovered in various other cases, all of which can be explained on the basis that there was a causal link between a loss sustained by the claimant and a gain received by the defendant.[114]

D. Unjust: Deficient Intent

(1) Lack of Consent and Want of Authority

The strongest example of deficient intent is no intent at all. The law recognizes two distinct **3.46** but overlapping types of claim in situations where the claimant did not intend the defendant to be enriched at his expense. One, which rests wholly on the claimant's lack of consent, is exemplified by a case of simple theft where the defendant takes the claimant's property without his knowledge. The other lies where a third party holds or controls property subject to duties and powers to deal with the property for the claimant's benefit, and he transfers the property to the defendant without the claimant's authority. In the latter case, the claimant may bring an action for restitution, but his agent may also have the power, and indeed may owe a duty, to do so,[115] relying on his own lack of authority as the ground of recovery (albeit that he may feel little enthusiasm for bringing a claim that requires him to plead facts that disclose his own breach of duty).[116]

(a) Common law

The simplest cases at common law concern the situation where the defendant takes property **3.47** directly from the claimant without his knowledge; on these facts the defendant is personally liable to make restitution of the value of the property.[117] Claims in unjust enrichment also lie where a third party takes the claimant's property and passes it on to the defendant without the claimant's consent or lawful authority. In *Criterion Properties plc v Stratford UK Properties LLC*,[118] Lord Nicholls said that such a claim lies to recover the value of benefits conferred on a defendant by a company as a result of the directors acting for an improper purpose and without authority. Another case of this kind is *Lipkin Gorman (a firm) v Karpnale Ltd*,[119] where a solicitor fraudulently stole cash from the claimant firm's client account and gambled it away at the defendant casino. The casino was ordered to make restitution of the value of the stolen money because it had been unjustly enriched at the firm's expense.[120]

---

[113] eg *Banque Belge pour l'Etranger v Hambrouck* [1921] 1 KB 321, CA; *Lipkin Gorman*, n 2.

[114] eg *Agip (Africa) Ltd v Jackson* [1990] Ch 265, affd [1991] Ch 547, CA; *BFC*, n 2, at 227; *Relfo* (Ch), n 108, at [86]–[88], affirmed *Relfo* (CA), n 107. cf Case C–35/05 *Reemtsma Cigarettenfabriken GmbH v Ministero delle Finanze* [2008] STC 3448, ECJ; Case C–94/10 *Danfoss A/S and Sauer-Danfoss ApS v Skatteministeriet* CJEU 20 October 2011.

[115] cf *Case v James* (1861) 3 De G F & J 256, 270; 45 ER 876, 883; *Morlea Professional Services Pty Ltd v Richard Walker Pty Ltd (in liq)* [1999] FCA 1820, (1999) 96 FCR 217, at [51]; *Evans v European Bank Ltd* [2004] NSWCA 82, (2004) 7 ITELR 19, at [116]. These concern the duty owed by trustees to recover misapplied trust funds.

[116] cf *Pitt v Holt* [2013] UKSC 26, [2013] 2 AC 108 ('*Pitt*'), at [69].

[117] *Holiday v Sigil* (1827) 2 Car & P 177, 172 ER 81; *Neate v Harding* (1851) 6 Ex 349, 155 ER 577.

[118] *Criterion*, n 2, at [3]–[4], followed in *Relfo* (Ch), n 108, at [86]–[89], affirmed *Relfo* (CA), n 107. cf *Guinness plc v Saunders* [1990] 2 AC 663, 698.

[119] *Lipkin Gorman*, n 2. See too *Clarke v Shee & Johnson* (1774) 1 Cowp 197, 98 ER 1041; *Marsh v Keating* (1834) 1 Bing NC 198, 131 ER 1094; *Corking v Jarrard* (1897) 1 Camp 36, 170 ER 867.

[120] *Lipkin Gorman*, n 2, at 559–560, 572, and 578.

3.48 In *Lipkin Gorman*, Lord Goff confused matters by holding that the claim could succeed only if the firm had been the legal owner of the money paid to the casino, and that this requirement was satisfied because this money had been the traceable proceeds of the firm's chose in action against its bank. This cannot be reconciled with his additional finding that legal title to the money withdrawn from the firm's account had passed to the fraudster at the time of the withdrawal: the firm and the fraudster cannot both have been the legal owners of the money.[121] Lord Goff seems to have thought that the firm had to establish a proprietary link between its chose in action against its bank and the cash received by the casino because otherwise it could not show that the casino had been enriched at its expense. This may have been to take too restricted view of the circumstances in which claims against remote recipients are permissible.[122]

3.49 Lord Goff's emphasis on the need to establish a proprietary link has led some courts and scholars to characterize the award made in *Lipkin Gorman* as a remedy which 'vindicated' (sc: responded directly to) the firm's right as property owner, reasoning that the firm's subsisting title made it impossible to say that the casino was enriched.[123] Support for this can also be drawn from *Trustee of the Property of FC Jones & Son (a firm) v Jones*,[124] where the defendant was liable to make restitution of the value of the traceable proceeds of the claimant's property, legal title to which had vested in the claimant firm by operation of the bankruptcy doctrine of 'relation back'. Millett LJ said that the claim was 'exclusively proprietary',[125] by which he meant that it was founded directly on the firm's property right and not on unjust enrichment.[126] Against this, it can be argued that a claimant's subsisting title does not prevent a finding that the defendant has been unjustly enriched at his expense. The claimant can renounce his title,[127] just as when he sues in tort.[128]

(b) Equity

3.50 Equity imposes a strict restitutionary liability on those who receive property out of a deceased person's estate, where the administrators lacked authority to transfer the property to them.[129] Again, where trust property and other property held subject to a fiduciary duty is misapplied to discharge a debt secured on a defendant's property, the beneficiaries or principal are entitled to a lien over the defendant's property via subrogation, to secure the defendant's strict personal liability to repay the value of the misapplied assets.[130] It follows inexorably from

---

[121] *Lipkin Gorman*, n 2, at 573–574. This would have been easier to understand if Lord Goff had instead held that the firm's title to the money had arisen in equity under a trust but he and Lord Templeman insisted that their analysis was solely concerned with legal title: at 565–566 and 572. For a trust-based analysis of similar facts, see *Armstrong*, n 101, at [127]–[129].

[122] See discussion at 3.42–3.45.

[123] eg *Armstrong*, n 101, at [84]–[94] and [287]; R Grantham and C Rickett, *Enrichment and Restitution in New Zealand* (2000) ch 12; Virgo, n 99, at 11–17 and ch 7. cf WJ Swadling, 'Ignorance and Unjust Enrichment: The Problem of Title' (2008) 28 OJLS 627.

[124] *Jones*, n 92.

[125] *Jones*, n 92, at 168.

[126] Lord Millett, '*Jones v Jones*: Property or Unjust Enrichment?' in Burrows and Rodger, n 30.

[127] P Birks, 'Property and Unjust Enrichment: Categorical Truths' [1997] NZ L Rev 623, 654–656.

[128] Torts (Interference with Goods) Act 1977, s 5. In tort the relevant moment at which C's title is extinguished is when D pays the damages. An inference can be indirectly drawn from *United Australia v Barclays Bank Ltd* [1941] AC 1, HL, that the same should be said of unjust enrichment.

[129] The leading case is *Re Diplock* [1948] Ch 465, CA, affirmed [1951] AC 251, HL, relying on a line of cases stretching back to the 17th century, surveyed in S J Whittaker, 'An Historical Perspective to the "Special Equitable Action" in *Re Diplock*' (1983) 4 JLH 3.

[130] *McCullough v Marsden* (1919) 45 DLR 645, 646–647, Alberta CA; *Boscawen v Bajwa* [1996] 1 WLR 328, CA; *Scotlife Home Loans (No 2) Ltd v Melinek* (1999) 78 P & CR 38, 398; *Primlake Ltd (in liq) v Matthews Associates* [2006] EWHC 1227 (Ch), [2007] 1 WLR 2489, at [337]–[340]; *Cook v Italiano Family Fruit Co Ltd (in liq)* [2010] FCA 1355, (2010) 190 FCR 474, at [81]–[99]. Subrogation is discussed at 3.278–3.282.

the availability of this remedy that equity must also impose a strict personal restitutionary liability on the recipients of misdirected trust property and other property held subject to a fiduciary duty.

The courts have been slow to recognize this because they have been slow to understand that **3.51** this liability in unjust enrichment differs from liability for knowing receipt of misdirected trust property.[131] That is a wrong-based compensatory liability arising when a defendant fails to perform a duty to hold and account for the property as though he were himself a trustee, which duty is imposed when he receives the property with sufficient knowledge of the circumstances to make it unconscionable for him to take the property for himself.[132] A defendant who receives misdirected trust property with this degree of knowledge is therefore concurrently liable for unjust enrichment and knowing receipt.[133]

Company shareholders who knowingly receive unlawful returns of capital are also personally **3.52** liable to account as constructive trustees of the property when they receive it with knowledge that makes it unconscionable for them to retain it.[134] This rule rests on the premise that directors who authorize a misapplication of company funds in breach of the capital mainte-nance rules are in a position analogous to that occupied by trustees who wrongfully distribute trust property to persons other than the beneficiaries.[135] Consistently with what has been said about recipients of misdirected trust funds, the recipients of unlawfully returned capital should also incur a concurrent, strict, restitutionary liability in unjust enrichment, either on the footing that the directors lacked the authority to make the payments, or alternatively on the policy ground that this would further the objectives of the capital maintenance rules, viz the protection of the company creditors.[136]

In *Foskett v McKeown*[137] the House of Lords held that trust beneficiaries had equitable pro- **3.53** prietary rights in the traceable proceeds of misapplied trust property which had arisen not to

---

[131] One reason is that the term 'restitutionary' is sometimes used to describe the compensatory liability incurred by knowing recipients: eg *Charter plc v City Index Ltd* [2007] EWCA Civ 1382, [2008] Ch 313, at [27]; *Brown v Innovatorone plc* [2012] EWHC 1321 (Comm) [1320]. cf n 43 and text.

[132] *Maundrell v Maundrell* (1805) 10 Ves Jun 246, 261, 32 ER 839, 844; *Wilson v Moore* (1834) 1 My & K 126, 146, 39 ER 629, 636; *Barnes v Addy* (1874) LR 9 Ch App 244, 251–252; *Gray v Johnston* (1868) LR 3 HL 1, 14; *John v Dodwell & Co Ltd* [1918] AC 563, 569, PC; *Green v Weatherill* [1929] 2 Ch 213; *Belmont Finance Corp v Williams Furniture Ltd (No 2)* [1980] 1 All ER 399, 405, CA; *Akindele*, n 39. See also J Story, *Commentaries on Equity Jurisprudence as Administered in England and America* (1836) vol I, 384 and vol II, 502–503; C Mitchell and S Watterson, 'Remedies for Knowing Receipt' in C Mitchell (ed), *Constructive and Resulting Trusts* (2010), endorsed in *Grimaldi v Chameleon Mining NL (No 2)* [2012] FCAFC 6, (2012) 200 FCR 296, at [253], *Independent Trustee Services Ltd v GP Noble Trustees Ltd* [2012] EWCA Civ 195, [2013] Ch 91, at [76]–[84], and *Arthur v AG of the Turks & Caicos Islands* [2012] UKPC 30, at [37].

[133] As held in *Re Esteem Settlement* 2002 JLR 53, at [148]–[161], Jersey Royal Ct. See too Lord Nicholls, 'Knowing Receipt: The Need for a New Landmark' in Cornish et al, n 4; P Birks, 'Receipt' in P Birks and A Pretto (eds), *Breach of Trust* (2002); Lord Walker, 'Fraud, Fault, and Fiduciary Liability' (2006) 10 Jersey Law Review [31]. And cf *Gold v Rosenberg* [1997] 3 SCR 767 and *Citadel General Assurance Co v Lloyds Bank Canada* [1997] 3 SCR 805, where these two types of liability are confusedly muddled together.

[134] *Russell v Wakefield Waterworks Co* (1875) LR 20 Eq 474, 479; *Precision Dippings Ltd v Precision Dippings Marketing Ltd* [1986] Ch 447, 457–458, CA; *Rolled Steel Products (Holdings) Ltd v British Steel Corp* [1986] Ch 246, 297–298, CA; *Allied Carpets Group plc v Nethercott* [2001] BCC 81. This rule is preserved by the Companies Act 2006, s 847(3); s 847(2) also places shareholders under a fault-based statutory liability to repay unlawful distributions.

[135] *Flitcroft's Case* (1882) 21 Ch D 519, 527, 534, and 535, CA; *Re Sharpe* [1892] 1 Ch 154, 165, CA; *Moxham v Grant* [1900] 1 QB 88, CA; *Selangor United Rubber Estates Ltd v Cradock (No 3)* [1968] 1 WLR 1555, 1575; *Bairstow v Queen's Moat Houses plc* [2000] 1 BCLC 549, 557–560, aff'd [2001] EWCA Civ 712, [2001] 2 BCLC 531.

[136] cf J Payne, 'Unjust Enrichment, Trusts and Recipient Liability for Unlawful Dividends' (2003) 119 LQR 583.

[137] [2001] 1 AC 102, HL.

reverse unjust enrichment, but to 'vindicate their property rights'.[138] To understand the reach of this principle, several situations must be distinguished. First, when a trustee wrongfully takes the original trust property for himself, or wrongfully transfers it to a recipient who is not a beneficiary, the property continues to be owned by the beneficiaries in equity unless it is transferred to a bona fide purchaser for value without notice of their interest.[139] There is no need for the law to generate new rights for the beneficiaries in such a case, because they are already the equitable owners of the property, and nothing happens to alter their subsisting rights.

3.54 Secondly, the same rule applies when the trustee uses the original trust property to acquire substitute property which he wrongfully takes for himself or transfers to the recipient.[140] This was the situation in *Foskett*. In cases of this kind, the beneficiaries' equitable interest in the original trust property is transmitted to the substitute property,[141] and, as in the first situation, only a bona fide purchaser without notice can take this property clear of the beneficiaries' subsisting interest. When the new property is acquired in an authorized transaction, the source of the beneficiaries' interest in the new property is the settlor's intention, agreed to by the trustee, that they should have such an interest following the trustee's authorized exercise of his powers of sale and investment. When the new property is acquired in an unauthorized transaction, the beneficiaries can choose whether to adopt or reject the transaction. If they adopt it, then, again, the new property is impressed with an equitable interest by a process which looks like an ad hoc variation of the trust that gives the beneficiaries rights whose source, again, is the settlor's intention, agreed to by the trustee, that they should have such rights, albeit in a form which is different from that which the settlor originally envisaged.[142]

3.55 A third situation can also arise, where trust property is transferred in breach of trust to a recipient other than a bona fide purchaser, who uses it to acquire new property. The beneficiaries have equitable proprietary rights in this new property, but these rights cannot be explained on the same basis as their rights in the first two situations. The reason is that the recipient owes the beneficiaries no pre-existing duty to hold the traceable proceeds of the trust property on the terms of the original trust, undertaken by agreement with the settlor. Where the recipient knows of the breach, such a duty might conceivably be imposed on him, and breach of this imposed duty might then constitute a wrong that justifies the imposition of a constructive trust of the new property for the beneficiaries. Alternatively, and necessarily in cases where the recipient has no knowledge of the breach, the beneficiaries' equitable proprietary interest in the new property may be attributed to his unjust enrichment at their expense, which occurs when he uses their property without their consent or authority to acquire new property for himself.[143]

(2) Mistake

3.56 Recent years have seen a radical reinterpretation of the law in this area. *Kelly v Solari*[144] exemplifies the way that things previously stood. Solari died. He had insured his life. His

---

[138] [2001] 1 AC 102, 129, HL.

[139] *Westdeutsche* (HL), n 2, at 705; *Noble Trustees*, n 132, at [77].

[140] *Foskett*, n 137, at 108–109 and 129.

[141] If their equitable interest in the original trust property were not transmissible in this way, the equitable doctrine of overreaching would be unsustainable: C Rickett, 'Old and New in the Law of Tracing' in S Degeling and J Edelman (eds), *Equity in Commercial Law* (2005) 140–144.

[142] R Chambers, 'Tracing and Unjust Enrichment' in J W Neyers et al (eds), *Understanding Unjust Enrichment* (2004) 267–268.

[143] R Chambers, 'Tracing and Unjust Enrichment' in J W Neyers et al (eds), *Understanding Unjust Enrichment* (2004) 279. See too Birks (1997), n 127, at 661.

[144] (1841) 9 M & W 54, 152 ER 24.

widow, as his executrix, claimed under the policy and was paid. The insurer later discovered that the policy had lapsed before Solari's death. Solari had omitted to pay a premium. The policy had been marked 'lapsed'. The office overlooked this fact. The insurer recovered. At the time the crucial elements were that the claimant could show that he had been mistaken as to fact, not law, and that the mistake had led him to believe that he owed a legal liability. Neither is now required.

(a) Mistakes of law

From the early nineteenth century onwards the English courts consistently denied restitution **3.57** for mistake of law. Then in 1999 the mistake of law bar was removed, in *Kleinwort Benson Ltd v Lincoln CC*.[145] The claimant bank and the defendant local authority had entered an interest rate swap contract under which payments had been made for the full term of the contract in the belief that it was valid. In an unconnected case, *Hazell v Hammersmith & Fulham BC*,[146] it was then declared that statutory local authorities lack the power to enter such contracts. The bank sought to recover its payments. To take advantage of section 32(1)(c) of the Limitation Act 1980,[147] it framed its action as a claim in mistake, arguing that it had mistakenly believed the parties' contract to be valid when it had been void. Because any such mistake must have been a mistake of law, the bank had to argue for the removal of the bar against recovery on this ground.

It had previously been assumed that the bar was a necessary restriction on recovery for mis- **3.58** take, because mistakes of law would be very common and easily fabricated, also because of serious anxieties as to the possibility that interpretative development of the law would from time to time release clouds of restitutionary claims. Events since 1999 show that the latter fear was well justified.[148] However the House of Lords considered that barring claims founded on mistake of law was not the best way to deal with these problems.

The court went very far. If mistake supposes wrong data fed into the claimant's decision- **3.59** making process, there can have been no mistake in *Lincoln* because the only data which could have falsified the claimant's belief by virtue of which the money was paid came into existence afterwards, in the form of the *Hazell* decision. The court also accepted the notion of a retro-spective mistake, holding that even where liability to make a payment has been established by judicial decision, parties who pay in line with this decision can recover on the ground of mistake if this decision is overruled.[149]

Subsequent authorities confirm that both of these findings are problematic. In *Dextra Bank* **3.60** *and Trust Co Ltd v Bank of Jamaica*,[150] the Privy Council emphasized the distinction between mistakes relating to currently verifiable facts (which give rise to a claim in unjust enrichment)

---

[145] *Lincoln*, n 24.
[146] [1992] 2 AC 1, HL.
[147] Discussed at 3.199ff.
[148] The 1990s saw a plethora of claims between the parties to void swap contracts brought in the wake of *Hazell*, n 146. The 2000s and 2010s have seen a similar wave of litigation triggered by ECJ findings that aspects of the UK taxation regime are contrary to EU law: Joined Cases C-397/98 and C-410/98 *Metallgesellschaft Ltd v IRC* and *Hoechst AG v IRC* [2001] ECR I-1727; Case C-169/04 *Abbey National plc v HMRC* [2006] ECR I-4027; Case C-446/04 *Test Claimants in the FII Group Litigation v IRC* [2006] ECR I-11753; Case C-363/05 *JP Morgan Fleming Claverhouse Investment Trust plc v HMRC* [2007] ECR I-5517; Case C-569/07 *HSBC Holdings plc v HMRC* [2009] ECR I-9047; and cf Case C-424/11 *Wheels Common Investment Fund Trustees Ltd v HMRC* [2013] Pens LR 149, CJEU. Much of this litigation can be traced to the activity of accountancy firms whose energies have been diverted from creating and marketing tax avoidance schemes (less saleable since the enactment of anti-avoidance legislation) into creating and marketing schemes to challenge aspects of the UK tax legislation with a view to obtaining restitution of money paid to HMRC.
[149] *Lincoln*, n 24, at 378–380 and 400–401.
[150] [2001] UKPC 50, [2002] 1 All ER (Comm) 193, affd in *Pitt*, n 116, at [104].

and mispredictions concerning future events that cannot be verified (which do not). The court may have misapplied this principle to deny recovery on the facts, which were little different from *RE Jones Ltd v Waring & Gillow Ltd*,[151] where recovery was allowed.[152] Nevertheless the court's clear statement that mispredictions do not generate rights in unjust enrichment undermines the *Lincoln* case, where the claimant's belief that the parties' contract was valid could only have been falsified by a later court decision. Hence there was no impairment of the claimant's decision-making processes, but only an exercise of judgment that turned out to be incorrect.

3.61 In *Deutsche Morgan Grenfell plc v IRC*,[153] money was paid as tax under a statutory regime, parts of which were later held by the European Court of Justice to have infringed the EC Treaty. The House of Lords held that the claimant could bring a claim founded on mistake of law,[154] and retrospectively deemed the claimant to have made such a mistake in line with the *Lincoln* case.[155] As Park J recognized at first instance, however, retrospective mistakes of this kind cannot have caused a claimant's payment on a 'but-for' basis unless other parties are deemed to have made the same mistake.[156] Otherwise, when the causative effect of the claimant's mistake is tested by posing the counter-factual question, 'Would the claimant have paid if he had known the true state of the law?', a positive answer must be given, because the defendant would have met the claimant's failure to pay by successfully suing to enforce his legal rights. In other words, it does the claimant no good for the court to deem that he alone knew the 'true' state of the law when he made his payment, because the defendant and the courts would only have let him withhold payment if they had known it too. This reinforces the view that retrospective mistakes of the kind recognized in *Lincoln* and *DMG* are fictional, and have nothing to do with the impairment of a claimant's thought processes. Indeed, Lord Hoffmann conceded this in *DMG* when he held that they are not actual but 'deemed' mistakes that ground recovery because of 'practical considerations of fairness'.[157]

(b) Causative mistakes

3.62 In *Barclays Bank Ltd v W & J Simms Son and Cooke (Southern) Ltd*,[158] decided in 1980, Robert Goff J showed that the requirement of a liability mistake produced arbitrary consequences and was not unequivocally supported in the cases. The bank had paid a stopped cheque, overlooking the stop. The judge held that the reason why the bank could recover from its immediate payee, a creditor of its customer, was not that it had contemplated itself as liable to its customer to make the payment to the creditor, but, more simply, because it had made a mistake which caused the payment.[159]

---

[151] [1926] AC 670, HL.

[152] *Re Griffiths (deceased)* [2008] EWHC 118 (Ch), [2009] Ch 162 also illustrates the ease with which the courts can manipulate the outcome of litigation by finding either that the claimant's mistake relates to a present fact or that it relates to a future fact.

[153] *DMG*, n 2.

[154] Overturning the CA's decision that the claimant could not rely on mistake because it could only rely on the ground of recovery recognized in *Woolwich*, n 2. This is discussed at 3.131–3.132. The claimant wished to ground its claim on mistake in order to take advantage of the Limitation Act 1980, s 32(1)(c) (as to which see 3.199ff).

[155] *DMG*, n 2, at [23].

[156] [2003] EWHC 1779 (Ch), [2003] STC 1017, at [25], holding that recovery could only be allowed by assuming that 'if the true state of the law had been understood, both DMG and the Revenue would have understood it'.

[157] *DMG*, n 2, at [23], echoed in *FII* (SC), n 2, at [167]. See too A Nair, '"Mistakes of Law" and Legal Reasoning: Interpreting *Kleinwort Benson v Lincoln City Council*' in Chambers et al, n 17. Lord Hoffmann did not spell out the considerations of fairness that he had in mind, but the probable nature of these is elaborated in C Mitchell, 'Retrospective Mistakes of Law' (1999) 10 KCLJ 121.

[158] [1980] QB 677.

[159] [1980] QB 677, 694. cf *David Securities*, n 15, at 376–378.

The appellate courts have confirmed that claims lie at common law for all 'causative mis- **3.63** takes', whether they be mistakes of fact[160] or mistakes of law.[161] However, a narrower test is used to decide whether mistaken gifts should be rescinded in equity: for this, according to Lord Walker in *Pitt v Holt*, there must have been 'a causative mistake of sufficient gravity' to make the defendant's enrichment unjust.[162] It is hard to predict when the courts will hold a mistake to have been sufficiently 'grave' to justify their intervention.[163] It is also unclear why the equitable rule governing the recovery of mistaken gifts should differ from the common law rule governing the recovery of other mistakenly transferred benefits. Conceivably, the law might place gifts in a different category from other types of transfer.[164] However, Lord Walker declined to hold that it is as difficult to rescind voluntary deeds of settlement as it is to rescind a contract.[165] If this means that mistaken gifts are to be treated no differently from other non-contractual mistaken transfers, then there is no good reason for the equitable and common law rules to differ, and a choice must be made between the two, the equitable test broadened or the common law test narrowed.[166]

In *Pitt*, Lord Walker also distinguished between 'incorrect conscious beliefs, incorrect tacit **3.64** assumptions, and true cases of mere causative ignorance ("causative" in the sense that but for his ignorance the person in question would not have acted as he did)'.[167] He noted that 'ignorance is not, as such, a mistake…[although] it can lead to a false belief or assumption which the law will recognise as a mistake', and he held that 'mere ignorance, even if causative, is insufficient' to trigger restitution.[168] There is no obvious justification for denying recovery in a case of causative ignorance but allowing it in a case of incorrect tacit assumption, and this may be nothing more than a pragmatic 'floodgates' rule. However that may be, the rule will surely generate litigation as the parties seek to characterize the facts in one way or the other.[168]

(c) Carelessness, doubts, and risk-taking

A claimant is not denied restitution for mistake merely because he was careless.[169] However, the **3.65** authorities for this proposition assume a claimant who was unconscious of the risk of error, ie a claimant who acted on the basis of an incorrect belief without any conscious appreciation that his belief might be wrong. They do not establish that a claimant can recover for mistake where

---

[160] *Rover*, n 72, at 933; *Dextra*, n 150, at [28].

[161] *DMG*, n 2, at [59]–[60] and [143]–[144]. See too *Nurdin & Peacock plc v D B Ramsden & Co Ltd* [1999] 1 WLR 1249, 1273.

[162] *Pitt*, n 116, at [122], reaffirming *Ogilvie v Littleboy* (1897) 13 TLR 399, 400, CA, which was approved sub nom *Ogilvie v Allen* (1899) 15 TLR 294, HL. Lord Walker added that 'the test will normally be satisfied only when there is a mistake either as to the legal character or nature of a transaction, or as to some matter of fact or law which is basic to the transaction'.

[163] A similar problem was created by the old common law test of 'fundamental' mistake that Robert Goff J abandoned in *Simms*, n 158, at 696–699, considering *Morgan v Ashcroft* [1938] 1 KB 49, CA. Litigation to test the boundaries of Lord Walker's test has begun: *Kennedy v Kennedy* [2014] EWHC 4129 (Ch), [2015] BTC 2; *Freedman v Freedman* [2015] EWHC 1457 (Ch).

[164] Tang Hang Wu, 'Restitution for Mistaken Gifts' (2004) JCL 1, 29–33. But cf B Häcker, 'Mistaken Gifts after *Pitt v Holt*' (2014) 67 CLP 333: by comparison with civilian systems English law has an underdeveloped notion of 'gift' as a legal category and significant conceptual work would be needed before an argument along these lines could be plausibly sustained.

[165] *Pitt*, n 116, at [115].

[166] Cf Neuberger J's suggestion in *Nurdin*, n 161, at 1273, that a 'but for' causal test should be 'coupled with a requirement for a close and direct connection between the mistake and the payment and/or a requirement that the mistake impinges on the relationship between payer and payee'.

[167] *Pitt*, n 116, at [108].

[168] *Pitt*, n 116, at [105] and [108].

[169] *Kelly*, n 144, at 59; *Imperial Bank of Canada v Bank of Hamilton* [1903] AC 49, 56, PC; *RE Jones Ltd v Waring & Gillow Ltd* [1926] AC 670, 688–689, HL; *BFC*, n 2, at 227, 235, and 243; *Lincoln*, n 24, at 399; *Dextra*, n 150, at [45]; *Pitt*, n 116, at [114].

he knows that he does not know the true circumstances, or doubts whether he knows them, and carelessly fails to establish the true position. In such cases restitution might be denied.

3.66 The reason is that the claimant may then be unable to show that his decision to benefit the defendant was caused by a mistake. This will certainly be the case where he positively intended the defendant to benefit in all events, irrespective of the truth or falsity of his beliefs.[170] A claimant with doubts may be in the same position, but whether he can show that his decision to benefit the defendant was caused by a mistake depends on the circumstances,[171] and it has been said that he will be denied relief when he has 'assumed the risk' of error.[172]

(3) Duress

3.67 Pressures endemic in ordinary life do not impair autonomy. They define the obstacles through which free will must pick its way. Decisions are only impaired when made under a pressure which is alien to society. The line is somewhat softer than that between lawful and unlawful.[173] Hence a payment made in response to illegitimate pressure applied by another is recoverable on the ground of duress. Duress is not restricted to particular categories of case,[174] but examples are actual or threatened violence to the person,[175] threats to take or retain a person's property,[176] and illegitimate commercial pressure that amounts to so-called 'economic duress'.[177] On the other side of the line, examples of legitimate pressure are a bona fide threat to sue[178] and a refusal to supply goods or credit in the absence of a contract to do so.[179] Illegitimate pressure does not become legitimate because the person applying it honestly thought he was entitled to do so. If I threaten to retain possession of your goods, it is no good my saying that I mistakenly thought I had a right to do so.[180]

3.68 In cases where the illegitimate pressure is a threat to break a contract, the courts have found it difficult to resolve the tension between the sanctity of the binding contract and the general interest in encouraging and upholding renegotiation to avoid a total collapse. If money obtained by a threat to break a contract were always recoverable there would be little room for renegotiation in any case where the initiative came from the likely contract breaker.[181]

---

[170] *Kelly*, n 144, at 59; *Simms*, n 158, at 695; *Scottish Equitable plc v Derby* [2001] EWCA Civ 369, [2001] 2 All ER (Comm) 274, [19]–[25]; *BP Oil International Ltd v Target Shipping Ltd* [2012] EWHC 1590 (Comm), [2012] 2 Lloyd's Rep 245, at [232].

[171] *DMG*, n 2, at [26]. See too *Marine Trade SA v Pioneer Freight Futures Co Ltd BVI* [2009] EWHC 2656 (Comm), [2010] 1 Lloyd's Rep 631, at [69]–[75].

[172] *DMG*, n 2, at [26]. See too *Pitt*, n 116, at [114].

[173] *Universe Tankships v ITWF (The Universe Sentinel)* [1983] AC 366, 385, HL; *Dimskal Shipping Co SA v ITWF (The Evia Luck)* [1992] 2 AC 152, 169, HL.

[174] *Borrelli v Ting* [2010] UKPC 21, [2010] Bus LR 1718.

[175] *Scott v Sebright* (1886) 12 PD 21; *Hussein v Hussein* [1938] P 159; *Barton v Armstrong* [1976] AC 104, PC.

[176] *Astley v Reynolds* (1731) 2 Str 915, 93 ER 939; *Somes v British Empire Shipping Co* (1860) 8 HLC 338, 11 ER 459; *Maskell v Horner* [1915] 3 KB 106.

[177] *Occidental Worldwide Investment Corp v Skibs A/S Avanti (The Siboen and The Sibotre)* [1976] 1 Lloyd's Rep 293; *North Ocean Shipping Co Ltd v Hyundai Construction Co Ltd (The Atlantic Baron)* [1979] AC 704; *Pao On v Lau Yiu Long* [1980] AC 614, PC; *The Universe Sentinel*, n 173, at 383–384 and 400–401; *The Evia Luck*, n 173, at 165.

[178] *Marriot v Hampton* (1797) 7 TR 269, 101 ER 969; *Unwin v Leaper* (1840) 1 M & G 747, 133 ER 533; *Goodall v Lowndes* (1844) 6 QB 464, 115 ER 173.

[179] *Smith v William Charlick* (1924) 34 CLR 38; *CTN*, n 26. Sometimes no more than lip service is paid to the difference between 'illegitimate' and 'unlawful': *Alf Vaughan & Co Ltd v Royscot Trust plc* [1999] 1 All ER (Comm) 856.

[180] *Maskell*, n 176; *Mason*, n 90.

[181] *Williams v Roffey Bros & Nicholls (Contractors) Ltd* [1991] 1 QB 1, CA, itself the rarer case in which the initiative in renegotiating the price comes from the client who would have to pay it, recognized the interest in renegotiation in its reinterpretation of the law on sufficiency of consideration.

Some cases of this kind have therefore sought to restrict restitution by stiffening the causal test, requiring an overbearing of the will.[182] But such a test is almost impossible to apply, and more recent cases have sought to achieve the same end by applying a 'but for' causal test and placing greater emphasis on the question whether the defendant acted in bad faith by opportunistically exploiting the claimant's commercial vulnerability.[183]

(4) Undue Influence

Prior to *Royal Bank of Scotland plc v Etridge (No 2)*,[184] the theory had developed that there were **3.69** two forms of undue influence: 'actual undue influence', comprising overt acts of improper pressure, and 'presumed undue influence', comprising excessive influence exercised by one party over another by reason of their relationship. These were understood to be substantively different, and the practice had grown up of pleading actual and presumed undue influence as alternative causes of action. In *Etridge*, the House of Lords held that this was a misunderstanding. There is only one type of undue influence, although there are two different ways of proving that it has occurred. 'Actual undue influence' is proved without the help of presumptions,[185] and 'presumed undue influence' is proved with the help of presumptions.[186] However the same thing is being proved in either case and so it would be inconsistent for a court to hold that a claimant had not established 'actual undue influence', but that he had established 'presumed undue influence'.[187]

It follows that the law of undue influence cannot be explained on the basis that cases of **3.70** 'actual undue influence' concern the improper application of pressure by a defendant (and might just as well be litigated as duress), while cases of 'presumed undue influence' concern the inability of a claimant to withstand the influence of another person.[188] An explanation of the doctrine must hold good for every case. Judicial opinions differ as to whether undue influence is a claimant-sided doctrine focused on the impairment of the claimant's intention,[189] or a defendant-sided doctrine focused on the defendant's unconscionable exploitation of the claimant's weakness.[190] This divergence of opinion needs to be resolved. Several

---

[182] *The Siboen and The Sibotre*, n 177, at 335–336; *Pao On*, n 177, at 636.

[183] *B & S Contracts and Design Ltd v Victor Green Publications Ltd* [1984] ICR 419, CA; *Huyton SA v Peter Cremer GmbH & Co* [1999] 1 Lloyd's Rep 620; *DSND Subsea Ltd v Petroleum Geo Services ASA* [2000] BLR 530; *Kolmar Group AG v Traxpo Enterprises Pvt Ltd* [2010] EWHC 113 (Comm), [2010] 2 Lloyd's Rep 653; *Progress Bulk Carriers Ltd v Tube City IMS LLC (The Cenk Kaptanoglu)* [2012] EWHC 273 (Comm), [2012] 1 Lloyd's Rep 501.

[184] [2001] UKHL 44, [2002] 2 AC 773. See too Sir K Lewison, 'Under the Influence' [2011] RLR 1.

[185] As in eg *Williams v Bayley* (1866) LR 1 HL 200, 209–210; *Re Craig (deceased)* [1971] Ch 95, 121; *Drew v Daniel* [2005] EWCA Civ 507, [2005] WTLR 807.

[186] The law raises a presumption of undue influence if the claimant can show, first, that he placed trust and confidence in the defendant, or was dependant on him, so that the parties were in a relationship of influence, and, secondly, that he entered a transaction at the defendant's behest that was not readily explicable by reference to the 'ordinary motives of ordinary persons': *Etridge* (HL), n 184, at [13]–[14]. Certain relationships are 'irrebuttably presumed' to be relationships of influence; there is no good reason for this and a rebuttable presumption would be a more principled rule: Lewison, n 184, at 9.

[187] *Etridge* (HL), n 184, at [92] and [210]–[228].

[188] As held by the CA in *Royal Bank of Scotland plc v Etridge (No 2)* [1998] 4 All ER 705, 711–712. The same argument had previously been made in P Birks and Chin NY, 'On the Nature of Undue Influence' in J Beatson and D Friedmann (eds), *Good Faith and Fault in Contract Law* (1994).

[189] *Inche Noriah v Bin Omar* [1929] AC 127, 135, PC; *Hammond v Osborn* [2002] EWCA Civ 885, [2002] WTLR 1125, at [32]; *Jennings v Cairns* [2003] EWCA Civ 1935, [2004] WTLR 361, at [40]; *Pesticcio v Huet* [2004] EWCA Civ 372, at [20].

[190] *Bank of Montreal v Stuart* [1911] AC 120, 137, PC; *National Westminster Bank plc v Morgan* [1985] AC 686, 705–706, HL; *Barclays Bank plc v O'Brien* [1994] AC 180, 189, HL; *Etridge* (HL), n 184, at [6]–[7] and [103]; *National Commercial Bank (Jamaica) Ltd v Hew* [2003] UKPC 51, at [28]–[33]; *R v Att-Gen for England and Wales* [2003] UKPC 22, [2003] EMLR 24, at [21]; *Samuel v Wadlow* [2007] EWCA Civ 155, at [40]; *Royal Bank of Scotland plc v Chandra* [2011] EWCA Civ 192, at [27]–[28].

issues are affected by it: does it suffice for a claimant to show that his relationship with the defendant disabled him from exercising a fully independent judgement, or must he prove that the defendant was at fault, and if so, then to what extent; must fault be proved against a defendant who receives a benefit from a claimant who was unduly influenced by a third party;[191] what test determines whether a claimant was caused by undue influence to enter an impugned transaction;[192] and is undue influence a wrong, the commission of which triggers a liability to pay compensation?[193]

(5) Personal Disadvantage

3.71 'If the party is in a situation, in which he is not a *free agent*, and is not *equal to protecting himself*, this court will protect him.'[194] A transfer may be attributable to some personal handicap which permanently or temporarily compromises the transferor's capacity to manage his own affairs. Two well-established cases are easily identified, namely the immaturity of the young[195] and mental illness or decline.[196] Inebriation might be said to be a transient species of the latter.[197] However, relief which the Chancery sparingly extended to the 'ignorant and poor'[198] has in modern times been extended to include numerous shades of special personal vulnerability impairing the autonomy ascribed to the typical adult. If some examples from the Commonwealth are included, the list comprises relational inequality falling short of undue influence,[199] serious stress, as for instance in the midst of a divorce,[200] serious illness,[201] social and educational deprivation,[202] imperfect command of the language,[203] isolation from advisers usually relied upon,[204] and acute lovesickness.[205]

3.72 In this area more than any other the courts proceed cautiously and insist on additional elements which restrict the incidence of relief and limit it to facts which either justify an

---

[191] Cases in point are *Bridgeman v Green* (1757) Wilm 58, 97 ER 22; *Huguenin v Baseley* (1807) 14 Ves Jun 273, 288–289, 33 ER 526, 533; *Barron v Willis* [1900] 2 Ch 121; *Goodchild v Bradbury* [2006] EWCA Civ 1868, [2007] WTLR 463; *Darjan Estate Co plc v Hurley* [2012] EWHC 189 (Ch), [2012] 1 WLR 1782; *Hart v Burbidge* [2014] EWCA Civ 992, [2014] WTLR 1361, at [41]–[44]. See too P Ridge, 'Third Party Volunteers and Undue Influence' (2014) 130 LQR 112.

[192] Compare *Bank of Credit and Commerce International SA v Aboody* [1990] 1 QB 923, 971, CA, and *UCB Corporate Services Ltd v Williams* [2002] EWCA Civ 555, [2003] 1 P & CR 12, at [86].

[193] As held in *Mahoney v Purnell* [1996] 3 All ER 61, deplored by P Birks, 'Unjust Factors and Wrongs: Pecuniary Rescission for Undue Influence' [1997] RLR 72, but applauded by L Ho, 'Equitable Compensation and Undue Influence' in P Birks and F Rose (eds), *Restitution and Equity* (2000).

[194] *Evans v Llewellin* (1787) 1 Cox 333, 340, 29 ER 1191, 1194 (emphasis in original).

[195] Under the Minors' Contracts Act 1987 a contract cannot be enforced against a minor but his right to recover value transferred is limited by, at least, a requirement of counter-restitution: *Valentini v Canali* (1889) 24 QBD 166; *Pearce v Brain* [1929] 2 KB 310.

[196] *Re Beaney* [1978] 1 WLR 770; *Hart v O'Connor* [1985] AC 1000, PC; *Williams v Williams* [2003] EWHC 742 (Ch), [2003] WTLR 1371. The common law test for mental incapacity, rather than the statutory test contained in the Mental Capacity Act 2005, governs the validity of inter vivos gifts: *Re Smith, deceased* [2014] EWHC 3926 (Ch), [2015] WTLR 579.

[197] *Matthews v Baxter* (1873) LR 8 Ex 132; *Blomley v Ryan* (1956) 99 CLR 362.

[198] *Fry v Lane* (1888) 40 Ch D 312, 322.

[199] *Crédit Lyonnais Bank Nederland NV v Burch* [1997] 1 All ER 144, CA; *Bridgewater v Leahy* [1998] HCA 66, (1998) 194 CLR 457.

[200] *Cresswell v Potter* [1978] 1 WLR 255.

[201] *Clarke v Malpas* (1862) 4 De GF & J 401, 405; 45 ER 1238, 1240; cf *Irvani v Irvani* [2000] 1 Lloyd's Rep 412.

[202] *Evans v Llewellin* (1787) 1 Cox 333, 29 ER 1191; *Mountford v Scott* [1974] 1 All ER 248, 252–253; *Chagos Islanders v A-G* [2003] EWHC 2222 (QB) [580].

[203] *Commercial Bank of Australia v Amadio* (1983) 151 CLR 447; *Singla v Bashir* [2002] EWHC 883 (Ch).

[204] *Boustany v Pigott* (1995) 69 P & CR 298, PC.

[205] *Louth v Diprose* (1992) 175 CLR 621.

inference of actual exploitation of the weakness or, at least, show that the impairment has seriously prejudiced the vulnerable person. It has been said that the doctrine might be triggered by the 'passive acceptance of a benefit',[206] but the weight of English authority holds that the defendant must have actively imposed oppressive terms on the other party in a morally reprehensible manner.[207] It seems preferable, however, to take the handicaps one by one, to rest such relief as may be available on the impairment which the handicap implies, and then to ask under what, if any, restrictions that relief should be allowed.

(6) Transactional Disadvantage

The law has always identified some transactions as especially sensitive, in that parties, however autonomous in other contexts, cannot protect their own best interests through negotiation and contract. Credit and security have attracted this kind of intervention throughout the ages. Usury was long forbidden. The equity of redemption owes its origin to equity's intervention to protect mortgagors from the severe forfeiture entailed by the common law mortgage. Outside mortgages, relief is available when penalties are promised against non-performance or parties rashly agree to forfeit proprietary interests.[208] Nowadays a fiercely protective regime is developing in relation to all means of tapping the home to fund business ventures.[209] Statutory protection for consumer credit is also in place.[210]   **3.73**

Other transactions catch people in desperate situations, where they have no room for manoeuvre. Market conditions have from time to time required would-be tenants to be protected from demands for premiums.[211] In insolvency those close to the debtor are protected from oppression by individual creditors seeking preferential treatment, but there the motivation is mixed and is clearly partly in the interest of the other creditors.[212] The social conditions in which a woman needed protection from marriage broking have passed, but it is still formally the law that a woman who pays someone to procure a marriage is entitled to recover her payment.[213]   **3.74**

It is a matter for debate whether these instances of transactional disadvantage are properly placed here as species of non-voluntariness or would be better considered below as examples of policy-motivated restitution, each dictated by its own species of protective policy. The argument for keeping them here is that the law intervenes because people who are otherwise autonomous lose their capacity for self-management when faced with transactions of this kind.   **3.75**

---

[206] *Hart*, n 196, at 1024.

[207] *Multiservice Bookbinding Ltd v Morden* [1979] Ch 84, 110; *Alec Lobb (Garages) Ltd v Total Oil Great Britain Ltd* [1983] 1 WLR 87, 94–95; *Boustany*, n 204, at 303; *Portman Building Society v Dusangh* [2000] 2 All ER 221, 229 and 232, CA; *Strydom v Vendside Ltd* [2009] EWHC 2130 (QB), [2009] 6 Costs LR 886, at [39]. Other jurisdictions take a less restrictive approach: D Capper, 'The Unconscionable Bargain in the Common Law World' (2010) 126 LQR 403.

[208] *Shiloh Spinners v Harding Ltd* [1973] AC 691, HL, considered in *On Demand Information plc v Michael Gerson (Finance) plc* [2002] UKHL 13, [2003] 1 AC 368 and *Cukurova Finance International Ltd v Alfa Telecom Turkey Ltd* [2013] UKPC 2, [2015] 2 WLR 875. cf *Andrews v Australia and New Zealand Banking Group Ltd* (2012) 247 CLR 205.

[209] The leading case is *Etridge* (HL), n 184, which effectively lays down a code of practice for lenders which is triggered whenever security for business borrowing is given by a person in a non-commercial relationship with the borrower. Only if they follow the code will lenders be insulated from undue influence and other vitiating factors arising between the borrower and the person giving security.

[210] Consumer Credit Act 1974, ss 140A–140D ('unfair relationships' between creditors and debtors).

[211] *Kiriri Cotton Co Ltd v Dewani* [1960] AC 192, PC.

[212] *Smith v Bromley* (1760) 2 Doug KB 696, 99 ER 441; *Smith v Cuff* (1817) 6 M & S 160, 105 ER 1203.

[213] *Hermann v Charlesworth* [1905] 2 KB 123.

E. Unjust: Qualified Intent

(1) Overview

(a) Introduction

3.76 The model is provided by *Fibrosa Spolka Akcyjna v Fairbairn Lawson Combe Barbour Ltd*.[214] Shortly before the outbreak of the Second World War, a Polish company bought machines in England. It made a part-payment in advance. With the German invasion of Poland, the contract was frustrated. The Polish company received nothing in exchange for its money. The House of Lords awarded restitution. The basis on which the money was paid had failed.

3.77 In cases of this kind the claimant does not rely on the fact that his intention to benefit the defendant was defective. He relies instead on the fact that the parties had a shared understanding that the defendant's enrichment was conditional. The basis for the transfer may materialize, and in that case the defendant can keep the benefit. But if the basis does not materialize, there is 'a failure in the fulfilment of the parties' expectations',[215] and restitution follows because 'the state of affairs contemplated as a basis for the [defendant's enrichment] has failed to sustain itself'.[216]

3.78 Claims of this kind can be made following the termination of a contract for repudiatory breach, whether by the innocent party[217] or by the party in breach.[218] Claims can also lie to recover benefits transferred under a void contract,[219] benefits transferred in anticipation of a contract that fails to materialize,[220] and benefits transferred on a non-promissory condition.[221] A claim may even lie to recover benefits transferred under a contract that has been fully performed, though only on the rare occasions when recovery will not upset the parties' agreed allocation of risk and benefit.[222]

3.79 *Fibrosa* shows that claims can also lie at common law to recover benefits transferred under a contract that has been frustrated. However the case was swiftly followed by the enactment of the Law Reform (Frustrated Contracts) Act 1943, which now governs the field. It has been said that the 1943 Act is a statutory embodiment of principles of the law of unjust enrichment.[223] However this is not borne out by all of the terms of the statute, whose creators intended both that it should mandate the reversal of unjust enrichment, and also that it should enable the courts to solve other problems created by the frustration of contracts.[224] Hence, while the reversal of unjust enrichment is one of its goals, it was also designed to

---

[214] *Fibrosa*, n 2.

[215] *Sharma v Simposh Ltd* [2011] EWCA Civ 1383, [2013] Ch 23, at [26].

[216] cf *Roxborough*, n 23, at [104]: 'Here, "failure of consideration" identifies the failure to sustain itself of the state of affairs contemplated as a basis for the payments [received by the defendant].'

[217] *Giles v Edwards* (1797) 7 TR 181, 101 ER 920; *Wilkinson v Lloyd* (1845) 7 QB 27, 115 ER 398; *DO Ferguson & Associates v Sohl* (1992) 62 Building LR 95, CA; *Baltic Shipping Co v Dillon (The Mikhail Lermontov)* (1993) 176 CLR 344.

[218] *Dies v British and International Mining and Finance Co Ltd* [1935] 1 KB 724; *Rover*, n 72.

[219] *Guinness Mahon*, n 29; *Haugesund*, n 10.

[220] *William Lacey*, n 71; *Countrywide Communications Ltd v ICL Pathway Ltd* (QBD 21 October 1999); *Vedatech*, n 71.

[221] *Re Ames' Settlement* [1946] Ch 217 (restitution of money settled on husband at time of marriage that was later annulled).

[222] *Roxborough*, n 23 (severable part of price paid for goods representing tax element recovered following discovery that tax not due).

[223] *BP*, n 51, at 805.

[224] P Mitchell, '*Fibrosa Spolka Akcyjna v Fairbairn Lawson Combe Barbour, Limited* (1942)' in C Mitchell and P Mitchell (eds), *Landmark Cases in the Law of Restitution* (2006); *Goff & Jones*, n 3, at ch 15.

apportion losses caused by the frustrating event, while allowing for the fact that one party may have been better placed than the other to protect himself against these, and preventing either party from renegotiating the basis on which benefits were agreed to be transferred.[225]

(b) Terminology

Since Lord Mansfield's time, the courts have spoken of restitution being ordered to reverse **3.80** transfers that were 'made upon a consideration which happens to fail'.[226] This language creates a constant risk of confusion with the doctrine of consideration in the law of contract. The risk is exacerbated by the fact that the failure of consideration on which claimants in unjust enrichment most often ground their claims is a failure of contractual reciprocation.[227]

Confusion between contract and unjust enrichment was largely responsible for the error that **3.81** had to be corrected in *Fibrosa*. The view had previously been taken that, if value were transferred under a contract rendered binding within the terms of the doctrine of consideration, then, unless the contract were rescinded *ab initio*, it could not be said afterwards that there had been a failure of consideration.[228] The House of Lords said that that was wrong.[229] For the purposes of a claim in unjust enrichment, the relevant consideration for a contractual pre-payment would generally be counter-performance rather than the promise of counter-performance. That did not mean that a legally binding promise of counter-performance can never be the relevant consideration,[230] nor that contractual counter-performance is the only type of consideration, failure of which can trigger restitution.[231] On the facts of *Fibrosa*, however, the claimant's payment had been made on the basis that the machines would be delivered, and that basis had failed.

In *Westdeutsche Landesbank Girozentrale v Islington LBC*[232] the same confusion resurfaced in **3.82** an inverted form. Hobhouse J, faced with facts in which value had passed under a void interest rate swap contract, decided that a claim based on failure of consideration could not lie. Such a claim, in his view, could only be brought in respect of transfers made under an initially valid contract.[233] He therefore turned to an alternative unjust factor that he called 'absence of consideration'. In the higher courts 'absence of consideration' was not repudiated, but it

---

[225] For further discussion of the 1943 Act, see 1.476–1.484.

[226] *Moses v Macferlan* (1760) 2 Burr 1005, 1013; 97 ER 676, 681. It has been said that Lord Mansfield identified actions for failure of consideration with the Roman *condictio causa data causa non secuta*: W Evans, *An Essay on the Action for Money Had and Received* (1802) 25; P Birks, 'English and Roman Learning in *Moses v Macferlan*' (1984) 37 CLP 1, 18. This is doubted in P Mitchell, 'Artificiality in Failure of Consideration' (2010) 29 University of Queensland Law Journal 190, 197–199, arguing that the *condictio* was concerned solely with failures of counter-performance, while the English action has never been so limited.

[227] The *OED* shows that 'consideration' is first the act of thinking about or reflecting on something and then the matter so thought about or reflected upon, whence the reason or motive for action of some kind. The connection with the contractual doctrine is that, to make a promise binding, quid pro quo became the only kind of 'consideration' which could count.

[228] *Chandler v Webster* [1904] 1 KB 493, CA. In the 18th and 19th centuries English law gave the innocent party the right to 'rescind' the contract *ab initio* for breach by the other party, and required him to exercise this right before bringing what would now be seen as a claim in unjust enrichment to recover benefits conferred under the contract: *Dutch v Warren* (1720) 1 Stra 406, 93 ER 598, discussed in *Moses*, n 226, at 1010–1011; 97 ER 676, 680; *Hochster v de la Tour* (1853) 2 E & B 678, 685; 118 ER 922, 924–925. That rule no longer forms part of English law: *Boston Deep Sea Fishing and Ice Co v Ansell* (1888) 39 Ch D 339, 365, CA; *Heyman v Darwins Ltd* [1942] AC 356, 399, HL; *Johnson v Agnew* [1980] AC 367, 393, HL.

[229] *Fibrosa*, n 2, esp at 52 and 65.

[230] cf *Guinness Mahon*, n 29 and *Haugesund*, n 10, where restitution was ordered on the ground that the claimant's payments were made on the unfulfilled basis that the defendant would make a legally binding promise to counter-perform.

[231] cf *Ames*, n 221.

[232] [1994] 4 All ER 890.

[233] [1994] 4 All ER 890, 921–923. See too *Benedetti* (SC), n 18, at [175].

was said that the claimant bank could have invoked failure of consideration as its ground for restitution.[234] It has since been held that Hobhouse J's 'absence of consideration' is merely 'failure of consideration' by another name.[235]

3.83 It is now indisputable that a restitutionary claim founded on failure of consideration is neither displaced where the transfer was made under an initially valid contract nor excluded where the parties never had a valid contract. However, in view of the history of error, a break must be made with the old language. It will be safer if the law of unjust enrichment leaves 'consideration' to the law of contract and speaks instead of 'failure of basis'.

(2) General Principles

(a) Objective determination of the parties' joint understanding

3.84 To determine whether there has been a failure of basis, the court must discover what the parties commonly understood the basis of the transfer to have been.[236] This is tested objectively and neither party's uncommunicated thoughts are relevant.[237] The court undertakes an interpretative process similar (though not identical) to that which is used to discover the meaning of contractual terms. The evidence to which the court can refer includes the terms of any contract between the parties, both where the contract was valid[238] and where it was never legally binding.[239] However it is not limited to this, and the court can take account of all the parties' communications,[240] including pre-contractual negotiations.[241]

3.85 It is tempting, but wrong, to suppose that the basis for a transfer must have failed where the claimant has received nothing of value. Perhaps the most common example is the payment of a non-returnable deposit, where the payer defaults: the basis for such a payment is that it shall be forfeited if the payer fails to proceed.[242] Again, in *Stocznia Gdanska SA v Latvian Shipping Co*,[243] the purchasers of six ships contracted to pay instalments of the price on the completion of certain stages of the design and construction. One instalment fell due after the keel of the vessel had been laid. At this point the purchasers had no property in the part-built

---

[234] [1994] 4 All ER 890, 960, CA; *Westdeutsche* (HL), n 2, at 683.

[235] *Guinness Mahon*, n 29, at 239–240; *Haugesund*, n 10, at [62].

[236] *Osborn v Governors of Guy's Hospital* (1726) 2 Str 728, 93 ER 812. *Barnes*, n 16, at [115], distinguishing such an agreed basis for the transfer of a benefit from a mere expectation that motivated one party to confer a benefit on the other.

[237] *Burgess v Rawnsley* [1975] 1 Ch 429, 442, CA; *Guardian Ocean Cargoes Ltd v Banco do Brasil SA (Nos 1 and 3)* [1994] 2 Lloyd's Rep 152, 158–159, CA; *Fostif Pty Ltd v Campbells Cash & Carry Pty Ltd* [2006] HCA 61, (2006) 229 CLR 386; *Giedo van der Garde BV v Force India Formula One Team Ltd* [2010] EWHC 2373 (QB), at [286]; *Killen v Horseworld Ltd* [2011] EWHC 1600 (QB), at [48].

[238] *Stocznia Gdanska SA v Latvian Shipping Co* [1998] 1 WLR 574, 588, HL; *ACG Acquisition XX LLC v Olympic Airlines Airlines SA* [2010] EWHC 923 (Comm), at [47]–[51].

[239] *Guinness Mahon*, n 29, at 240: 'the context of a supposed or expected contract is ... relevant as explaining what the parties are about.' Void contract: *Sharma*, n 215, at [27]–[52] considering *Gribbon v Lutton* [2002] QB 902, CA. Expected contract: *Chillingworth v Esche* [1924] 1 Ch 97, 107–108, CA.

[240] As in eg *Valencia v Llupar* [2012] EWCA Civ 396.

[241] There is no need to exclude these from the enquiry as the policy considerations in play are different from those which prevent the courts from examining them to determine the meaning of contractual terms: F Wilmot-Smith, 'Replacing Risk-Taking Reasoning' (2011) 127 LQR 610, 622.

[242] *Howe v Smith* (1884) 27 Ch D 89; *Monnickendam v Leanse* (1923) 39 TLR 445; *Mayson v Clouet* [1924] AC 980, PC; *Cadogan Petroleum Holdings Ltd v Global Process Systems LLC* [2013] EWHC 214 (Comm), [2013] 2 Lloyd's Rep 26. In some such cases, where the basis has not failed, the claimant may yet have some hope of restitution under the courts' jurisdiction to relieve from penalties and forfeitures. However the majority judgments in *Stockloser v Johnson* [1954] 1 QB 476, CA now have to be read in the restrictive light of *Shiloh*, n 208 and *Union Eagle Ltd v Golden Achievement Ltd* [1997] AC 514, HL; cf *Gerson*, n 208.

[243] *Stocznia Gdanska*, n 238. See too *Hyundai Heavy Industries Co Ltd v Papadopoulos* [1980] 1 WLR 1129, HL.

vessels. Yet the court held that the basis for the payment of that instalment had not failed, Lord Goff stating that 'the test is not whether the promisee has received a specific benefit, but rather whether the promisor has performed any part of the contractual duties in respect of which the payment is due'.[244]

Where the parties have bargained for work to be done and the worker fails to complete the **3.86** work, the court must decide whether the parties contemplated that, as it progressed, every part of the work should, on the analogy of a deposit, be regarded as security for completion. Where the contract specifies a single payment for the entire performance, it will not be difficult to reach that conclusion.[245] The customer is not lightly to be deprived of his most effective means of ensuring completion of the work: no completion, no money. On the other hand the mere fact that a single price has been fixed cannot be conclusive.[246]

(b) Multiple bases

A transfer can be made on more than one basis.[247] In *Guinness Mahon & Co Ltd v Kensington* **3.87** *and Chelsea Royal LBC*[248] a bank entered a swap transaction with a local authority that was void from the start. This was discovered only after full performance by both parties. The Court of Appeal awarded restitution on the ground that 'the consideration for each swap was the benefit of the contractual obligation'.[249] Suppose, however, that the contract had not been void, and that the bank had performed its obligations while the authority had not. In that case the bank could surely have terminated for breach and recovered its payments on the ground that they had been made on the basis that the authority would counter-perform. Hence there were at least two bases for the bank's payments in *Guinness Mahon*: that the local authority would make a legally binding promise to counter-perform and that counter-performance would in fact be rendered.

Another example is provided by contracts for the sale of goods. The basis on which buyers **3.88** usually make advance payments is that they will receive valid title to the goods and also that they will receive possession and use of the goods. In *Rowland v Divall*,[250] the claimant bought a car from the defendant, to which the defendant had no title. This came to light four months later and the claimant had to surrender the car to its true owner. The judge declined to order restitution of the sale price because the basis on which the money was paid had not totally failed: the claimant had paid for possession and use of the car, and he had had this for four months. The Court of Appeal disagreed. Atkin LJ said, 'He paid the money in order that he might get the property and he has not got it.'[251] This can be explained on the basis that there were at least two bases for the payment: that the claimant should receive possession and use of the car and that he should receive title to the car. Restitution was awarded because the latter basis totally failed.

---

[244] *Stocznia Gdanska*, n 238, at 588. cf *Systech International Ltd v PC Harrington Contractors Ltd* [2012] EWCA Civ 1371, [2013] Bus LR 970.

[245] *Sumpter v Hedges* [1898] 1 QB 673; *Bolton v Mahadeva* [1972] 1 WLR 1009; cf *Cutter v Powell* (1795) 6 TR 320, 1001 ER 573.

[246] Law Commission, *Pecuniary Breach of Contract* (Law Com No 121, 1983) paras 2.28–2.60. In *Segnit v Cotton* (CA, 9 December 1999) a contract to do work on a marketing project in exchange for a share of profits was construed to have been entire because profits could not be calculated until the project was completed.

[247] Mitchell (2010), n 226, at 209–210.

[248] *Guinness Mahon*, n 29.

[249] *Guinness Mahon*, n 29, at 227. See also *Westdeutsche* (HL), n 2, at 710; *Haugesund*, n 10, at [62].

[250] [1923] 2 KB 500. See too *Butterworth v Kingsway Motors Ltd* [1954] 1 WLR 1286; *Barber v NWS Bank plc* [1996] 1 WLR 641.

[251] [1923] 2 KB 500, 506.

(c) The requirement of total failure

3.89 Some bases for a transfer are all or nothing: either they are fulfilled or they are not. *Guinness Mahon* provides an example: either a promise of contractual counter-performance is legally binding or it is not. Other bases for transfer are capable of partial fulfilment. For example, in *Whincup v Hughes*[252] the claimant paid money on the basis that his son would be apprenticed to a watchmaker for six years. This basis only materialized in part, because the watchmaker died after one year. Restitution was denied because the basis on which the money was paid had not totally failed. This remains the basic rule: benefits are not recoverable if the basis on which they were transferred has only partially failed.[253] This rule is widely viewed as unsatisfactory because it enables a defendant to keep benefits although the basis on which they were transferred has not fully materialized.[254]

3.90 The rule does not apply where a claimant's contractual obligations to benefit the defendant can be apportioned and there is a total failure of basis of an apportioned part.[255] Nor does it apply where the claimant has received benefits from the defendant that are merely incidental to the parties' essential bargain.[256] Note, too, that it follows from the fact that there can be multiple bases for a transfer that recovery can be ordered on the total failure of one basis, although another has only partially failed, or, indeed, has fully materialized (as in *Guinness Mahon*).[257]

3.91 Some difficult cases award restitution where benefits were transferred on the basis that money would be paid to the claimant, and part of this money was paid.[258] A possible explanation is that where a claimant receives money, he could readily repay the money and then claim on the ground of total failure of basis, and it would be cumbersome and literal-minded to require him to do this when the benefits exchanged by the parties could more simply be set off against each other. As no insuperable difficulty attaches to the valuation of non-monetary benefits, however, this reasoning should also apply where the claimant has received benefits in kind—and in that case the 'total failure' rule would simply disappear.[259]

(d) Immediate and subsequent failure

3.92 Many cases concern the transfer of benefits on a basis that fails at some later point in time, eg because the recipient fails to render a contractual counter-performance when it falls due. Others concern the transfer of benefits on a basis that immediately fails, eg because its fulfilment has always been impossible, or has become impossible by the time of the transfer.

---

[252] (1871) LR 6 CP 78.

[253] *Yeoman Credit Ltd v Apps* [1962] 2 QB 508, 521 and 525, CA; *Baltic Shipping*, n 217, at 355–356; *Goss v Chilcott* [1996] AC 788, 797–798, PC; *Stocznia Gdanska*, n 238, at 590; *Roxborough*, n 23, at [105] and [173]; *Marks and Spencer plc v BNP Paribas Securities Services Trust Co (Jersey) Ltd* [2013] EWHC 1279 (Ch), [2013] L & TR 31, at [42]. cf F Wilmot-Smith, 'Reconsidering "Total" Failure' (2013) 72 CLJ 414, arguing for a different statement of the rule, that recovery is permitted only where there has been a substantial failure of basis.

[254] *Westdeutsche* (HL), n 2, at 682.

[255] *Stevenson v Snow* (1761) 3 Burr 1237, 1240; 97 ER 808, 810; *Devaux v Conolly* (1849) 8 CB 640, 137 ER 658; *Biggerstaff v Rowatt's Wharf, Ltd* [1896] 2 Ch 93; *Behrend & Co Ltd v Produce Brokers Co Ltd* [1920] 3 KB 530; *Fibrosa*, n 2, at 65; *Baltic Shipping*, n 217, at 375; *Goss*, n 253, at 798, PC; *Roxborough*, n 23, at [9]–[13], [109] and [195]–[196]. See too Sale of Goods Act 1979, s 30(1).

[256] *Rover*, n 72, at 924–925; *van der Garde*, n 237, at [284]–[285].

[257] Wilmot-Smith, n 253, 432–434.

[258] *Ebrahim Dawood Ltd v Heath (Est 1927) Ltd* [1961] 2 Lloyd's Rep 512; *Lusty v Finsbury Securities Ltd* (1991) 58 BLR 66, CA. This may also be the best explanation of *Pavey*, n 15, but see comments in n 77.

[259] As advocated by eg E McKendrick, 'Total Failure of Consideration and Counter-Restitution: Two Issues or One?' in P Birks (ed), *Laundering and Tracing* (1995).

Guinness Mahon[260] was a case of the first sort: the parties could never have legally bound themselves to perform their obligations under the swaps contract. *Neste Oy v Lloyds Bank plc*[261] was a case of the second sort: payments were made to a company on the basis that services would be rendered to ships arriving at a port, but by the time the last payment was made the company had decided to cease trading.

(e) Money and non-money benefits

Failure of basis was once thought to be a ground of recovery that would only lie to recover the value of money. There were never good reasons of principle for this,[262] and it is now beyond question that claims for non-money benefits, including services, can be brought in reliance on this ground.[263]   **3.93**

(3) Examples

(a) Wide range of possibilities

Many of the bases on which a benefit might be transferred are simple to identify and understand, eg the receipt of a money payment from the defendant. Others are more complex and identifying them may require careful analysis of the parties' dealings. For example, the court held that the basis on which the claimant's money was paid in *Fibrosa* was that the defendant would deliver the machinery; in contrast the court held that the basis on which money was payable in *Stocznia Gdanska* was that the ships would be designed, built and delivered. In *Fibrosa*, there was a failure of basis when the machinery was not delivered although the defendant had carried out some work; in *Stocznia Gdanska*, there was no failure of basis although no ships were delivered, because some design and construction had taken place. Lord Lloyd said that 'the distinction between a simple contract of sale, in which the only consideration is the transfer of title, and a contract of sale which also includes the provision of services prior to delivery, may sometimes be a fine one. But the distinction is sound in principle.'[264]   **3.94**

Benefits are sometimes transferred on the basis that the claimant will acquire legal rights. These may be legal rights to contractual counter-performance by the defendant,[265] in which case the basis will fail if the defendant does not make a legally binding promise to counter-perform. The void swaps cases are an example.[266] Other examples are cases where restitution has been ordered of money paid as premium under an illegal insurance policy or to an insurer who never went on risk,[267] money paid for an invalid annuity,[268] and money paid as premium for an invalid indenture.[269]   **3.95**

---

[260] *Guinness Mahon*, n 29.

[261] [1983] 2 Lloyd's Rep 658. See too *Re Farepak Food and Gifts Ltd (in admin)* [2006] EWHC 3272 (Ch), [2007] 2 BCLC 1; subsequent proceedings [2009] EWHC 2580 (Ch), [2010] 1 BCLC 444.

[262] The historical reason was that failure of consideration developed as a ground on which a plaintiff could bring an action for money had and received, an old form of action which could only be brought by plaintiffs seeking restitution of the value of money.

[263] *Pulbrook v Lawes* (1876) 1 QBD 284, 289 and 290, CA; *Cobbe*, n 2, at [43]; *Spencer v S Franses Ltd* [2011] EWHC 1269 (QB), at [237]; *Benedetti* (SC), n 18, at [86]; *Barnes*, n 16, at [116].

[264] *Stocznia Gdanska*, n 238, at 600.

[265] *Fibrosa*, n 2, at 82: 'There are cases where the payer pays not for the performance of the receiver's promise but for the promise itself - not for the doing of something but for the chance that it may be done.'

[266] *Westdeutsche* (HL), n 2, at 710; *Guinness Mahon*, n 29; *Haugesund*, n 10.

[267] *Stevenson v Snow* (1761) 1 Wm Bl 315, 96 ER 176; *Tyrie v Fletcher* (1777) 2 Cowp 666, 98 ER 1297; *Re Phoenix Life Assurance Co* (1862) 2 J & H 441, 70 ER 1131; *Flood v Irish Provident Assurance Co Ltd* [1912] 2 Ch 597 (Note).

[268] *Hicks v Hicks* (1802) 3 East 16, 102 ER 502.

[269] *Whincup*, n 252, at 82, considering *Stokes v Twitchen* (1818) 8 Taunt 492, 129 ER 475.

3.96 Benefits can also be transferred on the basis that the claimant will acquire rights in property. *Rowland* provides one example. Another is provided by cases where a defendant borrows money from the claimant to pay off a mortgage on his property and promises to execute a new one in the claimant's favour to secure repayment of the loan; when the new mortgage turns out to be invalid, or to have a different priority status from the one for which the claimant bargained, he can acquire an equitable lien on the property via subrogation, with the same priority status as the discharged mortgage.[270]

(b) Application of property to a purpose

3.97 A transfer of property may be tied to a particular application. The recipient may be bound by contract to apply it in a particular way. If the transferor intends that the recipient should hold the money on trust for the particular application, the recipient will become a trustee, although the trust will fail immediately if there are no beneficiaries. Either way, the transfer is made on the basis that the value in question be applied in the specified manner. If that basis fails, the transferee who does not or cannot make the application will be unjustly enriched.

(i) Where the transferee is bound by a contract

3.98 The transferor who obliges his transferee to apply value transferred in a particular manner can prevent misapplications by injunction. When the contract is discharged before the application is complete, the basis of the transfer will have failed and the transferor will be entitled to restitution. In *Barclays Bank Ltd v Quistclose Investments Ltd*[271] the House of Lords went further, and held that a trust will be imposed on money advanced for a particular purpose in the event that the purpose becomes impossible of fulfilment, or is repudiated by the recipient. On this view of the law, this is then a case in which the law gives proprietary effect to the transferor's right to restitution. But in *Twinsectra Ltd v Yardley*[272] the House of Lords then explained '*Quistclose* trusts' in a different way. They held that the money is impressed with a trust in the transferor's favour from the start,[273] subject to a power vested in the recipient to apply the fund to the agreed purpose. The failure of the purpose then terminates the power. The transferor's proprietary interest does not arise from this failure, but was in place all along under the trust.

3.99 It is not clear that a contract to lend money for a particular purpose will always be susceptible to the *Twinsectra* analysis. For example, where money is lent under a contract which places a positive obligation on the borrower to apply the money in a particular way, rather than a negative obligation not to use it for anything else, there is no obvious justification for downgrading the borrower's obligation to a power. In such cases, the court may prefer to say that the borrower owes a contractual obligation, and that failure of the purpose will lead to the imposition of a restitutionary trust for the lender, provided that an injunction would have been available to prevent the money being spent on other purposes.[274]

---

[270] *Anfield (UK) Ltd v Bank of Scotland plc* [2010] EWHC 2374 (Ch), [2011] 1 WLR 2414. See too the cases discussed in Mitchell and Watterson, n 5, at paras 6.73ff. Subrogation is discussed further at 3.278–3.282.

[271] [1970] AC 567, HL.

[272] [2002] UKHL 12, [2002] 2 AC 164.

[273] In 'The *Quistclose* Trust: Who Can Enforce It?' (1985) 101 LQR 269, Lord Millett seems to say that the trust is always express, but in his speech in *Twinsectra*, n 272, he seems to think that a resulting trust might be imposed in cases where the transferor does not declare an express trust for himself, and he also takes this position in 'The *Quistclose* Trust—a Reply' (2011) 17 T & T 7.

[274] R Chambers, 'Restrictions on the Use of Money' and P Birks, 'Retrieving Tied Money', both in W Swadling (ed), *The Quistclose Trust: Critical Essays* (2004).

On some facts superficially similar to those of the latter kind, the appropriate construction **3.100** may be that, in all or some events, the recipient was to take free of any fetter. That is to say, both the assets transferred and (which is a separate question) their value were to become freely his. A construction of this kind may show either that the fetter was merely precatory, and as such illusory,[275] or indicate circumstances in which the contractual fetter was intended to be struck off.[276]

(ii) Where the transferee is bound by a trust

Where the tie to a particular application is construed as creating a trust, the trust will fail **3.101** immediately if no beneficiary is named or no sufficiently certain class of such beneficiaries is identified. The basis of the transfer being that the transferee shall hold and apply the fund as a trustee, that basis then fails at once. If some but not all of the equitable beneficial interest is allocated under the trust, then it will fail as to the unallocated part.[277] In *Vandervell v IRC*,[278] it failed as to the whole fund. The problem arose from the mode in which Vandervell had chosen to make a benefaction to the Royal College of Surgeons. He meant to do it in a tax-efficient way by giving the RCS shares and declaring a dividend on them. The shares would then be transferred to his family's trust company. To achieve that purpose, the transfer to the RCS was made subject to an option in favour of the trust company. The RCS received its money, and the trust company exercised its option. However, the IRC then successfully maintained that Vandervell had failed to escape his surtax liability on the benefaction: he had not divested himself of his entire interest in the shares, because the option was all along held on trust for him. The trustee company was not intended to receive the option (and thus the shares) for itself, but to hold them for beneficiaries. However Vandervell had never declared who the beneficiaries were to be. Hence the basis of the transfer of the option to the trustee company failed, and a restitutionary trust arose in Vandervell's favour.

In cases where there is a giving upon trust and the trust fails, the imposition of a resulting **3.102** trust has traditionally been ascribed to a presumption that the transferor intended that the transferee should, on the failure of the intended basis, hold for the benefit of transferor.[279] That is a fiction of the same order as the fiction of implied contract which used to be relied upon to explain why mistaken payments and other unjust enrichments should be given back. Just as there is no contract in these cases, so there is manifestly no intent to create a resulting trust in many of the cases where express trusts have failed. As Harman J said in the *Gillingham* case the real fact is that the transferors never contemplated the contingency in question.[280] In *Vandervell* a trust for himself was the very last thing that Vandervell wanted: it contradicted his central purpose in structuring his benefaction as he did.[281] Just as the law has escaped the implied contract theory of quasi-contract, so it cannot but accept the reality

---

[275] *Re Osoba* [1979] 1 WLR 247, CA; cf *Re Bowes* [1896] 1 Ch 507.

[276] Where a gift is construed as having been made to members of an association beneficially, tied to the association's purposes by the contract between all the members, then, when that contract goes, the property, even that part of it which was donated by outsiders, will generally be construed as the unfettered property of the surviving members: *Re Bucks Constabulary Widows and Orphans' Fund Friendly Society (No 2)* [1979] 1 WLR 936; *Re Horley Town FC* [2006] EWHC 2386 (Ch), [2006] WTLR 1817; *Hanchett-Stamford v AG* [2008] EWHC 330 (Ch), [2009] Ch 173.

[277] As in eg *Re Abbott Fund Trusts* [1900] 2 Ch 326; *Re Gillingham Bus Disaster Fund* [1959] Ch 62, CA, affirming [1958] Ch 300.

[278] [1967] 2 AC 291, HL.

[279] Reasserted by Lord Browne-Wilkinson in *Westdeutsche* (HL), n 2, at 702 and 708–709.

[280] [1958] Ch 300, 310.

[281] As observed by Lord Millett in *Air Jamaica Ltd v Charlton* [2000] 1 WLR 1399, 1412, PC.

that 'the resulting trust arises by operation of law because the provider of the trust property did not intend to benefit the recipient'.[282]

3.103 It has been argued that these cases illustrate the proposition that the transferor retains that which he has not succeeded in giving away: the trustee holds for him that which he has failed to dispose of.[283] This 'retention' thesis once held sway in the English courts,[284] but the modern view is that it does not work because the transferor acquires, and does not retain, his equitable interest, so that cases of this kind are essentially identical with cases where a resulting trust is imposed for the benefit of a transferor who has successfully transferred the whole beneficial interest in his property to a recipient and received nothing in exchange.[285]

3.104 Another explanation is that the law presumes an intent to create the restitutionary trust.[286] The better view, though, is that where the defendant was intended to hold and apply the fund as a trustee, there is, when the trust fails, a prima facie failure of the basis of the transfer to him. The presumption which then comes into play is a presumption of non-beneficial intent. It is presumed, in the absence of contrary evidence, that the claimant-settlor did not intend in that event that the benefit of the fund should accrue to the trustee himself. In this way the familiar features of the law are accounted for without recourse to fiction.

F. Unjust: Policies Requiring Restitution

3.105 The law sometimes holds a defendant's enrichment at a claimant's expense to be unjust for policy reasons that are not concerned with the quality of the claimant's intention to benefit the defendant. Seven examples are considered here.

(1) Secondary Liability

3.106 It often happens that a claimant and a defendant are both legally liable to pay a third party in respect of the same debt or damage. The third party is forbidden to accumulate recoveries by enforcing his rights against both of them, but to maximize his chances of recovery, the law allows him to recover in full from either. If his choice falls on the claimant, who therefore pays him in full, the claimant may be entitled to recover some or all of his payment from the defendant, on the ground that the defendant has been unjustly enriched at his expense.

3.107 The claim brought in such cases varies according to whether the claimant's payment has discharged the defendant's liability to the third party. If it has not, then the claimant can take over the third party's subsisting right of action against the defendant by subrogation, and enforce this for his own benefit.[287] If it has, then the claimant can bring a direct claim

---

[282] R Chambers, *Resulting Trusts* (1997) 66. cf *Air Jamaica*, n 281, at 1412; *Twinsectra*, n 272, at [91]; *Lavelle v Lavelle* [2004] EWCA Civ 223, [2004] 2 FCR 418, at [13]–[14]; *Stack v Dowden* [2007] UKHL 17, [2007] 2 AC 432, at [60] and [114].

[283] eg *Re Vandervell's Trusts (No 2)* [1974] Ch 269, 289–297. cf Chambers (1997), n 282, at 51–55.

[284] As detailed in J Mee, '"Automatic" Resulting Trusts: Retention, Restitution, or Reposing Trust?' in Mitchell (2010), n 132.

[285] *Westdeutsche* (HL), n 2, at 706.

[286] See eg WJ Swadling 'A New Role for Resulting Trusts?' (1996) 16 LS 110; CEF Rickett and R Grantham, 'Resulting Trusts: A Rather Limited Doctrine' in Birks and Rose, n 193. Swadling continues to believe that 'presumed resulting trusts' respond to the transferor's intention to create a trust for himself; however he now considers that the 'automatic resulting trust' imposed on the failure of an express trust 'defies legal analysis': WJ Swadling, 'Explaining Resulting Trusts' (2008) 124 LQR 72, 102.

[287] The most important example in practice is where an insurer brings a subrogated action in the name of its insured against a third party seeking tort damages for the insured loss. For discussion see Mitchell and Watterson, n 5, at ch 10.

for contribution or reimbursement against the defendant, either under the Civil Liability (Contribution) Act 1978, or at common law.[288] There is no substantial difference between contribution claims and reimbursement claims; the quantum of the claimant's remedy is the only thing that distinguishes them.[289] If the claimant discharges securities over the defendant's property, then he may also be entitled to a lien over the defendant's property that mirrors the third party's extinguished rights as holder of the securities: the claimant is treated, by a legal fiction, as though the securities were not discharged, but were assigned to him.[290] Confusingly, the latter remedy is also termed subrogation.[291]

In the language of the cases, the claimant is entitled to these remedies if the defendant was 'primarily' and the claimant only 'secondarily' liable for the defendant's share of their common obligation to the third party.[292] To make out a cause of action, the claimant must establish several things. **3.108**

(a) Claimant and defendant both legally liable

The claimant must have paid the third party pursuant to an existing legal liability, but his payment need not have been compelled by legal process: it is enough that he was legally compellable to pay.[293] Often the claimant's liability is imposed by law, eg because he is a tortfeasor, and often it is voluntarily assumed at the defendant's request, eg because he is the defendant's surety. It is not automatically fatal if he voluntarily assumes his liability without any prior request from the defendant: this is merely one factor that may bear on a court's decision whether to allow a claim.[294] **3.109**

The defendant must also have owed a legal liability to the third party,[295] which existed at the time of the claimant's payment.[296] It may even be enough that the defendant would inevitably have incurred a liability but for the claimant's payment. This was rejected in *Metropolitan Police District Receiver v Croydon Corp*,[297] where the claimant paid statutory sick pay to its **3.110**

---

[288] Section 7(3) of the 1978 Act provides that rights conferred by the statute supersede any rights which the claimant would otherwise have at common law. Moreover different limitation rules apply to common law and statutory claims: the Limitation Act 1980, s 2 gives a claimant two years within which to claim under the 1978 Act, rather than the six years that he would otherwise have at common law. Claimants therefore need to know whether their case falls within the scope of the legislation, but unfortunately this is not always clear: *Goff & Jones*, n 3, at paras 19.30–19.34.

[289] *Edmunds v Wallingford* (1885) 14 QBD 811, 814–815, CA; *Whitham v Bullock* [1939] 2 All ER 310, 315, CA; *Ronex Properties Ltd v John Laing Construction Ltd* [1983] QB 398, 407, CA. Consistently with this, the courts can make 100% contribution awards, which are essentially identical with reimbursement awards: *Baynard v Woolley* (1855) 20 Beav 583, 585–586; 52 ER 729, 730; *Bahin v Hughes* (1886) 31 Ch D 390, 395, CA; *Nelhams v Sandells Maintenance Ltd* [1996] PIQR 52, CA.

[290] Mercantile Law Amendment Act 1856, s 5; *Duncan, Fox & Co v North and South Wales Bank* (1880) 6 App Cas 1, HL.

[291] See 3.278–3.282 for further discussion.

[292] *Duncan*, n 290, at 11; *Brook's Wharf and Bull Wharf Ltd v Goodman Bros* [1937] 1 KB 534, 544, CA; *Niru Battery Manufacturing Co v Milestone Trading Ltd (No 2)* [2004] EWCA Civ 487, [2004] 2 All ER (Comm) 289 ('*Niru (No 2)* (CA)'), at [68].

[293] *Stimpson v Smith* [1999] Ch 340, CA.

[294] Sureties: *Re a Debtor (No 627 of 1936)* [1937] 156, 166, CA. Co-sureties: *Deering v Earl of Winchelsea* (1787) 2 Bos & Pul 270, 126 ER 1276; *Smith v Wood* [1929] 1 Ch 14, 21, CA. Insurers: *Mason v Sainsbury* (1782) 3 Doug KB 61, 99 ER 538; *Caledonia North Sea Ltd v British Telecommunications plc* [2002] UKHL 4, [2002] 1 Lloyd's Rep 553. These all cast doubt on statements to the contrary in *England v Marsden* (1866) LR 1 CP 529 and *Owen v Tate* [1976] 1 QB 402, CA.

[295] *Bonner v Tottenham & Edmonton Permanent Investment Building Society* [1899] 1 QB 161, CA; *Wessex Regional Health Authority v John Laing Construction Ltd* (1994) 39 Con LR 56.

[296] But cf *Legal & General Assurance Soc Ltd v Drake Insurance Co Ltd* [1992] QB 887, CA; *Eagle Star Insurance Co v Provincial Insurance plc* [1994] AC 130, PC; *O'Kane v Jones (The Martin P)* [2003] EWHC 3470 (Comm), [2004] 1 Lloyd's Rep 389.

[297] [1957] 2 QB 154, CA.

employee, and sought reimbursement from the tortfeasor responsible for the employee's injuries. The Court of Appeal dismissed its claim, reasoning that the tortfeasor had never incurred a liability to the employee to the extent that he had received sick pay, and so the claimant's payments had not enriched the tortfeasor. However this analysis was rightly criticized as 'over-technical' by the Law Commission.[298] It may also be contrasted with the reasoning in *AMP Workers' Compensation Services (NSW) Ltd v QBE Insurance Ltd*,[299] where an injured party had a choice whether to sue one defendant or another or both. Both defendants carried liability insurance coverage. The injured party chose to sue one defendant only, whose insurer settled the claim. This insurer sought a contribution from the other insurer, which refused to pay, arguing that it had never owed a legal liability because the injured party had never sued its insured. The court found for the claimant, reasoning that its contribution right should not be defeated by the injured party's exercise of choice.

(b) Third party may not accumulate recoveries

3.111 If the third party can accumulate recoveries, the defendant will remain liable regardless of the claimant's payment, and the defendant cannot be enriched at the claimant's expense. When determining whether the third party may accumulate recoveries, the court must consider whether the liabilities owed by the claimant and defendant are assumed or imposed. Where they assumed their liabilities by agreement with the third party, the court must then look to their respective agreements to decide whether accumulation is permitted. For example, the terms of the parties' contracts explain why a creditor is allowed to accumulate recoveries from sureties who have guaranteed different debts, or different parts of the same debt, but not from sureties who have guaranteed the same debt subject to different limits which together exceed the total amount of the debt.[300]

3.112 Where the parties' liabilities are imposed by law, the court must consider whether it would be consistent with the policy which underpins their liabilities to allow the third party to accumulate recoveries. For example, the main purpose of imposing tort liability is to compensate tort victims for harm; it is not to make them better off than they were before the tort was committed. So tort victims are forbidden to recover more than the amount of their losses by accumulating recoveries from concurrent tortfeasors.[301]

(c) Third party may recover in full from either claimant or defendant

3.113 This is almost always the case where a third party may not accumulate recoveries from claimant and defendant. English law does not generally adopt a system of proportionate liability, under which the liability of claimant and defendant is limited to the amount of their proper share.[302] Instead, the third party can almost always recover from either claimant or defendant in full.[303] The unfairness which might be caused to a claimant who pays more than his proper share is redressed by giving him a claim in unjust enrichment against the defendant.

---

[298] Law Commission, *Damages for Personal Injury: Medical, Nursing and Other Expenses; Collateral Benefits* (Law Com No 262, 1999) para 12.30; cf paras 10.68–10.72, 12.7–12.10, and 12.28.
[299] (2001) 53 NSWLR 35, NSWCA, followed in *Zurich Australian Insurance Ltd v GIO General Ltd* [2011] NSWCA 47, (2011) 16 ANZ Ins Cas 61-880, and approvingly noted in *International Energy Group Ltd v Zurich Insurance plc UK Branch* [2015] UKSC 33, [2015] 2 WLR 1471, at [59].
[300] *Ellis v Emmanuel* (1876) 1 Ex D 157, 162.
[301] *Clarke v Newsam* (1847) 1 Exch 131, 140; 154 ER 55, 59; *Dingle v Associated Newspapers Ltd* [1961] 2 QB 162, 188–189, CA (not considered on appeal [1964] AC 371, HL).
[302] Law Commission, *Feasibility Investigation of Joint and Several Liability* (1996). An unprincipled move to proportionate liability has taken place in certain other jurisdictions, noted and criticized in K Barker and J Steele, 'Drifting Towards Proportionate Liability: Ethics and Pragmatics' [2015] CLJ 49.
[303] For a rare exception see *Barker v Corus (UK) Ltd* [2006] UKHL 20, [2006] 2 AC 572, immediately reversed by legislation: Compensation Act 2006, s 3. But not in Guernsey where *Barker* still applies: *International Energy*, n 299. See 2.71–2.72.

(d) Ultimate burden properly borne by defendant

As between the claimant and the defendant, some or all of the ultimate burden of paying **3.114**
the third party must rest on the defendant, so that it would be unjust if the defendant were
relieved of this burden by the claimant. Several principles emerge from the authorities. First,
where the relationship between the claimant and the defendant is affected by a contract that
allocates responsibility for paying the third party, effect is generally given to this contractual
allocation.[304] Secondly, where there is no contractual allocation, the courts have adopted
a default rule of equal apportionment.[305] Thirdly, this rule may be departed from, and a
defendant may have to bear a larger share of the burden of paying the creditor, where: (i) his
actions were a more potent cause of the creditor's loss than the claimant's actions;[306] (ii) his
actions were more morally blameworthy than the claimant's actions;[307] and/or (iii) he gained
a larger benefit than the claimant from the transactions which gave rise to their respective
liabilities to the creditor.[308]

In cases where they make an unequal apportionment because the actions of one party were **3.115**
more causatively potent than those of another, the courts often also hold that this party acted
in a more morally blameworthy way. However, while the ideas of causative potency and
moral blameworthiness are closely linked,[309] there have been cases where the courts have differentiated between the two, and have focused on the relative causative potency of the parties'
actions when apportioning liability between them.[310]

When assessing the relative moral blameworthiness of the parties' actions, the courts should **3.116**
not strive to achieve arithmetical perfection, or a 'nicely calculated less or more'.[311] In *Dubai
Aluminium Co Ltd v Salaam*,[312] Rix J took it to be a relevant factor going to the moral
blameworthiness of the various parties' actions that some had settled the third party's claims
quickly, while others had reprehensibly held out until after the initiation of proceedings.
However, obstructive (or co-operative) conduct when defending a third party's claim would
more properly be dealt with as a factor going to the apportionment of costs,[313] and should
be ignored when apportioning liability.[314]

Another issue in *Dubai* was whether a claimant who is vicariously liable for another's fraud- **3.117**
ulent wrongdoing should be treated as having acted in bad faith for the purposes of his
contribution claim against other wrongdoers, although he was personally innocent of any
dishonesty. The House of Lords held that he should, Lord Nicholls stating that otherwise the
employer of a dishonest employee would occupy 'a better position, vis-à-vis the co-defendants, than the employee for whose wrong [he] is vicariously liable'.[315] However, there would

---

[304] *Hutton v Eyre* (1815) 6 Taunt 289, 128 ER 1046; *Mawson v Cassidy* (CA 26 January 1995); *Morris v Breaveglen* (CA 9 May 1997).
[305] *Scholefield Goodman & Sons Ltd v Zyngier* [1986] AC 562, 575, HL; *Hampton v Minns* [2002] 1 WLR 1, at [58].
[306] *Schott Kem Ltd v Bentley* [1991] 1 QB 61, CA; *Australian Breeders Co-operative Soc Ltd v Jones* (1997) 150 ALR 488, FCA.
[307] *Betts v Gibbins* (1834) 1 A & E 57, 111 ER 22; *Baynard*, n 289, at 585–586; *J (a child) v Wilkins* [2001] RTR 19.
[308] *Butler v Butler* (1877) 7 Ch D 116, 121, CA; *Bonner*, n 295, at 176.
[309] *Miraflores v Owners of the George Livanos (The Miraflores, The Abadesa and The Livanos)* [1967] 1 AC 826, 845. See too HLA Hart and AM Honoré, *Causation in the Law* (2nd edn, 1985) 234.
[310] eg *Schott Kem*, n 306; *Webb v Barclays Bank plc* [2001] EWCA Civ 1411, [2002] PIQR 8, at [59]; *Crowley v Rushmoor BC* [2009] EWHC 2237 (TCC), at [133]–[134].
[311] *The Koningin Juliana* [1974] 2 Lloyd's Rep 353, 364, CA.
[312] [1999] 1 Lloyd's Rep 415.
[313] As in *Price v Price* (1880) 42 LT 626.
[314] *Furmedge v Chester-Le-Street DC* [2011] EWHC 1226 (QB), at [173].
[315] *Dubai* (HL), n 2, at [45].

be nothing wrong with this outcome if the employee and the co-defendants were dishonest conspirators. An employer is vicariously liable for his employee's fraud although he is not personally dishonest, because he has put the employee in a position to commit the wrong. But where the employee has conspired with another fraudster, the employer and the other fraudster are not equally at fault. Putting an employee in a position to commit a fraud is less reprehensible than choosing to participate in a dishonest scheme.

3.118 *Dubai* also establishes that the last of the three factors mentioned above carries more weight than the other two. The House of Lords agreed with Rix J's finding at first instance that two fraudsters who had received all of the money extracted from a third party should reimburse the other defendants who were also liable for the third party's loss because 'it cannot be just and equitable to require one party to contribute in a way which would leave another party in possession of his spoils.'[316] A similar finding was made in *Niru Battery Manufacturing Co v Milestone Trading Ltd (No 2)*,[317] where Clarke LJ held that the principle applies both where the recipient still has the money, and where he has paid it away other than in good faith. In *Charter plc v City Index Ltd*,[318] Morritt C was led by this dictum to conclude that there was no prospect of the claimant recovering a contribution and struck out the claim. On appeal, Carnwath LJ disagreed because he thought that a claimant who receives money and then pays it away is in a 'similar position' to a claimant who has never received anything.[319] This can only be true if the claimant has acted in good faith. If he has not, then why should he be able to recover some or all of his bad faith expenditure from the defendant?

(2) Necessity

3.119 In Roman law a stranger who undertook the unsolicited management of another person's affairs could recover his reasonable costs in some cases. *Negotiorum gestio*—'management of the affairs of another'—was a bilateral legal relationship that created rights and obligations on both sides. The Romans viewed the action of the party assisted against the intervener (the *actio negotiorum gestorum directa*) as the main action arising from their relationship, but also held that the intervener could bring an action to recover his expenses (the *actio (negotiorum gestorum) contraria*).[320] Modern civilian and mixed legal systems typically have a similar doctrine under which benevolent interveners can not only recover benefits conferred on the party assisted, but can also recover their expenses, and possibly also a reward for their intervention.[321]

3.120 In contrast, many common law jurisdictions, including England, have rejected any doctrine of *negotiorum gestio*, seemingly fearful that this would 'breed overnight a nation of busy-bodies anxious to perform useless and meddlesome services for others and to try their luck with the courts',[322] and contending that virtue should be its own reward.[323]

---

[316] *Dubai* (HC), n 312, at 475, following *K v P* [1993] Ch 140, 149.

[317] *Niru (No 2)* (CA), n 292, at [50]. See too *Burke v LFOT Pty Ltd* [2002] HCA 17, (2002) 209 CLR 282; *Cressman*, n 18, at [48].

[318] [2006] EWHC 2508 (Ch), [2007] 1 WLR 26, at [33]–[53].

[319] *Charter* (CA), n 131, at [59].

[320] F Schulz, *Classical Roman Law* (1951) 624; PG Stein (ed), WW Buckland, *Text Book of Roman Law from Augustus to Justinian* (4th edn, 2003) 537; J Kortmann, *Altruism in Private Law: Liability for Nonfeasance and Negotiorum Gestio* (2004) 44–47.

[321] JP Dawson, 'Negotiorum Gestio: The Altruistic Intermeddler' (1961) 74 Harvard LR 817 and 1073; R Zimmermann, *The Law of Obligations: Roman Foundations of the Civilian Tradition* (1996) ch 14 and 875–878; Kortmann, n 320, at ch 10.

[322] EW Hope, 'Officiousness' (1930) 15 Cornell LQ 25, 36, regarding this outcome as unlikely.

[323] CK Allen, 'Legal Duties' (1931) 40 Yale LJ 331, 373–377.

(a) The traditional position under English law

In *Nicholson v Chapman* Eyre CJ thought that a general right of recovery would encourage **3.121** 'the wilful attempts of ill-designing people to turn...floats and vessels adrift, in order that they may be paid for finding them'.[324] In *Falcke v Scottish Imperial Insurance Co Ltd*, Bowen LJ stated that 'liabilities are not to be forced on people behind their backs', and that 'the general principle is, beyond all question, that work or labour done or money expended by one man to preserve or benefit the property of another do not according to English law create any lien upon the property saved or benefited, nor even, if standing alone, create any obligation to repay the expenditure'.[325] In *The Tojo Maru*, Lord Reid said that 'on land a person who interferes to save property is not in law entitled to any reward'.[326] In *The Goring*, in the Court of Appeal, Ralph Gibson LJ thought that the English courts' reluctance to uphold a general right of recovery 'has not rested...only on a lack of prior authority and the fear of innovation but can be supported by reasons'.[327] In the same case, in the House of Lords, Lord Brandon considered this view to be quite as 'forceful'[328] as Sir John Donaldson MR's dissenting opinion in the Court of Appeal, that salvage awards in respect of rescues undertaken on non-tidal waters should be allowed pursuant to a general policy of encouraging rescuers.[329]

(b) Exceptional cases

Despite this antipathy, recovery has been allowed in some cases. Successful claimants include **3.122** the providers of medical and nursing care and/or the necessaries of life to the sick and mentally incapacitated;[330] voluntary carers of tort victims (to the extent that they can share in the fruits of tort actions in which damages have been awarded to reflect the cost of the care);[331] doctors and hospitals who have provided medical treatment to the victims of road traffic accidents;[332] private individuals and local authorities who have discharged another person's duty to bury the dead;[333] bailees who have incurred expenses in preserving the bailor's property;[334]

---

[324] (1793) 2 H Bl 254, 259; 126 ER 536, 539.

[325] (1886) 34 Ch D 234, CA.

[326] [1972] AC 242, 268, HL.

[327] [1987] QB 687, 708, CA.

[328] [1988] AC 831, 857, HL.

[329] [1987] QB 687, 706–707, CA.

[330] *Williams v Wentworth* (1842) 5 Beav 325, 329, 49 ER 603, 605; *Re Rhodes* (1890) 44 Ch D 94, 105, CA; *West Ham Union v Pearson* (1890) 62 LT 638; *Re Clabbon* [1904] 2 Ch 465. See also the Sale of Goods Act 1979, s 3(2).

[331] This portion of the damages must be held on trust for the carer: *Hunt v Severs* [1994] 2 AC 350, 358–363, HL; *H v S* [2002] EWCA 792, [2003] QB 965; *Hughes v Lloyd* [2007] EWHC 3133 (Ch), [2008] WTLR 473; *Drake v Foster Wheeler Ltd* [2010] EWHC 2004 (QB), [2011] 1 All ER 63, at [31]–[43]. Legislation was proposed to replace this trust with a personal liability: Department of Constitutional Affairs, *The Law on Damages* (CP 9/07, 2007) 48–50; Ministry of Justice, *Civil Law Reform Bill: Consultation* (CP 53/09, 2009) 64 and Annex A, Draft Civil Law Reform Bill, clause 7. But it was subsequently decided not to proceed with this legislation: Ministry of Justice, *Civil Law Reform Bill: Response to Consultation* (CP(R) CP 53/09, 2011) 40. Note that the principle does not apply in cases where the carer is herself the tortfeasor. For general discussion, see S Degeling, *Restitutionary Rights to Share in Damages: Carers' Claims* (2003).

[332] Road Traffic Act 1988, ss 158 and 159; Road Traffic (NHS Charges) Act 1999. The question whether the NHS should have a general right to recoup the cost of care from tortfeasors is discussed in Law Commission, *Damages for Personal Injury: Medical, Nursing and Other Expenses; Collateral Benefits* (Law Com No 262, 1999) paras 3.19–3.43. For discussion see R Lewis, 'Recovery of State Benefits from Tort Damages: Legislating For or Against the Welfare State?' in TT Arvind and J Steele (eds), *Tort Law and the Legislature* (2013).

[333] *Besfich v Cogil* (1628) 1 Palm 559, 81 ER 1219; *Jenkins v Tucker* (1788) 1 H Bl 90, 126 ER 55; *Ambrose v Kerrison* (1851) 10 CB 776, 138 ER 307; Public Health (Control of Disease) Act 1984, s 46(5).

[334] *Great Northern Railway v Swaffield* (1874) 9 Ex 132; *Sachs v Miklos* [1948] 2 KB 23, 35–36, CA; *The Winson* [1982] AC 939, 958, HL; *Guildford BC v Hein* [2005] EWCA Civ 979, at [33] and [80]; *ENE Kos 1 Ltd v Petroleo Brasileiro SA (The Kos) (No 2)* [2012] UKSC 17, [2012] 2 AC 164, at [18]–[30] and [55].

shipmasters who have incurred necessary expenditure to preserve the vessel;[335] salvors (who do not always, although they do often, enter a contract to render salvage services, and whose entitlement to a reward in the former case is restitutionary to the extent that its amount is calculated by reference to the benefit conferred);[336] cargo owners whose property has been sacrificed to save other cargo and/or the vessel;[337] recovery services who have removed vehicles from the public highway and stored them at the request of the police;[338] liquidators and trustees who have done more work than would normally be required;[339] and acceptors for honour *supra* protest of bills of exchange.[340]

(c) Possible emergence of a general doctrine

3.123 The time has come for the courts to recognize that these various 'exceptions' have swallowed up the general rule.[341] They should recognize that the cases are all underpinned by a policy of encouraging (or of not discouraging) intervention in emergency situations,[342] and they should generalize the principles disclosed by these cases into a coherent and rational doctrine analogous to the civilian doctrine of *negotiorum gestio*. This doctrine would only belong in part to the law of unjust enrichment, as the remedies awarded would include, but would not be limited to, the restitution of benefits. In appropriate cases, necessitous interveners might also be entitled to a reward or an indemnity for their costs.

3.124 Certain limitations disclosed by the existing case law might attach to any such generalized right of action. First, the likelihood of imminent harm to the defendant's property or person must have been great.[343] Secondly, it must have been impracticable for the claimant to communicate with the defendant,[344] and recovery should not usually be allowed where intervention 'was contrary to the known wishes of the assisted person'.[345] However, even here recovery might exceptionally be allowed if the defendant's rejection of the claimant's intervention was against the public interest.[346] Thirdly, the claimant must have been an appropriate person

---

[335] *The Argos* (1873) LR 5 PC 134, 165 (Sir Montagu Smith); *Hingston v Vent* (1876) 1 QBD 367; *Tetley v British Trade Corp* (1922) 10 Lloyd's List LR 678.

[336] For general discussion of civil salvage, see FD Rose, *Kennedy and Rose on Civil Salvage* (7th edn, 2010).

[337] FD Rose, 'General Average as Restitution' (1997) 113 LQR 569. General discussion: FD Rose, *General Average: Law and Practice* (2nd edn, 2005).

[338] *White v Troups Transport* [1976] CLY 33, County Ct; *Surrey Breakdown Ltd v Knight* [1999] RTR 84, CA. See too Road Traffic Regulation Act 1984, ss 99–103.

[339] *Re Duke of Norfolk's ST* [1982] 1 Ch 61, CA; *Re Berkeley Applegate (Investment Consultants) Ltd* [1989] 1 Ch 32; *Foster v Spencer* [1996] 2 All ER 672; *Polly Peck International plc v Henry* [1999] 1 BCLC 407. See too Trustee Act 2000, s 29.

[340] Bills of Exchange Act 1882, s 68(5), giving a right of recovery via subrogation to the position of the holder.

[341] cf *The Kos*, n 334, at [19] where Lord Sumption acknowledged that 'the exceptions have over the years become more important than the rule', but considered that the absence of a generalized right to recovery 'remains the general principle'.

[342] Kortmann observes that the present general rule disallowing interveners' claims 'does not *actively* discourage intervention but *merely fails to neutralize* the discouraging effect of the prospect that an intervention might prove costly': Kortmann, n 320, at 91, fn 2; see too A Honoré, 'Law, Morals, and Reason' in J Ratcliff (ed), *The Good Samaritan and the Law* (1966) 234.

[343] *The Bona* [1895] P 125, CA; *Sachs*, n 334, at 36; *Surrey*, n 338, at 88.

[344] *Springer v Great Western Railway Co* [1921] 1 KB 257; *The Winson*, n 334, at 961; *Industrie Chimiche Italia Centrale and Cerealfin SA v Tsavliris (Alexander G) Maritime Co (The Choko Star)* [1990] 1 Lloyd's Rep 516, 525.

[345] *Re F (Mental Patient: Sterilisation)* [1990] 2 AC 1, 75, HL; *Skibinski v Community Living British Columbia* [2012] BCCA 17, (2012) 346 DLR (4th) 688 [57].

[346] As in eg *Swaffield*, n 334; *The Kangaroo* [1918] P 327; *Matheson v Smiley* [1932] 2 DLR 787, Manitoba CA; *Hein*, n 334. cf BGB § 679, and other sources in Zimmermann, n 321, at 448, fn 118. But contrast *Soldiers' Memorial Hospital v Sanford* [1934] 2 DLR 334, Nova Scotia CA.

to act in the circumstances,[347] although he must not have owed a pre-existing duty to intervene, eg because he was a member of the emergency services, or a member of the crew of an imperilled ship.[348] Fourthly, a claimant should be able to recover only in respect of expenses reasonably incurred in all the circumstances.[349] Fifthly, it should be a bar to recovery that a claimant has acted for his own benefit and only incidentally conferred a benefit on the defendant in the course of doing so.[350] Sixthly, some cases suggest that the intervener must show that he intended to charge for his services.[351] However, it is illogical to conclude from the fact that it is good public policy to encourage intervention, that the burden of proving an intention to charge should be imposed on the intervener; the burden should rather lie on the assisted person to prove that the intervener intended to act gratuitously.

In the event that a general right of recovery is recognized, it will be necessary to distinguish three possible measures of recovery: reward, restitution of enrichment, and reimbursement of expenses. It seems possible that rewards will remain confined to maritime salvors, who are rewarded in order to provide a real incentive to 'seafaring folk to take risks for the purpose of saving property',[352] but who are rewarded only if their services are successful.[353] It is essential to encourage individuals to salvage property on the high seas, but doubtful that there is the same general need to encourage intervention elsewhere. Where a court decides to award reimbursement of the claimant's costs the best approach would be to follow French and German law in aiming to neutralize the whole cost of his intervention.[354] Where restitution of the defendant's enrichment is awarded, the relevant benefit should usually be the saved cost of employing someone else to perform the relevant service, rather than the value of preserved property that already belonged to the defendant.[355]   **3.125**

(3) Undue Payments to Public Bodies

(a) Statutory regimes

Various statutes provide for the recovery of money paid as tax that was not due. Most of these oust common law rights of recovery, expressly or impliedly.[356] Hence, in practice 'the number of cases [concerning the recovery of undue tax payments] where any principle of common law would need to be relied on is likely to be small',[357] and so is the number of cases where claimants will be allowed to rely on their common law rights in preference to their statutory rights, eg because they wish to take advantage of a more favourable limitation period or right   **3.126**

---

[347] *Rhodes*, n 330, at 107; *Macclesfield Corp v Great Central Railway Co* [1911] 2 KB 528, 541.

[348] *The Albionic* (1941) 70 Lloyd's List Rep 257, 263; *The Sava Star* [1995] 2 Lloyd's Rep 134, 142.

[349] *Jenkins*, n 333 (burial costs recoverable if suited to deceased's station in life); *Rhodes*, n 330, at 105 (cost of necessaries supplied to an incapax recoverable if suited to her station in life); *White*, n 338 (only hire cost of smallest crane needed to remove lorry from highway can be recovered).

[350] cf *Tanguay v Price* (1906) 37 SCR 657; *Warfel v Vondersmith* 101 A 2d 736 (1954). In *TFL*, n 23, the CA refused to recognize a general principle debarring recovery of 'incidental benefits'. Hence the best explanation of the rule stated in the text is that a claimant who acts in his own self-interest cannot establish a reason for restitution because he cannot bring himself within the policy grounding recovery in necessity cases.

[351] *Rhodes*, n 330.

[352] *The Sandefjord* [1953] 2 Lloyd's Rep 557, 561.

[353] *The Zephyrus* (1842) 1 W Rob 329, 330–331; 166 ER 596, 597; *The Renpor* (1883) 8 PD 115.

[354] Kortmann, n 320, at 179–183. See too RGZ 167, 83 (7 May 1941) and other cases in Dawson, n 321, at 148–154.

[355] Allowing the latter remedy would unacceptably subvert the defendant's pre-existing rights as property owner. cf *Cobbe*, n 2, at [41]: a locksmith who opens a locked cupboard containing silver cannot claim the value of the silver which already belongs to the owner.

[356] eg the Taxes Management Act 1970, s 33 and the Value Added Tax Act 1994, s 80. Further discussion: 3.221–3.222.

[357] *Woolwich*, n 2, at 200.

to interest. Even so, recent years have seen a number of high value common law claims proceed through the English courts.[358]

(b) Common law claims

3.127 Where money is paid as tax that is not due, the facts may disclose a cause of action in mistake or duress *colore officii*.[359] In *Woolwich Equitable Building Society v IRC*,[360] however, neither of these could be established. The claimant building society paid money in response to a tax demand issued under regulations that were later held to be ultra vires and void in judicial review proceedings.[361] The society had disputed the validity of the regulations from the outset, but had paid because it had wished to avoid penalties and unfavourable publicity. Following the outcome of the judicial review proceedings, the Revenue returned the capital sum together with interest from the date of judgment, but stated that it did so *ex gratia*, and refused to pay interest from the date of receipt. To make good its claim to this interest, the society had to show that it had been entitled to restitution as of right. The House of Lords held that it had been so entitled.[362]

(i) *The scope of the* Woolwich *principle*

3.128 One policy justification for this finding offered by Lord Goff was that a right to recover payments of tax levied without Parliamentary authority is needed to give full effect to the constitutional principle enshrined in article 4 of the Bill of Rights 1689, that the Crown and its ministers may not impose direct or indirect taxes without Parliamentary sanction.[363] Another, latent in their Lordships' speeches, is the wider public law principle of legality, that bodies invested with power by the state must respect the rule of law, and adhere to the limits of their authority. That would suggest that claims should lie not only against tax authorities which have been paid money as tax that is not due, but also against other public bodies which have been paid money as duties, fees, and other levies that are not due.[364] It also suggests that in this context the term 'public body' should be construed widely, to embrace both governmental bodies and also bodies such as privatized industries whose authority to charge is subject to and limited by public law principles.[365] At present, however, it is unclear how far the *Woolwich* principle extends beyond the core case of money paid as tax that is not due.[366]

---

[358] eg *DMG*, n 2; *Sempra*, n 2; *FII* (SC), n 2; *ITC* (CA), n 18. On the reasons for this phenomenon, see n 148. The provision for restitutionary liability in HMRC's latest accounts was £8.5 billion: HM Revenue & Customs, Annual Report and Accounts for 2013/14 (HC 19, 2014), 171.

[359] As to which see N Enonchong, 'Restitution from Public Authorities: Any Room for Duress?' in Elliott et al, n 30.

[360] *Woolwich*, n 2.

[361] In *R v Inland Revenue Commissioners, ex p Woolwich BS* [1990] 1 WLR 1400, HL.

[362] Drawing on arguments made in WR Cornish, '"Colour of Office": Restitutionary Redress against Public Authority' (1987) 14 Jo of Malaysian and Comparative Law 41, and P Birks, 'Restitution from the Executive: A Tercentenary Footnote to the Bill of Rights' in PD Finn (ed), *Essays on Restitution* (1990).

[363] *Woolwich*, n 2, at 172.

[364] eg charges to take extracts from a parish register (*Steele v Williams* (1853) Ex 625, 155 ER 1502); charges for the use of pier facilities (*Queens of the River SS Co v River Thames Conservators* (1889) 15 Times LR 474); stallage (cf *R v Birmingham CC, ex p Dredger* (1993) 91 LGR 532); charges for the provision of border control services (*Waikato Regional Airport Ltd v A-G of New Zealand* [2003] UKPC 50, [2004] 3 NZLR 1); sex shop licence fees (*R (Hemming (t/a Simply Pleasure Ltd)) v Westminster CC* [2012] EWHC 1260 (Admin), [2012] PTSR 1676; varied [2013] EWCA Civ 591, [2013] PTSR 1377; not considered on appeal [2015] UKSC 25, [2015] 2 WLR 1271). In such cases, the claimant may be able to recover no more than the difference between the sums paid and the sums that could legitimately been charged: *Waikato*, at [84]; *Hemming* (CA), at [110]; discussed in C Mitchell, 'Counter-Factual Arguments against *Woolwich* Liability' in A Dyson, J Goudkamp and F Wilmot-Smith (eds), *Defences in Unjust Enrichment* (2015).

[365] cf *South of Scotland Electricity Board v British Oxygen Co Ltd* [1959] 1 WLR 587 (HL Sc). See too Law Commission, *Restitution: Mistakes of Law and Ultra Vires Public Authority Receipts and Payments* (Law Com No 227, 1994) paras 6.42–6.45; J Beatson, 'Restitution of Taxes, Levies and Other Imposts: Defining the Extent of the *Woolwich* Principle' (1993) 109 LQR 401, 417–418.

[366] As stated by Lord Walker in *DMG*, n 2, at [140] and *FII* (SC), n 2, at [80].

In *Boake Allen Ltd v HMRC*[367] it appeared to be said that the *Woolwich* principle does not **3.129** authorize the recovery of money paid as tax unless it was paid in response to an official demand. This was denied in *Test Claimants in the FII Group Litigation v HMRC*, where Lord Walker and Lord Sumption held that a demand is not needed, although they thought that it must have been communicated to the taxpayer that a payment was required in circumstances where the tax authority had no power to require payment.[368] They both thought that for this purpose it suffices for a statute to exist which apparently requires the payment although in fact the payment is not due.[369] According to Lord Sumption, however, it does not suffice for a taxpayer to have paid money in the mistaken belief that a statute requires him to do so because he has miscalculated his tax liability or forgotten that he has already paid it.[370] Yet in such a case, the taxpayer pays only because he believes that he is required to do so by the legislation. So why should this situation fall outside the scope of the *Woolwich* rule as formulated in *FII*?

On Lord Sumption's conception of the rule, it responds only to positive steps taken by public **3.130** bodies to induce a claimant's mistaken belief that money is payable. It might alternatively be argued that the mischief against which the rule is directed is the receipt of money by public bodies to which they are not entitled, plain and simple, regardless of whether the defendant authority has induced the claimant's belief that he is liable to pay.[371] On this understanding of the rule, however, it looks identical to a rule that money paid as tax can be recovered simply on the ground that it is not due,[372] and in *FII* Lord Sumption made it clear that the court's decision did not change the law 'by allowing an action for the recovery of payments on the simple ground that they were not due'.[374]

(ii) Relationship with mistake of law

In *Kleinwort Benson Ltd v Lincoln CC* Lord Goff said that abolition of the mistake of law **3.131** bar[375] had left English law with 'two separate and distinct regimes in respect of the repayment of money paid under a mistake of law', namely '(1) cases concerned with repayment of taxes and other similar charges which, when exacted ultra vires, are recoverable as of right at common law on the principle in *Woolwich*, and otherwise are the subject of statutory regimes regulating recovery; and (2) other cases, which may broadly be described as concerned with repayment of money paid under private transactions, and which are governed by the common law'.[376]

In *Deutsche Morgan Grenfell plc v IRC*,[377] the Revenue argued that these words should be **3.132** interpreted to mean that a claimant who mistakenly pays money as tax, and who is not precluded from claiming at common law, may only rely on the *Woolwich* ground of recovery and may not base his claim on mistake of law. There is certainly something to be said for the view that claims to recover ultra vires payments to public authorities should be governed exclusively by public law principles, as these are best adapted to take account of the special

---

[367] [2006] EWCA 25, [2006] STC 606, at [84], [89] and [140]–[147]; not considered on appeal: [2007] UKHL 25, [2007] 1 WLR 1386.
[368] *FII* (SC), n 2, at [64]–[81] and [171]–[174].
[369] *FII* (SC), n 2, at [79] and [174].
[370] *FII* (SC), n 2, at [186].
[371] For an argument to this effect see R Williams, 'Overpaid Taxes: A Hybrid Public and Private Approach' in Elliott et al, n 30.
[372] cf the discussion of 'absence of basis' reasoning at 3.10–3.13.
[Footnote 373 has been deleted in the paperback edition.]
[374] *FII* (SC), n 2, at [162].
[375] See 3.10–3.13.
[376] *Lincoln*, n 24, at 362.
[377] *DMG*, n 2.

relationship between the parties.[378] However little attempt was made to argue the point from first principles before the House of Lords, which rejected the Revenue's reading of Lord Goff's words, and held that claimants are free to choose whether to rely on mistake of law or the *Woolwich* principle where both reasons for restitution are present on the facts of the case.[379]

(iii) Procedural issues

3.133 The claim in *Woolwich* was not brought until after the ultra vires nature of the Revenue's demand had been established in separate judicial review proceedings. At that time, restitution could not be awarded in public law proceedings, and so it was assumed that a claimant had to bring two separate sets of proceedings in order to recover his money. In *British Steel plc v Customs and Excise Commissioners (No 1)*,[380] it was then established that both the 'public' and the 'private' law aspects of *Woolwich* claims could be decided in a single set of private law proceedings. This was consistent with the relaxation of the *O'Reilly v Mackman*[381] exclusivity doctrine that took place at that time.[382] In 2004, section 31(4) of the Senior Courts Act 1981 was then amended to give the High Court the power to award restitution in judicial review proceedings.[383] This change has prompted some courts to hold that claimants should no longer be permitted to use *British Steel* to evade the three month time limit and other procedural requirements for judicial review proceedings, but Beatson LJ has said that although 'the factor making the payee's enrichment unjust is rooted in public law ... the right to restitution and the obligation to make restitution are part of the private law of obligations', and it follows that the time limit for judicial review should not apply to *Woolwich* claims.[384]

(4) Ultra Vires Payments by Public Bodies

(a) **Statutory regimes**

3.134 Many situations where money has been paid by a public body acting beyond its powers fall within the scope of exclusive statutory recovery regimes, such as those which enable the government to recover overpaid social security benefits,[385] overpaid housing benefit and council tax benefit,[386] and overpaid tax credits.[387]

(b) **Common law claims**

3.135 Payments made out of public funds without lawful authority are also recoverable at common law by virtue of their ultra vires nature. This rule can be traced back at least as far as the Privy

---

[378] As argued in R Williams, *Unjust Enrichment and Public Law* (2010), reprised in Williams (2013), n 371. Precisely such considerations led the Supreme Court of Canada to hold in *Kingstreet*, n 23, that common law claims to recover ultra vires tax payments are governed by a unique set of special principles. German law views such claims as lying within the province of public law: B Häcker, '"Public Law Restitutionary Claims": The German Perspective' in Elliott et al, n 30.
[379] In *FII* (SC), n 2, at [168] Lord Sumption acknowledged that there are reasons for thinking that the court would have done better to hold the opposite, but declined to reopen the debate.
[380] [1997] 2 All ER 366, CA.
[381] [1983] 2 AC 337, HL.
[382] *Clark v University of Lincolnshire and Humberside* [2000] 1 WLR 1988, CA; *Rhondda Cynon Taff CBC v Watkins* [2003] EWCA Civ 129, [2003] 1 WLR 1864; *Bunney v Burns Anderson plc* [2007] EWHC 1240 (Ch), [2008] Bus LR 22.
[383] Civil Procedure (Modification of Supreme Court Act 1981) Order, SI 2004/1033. See also Civil Procedure (Amendment No 5) Rules 2003, SI 2003/3361, para 13, amending CPR r 54.5.
[384] *Hemming* (CA), n 364, at [138]. See too *ITC* (CA), n 18, at [23], and *Littlewoods* (CA), n 36, at [8], both accepting that the limitation period for *Woolwich* claims is 6 years. cf *Jones v Powys Local Health Board* [2008] EWHC 2562 (Admin); *Hemming* (Admin), n 364. Both discussed in Williams (2013), n 371.
[385] Social Security Administration Act 1992, s 71.
[386] Social Security Administration Act 1992, ss 75 and 76.
[387] Income and Corporation Taxes Act 1988, s 813; Tax Credits Act 2002, s 28.

Council's decision in *Auckland Harbour Board v R*, where Viscount Haldane held that 'no money can be taken out of the Consolidated Fund into which the revenues of the State have been paid, excepting under a distinct authorisation from Parliament itself... Any payment out of the Consolidated Fund made without Parliamentary authority is simply illegal and ultra vires, and may be recovered.'[388]

Although the *Auckland Harbour* case was itself directed only to payments made out of the **3.136** Consolidated Fund, the Law Commission later observed that the rule stated in the case cannot rationally be confined in this way. It identified the underlying reason for the rule as 'the protection of public funds from unlawful dissipation', and contended that in line with this consideration, all unauthorized payments of central government funds should be recoverable as of right, by virtue of their ultra vires nature.[389] The Law Commission thought it 'unlikely' that the principle would apply to local authorities or semi-state bodies,[390] but there is no good reason for limiting its scope in this way either, and it has been successfully invoked in a case involving a local authority.[391]

It is curious that the *Auckland Harbour* rule was never identified by the courts as a ground **3.137** for recovery by local authorities in the swaps litigation of the 1990s which followed *Hazell v Hammersmith & Fulham LBC*.[392] There, interest rate swap contracts between banks and local authorities were held to be void because they were beyond the councils' statutory borrowing powers. In the wake of this decision many claims were made to recover payments that had been made under such contracts. Many of the contracts provided for 'upfront payments' by the banks, and so the councils were often the 'winners' of the contracts at the time when *Hazell* declared them to be void, and thus defendants to claims by banks. In some cases, however, the council was the 'loser', and thus the claimant,[393] and in these circumstances the council should have been able to invoke the *Auckland Harbour* rule.[394]

In *Hazell* Lord Templeman stressed that the object of the rule rendering the swaps contracts **3.138** void was 'the protection of the public',[395] and in one swaps case, *Guinness Mahon & Co Ltd v Kensington and Chelsea RLBC*,[396] Morritt LJ held that the law of unjust enrichment should be developed in a manner that was consistent with this policy. In *Guinness Mahon*, however, the council was the winner of the swap transaction and thus the defendant in the case, and as Waller LJ said, 'protection of council taxpayers from loss is to be distinguished from securing a windfall for them'.[397] In other words, the rule in *Hazell* was designed to protect taxpayers from unauthorized expenditure of public money, a rationale that does not obviously justify giving banks the right to recover money received by local authorities under ultra vires contracts. However, it might be said that if policy concerns demand that a local authority should recover money paid under a losing ultra vires contract, fairness demands that it should also

---

[388] [1924] AC 318, 326–327, PC.
[389] Law Com No 227, n 365, at paras 17.2 and 17.11.
[390] Law Com No 227, n 365, at para 17.11.
[391] *Charles Terence Estates Ltd v Cornwall Council* [2011] EWHC 2542 (QB), [2012] 1 P & CR 2; overruled on the basis that the council's payments were not ultra vires, without doubting the applicability of the *Auckland Harbour* rule: [2012] EWCA Civ 1439, [2013] 1 WLR 466.
[392] *Hazell*, n 146.
[393] eg *South Tyneside MBC v Svenska International plc* [1995] 1 All ER 545.
[394] As argued in E O'Dell, 'Incapacity' in P Birks and FD Rose (eds), *Lessons of the Swaps Litigation* (2000).
[395] *Hazell*, n 146, at 36.
[396] *Guinness Mahon*, n 29, at 229.
[397] *Guinness Mahon*, n 29, at 233, quoting Leggatt LJ's judgment in *Westdeutsche Landesbank Girozentale v Islington LBC* [1994] 1 WLR 938, 951, CA.

have to repay money received under a winning contract.[398] Also, if local authorities knew that they could recover money paid under ultra vires contracts, but keep money received, that would give them a perverse incentive to enter such contracts, subverting the policy of the ultra vires rule.[399]

(5) Illegality

3.139 If a claimant transfers a benefit to a defendant under an illegal agreement, the fact that the agreement is illegal might affect an unjust enrichment claim between them in several ways. If the claimant seeks restitution on a ground of recovery such as mistake or failure of basis, then the defendant may plead the illegality of the transaction as a defence.[400] In some classes of case, however, the claimant can rely on illegality itself as a ground of recovery.

(a) Protection of persons in the claimant's position

3.140 One such case is where the protection of persons in the claimant's position is the very reason for the rule rendering the transaction illegal: here restitution may be ordered pursuant to the policy of the rule, it being an overriding principle that 'if a transaction be objectionable on grounds of public policy, the parties to it may be relieved; the relief not being given for their sake, but for the sake of the public'.[401] An example is provided by *Re Cavalier Insurance Co Ltd*,[402] where purchasers of household appliances bought extended warranty cover from a company that was not authorized to do insurance business in the UK, as required by legislation. When the company became insolvent the policyholders could not enforce the contracts, but they were able to recover their premiums because the purpose of the rule requiring insurance companies to obtain authorization is the protection of policyholders.

(b) Encouraging withdrawal from illegal transactions

3.141 Pursuant to a policy of encouraging participants in illegal schemes to abandon them, the law allows a *locus poenitentiae*, or 'space for repentance': provided that the parties' illegal purpose has not been substantially carried into effect,[403] restitution is awarded to a claimant who withdraws from the transaction.[404] This long-standing rule[405] was reaffirmed in *Tribe v Tribe*,[406] although the facts of that case were not best suited to the application of the doctrine. The claimant was not so much aborting his illegal project as seeking help to carry through its second stage. He had transferred shares to his son to hide them from creditors (though none had in fact been defrauded). The time had come to resume full

---

[398] Krebs, n 30, at 183–184, observing that 'otherwise the bank would be "punished" twice, particularly if it had "hedged" its exposure under one swap by entering into the mirror image of it with another local authority'.

[399] Further discussion: Williams (2010), n 378, at 56–69.

[400] See 3.204ff.

[401] *Vauxhall Bridge Co v Earl Spencer* (1821) Jac 64, 67; 37 ER 774, 776.

[402] [1989] 2 Lloyd's Rep 430, 450. See too *Kiriri Cotton* (n 211); *Murray Vernon Holdings Ltd v Hassall* [2010] EWHC 7 (Ch), at [66].

[403] *Kearley v Thompson* (1890) 24 QBD 742, 747, CA doubting the more relaxed approach to this question previously taken in *Taylor v Bowers* (1876) 1 QBD 291, CA. See too *Symes v Hughes* (1870) LR 9 Eq 475; *Re National Benefit Insurance Co* [1931] 1 Ch 46; *Q v Q* [2008] EWHC 1874 (Fam), [2009] 1 FLR 935.

[404] Renuniciation is enough in itself and sincere repentance is not required: *Tribe v Tribe* [1996] Ch 107, 135, CA. cf *Parkinson v College of Ambulance Ltd* [1925] 2 KB 1, 16; *Harry Parker Ltd v Mason* [1940] 2 KB 590; *Bigos v Boustead* [1951] 1 All ER 92.

[405] eg *Roberts v Roberts* (1818) Dan 143, 159 ER 862; *Groves v Groves* (1829) 3 Y & J 163, 148 ER 1136.

[406] *Tribe*, n 404. See too *Patel v Mirza* [2014] EWCA Civ 1047, [2015] 2 WLR 405.

[407] See 3.223–3.225.

ownership. At this point he had been betrayed by the son's insistence on treating himself as their owner.

(6) Reversal of Judgments

A court may order the unsuccessful party to a suit to pay money or transfer property to the successful party, and this order may be complied with before any appeal is heard. In this situation, the successful party's enrichment is justified by the court order,[407] and so there is generally no prospect of the unsuccessful party recovering the benefit for as long as the order subsists, even if there are good reasons for thinking that the court has made a mistake. But if an appeal is heard, and the court's order is reversed, the appellate court will direct the respondent to return the money paid or property transferred under the original order.[408] **3.142**

Unless he has intentionally misled the court or otherwise abused court process,[409] a litigant commits no wrong by receiving money under a judgment that is later reversed. The law of unjust enrichment therefore provides the best explanation of the claimant's right of recovery. In *AB v British Coal Corp*[410] the reason for restitution was located in the fact that a payor does not truly intend to benefit the recipient where he is compelled to pay by legal process, because his intention is vitiated in the same way that a payor's intention is vitiated in cases of duress. Another possible explanation is that a payor makes a 'retrospective mistake' of the kind identified in *Kleinwort Benson Ltd v Lincoln CC*[411] when he pays pursuant to an understanding of the law that is falsified by the appellate court's decision.[412] A third is that the basis of the transfer fails when the judgment or order is set aside.[413] **3.143**

However, none of these explanations captures the essence of the claimant's right, because in cases where benefits are transferred pursuant to a judgment, the 'normal unjust enrichment models designed to protect the freedom of choice of the transferor do not apply; the judgment has rendered [his] consent irrelevant and the transferor cannot pick and choose the conditions of the transfer'.[414] Hence the best explanation of the claimant's right lies in the policy consideration that the courts' power to force litigants to transfer benefits to other litigants is partly justified by procedural mechanisms whose function is to reduce the risk of judicial error. These include the right to appeal, a necessary concomitant of which is the right to recover money paid under the initial judgment following a successful appeal.[415] Without **3.144**

---

[408] An order for recovery can be made in the appeal itself: *Nykredit plc v Edward Erdman Ltd* [1997] 1 WLR 1627, 1636–1637, HL. But a further order can also be applied for in new proceedings, if an unsuccessful respondent declines to repay what was received under the original order: *Lee v Mallam* (1910) 10 SR (NSW) 876, NSWSC.

[409] On the tort of abuse of process, see *Grainger v Hill* (1838) 4 Bing NC 212, 132 ER 769; *Varawa v Howard Smith Co Ltd* (1911) 13 CLR 35; *Metall und Rohstoff AG v Donaldson Lufkin & Jenrette Inc* [1990] 1 QB 391, 467–473, CA. On the tort of malicious prosecution (which extends to civil proceedings), see *Crawford Adjusters (Cayman) Ltd v Sagicor General Insurance (Cayman) Ltd* [2013] UKPC 17, [2014] AC 366.

[410] [2007] EWHC 1948 (QB). See too *Heydon v NRMA Ltd (No 2)* [2001] NSWCA 445, (2001) NSWLR 600, at [14].

[411] *Lincoln*, n 24, discussed at 3.57–3.61.

[412] Lord Cairns mentions mistake, probably without meaning to identify it as the ground for recovery, in *Rodger v Comptoir d'Escompte de Paris* (1871) LR 3 PC 465, 475. It was explicitly relied on as the ground of recovery in *Palmer v Blue Circle Southern Cement Ltd* [1999] NSWSC 697.

[413] *Vasailes v Robertson* [2002] NSWCA 177, at [5].

[414] B McFarlane, 'The Recovery of Money Paid Under Judgments Later Reversed' [2001] 9 RLR 1, 6, approved in *Woolworths Ltd v Strong (No 2)* [2011] NSWCA 72, at [35].

[415] A similar principle gives a defence or justification to defendants who are sued in the civil courts for acts that were legally validated by the initial judgment and undertaken in reliance on the judgment: eg *Wilde v Australian Trade Equipment Co Pty Ltd* (1981) 145 CLR 590, 603; *Battenberg v Union Club* [2005] NSWSC 242, (2005) 53 ACSR 263, at [41]–[67].

[416] *Commonwealth v McCormack* (1984) 155 CLR 273, 277.

this the legal system would be caught in self-contradiction and the appellate process would be rendered 'nugatory'.[416]

(7) Insolvency Policies

3.145 Certain sections of the Insolvency Act 1986 invalidate transactions entered by an insolvent company prior to insolvency, and empower the courts to make orders requiring the recipients of benefits from the company to repay them.[417] The policy goals of these statutory restitutionary regimes are fostering the collective insolvency process, enabling the equal distribution of an insolvent's assets, and deterring the dismemberment of companies on the verge of insolvency.[418]

G. Defences

(1) Change of Position

3.146 In *Lipkin Gorman (a firm) v Karpnale Ltd*,[419] money stolen from the claimant firm was used by the thief to gamble at the defendant casino. The casino incurred a prima facie liability in unjust enrichment. However, some of the thief's bets were successful and the court held that the casino's liability should be reduced by the total amount it had paid out as winnings.[420] Lord Goff held this to follow from the principle that a defendant can escape liability in unjust enrichment where his 'position has so changed that it would be inequitable in all the circumstances to require him to make restitution, or alternatively restitution in full'.[421] Lord Goff chose not to lay down a set of detailed rules about the scope and operation of this principle, as he thought it more appropriate for the courts to work matters out on a case-by-case basis.[422]

(a) Rationale

3.147 To develop the defence in a principled fashion the courts must understand its rationale. In most cases where the defence has succeeded, the benefit transferred from the claimant to the defendant has been irretrievably dissipated and the court must therefore decide which of the parties should bear this loss.[423] In making this choice, the court must strike a fair balance between the claimant's interest in restitution and the defendant's interest in making spending decisions freely, without fear that a claim in unjust enrichment might later invalidate the

---

[417] Insolvency Act 1986, ss 127, 238 and 423.

[418] Further discussion: EPL 19.69–19.80, 19.147–19.155. See too A Keay, 'The Recovery of Voidable Preferences: Aspects of Restoration' [2000] CFILR 1; S Degeling, 'Restitution for Vulnerable Transactions' in J Armour and HN Bennett (eds), *Vulnerable Transactions in Corporate Insolvency* (2003).

[419] *Lipkin Gorman*, n 2.

[420] *Lipkin Gorman*, n 2, at 581–583. This was generous to the defendant, since the fraudster had restaked much of this money and then lost it, but the court may have taken the pragmatic view that a stricter approach would have called for an excessively complex calculation.

[421] *Lipkin Gorman*, n 2, at 580.

[422] *Lipkin Gorman*, n 2, at 580. See too *Haugesund*, n 10, at [152]. In *Commerzbank AG v Price-Jones* [2003] EWCA Civ 1663, at [56] Munby J took Lord Goff to mean that the courts have a broad discretion to allow or to withhold the defence; however Lord Goff explicitly stated that 'the court [does not have] *carte blanche* to reject [a claim in unjust enrichment] simply because it thinks it unfair or unjust in the circumstances to grant recovery': at 578.

[423] This is different from the question that arises at the claim stage, viz which of the parties has the best right to the value of a benefit; hence it is misguided to argue that the situations where the defence is allowed are the same as the situations where a claim is allowed, as in J Edelman, 'Change of Position: A Defence of Unjust Disenrichment' (2012) 92 Boston Univ LR 1009.

[424] *Lincoln*, n 24, at 382: *Dextra*, n 150, at [38].

assumptions that he makes about the means at his disposal.[424] The courts could also conceivably aim to reduce litigation costs by withholding the defence from defendants who fail to take reasonable steps to check their receipts.[425] However, they have held that defendants owe no such duty.[426]

It has been said that the reason why restitution is withheld in cases where the defendant's enrichment has been lost is that in these circumstances the claimant can no longer establish the 'enrichment' element of his cause of action. Passages of Lord Templeman's speech in *Lipkin Gorman* can be read in this way, in particular his statement that 'in a claim for money had and received by a thief, the plaintiff victim must show that money belonging to him was paid by the thief to the defendant and that the defendant was unjustly enriched and remained unjustly enriched. An innocent recipient of stolen money may not be enriched at all; if [a thief paid] £20,000 derived from the [victim] to a car dealer for a motor car priced at £20,000, the car dealer would not have been enriched. The car dealer would have received £20,000 for a car worth £20,000.'[427] **3.148**

However, this analysis presupposes that the question whether a defendant has been enriched **3.149** is tested at the time of the action, and notwithstanding some loose dicta to the effect that a defendant must have 'retained' the relevant benefit,[428] the rule is clear that a claimant's cause of action is generally complete at the time when the defendant receives the benefit.[429] It follows that change of position is more accurately understood as a defence than as a denial that the claimant has established the enrichment element of his claim.[430] As it has developed in the English case law, however, it is still a defence that is strongly focused on 'disenrichment',[430a] ie it is most often successfully invoked by defendants relying on financially quantifiable detriment, and in this respect English law differs from the law of Australia, where the High Court has articulated a version of the defence that turns instead on the unconscionability of allowing the claim.[430b]

(b) Qualifying detriment

Most defendants suffer qualifying detriment because 'there has been a reduction in [their] **3.150** assets', but the defence can also be invoked by those who suffer other types of detriment,[431] such as lost earning opportunities[432] and even mental or physical harm.[433] The detriment must be 'extraordinary', in the sense that it would not have occurred had the defendant not been enriched.[434] This principle is wide enough to take in defendants who let their standard of living drift upwards to match their new wealth. These were the facts of *Philip Collins Ltd*

---

[425] E Bant, *The Change of Position Defence* (2009) 151–155.
[426] See 3.155.
[427] *Lipkin Gorman*, n 2, at 563, discussed in *Niru Battery Manufacturing Co v Milestone Trading Ltd (No 1)* [2003] EWCA Civ 1446, [2004] QB 985 ('*Niru (No 1)* (CA)'), at [145] and *Heperu Pty Ltd v Belle* [2009] NSWCA 252, (2009) 76 NSWLR 230, at [150]–[151].
[428] eg *Birmingham*, n 25, at 394; *Boake Allen* (CA), n 367, at [175]; *FII* (SC), n 2, at [162].
[429] See 3.22.
[430] See 3.16–3.17 for the difference between 'denials' and 'defences'.
[430a] *FII (No 2)*, n 53a, at [354].
[430b] *Australian Financial Services and Leasing Pty Ltd v Hills Industries Ltd* [2014] HCA 14, [2104] 307 ALR 512.
[431] *Commerzbank*, n 422, at [39].
[432] *Kinlan v Crimmin* [2006] EWHC 779 (Ch), [2007] 2 BCLC 67, at [60].
[433] *Scottish Equitable*, n 170, at [31]; *Commerzbank*, n 422, at [65]–[72].
[434] *Lipkin Gorman*, n 2, at 580; *Dextra*, n 150, at [38]; *Barons Finance Ltd v Kensington Mortgage Co Ltd* [2011] EWCA Civ 1592, at [28].
[435] [2000] 3 All ER 808, 827–830.

v Davis,[435] where two musicians with a 'relaxed and philosophical' propensity to overspend their income escaped liability to the extent that increases in their outgoings were referable to their receipts from the claimant.

3.151 It seems that transactions entered by a defendant do not count as detriment if they can readily be unwound.[436] Hence, eg, the defence has been refused in respect of tax payments made on a defendant's receipts, because they could be recovered from the Revenue.[437] It is unclear how much trouble and expense are expected of defendants, but in analogous tort damages cases concerning the duty to mitigate, the courts have held that claimants need not undertake difficult litigation but may be required to act against third parties where this would be straightforward.[438] Presumably the defendant should be able to offset the costs of any third party proceedings against his restitutionary liability, and so an outer limit would be set at the point where the costs of these would be greater than the amount due to the claimant.

3.152 It has been held that a defendant's detriment must have been incurred in reliance on his receipt of the relevant benefit.[439] However this creates the unsatisfactory outcome that a good faith defendant is unprotected where he receives a benefit that is stolen or destroyed.[440] The courts would therefore do better to hold that reliance is unnecessary provided that a causal link can be established.[441]

3.153 Assuming that the defendant's enrichment and detriment are causally linked, the enrichment need not precede the detriment: the defence is also available where detriment has been incurred in anticipation of an enrichment that arrives later. This was established by *Dextra Bank & Trust Co Ltd v Bank of Jamaica*.[442] Dextra Bank sent the Bank of Jamaica a cheque for $3 million. Both were the victims of a fraud. The Bank of Jamaica thought that it was buying foreign currency, and Dextra Bank thought that it was making a foreign currency loan. Even before it received Dextra Bank's cheque, the Bank of Jamaica paid third parties whom it mistakenly believed had paid Dextra Bank for the dollars on its behalf. This payment gave the Bank of Jamaica a complete defence to Dextra Bank's claim for the value of the cheque.

(c) Disqualifying conduct

3.154 In *Lipkin Gorman* Lord Goff said that defendants may not rely on the change of position defence where they have acted in bad faith, or are wrongdoers.[443]

---

[436] *Alpha Wealth Financial Services Pty Ltd v Frankland River Olive Co. Ltd* [2008] WASCA 119, (2008) 66 ACSR 594, at [202].
[437] *Hillsdown v Pensions Ombudsman* [1997] 1 All ER 862, 904; *Hinckley and Bosworth BC v Shaw* [2000] LGR 9, 51.
[438] *Pilkington v Wood* [1953] Ch 770; cf *Western Trust & Savings Ltd v Clive Travers & Co* [1997] PNLR 295, 303–304 CA.
[439] *Streiner v Bank Leumi (UK) plc* (QBD 31 October 1985); *Credit Suisse (Monaco) SA v Attar* [2004] EWHC 374 (Comm), at [98]. See too *David Securities*, n 15, at 386; *Rural Municipality of Storthoaks v Mobil Oil Canada Ltd* [1976] 2 SCR 147, 164; *State Bank of New South Wales Ltd v Swiss Bank Corp* (1995) 39 NSWLR 350, NSWCA; *Citygroup Pty Ltd v National Australia Bank Ltd* [2012] NSWCA 381, (2012) 82 NSWLR 391, at [67]–[86].
[440] As noted in *Scottish Equitable*, n 170, at [30]–[31]; *Cressman*, n 18, at [41].
[441] As in *Hua Rong Finance Ltd v Mega Capital Enterprises Ltd* [2000] HKCFI 1310; *National Bank of New Zealand Ltd v Waitaki International Processing (NI) Ltd* [1999] 2 NZLR 211, 228–229, NZCA. Under German law, too, the disenrichment rule in BGB §818 III applies eg where money received by a defendant is embezzled by his employee (RGZ 68, 269) or seized by a foreign power in wartime (RGZ 120, 297, 299).
[442] *Dextra*, n 150, at [38]. See too *Test Claimants in the FII Group Litigation v HMRC* [2008] EWHC 2893 (Ch), [2009] STC 254 ('*FII* (Ch)'), at [344].
[443] *Lipkin Gorman*, n 2, at 580.
[444] *Niru (No 1)* (Comm), n 112; aff'd *Niru (No 1)* (CA), n 427, at [164].

(i) Bad faith

In *Niru Battery Manufacturing Co v Milestone Trading Ltd (No 1)*,[444] Moore-Bick J discussed the **3.155** degree of fault needed to disqualify a defendant from pleading the defence, and his conclusions were endorsed by the Court of Appeal. He held that bad faith takes in dishonesty and is also 'capable of embracing a failure to act in a commercially acceptable way and sharp practice of a kind that falls short of outright dishonesty'.[445] This formulation does not include negligence, suggesting that a defendant can rely on the defence although he has negligently failed to recognize the flawed nature of the transfer by which he has been benefited.[446] Defendants can also rely on the defence although they have changed their position by making foolish investment decisions: if they honestly believe that money is theirs to spend as they choose, then they cannot be criticized for spending it unwisely.[447] Where a defendant does not know, but 'has grounds for believing that the [claimant's] payment may have been made by mistake',[448] Moore-Bick J thought that 'good faith may well dictate that an enquiry be made of the payer', an assessment that is borne out by several other authorities.[449]

The New Zealand Court of Appeal has twice held that where a claimant's money is lost **3.156** through the combined carelessness of claimant and defendant, the court should weigh up the relative fault of the parties when determining the extent to which the defendant's liability is reduced under section 94B of the New Zealand Judicature Act 1908, which establishes a statutory change of position defence for recipients of mistaken payments.[450] In the *Dextra* case,[451] however, the Privy Council declined to introduce the concept of 'relative fault' into the common law version of the defence.

The court gave two reasons. One was that the process of comparing the degrees of fault dis- **3.157** played by the parties was too uncertain. The other was that a claimant's fault does not prevent him from establishing a cause of action,[452] and so it would be 'very strange' if 'the defendant should find his conduct examined to ascertain whether he had been negligent'. The first of these reasons is more persuasive than the second. The claimant's fault is irrelevant when asking whether he has a claim, because this enquiry assumes that the benefit still exists and asks which of the parties has the better right to it. At the later stage when the defence of change of position is considered, this assumption no longer holds good. The benefit has been lost and a different question must be addressed, namely which of the parties should bear the loss. So there would be no inconsistency if the court ignored the claimant's fault at the first stage, but took it into account at the second stage.[453]

(ii) Wrongdoing

When Lord Goff said that wrongdoers could not rely on the change of position defence, he **3.158** may have had it in mind to prevent defendants from relying on the defence where claims are

---

[445] *Niru (No 1)* (Comm), n 112, at [135]. See too *Abou-Rahmah v Abacha* [2006] EWCA Civ 1492, [2007] Bus LR 220, at [49]; *Haugesund*, n 10, at [122].

[446] See too *Abacha*, n 445, at [42]; *Armstrong*, n 101, at [110]. These are stronger than the cases cited by Bant (2009), n 425, at 150–155 for the contrary proposition that negligence is a bar to relying on the defence: *Rose v AIB Group (UK) plc* [2003] EWHC 1737 (Ch), [2003] 2 BCLC 374; *Maersk Air Ltd v Expeditors International (UK) Ltd* [2003] 1 Lloyd's Rep 491; *Fea*, n 46.

[447] *Haugesund*, n 10, at [125].

[448] *Niru (No 1)* (Comm), n 112, at [135].

[449] *Maersk*, n 446; *Fea*, n 46; *Jones v Churcher* [2009] EWHC 772 (QB), [2009] 2 Lloyd's Rep 94; *Armstrong*, n 101, at [289].

[450] *Thomas v Houston Corbett & Co* [1969] NZLR 151, NZCA; *Waitaki*, n 441.

[451] *Dextra*, n 150, at [45].

[452] See 3.65.

[453] Bant (2009), n 425, at 179.

[454] [1998] 2 NZLR 481, 654 and 730, NZHC.

made to recover the profits of wrongdoing, ie in cases which are not concerned with unjust enrichment, but with wrongs. In later cases, however, his words have not been interpreted in this way, and in several of these the defence has been withheld from defendants to unjust enrichment claims on the ground that they have committed criminal offences.

3.159   In *Equiticorp Industries Group Ltd v R (No 47)*,[454] the New Zealand Government could not raise the defence in respect of payments which were made pursuant to a share purchase and buy-back scheme which infringed legislation prohibiting the purchase by a company of its own shares. In *Garland v Consumers' Gas Co Ltd*,[455] a regulated gas utility could not raise the defence against a claim to recover money which it had collected from customers as 'late payment penalties', contrary to a law prohibiting the recovery of interest at a criminal rate. In *Barros Mattos Junior v General Securities & Finance Ltd*,[456] the defendants could not raise the defence because although they had acted in good faith, they had converted US dollars which had been stolen from the claimant into Nigerian naira before paying the money away to third parties, in a transaction that infringed a Nigerian law that requires foreign exchange dealings in Nigeria to be conducted through authorized intermediaries. In *O'Neil v Gale*,[456a] the defendant could not raise the defence against a claim to recover money paid into her bank account for onward transmission to her husband who was running an unlawful collective investment scheme contrary to the Financial Services and Markets Act 2000.

3.160   The disparate nature of these cases suggests that the courts would do well to adopt a flexible attitude towards the question whether the illegality of the defendant's actions should debar him from raising the change of position defence. Yet in *Barros*, Laddie J denied that the courts have any such discretion, and held that, subject to a *de minimis* threshold, they must always disallow the change of position defence—even if this means imposing a heavy penalty on a defendant for a comparatively minor breach of the law.[457] In the result, the defendants were liable to pay US$8 million because they had changed the money into naira before paying it on to third parties, a liability they would not have incurred if they had paid over the money in US dollars. The harshness of this suggests that Laddie J's approach is unduly rigid.

(d) **Special cases**

3.161   In *Haugesund Kommune v Depfa ACS Bank (No 2)* Aikens LJ stated that 'the defence of change of position is a general defence to all restitution claims (for money or other property) based on unjust enrichment'.[458] However, this is not borne out by other cases, which indicate that the defence is not available in response to certain types of claim. Good reasons can be advanced for some, but not for all, of these findings.

(i) Lack of consent and want of authority

3.162   In *Ministry of Health v Simpson*,[459] Lord Simonds held that the Court of Chancery would make no decree against a defendant unless he had behaved unconscientiously, but said that this rule 'did not excuse the wrongly paid legatee from repayment because he had spent what he had been wrongly paid'. This was followed in *Gray v Richards Butler*,[460] where solicitors were not allowed to raise the change of position defence against a claim to recover money paid as fees by the executors of an invalid will. However, there is no good reason to withhold

---

[455] [2004] SCC 25, [2004] 1 SCR 629, at [63]–[66].
[456] [2004] EWHC 1188 (Ch), [2005] 1 WLR 247.
[456a] [2013] EWCA Civ 1554, [2014] Lloyd's Rep FC 202.
[457] [2004] EWHC 1188 (Ch), [2005] 1 WLR 247, at [22]–[30] and [42]–[43].
[458] *Haugesund*, n 10, at [122].
[459] [1951] AC 251, 276.
[460] [2001] WTLR 625.
[461] *Woolwich*, n 2, at 580.

the defence from the good faith recipients of misdirected funds, and in *Lipkin Gorman* Lord Goff attributed Lord Simonds' hostility towards the defence to 'the mistaken assumption that mere expenditure of money may be regarded as amounting to a change of position'.[461]

(ii) Undue influence

Where a wife is induced to give domestic security for business borrowing, the lender usually acts in good faith, since it has no more than an attenuated constructive notice of the fact that she has been unduly influenced by her husband. The lender inevitably changes its position by lending money or not calling in existing debts, but if it were allowed to invoke the defence, the wife's protection would be destroyed. This suggests that cases like *Barclays Bank plc v O'Brien*[462] and *Royal Bank of Scotland plc v Etridge (No 2)*[463] may be explained on the basis that the bank cannot invoke the defence because this would subvert the protective policies implemented by the cases.[464]

3.163

(iii) Failure of basis

When value is transferred to a recipient on an agreed basis, he knows that he may have to repay a like sum if the basis fails to materialize, suggesting that he cannot spend the money in the honest belief that the transferor had an unqualified intention to benefit him. *Goss v Chilcott*[465] was like this. The defendants borrowed money from the claimant under a void agreement, which was paid to a third party at the defendants' request. This arrangement did not constitute a change of position because the defendants knew that if the third party failed to repay the money then the claimant would require the defendants to repay it themselves. It seems, however, that a claimant may be entitled to the defence where he incurs expenses in the course of preparing for performance of a contract that is later frustrated.[466]

3.164

(iv) Undue tax payments

On several occasions, the courts have assumed that the Government commits to public expenditure in anticipation of tax revenue, with the result that it can argue change of position in reply to claims to recover money paid as tax that is not due.[467] However, central government spending plans are almost never tied to specific tax revenue streams and the better view is that 'the relationship between long-term spending commitments and short-term revenue raising measures is not sufficiently close to establish a causal link between taxation and Government expenditure'.[468] That point aside, it has since been held that in any case change of position should not be available as a response to *Woolwich* claims because this would 'unacceptably subvert, and be inconsistent with, the high principles of public policy

3.165

---

[462] *O'Brien*, n 190.

[463] *Etridge* (HL), n 184.

[464] M Chen-Wishart, 'In Defence of Unjust Factors: A Study of Recission for Duress, Fraud and Exploitation' in Johnston and Zimmermann, n 28, at 170–173.

[465] *Goss*, n 253, esp at 799; aff'd in *Haugesund*, n 10, at [127]. See too the finding at first instance in *Haugesund* that it was 'completely fatal' to the defence that 'the municipalities knew from the start that the amounts advanced by Depfa were to be repaid': [2009] EWHC 2227 (Comm), [2010] Lloyd's Rep PN 21, at [163].

[466] *BP*, n 51, at 800 and 804: the statutory allowance for such expenses given by the Law Reform (Frustrated Contracts) Act 1943, s 1(2) is a statutory example of the change of position defence. cf *Saba Yachts Ltd v Fish Pacific Ltd* [2006] NZHC 1452, at [58]–[63]: no defence where money spent on materials that do not actually help the defendant perform his contractual obligations.

[467] *FII* (Ch), n 442, at [344] (not considered on appeals to the CA and SC); *Bloomsbury International Ltd v Sea Fish Industry Authority* [2009] EWHC 1721 (QB), [2010] 1 CMLR 12, at [137].

[468] N Cleary, 'Property, Proportionality, and the Change of Position Defence' in Elliott et al, n 30, at 132. See too Law Com No 227, n 365, at para 11.12; E Bant, 'Change of Position as a Defence to Restitution of Unlawfully Exacted Tax' [2012] LMCLQ 122, 132.

[468a] *Test Claimants in the FII Group Litigation (No 2)* [2014] EWHC 4302 (Ch), [2015] BTC 3, at [315].

which led to recognition of the *Woolwich* cause of action as a separate one in the English law of unjust enrichment, with its own specific "unjust factor".'[468a]

(v) Insolvency policies

3.166 It has been held that that the change of position defence can be raised against a claim to recover benefits transferred under a transaction that is void by reason of section 127 of the Insolvency Act 1986,[469] and also against a claim to recover benefits conferred under a transaction defrauding creditors contrary to section 423.[470] Some Commonwealth statutory regimes analogous to the regime contained in sections 239–241 provide for such a defence in general terms.[471] However, it is arguable that the defence is contrary to the purpose of these sections, namely to claw back funds for the general body of creditors and maintain proper priority between them, and that the point of the 1986 Act is to place their interests above those of recipients who may have given little or nothing in exchange for the benefits they receive.

(2) Ministerial Receipt

3.167 If an agent receives a benefit from a claimant for the value of which he must immediately account to his principal, and he pays this value to the principal in good faith, then the agent can now rely on the change of position defence in response to any claim in unjust enrichment.[472] Even prior to the recognition of the change of position defence in *Lipkin Gorman*, however, an agent could escape liability if he paid the value of such a benefit over to his principal,[473] or applied it in accordance with his instructions,[474] provided that he acted in good faith and without notice of the claim.[475]

3.168 On one view, this rule should be understood as an early version of the change of position defence, which has now been subsumed by the wider version of the defence that was recognized in *Lipkin Gorman* (wider because it is not restricted to agents and is generally available).[476] On another, better view, an agent who receives a benefit for which he must account to his principal can escape liability in unjust enrichment whether or not he pays the value of the benefit over to his principal, and whether or not he takes good title to property which he then uses as his own, because his liability to account means that he never takes the value of the benefit for himself, and that the principal alone is enriched by the transaction.[477]

---

[469] *Rose*, n 446.
[470] *4Eng Ltd v Harper* [2009] EWHC 2633 (Ch), [2010] BPIR 1, at [14].
[471] T O'Sullivan, 'Defending a Liquidator's Claim for Repayment of a Voidable Transaction' (1997) 9 Otago LR 111; also *Re Ernst and Young Inc* (1997) 147 DLR (4th) 229, Alberta CA; *Countrywide Banking Corp Ltd v Dean* [1998] AC 338, PC; *Cripps v Lakeview Farm Fresh Ltd (in rec)* [2006] 1 NZLR 238, NZHC.
[472] As noted in *Churcher*, n 449, at [67].
[473] *D Owen & Co v Cronk* [1895] 1 QB 265, CA; *Kleinwort, Sons & Co v Dunlop Rubber Co* (1907) 97 LT 26, HL; *Admiralty Commissioners v National Provincial and Union Bank* (1922) 127 LT 452; *Gower v Lloyds and National Provincial Bank* [1938] 1 All ER 766, CA; *Transvaal and Delagoa Bay Investment Co Ltd v Atkinson* [1944] 1 All ER 579; *Australia and New Zealand Banking Group Ltd v Westpac Banking Corp* (1987) 164 CLR 662.
[474] *Holland v Russell* (1861) 1 B & S 424, 121 ER 773; aff'd (1863) 4 B & S 14, 122 ER 365.
[475] *Continental Caoutchouc & Gutta Percha Co v Kleinwort, Sons & Co* (1904) 90 LT 474, 477, CA; *Nizam of Hyderabad v Jung* [1957] Ch 185, 239 and 248, CA.
[476] Burrows (2011), n 99, at 565.
[477] This argument is made in JP Moore, *Restitution from Banks* (unpublished D Phil thesis, Oxford University, 2000). See too P Birks, 'The Burden on the Bank' in FD Rose (ed), *Restitution and Banking Law* (1998) 209–210.
[478] See 3.16–3.17 for the difference between denials and defences.

On this view, a claim in unjust enrichment lies against the principal, and no claim lies against **3.169** the agent, because the principal is enriched at the claimant's expense and the agent is not. If this is correct, then the results (though not the reasoning) of the cases where the 'payment over' defence was allowed can be explained on the basis that the agent came under an immediate accounting duty when he received the benefit and could therefore have escaped liability whether or not he had paid the value of the benefit over to the principal. If this argument is correct, then it may be that it should be understood as a denial that the agent is enriched rather than as a defence to the claim.[478]

Support for the view that English law enables defendants to escape liability where they have **3.170** received benefits ministerially can be drawn from a series of cases where agents have escaped liability for knowing receipt even though they have not paid the value of the benefits they have received to their principals;[479] liability for knowing receipt is not itself a liability in unjust enrichment,[480] but the logic of the courts' reasoning also applies to unjust enrichment claims. Agents have also escaped liability in some cases of this kind,[481] but the predominant view remains that payment over is required for the agent to escape liability,[482] and the courts would do well to develop the law by definitively dropping this requirement for payment over.

This would further the policy purposes which underpin the special treatment of ministerial **3.171** receipt. These are the protection of agents who would otherwise be caught in the middle of disputes between their principals and third parties, which would have the effect of reducing their ability to perform a valuable function as intermediaries.[483] It also makes the law simpler and reduces multiplicity of suits.

(3) Bona Fide Purchase

Most claims in unjust enrichment are made against direct recipients of benefits, but some are **3.172** made against remote recipients, ie recipients of benefits that have passed through the hands of a third party on their way from the claimant to the defendant.[484] In cases of the latter kind the defendant can escape liability if he can show that he received the benefit in good faith and without notice of the claim, and that he gave value to the third party in exchange for the benefit. In *Lipkin Gorman*,[485] the House of Lords clearly contemplated that bona fide purchase could be a defence to a common law claim in unjust enrichment against a remote recipient, although it was not available on the facts of the case; it can also operate as a defence to equitable claims, eg, those of the kind recognized in *Re Diplock*.[486]

---

[479] *Barnes*, n 132, at 254–255; *Westpac Banking Corp v Savin* [1985] 2 NZLR 41, 69; *Agip (Africa) Ltd v Jackson* [1990] Ch 265, 291–292; *Trustor AB v Smallbone (No 2)* [2001] 3 All ER 987, 994; *Twinsectra*, n 272, at [106].

[480] See 3.51.

[481] *Sadler v Evans* (1766) 4 Burr 1984, 1985; 98 ER 34, 35; *Greenway v Hurd* (1794) 4 TR 553, 555; 100 ER 1171, 1173–1174; *Duke of Norfolk v Worthy* (1808) 1 Camp 337, 339; 170 ER 977, 979; *Ellis v Goulton* [1893] 1 QB 350, 353–354, CA; *Jeremy D Stone Consultants Ltd v National Westminster Bank plc* [2013] EWHC 208 (Ch) [242]–[243].

[482] *Buller v Harrison* (1777) 2 Cowp 565, 568; 98 ER 1243, 1245–1246; *Cox v Prentice* (1815) 3 M & S 344, 105 ER 601; *Bavins & Sims v London & South Western Bank Ltd* [1900] 1 QB 270, CA; *British American Continental Bank v British Bank for Foreign Trade* [1926] 1 KB 328, CA; *Portman Building Society v Hamlyn Taylor Neck (a firm)* [1998] 4 All ER 202, 207, CA.

[483] As recognized in German law: H Dörner, 'Change of Position and *Wegfall der Bereicherung*' in WJ Swadling (ed), *The Limits of Restitutionary Claims: A Comparative Analysis* (1997) 65–66.

[484] See 3.51.

[485] *Lipkin Gorman*, n 2.

[486] *GL Baker Ltd v Medway Building and Supplies Ltd* [1958] 3 All ER 540, 543; *Re J Leslie Engineers Co Ltd* [1976] 1 WLR 292, 299. For discussion of *Diplock* claims see 3.50.

[487] Sir P Millett, 'Tracing the Proceeds of Fraud' (1991) 107 LQR 71, 82.

(a) Rationale

3.173 It has been said that the defence of bona fide purchase is 'simply the paradigm change of position defence',[487] but the better view is that these defences are distinct. One reason, identified by Lord Goff in *Lipkin Gorman*, is that 'change of position will only avail a defendant to the extent that his position has been changed; whereas, where bona fide purchase is invoked, no inquiry is made (in most cases) into the adequacy of the consideration'.[488] Hence, the change of position defence only operates pro tanto, to the extent that the defendant has suffered detriment, whereas the bona fide purchase defence operates as an absolute bar: provided that the defendant has given some consideration in exchange for the relevant property, the claim will fail completely, whatever the value of the consideration given.

3.174 This difference reflects the different rationales of the defences. The change of position defence protects the defendant's interest in making spending decisions freely, without fear that a claim in unjust enrichment might later invalidate his assumptions about the means at his disposal. The bona fide purchase defence protects the security of certain classes of purchase transaction. The rules of property law provide that a bona fide purchaser for value can acquire clear legal title although the vendor's title is defective,[489] and the function of the defence may simply be to prevent the law of unjust enrichment from stultifying these property law rules by preventing a claimant from recovering the value of property, title to which has passed to a defendant who is a bona fide purchaser.[490] Alternatively, the defence may have the wider function of preventing claims in unjust enrichment from stultifying the contractual arrangements made between the defendant and the vendor from whom the defendant has received the claimant's property.[491] If the latter explanation is correct, then there is no reason to limit the availability of the defence to situations where an exception to the *nemo dat* principle is engaged.

(b) Giving value

3.175 In *Lipkin Gorman*,[492] the claimant firm had a claim in unjust enrichment against the defendant casino, which had received money stolen from the firm by a fraudulent partner. The casino could not plead bona fide purchase. The casino had received the money in good faith. It had also given value. But, because the contracts of licensed casinos with their customers were void,[493] there was no legal nexus between what the casino gave and what it received from the gambler. This defines one important limitation on the defence. Even where it would otherwise be effective, it does not work unless value passes under a valid contract between the defendant and the third party. A factual exchange will not suffice.[494]

---

[488] *Lipkin Gorman*, n 2, at 580–581.

[489] The most prominent example at common law is that one who gives value for money in good faith becomes owner of that money: *Miller v Race* (1758) 1 Burr 452, 97 ER 398; *Clarke*, n 119; D Fox, *Property Rights in Money* (2008) paras 8.20–8.83. In equity, the rule that a bona fide purchaser of legal title takes free of any equitable title or interest in the property was largely settled in the late seventeenth century: DEC Yale, 'Introduction' in *Lord Nottingham's Chancery Cases, vol II* (Selden Society, Vol 79 for 1961) 160–194. For the current law, see C Harpum et al, *Megarry & Wade: The Law of Real Property* (8th edn, 2012) paras 8.05–8.25; D Hayton et al, *Underhill and Hayton: Law Relating to Trusts and Trustees* (18th edn, 2010) paras 99.14–99.58.

[490] Birks (2005), n 7, at 240–244; Swadling (2008), n 123, at 656–657.

[491] K Barker, 'Bona Fide Purchase as a Defence to Unjust Enrichment Claims: A Concise Restatement' [1999] RLR 75; Burrows (2011), n 99, at 577–580. For discussion of contract as a legal ground for a defendant's enrichment, see 3.226ff.

[492] *Lipkin Gorman*, n 2.

[493] A rule that has since been altered by legislation: Gambling Act 2005, ss 334 and 335.

[494] See too *Hambrouck*, n 113, at 326 and 329: no defence in respect of money paid to a mistress for past or future cohabitation because this was paid in exchange for an immoral consideration that was not

Lord Templeman and Lord Goff also held that executory consideration, in the form of **3.176** a promise to repay money in the future, does not count as value for the purpose of the defence.[495] However, their comments on this point were obiter, and are out of line with older authorities which hold that a bank which accepts the deposit of a cheque from its customer and irrevocably credits his account may qualify as a holder for value of the instrument.[496] Hence the best view is that executory consideration can count as value for the purposes of the bona fide purchase rule, and their Lordships' dicta should be understood to mean only that a bank gives no value where it accepts money on deposit but merely makes a provisional credit entry to its customer's account.[497]

(c) Disqualifying conduct

The dishonest are clearly excluded from the defence of bona fide purchase. They cannot be **3.177** said to have given value in good faith.[498] However this defence has traditionally required not only good faith but also absence of notice of the adverse rights. In *Nelson v Larholt*[499] the defendant cashed cheques for a third party. The money which he received in return when he presented the cheques came from the estate of a deceased person which the third party was administering. After he had been replaced, the estate sought restitution. Denning J found that the defendant had honestly given value but had no defence because it was apparent on the face of the cheques that they were drawn on an estate account.

The question is what standard should apply. The Chancery doctrine, now in section 199 of the **3.178** Law of Property Act 1925, was evolved in relation to conveyancing.[500] 'Without notice' meant 'without failing to make the inquiries that a reasonable person would make' and was made yet stricter by the assumption that the reasonable person always made the well-understood inquiries known to conveyancers. Outside the conveyancing context, the same strictness would bring commerce to a halt.[501] It is clear that this rigour does not apply to ordinary dealing where no fixed procedures are customary. Whether we say that a different standard applies or, letting the standard take the strain, that the reasonable man behaves very differently in different contexts, it is probable that 'without notice' now adds little if anything to the requirement of good faith. The reasonable person must not shut his eyes to obvious evidence of impropriety.[502]

It was unequivocally laid down in *Re Nisbet and Potts' Contract*,[503] albeit still within the **3.179** conveyancing context, that the onus of proving every element of the defence lay on the

---

recognized by law; *Noble Trustees*, n 132, at [113]: no bona fide purchase defence in respect of money paid to divorced wife pursuant to consent order that was later set aside, because the transaction then had 'to be treated, as far as possible, as if it had never happened, or at any rate had never had any legal effect'.

[495] *Lipkin Gorman*, n 2, at 562 and 577.

[496] *Pease v Hirst* (1829) 10 B & C 122, 109 ER 396; *Hulse v Hulse* (1856) 17 CB 711, 139 ER 1256; *ex parte Richdale* (1881) 19 Ch D 409, 417 and 418, CA; *Capital and Counties Bank Ltd v Gordon* [1903] AC 240, 245, HL. See too Bills of Exchange Act 1881, ss 27 and 29.

[497] Fox, n 489, at paras 8.33–8.38.

[498] cf Sale of Goods Act 1979, s 61: 'A thing is deemed to be done in good faith within the meaning of this Act when it is in fact done honestly, whether it is done negligently or not.'

[499] [1948] 1 KB 339.

[500] The doctrine of notice now has only a very limited role to play in registered conveyancing. For discussion of the extent to which the registration of interests in land can operate as a defence to claims in unjust enrichment under English law, see E Bant, 'Registration as a Defence to Claims in Unjust Enrichment: Australia and England Compared' [2011] Conv 309, 322–326.

[501] '[I]f we were to extend the doctrine of constructive notice to commercial transactions we should be doing an infinite mischief and paralysing the trade of the country': *Manchester Trust v Furness* [1895] 2 QB 539, 545, CA.

[502] *Eagle Trust plc v SBC Securities Ltd* [1993] 1 WLR 484, 505–506.

[503] [1906] 1 Ch 386 at 404, 409 and 410, CA. See too *Pilcher v Rawlins* (1872) LR 7 Ch App 259, 268–269, CA.

defendant. Although the onus is easily shifted, contrary dicta cannot throw doubt on that proposition.[504]

(4) Estoppel

3.180 Before the formal recognition that a change of position would operate as a defence to claims in unjust enrichment, some of its work was done by estoppel. This depended on establishing that the claimant had made a representation to the effect that payments might once and for all be relied on or had been finally checked and, further, that that representation had become binding by detrimental reliance.[505] *Avon County Council v Howlett*[506] confirmed that such an estoppel provided complete defence. The reliance need not have consumed the entirety of the enrichment received.

3.181 It was predictable thereafter that, armed with change of position, which diminishes the liability pro tanto, the courts would lean against finding the facts necessary to support an estoppel. The Court of Appeal has twice shown itself unwilling to apply the logic of the *Avon* case to create a total defence regardless of the scale of the recipient's reliance. In each case the court invoked an exception to cover, and prevent, gross disproportion.[507] 'Gross' will soon mean 'any'. Under such a regime it will be impossible to effect a permanent, binding estoppel which will be stronger than the defence of change of position. Yet the two defences are different and estoppel has a role to play that is not performed by change of position. Change of position is about the fair allocation of loss where the value transferred from the claimant to the defendant has been dissipated through no fault of the defendant's, while estoppel is about holding the claimant to his undertakings where these have been detrimentally relied upon by the defendant.[508]

3.182 In the *Scottish Equitable* case,[509] Robert Walker LJ was attracted to the argument that the court should assess the detriment suffered by the defendant at the date of trial, and that application of the change of position defence at this date would always negative the defendant's detriment, leaving him unable to raise the defence of estoppel. This argument was misconceived because it makes the application of the estoppel defence conditional on the prior application of the change of position defence. There is no justification for this. It is a matter for the defendant to decide which defences he chooses to rely upon, and it does not follow from the fact that a defendant *could* invoke the change of position defence if he chose that he *must* invoke it, and is therefore disabled from invoking the defence of estoppel instead.[510]

(5) Counter-Restitution Impossible

3.183 A claimant who seeks restitution of an unjust enrichment must make counter-restitution of benefits received from the defendant in exchange. If counter-restitution is impossible, the

---

[504] *Polly Peck International plc v Nadir (No 2)* [1992] 4 All ER 769, 781, CA; *Barclays Bank plc v Boulter* [1999] 1 WLR 513, 518, HL.

[505] *Skyring v Greenwood* (1825) 4 B & C 281, 107 ER 1064; *Holt*, n 14; *Waring & Gillow*, n 169, at 692–694.

[506] [1983] 1 WLR 605, CA.

[507] *Scottish Equitable*, n 170, at [44]; *National Westminster Bank Plc v Somer International (UK) Ltd* [2001] EWCA Civ 970, [2002] QB 1286, at [46]–[48] and [67].

[508] Birks (2005), n 7, at 235–236 where he argues that 'the legitimate way to prevent overkill is…to construe [the claimant's representations] as prospectively revocable in the event of the representor's making a mistake.' Bant (2009), n 425, at 228–229 rightly doubts that the courts would be willing to find implied terms of this kind.

[509] *Scottish Equitable*, n 170, at [45]–[47].

[510] Bant (2009), n 425, at 226–227, endorsed in *TRA Global Pty Ltd v Kebakoska* [2011] VSC 480, (2011) 209 IR 453, at [37].

claim to restitution will be barred. However, the courts are nowadays increasingly content to see counter-restitution made in money, as the flexible approach which they have long taken in equity is now also taken at common law.[511] Cases in which counter-restitution is thought to be impossible have therefore become vanishingly rare,[512] and it has become inaccurate to say that 'counter-restitution impossible' is a general defence to claims in unjust enrichment; it is, rather, a pre-condition for recovery that the amount recoverable by a claimant should be reduced by the amount of the benefits that he received from the defendant.[513]

There is an overlap between the counter-restitution requirement and the change of position defence, to the extent that both rules enable a defendant to escape liability where he has incurred the cost of conferring a benefit on the claimant. However there are differences between them that make it impossible to say that the counter-restitution requirement is simply a manifestation of the change of position defence. One is that a defendant who has induced a claimant to transfer a benefit by a threat or a fraudulent misrepresentation is entitled to counter-restitution,[514] although he would be disqualified from pleading change of position.[515] Another is that in cases where the cost to the claimant of conferring a benefit on the defendant is greater than the value of the benefit to the defendant, the claimant's cost will count as detriment under the change of position defence, but the defendant need not make counter-restitution of more than the value of the benefit. **3.184**

It follows that the best explanation of the counter-restitution requirement does not go to the defendant's disenrichment in the same way as the change of position defence. Instead the rule rests on the fact that, where there has been an exchange between the parties, and the claimant recovers the benefit he has conferred on the defendant, the basis on which he received the benefit from the defendant fails. Were he to recover without making counter-restitution, the defendant would therefore have a claim against him on the ground of failure of basis.[516] **3.185**

This still does not explain why the law makes counter-restitution a pre-condition for the claimant's right of recovery, rather than simply allowing the claim and leaving the defendant to bring a counter-claim. There are two ways to understand this rule. One is to see it as a rule of convenience that understands the parties to have a claim and counter-claim, and requires these to be set off against one another in order to avoid a multiplicity of suits. The other is to see it as a special rule applying to benefits acquired in exchange for other benefits, the purpose of which is to ensure that the mutual reciprocity of the parties' performances is reflected in the unwinding process that follows a failure of the basis for their exchange. To achieve this, the benefits each has transferred to the other are netted off, so that as they go **3.186**

---

[511] Equity: *Erlanger v New Sombrero Phosphate Co* (1878) 3 App Cas 1218, 1278–1279, HL; *Alati v Kruger* (1955) 94 CLR 216, 223–224; *O'Sullivan v Management Agency and Music Ltd* [1985] QB 428, CA. Common law: *Atlantic Lines & Navigation Co Inc v Hallam Ltd (The Lucy)* [1983] 1 Lloyd's Rep 188, 202; *Halpern v Halpern (Nos 1 and 2)* [2007] EWCA Civ 291, [2008] QB 195.

[512] For a modern case in which the relationship between the parties would have made counter-restitution exceptionally difficult to quantify, see *Crystal Palace (2000) Ltd v Dowie* [2007] EWHC 1392 (QB), [2007] IRLR 682, at [210]–[218].

[513] *Dunbar Bank plc v Nadeem* [1998] 3 All ER 876, 884, CA; Birks (2005), n 7, at 228.

[514] *Halpern*, n 511.

[515] As he would have acted in bad faith: 3.155. An exception to the principle that even a fraudster is entitled to counter-restitution is established by the Marine Insurance Act 1906, s 84, which provides that an insurer which avoids a policy for fraud need not return any premium. Whether this punitive rule is justified by the special circumstances of insurance business is questionable.

[516] *Spence v Crawford* [1939] 3 All ER 271, 288–289, HL; *Hew*, n 190, at [43]; *Halpern*, n 511, at [74] citing GH Treitel, *The Law of Contract* (11th edn, 2003) 380: 'the essential point is that the representee should not be unjustly enriched at the representor's expense; that the representor should not be prejudiced is a secondary consideration, which is only taken into account when some benefit has been received by the representee.'

back and forth between the parties, there is only ever one single rolling enrichment consisting in the difference between them, and thus only ever one possible claim.[517] On this view of the rule, it enables the defendant to deny that the claimant has established the enrichment element of his claim.[518]

3.187 In *Kleinwort Benson Ltd v Sandwell BC*,[519] Hobhouse J effectively adopted the latter analysis. The case concerned an interest rate swap contract that had been performed for more than six years before the commencement of the action. The question arose whether the claimant bank should have to make counter-restitution of payments received more than six years previously, given that an independent claim by the defendant council to recover these payments would now be time-barred. The judge held that all payments both ways should be taken into account when quantifying the claim, proceeding on the basis that, as interest rates fluctuated and payments went back and forth between the parties, there was one single rolling enrichment consisting in the difference between the value of their performances. It followed that the bank's claim was only for the net amount that it was owed following the most recent payment under the contract (which had been made within the limitation period).[520]

3.188 Note, finally, that there are situations where the claimant is exempt from the counter-restitution requirement. Such exemptions arise in respect of benefits that the defendant ought never to have transferred to the claimant. In *Guinness plc v Saunders*,[521] eg, the House of Lords held that a company could recover money paid to a director for special services in connection with a takeover bid without making counter-restitution of the value of the services. These should have been performed by the director qua director, and he was in breach of fiduciary duty in taking special payment for them. The court was anxious to give no encouragement to those who breach their fiduciary duties, but it is hard to reconcile its approach with the allowance for work and skill that has been made in other cases in favour of fiduciaries who are ordered to disgorge unauthorized profits in actions founded on breach of fiduciary duty.[522]

(6) Passing On

3.189 The term 'passing on' describes the argument that a claimant is not entitled to restitution because he has passed on the loss he suffered when he transferred a benefit to the defendant. There are two ways in which this argument could be understood. It could be said that restitution is denied where the claimant has passed on his loss to a third party because in such a case the cost to the claimant of conferring the benefit on the defendant is zero. On this view, the defendant escapes liability because the claimant cannot establish one of the ingredients of his action, namely that the defendant's enrichment was gained at his expense.[523]

---

[517] The difference between these two conceptualizations has been extensively discussed by German legal scholars. For a summary of their debates, see B Häcker, *Consequences of Impaired Consent Transfers* (2009) 71–77.

[518] For the difference between 'denials' and 'defences', see 3.16–3.17.

[519] *Sandwell*, n 29.

[520] *Sandwell*, n 29, at 941. See too *South Tyneside*, n 47, at 978–979; *Goss*, n 253, at 798; *Skandinaviska Enskilda Banken AB (Publ), Singapore Branch v Asia Pacific Breweries (Singapore) Pte Ltd* [2011] SGCA 22, [2011] 3 SLR 540, at [126]–[130].

[521] [1990] 2 AC 663, HL.

[522] As in *Boardman v Phipps* [1967] 2 AC 46, HL. After Lord Goff's statement in *Guinness*, n 521, at 701, that allowances should be restricted to cases where an award would not encourage fiduciaries to put themselves in a position of conflict, the English courts have become less generous: *Quarter Master UK Ltd (in liq) v Pyke* [2004] EWHC 1815 (Ch), [2005] 1 BCLC 245, at [76]–[77]; *Cobbetts LLP v Hodge* [2009] EWHC 786 (Ch), at [118]; *Imageview Management Ltd v Jack* [2009] EWCA Civ 63, [2009] Bus LR 1034, at [54]–[61].

[523] See 3.37ff.

This presupposes that the 'loss' which a claimant must have sustained in order to satisfy the requirement that the defendant was enriched at his expense is not an initial loss sustained at the time of the transfer, but a subsisting loss that continues up to the time of the action. This is hard to reconcile with the rule that a cause of action in unjust enrichment generally accrues at the time when the defendant is enriched.[524]

A second version of the argument conceives it to be a defence rather than a denial that the defendant's enrichment was gained at the claimant's expense. This version locates the reason for withholding restitution in the following considerations.[525] Where a third party to whom the claimant passes on his loss is thereby the remote source of the defendant's enrichment, it may be that the third party does not mean to enrich the claimant and thus the defendant, in which case the best outcome would be to return the benefit received by the defendant to the third party, either directly by allowing the third party to sue the defendant himself,[526] or indirectly by allowing the claimant to sue the defendant on the condition that he accounts for the fruits of his action to the third party.[527] If this is impossible, eg, because the third party can no longer be identified, the benefit must either be left in the hands of the defendant, or returned to the claimant, and since neither party deserves it, the preferable option is to let the gain lie where it falls, in the defendant's hands. The defendant therefore escapes liability because ordering restitution would produce the right result as between the claimant and the defendant, but the wrong result as between the claimant and the third party, since it would result in the claimant's unjust enrichment at the third party's expense. Denying restitution also produces a wrong result, as between the defendant and the third party, but there is no social interest in using scarce judicial resources to replace one wrong result with another by redirecting an unjust enrichment at the third party's expense from the defendant to the claimant. **3.190**

If this explanation is correct, then there are two cases in which passing on does not prevent restitution, although the claimant suffers no subsisting loss. The first is where the third party does not mean to benefit the claimant and thus the defendant, and the defendant's enrichment can be returned to him indirectly by allowing the claim on the condition that the claimant account to him for the fruits of the action. In this case, allowing the passing on defence would prevent the law from reaching the best result since it would leave a benefit in the defendant's hands that should go to the third party. The second case is where the third party meant the claimant to be enriched in all events and regardless of whether he also recovers from the defendant. In this case passing on should not be a defence because awarding restitution will not produce the wrong result as between the claimant and the third party. **3.191**

This second version of passing on was adopted by the legislature when enacting section 80(3) of the Value Added Tax Act 1994.[528] VAT is an indirect tax on consumers collected from businesses which can choose whether to include a VAT element in the charges they make for their products or services. If a business does this, and it transpires that the VAT was not due, then allowing the business to recover its VAT payment would unjustly enrich the business at the expense of the customers who effectively provided the money, unless secure mechanisms are put in place to ensure that the repayment is passed back to them.[529] Otherwise, the **3.192**

---

[524] For which see 3.22.

[525] Further discussion: Rush, n 97, esp at ch 10.

[526] See the cases discussed in 3.42–3.45, esp *ITC* (Ch), n 40; and cf *Niru (No 1)* (Comm), n 112, at [145].

[527] cf *Commissioner of State Revenue (Vic) v Royal Insurance Australia Ltd* (1994) 182 CLR 51, 78.

[528] M Chowdry, 'Unjust Enrichment and Section 80(3) of the Value Added Tax Act 1994' [2004] BTR 620.

[529] *Lamdec Ltd v C & E Commissioners* [1991] VATTR 296; *C & E Commissioners v McMaster Stores (Scotland) Ltd* 1996 SLT 935; *C & E Commissioners v National Westminster Bank plc* [2003] EWHC 1822 (Ch), [2003] STC 1072. And note VATA 1994, s 80A.

business cannot recover the money because it has no better claim to it than HMRC. Note that if the business does not adjust its prices to include the VAT element, but absorbs the cost of paying output tax into its overheads, then allowing it to reclaim the payments would not result in its unjust enrichment at its customers' expense as they cannot have been the source of the money, and in this case the defence is not available.[530]

3.193 The question whether passing on is a defence to common law claims in unjust enrichment arose in the litigation spawned by the discovery that many interest rate swap contracts between local authorities and banks in the late 1980s and early 1990s were void because beyond the authorities' powers. To cover their payments out on interest swaps which later turned out to be void, some banks had entered valid back-to-back swap contracts with other banks in which the risks were reversed. These hedge contracts ensured that money lost under the void swap contract came back to the bank under the hedge. In response to claims in unjust enrichment by certain banks which had entered hedge contracts, some defendant councils argued that the claims should fail because the banks' losses had been passed on.

3.194 In *Kleinwort Benson Ltd v Birmingham CC*[531] the Court of Appeal rejected this argument for two reasons: first, because the payments received by the claimant bank from another bank under the hedge contract were not relevantly connected with the payments made by the claimant to the defendant under the swaps contract;[532] and, secondly, because a claimant need not show that he has suffered a loss that exactly corresponds with the defendant's gain provided he can show a causal link between the defendant's gain and some loss to the claimant.[533] The first reason was a finding of fact that the claimant had not passed on its loss to its counter-party under the hedge contract; if that was the ground for the court's decision then its second, broader reason for denying the defence was not the ratio of the case.[534] Also, the proposition that a claimant need not show that his loss corresponded to the defendant's gain has not been universally accepted. Some courts have held that a claimant's entitlement is capped at the amount of his loss if this is lower than the amount of the defendant's gain, and there are good reasons for thinking that this narrower rule should be preferred.[535]

(7) Limitation

(a) Limitation periods

3.195 The primary source for time limits is now the Limitation Act 1980. This statute contains nothing explicitly about unjust enrichment. In this it reflects the earlier cast of mind which hid this area of law under the corners of contract and trusts. Section 5 says: 'An action founded on simple contract shall not be brought after the expiration of six years from the date on which the cause of action accrued.' In *Kleinwort Benson Ltd v Sandwell BC*,[536] an elaborate exercise in statutory interpretation allowed Hobhouse J to conclude that this rule applied to actions for money had and received. Common law claims in unjust enrichment

---

[530] *National Provincial BS v C & E Commissioners* [1996] V & DR 153; *Baines & Ernst Ltd v HMRC* [2006] EWCA Civ 1040, [2006] STC 1632, stressing that the burden of proof is on HMRC to show that there has been no absorption.

[531] *Birmingham*, n 25. See too *South Tyneside*, n 47, at 984–985 and 987.

[532] *Birmingham*, n 25, at 399.

[533] *Birmingham*, n 25, at 394–395. See too *Mason*, n 90, at 146; *Royal Insurance*, n 527, at 75; *Roxborough*, n 23, at [25]–[26].

[534] *Rush*, n 97, at 39.

[535] See 3.41.

[536] *Sandwell*, n 29, at 942–943. See too *Diplock*, n 129, at 514.

are thus generally barred after six years,[537] unless a different period is prescribed by the 1980 Act or other legislation.

Equitable claims for which no period is prescribed by statute, eg claims to avoid transactions **3.196** for undue influence, are barred only by laches,[538] but where an equitable claim is similar to a common law claim that is governed by a statutory limitation period, the court has a discretion to proceed by way of analogy by applying the statutory limitation period.[539]

Statutory limitation periods are laid down for the following claims: six years for claims under **3.197** the Law Reform (Frustrated Contracts) Act 1943;[540] two years for claims under the Civil Liability (Contribution) Act 1978;[541] twelve years for claims for restitution of a deceased person's estate;[542] and six years for claims by beneficiaries to recover misdirected trust property from third parties to whom the trustees have conveyed it.[543] Also, many statutory restitutionary regimes make special provision for limitation that differs from the usual six-year rule at common law.[544]

(b) Date of commencement

Limitation periods generally run from the date when the claimant's cause of action accrues, **3.198** and a cause of action in unjust enrichment normally accrues at the date when the defendant receives a benefit from the claimant.[545] Special rules for ascertaining the date when time starts to run on a claim under the Civil Liability (Contribution) Act 1978 are set down in section 10(3) and (4) of the Limitation Act 1980.[546]

---

[537] *ITC* (CA), n 18, at [23].

[538] As in eg *Wright v Vanderplank* (1856) 8 De GM & G 133, 44 ER 340; *Allcard v Skinner* (1887) 36 Ch D 145; *Azaz v Denton* [2009] EWHC 1759 (QB), at [106]–[122]; *Evans v Lloyd* [2013] EWHC 1725 (Ch), [2013] WTLR 1137, at [79].

[539] *Molloy v Mutual Reserve Life Insurance Co* (1906) 94 LT 756, 762, CA; *Diplock*, n 129, at 514; *Sandwell*, n 29, at 943; *Hampton*, n 305, at [115]. The rationale for applying statutory limitation periods to equitable claims by analogy is obscure.

[540] Limitation Act 1980, s 9. This section applies to actions to recover any sum recoverable by virtue of any enactment other than the Civil Liability (Contribution) Act 1978.

[541] Limitation Act 1980, s 10. This rule does not apply to contribution claims at common law which are governed by the usual six-year rule, nor to contribution claims in equity which are governed by the same rule by way of analogy: *Hampton*, n 305, at [115]. There is no good reason for statutory and common law claims for contribution and reimbursement to be governed by different limitation rules.

[542] Limitation Act 1980, s 22(a), considered in *Davies v Sharples* [2006] EWHC 362 (Ch), [2006] WTLR 839; *Re Loftus (deceased)* [2006] EWCA Civ 1124, (2006) 9 ITELR 107.

[543] Limitation Act 1980, s 21(3). Section 21(1) provides that there is no statutory limitation period for claims against trustees (a) in respect of fraud to which the trustees were privy and (b) against trustees to recover trust property held by the trustees or previously converted to their use. Section 21(1) does not affect claims against third parties, which are governed exclusively by s 21(3): *Williams v Central Bank of Nigeria* [2014] UKSC 10, [2014] AC 1189.

[544] eg four-year periods apply to claims under the Inheritance Tax Act 1984, s 241, and the Taxes Management Act 1970, s 33; and three-year periods apply to claims under the Customs and Excise Management Act 1979, s 137A (4) and (5), the Value Added Tax Act 1994, s 80, and the Finance Act 1996, Sched 5, para 14 (4) and (6).

[545] See 3.22; also *Jim Ennis Construction Ltd v Premier Asphalt Ltd* [2009] EWHC 1906 (TCC), (2009) 125 Con LR 141, at [31]. Exceptionally, a cause of action to recover benefits transferred on a basis that subsequently fails does not accrue until the basis fails; and claims based on undue influence can be brought for as long as the undue influence persists, and within a reasonable period after it has ended: *Humphreys v Humphreys* [2004] EWHC 2201 (Ch), at [99].

[546] On which: *Knight v Rochdale Healthcare NHS Trust* [2003] EWHC 1831 (QB), [2004] 1 WLR 371; *Baker & Davies plc v Leslie Wilks Associates* [2005] EWHC 1179 (TCC), [2006] PNLR 3; *Aer Lingus plc v Gildacroft Ltd* [2006] EWCA Civ 4, [2006] 1 WLR 1173.

(c) Postponement of the date of commencement

3.199   The Limitation Act 1980 contains various provisions that postpone the date from which a limitation period starts to run in particular cases.[547] Section 28 prevents time running against a person under a disability such as mental illness or minority, and section 32 provides that in cases of fraud, concealment, or mistake, the clock will not start to run until the claimant has discovered the true facts or could with reasonable diligence have done so.[548] The fraud or concealment may have been done by the defendant's predecessor in title, but in that case the extension of the limitation period will not be extended against a bona fide purchaser for value.[549]

3.200   It was to obtain the benefits of the extended limitation period under section 32(1)(c) that the claimants in both *Kleinwort Benson Ltd v Lincoln CC*[550] and *Deutsche Morgan Grenfell plc v IRC*[551] sought to ground their claims on mistake of law. Both cases were fought on the basis that the claimant could only take advantage of the provision if mistake were a necessary component of its cause of action. When *DMG* reached the House of Lords, however, the claimant amended its pleadings to argue that mistake did not need to be an essential element of its cause of action for the sub-section to apply, provided that a mistake could be discovered in the facts of the case. In the event, the court did not have to decide this point, but in obiter dicta Lord Walker and Lord Hoffmann favoured the claimant's contention,[552] while Lord Scott preferred Pearson J's previous finding in *Phillips-Higgins v Harper*,[553] that the subsection 'applies only where the mistake is an essential ingredient of the cause of action'.[554]

3.201   The point was revisited in *Test Claimants in the FII Group Litigation v HMRC*. The Court of Appeal followed Aldous LJ's earlier finding in *Malkin v Birmingham CC*[555] that the subsection applies only in cases 'where the plaintiff can establish that the mistake was part of or an element of the cause of action'. The court was influenced by the consideration that any broader formulation would lead to 'undesirable uncertainty as to its scope' and stated that 'extending the scope of liabilities of indefinite duration, the existence of which after the expiration of the normal limitation period may be unknown to the obligor, is not obviously desirable'.[556] The Supreme Court agreed.[557] Consequently, it is not open to a claimant who wishes to bring a claim founded on the *Woolwich* principle, eg, to take advantage of section 32(1)(c) by arguing that he made a mistake although that fact forms no part of his cause of action.

3.202   *DMG* was one of many claims brought against the Revenue following the ECJ's decision in *Metallgesellschaft Ltd v IRC*[558] that tax paid by many corporate groups had not been due because the statutory scheme under which it had been levied had infringed the EC Treaty. Following Park J's decision for the claimant at first instance,[559] it became clear that many

---

[547] Including s 29(5), considered in *FJ Chalke Ltd v HMRC* [2009] EWHC 952 (Ch), [2009] STC 2027, at [157].

[548] On reasonable diligence: *Peco Arts Inc v Hazlitt Gallery Inc* [1983] 1 WLR 1315; *Davies*, n 542, at [57]–[59]; *Bloomsbury*, n 467, at [129]–[132].

[549] Section 32(2) and (3); *GL Baker Ltd v Medway Building and Supplies Ltd* [1958] 2 All ER 532 (Danckwerts J), [1958] 1 WLR 1216, CA: the defendant was a donee from a fraudster.

[550] *Lincoln*, n 24.

[551] *DMG*, n 2.

[552] *DMG*, n 2, at [22] and [147].

[553] [1954] 1 QB 411, 419, considering the statutory precursor to s 32(1)(c), the Limitation Act 1929, s 26(c).

[554] *DMG*, n 2, at [91]–[92].

[555] CA 12 January 2000, at [23].

[556] *FII* (CA), n 67, at [245].

[557] *FII* (SC), n 2, at [42]–[63] and [177]–[185].

[558] *Metallgesellschaft*, n 148.

[559] [2003] EWHC 1779 (Ch), [2003] STC 1017.

claims would be brought by claimants relying on section 32(1)(c), whose mistake had not been reasonably discoverable until the date of the ECJ's decision.[560] Legislation was therefore enacted to disapply the sub-section in relation to mistakes of law relating to taxation matters: section 320 of the Finance Act 2004, and section 107 of the Finance Act 2007.

In *FII* the validity of these sections was challenged. It was argued that they were contrary   **3.203**
to the EU law principles of effectiveness and legitimate expectations. The claimants were entitled under EU law to recover money paid as tax to HMRC. Yet the sections curtailed the limitation period applicable to any claim in mistake without making transitional arrange-ments to protect the claimants' accrued restitutionary rights. HMRC replied that this was not contrary to EU law because the claimants could also have brought *Woolwich* claims, and these were unaffected by the change, albeit that they were now time-barred. A majority of the Supreme Court provisionally concluded that as a matter of EU law a mistake claim had to be available to the claimants alongside their *Woolwich* claim, and so the legislature's failure to make transitional arrangements meant that the enactment of sections 320 and 107 had violated the principle of effectiveness.[561] However, a minority disagreed that section 320 was incompatible with EU law,[562] and so a reference was made to the CJEU which confirmed the majority's view.[563] The UK government has responded by enacting legislation to remedy the incompatibility of section 107, although not that of section 320.[563a]

(8) Illegality

(a) Stultification and turpitude

A party who has transferred value under an illegal contract may be able to make out a claim   **3.204**
in unjust enrichment, eg on the ground of mistake or failure of basis. The question then arises whether allowing that claim would make nonsense of the law's refusal to enforce the contract. If it would, then the action in unjust enrichment will be barred. It is a separate ques-tion whether the claim in unjust enrichment is independently obstructed by grave turpitude.

The law is nowadays more easily explained by stultification than by turpitude. The reason is   **3.205**
that, even up to and including crimes of dishonesty, the courts no longer react to illegality with the decisive revulsion which they once were wont to show. No formal explanation of the results can conceal this truth in cases in which people bent on defrauding the social security system or deceiving their creditors have been allowed to recover.[564]

Any non-contractual action in respect of value which has passed under an illegal contract   **3.206**
will prima facie be barred on the ground of stultification. A claimant pays a defendant for an honour, and no honour is forthcoming.[565] There is a failure of basis, but restitution is not awarded. It suffices to say, without entering into judgments on turpitude, that recovery of the

---

[560] The HL later confirmed that the date when the ECJ had handed down its decision in *Metallgesellschaft* was the date when the claimant in *DMG* could first reasonably have discovered its mistake: *DMG*, n 2, at [34], [71] and [144].

[561] *FII* (SC), n 2, at [22], [120], [126]–[139], [140] and [246].

[562] *FII* (SC), n 2, at [121]–[125] and [142].

[563] *Test Claimants in the FII Group Litigation v HMRC* (Case C-362/12) [2014] STC 638. For discussion of the EU law aspects of the case, see M Schlote, 'The Principle of Effectiveness and Restitution of Overpaid Tax' in Elliott et al, n 30.

[563a] Finance Act 2014, s 299. For critical comment, see P Baker [2014] BTR 424.

[564] *Tinsley v Milligan* [1994] AC 340, HL; *Tribe*, n 404. In the light of these cases *Berg v Sadler and Moore* [1937] 2 KB 158 (money paid to obtain goods on false pretences) could not possibly be explained in terms of turpitude and probably cannot be explained at all.

[565] *Parkinson v College of Ambulance Ltd* [1925] 2 KB 1.

money would stultify the invalidity of the contract. It would provide both a lever to compel performance and a safety net against the event of non-performance, reducing the risks of entering the illegal contract.

3.207   The lever argument and the safety net argument routinely indicate a prima facie stultification, and this may be confirmed if it is found on closer inspection that the policy behind the illegality in question would indeed be stultified if the claimant were allowed non-contractual recourse.[566] But stultification can also be negatived in two ways, by flat denial or by confession and avoidance.

3.208   It can be flatly denied where restitution would assist the underlying policy. A prohibition on taking premiums for leases is likely to arise from a policy of protecting tenants from market forces. Restitution of illegal premiums positively helps. Once a court concludes that restitution would further the protective policy underlying the invalidity, there will be no question of stultification. Indeed the policy may itself constitute the unjust factor—the very reason why the enrichment must be returned.[567]

3.209   The prima facie stultification can be confessed and avoided in two ways. First, those who can demonstrate their innocence of the illegality can be allowed to recover, because the innocent as a class will never be encouraged to enter illegal transactions. Hence, restitution is allowed where a mistake concealed the illegality[568] or oppression compelled it.[569]

3.210   Secondly, the law will not be stultified even where the guilty are allowed to recover if it the denial of restitution would entail some greater evil. Stultification is unexplained contradiction. The greater evil which is avoided provides the explanation. Thus, to allow an illegal immigrant to sue for the value of his work seems to stultify the refusal to enforce his contract, but to refuse the non-contractual action would leave the immigrant with no remedy at all and open the way to slave labour.[570] In such a case the law prefers the lesser evil.

(b) Proprietary claims

3.211   In *Tinsley v Milligan*,[571] a majority of the House of Lords held that a participant in an illegal scheme to defraud the Department of Social Security could assert a claim under a resulting trust to a share in a house which had been bought with her financial assistance, but put into her lover's name pursuant to the fraudulent scheme. The majority reasoned that the claim was based on evidence that the claimant had contributed to the purchase price, that she had received nothing in exchange, and that legal title to the house was vested in the defendant alone. These facts were enough to raise a presumption in the claimant's favour, failure to rebut which led to the imposition of the trust. Hence the claimant did not need to rely on evidence of her illegal behaviour to make out her claim, and the illegality emerged only because the defendant sought to raise it. In these circumstances the claim should be allowed.

3.212   There are several problems with this analysis. First, it rested on an analogy with common law cases that permitted claims in tort founded on the claimant's subsisting legal title, which

---

[566] As in *Wilson v First County Trust Ltd (No 2)* [2003] UKHL 40, [2004] 1 AC 816; *Equuscorp*, n 15, at [45]. cf *Dimond v Lovell* [2002] 1 AC 384, HL.

[567] See 3.140.

[568] *Oom v Bruce* (1810) 12 East 225, 104 ER 87; *Hughes v Liverpool Victoria Friendly Society* [1916] 2 KB 482; *Lehman Commercial Mortgage Conduit Ltd (in administration) v Gatedale Ltd* [2012] EWHC 3083 (Ch).

[569] *Smith v Cuff* (1817) 6 M & S 160, 105 ER 1203.

[570] *Nizamuddowlah v Bengal Cabaret, Inc* 399 NYS 2d 854 (1977). And cf *Hounga v Allen* [2014] UKSC 47, [2014] 1 WLR 2889.

[571] *Tinsley*, n 564.

pre-dated the parties' illegal dealings and needed no special justification.[572] In contrast the claimant in *Tinsley* argued that she had acquired a new equitable title under a resulting trust. This meant extending the principle disclosed by the tort cases in a way that was not obviously justified.

Secondly, this extension of the principle was limited to cases where there was no special **3.213** relationship between the parties of a kind that would lead the law to make a presumption of advancement.[573] It was unsatisfactory to make the transferor's ability to recover property transferred for an illegal purpose turn on the irrelevant question of whether she and the transferee are in a special relationship giving rise to a presumption of advancement.[574]

Thirdly, the majority's approach was highly formalistic. Whether a claim in unjust enrich- **3.214** ment should be permitted to recover benefits conferred under an illegal contract is a question that ought to be addressed by examining the policy underlying the rule that renders the contract illegal, and asking whether this would be stultified if recovery were allowed. Arguably, the courts should also consider a wider range of issues, such as whether the illegality is sufficiently serious to make it inappropriate for the court to assist the claimant, whether disallowing the claim will deter other parties from committing similar acts, and whether disallowing the claim would be an appropriate or excessive punishment.

In 1999, the Law Commission recommended legislation to give the courts a structured statu- **3.215** tory discretion to take precisely such factors into account when deciding the effects of illegality on private law claims.[575] This recommendation was not followed. In 2010, the Law Commission published another report,[576] noting that the courts have begun to develop a similar discretion to deal with the effect of illegality on tort claims,[577] and concluding that there is no need for general legislation in this area because the existing rules are largely amenable to common law development that will set them on a clearer and more rational footing. However, they still considered that legislation is needed to abolish the *Tinsley* principle. Since then, the Supreme Court has held, once, that the courts can legitimately take public policy considerations into account on a case-by-case basis when deciding the effect of illegality on private law claims,[577a] and, twice, that they cannot do this, and that it is desirable for them to take the approach laid down in *Tinsley*.[577b]

H. Legal Grounds for Enrichment

A defendant can escape liability in unjust enrichment if he can show that another source **3.216** of legal rights entitles him to receive the relevant benefit, and this overrides the conclusion that would otherwise be generated by the law of unjust enrichment, that he should make

---

[572] *Tinsley*, n 564, at 369, citing *Bowmakers Ltd v Barnet Instruments Ltd* [1945] KB 65; *Feret v Hill* (1854) 15 CB 207, 139 ER 400; *Taylor v Chester* (1869) LR QB 309; *Alexander v Rayson* [1936] 1 KB 169.

[573] *Tinsley*, n 564, at 371–372. The presumption of advancement will be abolished in English law (with prospective effect) if the Equality Act 2010, s 199 is brought into force.

[574] As noted in *Nelson v Nelson* (1995) 184 CLR 538, 609; *Tribe*, n 404, at 118; *Silverwood v Silverwood* (1997) 74 P & CR 453, 458–9; *Lowson v Coombes* [1999] Ch 373, 385. See too Law Commission, *Illegal Transactions: The Effect of Illegality on Contracts and Trusts* (Law Com No 154, 1999) paras 3.19–3.24.

[575] Law Com No 154, n 574, at para 8.63.

[576] Law Commission, *The Illegality Defence* (Law Com No 320, 2010).

[577] *Stone & Rolls Ltd (in liq) v Moore Stephens (a firm)* [2009] UKHL 39, [2009] 1 AC 1391; *Gray v Thames Trains Ltd* [2009] UKHL 33, [2009] 1 AC 1339.

[577a] *Hounga*, n 570.

[577b] *Les Laboratoires Servier v Apotex Inc* [2014] UKSC 55, [2015] AC 430; *Bilta (UK) Ltd (in liq) v Nazir* [2015] UKSC 23, [2015] 2 WLR 1168.

restitution.[578] Three possibilities are considered here: that the defendant is entitled to receive the benefit under a statute, under a judgment, or under a contract.[579]

(1) Statutes

3.217 Legislation might require a claimant to benefit a defendant or it might extinguish his rights in unjust enrichment.

(a) Statute requires claimant to benefit defendant

3.218 An example is where a taxpayer overlooks an opportunity to rearrange his affairs in a more tax-efficient way. Even if he can show that he failed to do this by mistake, he cannot recover the difference between the tax he pays and the amount he would have paid if he had arranged his affairs more efficiently.[580] HMRC has the right to receive tax calculated under the relevant statutory rules by reference to the taxpayer's affairs as they are, and not as they might have been.[581]

3.219 This principle was misapplied in *FII*.[582] The claimants used tax reliefs to offset invalid tax liabilities that they would otherwise have used to offset valid tax liabilities. Arden LJ denied restitution because the claimants' valid tax payments were payments that HMRC had been entitled to receive.[583] However the enrichment in respect of which the claim was made was not the value of the money paid by the claimants to HMRC in respect of lawful tax liabilities, but the value of HMRC's discharged obligation to allow the claimants a credit against lawfully due tax. That enrichment accrued in HMRC's hands at the time when the reliefs were used, albeit that its value could not be calculated until afterwards.

3.220 Arden LJ's analysis is also difficult to reconcile with *Deutsche Morgan Grenfell plc v IRC*.[584] There money was paid as tax under a statutory scheme that was contrary to EU law because it gave the claimants no option to avoid paying the tax by making an election. Restitution was awarded although the claimants had a statutory duty to pay the tax unless and until they validly exercised an election, something which they never did. In his dissenting speech Lord Scott argued that restitution should therefore be denied because the money paid by the claimants had been due under the relevant statute.[585] Lord Walker thought that this objection was 'over-analytical',[586] and it has been suggested that restitution should be awarded although the defendant has a statutory right to be enriched in cases where his right arises 'in a technical sense only'.[587] However it is difficult to make out the contours of this projected exception to the general rule.

---

[578] It is unclear whether a defendant's argument to this effect operates as a defence or a denial: see 3.16–3.17.

[579] On gifts, note 3.63; and on the question whether natural obligations ever entitle a defendant to a benefit, see D Sheehan, 'Natural Obligations in English Law' [2004] LMCLQ 170; M McInnes, 'Natural Obligations and Unjust Enrichment' in E Bant and M Harding (eds), *Exploring Private Law* (2010).

[580] A significant exception to this is created by the rule in *Re Hastings-Bass (deceased)* [1975] Ch 25, CA, as reformulated in *Pitt*, n 116.

[581] *FII* (Ch), n 442, at [257]: if inheritance tax is received by HMRC due to a failure to make an election in a deed of variation pursuant to the Inheritance Tax Act 1984, s 142, the taxpayer cannot recover even if the failure to make the election was due to a mistake.

[582] *FII* (CA), n 67. This aspect of the CA's decision was not considered on appeal: *FII* (SC), n 2.

[583] *FII* (CA), n 67, at [178]–[184].

[584] *DMG*, n 2.

[585] *DMG*, n 2, at [84]–[85].

[586] *DMG*, n 2, at [143].

[587] A Burrows, 'Restitution of Mistaken Payments' (2012) 92 Boston University LR 767, 777.

(b) Statute expressly or impliedly extinguishes claimant's rights

A statute may expressly prohibit common law claims in unjust enrichment, and give a claim- **3.221** ant no other rights, leaving him without a remedy. For example, a claimant's rights may effectively be extinguished by a limitation statute.[588] Alternatively a statute may give him a set of statutory rights and either expressly or impliedly remove his common law rights. In such cases, a careful exercise of statutory interpretation may be needed to determine the legislation's effect.[589] Some statutes use vague language that makes it hard to discern whether it is intended to extinguish the claimant's rights at common law.[590] Others fail to make it clear whether particular claimants fall within the scope of a provision that forbids common law claims.[591] Others fail to make it clear whether a claimant's statutory recovery rights are intended to run alongside, or supersede, his common law rights.[592]

In cases of the last kind, the courts can baulk at depriving claimants of their common law **3.222** rights where there is little or no evidence that Parliament positively intended to take them away. It has been said that that 'first principles in statutory interpretation...rule out the dismantling of judge-made law by stealth',[593] and that the court 'should not be too ready to find that a common law remedy has been displaced by a statutory one, not least because it is always open to Parliament to make the position clear by stating explicitly whether the statute is intended to be exhaustive.'[594] However it is unpredictable how much weight the courts will lend to this consideration,[595] and they have sometimes held that a claimant's common law rights are excluded by necessary implication because it is 'inconceivable' that Parliament would enact a limited statutory recovery regime that could be simply sidestepped by a claim- ant relying on his common law rights.[596]

(2) Judgments

Benefits transferred pursuant to a court order are irrecoverable for as long as the order sub- **3.223** sists,[597] but there is an exception to this principle where the order has been obtained by fraud.[598]

---

[588] See 3.195–3.197.

[589] For a summary of the operable principles, see *Legal Services Commission v Henthorn* [2011] EWHC 258 (QB), at [72].

[590] See eg *Friends' Provident Life Office v Hillier Parker May & Rowden (a firm)* [1997] QB 85, CA; *Royal Brompton Hospital NHS Trust v Hammond* [2002] 1 WLR 1397, HL; *Niru (No 2)* (CA), n 292; *Charter*, n 131; all considering whether the parties owed a common liability for 'damage' for the purposes of the Civil Liability (Contribution) Act 1978, ss 1 and 6, with the result that their contribution rights inter se arose exclusively under the 1978 Act as a result of s 7(3). See also *Littlewoods* (CA), n 36, at [15]–[50], holding that the Value Added Tax Act 1994, s 78(1) and s 80(7) exclude common law claims to recover the use value as well as the face value of money paid as VAT that was not due.

[591] See eg *ITC* (CA), n 18, reversing the finding in *ITC* (Ch), n 40, that the Value Added Tax Act 1994, s 80(7) excludes common law claims to recover overpaid VAT not by a taxable person but by a final consumer of services on which VAT has been incorrectly charged.

[592] See eg *Woolwich*, n 2, at 169 and 199–200; *DMG*, n 2, at [19], [55], and [135]; *Monro v HMRC* [2008] EWCA Civ 306, [2009] Ch 69; all considering the Taxes Management Act 1970, s 33. See too *CPAG*, n 2, considering the Social Security Administration Act 1992, s 71.

[593] *Green v Associated Newspapers Ltd* [2005] QB 972, 991–992, CA. See too *Pyx Granite Co Ltd v Ministry of Housing and Local Government* [1960] AC 260, 286, HL; *Black Clawson International Ltd v Papierwerke Waldhof-Aschaffenburg AG* [1975] AC 591, 614, HL; *R (Rottman) v Metropolitan Police Commissioner* [2002] UKHL 20, [2002] 2 AC 692, at [75].

[594] *CPAG*, n 2, at [34].

[595] Compare *Henthorn*, n 589 and *Legal Services Commission v Loomba* [2012] EWHC 29 (QB), [2012] 1 WLR 2461.

[596] *CPAG*, n 2, at [14].

[597] If the order is successfully appealed then the benefits can be recovered: 3.142–3.144.

[598] In cases of fraud the claimant may alternatively be entitled to recover damages for the torts of abuse of process or malicious process. See n 409.

3.224 The general rule is established by *Marriot v Hampton*.[599] The claimant paid the defendant for goods. The defendant then sued for the price, alleging that he had not been paid. The claimant could not find the receipt he had been given, and was ordered by the court to pay again. He then found the receipt and brought an action for restitution of the second payment. He was non-suited, Lord Kenyon CJ stating that, 'If this action could be maintained I know not what cause of action could ever be at rest. After a recovery by process of law there must be an end of litigation, otherwise there would be no security for any person.'[600]

3.225 The exception was established by *Duke de Cadaval v Collins*.[601] The claimant was arrested by the defendant on the false basis that he owed him money. He paid £500 to secure his release and then successfully sued to recover his payment.

(3) Contracts

(a) Subsisting contracts

3.226 Where a contract between the parties confers the right to be enriched on the defendant, a claim in unjust enrichment will normally be disallowed for as long as the contract subsists.[602] The point of this rule is that the law should give effect to the parties' agreed allocation of risk and benefit, and should not allow this allocation to be subverted by a claim in unjust enrichment.[603] Consistently with this, however, there is no need to debar a claim in unjust enrichment that does not have this effect.[604]

(b) Contracts discharged by performance

3.227 For the same reason, where a contract has been discharged by performance, there is generally no remedy in unjust enrichment in respect of benefits transferred under the contract. So, in in *Taylor v Motability Finance Ltd*,[605] the claimant was a director of the defendant company. While working in this capacity he brought about the settlement of an £80 million insurance claim, and was rewarded for this work by the maximum possible award under the company's bonus scheme. Following his dismissal, he brought a claim in unjust enrichment for his services in obtaining the settlement, which he valued at a significantly higher figure. Cooke J rejected the claim, stating that 'if it were otherwise, not only would the claimant be able to recover more than his contractual entitlement in respect of bonus, but he could also seek to establish that he was underpaid in terms of salary, despite his agreement thereto'.[606]

3.228 In *Roxborough v Rothmans of Pall Mall Australia Ltd*[607] the High Court of Australia held that a claim in unjust enrichment did not subvert the parties' allocation of risks under a contract that was fully performed. Under a contract for the sale of cigarettes by a wholesaler

---

[599] (1797) 7 TR 269, 101 ER 969. This is hard to reconcile with *Moses*, n 226, which was said to be wrong in *Phillips v Hunter* (1795) 2 H Bl 402, 416; 126 ER 618, 626; and *Brisbane v Dacres* (1813) 5 Taunt 143, 160; 128 ER 641, 649.

[600] (1760) 7 TR 269, 269; 101 ER 969, 969.

[601] (1836) 4 Ad & El 858, 111 ER 1006. See too *Wilson v Ray* (1839) 10 Ad & El 82, 88–89; 113 ER 32, 35–36; *De Medina v Grove* (1846) 10 QB 152, 171; 116 ER 59, 68; *Ward & Co v Wallis* [1900] 1 QB 675.

[602] *Weston v Downes* (1778) 1 Doug 23, 99 ER 19; *Hulle v Heightman* (1802) 2 East 145, 102 ER 324; *De Bernardy v Harding* (1853) 8 Exch 822, 155 ER 1586; *Kwei Tek Chao v British Traders and Shippers Ltd* [1954] 2 QB 459.

[603] J Beatson, 'Restitution and Contract: Non-Cumul?' (2000) 1 Theoretical Inquiries in Law 83.

[604] cf *Miles v Wakefield MDC* [1987] 1 AC 539, 552–553 and 561, HL. Further discussion: T Baloch, *Unjust Enrichment and Contract* (2009) ch 6.

[605] *Motability*, n 72. See too *Stoomvaart Maatschappij Nederlandsche Lloyd v General Mercantil Company Ltd (The Olanda)* [1919] 2 KB 728n.

[606] *Motability*, n 72, at [25].

[607] *Roxborough*, n 23.

to a retailer, the price included a sum representing a tax liability which the parties expected the wholesaler to incur. The tax was then held to be unconstitutional. The court ordered the wholesaler to repay the tax element of the purchase price to the retailer, reasoning that the risk that the tax was not payable had been allocated to the wholesaler because the amount of the tax element was fixed from the outset, and was not the product of negotiation.

(c) Contracts terminated for breach

Once a contract has been terminated for breach, either party is free to claim in unjust enrich- **3.229** ment and there is no rule that prevents the party in breach from doing so.[608] It is open to debate whether the defendant's enrichment should be valued by reference to the market price or the contract price for the purposes of such a claim.[609] Since no claim in unjust enrichment will lie unless the contract is terminated, it appears that the innocent party can prevent the party in breach from bringing such a claim by refusing to accept his repudiatory breach and affirming the contract.[610]

(d) Multiple parties

The foregoing principles do not merely affect claims in two-party cases; they also affect claims **3.230** in cases involving multiple parties. *MacDonald Dickens & Macklin (a firm) v Costello*[611] is a representative example. The claimant builders worked on land owned by the defendants. There was no contract between them, because for tax reasons the defendants wished to pay for the work through a company of which they were the shareholders. The builders agreed. A dispute then arose about the standard of the works. The company refused to pay for some work done under the contract, and for other work done outside the contract. The builders won judgment against the defendants for the outstanding amount, on the basis that they had been unjustly enriched at the builders' expense. This was overturned on appeal. Etherton LJ accepted that the defendants had been enriched at the claimants' expense, but held that restitution would undermine the parties' choices with regard to the way in which they had arranged their affairs, including their decision that the builders should contract with the company and their decision that the builders should not contract with the defendants.[612]

I. Rights to Restitution

(1) The Personal Restitutionary Right Arising from Unjust Enrichment

Almost every unjust enrichment gives rise to a personal restitutionary right.[613] That is to **3.231** say, the defendant comes under a liability to pay the claimant the value of the enrichment received. The enrichment is measured at the moment of receipt, although the obligation to return it may be reduced or indeed extinguished by the operation of defences.

---

[608] See cases cited in n 217. Restitution may be excluded by a term of the contract: *Cadogan*, n 242, at [27].
[609] See 3.31.
[610] A rule with the potential to create injustice where a buyer under an instalment contract cannot raise the funds needed to complete the purchase, since the seller might then prevent him from recovering his payments by continuing to affirm the contract: A Tettenborn, 'Subsisting Contracts and Failure of Consideration— A Little Scepticism' [2002] RLR 1, 2–3.
[611] *Costello*, n 102. See too *Galbraith*, n 111; *Lumbers* (HCA), n 77; *Yew*, n 103.
[612] *Costello*, n 102, at [21] and [23].
[613] Rescission of voidable transactions arguably constitutes an exception, but, in the light of (a) the rise of pecuniary rescission as in *Mahoney* (n 193) and (b) long-established practice where the claimant has paid money rather than transferred a thing, it is difficult to deny the initial personal obligation to repay the value obtained, so long as the defendant can be shown to have been enriched.

3.232 The claimant's personal right to restitution of the value received is not an alternative held in reserve for the case in which the specific asset can no longer be given up. The old actions reveal this.[614] In the action for money had and received the claimant declared that the defendant was indebted to him in such and such a sum, the *causa debendi* being the receipt of that much money to the claimant's use. The claim was not for the coins or notes received but in respect of the abstract debt thus created in that sum. The same is true of related actions within the *assumpsit* family. It is true, eg, of money paid to the use of the defendant, *quantum meruit*, and *quantum valebat*. All these go directly for the money value of that which the defendant received. This marks a major point of difference between English and German law. Under the latter the obligation is expressed as in the first instance an obligation to surrender the specific asset received. The right to the value arises only when it has become impossible to surrender (*herausgeben*) the specific thing.[615]

3.233 In equity, free-standing obligations arising from unjust enrichment are also obligations to pay value, not to transfer any specific thing.[616] Furthermore, while common law proceedings had to be pursued through forms of action which obscured the nature of restitutionary awards, the Chancery courts always simply ordered a payment of money.[617]

(2) Proprietary Restitutionary Rights Arising from Unjust Enrichment

3.234 In most cases the only response in question is the personal right to restitution of enrichment received. But in some contexts, above all in insolvency, it becomes necessary to ask whether the law responds to a defendant's unjust enrichment by raising a property right in the claimant.

3.235 Whereas a personal right is a means to effecting restitution by the realization of an obligation incumbent on the enriched person, a proprietary right is a means of effecting restitution by the realization of a right in an asset held by the enriched person, whether the very asset which carried the enrichment to him or, more likely, an asset which is its traceable substitute. Personal rights, though diverse in content, are all of one kind in that they require a defendant to do something. Rights *in rem* (proprietary rights) by contrast cannot be considered without being sub-divided into different kinds.

3.236 A right *in rem* may be a power to alter the legal condition of a thing or a substantive interest in that thing; and, again, a right *in rem* which is a substantive interest may be a beneficial interest or a security interest. 'Substantive' underscores the contrast with a power. A power *in rem* is an interest in the thing, but it is an instrument for creating vested beneficial and security interests.

3.237 The most convenient strategy is to ask first whether any species of proprietary interest is raised by any instance of unjust enrichment and afterwards to ask what kind of proprietary right it might be.

(a) When will a claimant in unjust enrichment have a proprietary interest?

3.238 We have seen that an enrichment at the expense of the claimant will be unjust where the claimant's intent to part with it was deficient, where his intent was qualified, and where,

---

[614] For the words of the action for money had and received, and of the other counts in *indebitatus assumpsit*, see *Stephen on Pleading* (2nd edn, 1827) 312.

[615] BGB § 818(2).

[616] 'Free-standing' here indicates an obligation which is independent of any proprietary interest in the thing.

[617] eg *A-G ex rel Ethery v Hunton* (1739) West t Hard 703, 25 ER 1158. See too *Ministry of Health v Simpson* [1951] AC 251, HL.

independently of his intent, there is a policy reason requiring restitution. Each of these three will be considered in turn, but first must come three general propositions which apply throughout.

(i) Three general doctrines

Substitution. If, immediately after the defendant's receipt, the claimant has a proprietary **3.239** interest in the *res* received, he will later be able to claim a proprietary interest in any substitute for that original still traceably held by the recipient.

The recipient of money or other assets may later exchange them for other things. Money **3.240** is likely to be exchanged almost immediately. Even putting it in the bank, or taking it out, entails a substitution, cash for personal claim, or vice versa. The chain of substitutions may be long or short. It may involve only clean substitutions but it is more likely to include mixed substitutions. A mixed substitution happens when someone acquires an asset with value derived from more than one source, as for instance £1,000 of his own and £2,000 received from another.

If each link in a chain of substitutions had to be proved by evidence, the chain would often **3.241** break after the first or second exchange. However, it is saved from so easily breaking by the rules of tracing.[618] Tracing is 'the process of identifying [a] new asset as the substitute for [an old asset]'.[619] When a defendant receives Asset One from a claimant, a tracing exercise which shows that Asset Ten in the defendant's hands is its traceable substitute will only give the claimant rights in Asset Ten if other facts establish his entitlement.

The question whether a claimant has proprietary rights in traced substitutes depends on his **3.242** having had such rights in the asset at the head of the chain. The asset at the head of the chain is the asset received by the defendant, contemplated at the moment after its receipt. It is there that the claimant must establish his proprietary base. He may establish this proprietary base by the operation of the law of unjust enrichment as described below or by reference to doctrines which have nothing to do with the law of unjust enrichment. The efficacy of substitution in raising proprietary rights in the substitute depends on the establishment of a proprietary base at the first link of the chain, not on the nature of the facts relied on to establish that proprietary base. For example, the defendant may have committed an acquisitive wrong which, exceptionally, turned him into a trustee for his victim.[620] Again it may be that he held as bailee, as where a solicitor was a depositee for safe-keeping of his client's bonds and sold them out.[621]

In such cases, just as much as in those in which the proprietary base itself arises directly from **3.243** unjust enrichment, the claimant's interest in the substitute arises from unjust enrichment.[622] The reason is that the defendant has used the claimant's property to acquire a benefit for himself without the claimant's consent.[623] As for the proprietary nature of the response, that derives simply from the choice made by English law in favour of responding to every substitution by, inter alia, according to the claimant as nearly as possible the same rights in relation

---

[618] Comprehensively treated by LD Smith, *The Law of Tracing* (1997).

[619] *Foskett*, n 137, at 127.

[620] eg *LAC Minerals Ltd v International Corona Resources Ltd* [1989] 2 SCR 574; *Minera Aquiline Argentina SA v IMA Exploration Inc* [2007] BCCA 319, (2007) 10 WWR 648. These cases hold that a constructive trust will be imposed on the profits of a breach of confidence. cf *A-G v Guardian Newspapers Ltd (No 2)* [1990] 1 AC 109, 288, HL, and *United Pan-Europe Communications NV v Deutsche Bank AG* [2000] 2 BCLC 461, 482–483, CA.

[621] *Re Hallett's Estate* (1879) 13 Ch D 696, CA.

[622] So also Smith, n 618, at 300–301.

[623] cf 3.55.

to the substitute as he enjoyed in the original at the moment when the original was received by the defendant. Many systems do not make that choice.

3.244 In *Foskett v McKeown* Lord Millett said that '[t]he transmission of a claimant's property rights from one asset to its traceable proceeds is part of our law of property, not of the law of unjust enrichment'.[624] That statement falsely opposes unjust enrichment (a source of rights) and property (a type of right). It conceals the events from which proprietary rights in substitute assets might conceivably arise. Suppose that a claimant loses £5 and a defendant finds it, and that he uses it to buy a cake. The law may say that the claimant is now the owner of the cake, but if it does so then his property in the cake cannot be regarded as arising from the same event as his property in the £5. Something must have happened which made him owner of the cake.

3.245 In *Foskett*, a trustee committed a breach of trust when he used trust funds to pay some of the premiums for a life assurance policy, nominating his children as the policy beneficiaries. Following his death, the trust beneficiaries were held to have acquired proprietary rights in a proportionate share of the policy proceeds which were the traceable substitute of the misapplied trust money. The reason was that the trustee had previously agreed that he would hold any assets acquired with trust money for the trust beneficiaries and the court would not allow the trustee (and thus, donees of from the trustee) to go back on this agreement once the trust beneficiaries had retrospectively ratified the transaction. In other words, the trust beneficiaries' rights in the substitute assets derived not from 'property law' but from consent.[625]

3.246 In other cases, this explanation is not available. Suppose that a trustee gives his son cash stolen from the trust bank account, and that in good faith the son uses this money to buy shares. The trust beneficiaries would then be entitled to the shares, but this cannot be explained on the basis that the son had consented to their acquiring rights to the shares. Their rights would derive instead from unjust enrichment: the son would have used their money to enrich himself without their consent.

3.247 **Immediate knowledge.** Several cases hold that a trust is imposed on assets if they are transferred to a recipient who knows at the moment of receipt that the transferor is entitled to restitution. However the scope of this doctrine has been uncertain since the Court of Appeal sought to confine it to cases where the recipient has acted with a high degree of improbity.

3.248 In *Neste Oy v Lloyds Bank plc*[626] some ships' chandlers were in financial trouble. They were wont to receive payments in advance in respect of ships which they were to look after. One such payment arrived when they already knew that they would be unable to fulfil the contract. That is, they knew the basis on which they received was going to fail. Bingham J held that they became trustees of that payment. In their insolvency that payment was therefore not a part of the fund available to creditors and, equally important, as they fell into insolvency it would have been proper, and not a voidable preference, for them to have returned it. The recipients knew at the moment of their receipt that the basis of the payment was going to fail.

3.249 In this case none of the five payments was tied to a particular application so as trigger a *Quistclose* trust.[627] Apart from the one payment caught by the immediate knowledge doctrine, the others all illustrate a situation in which there never will be a proprietary response.

---

[624] *Foskett*, n 137, at 127.
[625] See 3.54.
[626] *Neste Oy*, n 261, followed in *Farepak*, n 261.
[627] See 3.98.

They were payments made on a basis which failed but where the money was in the meantime freely at the disposal of the recipients.

Hodgson v Marks[628] is also amenable to a *Neste Oy* explanation, although the immediate knowledge doctrine was not invoked in the case. An old lady conveyed her house to her lodger, Evans. He knew from the start that he was not meant to benefit. It was a contrivance, part of a scheme to make his position secure as against her nephew who wanted him out. Similarly, in *Tribe v Tribe*[629] the son knew from the start that he was not meant to benefit. The shares had only been transferred in order to keep them out of sight of any creditor in the event of the father's insolvency. The father's claim that the son was a trustee might have run into serious difficulties on the ground of illegality, but the Court of Appeal held that it did not.

3.250

In *National Bank of New Zealand v Waitaki International Processing (NI) Ltd*[630] the bank persuaded itself that it owed Waitaki $500,000. It insisted on paying it over, in the teeth of warnings and protests. Waitaki knew that the bank had made a mistake. It knew that the money would have to go back. There was no word of trusteeship in the judgments, but the courts treated Waitaki exactly as though it were a trustee. It was found to have been honest, but, knowing that it was not entitled, it was under a duty to look after the money and invest it on good security. It had not taken a good security and it was in principle liable to the extent that the security had been inadequate at the time of the investment. This is an application of the rule that would have applied to a trustee.

3.251

The *Neste Oy* principle was revisited in *Triffit Nurseries (a firm) v Salads Etcetera Ltd (in admin rec)*.[631] The claimants' vegetables were distributed by an agent company, which billed customers and remitted the proceeds, deducting commission. The company was free to mix the sums collected with its own funds and use them for its own purposes, and did not hold them on an express trust for the claimants. The company went into administrative receivership at a time when there were amounts outstanding in respect of sales of the claimants' produce. The receivers collected the outstanding sums and the question arose whether this money should go to the claimants or to the company's bank which held a charge over its book debts. Consistently with the foregoing cases one might have expected the court to impose a trust, because the company could not conscionably have received the customers' money, knowing that it would not perform its contractual duty to account for an equivalent sum to the claimants. However the Court of Appeal held that this was an insufficient degree of improbity to convert the company into a trustee. It is hard to see what distinguishes the recipients in *Neste Oy* from the recipient in *Triffit*. In the former case the relevant funds came from the claimants, while in the latter they came from third parties, but it is unclear why this should have made a difference.

3.252

Further uncertainty is created by *Westdeutsche Landesbank Girozentrale v Islington LBC*.[632] The bank made payments to Islington under an interest rate swap that was interrupted when the contract turned out to have been void *ab initio*. In the lower courts it was held, following *Sinclair v Brougham*,[633] that the bank had both a personal claim to restitution and a proprietary interest in the money paid to the council. The House of Lords said that was wrong. The bank had no proprietary interest. *Sinclair*, which suggested the contrary, was overruled. The

3.253

---

[628] [1971] Ch 892, CA.
[629] *Tribe*, n 404.
[630] *Waitaki*, n 441.
[631] [2000] 1 BCLC 761, CA.
[632] *Westdeutsche* (HL), n 2.
[633] *Sinclair*, n 9.

bank had not known at the start that the basis would fail. Hence it was certainly not within the *Neste Oy* doctrine.[634] However, Lord Browne-Wilkinson enunciated a doctrine which would enlarge *Neste Oy*. He said that a recipient might be turned into a trustee if he acquired knowledge of the restitutionary obligation at any time while proceeds remained traceable in his hands.[635] This would cause proprietary interests to arise in many cases. It would have produced a different result in the *Westdeutsche* case itself if the defendants had held assets traceably derived from the original.

3.254 If Lord Browne-Wilkinson's doctrine is too generous, then the *Neste Oy* doctrine must be limited to knowledge of non-entitlement concurrent with knowledge of the receipt, at the first opportunity to accept or reject. Just possibly it might be extended to cases in which the recipient acquires knowledge while he still has the specific *res* received as opposed to traceable substitutes.

3.255 Judicial discretion. In *Westdeutsche* Lord Browne-Wilkinson indicated that a day might come when English courts would claim a discretion to turn defendants into trustees and to tailor the attendant proprietary interests to the circumstances of the case. This might be done, he thought, by introducing the 'remedial constructive trust'.[636] That step has not been taken. The English Court of Appeal has since repudiated any such discretion. 'It is not that you need an Act of Parliament to prohibit a variation of property rights. You need one to permit it: see the Variation of Trusts Act 1958 and the Matrimonial Causes Act 1973.'[637] However, in the unlikely event that the Supreme Court comes to take a different view, judicial discretion will have to take its place as the third general way in which a claimant in unjust enrichment can acquire a proprietary interest.

(ii) The three types of unjust factor

3.256 In sections D to F, the reasons for restitution were categorized into three groups: deficient intent, qualified intent, and policy grounds for recovery. The paragraphs which follow deal with the effect of each of these three types of unjust factor in engendering a proprietary response independently of the three general doctrines just discussed. Discussion of the kind of proprietary right engendered is so far as possible postponed to the next section.

3.257 Deficient intent. The strongest type of deficient intent is no intent at all. Here the pre-existing proprietary right in general survives, and that surviving right does not arise from the unjust enrichment of the recipient. If a claimant loses his money, and a defendant finds it, the defendant takes subject to the claimant's property in it. On these facts the law of unjust enrichment has nothing to say about the specific asset received, the note in the finder's hands. On the other hand it does put the recipient under an obligation to make restitution of the value.[638] The right *in rem* does not arise from unjust enrichment. The debt measured by the value received does.[639]

---

[634] Chambers (1997), n 282, at 158–163 reviews all the reasons why it might be said that Islington did not become a trustee for the bank and concludes that the key fact was that the money was freely at the disposition of the recipient before the basis for the receipt failed.

[635] *Westdeutsche* (HL), n 2, at 714–715, followed in *Commerzbank AG v IMB Morgan plc* [2004] EWHC 2771 (Comm), [2005] 2 All ER (Comm) 564, at [36]; *Deutsche Bank AG v Vik* [2010] EWHC 551 (Comm), at [4]. But cf cases cited in n 675.

[636] *Westdeutsche* (HL), n 2, at 714–716.

[637] *Re Polly Peck (No 2)* [1998] 3 All ER 812, 831, CA. See too *Sinclair Investments (UK) Ltd v Versailles Trade Finance Ltd (in admin rec)* [2011] EWCA Civ 347, [2012] Ch 453, at [37]; *Crossco No 4 Unlimited v Jolan Ltd* [2011] EWCA Civ 1619, [2012] 1 P & CR 16, at [84]; *FHR European Ventures LLP v Cedar Capital Partners LLC* [2014] UKSC 45, [2015] AC 250, at [47].

[638] *Holiday*, n 117; *Neate*, n 117; *Moffatt v Kazana* [1959] 2 QB 152; *Lipkin Gorman*, n 2.

[639] For differences between common law and equity in this context, see 3.47–3.55.

In some cases of 'no intent' this survival model cannot apply. Instead a new equitable pro-   **3.258**
prietary interest arises from the unjust enrichment of the recipient. In the normal course
a company has full legal ownership of its assets. If the directors, being fiduciaries, transfer
assets without authority, then, unless that recipient has dealt with the company in good faith,
equity treats the recipient in the same way as a person who receives trust property from a
trustee acting without the authority of the trust deed or the consent of his beneficiaries.[640] In
the latter case the recipient takes subject to the pre-existing equitable interest of the beneficiaries. The survival model applies.[641] But in the former case there is no pre-existing equitable
interest in the company. Equity therefore completes the analogy by raising a new interest in
the assets received from the unauthorized fiduciary. Though it is tempting to attribute that
new interest to a breach of fiduciary duty and hence to locate it in the law of wrongs, it is
unnecessary to do so.

Though not sufficient, intent is in general necessary to the passing of property.[642] Just as in   **3.259**
absolutely involuntary transfers the property does not pass, so in some instances of severely
impaired transfer the transferee takes subject to the transferor's pre-existing proprietary rights,
as where the latter has laboured under a fundamental mistake.[643] However, the law generally gives the defectively intending transferor a more limited proprietary right as a means to
restitution. Thus, at common law, contracts may be rescinded for fraudulent misrepresentation,[644] duress,[645] and mental incapacity,[646] and insurance contracts may also be rescinded
for non-disclosure and non-fraudulent misrepresentation.[647] In equity, contracts may be
rescinded for fraudulent and non-fraudulent misrepresentation,[648] undue influence,[649]
unconscionable dealing,[650] and non-compliance with the fiduciary dealing rules[651]—though
they may not be rescinded for common mistake[652] or unilateral mistake known to the other
party.[653] This all implies at the very least that the transferor has a power *in rem*, a power to

---

[640] See 3.52.

[641] See 3.53–3.54.

[642] Thus, when the facts indicate a sale of specific goods, the Sale of Goods Act 1979, s 17(1), provides
that property passes when it is intended to pass.

[643] *Cundy v Lindsay* (1878) 3 App Cas 459, HL (fundamental mistake of identity). In *Simms*, n 158, at
686, Robert Goff J expressly took account of the fact that in some restitutionary claims for mistake the property would not have passed.

[644] *Load v Green* (1846) 15 M & W 216, 153 ER 828; *Clarke v Dickson* (1858) El Bl & El 148, 120 ER
463; *Car and Universal Finance Co Ltd v Caldwell* [1965] 1 QB 525, CA.

[645] *The Evia Luck*, n 173; *Halpern*, n 511.

[646] *Imperial Loan Co Ltd v Stone* [1892] 1 QB 599, CA; *Hart*, n 196.

[647] *Carter v Boehm* (1766) 3 Burr 1909, 97 ER 1162; *Pan Atlantic Insurance Co Ltd v Pine Top Insurance
Co Ltd* [1995] 1 AC 501, HL; *Manifest Shipping Co Ltd v Uni-Polaris Insurance Co Ltd (The Star Sea)* [2003]
1 AC 469, HL.

[648] *Peek v Gurney* (1871) LR 13 Eq 79; *Redgrave v Hurd* (1881) 20 Ch D 1, CA; *Newbigging v Adam*
(1886) 34 Ch D 582, CA; *O'Brien*, n 190.

[649] *O'Brien*, n 190; *Etridge* (HL), n 184.

[650] *Cresswell*, n 200; *Burch*, n 199; *Dusangh*, n 207.

[651] *Daly v Sidney Stock Exchange* (1986) 160 CLR 371; *Saunders*, n 118.

[652] *Great Peace Shipping Ltd v Tsavlisis Salvage (International) Ltd (The Great Peace)* [2002] EWCA Civ
1407, [2003] QB 679, disapproving *Solle v Butcher* [1950] 1 KB 671, CA.

[653] D O'Sullivan, S Elliott, and R Zakrzewski, *The Law of Rescission* (2008) paras 7.07–7.26 argue that
this is a ground for rescission in equity under English law, citing *Riverlate Properties Ltd v Paul* [1975] 1 Ch
133, 145, CA, and *Huyton SA v Distribuidora Internacional De Productos Agricolas SA de CV* [2002] EWHC
2088 (Comm), [2003] 2 Lloyd's Rep 780. But it is hard to see how this ground can have survived *The Great
Peace*, n 652, as Aikens J observed in *Statoil ASA v Louis Dreyfus Energy Services LP (The Harriette N)* [2008]
EWHC 2257 (Comm), [2009] 1 All ER (Comm) 1035, at [105].

vest in himself that with which he has parted. We will return below to the question whether that is all that such a transferor obtains.[654]

3.260 Qualified intent. The commonest qualified transfers do not generate proprietary rights. To determine which do and which do not, it is necessary to insist on the distinction between the abstract value received and the thing itself which carries that value to the defendant. Ex hypothesi, no qualified transfer can put the abstract value finally at the disposition of the transferee until the basis on which the transfer was made has materialized. However, the failure of the basis of the transfer will generate no proprietary interest unless an exercise of construction concludes that the qualification was such as also to ring-fence the thing received.[655] 'Thing' here includes money or, if no corporeal money actually passes, the fund or credit. As Robert Chambers says, there will be no proprietary interest if, before the basis fails, the recipient obtains the unrestricted use of the property.[656]

3.261 If money is construed to have been transferred solely for a particular purpose, that construction easily carries with it the secondary conclusion that the money itself, or the credit, was never to be at the disposition of the recipient or, in short, that it was ring-fenced from the beginning. In these circumstances, it may be that an express trust in favour of the transferor arises from the moment of receipt, subject to a power vested in the transferee to apply the money[657]—in which case there is no room for the law of unjust enrichment to operate. But in some situations where a claimant transfers property to a defendant on the basis that the defendant will never treat himself as entitled to the benefit normally inherent in such a transfer, an express trust is excluded on the facts. Here, the law of unjust enrichment will turn the transferee into a trustee for the transferor.[658]

3.262 In *Hussey v Palmer*[659] an elderly lady advanced money for her son-in-law to extend his house and provide her with accommodation. If he had not extended the house, it would have been easy to conclude that the money had been ring-fenced for that purpose. What actually happened was that the house was extended but the relationship broke down so that the mother-in-law had to find accommodation elsewhere. She wanted her money back and would have been content with a personal claim. The court insisted that she had a trust interest in the house. It makes perfect sense to say that the abstract value of the mother's money was not to be at her son-in-law's disposition if the accommodation limb of the arrangement broke down. There was a failure of basis. But it is difficult to follow this line of reasoning to any conclusion that she had a proprietary interest in the house.

3.263 Many cases in which the failure of the intended basis of a transfer does turn the defendant into a trustee, and thus raises a proprietary interest in the transferor, could be decided on the *Neste Oy* basis, that the recipient knew from the moment of the receipt that he was not entitled to treat the asset as his own.[660] However, the proprietary response can be independently explained by the combination of the qualification and the construction of that qualification as requiring the segregation of the asset.

---

[654] See 3.266–3.273.
[655] *Westdeutsche* (HL), n 2, at 709–712, in overruling the proprietary aspect of *Sinclair*, n 9, classifies it as a case in which there was no ring-fencing. cf *Re Goldcorp Exchange Ltd* [1995] 1 AC 74, PC and all the payments except the last in *Neste Oy*, n 261.
[656] Chambers (1997), n 282, at 148–151 and 169. Note especially the passage in *Re Nanwa Goldmines Ltd* [1955] 1 WLR 1080, 1083–1084, cited by Chambers at 150.
[657] *Quistclose*, n 271, as interpreted in *Twinsectra*, n 272.
[658] *Tinsley*, n 564.
[659] [1972] 1 WLR, 1286, CA. Similarly problematic is *Muschinski v Dodds* [1985] 160 CLR 583.
[660] See 3.247ff.

This independent explanation shows up in cases where the transferor's qualified intent is **3.264** established by evidence or by presumption. In *Re Vinogradoff*[661] securities were transferred into the name of a four-year-old child, and the presumption of non-beneficial intent operated to turn the child into a trustee for the transferor. The *Neste Oy* doctrine could not run against a child. Again, in *Tinsley v Milligan*[662] a woman contributed to the price of a house which went into the name of her lesbian partner. No question arose of her having to prove that the partner knew from the start that she was not intended to take the benefit of the claimant's contribution. On the particular facts, the claimant could take advantage of a presumption that she did not intend this. The *Neste Oy* doctrine could not work through presumptions. Yet the contributor's qualified intent, established by unrebutted presumption, was enough to raise a resulting trust.

Policy-motivated unjust factors. The three general propositions considered above can **3.265** apply to policy-motivated unjust factors, but the special propositions relevant to the different kinds of non-voluntary transfer cannot. This might suggest that policy-motivated unjust factors should meet only a personal response. However, a surety is always entitled to a proprietary right via subrogation, where he has discharged a creditor's security.[663] Again, if an insured person receives money or some other valuable asset in diminution of a loss which the insurer has already made good, the insurer has not only a personal claim to be repaid the over-indemnity, but also an equitable lien over that money or other asset so received.[664] It is not easy to detect the principle which determines that proprietary response. Similarly, arguments as to the proprietary consequences of payment of taxes not due are unlikely to rest on any principled foundation.[665] In this sector the policy which dictates restitution must be expected also to determine the nature of the response.

(3) What Kind of Proprietary Right?

(a) Power or substantive interest?

Three models exist: the survival model, the power model, and the immediate interest model. **3.266** The first supposes the survival of the pre-existing interest, itself not the creature of the recipient's unjust enrichment. In the second the claimant obtains a power to crystallize an interest in the thing received. The substantive interest will not arise till the power is exercised. In the third the law raises a new substantive interest as soon as the unjust enrichment happens.

(i) Traceable substitutes

Suppose that a defendant receives £10,000 from a claimant, buys a painting with the money, **3.267** then exchanges the painting for a car. Even if the money came to the defendant in circumstances in which the claimant acquired, or retained, an immediate substantive interest in it, the claimant would have only a power to crystallize a similar interest in first the painting, and then the car. This power floats over the chain of substitutions. Only when the claimant exercises the power by asserting his entitlement to the thing at the end of the chain does he

---

[661] [1935] WN 68.

[662] *Tinsley*, n 564.

[663] Mercantile Law Amendment Act 1856, s 5. The nature of the surety's proprietary right is discussed at 3.279–3.281.

[664] *Lord Napier and Ettrick v Hunter* [1993] AC 713, HL. The insurer's lien probably extends only to assets recovered from third parties, and not to any cause of action which the insured may have against them: *Re Ballast plc* [2006] EWHC 3189 (Ch), [2007] BPIR 117.

[665] *Zaidan Group Ltd v City of London* [1990] 64 DLR (4th) 514, Ontario CA.

acquire his substantive interest in that thing. The applicability of the power model here is controversial,[666] but the other model leads to very grave practical difficulties.[667]

(ii) The original asset received

3.268 Where the *Neste Oy* doctrine bites,[668] it produces an immediate trust and, necessarily, an immediate interest in the claimant. The *Neste Oy* doctrine apart, in cases of qualified intent there is either no proprietary response at all or, in those cases where the asset received is ring-fenced, the immediate interest model again applies. For example, if a fund is transferred upon trust and the trust fails, there will be an immediate resulting trust.[669]

3.269 In cases of deficient intent, the transfer is either voidable or void. If it is void, the recipient takes subject to the pre-existing proprietary right.[670] If the common law regards the transaction as voidable, as for fraudulent misrepresentation or duress, the power can be exercised at law without communication with the transferee, merely by manifesting in a suitably public manner the intention to rescind.[671] If the transaction is voidable only in equity, the transferor now appears to obtain a similar power to crystallize an equitable beneficial interest. Once that power is exercised, there will be a trust.[672] The beneficial owner in equity will then be in a position to demand the transfer of the legal title.

3.270 Some cases apply the immediate interest model to transfers voidable in equity. On this view the legal title passes voidably, in the sense that the court will order the transfer to be reversed but, from the moment of the transfer, the transferee already holds on trust for the transferor. No further act is required of the impaired transferee.[673] This model has never been repudiated. It has simply been departed from.

3.271 *Chase Manhattan Bank NA v Israel-British Bank (London) Ltd*[674] is a lone modern survival of that line of cases, not obviously aware of its ancestry. The bank mistakenly made the same payment twice. It transferred $2 million and then sent it again. The payee became insolvent. The personal claim, which undoubtedly lay, would have yielded little or nothing. A proprietary claim would give priority over unsecured creditors. Goulding J held that the effect of the mistake was immediately to turn the payee into a trustee of the second payment.

---

[666] In *Cave v Cave* (1880) 15 Ch D 639, Fry J came down in favour of the immediate interest model, a view preferred by the leading treatise on tracing: Smith, n 618, at 358–361. *Cave* was criticized in *Re Ffrench's Estate* (1887) 21 LR Ir 83, CA (Ir) and is doubtfully compatible with *Re J Leslie (Engineers) Co Ltd* [1976] 1 WLR 292. The House of Lords applied the power model in *Lipkin Gorman*, n 2, which concerned a legal interest. It would be intolerable to encourage different analyses at law and in equity.
[667] Vividly illustrated on the facts of *Jones*, n 92.
[668] See 3.247–3.254.
[669] *Air Jamaica*, n 281.
[670] Nullity does not necessarily prevent the property passing, but nullity from seriously impaired intent does: *Cundy*, n 643; *Shogun Finance Ltd v Hudson* [2003] UKHL 62, [2004] 1 AC 919.
[671] *Caldwell*, n 644.
[672] *Lonrho plc v Fayed* [1992] 1 WLR 1, 11–12; *Twinsectra Ltd v Yardley* [1999] Lloyd's Rep Bank 438, 461–462, CA; *Shalson v Russo* [2003] EWHC 1637 (Ch), [2005] Ch 281, at [121]–[127]. Very influential in this has been Brennan J's judgment in *Daly*, n 651. More recent Australian authorities have identified the trust arising in such cases as a 'remedial constructive trust' (which are not recognized in England: 3.255): *Robins v Incentive Dynamics Pty Ltd (in liq)* (2003) 175 Fed LR 286 at [74]; *Grimaldi*, n 132, at [277].
[673] This model is strongly defended by Robert Chambers in his discussion of the emergence of 'mere equities': Chambers (1997), n 282, at 171–181, relying on *Stump v Gaby* (1852) 2 De GM & G 623, 42 ER 1015; *Gresley v Mousley* (1859) 4 De G & J 78, 45 ER 31; *Dickinson v Burrell* (1866) LR 1 Eq 377, CA; *Melbourne Banking Corp v Brougham* (1882) 7 App Cas 307, PC; *Blacklocks v JB Developments (Godalming) Ltd* [1982] Ch 183.
[674] [1981] Ch 105, applied in *Bank Tejerat v Hong Kong and Shanghai Banking Corp* [1995] Lloyd's Rep 239.

This case later came under heavy pressure. Lord Browne-Wilkinson said that he could only **3.272** reach the same result if he could find that the recipient bank knew that it was not entitled.[675] Lord Millett, writing extra-judicially, argued that an immediate trust can only be found where the payee is or receives through a fiduciary. For the rest he espoused the power model of the proprietary reaction to transfers that are unjust by reason of the claimant's impaired consent. The trust must await the act of rescission: 'Pending rescission the transferee has the whole legal and beneficial interest in the property, but his beneficial interest is defeasible . . . It is not inappropriate to describe the transferee as holding the property on a constructive trust for the transferor, but only after rescission.'[676]

For impaired transfers, therefore, the power model is now in the ascendant.[677] So far as it **3.273** turns simply on mistake, the *Chase Manhattan* case will have to be reinterpreted as having generated a power, and not an immediate substantive interest. Only if the recipients could have been found to know from the start that the money would have to be repaid will they, on this view, have been immediate trustees, under the *Neste Oy* doctrine.[678]

(b) Beneficial or security interest?

When the claimant's substantive interest accrues, whether immediately or by the exercise of **3.274** a power, the question arises whether it should be a beneficial interest or a lien securing the personal claim. The basic principle which governs this difficult question is that the claimant's proprietary right should be as nearly as possible identical to that which he had at the beginning of the story. A supporting principle leaves it to the claimant to choose between multiple rights which the law accords to him. English law now clearly gives effect to this principle and allows the claimant to choose between a beneficial interest proportionate to his contribution and a security interest for the amount of his contribution.[679]

This principle of free choice cannot operate where the law has specified the nature of the **3.275** interest which arises on the particular facts. In some areas it has done so, not always for a discernible reason. The House of Lords decided that money which diminishes a loss for which an insured person had already been indemnified is held subject to an equitable lien in favour of the insurer, but does not turn the insured into a trustee so as to confer a beneficial interest on the insurer.[680] Where money is traced into improvements, it is also said that this generates at most a lien.[681] However, in such a case there will be no claim at all unless the circumstances are such as to bar the argument from subjectivity of value.[682]

(c) Vulnerability to defences

All rights arising from unjust enrichment, not excluding proprietary rights, are vulnerable to **3.276** defences.[683] The defence of change of position is open even to the immediate recipient. If the

---

[675] *Westdeutsche* (HL), n 2, at 715. This dictum has itself been treated with some circumspection: *Barclays Bank plc v Box* [1998] Lloyd's Rep Bank 185, 200–201; *Papamichael v National Westminster Bank plc* [2003] EWHC 164 (Comm), [2003] 1 Lloyd's Rep 341, at [232]–[242]; *Shalson*, n 672, at [108]–[127]; *London Allied Holdings Ltd v Lee* [2007] EWHC 2061 (Ch), at [268]–[272]; *Fitzalan-Howard v Hibbert* [2009] EWHC 2855 (QB), [2010] PNLR 11, at [49]; *Maqsood v Mahmood* [2012] EWCA Civ 251, at [35]–[38].

[676] 'Restitution and Constructive Trust' (1998) 114 LQR 399, 416.

[677] Further discussion: Häcker, n 517, at 125–159; E Bant, 'Reconsidering the Role of Election in Rescission' (2012) 32 OJLS 467.

[678] See 3.247–3.254.

[679] *Foskett*, n 137, at 130.

[680] *Napier and Ettrick*, n 664.

[681] *Foskett*, n 137, at 109. cf *Esteem*, n 133, at 105–106.

[682] *Diplock*, n 129, at 546–548. Contrast *Unity Joint Stock Mutual Banking Association v King* (1858) Beav 72, 44 ER 1192. And see 3.27ff.

[683] For discussion of which, see 3.146ff.

assets pass to a third party, the defence of bona fide purchase will destroy the claimant's right in all cases if the claimant has only a power or if money is in question. A substantive legal proprietary interest will otherwise be exigible against anyone, and a substantive equitable interest will be exigible against anyone but a bona fide purchaser of a legal interest. Assets which pass to a donee will be recoverable,[684] although nowadays such a donee will always be entitled to have any change of position taken into account.

3.277 Obiter dicta in the House of Lords suggest that, where a claimant purports to exercise a power to crystallize an interest in an asset which has passed to a third party, and the latter contests his right to do so, the onus is on the claimant to show that the third party was not a bona fide purchaser.[685] This must be regarded as controversial. A third party seeking to rely on change of position will certainly not be entitled to any such shift of the onus of proof.

(4) Subrogation

3.278 The word 'subrogation' means 'substitution'; it comes from the same Latin root as the more familiar word 'surrogate'. Thus the term envisages the substitution of one person for another for the purpose of exercising rights initially held by that other. In some cases, this language accurately reflects the operation of the remedy: eg, where an insurer acquires its insured's subsisting rights against a third party responsible for causing an insured loss.[686] In another class of case, however, this language is misleading.

3.279 When a claimant's money is used to discharge a creditor's rights against a defendant, the law may give him the right to be treated, by a legal fiction, as though the creditor's rights have been 'kept alive' and transferred to him so that he can enforce them for his own benefit.[687] The language of 'revival' and 'transfer' used in these cases is metaphorical. In fact the law of unjust enrichment generates new rights in the claimant's favour, whose content and characteristics resemble those of the creditor's extinguished rights, but are not identical with them.[688]

3.280 The imagery used in cases of this type has sometimes led the courts into error. They have worried unnecessarily about the mechanisms by which the creditor's extinguished rights might be revived and transferred, when no revival and transfer actually occur.[689] And they have forgotten that a claimant cannot be entitled to subrogation in this sort of case unless he also has a direct personal claim in unjust enrichment deriving from the fact that he has discharged the defendant's debt. Hence the fictional 'acquisition' of the creditor's rights is redundant unless these rights were secured.[690] The courts have sometimes failed to recognize

---

[684] *Bridgeman*, n 191; *Huguenin*, n 191. In the latter case Lord Eldon LC said (at 289), invoking the former, 'I should regret that any doubt could be entertained that, whether it is not competent to a Court of equity to take away from third persons the benefits which they have derived from the fraud, imposition, or undue influence of others'.

[685] *Boulter*, n 504, at 1926. The dicta go beyond the facts, on which it was rightly held that the party seeking relief bore the onus of proving that the other had notice of her disability.

[686] Mitchell and Watterson, n 5, at ch 10.

[687] For the language of fictional revival see eg *Butler*, n 106, at 282; *UCB Group Ltd v Hedworth (No 2)* [2003] EWCA Civ 1717, [2003] 3 FCR 739, at [146].

[688] *BFC*, n 2, at 236; *Cheltenham & Gloucester plc v Appleyard* [2004] EWCA Civ 291, at [49]; *Filby*, n 106, at [63]; *Day v Tiuta International Ltd* [2014] EWCA Civ 1246 at [43].

[689] *Diplock*, n 129, at 549, corrected in *Boscawen*, n 130, at 340.

[690] A point which was apparently overlooked in *Filby*, n 106, where much time was spent discussing whether the claimant should have a subrogated claim, but it never seems to have been considered whether it might simply have a direct claim.

this, or have chosen to ignore it, and have awarded a personal remedy in the form of a sub-rogation order while simultaneously denying the claimant a direct personal claim.[691] This is self-contradictory.

Unless the courts clearly recognize that the law of unjust enrichment generates new rights **3.281** for claimants in this class of subrogation case, they will struggle to answer some of the dif-ficult questions thrown up by the case law.[692] Examples are: whether the remedy should be awarded to a claimant who has paid only part of the defendant's debt;[693] whether a claimant who has paid off a mortgage debt can obtain an order for sale of the mortgaged property, after he has been repaid more than the amount of the mortgage debt;[694] whether interest awarded on a subrogation claim should be assessed on an independent basis,[695] or by reference to the interest that was previously payable on the defendant's extinguished debt;[696] and whether the priority status of a claimant's new proprietary right should mirror the priority status of the creditor's discharged security, or reflect the fact that the claimant has acquired a com-pletely new equitable interest.[697]

The courts have been slow to appreciate that the same rules should govern the acquisition **3.282** of proprietary rights in subrogation cases as govern other proprietary responses to unjust enrichment. Thus, only obscure language conceals the fact that, if a successful tracing exercise identifies, not shares or a yacht, but an extinguished security interest, the conditions which dictate the transfer of the shares or yacht will be the same conditions as will justify giving the claimant a new security that mirrors the extinguished charge. As the previously scattered fragments of the law of unjust enrichment become better integrated, common principles are more easily asserted. When contemplating whether to impose a trust or lien on the ground of unjust enrichment, the courts can usefully look across to subrogation cases where the remedy has been awarded on the ground of mistake, failure of basis, or absence of consent.[698] They can also take note of the subrogation cases which hold that a claimant who lends money to a defendant may not acquire better rights than the ones he has bargained for,[699] and may not obtain a proprietary right at all where he has expressly agreed not to take security or has intended to make an unsecured loan.[700]

[691] *Marlow v Pitfeild* (1719) 1 P Wms 558, 24 ER 516; *Jenner v Morris* (1861) 3 De G F & J 45, 45 ER 795; *Baroness Wenlock v River Dee Co* (1888) 38 Ch D 534; *Re Walter's Deed of Guarantee* [1933] 1 Ch 321; *Niru Battery Manufacturing Co v Milestone Trading Ltd (No 2)* [2003] EWHC 1032 (Comm), [2003] 2 All ER (Comm) 365 ('*Niru (No 2)* (Comm)'), corrected on appeal: *Niru (No 2)* (CA), n 292.
[692] For discussion of which, see Mitchell and Watterson, n 5, at chs 7, 8, and 9.
[693] *Gedye v Matson* (1858) 25 Beav 310, 53 ER 655; *ex p Brett* (1871) LR 6 Ch App 838, 841; *Chetwynd v Allen* [1899] 1 Ch 353; *McCullough v Elliott* (1922) 62 DLR 257, Alberta CA; *BFC*, n 2, at 236.
[694] *Halifax Mortgage Services Ltd v Muirhead* (1997) 76 P & CR 418, CA; *UCB*, n 192, at [70]–[75] and [101]–[103].
[695] As in eg *Thurstan v Nottingham Permanent Building Society* [1902] 1 Ch 1, CA, aff'd [1903] AC 6, HL; *Congresbury Motors Ltd v Anglo-Belge Finance Co Ltd* [1970] Ch 294, aff'd [1971] Ch 81, CA; *Re Tramway Building & Construction Co Ltd* [1988] Ch 293.
[696] As in eg *Western Trust & Savings Ltd v Rock* [1993] NPC 89, CA; *Castle Phillips Finance Ltd v Piddington* (1995) 70 P & CR 592, CA; *Filby*, n 106.
[697] The latter, according to *Appleyard*, n 688, at [44], citing *Halifax plc v Omar* [2002] EWCA Civ 940. See also *National Westminster Bank plc v Mayfair Estates Property Investments Ltd* [2007] EWHC 287 (Ch).
[698] For discussion of which, see Mitchell and Watterson, n 5, at ch 6.
[699] *BFC*, n 2, at 235 and 236–237; *Appleyard*, n 688, at [41]; *Filby*, n 106, at [62] and [63].
[700] *Boscawen*, n 130, at 338; *Muirhead*, n 694, at 426–427; *Eagle Star plc v Karasiewicz* [2002] EWCA Civ 940, at [19]; *Appleyard*, n 688, at [38]; *Filby*, n 106, at [39].

4

JUDICIAL REMEDIES

A. A General Survey

(1) Introduction

The concept of a remedy has rarely been subjected to rigorous analysis.[1] Views may differ as **4.01** to precisely what one is talking about. In this chapter, a remedy is used to denote the relief (whether an order or a pronouncement) that a person can seek from a court. The focus is therefore entirely on judicial remedies and not on what are sometimes termed 'self-help' remedies (which are available without coming to court). There is a wide range of judicial remedies. It is helpful to distinguish between those available pre-trial, those available at trial, and those available post-trial. Although we shall briefly mention the first and the last,[2] our concern in this chapter will essentially be with judicial remedies available at trial.

Within the law of obligations (and leaving aside specialist areas such as family law)[3] a judicial **4.02** remedy granted at trial can be said to be a response to a cause of action. For example, contractual remedies respond to a breach of contract; tort remedies respond to a tort; restitutionary remedies respond to an unjust enrichment. It follows that judicial remedies at trial cannot be fully understood in isolation from—and an exposition must to some extent be structured by—the relevant cause of action. An alternative way of expressing this is to say that there is a division—albeit one where the two sides of the division are closely connected—between issues going to liability (eg, has the defendant committed a breach of contract or tort against the claimant or has the defendant been unjustly enriched at the claimant's expense?) and

---

[1] Notable exceptions include P Birks, 'Rights, Wrongs, and Remedies' (2000) 20 OJLS 1; and R Zakrzewski, *Remedies Reclassified* (2005).

[2] See 4.03–4.05.

[3] For judicial remedies in respect of family law (eg divorce decrees, decrees of nullity of marriage, separation orders and adoption orders) see EPL ch 2. Other examples of judicial remedies in specialist areas—and not covered in this chapter—include the appointment of an administrative receiver or a liquidator and the winding-up of a company (see EPL ch 19); and the dissolution of a partnership.

issues going to remedies (eg, what will the courts award or grant to redress a breach of contract or tort or to reverse an unjust enrichment?).

(2) Pre-trial and Post-trial Judicial Remedies

4.03 These are further examined in EPL chapter 22. Only the barest of outlines is therefore called for here.

4.04 Pre-trial judicial remedies can be helpfully categorized into remedies designed to assist a litigant's preparation for trial; and remedies designed to protect a claimant's rights against pre-trial delay. The former includes, eg, orders for disclosure,[4] orders for further information,[5] and search orders (*Anton Piller* orders).[6] The latter includes interim injunctions,[7] freezing injunctions (*Mareva* injunctions),[8] and interim payments.[9] In many cases, the time factor and circumstances are such that by giving a claimant an interim injunction, which protects its rights against delay pre-trial, or by refusing that remedy, the need for a trial is avoided. That is, the decision regarding the pre-trial remedy in practice resolves the dispute. This is one of the reasons why the House of Lords' approach to interim injunctions in the leading case of *American Cyanamid Co v Ethicon Ltd*[10] has been criticized. In that case, their Lordships laid down that the courts should decide whether or not an interim injunction should be granted on the basis of what is more convenient pending trial. The merits of the claim should not be looked at except as a last resort where it is otherwise unclear where the balance of convenience lies. The objection to this is that, where the decision on the interlocutory application will effectively decide the dispute, the courts cannot fairly decide the interlocutory application without taking a view on the merits of the claim.[11]

4.05 Post-trial judicial remedies are concerned with the enforcement or execution of the remedies ordered at trial. For some non-monetary remedies, such as injunctions and specific performance, enforcement is by proceedings for contempt of court, with the ultimate sanction being imprisonment;[12] whereas for monetary remedies, such as damages and the award of an agreed sum, there are several post-trial judicial remedies concerned to enforce payment, examples being a warrant of execution,[13] an attachment of earnings order,[14] a third party debt order,[15] a charging order,[16] or a post-trial freezing injunction.[17]

(3) Judicial Remedies Available at Trial

(a) General

4.06 In examining judicial remedies available at trial, a number of distinctions can be drawn. One can contrast orders (ie, coercive remedies) such as damages, specific performance, injunctions,

---

[4] See EPL 22.53–22.60.
[5] CPR Part 18.
[6] See EPL 22.28–22.29.
[7] See EPL 22.35–22.37.
[8] See EPL 22.20–22.27.
[9] See EPL 22.34.
[10] [1975] AC 396. See EPL 22.36–22.37.
[11] This objection has been recognized and the *American Cyanamid* test rejected or modified or reinterpreted in, eg, *Cayne v Global Natural Resources plc* [1984] 1 All ER 225, CA; *Cambridge Nutrition Ltd v BBC* [1990] 3 All ER 523, CA; *Series 5 Software v Clarke* [1996] 1 All ER 853.
[12] See EPL 22.130–22.131.
[13] See EPL 22.127.
[14] CCR Ord 27 in CPR Sch 2.
[15] See EPL 22.127.
[16] See EPL 22.127.
[17] See *Orwell Steel Ltd v Asphalt and Tarmac (UK) Ltd* [1984] 1 WLR 1097.

the award of money had and received, the award of an agreed sum, or delivery up of goods; with pronouncements (ie, non-coercive remedies) such as declarations, rescission, rectification, constructive and resulting trusts, and liens.[18] One can further contrast monetary remedies (ie, awards of money) such as an account of profits, damages, and the award of an agreed sum; with non-monetary remedies (eg, injunctions). Another distinction is between specific remedies, which order the defendant to comply with his primary duty or to 'undo' breach of a primary duty (eg, injunctions, specific performance, the award of an agreed sum) and substitutionary remedies, which order the defendant to pay a 'substitute sum' for having failed to comply with a primary duty (eg, damages). Some remedies are personal remedies, which are not tied to particular property in the defendant's possession and hence do not give priority to the claimant on the defendant's insolvency (eg, damages, the award of an agreed sum, the award of money had and received, and an account of profits); while others are proprietary remedies, which are concerned to return property owned by the claimant or to confer proprietary rights on the claimant over property in the defendant's possession, and which do give priority to the claimant on the defendant's insolvency (eg, delivery up of goods, recovery of land, some constructive and resulting trusts and, in some situations, rescission). Then there is the historical division, reflecting the organization of the courts before the Judicature Acts 1873–1875, between common law remedies (eg, damages and the award of an agreed sum) and equitable remedies (eg, an account of profits, specific performance and injunctions). Common law remedies are those awarded pre-1875 by the common law courts. Equitable remedies are those awarded pre-1875 by the Court of Chancery. Table 4.1 shows the main judicial remedies available at trial categorized according to the major remedial distinctions referred to in this paragraph.

4.07 Some of these major distinctions can be further subdivided. For example, monetary remedies are sometimes subdivided—and for some rules of law must be subdivided[19]—into (unliquidated) damages, on the one hand, and debts or liquidated claims on the other. The latter include, eg, the award of an agreed sum, the award of money had and received, and a *quantum meruit*.[20]

4.08 Some of the above distinctions, while commonly made, do not appear particularly significant or illuminating. Moreover, in contrast to remedies for wrongs, there is relatively little to say (see 4.09–4.13) in relation to remedies for the cause of action of unjust enrichment that has not already been said in discussing that cause of action.[21] The treatment of judicial remedies in this chapter therefore concentrates on remedies for civil wrongs, whether the wrong be a breach of contract, a tort or an equitable wrong.[22] A primary aim is to expose and analyse the purposes pursued by remedies for wrongs. *Broadly speaking, the purposes are as follows: (1) compensation; (2) restitution and punishment; (3) compelling performance or preventing (or compelling the undoing of) a wrong; and (4) declaring rights. These purposes form the structure for the bulk of this chapter.* Table 4.2 shows the purposes of the main judicial remedies available at trial for wrongs.

---

[18] With the exception of declarations, pronouncements by a court alter the legal rights of the parties: FH Lawson, *Remedies of English Law* (2nd edn, 1980) ch 17 refers to such pronouncements as 'constitutive remedies'.

[19] See eg Limitation Act 1980, s 29(5) (acknowledgement or part payment).

[20] *Amantilla Ltd v Telefusion plc* (1987) 9 Con LR 139.

[21] See ch 3.

[22] Equitable wrongs can be regarded as comprising breach of fiduciary duty (including breach of trust), breach of confidence, assisting or procuring a breach of fiduciary duty, and breach of a duty arising under the doctrine of proprietary estoppel.

Table 4.1 Main judicial remedies available at trial categorized by principal remedial distinctions

Remedy	Coercive/non-coercive	Monetary/non-monetary	Specific/substitutionary	Personal/proprietary	Common law/equitable
Damages	Coercive	Monetary	Substitutionary	Personal	Normally common law but can be equitable
Equitable compensation	Coercive	Monetary	Substitutionary	Personal	Equitable
Award of an agreed sum	Coercive	Monetary	Specific	Personal	Common law
Specific performance	Coercive	Non-monetary	Specific	Normally personal	Equitable
Injunction	Coercive	Non-monetary	Specific	Normally personal	Equitable
Delivery up of goods	Coercive	Non-monetary	Specific	Proprietary	Statutory (equitable roots)
Delivery up for destruction	Coercive	Non-monetary	Specific	Proprietary	Equitable
Recovery of land	Coercive	Non-monetary	Specific	Proprietary	Common law
Award of money had and received	Coercive	Monetary	Normally specific	Personal	Common law
Award of money paid to defendant's use	Coercive	Monetary	Specific	Personal	Common law
Quantum meruit/quantum valebat	Coercive	Monetary	Specific	Personal	Common law
Account of money received/account of profits	Coercive	Monetary	Normally substitutionary	Personal	Equitable
Declaration	Non-coercive	Non-monetary	–	–	Statutory (equitable roots)
Rescission	Non-coercive	Non-monetary	–	Both	Normally equitable but can be common law
Rectification	Non-coercive	Non-monetary	–	Both	Equitable
Constructive/resulting trusts	Non-coercive	Non-monetary	–	Proprietary	Equitable
Liens	Non-coercive	Non-monetary	–	Proprietary	Equitable

Table 4.2 Purposes of main judicial remedies available at trial for wrongs

Purpose	Remedy
Compensation	Compensatory damages. Equitable compensation.
Restitution	Restitutionary damages. Account of profits. Award of money had and received. Constructive trust.
Punishment	Punitive damages.
Compelling performance (of positive obligations)	Specific performance. Award of an agreed sum. Mandatory enforcing injunction.
Preventing a wrong	Prohibitory injunction. Delivery up for destruction or destruction on oath.
Compelling the undoing of a wrong	Mandatory restorative injunction. Delivery up of goods.
Declaring rights	Declaration. Nominal damages.

(b) Restitutionary remedies to reverse unjust enrichment

As will have been apparent from chapter 3, there is a range of judicial remedies which seek **4.09**
to reverse an unjust enrichment. They include both common law remedies (eg, the award of money had and received, the award of money paid to the claimant's use, and a *quantum meruit*) and equitable remedies (eg, an account of money received or a resulting trust); coercive remedies (eg, an award of money had and received) and non-coercive remedies (eg, rescission, a resulting trust, and a lien); monetary remedies (eg, an award of money had and received) and non-monetary remedies (eg, rescission of an executed contract which revests goods or land in the claimant); personal remedies (eg, the award of money had and received, a *quantum meruit* and an account of money received) and proprietary remedies (eg, a resulting trust and a lien).

Some of the restitutionary remedies overlap and could be rationalized and reduced. In par- **4.10**
ticular, the award of money had and received and its equitable equivalent—an account of money received—perform precisely the same role and it appears that history alone explains their dual existence. Similarly, within the realm of personal common law remedies, it is not clear that one needs the separate remedies of an award of money had and received, the award of money paid to the defendant's use, a *quantum meruit*, and a *quantum valebat*. Admittedly each of these remedies has come to be associated with particular factual situations. For example, the award of money had and received is the standard remedy for restitution of money paid by the claimant to the defendant under mistake or duress or for a consideration that has failed;[23] the award of money paid to the defendant's use is the conventional remedy for compulsory discharge of another's debt;[24] and a *quantum meruit* and a *quantum valebat* effect restitution of the value of services and goods respectively.[25] The law would be simplified and, arguably, improved if one swept away these different remedies and talked instead of a single personal remedy of a 'monetary restitutionary award'.[26]

---

[23] See 3.07, 3.56–3.68 and 3.76ff.
[24] See 3.07 and 3.106ff.
[25] See 3.07.
[26] A Burrows, *A Restatement of the English Law of Unjust Enrichment* (2012) 38.

4.11 The remedy of rescission of a contract (or deed of gift) is one of the most difficult remedies to analyse. Rescission (or as one can otherwise term it 'setting aside' a contract) is a remedy available where a party has entered into a voidable contract under, eg, duress[27] or undue influence;[28] or as a result of a misrepresentation or non-disclosure.[29] It wipes away a contract ab initio. It is both a self-help and a judicial remedy. It is normally subject to four bars: lapse of time, affirmation, third party rights and *restitutio in integrum* being impossible.[30] While one can regard it as always being a contractual remedy in the sense that it wipes away and allows escapes from a contract, it is also a restitutionary remedy reversing unjust enrichment where a contract has been wholly or partly executed and where the effect of the rescission is therefore to restore benefits to the contracting parties. The rescission may effect personal restitution (eg, by entitling the payor to the repayment of a purchase price);[31] but it is also commonly a proprietary restitutionary remedy in that it revests the proprietary rights to goods or land transferred under the contract.[32] Rescission is, therefore, difficult to analyse because it may involve contract and unjust enrichment, personal and proprietary restitution, and restitution of payments and restitution for benefits in kind.

4.12 An unresolved, yet fundamental, question is the extent to which, if at all, restitutionary remedies reversing unjust enrichment are, or should be, proprietary rather than merely personal.[33] A personal restitutionary remedy reverses an unjust enrichment received by the defendant irrespective of whether he or she still retains particular property. It does not afford priority on the defendant's insolvency. In contrast, a proprietary restitutionary remedy affords priority on the defendant's insolvency and is dependent on the defendant's retention of particular property.

4.13 If one puts to one side those proprietary remedies which are concerned to enable an owner to recover property which he continues to own, such as the remedy of ejectment from land or delivery up of goods,[34] and concentrates instead on the creation of new proprietary rights in response to unjust enrichment, the following may be regarded as examples of restitutionary proprietary rights.[35]

---

[27] See 1.203, 3.67–3.68.

[28] See 1.204–1.210 and 3.69–3.70.

[29] See 1.159–1.201.

[30] See 1.180–1.187. Furthermore, where rescission is thought too harsh a remedy against the *misrepresentor* (eg where the misrepresentation was wholly innocent and relatively trivial), damages can be awarded for a non-fraudulent misrepresentation in lieu of rescission under s 2(2) of the Misrepresentation Act 1967: see *William Sindell plc v Cambridgeshire CC* [1994] 1 WLR 1016, CA; *Govt of Zanzibar v British Aerospace (Lancaster House) Ltd* [2000] 1 WLR 2333 (laying down that, if rescission is barred, so are damages under s 2(2)).

[31] eg *Redgrave v Hurd* (1881) 20 Ch D 1. Rescission sometimes carries with it the award of a restitutionary indemnity indemnifying the claimant against expenses incurred that the defendant would otherwise have had to incur: see, eg, *Newbigging v Adam* (1886) 34 Ch D 582; *Whittington v Seale-Hayne* (1900) 82 LT 49. For rescission plus equitable compensation to the claimant, see *Mahoney v Purnell* [1996] 3 All ER 61; 4.133.

[32] eg *Erlanger v New Sombrero Phosphate Co* (1878) 3 App Cas 1218, HL. This case shows that, where property is revested in the claimant, the claimant may have to give counter-restitution, through an equitable account of profits, for benefits derived from use of the property. More problematic is the extent to which, if at all, a claimant should be required to give the other party an equitable allowance for a deterioration in the property returned by the claimant: see the *Erlanger* case, (1878) 3 App Cas 1218, 1278–1279.

[33] See 3.234–3.265. For the same question in respect of restitution for wrongs, see 4.158.

[34] See 2.317, and 4.225–4.227.

[35] See A Burrows, *The Law of Restitution* (3rd edn, 2011) ch 8; P Birks, *Unjust Enrichment* (2nd edn, 2005) ch 8.

(1) Equitable proprietary rights created following equitable tracing.[36] Although it may be tempting to regard those equitable rights as responding to the defendant retaining property that previously belonged in equity to the claimant, they are better viewed as restitutionary proprietary rights. They involve the creation of new proprietary rights over property which does not already belong to the claimant but is rather a substitution of property previously owned in equity by the claimant. So if one is entitled to trace from one's pig to a horse to a car one cannot say, without invoking fiction or a leap in reasoning, that one has proprietary rights in the car merely because one owned the pig that is now represented by the car. The most convincing analysis is that one's ownership of the pig, which has been substituted by the car, entitles one to claim new ownership of the car because the owner of the car is unjustly enriched at one's expense. The tracing rules are being invoked to show that the subtraction of one's pig has become the defendant's enrichment in the form of the car so that the car has been gained at the claimant's expense. It should be stressed, however, that this unjust enrichment analysis of rights after tracing was rejected by the House of Lords in *Foskett v McKeown* [37] which thought that the pre-existing proprietary rights were a sufficient explanation of the proprietary rights in the traced substitute.

(2) Some examples of subrogation: ie situations where the claimant is entitled to take over the third party's proprietary, rather than merely personal, rights against the defendant.[38]

(3) Equitable liens over land for the value of improvements mistakenly made to it.[39]

(4) Rescission of an executed contract which revests the proprietary rights to goods or land transferred under the contract.[40]

(5) Some resulting (or constructive) trusts.[41] But the role of resulting (and constructive) trusts in reversing unjust enrichment is a matter of continuing controversy. On one view, the equitable proprietary interest held to exist prior to tracing in *Chase Manhattan Bank v Israel-British Bank (London) Ltd*[42] is a valid example of proprietary restitution being granted in respect of payments made under a mistake of fact.[43] But in *Westdeutsche Landesbank Girozentrale v Islington London BC*[44] the House of Lords, in laying down that payments made under a void 'interest rate swap' transaction were not held by the payee on a resulting trust for the payor, rejected the reasoning (although, possibly, not the result) in the *Chase Manhattan* case.

B. Compensation

Compensation means the award of a sum of money which, so far as money can be so, is **4.14** equivalent to the claimant's loss. The loss may be pecuniary (ie, a loss of wealth) where the equivalence to the claimant's loss can be precise; or non-pecuniary (eg, pain and suffering

---

[36] eg *Re Hallett's Estate* (1880) 13 Ch D 696, CA; *Re Oatway* [1903] 2 Ch 356; *Re Diplock* [1948] Ch 465, CA; *Barlow Clowes International Ltd v Vaughan* [1992] 4 All ER 22, CA; *Bishopsgate Investment Management Ltd v Homan* [1995] Ch 211, CA; *Foskett v McKeown* [2001] 1 AC 102, HL. See 3.239–3.246, and 3.267.

[37] [2001] 1 AC 102, HL.

[38] eg Mercantile Law Amendment Act 1856, s 5; *Nottingham Permanent Benefit Building Society v Thurstan* [1903] AC 6; *Butler v Rice* [1910] 2 Ch 277; *Lord Napier & Ettrick v Hunter* [1993] AC 713, HL; *Boscawen v Bajwa* [1996] 1 WLR 328, CA. See 3.278–3.292.

[39] eg *Cooper v Phibbs* (1867) LR 2 HL 149.

[40] eg *Car and Universal Finance Co Ltd v Caldwell* [1965] 1 QB 525, CA.

[41] See EPL 4.317–4.324, and 3.234–3.277.

[42] [1981] Ch 105.

[43] See P Birks, *Unjust Enrichment* (2nd edn, 2005) ch 8; R Chambers, *Resulting Trusts* (1997).

[44] [1996] AC 669, HL.

and loss of amenity, loss of reputation, and mental distress generally) where the sum to be awarded as compensation cannot be precisely equivalent to the loss and where the only way to ensure consistency of awards is through conventionally accepted tariffs of value.

4.15 Compensation is generally achieved for the common law civil wrongs comprising torts and breach of contract through the remedy of compensatory damages (ie, damages designed to compensate). For equitable wrongs[45] the equivalent remedy is equitable compensation. For all civil wrongs, there is also the notion of equitable damages, which are awarded in addition to, or in substitution for, specific performance or an injunction under section 50 of the Senior Courts Act 1981.[46] Equitable damages are normally concerned to compensate the claimant. The rules applicable to compensatory damages, equitable compensation and equitable (compensatory) damages are not in all respects identical, so that it is still necessary to distinguish them, even though they are concerned with the common function of compensation. This is an unfortunate consequence of the historical divide between common law and equity.

4.16 This section primarily examines (common law) compensatory damages, which are available for torts and breach of contract.[47] It examines more briefly equitable compensation[48] and equitable (compensatory) damages.[49]

(1) Compensatory Damages: Breach of Contract

(a) The compensatory aim

(i) Protection of the expectation interest

4.17 The general aim of damages for breach of contract is to put the claimant into as good a position as if the contract had been performed. The classic authority for this is *Robinson v Harman* where Parke B said, 'The rule of common law is that where a party sustains a loss by reason of a breach of contract he is, so far as money can do it, to be placed in the same situation, with respect to damages as if the contract had been performed.'[50] This central aim is often referred to as the protection of the claimant's expectation interest.[51]

4.18 Theoretically an alternative aim of compensation for a breach of contract would be to put the claimant into as good a position as if no contract had been made. This would be to protect the claimant's reliance interest.[52] But while a claimant can opt to frame the claim in this way, the courts regard this as subservient to the expectation interest, so that the claimant cannot escape from a proven bad bargain by claiming the reliance interest.[53] The advantage to a

---

[45] See n 22.

[46] Formerly this power was contained in the Chancery Amendment Act 1858 (Lord Cairns's Act), s 2.

[47] See 4.17–4.132. For (compensatory) damages under s 8 of the Human Rights Act 1998 see *R (on the application of Greenfield) v Secretary of State for the Home Department* [2005] UKHL 14, [2005] 1 WLR 673 (laying down that such damages are sui generis and should not be equated to damages for domestic torts). See also D Feldman (ed), *English Public Law* (2nd edn, 2009) paras 19.39–19.44.

[48] See 4.133–4.137.

[49] See 4.138–4.142.

[50] (1848) 1 Exch 850, 855. The date for assessing damages is normally the date of the breach of contract but this is not an inflexible rule and will be departed from if, on facts known at trial and taking into account the duty to mitigate, that would not effect true compensation: *Johnson v Agnew* [1980] AC 367, HL; *Golden Strait Corp v Nippon Yusen Kubishika Kaisha, The Golden Victory* [2007] UKHL 12, [2007] 2 AC 353.

[51] The term was coined by L Fuller and WR Perdue, 'The Reliance Interest in Contract Damages' (1936–37) 46 Yale LJ 52. It is also sometimes referred to as the 'performance interest'.

[52] L Fuller and WR Perdue, 'The Reliance Interest in Contract Damages' (1936–37) 46 Yale LJ 52.

[53] *C and P Haulage v Middleton* [1983] 1 WLR 1461, CA; *CCC Films (London) v Impact Quadrant Films Ltd* [1985] QB 16. See also *Anglia Television Ltd v Reed* [1972] 1 QB 60, CA; *Commonwealth of Australia v Amann Aviation Pty Ltd* (1991) 66 ALJR 123, High Court of Australia.

claimant of framing the claim in this alternative way is, therefore, that it throws onto the defendant the burden of proving that the claim for reliance loss would put the claimant into a better position than if the contract had been performed; or, put another way, the claimant has the benefit of a rebuttable presumption that it would, at the very least, have made gains to cover its proven reliance expenses (which can include pre-contractual expenses). It has recently been accepted that the one and only compensatory aim for breach of contract is the protection of the expectation interest and that protection of the so-called 'reliance interest' is not independent of, but merely an alternative method of protecting, the expectation interest.[54]

(ii) Difference in value or cost of cure

In compensating the claimant for a breach of contract, the courts often face a choice between **4.19** awarding the difference in value or the cost of cure. The former directly awards the claimant the financial advantage it has lost by being deprived, partially or wholly, of the benefit to which it was contractually entitled. The cost of cure, on the other hand, seeks to award the claimant the additional financial sacrifice it would have to incur to put itself into as good a position as if it had received the benefit to which it was contractually entitled. In many situations the difference in value is in practice the only possible measure because no replacement benefit is available at any cost: eg, the party in breach may alone be capable of performing the contract or the delay may have made the performance impossible. But where both are possible measures, which will be awarded?

The answer turns on a range of factors, including the reasonableness of the claimant's conduct **4.20** in response to the breach and, most importantly, whether the claimant has cured or genuinely intends to cure. To illustrate this, let us take an example of a building contract where a builder, in breach of contract, refuses to carry out work or carries it out defectively.[55] Is the owner entitled to the difference in value of the property (ie, the value that the property would have had if the work had been properly completed minus its present value) or is the owner instead entitled to the cost of cure (ie, the cost of repairing any defects and having any remaining work completed)? Two cases repay examination.

In *Radford v De Froberville*,[56] the claimant had sold a plot of land to the defendant on condi- **4.21** tion that the defendant erected a wall on the plot so as to divide it from the claimant's land. The defendant had failed to build the wall. One question was whether the claimant was entitled to damages assessed according to the cost of cure (ie, the cost of building a wall on his land) which at the time of trial would have cost £3,400; or according to the difference

---

[54] *Omak Maritime Ltd v Mamola Challenger Shipping Co, The Mamola Challenger* [2010] EWHC 2026 (Comm), [2011] 1 Lloyd's Rep 47

[55] See also, eg, contracts for the sale of goods where general measures are set out in the Sale of Goods Act 1979 and are tied to what it is reasonable for the claimant to do. For a seller's breach in failing to deliver goods, Sale of Goods Act 1979, s 51(3) lays down that the generally appropriate measure is market price at time fixed for delivery minus contract price. This refers to the market buying price (for buying substitute goods) and is a cost of cure measure. For the ignoring of the resale price in this context, see *William Bros Ltd v Agius Ltd* [1914] AC 510, HL. Where a seller is in breach in delivering defective goods, the Sale of Goods Act 1979, s 53(3), lays down that the generally appropriate measure is the market price that the goods would have had if the contracted-for quality minus the market price of the goods delivered. This refers to the market selling price and is a difference in value measure. For the ignoring of resale prices in this context, see *Slater v Hoyle and Smith* [1920] 2 KB 11, CA, although doubt was cast on this in *Bence Graphics Int Ltd v Fasson UK Ltd* [1998] QB 87, CA. For breach by a buyer in refusing to accept goods, the Sale of Goods Act 1979, s 50(3) lays down that the general measure is the contract price minus the market price at the date of breach. This refers to the market selling price and is a difference in value measure. For the ignoring of a resale price here, see *Campbell Mostyn (Provisions) Ltd v Barnett Trading Co* [1954] 1 Lloyd's Rep 65. For an exception to s 50(3), see *Thompson Ltd v Robinson (Gunmakers) Ltd* [1955] Ch 177. See generally EPL 10.61, 10.65–10.68.

[56] [1977] 1 WLR 1262.

in the land's value with and without the wall, which was almost nil. Oliver J, applying *Tito v Waddell (No 2)*,[57] held that the claimant was entitled to the cost of cure. He said, 'In the instant case, I am entirely satisfied that the plaintiff genuinely wants this work done, and that he intends to expend any damages awarded on carrying it out.'[58]

4.22 In the leading case of *Ruxley Electronics and Construction Ltd v Forsyth*,[59] the claimant contracted to have a swimming pool built with the depth at the deep end of 7ft 6ins. When built the pool was in fact only 6ft 9ins at the deep end. Nevertheless, it was still perfectly safe for swimming and diving so that the difference in resale value of the property was not affected by the admitted breach of contract. To increase the depth of the pool to the agreed depth would cost £21,460 (nearly a third of the total price of the pool). Overturning the Court of Appeal, the House of Lords refused to award the claimant the cost of cure of £21,560; that would be unreasonable, because of the contrast with the nil difference in value. Moreover, the first instance judge had found that the claimant had no intention to use the damages to rebuild the pool. But rather than awarding the claimant no damages at all for the breach the House of Lords upheld the first instance judge's award of damages of £2,500 for loss of amenity.

4.23 We can therefore see from these decisions that the courts may award damages measured by a cost of cure that is higher than the difference in value but will not do so where the claimant has not cured and does not intend to cure; and, although this is more controversial (and seems unsatisfactory given that the claimant contracted for performance) a cost of cure measure may possibly be denied, even though the claimant has cured or intends to cure, if to do so would be unreasonable (ie economically wasteful) because of a disparity with the difference in value.

(iii) Loss of a chance

4.24 What happens when all that the claimant can establish is that he has lost the chance to make a gain? The leading case in relation to contract damages is *Chaplin v Hicks*.[60] The claimant entered a beauty competition organized by the defendant. Fifty of the entrants were to be selected for interview and, from those, 12 were to be offered theoretical engagements. The claimant was selected as one of the 50 for interview but, through the defendant's breach of contract, she was not informed in time. It was held by the Court of Appeal that, while the claimant was not entitled to damages on the basis that she would have won an engagement, nevertheless she was entitled to damages for the lost chance of winning an engagement. That is, she was entitled to damages scaled down proportionately in accordance with what the chances of gain were thought to be.

4.25 It is important to clarify that the approach of awarding damages according to the chances of gain is appropriate only where the uncertainty relates to hypothetical or future events, rather than a past fact.[61] In *Chaplin v Hicks*, the uncertainty was over whether those conducting the interview would have chosen the claimant for a theatrical engagement if she had been interviewed.[62] But where the uncertainty is in relation to past fact (or, it would seem, the

---

[57] [1977] Ch 106.

[58] [1977] 1 WLR 1262, 1284.

[59] [1996] AC 344.

[60] [1911] 2 KB 786, CA. A leading case in relation to tort damages is *Davies v Taylor* [1974] AC 207, HL. See also *Allied Maples Group Ltd v Simmons & Simmons* [1995] 1 WLR 1602, CA (action in contract and tort for solicitor's negligence).

[61] See 4.77–4.80.

[62] It is normally assumed that the interviewing panel was a third party. However, close scrutiny of the facts reveals that the rules had been changed so that the sole decision-maker was the defendant himself. Normally a minimum obligation rather than a 'chances' approach is applied to hypothetical conduct of the defendant: see 4.62–4.65.

hypothetical conduct of the claimant) the courts apply an all-or-nothing 'balance of prob-abilities' test. If the claimant cannot meet that standard of proof, the claim for that head of loss fails entirely; whereas if it can meet that standard of proof, it is entitled to full damages on the basis that that past fact was definitely true.

(b) Limiting principles

There are a number of principles which limit compensatory damages for breach of contract **4.26** and mean that the claimant is not put fully into as good a position as if the contract had been performed. Most of these principles, albeit sometimes with differences, apply also to compensatory damages for torts.[63]

(i) Remoteness

A principal restriction is that a defendant will not be liable for loss suffered by the claimant **4.27** that is too remote from the breach of contract. In policy terms, the remoteness restriction is based on the view that it is unfair to a defendant, and imposes too great a burden, to hold him responsible for losses however unusual and however far removed from the breach of contract. It has also been regarded as having an economic efficiency rationale in encouraging the disclosure of information regarding unusual potential losses, so that the defendant, with full knowledge of the risk involved, can plan and act rationally.

The traditional test. The traditional test for remoteness in contract was laid down in, **4.28** perhaps the best-known of all English contract cases, *Hadley v Baxendale*.[64] The claimant's mill was brought to a standstill by a broken crank-shaft. The claimant engaged the defend-ant's carrier to take it to Greenwich as a pattern for a new one, but in breach of contract the defendant delayed delivery. The claimant sought damages for loss of profit arising from the fact that the mill was stopped for longer than it would have been if there had been no delay. The court held that the loss of profit was too remote and that therefore the carriers were not liable for it.

The test for remoteness was regarded as comprising two rules by Alderson B. He said: **4.29**

> Where two parties have made a contract which one of them has broken, the damages which the other party ought to receive in respect of such breach of contract, should be such as may fairly and reasonably be considered, either arising naturally, ie according to the usual course of things from such breach of contract itself, or such as may reasonably be supposed to have been in the contemplation of both parties, at the time they made the contract as the probable result of the breach of it.[65]

On the facts neither of these two rules was satisfied. The loss was not the natural consequence **4.30** of the delay because it was felt that in the vast majority of cases the absence of a shaft would not cause a stoppage at a mill as usually a mill-owner would have another shaft in reserve or be able to get one. Nor was the loss in the contemplation of both parties because the special circumstance that the mill could not restart until the shaft came back was not known to the defendant.

The *Hadley v Baxendale* test was subsequently refined in two well-known cases. In *Victoria* **4.31** *Laundry (Windsor) Ltd v Newman Industries Ltd*,[66] the claimants decided to extend their laundry business and contracted to buy a boiler from the defendants. The defendants knew that the claimants wanted the boiler for immediate use in their business, but in breach of

---

[63] See 4.81–4.93.
[64] (1854) 9 Exch 341.
[65] (1854) 9 Exch 341, 354.
[66] [1949] 2 KB 528, CA.

contract delivered the boiler five months late. The claimants sought damages for the ordinary loss of profit that would have resulted from using the boiler during those months, including damages for the exceptional loss of profits that they would have been able to gain from contracts with the Ministry of Supply. The Court of Appeal held that, applying *Hadley v Baxendale*, damages should be awarded for the ordinary loss of profits but not for the exceptional loss of profits. The exceptional profits were too remote because they did not arise naturally and were not in the contemplation of the parties at the time of contracting because the defendants knew nothing about the Ministry of Supply contracts. Most significantly, Asquith LJ took the view that the two rules of *Hadley v Baxendale* could be reformulated as comprising a single rule (centring on reasonable contemplation or, as he preferred, reasonable foreseeability).

4.32 In *Koufos v Czarnikow Ltd, The Heron II*[67] a ship was chartered to carry sugar from Constanza to Basrah. At the time of contracting the claimant charterer intended to sell the sugar as soon as it reached Basrah. The defendant shipowner did not actually know this but did know that there was a market for sugar at Basrah. In breach of contract the shipowner reached Basrah nine days late. During those nine days the market price of sugar at Basrah fell and the claimant sought damages for the profit lost by reason of that fall. The House of Lords held that he should recover such damages because the loss of profit was not too remote. Concentration in the case was focused on what degree of likelihood of the loss occurring was required to have been reasonably contemplatable by the defendant at the time of the contract and, in particular, was it the same degree of likelihood of loss occurring that was required to be reasonably foreseeable under the tort test of remoteness laid down in *The Wagon Mound*?[68] The Law Lords agreed that a higher likelihood of the loss occurring was required in contract than in tort, so that losses may be too remote in contract that are not too remote in tort. Unfortunately, there was no clear consensus as to how the degree of likelihood required in contract should be expressed. Perhaps the clearest way of expressing the essence of the reasoning is that, while a slight possibility of the loss occurring is required in tort, a serious possibility of the loss occurring is required in contract. Taking this interpretation the traditional contract test, derived from *Hadley v Baxendale* and applied in *Heron II*, can be expressed as follows: a loss is too remote if the defendant did not contemplate, or could not reasonably have contemplated, that loss as a serious possibility, if he had thought or did think about the breach at the time the contract was made.[69]

4.33 **Type of loss?** Is it the actual loss or the type of loss that one is focusing on in applying the traditional test? This was the issue in *Parsons v Uttley Ingham & Co Ltd*[70] in which it was held that the supplier of a defective pig hopper was liable in contract for the loss of 254 pigs that had died from a rare intestinal decease after eating nuts that had gone mouldy in the hopper. The Court of Appeal decided that the loss of the pigs was not too remote, but the judges found this difficult to reconcile with the traditional *Hadley v Baxendale* approach. The majority, Scarman and Orr LJJ, said that the crucial question was whether the type of loss, not the extent or precise nature of the loss, was reasonably contemplatable; and that as illness of pigs and death of pigs were both the same type of loss, and the former was reasonably contemplatable, the death of the 254 pigs was not too remote. The majority judges also went out of their way to try to equate the remoteness tests in contract and tort. Scarman LJ

---

[67] [1969] 1 AC 350, HL.

[68] [1961] AC 388, PC. See 2.81.

[69] *Jackson v Royal Bank of Scotland plc* [2005] UKHL 3, [2005] 1 WLR 377 provides an excellent illustration of the application of the traditional contract remoteness test. It was stressed that the relevant date in applying the test is when the contract was made not the date of breach.

[70] [1978] QB 791, CA.

said, '... The law must be such that in a factual situation where all have the same actual or imputed knowledge... the amount of damages recoverable does not depend on whether, as a matter of legal classification, the plaintiff's cause of action is breach of contract or tort.'[71]

In *Brown v KMR Services Ltd*,[72] one of the questions, in claims by Lloyd's names against their **4.34** members' agents for breach of contract (and the tort of negligence), was whether the loss was too remote. The defendants' argument was that the magnitude of the financial disasters that had struck, and the consequent scale of the loss, was unforeseeable and uncontemplatable. The Court of Appeal held that the loss was not too remote because it was the type and not the extent of the loss that needed to be foreseen or contemplated: here the relevant type of loss was underwriting loss and that was clearly foreseeable. *Parsons v Uttley Ingham* was cited with approval.

In the light of the *Brown* case, it is clear that the traditional remoteness test in contract, as **4.35** in tort, focuses on the type of loss in question and not the specific loss that occurred. The difficult issue is not whether the emphasis on the type of loss is appropriate, but how types of loss should be divided up. If, as the *Parsons* and the *Brown* cases indicate, the courts are taking a broad view of types of loss, it may well be that the distinction drawn in the *Victoria Laundry* case, between recoverable loss of ordinary profits and irrecoverable loss of exceptional profits, can no longer stand (albeit that the *Victoria Laundry* case was distinguished in the *Brown* case).

Two additional points on the traditional test. First, the traditional test of remoteness **4.36** does not take into account the amount of the contractual consideration to be received by the defendant. In other words, the fact that the claimant's losses are out of all proportion to what the defendant was to receive under the contract is irrelevant. For example, in *Hadley v Baxendale*[73] itself, the fact that the claimant's loss of profits from delay was out of all proportion to the price to be paid to the defendant for carrying the mill-shaft was irrelevant. Secondly, where the claimant's actual loss of profits is too remote, and irrecoverable, it is still entitled to a lesser sum of damages measured by the loss of profit that would have been non-remote.[74]

Departure from the traditional test. In *Transfield Shipping Inc v Mercator Shipping Inc,* **4.37** *The Achilleas*[75] at least two members of the House of Lords departed from the *Hadley v Baxendale* test. The defendant charterers had redelivered a ship to the claimant owners nine days late. As a result the owners had to renegotiate a follow-on fixture at a loss of $8,000 a day. The defendants accepted that they were liable for the difference between the market rate and the charter rate for the nine-day overrun period but the dispute was as to whether the claimants were entitled to their full loss, namely $8,000 a day for the whole period of the follow-on fixture. The House of Lords unanimously held they were not because that loss was too remote. Lord Rodger and Baroness Hale applied the traditional *Hadley v Baxendale* test but came to a surprising result on the facts. In contrast, Lords Hoffmann and Hope[76] moved away from the traditional test by adding the requirement that the defendants must have accepted liability (or assumed responsibility) for the loss; and here they had not done so

---

[71] [1978] QB 791, 807, CA.
[72] [1995] 4 All ER 598, CA.
[73] (1854) 9 Exch 341.
[74] *Cory v Thames Iron Works Co* (1868) LR 3 QB 181.
[75] [2008] UKHL 48, [2009] 1 AC 61.
[76] One cannot say that this was the majority view because Lord Walker appeared to agree with both (conflicting) lines of reasoning. For a clarification of Lord Hoffmann's reasoning, see his article '*The Achilleas*: Custom and Practice or Foreseeability?' (2010) 14 Edinburgh LR 47.

because, apparently, the understanding of the shipping industry was that charterers were only liable for the loss of a follow-on fixture during the period until redelivery.

4.38 In trying to work out the precise impact of *The Achilleas*, the most important subsequent case has been *Supershield Ltd v Siemens Building Technologies FE Ltd.*[77] In the context of deciding that a settlement reached by the parties was reasonable, Toulson LJ (with whom Richards and Mummery LJJ agreed) said that, while *Hadley v Baxendale* remains the standard test, it can be overridden if, on examining the contract and the commercial background, the loss in question was within or outside the scope of the contractual duty. In other words, the approach of Lord Hoffmann in *The Achilleas* might override the standard test by making loss that would be recoverable under *Hadley v Baxendale* too remote (an 'exclusionary' effect)[78]—as on the facts of *The Achilleas* itself—or by making loss that would be non-recoverable under *Hadley v Baxendale* not too remote (an 'inclusionary' effect). On the facts, the latter was in question. Although it was unlikely that loss by flooding would occur as a consequence of the defendant's breach in failing properly to install a float valve in a fire-sprinkler water storage system—because normally the drains would have taken the overflow water but here the drains were blocked—that loss was thought not to be too remote because it was within the scope of the installer's duty.

4.39 As regards the exclusionary effect of *The Achilleas*, Hamblen J's rationalization in *Sylvia Shipping Co Ltd v Progress Bulk Carriers Ltd* is also helpful. He said:

> The orthodox [*Hadley v Baxendale*] approach remains the general test of remoteness applicable in the great majority of cases. However, there may be 'unusual' cases, such as *The Achilleas* itself, in which the context, surrounding circumstances or general understanding in the relevant market make it necessary specifically to consider whether there has been an assumption of responsibility. This is most likely to be in those relatively rare cases where the application of the general test leads or may lead to an unquantifiable, unpredictable, uncontrollable or disproportionate liability or where there is clear evidence that such a liability would be contrary to market understanding and expectations.[79]

The overall impact of *The Achilleas* has been to make the law on remoteness in contract far less certain than it previously was thought to be. The precise factors that permit the courts to override the traditional remoteness test are unclear and the uncertainty is not assisted by Lord Hoffmann's underlying assumption that in applying remoteness one is construing the parties' agreement.

(ii) Intervening cause

4.40 The limiting principle of 'intervening cause' has been discussed far less in the context of breach of contract than in respect of torts.[80] But the idea is the same. Although the defendant's breach of contract has been a cause of the claimant's loss, the claimant should not be able to recover damages for that loss where another intervening cause has been so much more responsible for the loss that it can be regarded as having broken the chain of causation between the breach and the loss.

4.41 The intervening cause may be a natural event, the conduct of a third party, or the conduct of the claimant. There is no clear test to which one can turn to decide whether any of these intervening causes is regarded as breaking the chain of causation. But one can say that it will be rare for a natural event to break the chain of causation; that, in the context of intervention

---

[77] [2010] EWCA Civ 7, [2010] 1 Lloyd's Rep 349.
[78] [2010] EWCA Civ 7, [2010] 1 Lloyd's Rep 349, at [43].
[79] [2010] EWHC 542 (Comm), [2010] 2 Lloyd's Rep 81, at [40].
[80] For intervening cause in respect of torts, see 2.75–2.77.

by a third party, the courts will tend to ask themselves whether or not the defendant had a duty to prevent the third party's intervention;[81] and, in the context of the claimant's own conduct, it will be important to ascertain how unreasonable the conduct has been. The last point is illustrated by *Quinn v Burch Bros (Builders) Ltd*.[82] The defendants in breach of contract failed to supply a step-ladder to the claimant. The claimant was injured when he fell from an unfooted trestle which he had made use of instead. The Court of Appeal held that the defendants were not liable for the claimant's injuries because their breach of contract did not cause them: the claimant's own unreasonable acts broke the chain of causation.

The concept of intervening cause has figured prominently in cases in which it has been held **4.42** that an auditor's breach of contract in negligently auditing the claimant company's accounts was not the effective cause of the company's trading losses and insolvency. In other words, market forces and the company's own decisions have been treated as intervening causes thereby cutting back the liability of auditors for (contractual or tortious) negligence.[83]

(iii) The duty to mitigate

The idea behind the duty to mitigate is that a claimant should not sit back and do nothing **4.43** to minimize loss flowing from a breach of contract but should rather use its resources to do what is reasonable to put itself into as good a position as if the contract had been performed. On the other hand, it should not unreasonably incur expense subsequent to the breach. The policy is one of encouraging the claimant, once a breach has occurred, to be to a reasonable extent self-reliant or efficient, rather than pinning all loss on the defendant.

The main rule encompassed by the duty to mitigate is that a claimant must take all reasonable **4.44** steps to minimize its loss so that it cannot recover for any loss which it could reasonably have avoided but has failed to avoid.[84] Clearly whether a step should reasonably have been taken to minimize loss depends on the particular facts in question. Nevertheless, some indication can be given of the sort of factors that have been considered important in past contract cases in deciding this.

(1) Where the claimant has been wrongfully dismissed, he need not accept an offer of re-employment from his former employer if, eg, the new work would involve a reduction of status; and/or employment elsewhere would be more likely to be permanent; and/or the claimant has no confidence in his employers because of their past treatment of him.[85]

(2) In relation to a contract of sale, if the defendant makes an offer of alternative performance, it will generally be unreasonable for the claimant to turn it down if acceptance would reduce its loss.[86]

(3) The claimant need not take action which would put its commercial reputation or good public relations at risk.[87]

(4) The claimant need not take steps which would involve it in complicated litigation.[88]

---

[81] *Stansbie v Troman* [1948] 2 KB 48, CA; cf *Weld-Blundell v Stephens* [1920] AC 956, HL.

[82] [1966] 2 QB 370, CA. See also *Lambert v Lewis* [1982] AC 225, HL.

[83] See eg *Galoo v Bright Grahame Murray* [1994] 1 WLR 1360.

[84] The classic expression of this rule is by Viscount Haldane LC in *British Westinghouse Electric and Manufacturing Co Ltd v Underground Electric Rlys Co of London Ltd* [1912] AC 673, 689, HL.

[85] *Yetton v Eastwoods Froy Ltd* [1967] 1 WLR 104; *Brace v Calder* [1895] 2 QB 253, CA.

[86] *Payzu Ltd v Saunders* [1919] 2 KB 581, CA; *Strutt v Whitnell* [1975] 1 WLR 870, CA.

[87] *James Finlay & Co Ltd v Kwik Hoo Tong* [1929] 1 KB 400, CA; *London and South of England Building Society v Stone* [1983] 1 WLR 1242, CA.

[88] *Pilkington v Wood* [1953] Ch 770. cf *Walker v Medlicott* [1999] 1 All ER 685, CA.

(5) The claimant need not take steps which it cannot financially afford; ie impecuniosity is an excuse for failure to mitigate.[89]

4.45 It is a corollary of the above main rule of the duty to mitigate that, where the claimant does take reasonable steps in an attempt to minimize its loss, it can recover for loss incurred in so doing even though the resulting loss is in the event greater than it would have been had the mitigating steps not been taken.[90]

(iv) Contributory negligence

4.46 If applicable as a defence, contributory negligence (which means that the claimant has been at fault for his own loss) leads to a reduction of damages. This is in contrast, eg, to the duty to mitigate and intervening cause, which are all or nothing restrictions.[91] The contributory negligence defence is enshrined in the Law Reform (Contributory Negligence) Act 1945 and, while the defence applies to nearly all torts and, in particular, to the most important tort of negligence, the courts have taken the view that, subject to where there is concurrent liability with tort, it does not apply to breach of contract.

4.47 In *Forsikringsaktieselskapet Vesta v Butcher*[92] it was said that contract cases should be divided, for the purposes of construing section 4 of the 1945 Act, into three categories. A category 1 case is where the defendant has been in breach of a strict contractual duty. A category 2 case is where the defendant has been in breach of a contractual duty of care. A category 3 case is where the defendant has been in breach of a contractual duty of care and is also liable in the tort of negligence.

4.48 According to *Vesta v Butcher* (where, strictly speaking, the discussion was obiter dicta) and *UCB Bank plc v Hepherd Winstanley & Pugh*[93] it is in a category 3 case only that section 4 of the 1945 Act allows contributory negligence to be a defence to breach of contract. While the Court of Appeal in *Barclays Bank Ltd v Fairclough Building Ltd*[94] accepted that contributory negligence is applicable in a category 3 case, the main point of that decision was that it is not applicable in a category 1 case.

4.49 This state of affairs is most unsatisfactory. It stems from the fact that the definition of fault in the 1945 Act is geared towards tort and not contract. While it is true that, since the House of Lords' acceptance of concurrent liability in *Henderson v Merrett Syndicates Ltd*,[95] there should be little prospect of a case falling within category 2 but outside

---

[89] *Clippens Oil Co Ltd v Edinburgh and District Water Trustees* [1907] AC 291, 303, HL (Sc); *Lagden v O'Connor* [2003] UKHL 64, [2004] 1 AC 1067.

[90] *Banco de Portugal v Waterlow & Sons Ltd* [1932] AC 452, HL; *Bacon v Cooper (Metals) Ltd* [1982] 1 All ER 397. In the first of these cases, Lord MacMillan also stressed, at 506, that the courts will not treat too favourably an argument by a defendant that the claimant has been unreasonable because it could have taken less expensive steps than it has taken to mitigate its loss: see also *London and South of England Building Society v Stone* [1983] 1 WLR 1242, CA.

[91] ie if one focuses on particular loss, a failure in the duty to mitigate that loss means that no damages will be awarded for it. In contrast, contributory negligence in relation to a loss means that damages are reduced, not eliminated, for that loss.

[92] [1989] AC 852, CA, aff'd on a different point [1989] AC 880, HL.

[93] [1999] Lloyd's Rep PN 963, CA.

[94] [1994] 3 WLR 1057.

[95] [1995] 2 AC 145, HL. But this was distinguished, with respect incorrectly, in *Robinson v PE Jones (Contractors) Ltd* [2011] EWCA Civ 9, [2012] QB 44, in deciding that a building contractor owes contractual duties only to its client.

category 3,[96] there is much to be said in principle for contributory negligence applying to all three categories.[97]

(v) Mental distress

Traditionally, the House of Lords' decision in *Addis v Gramophone Co Ltd*[98] was regarded **4.50** as barring damages for mental distress in an action for breach of contract. In that case, no damages were awarded for the harsh and humiliating manner of the claimant's wrongful dismissal. But this restrictive approach was departed from by a series of cases in the 1970s; and the situations in which one can recover damages for mental distress for breach of contract have stabilized in recent years. It is now clear that they are recoverable in two categories but two categories only.[99]

The first, and most important, is where the predominant, or an important, object of the **4.51** contract from the claimant's point of view was to obtain mental satisfaction whether enjoyment or relief from distress. The ruined holiday cases such as *Jarvis v Swan's Tours Ltd* [100] and *Jackson v Horizon Holidays Ltd* [101] most obviously fall within this. So does *Heywood v Wellers*[102] where the defendant solicitors, in breach of their contractual duty of care, failed to gain an injunction to stop molestation of the claimant by her former boyfriend. Also within this category is the House of Lords' decision in *Ruxley Electronics & Construction Ltd v Forsyth*,[103] in which the damages of £2,500 for loss of amenity is best rationalized as flowing from the fact that the claimant's primary object in specifying the particular depth for the swimming pool was mental satisfaction.

In *Farley v Skinner* [104] the House of Lords examined the width of this first category and **4.52** decided that it extended to where *an important object* of the contract was mental satisfaction or freedom from distress even though that was not the very, or predominant, object. The claimant was considering buying a house 15 miles from Gatwick Airport and engaged the defendant as his surveyor. He specifically asked him to investigate whether the property was affected by aircraft noise and the surveyor reported that it was unlikely that the property would suffer greatly from such noise. In fact aircraft noise substantially affected the property. Having decided not to sell, the claimant sued the surveyor in the tort of negligence and for breach of contract. It was held that although the claimant had suffered no financial loss, he

---

[96] For an unusual example, see *Raflatac Ltd v Eade* [1999] 1 Lloyd's Rep 506 (Colman J said that it was a category 2 case, and hence contributory negligence was inapplicable, where the head-contractor was under a contractual duty (of care) to procure work by a sub-contractor but did not owe a duty of care in relation to the sub-contractor's performance).

[97] But the Law Commission in *Contributory Negligence as a Defence in Contract* (Law Com No 219, 1993) recommended merely extending contributory negligence to category 2.

[98] [1909] AC 488, HL. In *Johnson v Unisys Ltd* [2001] UKHL 13, [2003] 1 AC 518, which was confirmed in *Edwards v Chesterfield Royal Hospital NHS Foundation Trust* [2011] UKSC 58, [2012] 2 AC 22, it was held that, whatever the normal position at common law, there is a special reason to deny damages for mental distress (and psychiatric illness and loss of reputation) *for wrongful dismissal* because of the need to avoid undermining the statutory cap on compensation for unfair dismissal. For the drawing of the line between wrongful dismissal and a breach of the employment contract that is sufficiently distinct from wrongful dismissal as to fall outside the *Johnson v Unisys* bar to damages, see *Eastwood v Magnox Electric plc* [2004] UKHL 35, [2005] 1 AC 503.

[99] For examples of cases falling outside the two categories and therefore denying mental distress damages, see *Bliss v South East Thames Regional Health Authority* [1985] IRLR 308, CA; *Hayes v James & Charles Dodd* [1990] 2 All ER 815, CA; *Johnson v Gore Wood & Co* [2002] 2 AC 1, HL.

[100] [1973] QB 233, CA. See also *Diesen v Samson* 1971 SLT 49.

[101] [1975] 1 WLR 1468, CA.

[102] [1976] QB 446, CA.

[103] [1996] AC 344, HL. See 4.22.

[104] [2001] UKHL 49, [2002] 2 AC 732.

was entitled to mental distress damages of £10,000 because an important object of the contract with the surveyor, albeit not its very object, was peace of mind in relation to the aircraft noise.[105]

4.53 The second category is where the claimant's mental distress is directly consequent on physical inconvenience caused by the defendant's breach of contract. Hence in *Perry v Sidney Phillips & Son*[106] and *Watts v Morrow*[107] mental distress damages for the distress and inconvenience of living in poor accommodation, purchased as a result of negligent surveys, were awarded against surveyors for breach of contract. In *Farley v Skinner* it was decided that the award of mental distress damages could be justified as falling within this second category as well as the first: aircraft noise causes physical inconvenience because that phrase should be interpreted in a wide sense to include matter detrimentally affecting sight, hearing or smell.

4.54 Having decided that mental distress damages should be awarded, it is not easy to fix the quantum of those damages. Given that there can be no mathematically correct answer, it seems crucial to seek consistency with the level of awards in similar cases. In *Milner v Carnival plc*[108] the claimants' luxury cruise was ruined as a result of structural noise problems in their cabin. In awarding contractual damages for inconvenience and mental distress of £4,000 to Mr Milner and £4,500 to Mrs Milner, Ward LJ emphasized that the level of such damages should be fixed not only by looking at other holiday awards for breach of contract but also at 'comparable awards for psychiatric damage in personal injury cases, for injury to feelings in cases of sex and race discrimination and damages for bereavement'.[109]

(vi) Loss of reputation

4.55 Until recently, *Addis v Gramophone Co Ltd*[110] was also the leading authority denying contractual damages for loss of reputation. The House of Lords held that, in the claimant's action for wrongful dismissal, he should be confined to damages for his direct pecuniary loss, such as loss of salary, and should not be compensated for any loss of his reputation or for the fact that the dismissal might make it more difficult for him to obtain another job.

4.56 Yet in many cases outside the context of wrongful dismissal, damages for loss of reputation have been awarded in respect of the pecuniary loss flowing from a loss of reputation. The distinction between the irrecoverable non-pecuniary loss constituted by the loss of reputation itself and the recoverable pecuniary loss consequent on the loss of reputation was particularly clearly applied in *Aeriel Advertising Co v Batchelors Peas Ltd*.[111] There the defendants had

---

[105] For a case falling within the first category, as expanded by *Farley v Skinner*, see *Hamilton Jones v David & Snape* [2003] EWHC 3147 (Ch), [2004] 1 All ER 657 (solicitor's breach of contract and tortious negligence leading to a mother's loss of custody of her children).

[106] [1982] 1 WLR 1297, CA.

[107] [1991] 1 WLR 1421, CA.

[108] [2010] EWCA Civ 389, [2010] 3 All ER 701.

[109] [2010] EWCA Civ 389, [2010] 3 All ER 701, at [57]. For discussion of the quantum of damages for discomfort and inconvenience consequent on the breach by a landlord of his obligations to keep the property in good repair, see *Shine v English Churches Housing Group* [2004] EWCA Civ 434; *Earle v Charalambous* [2006] EWCA Civ 1090, [2007] HLR 8. See also n 203.

[110] [1909] AC 488, HL. See also, eg, *O'Laoire v Jackel International Ltd (No 2)* [1991] ICR 718, CA.

[111] [1938] 2 All ER 788. See also, eg, *Rolin v Steward* (1854) 14 CB 595 (refusal to honour cheque causing damage to credit and reputation); *Wilson v United Counties Bank Ltd* [1920] AC 102, HL (breach of contract in proper vision leading to claimant's bankruptcy); *Marbé v George Edwardes (Daly's Theatre) Ltd* [1928] 1 KB 269, CA; *Herbert Clayton v Oliver* [1930] AC 209, HL; *Tolnay v Criterion Films Productions Ltd* [1936] 2 All ER 1625; *Joseph v National Magazine* Co [1959] Ch 14 (all an actor's or author's loss of publicity); *Anglo-Continental Holidays Ltd v Typaldos Lines (London) Ltd* [1967] 2 Lloyd's Rep 61, CA; *GKN Centrax Gears Ltd v Matbro Ltd* [1976] 2 Lloyd's Rep 555, CA (supplying of defective goods and services damaging claimant's reputation with customers).

contracted with the claimants to advertise their peas by trailers from a plane. In breach of contract the claimants flew the plane with the advertising trailers over a city centre during minutes of silence in armistice services. The public was horrified and the defendants' sales dropped. Atkinson J held that, while they were not entitled to damages for loss of reputation itself, they were entitled to damages for loss of sales following on that loss of reputation.

It is clear therefore that, outside the context of wrongful dismissal, the courts have been **4.57** prepared to award contractual damages compensating pecuniary loss (but not non-pecuniary loss) flowing from loss of reputation. The general position can therefore be regarded as that so clearly expressed by Hallett J in *Foaminol Laboratories v British Artid Plastic Ltd*:[112] '...if pecuniary loss be established, the mere fact that the pecuniary loss is brought about by the loss of reputation caused by a breach of contract is not sufficient to preclude the plaintiffs from recovering in respect of that pecuniary loss'.

That that is a correct statement of the law was authoritatively established in *Malik v Bank* **4.58** *of Credit and Commerce International SA*.[113] Former employees of the corrupt bank, BCCI, claimed damages from the bank for loss of reputation: ie they sought compensation for their handicap in the labour market flowing from the dishonesty stigma that attached to employees of BCCI. It was laid down that damages were recoverable for the pecuniary loss of reputation flowing from the employer's breach of the implied term not to undermine the employee's trust and confidence.[114] Lord Nicholls specifically cited with approval Hallett J's statement in *Foaminol*.

(vii) The only obligation broken is to pay money

It was laid down in *London, Chatham and Dover Railway Company v South Eastern Railway*[115] **4.59** that, where the only obligation broken is to pay money, no damages can be awarded and the sole remedy is for the unpaid sum in an action for the award of the agreed sum. The main practical consequence of this rule[116] has been that no damages can be awarded for the general loss of the use of money (ie, traditionally damages could not be awarded for loss of interest). In *Wadsworth v Lydall*[117] the *London, Chatham and Dover Railway* case was distinguished on the ground that, while it prevents general damages for failure to pay a sum of money, it does not prevent special damages (ie if the claimant can show a special loss, damages are recoverable).

However, interest is recoverable by statute. By section 35A of the Senior Courts Act 1981, a **4.60** court has a discretion to award simple interest on an agreed sum from the date of the cause of action until the date of the judgment or payment. And, although section 35A does not apply where the agreed sum was paid in advance of proceedings to recover it, the Late Payment of Commercial Debts (Interest) Act 1998 gives a creditor an automatic right to simple interest after a specified period of time on an unpaid commercial debt.[118]

---

[112] [1941] 2 All ER 393, 400.

[113] [1998] AC 20, HL.

[114] The *Addis* case was departed from. But as laid down in *Johnson v Unisys Ltd* [2001] UKHL 13, [2003] 1 AC 518, the need to avoid undermining the cap on compensation for unfair dismissal is a special reason to maintain the bar on damages for loss of reputation for wrongful dismissal: see n 98.

[115] [1893] AC 429, HL.

[116] This rule has never been regarded as affecting the claimant's right to terminate the contract and to recover damages for the defendant's repudiatory breach, presumably because a repudiatory breach always goes beyond being the breach of an obligation to pay money (eg a seller of goods can sue the buyer for non-acceptance).

[117] [1981] 1 WLR 598, CA.

[118] The Act applies to contracts for the supply of goods or services (other than excluded contracts) where the purchaser and supplier are each acting in the course of business. The rate of interest has been fixed at the base rate plus 8%. By s 5 the interest may be remitted, wholly or in part, because of the creditor's conduct.

4.61 Moreover, in *Sempra Metals Ltd v Commissioners of Inland Revenue*[119] the House of Lords has effectively buried the rule in the *London, Chatham and Dover Railway* case by accepting that damages can be awarded for a proved general loss of interest (including compound interest) subject to normal limiting principles, such as remoteness and the duty to mitigate.

(viii) No damages beyond the defendant's minimum contractual obligation

4.62 Where a contract entitles the defendant to perform in alternative ways or, as it is sometimes expressed, the defendant has a discretion as to the contractual benefits to be conferred on the claimant, damages have traditionally been assessed on the basis that the defendant would have performed in the way most favourable to itself. As Diplock LJ said in *Lavarack v Woods of Colchester Ltd*, 'The first task of the assessor of damages is to estimate as best he can what the plaintiff would have gained... if the defendant had fulfilled his legal obligation and had done no more'.[120]

4.63 So, eg, if in a contract for the carriage of goods by sea the cargo-owner has the right to choose between a number of different ports for the cargo to be unloaded, damages for his failure to provide the cargo to the carrier will be based on the assumption that he would have chosen the most distant port for unloading.[121] In a contract for the sale of goods, where the seller has an option as to the exact quantity to be delivered, damages for non-delivery are based on the assumption that he would have delivered the smallest quantity.[122] And in the *Lavarack* case itself no damages were awarded in relation to bonuses under a service contract that still had two years eight months to run because it was at the employer's discretion whether such payments should be made.

4.64 Two qualifications should be borne in mind. The first is that where, on the construction of the contract, it was the parties' intention that the defendant's discretion should be exercised reasonably, damages will be assessed on the basis of the defendant's minimum reasonable performance.[123] A second qualification is that, while a particular performance may be the least burdensome to the defendant when judged solely according to the contract, this may not be the basis upon which damages are assessed because the courts judge the defendant's least burdensome performance by taking all other potential losses into account. So in the *Lavarack* case Diplock LJ said that, '... one must not assume that he [the defendant] will cut off his nose to spite his face and so [act] as to reduce his legal obligation to the plaintiff by incurring greater loss in other respects'.[124]

4.65 It would seem that the rationale for giving no damages beyond the defendant's minimum contractual obligation is that that is all that the claimant is legally entitled to. Had the contract been on foot, the claimant could not have complained if the defendant had merely performed its bare contractual obligation. But it is not clear that this is the correct approach in contrast to an assessment of how the defendant was likely to have performed (which may or may not coincide with its minimum legal obligation). The latter approach was adopted, and *Lavarack* distinguished, by the Court of Appeal in *Horkulak v Cantor Fitzgerald International*.[125] In assessing damages for a wrongful dismissal, the claimant employee was

---

[119] [2007] UKHL 34, [2008] 1 AC 561.

[120] [1967] 1 QB 278, 294.

[121] *Kaye Steam Navigation Co v W & R Barnett* (1932) 48 TLR 440. See also, eg, *Kurt A Becher GmbH v Roplak Enterprises SA (The World Navigator)* [1991] 2 Lloyd's Rep 23, CA.

[122] *Re Thornett & Fehr and Yuills Ltd* [1921] 1 KB 219.

[123] *Abrahams v Herbert Reiach Ltd* [1922] 1 KB 477, CA; *Paula Lee Ltd v Robert Zehil & Co Ltd* [1983] 2 All ER 390.

[124] [1967] 1 QB 278, 295.

[125] [2004] EWCA Civ 1287, [2005] ICR 402. See also *Lion Nathan Ltd v C-C Bottlers Ltd* [1996] 1 WLR 1438, PC (although there the reasoning was ultimately that there was no discretion).

held entitled to the bonus that the defendant company would have paid rather than the minimum that the company acting reasonably and in good faith could have paid.

(c) Additional issues

(i) Compensating advantages

An issue that has received relatively little attention in relation to claims for breach of contract, as opposed to claims in tort for personal injury and death,[126] is the extent to which benefits accruing to the claimant as a result of the breach of contract are to be taken into account in assessing damages. **4.66**

In general, it would seem that where the benefit arises from what the claimant has done in response to the breach (ie, it arises out of an act of mitigation even though there was no duty to act), that benefit will be taken into account in assessing damages. A leading case is *British Westinghouse v Underground Electric Railways Company of London Ltd*.[127] The defendants in breach of contract supplied to the claimants turbines which were defective. The claimants subsequently replaced them with other turbines. The replacement turbines turned out to be more efficient and profitable than the old turbines would have been if non-defective. The House of Lords held that the greater efficiency of the replacements should be taken into account as mitigating the defendants' loss. **4.67**

But indirect compensating advantages will not be taken into account. This is shown by *Lavarack v Woods of Colchester Ltd*.[128] The claimant was wrongfully dismissed from his employment with the defendants and so freed from the provision in his contract with them that he should not, without their written consent, be engaged or interested in any other business. After his dismissal the claimant took employment with a company called Martindale at a lower salary than he had earned with the defendants, acquired half the shares in Martindale and bought shares in a company called Ventilation. The value of both the Martindale and Ventilation shares increased. The Court of Appeal held that, while his new salary and the profit from the Martindale shares should be deducted in assessing his damages for wrongful dismissal, the profits from the Ventilation shares should not be. The latter were too indirect to be taken into account. **4.68**

It can be seen from this that 'directness' puts a limit on the extent to which compensating advantages are deducted. It operates in an analogous, but reverse, way to 'remoteness' and 'intervening cause'. They counter the compensatory principle by limiting the claimant's damages; whereas directness here counters compensation, as strictly applied, by allowing the claimant to recover more than his loss. **4.69**

It must be stressed that to be relevant as a compensating advantage the benefit that the claimant has subsequently gained must have accrued from the breach. That is, it must have been factually caused by the breach. If the claimant would have made the gain even if there had been no breach, it will not be taken into account in assessing damages.[129] **4.70**

---

[126] See 4.109–4.110 and 4.128.

[127] [1912] AC 673, HL.

[128] [1967] 1 QB 278, CA. For other examples of the non-deduction of compensating advantages in assessing contractual damages, see *Hussey v Eels* [1990] 2 QB 227, CA; *Gardner v Marsh & Parsons* [1997] 1 WLR 489, CA; *Needler Financial Services Ltd v Taber* [2002] 3 All ER 501; *Primavera v Allied Dunbar Assurance plc* [2002] EWCA Civ 1327, [2003] PNLR 12.

[129] *Thompson Ltd v Robinson (Gunmakers) Ltd* [1955] Ch 177 can be regarded as an illustration of this. As supply exceeded demand, the subsequent sale of a car was not a compensating advantage to the vendor and the purchaser had to pay damages for the vendor's loss of profit on the sale between them.

(ii) Damages in a contract for the benefit of a third party

4.71   What is the measure of damages if the promisee chooses to sue on a contract made for another's benefit? Applying the normal expectation principle, the claimant is entitled to be put into as good a position as it would have been if the contract had been performed; ie the relevant loss is the claimant's not the third party's. However, this does not mean that the promisee is necessarily restricted to nominal damages.[130] One would expect that in some contracts made for a third party's benefit, the defendant's failure to benefit the third party would also constitute a substantial pecuniary loss to the promisee. This may be, eg, because the promisee required the defendant to pay the third party in order to pay off a debt owed by the promisee to the third party. Or the promisee may have stood to gain from the use to be made by the third party of the promised benefits. Moreover, by analogy to the cases allowing a cost of cure in excess of a difference in value,[131] the claimant should be entitled to substantial damages (measured by the cost of cure) where it has subsequently conferred the benefit on the third party or intends to do so.

4.72   Moreover, there have been a number of important cases on construction contracts in which, contrary to the general rule, it has been held that a promisee can recover the third party's loss rather than its own loss. In *Darlington BC v Wiltshier Northern Ltd*[132] the principle applied by the Court of Appeal was in effect as follows: wherever the breach of a contract for work on property causes loss to a third party, who is an owner of that property, and it was known or contemplated by the contracting parties that the third party was, or would become, owner of the property and the third party has no direct right to sue for breach of contract, the promisee, who has the right to sue, can recover substantial damages compensating the third party's loss.[133]

4.73   In *Alfred McAlpine Construction Ltd v Panatown Ltd*[134] the House of Lords, by a majority, dismissed a promisee's claim for substantial damages emphasizing that the above exceptional principle does not apply where, as in the case at hand, the third party has a direct contractual right to sue the promisor.

(2)   Compensatory Damages: Torts

4.74   In relation to torts, as opposed to breach of contract, it is not straightforward to distinguish matters going to liability from matters going to damages. A breach of contract is actionable without proof of loss or damage so that the liability question is simply one of whether the defendant has committed a breach of contract. The same can be said of torts actionable per se, such as trespass and libel. In contrast, the most important tort, the tort of negligence, along with, eg, the tort of nuisance is actionable only on proof of damage; and for such torts the line between liability and quantum is less easy to draw and has to be drawn in a different place than for wrongs actionable per se. In particular, for torts actionable only on proof of damage, remoteness of damage and intervening cause will normally be matters going to liability (ie, to the question whether the tort has been committed) rather than to damages.

---

[130] See eg *Woodar Investment Development Ltd v Wimpey Construction UK Ltd* [1980] 1 WLR 277, HL.

[131] See 4.19–4.23.

[132] [1995] 1 WLR 68, CA.

[133] This is an extension to the approach of the House of Lords in *Linden Gardens Trust Ltd v Lenesta Sludge Disposals Ltd* [1994] 1 AC 85 which in itself had applied to real property the exceptional principle applicable to a changed ownership of goods established in *Dunlop v Lambert* (1839) 6 CL & F 600 and *The Albazero* [1977] AC 774.

[134] [2001] 1 AC 518, HL. For contrasting views of this controversial decision, see B Coote, 'The Performance Interest, *Panatown*, and the Problem of Loss' (2000) 117 LQR 81; A Burrows, 'No Damages for a Third Party's Loss' (2001) OUCLJ 107.

For this reason, remoteness and causation have been dealt with in the general examination of the law of tort above and will only be briefly mentioned again here.

(a) The compensatory aim and limiting principles

(i) The compensatory aim

The general aim of damages for a tort is to put the claimant into as good a position as he **4.75** would have been in if no tort had been committed. Lord Blackburn's statement in *Livingstone v Rawyards Coal Co*,[135] a case concerning trespass to goods, is the most cited authority on this. He said that the measure of damages was: '...that sum of money which will put the party who has been injured, or has suffered, in the same position as he would have been in if he had not sustained the wrong for which he is now getting his compensation or reparation'.

This aim applies even in relation to the tort of deceit or negligent misrepresentation: so the **4.76** claimant is entitled to be put into as good a position as if no representation had been made but is not entitled to be put into as good a position as if the statement had been true.[136] Given that the compensatory aim differs as between a claim for misrepresentation and a claim for breach of contract, it is essential to distinguish between mere representations, where the sole action is for tortious misrepresentation, and warranties, where the claimant can sue for breach of contract; or, to put it another way, between statements inducing the making of a contract and the terms of the contract.

In seeking to put the claimant into as good a position as if no tort had been committed, the **4.77** courts inevitably encounter the question of how to deal with uncertainties (eg, whether a consequential loss will or will not be suffered in the future). Where the uncertainty relates to future events, the courts will award damages in proportion to their assessment of the chances provided those chances are not so small as to be dismissed as 'entirely speculative'.[137] In contrast, where the uncertainty relates to a past fact (or, it would seem, the hypothetical conduct of the claimant), the courts decide the issue on the balance of probabilities. In *Mallett v McMonagle*[138] Lord Diplock summarized the law as follows:

> In determining what did happen in the past a court decides on the balance of probabilities. Anything that is more probable than not it treats as certain. But in assessing damages which depend upon its view as to what will happen in the future or would have happened in the future if something had not happened in the past, the court must make an estimate

---

[135] (1880) 5 App Cas 25, 39.

[136] *Smith New Court Securities Ltd v Scrimgeour Vickers (Asset Management) Ltd* [1997] AC 254, HL (deceit). See also *Doyle v Olby (Ironmongers) Ltd)* [1969] 2 QB 158, CA (deceit); *East v Maurer* [1991] 1 WLR 461, CA (deceit); *Esso Petroleum Co Ltd v Mardon* [1976] QB 801, CA (negligent misrepresentation); *Cemp Properties (UK) Ltd v Dentsply Research & Development Corpn* [1991] 2 EGLR 197, 201, CA (Misrepresentation Act 1967, s 2(1)); *Royscot Trust Ltd v Rogerson* [1991] 2 QB 297, 304–305, CA (Misrepresentation Act 1967, s 2(1)). Much needless confusion has been caused by *South Australia Asset Management Corpn v York Mantague Ltd* [1997] AC 191, HL ('SAAMCO') which concerned contractual and tortious claims for negligent property valuations. The reasoning appears to cut across long-established principles of compensation, legal causation and remoteness and, although courts have felt obliged to apply it generally in contract and tort cases on negligent misrepresentation and negligent failure to provide information, it is best viewed as a specific policy decision that valuers should not normally be held liable for falls in the property market (or possibly as a forerunner of the new approach to remoteness put forward in *The Achilleas* [2008] UKHL 48, [2009] 1 AC 61: see 4.37–4.39). For examples of the difficulties in applying it, see, eg, *Platform Homes Loans Ltd v Oyston Shipways Ltd* [2000] 2 AC 190, HL; *Aneco Reinsurance Underwriting Ltd v Johnson & Higgins Ltd* [2001] UKHL 51, [2001] 2 All ER (Comm) 929. For detailed criticism of the reasoning in *SAAMCO* see A Burrows, *Remedies for Torts and Breach of Contract* (3rd edn, 2004) 109–122.

[137] See eg *Davies v Taylor* [1974] AC 207, HL.

[138] [1970] AC 166, 176. See also *Brown v Ministry of Defence* [2006] EWCA Civ 546, [2006] PIQR Q9.

as to what are the chances that a particular thing will or would have happened and reflect those chances, whether they are more or less than even, in the amount of damages which it awards.

4.78 A leading case is *Hotson v East Berkshire Area Health Authority*.[139] The claimant injured his hip in a fall and later developed a permanent hip disability. He brought an action for negligence against the defendant claiming that, if his injury had been properly diagnosed at the start, his permanent disability would have been avoided. The trial judge found that, even if the defendant had treated the claimant properly, there was still a 75 per cent chance that his disability would have developed. Nevertheless, he awarded the claimant damages (of 25 per cent of the full damages) for being deprived by the defendant's negligence of the 25 per cent chance of avoiding the disability. But that award was overturned by the House of Lords. Their Lordships stressed that what was in question was a matter of past fact to which the all or nothing balance of probabilities standard of proof applied. Applying that test, their Lordships concluded that the claim failed because the claimant had not established that the negligence of the defendant had caused his hip disability.

4.79 This area of the law was reviewed in the difficult case of *Gregg v Scott*[140] where it would appear that the uncertainty could not be clearly isolated as one of past fact as opposed to the hypothetical or future medical condition of the claimant. A doctor negligently diagnosed a lump under the claimant's left arm as benign when it was in fact cancerous. This led to a delay of nine months in the claimant receiving proper treatment. It was found that, on the balance of probabilities, the claimant would not have been 'cured' of cancer (with 'cure' meaning surviving for more than 10 years) even if there had been no delay. It was also found that the delay had reduced the claimant's chances of cure from 42 per cent to 25 per cent. The majority of the House of Lords (Lord Hoffmann, Lord Phillips and Baroness Hale) refused to award the claimant damages for the reduction in the chances of cure. The case has left at least two troubling uncertainties. The first is that no clear justification was given as to why a loss of the chance approach is thought appropriate—as many past cases have established that it is[141]—for professional negligence cases causing pure economic loss but not for medical negligence.[142] The second is that the precise status of Stuart-Smith LJ's influential judgment in *Allied Maples Group Ltd v Simmons & Simmons* is left unclear. Stuart-Smith LJ had there attempted to rationalize the law on hypothetical events by laying down that a loss of the chance approach was appropriate where the uncertainty was as to the hypothetical conduct of third parties, but not the hypothetical conduct of the claimant who could be expected to prove, on the balance of probabilities, one way or the other, what he would have done had there been no breach of duty by the defendant.

4.80 A further complication has been added by *Barker v Corus (UK) Plc*.[143] The relevant damage in question (in applying the exception to causation recognized in *Fairchild v Glenhaven Funeral Services Ltd*)[144] was treated as the material increase of risk of contracting mesothelioma

---

[139] [1987] AC 750, HL.

[140] [2005] UKHL 2, [2005] 2 WLR 268.

[141] eg *Kitchen v Royal Air Force Association* [1948] 1 WLR 563; *Allied Maples Group Ltd v Simmons & Simmons* [1995] 1 WLR 1602, CA; *Sharif v Garrett & Co* [2001] EWCA Civ 1269, [2002] 1 WLR 3118; *Dudarec v Andrews* [2006] EWCA Civ 256, [2006] 1 WLR 3002.

[142] Probably the best explanation is to be built from Baroness Hale's point, in *Gregg v Scott* at [212], that 'wait and see' makes sense for uncertainty as to whether a disease or injury will eventuate in the future but makes little sense in relation to pure economic loss.

[143] [2005] UKHL 20, [2006] 2 WLR 1027. For mesothelioma, the effect of the decision was reversed by the Compensation Act 2006, s 3. See also *Sienkiewicz v Greif (UK) Ltd* [2011] UKSC 10, [2011] 2 AC 229; *Durham v BAI (Run off) Ltd* [2012] UKSC 14, [2012] 1 WLR 867; *Zurich Insurance Plc UK Branch v International Energy Group Ltd* [2015] UKSC 33. See generally 2.69–2.73.

[144] [2002] UKHL 20, [2003] 1 AC 32.

(ie the loss of the chance of avoiding the disease). But it was stressed that this applied only because there was a single causal agent (asbestos) and the outcome was known, ie the relevant disease had been contracted. Their Lordships did not see themselves as opening the door to the recovery of damages simply because a defendant had negligently materially increased the risk of a claimant suffering a particular disease or injury.

(ii) Limiting principles

Remoteness.   As we have seen above,[145] the leading case is *Overseas Tankship (UK) Ltd*   **4.81**
v Morts Dock & Engineering Co Ltd (The Wagon Mound)[146] which established that a loss is too remote if it was not reasonably foreseeable at the time of the breach of duty. Subsequent cases show that it is a slight possibility (ie a low degree of likelihood) of the loss occurring that needs to be reasonably foreseeable;[147] and that it is the type of loss suffered, and not the specific loss suffered, that needs to have been reasonably foreseeable.[148] Although at one time it was thought that the tort remoteness test was significantly different from the contract test, the emphasis in applying the traditional contract test on it being the type of loss, rather than the specific loss, that needs to be reasonably contemplated has brought the two closer together.[149] But there still appears to be a higher degree of likelihood required under the traditional contract 'reasonable contemplation' test than under the tort 'reasonable foreseeability' test.[150]

The Wagon Mound lays down the remoteness test for most, but not all, torts. An exception is   **4.82**
the tort of deceit where the remoteness test is wider and, as authoritatively laid down in *Smith New Court Securities Ltd v Scrimgeour Vickers (Asset Management) Ltd*[151] is one of 'direct consequence' irrespective of whether the loss is reasonably foreseeable.

Intervening cause.   The operation of intervening causation in relation to tort has been   **4.83**
considered above.[152] Suffice it to say here that there is no clear test for deciding whether or not a natural event, the conduct of a third party, or the conduct of the claimant breaks the chain of causation.

The duty to mitigate.   The duty to mitigate applies in much the same way to damages   **4.84**
for torts as it does to damages for breach of contract. As we have seen in relation to breach of contract,[153] a claimant must take all reasonable steps to minimize the loss to him so that he cannot recover for any loss which he could so have avoided but has failed to avoid. Whether a step should reasonably have been taken depends on the particular facts in question. Some of the factors which have been considered important in past tort cases are as follows:

---

[145] See 4.32, and see also 2.82–2.83.
[146] [1961] AC 388, PC.
[147] *Overseas Tankship (UK) v Miller SS Co Pty Ltd (The Wagon Mound) (No 2)* [1967] 1 AC 617, PC.
[148] *Hughes v Lord Advocate* [1963] AC 837, HL.
[149] See 4.33–4.35.
[150] For an argument that the 'stricter' contract test applies to a concurrent claim in the tort of negligence, see A Burrows, 'Comparing Compensatory Damages in Tort and Contract: Some Problematic Issues' in S Degeling, J Edelman and J Goudkamp (eds), *Torts in Commercial Law* (2011) 367, 370–375.
[151] [1997] AC 254, HL. This confirmed *Doyle v Olby (Ironmongers) Ltd* [1969] 2 QB 158, CA. In *Royscot Trust Ltd v Rogerson* [1991] 2 QB 297, CA, it was held that the wider remoteness test for deceit also applied to damages under s 2(1) of the Misrepresentation Act 1967. In the *Smith New Court* case it was left open whether the *Royscot* case was correctly decided on this point: [1997] AC 254, 267, 283.
[152] See 2.75–2.77.
[153] See 4.44.

(1) An injured claimant acts unreasonably if he refuses an operation contrary to firm medical advice.[154] But the claimant need not submit himself to a surgical operation involving substantial risk or where the outcome is uncertain.[155]

(2) It will generally be unreasonable for the claimant to refuse offers of help which would have prevented further property damage.[156]

(3) The claimant need not take action which will put its good public relations at risk.[157]

(4) The claimant need not take steps which it cannot financially afford.[158]

4.85 It follows from the main rule of the duty to mitigate that, where the claimant does take reasonable steps in an attempt to minimize loss, it can recover for loss incurred in so doing even though the resulting loss is in the event greater than it would have been had the mitigating steps not been taken.[159] As has been noted in relation to the duty to mitigate in relation to breach of contract, the courts will lean in favour of the claimant in deciding whether or not expenses were reasonably incurred.[160]

4.86 Contributory negligence. In contrast to claims for breach of contract, it is clear that contributory negligence applies to most torts and, in particular, to the tort of negligence. The defence applies where the defendant can establish three elements. First, the claimant must have been at fault or negligent towards herself. To illustrate this by reference to cases of personal injury or death, the claimant is most obviously negligent towards herself if she negligently causes an accident involving herself,[161] or puts herself in an inherently dangerous position,[162] or renders an inherently non-dangerous position dangerous by failing to take safety precautions.[163] Secondly, the claimant's negligence must have been a factual cause of the claimant's loss. Thirdly, the claimant's negligence must have exposed the claimant to the particular risk of the type of injury suffered.[164]

4.87 Once it has been decided that contributory negligence applies to the case in hand, the court must decide the extent of the reduction in damages by reason of that contributory negligence. Section 1(1) of the Law Reform (Contributory Negligence) Act 1945 lays down that the damages '…shall be reduced to such extent as the court thinks just and equitable having regard to the claimant's share in the responsibility for the damage'. How exactly the courts apply these words is difficult to clarify; but what can be said, as stressed by Denning LJ in *Davies v Swan Motor Co (Swansea) Ltd*,[165] is that the courts consider both the causal potency and the comparative blameworthiness of the parties' conduct.

4.88 In *Froom v Butcher*[166] Lord Denning, recognizing the difficulty of deciding to what extent to reduce damages and in his desire to avoid prolonging cases, suggested standard figures

---

[154] *McAuley v London Transport Executive* [1957] 2 Lloyd's Rep 500, CA.

[155] *Geest plc v Lansiquot* [2002] UKPC 48, [2002] 1 WLR 3111.

[156] *Anderson v Hoen (The Flying Fish)* (1865) 3 Moo PCCNS 77, PC.

[157] *London and South of England Building Society v Stone* [1983] 1 WLR 1242, CA (where the action against the defendant valuer was brought in both contract and tort).

[158] *Clippens Oil Co Ltd v Edinburgh & District Water Trustees* [1907] AC 291, 303, HL; *Lagden v O'Connor* [2003] UKHL 64, [2004] 1 AC 1067.

[159] *Esso Petroleum Co Ltd v Marden* [1976] QB 801.

[160] *London and South of England Building Society v Stone* [1983] 3 All ER 105, 121. See also 4.45.

[161] eg where two motorists negligently collide.

[162] See, eg, *Jones v Livox Quarries Ltd* [1952] 2 QB 608, CA; *Owens v Brimmell* [1977] QB 859; *Gregory v Kelly* [1978] RTR 426.

[163] See, eg, *Froom v Butcher* [1976] QB 286, CA (failing to wear a seat-belt); *O'Connell v Jackson* [1972] 1 QB 270, CA (failing to wear a crash helmet on a motor-bike).

[164] *Jones v Livox Quarries Ltd* [1952] 2 QB 608.

[165] [1949] 2 KB 291, 326. See also *Jackson v Murray* [2015] UKSC 5 (Sc), 2015 SLT 151.

[166] [1976] QB 286, cf *Capps v Miller* [1989] 1 WLR 839, CA (not fastening a chin-strap on a helmet led to a 10% reduction for contributory negligence).

for reducing damages where the claimant has been contributorily negligent by not wearing a seat-belt. If the damage would have been prevented altogether a reduction of 25 per cent should be made and if it would have been considerably less severe a reduction of 15 per cent should be made.

In deciding on the appropriate reduction, one must keep contributory negligence distinct **4.89** from the issue of contribution between tortfeasors. In the leading case of *Fitzgerald v Lane*[167] the claimant was hit by two cars one after the other on a pelican crossing. The claimant and each of the drivers was found to have been equally to blame for the claimant's injuries. It was held by the House of Lords that the appropriate reduction for contributory negligence should have been 50 per cent and not 33.3 per cent. What has to be contrasted is the claimant's conduct on the one hand with the totality of the tortious conduct of the defendants on the other.

It was held by the House of Lords in *Standard Chartered Bank v Pakistan National Shipping* **4.90** *Corp (No 2)*[168] that contributory negligence does not apply to the tort of deceit. The same applies to other 'intentional torts', such as trespass to the person.[169] In addition, the Torts (Interference with Goods) Act 1977, section 11,[170] specifically lays down that contributory negligence is not a defence to conversion or intentional trespass to goods.

Damages for mental distress and loss of reputation. In contrast to damages for breach **4.91** of contract, restrictions on the type of damages recoverable in tort tend to be issues going to liability rather than to quantum. For example, there is generally no liability in the tort of negligence for the infliction of mere mental distress which falls short of a recognizable psychiatric illness.[171] However, once liability has been established (ie, once the tort has been made out) damages for mental distress are commonly recoverable. So, eg, a person who has been physically injured by the defendant's negligence can recover damages for pain and suffering. And damages for loss of reputation are, of course, recoverable for the tort of defamation, the very essence of which is to protect a person's reputation.[172]

Damages for mental distress are also often recoverable under the head of 'aggravated damages'.[173] **4.92** In *Rookes v Barnard*[174] aggravated damages were stressed to be compensatory—albeit

---

[167] [1989] AC 328, HL.

[168] [2002] UKHL 43, [2003] 1 AC 959.

[169] *Co-operative Group (CWS) Ltd v Pritchard* [2011] EWCA Civ 329, [2012] QB 320. See also *Corporacion Nacional del Cobre de Chile v Sogemin Metals Ltd* [1997] 1 WLR 1396 in which contributory negligence was held to be inapplicable in a bribe case founded on various dishonestly-committed torts (including deceit, conspiracy, and inducing breach of contract) and the equitable wrong of assisting a breach of fiduciary duty.

[170] This must be read subject to the Banking Act 1979, s 47.

[171] *Alcock v Chief Constable of South Yorkshire Police* [1992] 1 AC 310, 401, 409–410, 416, HL. As recognized in eg *Perry v Sidney Phillips & Son* [1982] 1 WLR 1297 and *Hamilton Jones v David & Snape* [2003] EWHC 3147 (Ch), [2004] 1 WLR 924 an exception is where there is concurrent liability in tort and contract: mental distress damages are recoverable in the tort action if they are, or would be, recoverable for breach of contract because falling within one of the two categories (see 4.50–4.53) where such damages are recoverable.

[172] In *John v MGN Ltd* [1997] QB 586, CA, it was held that, in defamation cases, the scale of awards for non-pecuniary loss in personal injury cases (see 4.108) could be drawn to the attention of juries and that the level of an appropriate award could be indicated by the judge. For guidelines on the level of compensatory (and punitive) damages for false imprisonment and malicious prosecution actions against the police, see *Thompson v Commissioner of Police for the Metropolis* [1998] QB 498, CA.

[173] eg for the torts of trespass to the person, malicious prosecution, defamation, and sex or race discrimination. See, eg, *Walter v Alltools Ltd* (1944) 61 TLR 39, CA (false imprisonment); *Savile v Roberts* (1698) 1 Ld Raym 374 (malicious prosecution); *McCarey v Associated Newspapers Ltd* [1965] 2 QB 86, CA (libel); *Vento v Chief Constable of West Yorkshire Police (No 2)* [2002] EWCA Civ 1871, [2003] IRLR 102 (sex discrimination).

[174] [1964] AC 1129, HL. See also 4.163–4.165.

compensating for mental distress—and not punitive. But the confusion between the two lingers on. This is not surprising since aggravated damages have traditionally only been awarded where the defendant's behaviour has been particularly reprehensible.[175] All confusion would be avoided by abandoning the label of 'aggravated damages' and by referring only to 'damages for mental distress' or 'damages for injured feelings'.[176]

4.93 Although damages for mental distress or loss of reputation are widely recoverable for torts, there are exceptional torts for which only pecuniary loss—and not mental distress or loss of reputation—is recoverable. The clearest illustration is lawful means conspiracy.[177]

(b) Damages for personal injury

4.94 In practice, the commonest and most important area in which tort damages have to be assessed is for personal injury, caused usually by the tort of negligence or breach of statutory duty.[178] The area of damages for personal injury has developed its own scheme of rules and principles, which we will now set out in some detail. But it must be remembered that this scheme is in line with the general principles set out above: in particular, the guiding aim is to compensate the claimant by putting him into as good a position as if the personal injury had not occurred.

(i) Damages for pecuniary loss

4.95 **The different types of recoverable pecuniary loss.** The claimant is entitled to recover his loss of net earnings.[179] He can also recover all medical, nursing and hospital expenses which have been, or will be, reasonably incurred.[180] It follows that if the claimant does not, or will not, incur those expenses because he makes use of, or is likely to make use of, the NHS, he cannot recover what he would have been paid had he had private treatment.[181] So as not to overcompensate, ordinary living expenses saved are deducted from the cost of staying in a private hospital or home;[182] and by section 5 of the Administration of Justice Act 1982 any saving to the claimant, which is or will be attributable to his maintenance by the NHS,

---

[175] If a court combines aggravated damages with (ordinary) mental distress damages, it must be astute to avoid double compensation: see *McConnell v Police Authority of Northern Ireland* [1997] IRLR 625, 629; *Gbaja-Biamila v DHL International (UK) Ltd* [2000] ICR 730, at [32]; *Richardson v Howie* [2004] EWCA Civ 1127, [2005] PIQR Q3; *Rowlands v Chief Constable of Merseyside Police* [2006] EWCA Civ 1773, [2007] 1 WLR 1065; *Martins v Choudhary* [2007] EWCA Civ 1379, [2008] 1 WLR 617.

[176] This was recommended by the Law Commission in its report on *Aggravated, Exemplary and Restitutionary Damages* (Law Com No 247, 1997) para 2.42. See also *Richardson v Howie* [2004] EWCA Civ 1127, [2005] PIQR Q3, where it was said, in a trespass to person case, that a court should not characterize as aggravated damages an award of damages for injury to feelings except possibly in a wholly exceptional case.

[177] *Lonrho plc v Fayed (No 5)* [1994] 1 All ER 188, CA.

[178] Although rare, a claim for personal injury and death can be founded on a breach of contract: see eg *Summers v Salford Corporation* [1943] AC 283, HL; *Matthews v Kuwait Bechtel Corporation* [1959] 2 QB 57, CA. If so, the same basic principles apply in respect of the assessment of damages for the personal injury and death as where the claim is brought in tort.

[179] One deducts the tax (*British Transport Commission v Gourley* [1956] AC 185, HL) and national insurance contributions (*Cooper v Firth Brown Ltd* [1963] 1 WLR 418) that the claimant would have paid out of the gross earnings. The claimant may additionally (or alternatively) be awarded loss of earnings for being 'handicapped in the labour market': *Smith v Manchester Corpn* [1974] 17 KIR 1.

[180] See, eg, *Sowden v Lodge* [2004] EWCA Civ 1370, [2005] 1 WLR 2129.

[181] *Cunningham v Harrison* [1973] QB 942, CA; *Lim Poh Choo v Camden and Islington Area Health Authority* [1980] AC 174, HL; *Woodrup v Nicol* [1993] PIQR Q104 CA. The same applies to social services provided free by a local authority: *Eagle v Chambers* [2004] EWCA Civ 1033, [2004] 1 WLR 3081. Where a claimant will receive direct payments from a local authority for care, they must be deducted in assessing damages for the cost of care: *Crofton v NHS Litigation Authority* [2007] EWCA Civ 71, [2007] 1 WLR 923.

[182] *Shearman v Folland* [1950] 2 KB 43, CA; *Lim Poh Choo v Camden and Islington Area Health Authority* [1980] AC 174, HL.

is to be set-off against his loss of earnings.[183] By section 2(4) of the Law Reform (Personal Injuries) Act 1948 the possibility that the claimant could have avoided expenses by using the facilities of the NHS is to be disregarded.

There is still a valid claim for nursing expenses even though they have been rendered gra-   **4.96**
tuitously by a third party. In *Donnelly v Joyce*[184] this was rationalized as compensating the claimant's loss. But in *Hunt v Severs*[185] the House of Lords decided that it was unrealistic to regard the claimant as suffering any pecuniary loss. Rather it was the gratuitous carer who suffered the loss. The claimant was entitled to recover damages in respect of the gratuitous care but should hold them on trust for the carer. It followed, and this was the actual decision in the case, that where the nursing services were gratuitously rendered by the tortfeasor, no damages for that gratuitous care should be awarded. To award such damages would be circular; the defendant would be paying them only for the claimant to hold them on trust for the defendant.

The principle established in *Hunt v Severs*, that a claimant can recover damages for the loss   **4.97**
incurred by a third party in gratuitously caring for the claimant, was applied in *Drake v Foster Wheeler Ltd*[186] so as to allow the cost of care provided by a charitable hospice to be compensated. The claimant was the estate of the deceased who had been cared for, prior to his death, by the hospice. As the damages awarded for that care were subject to a trust in favour of the hospice, it was ordered that the tortfeasor should pay the damages direct to the hospice.

A claimant can also recover for loss of housekeeping capacity. In *Daly v General Steam*   **4.98**
Navigation Co Ltd,[187] it was held that, while loss of housekeeping capacity could be compensated for the future, even though a third party would gratuitously carry out the duties, it was only recoverable for the past either where the claimant actually had employed someone or where a third party had given up earnings so as to help gratuitously with the housekeeping. Otherwise the Court of Appeal thought that the past loss of housekeeping capacity should be regarded as a non-pecuniary loss, which was recoverable at least where the claimant had struggled on with the housekeeping despite injury.

The claimant can also recover the cost of buying, fitting out and moving to special accom-   **4.99**
modation. But the capital cost of a new house, as opposed to the cost of the capital, is not awarded since the claimant still has that capital in the form of the house. In the leading case of *Roberts v Johnstone*[188] it was laid down that the claimant can recover 2 per cent per annum of the capital cost of the purchase as the cost of the capital. More recently, in *Wells v Wells*[189] the House of Lords decided that the appropriate interest rate is that on index-linked government stock (ILGS) and for the time being that rate was regarded as being 3 per cent.[190]

Most other expenses and pecuniary losses consequent on the injury are recoverable, provided   **4.100**
they are not too remote or do not infringe the duty to mitigate. An exception is losses consequent on a divorce caused by the personal injury.[191]

---

[183] The same approach was applied in *O'Brien v Independent Assessor* [2007] UKHL 10, [2007] AC 312 in the different context of the statutory compensation scheme for those whose convictions have been quashed for a miscarriage of justice: the saved cost of food, clothing and accommodation while in prison was held to be deductible from the compensation for loss of earnings.

[184] [1974] QB 454, CA.

[185] [1994] 2 AC 350, HL.

[186] [2010] EWHC 2004 (QB), [2011] 1 All ER 63.

[187] [1979] 1 Lloyd's Rep 257, CA.

[188] [1989] QB 878, CA.

[189] [1999] 1 AC 345, HL.

[190] The figure applied should now be 2.5% as that is the discount rate fixed by the Lord Chancellor: see 4.103.

[191] *Pritchard v JH Cobden Ltd* [1988] Fam 22, CA.

4.101 **Calculating damages for pecuniary loss.** The calculation of damages for pre-trial pecuniary loss is relatively straightforward. It is essentially merely a question of adding together the expenses that the claimant has incurred; or multiplying the claimant's pre-injury monthly earnings by the number of months during which the claimant could not work. The latter calculation clearly depends upon the assumption that, but for the injury, the claimant would have continued to earn at the same rate. If this assumption is not justified (eg, because the claimant would have been promoted and had higher earnings) an adjustment must be made.

4.102 The calculation of damages for future pecuniary loss is more complex. Elements of uncertainty inevitably enter into the calculation, such as the claimant's life expectancy, and what would have happened to the claimant had he not been injured. The standard method of assessment (the so-called 'multiplier' method) is to multiply the assessed net annual loss by a multiplier.[192] The starting point for the multiplier is the number of years during which the loss is likely to endure and thus, typically, the remaining period that the claimant would have worked. This figure is then reduced to take account not only of the element of uncertainty (eg, would the claimant in any event have been unemployed or sick) but, more importantly for the fact that the claimant receives a lump sum which he can invest. The basis of the award is that the total sum will be exhausted at the end of the period contemplated and that during the period the claimant will draw upon both the income derived from the investment of the sum awarded and the capital.

4.103 The courts conventionally used multipliers based on a discount of about 4.5 per cent. But in *Wells v Wells*,[193] the House of Lords held that this was incorrect and that the claimant was entitled to be treated as risk-averse. It was therefore appropriate that the (relatively low) rate of interest on ILGS should be taken as the appropriate discount rate for calculating multipliers. At the time of the decision, the ILGS rate was 3 per cent (net of tax) and this was therefore laid down as the appropriate basis for multipliers for the time being. This meant that significantly higher multipliers would be used than where the discount rate was 4.5 per cent. Exercising his powers under section 1(1) of the Damages Act 1996, the Lord Chancellor has since set a discount rate of 2.5 per cent.[194] Although by section 1(2) of the Damages Act 1996, a court may apply a different rate from that set if it is 'more appropriate in the case in question', the Court of Appeal has shown no willingness to depart from the 2.5 per cent rate.[195]

4.104 One should also note that, despite earlier judicial reluctance to take account of actuarial evidence, it was laid down in *Wells v Wells* that it is appropriate in working out the correct multiplier to make use of the Ogden actuarial tables.[196]

4.105 As the calculation is now being based on ILGS, this neatly takes account of future inflation.[197] It also follows that the costs of investment advice are irrecoverable: the assumed ILGS

---

[192] Sometimes, especially where fixing a multiplicand is difficult, the courts will estimate future pecuniary loss by roughly assessing a general global figure: see, eg, *Joyce v Yeomans* [1981] 1 WLR 549, CA.

[193] [1999] 1 AC 345, HL.

[194] Damages (Personal Injury) Order 2001, SI 2001/2301.

[195] *Warriner v Warriner* [2002] EWCA Civ 81, [2002] 1 WLR 1703; *Cooke v United Bristol Health Care* [2003] EWCA Civ 1370, [2004] 1 WLR 251. But it is significant that in *Simon v Helmot* [2012] UKPC 5, on an appeal from Guernsey, where there is no legislation governing the discount rate so that the courts must decide that rate, it was held that, on the present economic evidence, a 'negative discount rate' of minus 1.5% should be applied in assessing damages for loss of future earnings (ie, in calculating the multiplier, there should be an addition to, rather than a deduction from, the number of years during which the loss would be suffered).

[196] *Actuarial Tables for Use in Personal Injury and Fatal Accident Cases* (7th edn, 2011). These are produced by a working party of lawyers and actuaries. The first chairman was the late Sir Michael Ogden QC.

[197] Prior to reliance on ILGS, the courts ruled that no adjustment should be made for future inflation: *Cookson v Knowles* [1979] AC 556, HL: *Lim Poh Choo v Camden and Islington Area Health Authority* [1980] AC 174, HL.

investment is straightforward and does not require the sort of advice that investing in gilts and equities would do.[198] The standard multipliers assume that standard rate tax will be paid on the investment income but, according to *Hodgson v Trapp*,[199] no further uplift of the multiplier is normally appropriate to account for any higher rate tax that the claimant has to pay.

Where the injury has reduced the claimant's life expectancy, the multiplier is calculated **4.106** according to his life expectancy prior to the injury, with a deduction for the living expenses which he would have incurred during the 'lost years' that he will no longer live through. That damages can be recovered for the 'lost years' was laid down in *Pickett v British Rail Engineering Ltd*.[200] The living expenses deducted are what the claimant spent on maintaining himself at the standard of living appropriate to his case and includes a pro-rata amount of his family expenditure on, eg, housing, heating and lighting.

(ii) Damages for non-pecuniary loss

In addition to the claimant's pecuniary losses which, at least in theory, can be mathematically **4.107** assessed, the claimant is entitled to damages for his non-pecuniary loss. That is, he is entitled to damages for the pain and suffering and loss of amenity[201] consequent on the injury. The amount of damages is awarded in accordance with a tariff system whereby the courts are guided by awards made in past cases for similar personal injuries. This system has traditionally depended on the publication (in, eg, Kemp and Kemp, *The Quantum of Damages*) of judicial awards listed under the different types of personal injury (such as deafness, loss of thumb, loss of leg, quadriplegia) with brief details of the claimant's circumstances. The tariff or bracket of damages for that injury will provide the basic range of award in the instant case; but it will be adjusted flexibly by the judge to take account of the claimant's particular circumstances. For example, the injury may have been accompanied by a great deal of pain in one case but not so in another. There may also be particular deprivations brought about by the injury. For example, the claimant who has lost a hand may have been a pianist. The loss of amenity aspect of the award is assessed objectively in the sense that it is made irrespective of the claimant's own appreciation of his condition; in contrast, pain and suffering is subjectively assessed so that if the claimant is not capable of experiencing the pain or suffering no damages should be awarded for them.[202]

In an attempt to produce greater consistency of awards, and in generally seeking to make **4.108** the judicial tariff of values more accessible, the Judicial Studies Board in 1992 produced *Guidelines for the Assessment of General Damages in Personal Injury Cases*. The twelfth edition of the *Guidelines* was published in 2013. They set out, in easily understood form, the range of awards for various injuries. As at that date, the range runs from £670 for minor hand injuries through to £297,000 for the most serious injuries.[203] The courts have laid down that past

---

[198] *Page v Plymouth Hospital NHS Trust* [2004] EWHC 1154, [2004] 3 All ER 367; *Eagle v Chambers* [2004] EWCA Civ 1033, [2004] 1 WLR 3081.

[199] [1989] AC 807, HL.

[200] [1980] AC 136, HL.

[201] ie loss of enjoyment of life.

[202] *Wise v Kaye* [1962] 1 QB 638, CA; *West v Shepherd* [1964] AC 326, HL; *Lim Poh Choo v Camden and Islington Area HA* [1980] AC 174, HL.

[203] In *Heil v Rankin* [2001] QB 272, CA, awards for more serious injuries were increased because they had fallen behind what was considered fair, just and reasonable. From 1 April 2013, when the legislative changes to the costs regime recommended by Sir Rupert Jackson came into force, damages for pain, suffering and loss of amenity (and indeed all awards of damages for non-pecuniary loss including physical inconvenience and mental distress in contract cases) should be increased by 10% (unless the claimant falls within s 44(6) of the Legal Aid, Sentencing and Punishment of Offenders Act 2012): *Simmons v Castle* [2012] EWCA 1039, [2012] EWCA Civ 1288, [2013] 1 All ER 334.

awards must be increased to allow for inflation by taking into account changes in the retail prices index since the past award was made.[204]

(iii) Compensating advantages

4.109   What happens where, as a result of the injury, the victim receives benefits from other sources (often referred to as collateral benefits)? For example, he may receive sick pay or charitable payments or payments from a personal accident insurance policy or social security benefits. Adherence to the compensatory principle would suggest that, provided the benefit is not too indirectly related to the injury, it should be deducted. But it is clear that English law does not rigidly apply the compensatory principle in this regard. Rather some collateral benefits are deducted and others are not. In particular, while sick pay is deducted,[205] the proceeds of an accident insurance policy,[206] sums received under a disability pension,[207] and charitable payments[208] are not deducted.

4.110   In respect of social security benefits the law is now largely contained in the Social Security (Recovery of Benefits) Act 1997.[209] This basically lays down that social security benefits paid, as a result of the injury, or likely to be so paid, for a maximum period of five years from the accident[210] are to be deducted but that the state (through the Compensation Recovery Unit) is entitled to recoup the amount of the benefits paid from the tortfeasor. However, there is to be no deduction from damages awarded for non-pecuniary loss.[211]

(iv) Interest

4.111   Simple interest on damages for personal injury and death (exceeding £200) must be awarded (unless there are special reasons for it not to be).[212] It was laid down in *Jefford v Gee*[213] that, for the purposes of interest, personal injury awards must be itemized into non-pecuniary loss, pre-trial pecuniary loss, and future pecuniary loss. As regards non-pecuniary loss, interest on damages is awarded at the rate of 2 per cent[214] from the date of service of the claim form to the date of trial.[215] Interest on pre-trial pecuniary loss awards is normally payable from the date of the accident until trial on the full sum awarded and the normal rate is half the average

---

[204]   *Wright v British Railways Board* [1983] 2 AC 773, HL; *Heil v Rankin* [2001] QB 272, CA.

[205]   *Hussain v New Taplow Paper Mills Ltd* [1988] AC 514, HL.

[206]   *Bradburn v Great Western Railway Co* (1874) LR 10 Exch 1.

[207]   *Parry v Cleaver* [1970] AC 1, HL; *Smoker v London Fire and Civil Defence Authority* [1991] 2 AC 502, HL.

[208]   *Redpath v Belfast and County Down Rly* [1947] NI 167. But the policy of not discouraging benevolence means that gratuitous payments made by the tortfeasor will be deducted: *Gaca v Pirelli General plc* [2004] EWCA Civ 373, [2004] 1 WLR 2683.

[209]   The common law position, which applies to state benefits not covered by the 1997 Act, is that state benefits should be deducted: *Hodgson v Trapp* [1989] AC 807, H; *Clenshaw v Tanner* [2002] EWCA Civ 1848.

[210]   Benefits after the five years are to be ignored: see ss 3 and 17 of the 1997 Act.

[211]   By s 8 of, and Sch 2 to, the 1997 Act, recoupment shall only be against compensation for loss of earnings, cost of care and loss of mobility, and then only 'like for like'. The tortfeasor is therefore being held liable for the pure economic loss caused to the state by the tort. See analogously the right of hospital authorities to charge the costs of treatment to tortfeasors under the Health and Social Care (Community Health and Standards) Act 2003, Part 3.

[212]   Senior Courts Act 1981, s 35A(2); County Courts Act 1984, s 69(2).

[213]   [1970] 2 QB 130.

[214]   After *Wells v Wells* [1999] 1 AC 345, HL, one might have thought that the appropriate rate should be the ILGS rate. But this argument was rejected in *Lawrence v Chief Constable of Staffordshire* [2000] PIQR Q349, CA.

[215]   *Wright v British Railways Board* [1983] 2 AC 773.

rate on the special account over that period.[216] No interest is payable on damages for future pecuniary loss.[217]

(v) Provisional damages

By section 32A of the Senior Courts Act 1981, and the accompanying rules of court, the **4.112** courts have power to award provisional damages in actions 'for damages for personal injuries in which there is proved or admitted to be a chance that at some definite or indefinite time in the future the injured person will, as a result of the act or omission which gave rise to the cause of action, develop some serious disease or suffer some serious deterioration in his physical or mental condition'. In such a case the court is able to assess the damages on the assumption that the injured person will not develop the disease or suffer deterioration but can then award further damages at a future date if the risk should in fact materialize. However, the power can only be used if the claimant has pleaded a claim for provisional damages. The order for an award of provisional damages must specify the disease or type of deterioration in respect of which an application may be made at a future date and will normally specify the period within which such application may be made, although the period may be extended on an application by the claimant. Only one application for further damages may be made in respect of each disease or type of deterioration specified in the order for the award of provisional damages.

The introduction of provisional damages marked an important theoretical break with the **4.113** once-and-for-all lump sum system. However, they represented only a small departure from the traditional approach and are different from (reviewable) periodical payments. In practice, most claimants do not claim provisional damages. That is, they choose to forgo the possibility of higher damages in the long term, by taking what at trial is a higher award under the traditional once-and-for-all approach.

(vi) (Reviewable) periodical payments

On 1 April 2005 a fundamental departure from lump sums was introduced by the Courts **4.114** Act 2003, sections 100–101 (amending the Damages Act 1996), the Damages (Variation of Periodical Payments) Order 2005[218] and accompanying Civil Procedure Rules.[219] In the case of damages for future pecuniary loss in respect of personal injury or death, the courts are empowered (and are required to consider whether) to make an order that the damages are to take the form of periodical payments.[220] Moreover, the periodical payments order (PPO) may be made variable so that it can be reviewed by the courts.[221] These provisions, therefore, give the courts, for the first time, the power to order (reviewable) periodical payments. It is clear that a particularly influential 'political' factor behind the introduction of the new regime was that, in respect of litigation against the National Health Service, periodical payments are more attractive to the NHS (at least in the short term) than having to find large capital sums.[222] However, before such an order can be made, a court has to be

---

[216] *Jefford v Gee* [1970] 2 QB 130, CA; *Cookson v Knowles* [1979] AC 556, HL. Half-rate on the full sum is a rough-and-ready substitute for calculating the full average rate on each loss from when it occurred until trial. In exceptional cases, a more precise calculation is appropriate: see, eg, *Dexter v Courtaulds Ltd* [1984] 1 WLR 372, CA. The special account (sometimes referred to as the special investment account) is an investment account used for court funds.

[217] *Jefford v Gee* [1970] 2 QB 130, CA.

[218] SI 2005/841.

[219] CPR, r 41.4–41.10.

[220] Damages Act 1996, s 2(1), as substituted by the Courts Act 2003, s 100.

[221] Damages Act 1996, s 2B, as substituted by the Courts Act 2003, s 100; and Damages (Variation of Periodical Payments) Order 2005.

[222] The Explanatory Notes to the Act make this clear.

satisfied that the continuity of payment is reasonably secure.[223] Other than in respect of public sector defendants, this will essentially be so where the defendant's insurer purchases an annuity.[224] Protection for claimants in the event of an insurer's insolvency or a public body's non-existence is provided by the Damages Act 1996, sections 4 and 6, as amended by the Courts Act 2003, section 101. By section 2(8) periodical payments are to be updated by reference to the retail prices index although this can be modified under section 2(9). It has been decided that section 2(9) allows a different index than the RPI to be applied.[225] The reviewability provisions closely match those on 'provisional damages'. The original court can make a variable order but only to deal with the development of some serious disease or the suffering of some serious deterioration or significant improvement in the claimant's condition. Moreover, only one application to vary a variable order can be made in respect of each specified disease or type of deterioration or improvement.

(vii) Claims by the deceased's estate

4.115   The Law Reform (Miscellaneous Provisions) Act 1934, section 1(1) provides that, on the death of any person, causes of action vested in him, subject to certain exceptions,[226] survive for the benefit of his estate.[227] The most important consequence of this is that the deceased's action for personal injury survives for the benefit of his estate.

4.116   Thus the deceased's personal representatives will be awarded damages for all the deceased's recoverable loss, both non-pecuniary[228] and pecuniary,[229] but only until the time of the death, applying the normal principle that all events known about at trial are taken into account.

4.117   In one respect, however, the principles governing compensatory damages for the deceased's estate differ from those governing the injured claimant's damages. By section 4(2) of the Administration of Justice Act 1982, amending section 1(2) of the Law Reform (Miscellaneous Provisions) Act 1934, no damages may be awarded for lost income in respect of any period after the death of the injured person; ie the claim for loss of earnings in the 'lost years'[230] does not survive for the benefit of the estate.

(c) Damages for death: Fatal Accidents Act 1976

4.118   At common law no action could be brought for loss suffered through the killing of another. This was altered by the Fatal Accidents Act 1846. The governing statute is now the Fatal Accidents Act 1976. This gives a statutory action '...if death is caused by any wrongful act, neglect or default...'.[231]

---

[223] Damages Act 1996, s 2(3).

[224] The new system therefore builds on and absorbs the 'structured settlement' which was introduced in the 1980s as a consequence of the acceptance by the Inland Revenue that, if the defendant's insurer purchased an annuity for the claimant, payments received were tax free. But structured settlements could not be imposed by the courts.

[225] *Flora v Wakom (Heathrow) Ltd* [2006] EWCA Civ 1103, [2007] 1 WLR 482; *Tameside and Glossop Acute Services NHS Trust v Thompstone* [2008] EWCA Civ 5, [2008] 1 WLR 2207 (using the Annual Survey of Hours and Earnings ('ASHE' 6115) for updating future care costs).

[226] ie actions for defamation, bereavement damages, and exemplary damages.

[227] By s 1(2)(c) of the 1934 Act, where the defendant was responsible for the death, damages may be awarded to the estate for funeral expenses incurred: plainly this is distinct from the survival of the deceased's cause of action.

[228] See *Rose v Ford* [1937] AC 826, HL; *Andrews v Freeborough* [1967] 1 QB 1, CA; *Murray v Shuter* [1976] QB 972, CA.

[229] *Murray v Shuter* [1976] QB 972 (deceased's loss of earnings); *Rose v Ford* [1937] AC 826 (deceased's medical expenses).

[230] See 4.106.

[231] Normally such statutory actions are founded on a tort by the defendant. But the basis may be breach of contract: *Grein v Imperial Airways Ltd* [1937] 1 KB 50.

(i) Actionability by injured person

By section 1(1) of the 1976 Act, an action can only succeed if the wrongful act, neglect or **4.119** default which caused the death 'is such as would (if death had not ensued) have entitled the person injured to maintain an action and recover damages in respect thereof'. Therefore if the deceased was killed entirely through his own fault,[232] or if the defendant had validly excluded all liability to the deceased, or if the deceased's action had become time-barred before his death, or if the deceased had settled his claim or obtained judgment against the defendant, the dependants will have no action.

By section 5 of the 1976 Act, where the deceased was contributorily negligent in relation to **4.120** his death, and hence his damages would have been reduced by a certain amount under the Law Reform (Contributory) Negligence Act 1945, the damages recoverable by the dependants under the 1976 Act are to be reduced to a proportionate extent.[233]

(ii) Loss of dependency

Damages are primarily awarded under the 1976 Act to dependants for the loss of their **4.121** expected non-business pecuniary benefits consequent on the death. This most obviously covers loss of support from the deceased's earnings. It also covers loss of 'services'; eg, a husband will be awarded damages in respect of his wife's housekeeping in the home;[234] children will be compensated for the loss of their mother's daily care and work on their behalf;[235] and a wife and children will be compensated for the loss of a husband's and father's services as a handyman around the house.[236]

As laid down in section 1(2), the action under the 1976 Act is for the benefit of the dependants **4.122** of the deceased (subject to a narrower restriction on who can be awarded bereavement damages).[237] The meaning of 'dependant' is laid down in a list (the present list being an extension of previous lists). By section 1(3) the list now comprises the spouse or former spouse of the deceased, including a person whose marriage has been annulled or declared void; a civil partner or former civil partner of the deceased; any person who was living as the husband or wife or civil partner of the deceased in the same household immediately before the date of the death and has been so living for at least two years before the death; any parent or ascendant of the deceased; any person who was treated by the deceased as his parent; any child or other descendant of the deceased; any person who has been treated by the deceased as a child of the family in relation to any marriage or civil partnership of the deceased; and any person who is, or is the issue of, a brother, sister, uncle or aunt of the deceased. A relationship by marriage or civil partnership is treated as a relationship by consanguinity, a relationship of the half-blood as a relationship of the whole blood and the stepchild of any person as his child. An illegitimate person is to be treated as the legitimate child of his mother and reputed father or, in the case of a person who has a female parent by virtue of section 43 of the Human Fertilisation and Embryology Act 2008, the legitimate child of his mother and that female parent.

---

[232] cf *Corr v IBC Vehicles Ltd* [2008] UKHL 13, [2008] 1 AC 884 in which it was held that the deceased's suicide, caused by the defendant's negligence or breach of statutory duty, was actionable by his widow under the 1976 Act.

[233] See, eg, *Reeves v Commissioner of Police of the Metropolis* [2000] 1 AC 360, HL (50% reduction for suicide). In accordance with normal principle, under the Law Reform (Contributory Negligence) Act 1945, a dependant's contributory negligence in relation to the death will reduce that dependant's damages for pecuniary loss: see *Mulholland v McCrea* [1961] NI 135.

[234] *Berry v Humm & Co* [1915] 1 KB 627.

[235] *Hay v Hughes* [1975] QB 790, CA; *Spittle v Bunney* [1988] 1 WLR 847; *Stanley v Saddique* [1992] QB 1, CA.

[236] *Clay v Pooler* [1982] 3 All ER 570.

[237] See 4.131.

4.123 Although the list of dependants is now a wide one, it is still capable of causing hardship, which calls into question the need for a restriction beyond financial dependency. For example, a financially dependent friend and companion of the deceased remains excluded.

4.124 As with damages for future pecuniary loss consequent on a personal injury, damages for loss of a pecuniary benefit under the 1976 Act are calculated using a multiplier method. However, in the context of fatal accident claims, in contrast to personal injury claims, the multiplier is used to assess all the pecuniary loss from the date of death and not merely the post-trial pecuniary loss. In *Cookson v Knowles*[238] the House of Lords laid down that the dependant's pecuniary loss prior to trial should be assessed separately from that after the trial. This is essentially because the former is less speculative and because no interest is to be paid on the future loss but is payable on the pre-trial loss. In *Graham v Dodds*[239] it was clarified that that itemization does not entail that the multiplier method should be abandoned for pre-trial loss. Rather the multiplier should continue to be calculated from the date of death, rather than from the date of trial, on the basis that, in contrast to a personal injury case, there can be no certainty even that the deceased would have survived until trial. So if, eg, the multiplier is 14, and four years have elapsed between death and trial, the pre-trial loss will be calculated using a multiplier of 4 and the post-trial loss will be calculated using a multiplier of 10. But a separate pre-trial and post-trial multiplicand is generally appropriate to take account of facts known at trial (eg, the rate of wages for the job that the deceased had). The multiplicands will be the pre-trial and post-trial annual pecuniary loss to the dependant calculated by, eg, deducting from the deceased's notional annual net earnings his living expenses; and living expenses here means expenses for the deceased's own purposes exclusively.[240] There will then be an adjustment to take account, eg, of the prospects of promotion that the deceased had.

4.125 It is strongly arguable that it would be more accurate to calculate multipliers for post-trial pecuniary loss from the date of death with pre-trial loss being calculated in much the same straightforward way as in personal injury cases (with the qualification that there would need to be a general discount for the uncertainty as to whether the deceased would have lived to trial). The difficulties of the present approach are illustrated by *Corbett v Barking, Havering & Brentwood HA*,[241] where there had been a long delay between death and trial (eleven and a half years). Controversially, the Court of Appeal (Ralph Gibson LJ dissenting) held that it did not contradict *Graham v Dodds* to increase the normal multiplier, calculated from the date of the death, to take into account the known fact that the child dependant had survived to the age of 11½. In *White v ESAB Group (UK) Ltd*[242] Nelson J, in the light of the views of the Law Commission and the Ogden Working Party, would have preferred to calculate the multiplier from the date of trial, but held himself precluded from doing so by *Cookson v Knowles* and *Graham v Dodds*. In his view, those decisions had not been expressly or impliedly overruled by *Wells v Wells*. The decision in the *Corbett* case was held not to be applicable since, in contrast to that case, there were, in this case, no unusual significant facts that had arisen between the date of death and the trial. In *H v S*[243] the Court of Appeal approved Nelson J's refusal to depart from the traditional 'date of death' approach. In *Fletcher v A Train & Sons Ltd*[244] the Court of Appeal again criticized *Cookson v Knowles*—and called for a reconsideration of it by the House of Lords—while holding itself bound to apply it. In this case, the question at

[238] [1979] AC 556, HL.
[239] [1983] 1 WLR 808, HL.
[240] Contrast the living expenses deducted in calculating the injured person's 'lost years' damages: see 4.106.
[241] [1991] 2 QB 408.
[242] [2002] PIQR Q6.
[243] [2002] EWCA Civ 792, [2003] QB 965, at [36].
[244] [2008] EWCA Civ 413, [2008] 4 All ER 699.

issue was not directly about the date from which the multiplier should be calculated. Instead the central, linked question was whether courts were free to depart from the approach to calculating interest in Fatal Accident Act cases put forward in *Cookson v Knowles*. It was held that that approach to interest was binding and, unless and until reconsidered by the House of Lords, it could not be departed from.

The starting point for the multiplier is the estimated number of years (taking into account, eg, the deceased's and dependant's life expectancies) from the date of death that the dependant would have received the pecuniary benefits. The starting figure is then discounted by 2.5 per cent because the dependant receives a capital sum now, which he can invest, rather than periodical payments over the years. There may then be a small adjustment for the contingencies of life other than mortality (such as the deceased's possible unemployment). The basis of the award is that the total sum will be exhausted at the end of the period contemplated and that during the period the dependant will draw upon both the income derived from the investment of the sum awarded and the capital itself. **4.126**

In calculating the dependant's loss of pecuniary benefit the court must make its best estimate of the future. However, by section 3(3) of the Fatal Accidents Act 1976, in assessing a widow's claim in respect of her husband's death, 'there shall not be taken into account the remarriage of the widow or her prospects of remarriage'. Parliament introduced this provision primarily to put a stop to the degrading judicial 'guessing game' of assessing a widow's prospects of remarriage. But this is at the expense of not deducting what is a direct compensating advantage and the effect can be that, eg, a widow who marries a very wealthy husband, even prior to trial, is still entitled to damages in respect of her dependency on her former husband. It should also be noted that section 3(3) applies only to a widow's claim and therefore a mother's remarriage or prospects of remarriage must still be taken into account in assessing a child's claim. Similarly, where the claim is brought by a cohabitee her marriage or prospects of marriage are to be taken into account. Also outside the scope of section 3(3) is a widower's remarriage or prospects of remarriage which therefore are relevant in assessing damages. **4.127**

By section 4 of the 1976 Act, 'in assessing damages in respect of a person's death in an action under this Act, the benefits which have accrued or will or may accrue to any person from his estate or otherwise as a result of his death shall be disregarded'. So, eg, charitable payments, payments under a life assurance policy, a widow's pension, and social security benefits are not to be deducted in assessing damages under the 1976 Act. The width of section 4 is a cause of uncertainty[245] although, as regards gratuitous care provided to the dependant consequent on the death, the law has been made more rational by the application to a Fatal Accidents Act case in *H v S*[246] of the approach in *Hunt v Severs*[247] (the leading personal injury case on gratuitous services). Infant children, following the death of their mother, were receiving care from their father, who was not the tortfeasor and had not previously provided them with any care or support. Although under section 4 of the Fatal Accidents Act 1976 the value of such gratuitous services was not to be deducted, the damages in respect of the lost services of the deceased mother were to be held on trust for the gratuitous carer (the father). **4.128**

It should be emphasized that the 1976 Act is concerned only to compensate dependants for non-business pecuniary benefits consequent on the death. Benefits flowing from the business relationship between the dependant and the deceased are irrecoverable. For example, in **4.129**

---

[245] See eg the contrast between the decisions in *Stanley v Saddique* [1992] QB 1, CA; and *Hayden v Hayden* [1992] 1 WLR 986, CA. See also *R v Criminal Injuries Compensation Board, ex p K* [1999] 2 WLR 948.
[246] [2002] EWCA Civ 792, [2003] QB 965.
[247] [1994] 2 AC 350, HL: see 4.96.

Burgess v Florence Nightingale Hospital For Gentlewomen [248] it was held that a husband could not recover damages for his loss of income as a dancer resulting from the death of his dancing partner wife.

4.130 Although not a loss of pecuniary benefit, but rather an expense necessary as a consequence of the death, section 3(5) of the 1976 Act lays down that funeral expenses incurred by dependants in respect of the deceased are recoverable.

(iii) Bereavement damages

4.131 By section 1A of the 1976 Act damages are to be awarded for the mental distress (ie, the sorrow, grief and loss of enjoyment) consequent on the death. Called 'damages for bereavement', a fixed sum, at present £12,980,[249] can be claimed for the benefit of the spouse of the deceased or, where the deceased was a minor who was never married or a civil partner, the parents of the deceased (or, if the child was illegitimate, his mother).[250] By section 1A(4) if both parents claim bereavement damages, the fixed sum is to be divided equally between them.

(iv) Relationship between actions under the Law Reform (Miscellaneous Provisions) Act 1934 and the Fatal Accidents Act 1976

4.132 Where the defendant's wrong has caused a death, an action may be brought under both the Law Reform (Miscellaneous Provisions) Act 1934 and the Fatal Accidents Act 1976. Where the death is not instantaneous, the survival action enables recovery, on behalf of the estate, of damages for the deceased's pre-death losses both pecuniary and non-pecuniary, while the Fatal Accidents Act action enables dependants to recover for their loss of dependency and a spouse or parent to recover damages for bereavement. Funeral expenses may be recovered in either action (although clearly they will not be awarded twice over). On the other hand, where the death is instantaneous, and there has been no property damage, no damages can now be recovered under the 1934 Act, other than where the estate has incurred the funeral expenses.[251]

(3) Equitable Compensation

4.133 Although, until recently, there has been surprisingly little examination of it, a major remedy for equitable wrongs—of which the prime example is breach of fiduciary duty—is equitable compensation.[252] This is a monetary personal remedy the purpose of which is to compensate

---

[248] [1955] 1 QB 349.
[249] Damages for Bereavement (Variation of Sum) Order 2013, SI 2013/510. The Minister for Justice's power to alter the amount is conferred by s 1A(5) of the 1976 Act.
[250] But note that there may now be a claim under the Human Rights Act 1998 if the death has been caused by a public authority's breach of a convention right and in that situation the claimants who may be awarded damages for non-pecuniary loss are not restricted to those falling within s 1A of the 1976 Act: *Rabone v Pennine NHS Foundation Trust* [2012] UKSC 2, [2012] 2 AC 72.
[251] Formerly a claim for loss of earnings in the 'lost years' survived for the benefit of the estate, but this is no longer so: see 4.117.
[252] eg *Re Dawson* [1966] 2 NSWR 211; *Bartlett v Barclays Bank Trust Co (No 2)* [1980] Ch 515; *Target Holdings Ltd v Redfern* [1996] AC 421, HL; *Bristol & West Building Society v Mothew* [1998] Ch 1, CA; *Swindle v Harrison* [1997] 4 All ER 705, CA; *AIB Group (UK) Ltd v Mark Redler & Co* [2014] UKSC 58, [2014] 3 WLR 1367. I Davidson, 'The Equitable Remedy of Compensation' (1982) 13 Melbourne UL Rev 349. For equitable compensation for dishonestly assisting a breach of fiduciary duty, see *Twinsectra v Yardley* [2002] UKHL 12, [2002] 2 AC 164; *Barlow Clowes International Ltd v Eurotrust International* Ltd [2005] UKPC 37, [2006] 1 WLR 1476. Monetary compensation, best viewed as the remedy of equitable compensation, has been awarded under the doctrine of proprietary estoppel: *Dodsworth v Dodsworth* (1973) 228 EG 1115 (the compensation was 'secured' by giving the claimant possession of the land until payment by the defendant); *Baker & Baker v Baker* (1993) 25 Housing LR 408, CA; *Gillett v Holt* [2001] Ch 210, CA; *Jennings v Rice* [2002] EWCA Civ 159, [2003] 1 P & CR 8; cf *Hussey*

the claimant. Although sometimes referred to as 'accounting for loss' (or, very misleadingly, 'restitution') this contrasts with 'accounting for profits' which is the other main monetary remedy for equitable wrongs.[253] Accounting for profits is concerned to effect restitution, whereas equitable compensation is concerned to effect compensation.[254] Equitable compensation therefore equates to (common law) compensatory damages; and a topical question is the extent to which, if at all, the principles governing equitable compensation differ from those applicable to (common law) compensatory damages.[255]

The courts have recently recognized that, in general terms, there is little difference between equitable compensation and compensatory damages. In particular, the House of Lords in *Target Holdings Ltd v Redfern*,[256] affirmed by the Supreme Court in *AIB Group (UK) Ltd v Mark Redler & Co*,[256a] rejected the argument that a breach of trust required loss to the trust to be restored even though that loss would have been suffered even if there had been no breach of duty.[257] In other words, it was accepted that equitable compensation will not be awarded unless loss has been factually caused (applying a 'but for' test) by the breach of duty. On the other hand, Lord Browne-Wilkinson, giving the leading speech, said that the common law rules of remoteness of damage and legal causation do not apply to equitable compensation.[258] But it is not obvious that this is correct, particularly given the flexibility of the common law rules relating to legal causation and remoteness. So, eg, Lord Browne-Wilkinson seemed to have it in mind that a contrast with the common law position was shown where the immediate cause of the loss was the dishonesty or failure of a third party. In that situation, the trustee would still be liable to compensate the trust estate if loss was factually caused by the breach of duty. However, the same might be true at common law in respect of the tort of negligence if the purpose of the duty of care was to guard against the very risk of third party intervention that has occurred. Moreover, it is clear that at common law the test of remoteness is wider (and does not require the loss to have been reasonably foreseen) in respect of the tort of deceit than in respect of the tort of negligent misrepresentation.[259] And it has long been open to question whether the normal foreseeability test of remoteness applies to torts of strict liability.

4.134

---

v Palmer [1972] 1 WLR 1286. There appears to be no English case in which equitable compensation has been awarded for breach of confidence. It was suggested in *Mahoney v Purnell* [1996] 3 All ER 61 that rescission plus equitable compensation could be awarded for undue influence. But undue influence is not a wrong and the better view is that it triggers rescission and restitution not compensation: see P Birks, 'Unjust Factors and Wrongs: Pecuniary Rescission for Undue Influence' (1997) Restitution Law Review 72.

[253] See 4.156–4.158.

[254] See 4.163 for consideration of whether equitable compensation can ever be awarded to punish the equitable wrongdoer.

[255] Equitable damages—awarded in substitution for an injunction or specific performance—can be awarded for equitable wrongs just as they can for common law wrongs: see 4.138–4.142.

[256] [1996] AC 421, HL.

[256a] [2014] UKSC 58, [2014] 3 WLR 1367.

[257] See also *Gwembe Valley Development Co Ltd v Koshy* [2003] EWCA Civ 1048, [2004] 1 BCLC 131, at [142]–[160] (no loss caused by breach of fiduciary duty by director and therefore no equitable compensation could be awarded). For criticism of this approach, on the ground that the trustee's liability was to account for the course of his trusteeship and that the account remedy is analogous to an action in debt which should not be equated to compensation, see P Millett, 'Equity's Place in the Law of Commerce' (1998) 114 LQR 214, 224–227; S Elliott and C Mitchell, 'Remedies for Dishonest Assistance' (2004) 67 MLR 16, 23–36; C Mitchell, 'Equitable Rights and Wrongs' (2006) 59 CLP 267; C Mitchell and S Watterson, 'Remedies for Knowing Receipt' in C Mitchell (ed), *Constructive and Resulting Trusts* (2010) 115.

[258] See also *Swindle v Harrison* [1997] 4 All ER 705 (*per* Mummery LJ).

[259] See 4.82. For the drawing of an analogy between the remoteness rules for deceit and the remoteness rules for equitable compensation using, in relation to the latter, a general concept of equitable fraud, see *Canson Enterprises Ltd v Boughton* [1991] 3 SCR 534; cf *Swindle v Harrison* [1997] 4 All ER 705 (*per* Evans LJ).

4.135   In *Bristol & West Building Society v Mothew*[260] Millett LJ argued that one could assimilate equitable compensation and damages in respect of breach of an equitable duty of skill and care. He said:

> Although the remedy which equity makes available for breach of the equitable duty of skill and care is equitable compensation rather than damages, this is merely the product of history and in this context is in my opinion a distinction without a difference. Equitable compensation for breach of the duty of skill and care resembles common law damages in that it is awarded by way of compensation to the plaintiff for his loss. There is no reason in principle why the common law rules of causation, remoteness of damage and measure of damages should not be applied by analogy in such a case.[261]

4.136   On the other hand, Millett LJ, more controversially, went on to say that the same assimilation could not be made in respect of other types of breach of fiduciary duty. 'This leaves those duties which are special to fiduciaries and attract those remedies which are peculiar to the equitable jurisdiction and are primarily restitutionary or restorative rather than compensatory.'[262]

4.137   Apart from the controversy over the applicability of causation and remoteness to equitable compensation, there is some doubt whether contributory negligence applies where equitable compensation is being claimed.[263] But again, even if often not applicable, this is not necessarily different from the position at common law where contributory negligence is not a defence to the tort of deceit or, it would seem, other intentional torts.[264]

(4) Equitable (Compensatory) Damages

4.138   By section 50 of the Senior Courts Act 1981, where the High Court 'has jurisdiction to entertain an application for an injunction or specific performance, it may award damages in addition to, or in substitution for, an injunction or specific performance'. This power was formerly contained in section 2 of the Chancery Amendment Act 1858 (Lord Cairns's Act).

4.139   As regards additional damages, the power is self-explanatory. But, for the purpose of 'damages in substitution for an injunction or specific performance', there has been some difficulty in deciding what is meant by the court having 'jurisdiction to entertain an application for an injunction or specific performance'. The traditional approach has been to decide whether the particular reason for denying specific performance or the injunction is jurisdictional or discretionary and only if it is the latter can damages in substitution be awarded.[265] A simpler and preferable approach, and one which could equally well justify past decisions, is to ask whether the claimant had an arguable case for specific performance or an injunction at the time the claim was brought; if so, equitable damages in substitution can be awarded. It should also be noted that, as laid down in *Horsler v Zorro*,[266] section 50 does not allow the award of equitable damages in substitution in the unusual case where the claimant would

---

[260] [1998] Ch 1, CA.

[261] [1998] Ch 1, 17. See also *Bank of New Zealand v New Zealand Guardian Trust Co Ltd* [1999] 1 NZLR 664.

[262] [1998] Ch 1, 18.

[263] See *Day v Mead* [1987] 2 NZLR 443. cf *Pilmer v The Duke Group Ltd* (2001) 75 AJLR 1067, High Court of Australia.

[264] See 4.90. In *Corporacion Nacional del Cobre de Chile v Sogemin Metals Ltd* [1997] 1 WLR 1396 contributory negligence was held to be inapplicable to various dishonestly committed wrongs, whether common law or equitable: see n 169.

[265] *Price v Strange* [1978] Ch 337.

[266] [1975] Ch 302.

have been granted specific performance or an injunction had he claimed it but he has made no such claim because what he wants is damages in substitution.

Why should a claimant want equitable damages rather than normal common law damages? **4.140** After all, section 49 of the Senior Courts Act 1981 allows the claimant to combine a claim for common law damages with an action for specific performance or an injunction. Moreover, it was clearly laid down in *Johnson v Agnew*[267] that the assessment of equitable damages is no different from that for normal common law damages. The normal measure of equitable damages will therefore be compensatory and they will be assessed in the same way as common law compensatory damages.

But there is one major advantage of equitable damages. This is that they may be awarded **4.141** even though there is no cause of action at common law and hence no possible award of common law damages. In particular this means that damages can be awarded in addition to, or in substitution for, a '*quia timet*' injunction, which is an injunction to prevent a threatened wrong where no wrong has yet been committed.[268] For example, in *Leeds Industrial Co-operative Society Ltd v Slack*[269] damages were held recoverable in substitution for a *quia timet* injunction to prevent the defendant constructing buildings which, when complete, would have obstructed the claimant's ancient lights but as yet were causing no obstruction. Similarly, in respect of continuing torts or a continuing breach of contract equitable damages in substitution for an ordinary (ie not a *quia timet*) injunction are more advantageous than common law damages in compensating for an anticipated rather than just an accrued cause of action.[270] Common law damages, in contrast, compensate only for loss (whether past or prospective) caused by a tort or breach of contract that has already been committed.

Three other illustrations may be given of the application of this major advantage offered by **4.142** equitable damages. First, a third party can be awarded damages in addition to or in substitution for an injunction, available under the principle laid down in *Tulk v Moxhay*[271] for the breach of a restrictive covenant concerning land, although he would have no cause of action at common law because of the doctrine of privity of contract. Secondly, equitable damages can be awarded for an anticipatory breach of contract that has not been accepted because specific performance can be awarded for such a breach even though there is no cause of action at common law.[272] Thirdly, while common law damages cannot yet be awarded for breach of confidence, because that is still regarded as an equitable wrong and not a tort,[273] equitable damages can be:[274] presumably the same also applies in respect of other equitable wrongs, such as breach of fiduciary duty.

---

[267] [1980] AC 367, HL.

[268] See 4.201.

[269] [1924] AC 851, HL.

[270] See eg *Bracewell v Appleby* [1975] Ch 408 and *Jaggard v Sawyer* [1995] 1 WLR 269, CA (damages in substitution for an injunction to prevent the defendant continuing to trespass over the claimant's land).

[271] (1848) 18 LJ Ch 83.

[272] *Oakacre Ltd v Claire Cleaners (Holdings) Ltd* [1982] Ch 197.

[273] *Wainwright v Home Office* [2003] UKHL 53, [2004] 2 AC 406, at [18].

[274] *Saltman Engineering Co Ltd v Campbell Engineering Ltd* (1948) 65 Reports of Patents Cases 203, CA; *Seager v Copydex Ltd* [1967] 1 WLR 923, CA. In *Campbell v MGN Ltd* [2004] UKHL 22, [2004] 2 AC 457, the House of Lords upheld an award for breach of confidence of £2,500 damages for mental distress plus £1000 aggravated damages without making any comment as to the jurisdictional basis of those damages.

C. Restitution and Punishment

4.143   This section examines exceptional monetary remedies for wrongs that are concerned not to compensate the innocent party but to strip away gains made by the wrongdoer (restitution)[275] or to punish the wrongdoer (punishment). Restitution for common law wrongs, stripping away gains made by the wrongdoer, has only been judicially recognized relatively recently and remains controversial; and, since *Rookes v Barnard*[276] in 1964, punishment of the wrongdoer, through 'exemplary' or 'punitive' damages, has been treated as an unusual and peripheral remedy in English civil law.

4.144   But to accept that restitution and punishment are less central responses to a wrong than compensation should not lead one to pretend that they do not exist. One must therefore view with scepticism attempts that are commonly made to analyse all awards of 'restitutionary damages' as if they were really awards of 'compensatory damages'.[277] On the contrary, one can argue that, to ensure proper protection of victims, the law should recognize as wide a range of remedial responses to civil wrongs as possible. It is also important to realize that, through the remedy of an 'account of profits', restitution for equitable wrongs, such as breach of fiduciary duty and breach of confidence, has long been awarded without being questioned. On the contrary, it is the remedy of equitable compensation that has been undeveloped for equitable wrongs.[278] The contrast with the controversy generated by the notion of restitution for common law wrongs is a stark one. It is yet another example of the unacceptable inconsistency between common law and equity.

(1) Restitution for Wrongs

4.145   The most obvious reason why a claimant may seek restitution for a wrong, rather than compensation, is in order to recover a higher award. This is so where the gain the defendant has made by the wrong exceeds loss caused to the claimant by the wrong.[279] It is also conceivable that bars (eg, limitation periods) to compensation may apply differently than to restitution.[280]

4.146   Historically a number of differently labelled remedies have performed the role of stripping away gains made by a civil wrongdoer: eg, the award of money had and received (especially in

---

[275] This is sometimes referred to as 'disgorgement'.

[276] [1964] AC 1129.

[277] A well-known example is the article by R Sharpe and S M Waddams, 'Damages for Lost Opportunity to Bargain' (1982) 2 OJLS 290.

[278] See 4.133.

[279] This is most clearly illustrated by cases awarding restitution of bribes: eg *Reading v A-G* [1951] AC 507; *A-G for Hong Kong v Reid* [1994] 1 AC 324, PC. See 4.158.

[280] See *Chesworth v Farrar* [1967] 1 QB 407. But the Limitation Act 1980 is largely drafted in terms of causes of action not remedies. Unless one takes the view that restitution for wrongs rests on a different cause of action than compensation for wrongs, the six-year time limit applicable, eg, to 'an action founded on tort' (s 2 of the 1980 Act) should apply to restitution for torts as well as compensation for torts. By s 23 of the 1980 Act, an action for an account of profits 'shall not be brought after the expiration of any time limit under this Act which is applicable to the claim which is the basis of the duty to account', which appears to mean that, if the basis is tort, tort limitation periods should apply. The limitation periods for breach of trust are laid down in s 21 of the 1980 Act although, by s 21(1), there is no limitation period for fraudulent breach of trust or to recover trust property or its proceeds. Section 21 may also apply to breach of fiduciary duty (other than breach of trust) but, if not, a six-year period will be applied by analogy under s 36(1) of the 1980 Act (*Paragon Finance plc v DB Thakerar & Co* [1999] 1 All ER 400, CA; *Gwembe Valley Development Co Ltd v Koshy* [2003] EWCA Civ 1048, [2004] 1 BCLC 131). In *Williams v Central Bank of Nigeria* [2014] UKSC 10, [2014] AC 1189, it was held that

the so-called 'waiver of tort' cases), an account of profits, and 'restitutionary damages' (where the damages are assessed according to the gains made by the wrongdoer rather than the loss to the claimant). The Law Commission has recommended that, as there is no rational reason for having these different personal restitutionary remedies, rather than a single remedy, it would be appropriate, in the context of restitution for wrongs, for judges and practitioners to abandon the labels 'action for money had and received' and 'account of profits' in favour of the single term 'restitutionary damages'.[281]

Although it is arguable that, in principle, there is no justification for this, a claimant cannot **4.147** be awarded both a restitutionary remedy (eg, an account of profits or the award of money had and received) and compensatory damages for a wrong.[282] Restitutionary and compensatory remedies are regarded as 'alternative and inconsistent' and cannot be combined: the claimant must elect between them, albeit that the election need not be made until judgment and even then it can be changed if the judgment is unsatisfied.[283]

It is convenient to examine the present law on restitution for wrongs in three parts: resti-   **4.148** tution of enrichments gained by a tort: restitution of enrichments gained by an equitable wrong; and restitution of enrichments gained by a breach of contract.

(a) Enrichments gained by a tort

One first needs to explain what is meant by 'waiver of tort'. This is a confusing concept and   **4.149** it carries more than one meaning. It is normally used to refer to a situation in which a claimant seeks a restitutionary remedy for a tort (ie the cause of action is the tort) rather than compensatory damages. For example, in the leading case of *United Australia Ltd v Barclays Bank Ltd*,[284] the claimant brought an action for money had and received by conversion of a cheque. This was a claim for restitution of the gains made by the tort of conversion and the claimant was described as 'waiving the tort'. Yet this did not mean that the claimant was excusing the tort, so that, when that claim was abandoned prior to judgment, the claimant was nevertheless entitled to bring an action claiming compensatory damages for conversion of the cheque by another party. There are two other meanings of the phrase 'waiver of tort'. One refers to a principle of agency law whereby the victim of a tort can choose to give up his right to sue for a tort by treating the tortfeasor as having been authorized to act as the claimant's agent and then relying on the standard remedies against an agent to recover the profits made. In this situation, the tort is truly extinguished.[285] The other meaning refers to where the claimant chooses to ignore the tort and instead rests his claim to restitution on the cause of action of unjust enrichment; eg, a claimant, who has been induced to transfer money to the defendant by the defendant's fraudulent misrepresentation, may ignore the tort of deceit

---

a six-year limitation period applies to the equitable wrongs of dishonest assistance and knowing receipt. There is no limitation period explicitly laid down for breach of confidence but the equitable doctrine of laches will apply.

[281] *Aggravated, Exemplary and Restitutionary Damages* (Law Com No 247, 1997) paras 3.82–3.84. (For a similar argument in respect of restitution for the cause of action of unjust enrichment, see 4.10.) J Edelman, *Gain-Based Damages* (2002) prefers, as a general label, 'gain-based damages' with a subdivision between 'disgorgement damages' and 'restitutionary damages'.

[282] *Neilson v Betts* (1871) LR 5 HL 1, HL; *De Vitre v Betts* (1873) LR 6 HL 319, HL; *Colbeam Palmer Ltd v Stock Affiliates Pty Ltd* (1968) 122 CLR 25, HC; *Mahesan v Malaysia Government Officers' Co-op Housing Society Ltd* [1979] AC 374; *Island Records Ltd v Tring International plc* [1996] 1 WLR 1256; *Tang Min Sit v Capacious Investments Ltd* [1996] AC 514, PC. See also Patents Act 1977, s 61(2). For analysis of the 'election' requirement, see A Burrows, *Remedies for Torts and Breach of Contract* (3rd edn, 2004) 14–16, 388–390.

[283] *United Australia Ltd v Barclays Bank Ltd* [1941] AC 1, HL.

[284] [1941] AC 1.

[285] For a rare example of this, see *Verschures Creameries Ltd v Hull & Netherlands SS Co Ltd* [1921] 2 KB 608.

and seek restitution of the payment from the defendant on the basis that it was made by mistake. In this section we are essentially concerned with 'waiver of tort' in its first, and usual, sense. That is, we are concerned with restitution *for* a tort.

4.150   In examining restitution for torts, it is helpful to divide between proprietary torts, excluding the protection of intellectual property; intellectual property torts; and other torts.

(i) Proprietary torts other than those protecting intellectual property

4.151   The restitutionary remedy of an award of money had and received has long been granted for proprietary torts, such as conversion,[286] trespass to goods,[287] and trespass to land.[288] Moreover, damages which are arguably best analysed as restitutionary being concerned to strip away some or all of the defendant's gains (although the prevailing view remains that these are compensatory damages for loss of an opportunity to bargain or to prevent the wrong) have been awarded for trespass to goods,[289] trespass to land[290] and nuisance.[291] In assessing damages, the courts have usually found it helpful to think of a hypothetical bargain that the parties might reasonably have struck for a 'purchase' of the right.[292] Important to the restitutionary analysis is that in deciding on that hypothetical price the courts have generally taken a fair percentage of the wrongdoer's anticipated profits; and that it has been irrelevant that the claimant would not have been willing to sell the right. It is also significant that, in the contract case of *Attorney-General v Blake*,[293] Lord Nicholls appeared to take a restitutionary, rather than a compensatory, analysis of the relevant proprietary tort cases.

4.152   A significant feature of restitution for proprietary torts is that it is not a pre-condition that the defendant was acting dishonestly or in bad faith or cynically. While it may be said that the proprietary torts normally require intentional conduct (eg, the tort of conversion normally requires that the defendant intended to deal with the goods in question), it is no defence to the tort, including a restitutionary remedy for the tort, that the defendant honestly and reasonably believed that the property was his rather than the claimant's. So if the defendant commits the tort of conversion by selling the claimant's goods, the claimant is entitled to restitution of the sale profits in an action for money had and received even though the defendant honestly believed them to be his own. Similarly if the defendant commits the tort of trespass to goods by using another's goods, it would seem that the owner is entitled to damages assessed according to a reasonable hiring charge, even though the defendant honestly believed them to be his own.

---

[286]   *Lamine v Dorrell* (1705) 2 Ld Raym 1216; *Chesworth v Farrar* [1967] 1 QB 207.
[287]   *Oughton v Seppings* (1830) 1 B & Ad 241.
[288]   *Powell v Rees* (1837) 7 Ad & El 426.
[289]   *Strand Electric and Engineering Co Ltd v Brisford Entertainments Ltd* [1952] 2 QB 246, 254–255 (*per* Denning LJ; cf Somervell and Romer LJJ, who analysed the award as compensatory).
[290]   *Penarth Dock Engineering Co Ltd v Pounds* [1963] 1 Lloyd's Rep 359; *Bracewell v Appleby* [1975] Ch 408; *Ministry of Defence v Ashman* (1993) 66 P & CR 195, CA; *Jaggard v Sawyer* [1995] 1 WLR 269, CA; *Inverugie Investments Ltd v Hackett* [1995] 1 WLR 713, PC; *Severn Trent Water Ltd v Barnes* [2004] EWCA Civ 570; *Sinclair v Gavaghan* [2007] EWHC 2256; *Field Common Ltd v Elmbridge BC* [2008] EWHC 2079 (Ch), [2009] 1 P & CR 1; *Stadium Capital Holdings (No 2) Ltd v St Marylebone Property Co Plc* [2010] EWCA Civ 952; *Jones v Ruth* [2011] EWCA Civ 804, [2012] 1 WLR 1495, at [36]–[41]; *Ramzan v Brookwide Ltd* [2011] EWCA Civ 985, [2012] 1 All ER 903.
[291]   *Carr-Saunders v Dick McNeill Associates Ltd* [1986] 1 WLR 122; *Tamares (Vincent Square) Ltd v Fairpoint Properties (Vincent Square) Ltd* [2007] EWHC 212. cf *Stoke-on-Trent City Council v W & J Wass Ltd* [1988] 1 WLR 1406, CA (nominal damages only for the deliberate commission of the tort of nuisance by operating a market within a distance infringing the claimant's proprietary market right); *Forsyth Grant v Allen* [2008] EWCA Civ 505 (*Wass* applied in holding that no account of profits could be awarded for the tort of nuisance).
[292]   These are often referred to as '*Wrotham Park* damages': see 4.160.
[293]   [2001] 1 AC 268, HL: see 4.161.

(ii) Intellectual property torts

These are civil wrongs which are either statutory torts (eg, infringement of a patent, infringe- **4.153** ment of copyright, infringement of design right) or common law torts (eg, passing off). The reason why it is convenient to treat them separately from other proprietary torts is that restitution for these torts, through the equitable remedy of an account of profits, is very well-established.[294] This reflects the fact that these torts started life as equitable wrongs.

So an account of profits may be ordered for passing off[295] or infringement of trade mark,[296] **4.154** although it appears that dishonesty is here a pre-condition of an account of profits,[297] albeit not of a claim for damages.[298] It is explicitly laid down in statute that an account of profits may be ordered for infringement of a patent,[299] infringement of copyright,[300] infringement of design right,[301] and infringement of performer's property right.[302] Statutory provisions further lay down that negligence is required to trigger an account of profits for patent infringement,[303] whereas for infringement of copyright,[304] primary infringement of a design right,[305] and infringement of a performer's property right,[306] an account of profits may be ordered on a strict liability basis: ie it is not a defence that the defendant did not know, and had no reason to believe, that copyright or design right or performer's right existed in the work to which the action relates. As we have seen above, a strict liability approach to restitutionary remedies for the tort is applied in respect of other proprietary torts;[307] although, as noted at the start of this paragraph, it clashes with what appears to be the approach in respect of passing off and infringement of trade mark.

(iii) Non-proprietary torts

When one moves to non-proprietary torts, it is much more difficult to find examples of **4.155** cases illustrating the award of restitution for a tort. In particular, 'waiver of tort' cases that are sometimes cited as illustrations[308] turn out on closer inspection to be better (or, at least, equally well) interpreted as cases on restitution for the cause of action of unjust enrichment: ie 'waiver of tort' is being used in the third sense set out above.[309] In *Devenish Nutrition Ltd v Sanofi-Aventis SA*[310] an account of profits for the tort of breach of statutory duty was denied on the facts and the majority (Arden and Tuckey LJJ) held that, applying *Stoke-on-Trent City Council v W & J Wass Ltd*,[311] a restitutionary award (whether damages or an account

---

[294] One can argue that, while 'reasonable licence fee' damages are usually compensatory, sometimes they are better analysed as restitutionary: see Edelman, *Gain-Based Damages* (2002) 224–231.

[295] *Lever v Goodwin* (1887) 36 Ch D, CA; *My Kinda Town Ltd v Soll* [1982] FSR 147, reversed on liability [1983] RPC 407, CA.

[296] *Edelsten v Edelsten* (1863) 1 De GJ & Sm 185; *Slazenger & Sons v Spalding & Bros* [1910] 1 Ch 257; *Colbeam Palmer Ltd v Stock Affiliates Pty Ltd* (1968) 122 CLR 25, HC; cf Trade Marks Act 1994, s 14(2).

[297] See especially the decision of Windeyer J in the High Court of Australia in *Colbeam Palmer Ltd v Stock Affiliates Pty Ltd* (1968) 122 CLR 25.

[298] *Gillette UK Ltd v Edenwest Ltd* [1994] RPC 279.

[299] Patents Act 1977, s 61(1)(d).

[300] Copyright, Designs and Patents Act 1988, s 96(2). See *Potton Ltd v Yorkclose Ltd* [1990] FSR 11.

[301] Copyright, Designs and Patents Act 1988, s 229(2).

[302] Copyright, Designs and Patents Act 1988, s 191I(2).

[303] Patents Act 1977, s 62(1). The same approach applies to damages.

[304] Copyright, Designs and Patents Act 1988, s 97(1). A different approach applies to damages.

[305] Copyright, Designs and Patents Act 1988, s 233(1). A different approach applies to damages.

[306] Copyright, Designs and Patents Act 1988, s 191J(1). A different approach applies to damages.

[307] See 4.152.

[308] eg *Hill v Perrott* (1810) 3 Taunt 274 (deceit); *Universe Tankships of Monrovia v International Transport Workers Federation (The Universe Sentinel)* [1983] 1 AC 366, HL (duress).

[309] See 4.149.

[310] [2008] EWCA Civ 1086, [2009] Ch 390.

[311] [1988] 1 WLR 1406, CA: see n 291.

of profits) could not be made for a non-proprietary tort. It is also significant that in *Halifax Building Society v Thomas*[312] the Court of Appeal denied a claimant a restitutionary claim to the gains made by the tort of deceit, albeit in a situation where the defendant was the subject of a criminal conviction and confiscation order which was sufficient to reverse the gains he had made from civil fraud and to punish him for that fraud. Yet, as we shall see below,[313] Lord Devlin's second category of punitive damages is concerned to punish those who cynically commit torts with a view to making profits. If the courts are prepared to award punitive damages against the cynical profit-seeking tortfeasor, they must be willing to go to the less extreme lengths of awarding restitution against such a tortfeasor. This is particularly obvious when one realizes that a restitutionary remedy need not strip away all the gains made by the tortfeasor; rather the remedy can be tailored to remove a fair proportion of the gains, taking into account, eg, the skill and effort expended by the defendant.[314]

(b) Enrichments gained by an equitable wrong

4.156 It is a surprising fact, which reflects the unfortunate influence still exerted by the common law/equity divide, that when one turns one's attention from torts to equitable wrongs, such as breach of fiduciary duty and breach of confidence, the availability of restitution, through the remedy of an account of profits, is well-established. The account of profits is, therefore, standardly awarded to ensure that a fiduciary does not make secret unauthorized profits out of his position,[315] and to ensure the disgorgement to principals of bribes made to their fiduciaries.[316] The account of profits may be awarded even if (as shown in the secret profit cases) the fiduciary was not acting dishonestly or in bad faith. Similarly, it is well-established that an account of profits can be awarded for breach of confidence. For example, in the leading case of *Attorney-General v Guardian Newspapers Ltd (No 2)*[317] the Sunday Times was held liable to an account of profits, for breach of confidence to the Crown, in publishing extracts of Peter Wright's book, *Spycatcher*, at an early stage before the information had reached the public domain.

4.157 In the context of breach of confidence, it may be that the courts will award damages, whether restitutionary or compensatory, rather than an account of profits, if the breach of confidence was committed without dishonesty. This is one explanation for *Seager v Copydex Ltd* [318] in which the defendants had manufactured a carpet grip, honestly and unconsciously making use of confidential information given to them by the claimant. The Court of Appeal ordered damages to be assessed apparently on a restitutionary basis.[319]

4.158 Restitution for breach of fiduciary duty and breach of confidence is so well-established that the area of debate focuses, not on whether restitution rather than compensation should be

---

[312] [1996] Ch 217, CA.

[313] See 4.163.

[314] See eg *Boardman v Phipps* [1967] 2 AC 46, HL (breach of fiduciary duty); *Redwood Music Ltd v Chappell & Co Ltd* [1981] RPC 109, 132 (copyright infringement); cf *Guinness plc v Saunders* [1990] 2 AC 663, HL.

[315] eg *Regal (Hastings) Ltd v Gulliver* [1942] 1 All ER 378, HL; *Boardman v Phipps* [1967] 2 AC 46, HL; *Murad v Al-Saraj* [2005] EWCA Civ 959. An account of profits may also be granted for the equitable wrongs of dishonest assistance and knowing receipt: *Novoship (UK) Ltd v Mikhaylyuk* [2014] EWCA Civ 908, [2015] 2 WLR 526.

[316] eg *Reading v A-G* [1951] AC 507, HL.

[317] [1990] 1 AC 109, HL. See also, eg, *Peter Pan Manufacturing Corpn v Corsets Silhouette Ltd* [1964] 1 WLR 96.

[318] [1967] 1 WLR 923, CA. See also *Seager v Copydex Ltd (No 2)* [1969] 1 WLR 809, CA. See further the award of '*Wrotham Park* damages' for breach of confidence and breach of contract in *Vercoe v Rutland Fund Management Ltd* [2010] EWHC 424 (Ch).

[319] Another explanation is that the court awarded damages, rather than an account of profits, because, as a matter of factual causation, the contribution of the confidential information to the profits made was relatively minor.

awarded, but rather on whether restitution should be effected by merely a personal remedy (account of profits) or by a proprietary remedy (constructive trust). *Lister v Stubbs*[320] denied that a proprietary remedy should be awarded in respect of a bribe and sought to maintain a clear divide between obligation and ownership. In contrast, the Privy Council in *Attorney-General for Hong Kong v Reid*[321] decided that, contrary to *Lister v Stubbs*, a bribe was held on constructive trust. This had the result that the claimant was entitled to land bought with the bribe. Most recently, after a detailed analysis, the Supreme Court in *FHR European Ventures LLP v Cedar Capital Partners LLC*[322] has preferred *Reid* to *Lister v Stubbs*.

(c) Enrichments gained by a breach of contract

Until recently, restitution could not be awarded for a breach of contract. Admittedly, it **4.159** has long been the law that restitutionary remedies, such as the recovery of money had and received where there has been a total failure of consideration[323] or a *quantum meruit*,[324] can be claimed by an innocent party once it has validly terminated a contract for breach. But they are remedies for the cause of action of unjust enrichment; they are not remedies for the cause of action of breach of contract.[325] So, eg, in *Surrey County Council v Bredero Homes Ltd*[326] the Court of Appeal declined to award restitutionary damages for a breach of contract where the defendants, to whom the claimant had sold land for a housing estate, had built more houses on the site than they had covenanted to build, thereby making a greater profit. Nominal damages were awarded on the ground that the claimant had suffered no loss. Restitutionary damages were held to be inappropriate because this was an action for ordinary common law damages for breach of contract: it involved neither a tort nor an infringement of proprietary rights nor equitable damages.

The reference to proprietary rights and equitable damages reflects the fact that in *Wrotham* **4.160** *Park Estate Co Ltd v Parkside Homes Ltd*[327] Brightman J, using a 'hypothetical bargain' approach, did award damages that are arguably best rationalized as restitutionary[328] for breach of restrictive covenants preventing the building of houses that were enforceable in equity by the claimants.

However, this traditional approach to restitution for breach of contract was shattered by the **4.161** House of Lords in *Attorney-General v Blake*.[329] It was there recognized that, in exceptional cases, an account of profits can be ordered for a breach of contract. Such an order was made to deprive George Blake, the spy, of profits made or to be made from a book that he had written in breach of his undertaking to the Crown. Lord Nicholls, giving the leading speech, said that exceptionally an account of profits is appropriate where other contractual remedies are inadequate. 'A useful general guide . . . is whether the plaintiff had a legitimate interest in preventing the defendant's profit-making activity . . .'[330]

---

[320] [1890] 45 Ch D 1, CA.
[321] [1994] 1 AC 324, PC. See also *LAC Minerals Ltd v International Corona Resources Ltd* (1989) 61 DLR (4th) 14, SC (breach of confidence). See generally EPL 4.302–4.313, 4.315–4.316.
[322] [2014] UKSC 45, [2015] AC 250.
[323] eg *Giles v Edwards* (1797) 7 Term Rep 181; *Rowland v Divall* [1923] 2 KB 500, CA.
[324] eg *De Bernardy v Harding* (1853) 8 Exch 822.
[325] See 3.78.
[326] [1993] 1 WLR 1361, CA.
[327] [1974] 1 WLR 798.
[328] This is not only because of Brightman J's general reasoning but because he made clear that the claimants would not have accepted that sum for relaxing the covenant. See Steyn LJ in *Surrey CC v Bredero Homes Ltd* [1993] 1 WLR 1361. But the Court of Appeal in *Jaggard v Sawyer* [1995] 1 WLR 269 has said that the damages in the *Wrotham Park* case were compensatory and not restitutionary.
[329] [2001] 1 AC 268, HL.
[330] [2001] 1 AC 268, 285, HL.

4.162 Although *Blake* has only been directly applied in one subsequent case to order an account of profits for breach of contract,[331] it has been influential in encouraging courts to assess contractual damages, albeit exceptionally, on the hypothetical bargain approach favoured in the *Wrotham Park* case. Those damages are, arguably, best analysed as restitutionary. For example, in *Experience Hendrix LLC v PPX Enterprises Inc* [332] the defendant record company, in breach of a contractual settlement with Jimi Hendrix, used certain master tapes that should have been delivered up to Jimi Hendrix. Although *Blake* was distinguished—in the sense that an account of profits, stripping the defendant of all its gains made from the breach of contract, was not awarded—*Wrotham Park*, as endorsed by *Blake* was applied in holding that the claimant was entitled to damages based not on compensating loss but on what was a reasonable sum to pay taking into account the gains made by the defendant from its use of the forbidden tapes. Although the Court of Appeal was not required to assess that reasonable sum, it thought that one-third of the defendant's royalties on the retail selling price of records made from the forbidden tapes would probably be an appropriate reasonable sum.

(2) Punishment

4.163 A remedy concerned to punish a defendant for a civil wrong is rare in English law. The exception is 'punitive' (or 'exemplary') damages which, as laid down in *Rookes v Barnard* [333] and *Kuddus v Chief Constable of Leicestershire* [334] can be awarded in certain limited categories for some torts but not, as yet, for breach of contract[335] or equitable wrongs (such as breach of fiduciary duty or breach of confidence).[336] The House of Lords in *Rookes v Barnard* laid down that punitive damages can be awarded in only three categories of case. First, where there has been oppressive, arbitrary or unconstitutional wrongdoing by a servant of government;[337] secondly, where the defendant has committed a wrong cynically

---

[331] *Esso Petroleum Co Ltd v Niad Ltd* [2001] 1 All ER (D) 324 (Nov).

[332] [2003] EWCA Civ 323, [2003] 1 All ER (Comm) 830. See also *Lane v O'Brien Homes Ltd* [2004] EWHC 303 (QB); *Pell Frischmann Engineering Ltd v Bow Valley Iran Ltd* [2009] UKPC 45, [2011] 1 WLR 2370; *Vercoe v Rutland Fund Management Ltd* [2010] EWHC 424 (Ch); *Van der Garde v Force India Formula One Team Ltd* [2010] EWHC 2373 (QB). In *WWF World Wide Fund for Nature v World Wrestling Federation Entertainment Inc* [2007] EWCA Civ 286, [2008] 1 WLR 445, *Wrotham Park* damages were conceptualized as compensatory and a restitutionary analysis was rejected. The force of this is undermined by the CA's view that even an account of profits is a compensatory and not a gains-based award.

[333] [1964] AC 1129, HL. For a wide-ranging review of the law on exemplary damages, see *Aggravated, Exemplary and Restitutionary Damages* (Law Com No 247, 1997).

[334] [2001] UKHL 29, [2002] 2 AC 122.

[335] *Addis v Gramophone Company Ltd* [1909] AC 488, HL; *Perera v Vandiyar* [1953] 1 WLR 672, CA; *Newcastle-upon-Tyne CC v Allan* [2005] ICR 1170, EAT. For an interesting example of punitive damages being awarded for breach of contract by the Supreme Court of Canada, see *Whiten v Pilot Insurance Co* (2002) 209 DLR (4th) 257.

[336] *Mosley v News Group Newspapers Ltd* [2008] EWHC 1777 (QB), [2008] EMLR 20 (breach of confidence/privacy); *Harris v Digital Pulse Pty Ltd* (2003) 56 NSWLR 298, NSWCA. This denial is perhaps surprising given the standard willingness of the courts to award restitution, through an account of profits, for equitable wrongs. Contrast *Acquaculture Corp v New Zealand Green Mussel Co Ltd* [1990] 3 NZLR 299, NZCA.

[337] eg *Huckle v Money* (1763) 2 Wils 205; *Wilks v Wood* (1763) Lofft 1; *White v Metropolitan Police Commissioner* The Times, 24 April 1982; *Holden v Chief Constable of Lancashire* [1987] QB 380; *Treadaway v Chief Constable of West Midlands* The Times, 25 October 1994; *Thompson v Commissioner of Police for the Metropolis* [1998] QB 498, CA; *Muuse v Secretary of State for the Home Department* [2010] EWCA Civ 453. cf *Lumba v Secretary of State for the Home Department* [2011] UKSC 12, [2011] 2 WLR 671(no exemplary damages for false imprisonment because the claimant would have been detained in any event even if the correct procedures had been followed).

calculating that it will be profitable so to do;[338] and, thirdly, where expressly authorized by statute.[339] The Court of Appeal in *AB v South West Water Services Ltd*[340] added a second restriction, namely that punitive damages could only be awarded if they were awarded for that particular wrong pre-1964 (ie, before *Rookes v Barnard* was decided). However, this 'cause of action' test was removed by the House of Lords in *Kuddus v Chief Constable of Leicestershire*. On the facts of the case this meant that, if the other requirements for the award of punitive damages were satisfied, punitive damages could be awarded for the tort of misfeasance in public office. It was noted that the need to search through old authorities to find a pre-1964 award of punitive damages was unfortunate, especially since aggravated and punitive damages have only been clearly distinguished since *Rookes v Barnard* itself, and it may well be difficult to determine the characterization of an award of damages in an older case. The removal of the cause of action test in *Kuddus* means that punitive damages can be awarded for any tort provided the facts fall within the *Rookes v Barnard* categories.[341]

Even if a claimant can show that the defendant's wrong falls within one of the three categories punitive damages may still not be awarded for a number of reasons. For example, they will not be awarded unless a court is satisfied that the sum which it seeks to award as compensation is inadequate to punish the defendant for his outrageous conduct, to deter him and others from engaging in similar conduct, and to mark the court's disapproval of such conduct. This is the so-called 'if, but only if' test.[342] In general, punitive damages will also not be awarded where a defendant has already been punished by the criminal law in respect of the facts upon which the claimant now founds his tortious action because a person should not be punished twice for the same offence.[343] Punitive damages may also be denied where the claimant has provoked the wrongful action by his own conduct.[344]   **4.164**

If it has been decided that punitive damages are to be awarded, there are a number of factors which the courts have considered relevant in assessing those damages. Punitive awards should be moderate.[345] The means of the defendant and all mitigating circumstances should be   **4.165**

---

[338] *Bell v Midland Rly Co* [1861] 10 CBNS 287; *Broome v Cassell* [1972] AC 1027, HL; *Drane v Evangelou* [1978] 1 WLR 455, CA; *Guppys (Bridport) Ltd v Brookling and James* (1983) 14 HLR 1, CA; *McMillan v Singh* [1984] HLR 120, CA; *Design Progression v Thurloe Properties Ltd* [2004] EWHC 324 (Ch); [2004] 10 EG 184 (CS) (breach of statutory duty under Landlord and Tenant Act 1988, s 1(3)); *Borders (UK) Ltd v Commissioner of Police of the Metropolis* [2005] EWHC Civ 197; *AT v Gavril Dulghieru* [2009] EWHC 825 (QB); *Ramzan v Brookwide Ltd* [2011] EWCA Civ 985, [2012] 1 All ER 903.

[339] The only clear example is the Reserve and Auxiliary Forces (Protection of Civil Interests) Act 1951, s 13(2). Perhaps the Copyright, Designs and Patents Act 1988, s 97(2) does so but in *Redrow Homes Ltd v Bett Brothers plc* [1999] 1 AC 197 HL (Sc), Lord Clyde said that 'additional damages' under s 97(2) were more probably aggravated rather than punitive damages.

[340] [1993] QB 507, CA.

[341] Punitive damages probably cannot be awarded for infringement of a convention right under the Human Rights Act 1998 (best conceptualized as a sui generis public law wrong rather than as a tort). This is because s 8(3) of the Human Rights Act 1998 refers to the award being necessary to afford 'just satisfaction' to the claimant which appears to be a reference to compensation alone; and the jurisprudence of the European Court of Human Rights indicates that no exemplary damages can be awarded. See *Anufrijeva v London Borough of Southwark* [2003] EWCA Civ 1406, [2004] QB 1124.

[342] *Rookes v Barnard* [1964] AC 1129, 1228, HL; *Broome v Cassell* [1972] AC 1027, 1062, 1089, 1096, 1104, 1118, 1121–1122, 1134, HL.

[343] *Archer v Brown* [1985] QB 401, CA. For departures from the general rule, see *Borders (UK) Ltd v Commissioner of Police of the Metropolis* [2005] EWHC Civ 197; *AT v Gavril Dulghieru* [2009] EWHC 825 (QB).

[344] *Holden v Chief Constable of Lancashire* [1987] QB 380, CA.

[345] *Rookes v Barnard* [1964] AC 1129, HL; *John v MGN Ltd* [1997] QB 586, CA; *Thompson v MPC* [1998] QB 498, CA. In the *Thompson* case, the Court of Appeal laid down guideline figures for juries on quantum (including punitive damages) in false imprisonment and malicious prosecution actions against the police.

taken into account.[346] Where there are joint defendants punitive damages must not exceed the lowest sum that any of the defendants ought to pay.[347] And where there are multiple claimants the total amount of punitive damages considered fair for the defendant to pay should first be decided on and then divided among the claimants.[348]

D. Compelling Performance or Preventing (or Compelling the Undoing of) a Wrong

4.166   In this section, we examine what may be termed 'specific' remedies for wrongs. In general, these are orders requiring a defendant to comply with his primary duty not to commit a wrong. Where the duty in question is a positive one (as, eg, with most contractual duties) the remedies (eg, specific performance or the award of an agreed sum) order the defendant to perform his positive duty. In other words, the remedies seek to compel performance.[349] Where the duty in question is a negative one (as, eg, with most duties imposed by tort) the remedies (eg, a prohibitory injunction) order the defendant not to act in such a way as to commit, or to continue to commit, a wrong. In other words, the remedies seek to prevent a wrong. Also covered in this section are remedies (eg, a mandatory restorative injunction or delivery up of goods) which seek to stop the continuing effects of a wrong by compelling a defendant to 'undo' the wrong.

4.167   It should be noted that specific remedies for wrongs, with the exception of the award of an agreed sum, are equitable rather than common law remedies. As equitable remedies, they are discretionary rather than being available as of right. But it would be a mistake to imagine that this means that the law on equitable specific remedies is not clear and certain. In truth, all that is meant is that, in contrast to common law remedies, there are numerous, albeit clearly established, bars to the equitable remedies.

4.168   A central underlying question is the extent to which a claimant can choose a specific remedy rather than compensation. On the face of it, one might expect the claimant to have a free choice. After all, the specific remedies more directly protect the claimant's right not to be the victim of a wrong than does compensation. But while in relation to negative duties, the prohibitory injunction is freely available—and can be regarded as the primary remedy as against compensatory damages—the same cannot be said of the enforcement of positive duties through specific performance and mandatory injunctions. They are secondary remedies to compensatory damages in the sense that they will not be awarded unless damages are inadequate. Whether this approach is rationally justified, as opposed to being a product of the historical divide between common law and equity, is a matter which we shall discuss below.

---

[346] *Rookes v Barnard* [1964] AC 1129.

[347] *Broome v Cassell* [1972] AC 1027, HL.

[348] *Riches v News Group Newspapers* [1986] QB 256, CA. In *Lumba v Secretary of State for the Home Department* [2011] UKSC 12, [2011] 2 WLR 671, at [167], one of the reasons for not awarding exemplary damages was that there were others in the same position as the claimants who were not before the court.

[349] A further judicial remedy concerned to 'enforce' a defendant's positive duties (but which goes one step beyond ordering the defendant to do something) is the court's appointment of a receiver and manager. Apart from the specialist area of insolvency (see EPL ch 19), the High Court has long had an equitable jurisdiction to appoint a receiver and this is now embodied in the Senior Courts Act 1981, s 37(1). For examples of such an order (which may be interim or final), being made in response to a wrong, see *Riches v Owen* (1868) 3 Ch App 820; *Leney & Sons Ltd v Callingham and Thompson* [1908] 1 KB 79, CA; *Hart v Emelkirk Ltd* [1983] 1 WLR 1289.

(1) Award of an Agreed Sum

This contractual remedy can be regarded as a hybrid, being like damages in that it is a common law and monetary remedy, but like specific performance in that its function is to compel performance of a positive contractual duty. It plainly protects the claimant's expectation interest.[350]   **4.169**

(a) Award of an agreed price

The most important agreed sum is an agreed 'price', whether for, eg, goods, services, real property, or a loan of money. Indeed an action for the price (ie, the standard action for a debt owed) is the commonest claim brought for breach of contract.   **4.170**

For a claimant to be entitled to this remedy, the defendant must plainly be in breach of a valid contractual obligation to pay the agreed price. The contract must not, therefore, be void or unenforceable, and must not have been rescinded; nor must the obligation to pay be one that has been wiped away by termination of the contract for frustration or breach. Also the sum must be due. An agreed price is only regarded as due, in the absence of any express provision as to advance payment, where the claimant has completed or substantially completed what it is being paid for: eg, a seller of goods is generally not entitled to the agreed price until property in the goods has passed to the buyer, as laid down in section 49(1) of the Sale of Goods Act 1979; and a builder is generally not entitled to the agreed price until he has completed or substantially completed the stage of the building to which the payment relates.[351]   **4.171**

An issue of great controversy is whether an action for the agreed price may fail where the defendant has clearly repudiated the contract but the claimant, instead of accepting the repudiation and suing for damages, has kept the contract open.   **4.172**

There are two major contradictory approaches to this issue. First, one might say that the claimant has an unfettered option to hold the contract open and recover the agreed price; ie that the duty to mitigate does not apply to an action for the agreed price and that it is no bar that damages are adequate. The alternative view is that the claimant may not be entitled to hold a contract open and recover the agreed price; the duty to mitigate does apply to an action for the agreed price and, where damages are adequate to compensate a claimant for his loss, it is contrary to that duty for the claimant to carry on with his unwanted performance and claim the agreed price: rather, he should accept the repudiation, claim damages and make substitute contracts.   **4.173**

The leading case is *White and Carter (Councils) Ltd v McGregor*.[352] The claimants supplied to local authorities litter bins on which they let advertising space. The defendants contracted to pay for the display of adverts, but later that day they repudiated the contract. The claimants refused to accept the repudiation and went ahead and displayed the adverts for the three year period of the contract. They then claimed the agreed price. The House of Lords held, by a 3–2 majority, that they were entitled to the agreed price. Two of the majority (Lords Hodson and Tucker) adopted the first of the two views set out in 4.173. The third, Lord Reid, while basically taking that view, suggested a possible qualification. He said, '[I]t may well be that, if it can be shown that a person has no legitimate interest, financial or otherwise, in performing the contract, rather than claiming damages, he ought not be allowed to saddle the other party with an additional burden with no benefit to himself.'[353] Lords Morton and Keith, dissenting, took the second of the two views set out above.   **4.174**

---

[350] See 4.17.
[351] *Hoenig v Isaacs* [1952] 2 All ER 176, CA.
[352] [1962] AC 413, HL.
[353] [1962] AC 413, 431, HL.

4.175 In a few subsequent cases, courts have shown a reluctance to follow the *White and Carter* case. It has been distinguished on one of two main grounds. The first is that, as Lord Reid himself observed, the *White and Carter* case can only apply where the claimant is able to carry on with his performance without the defendant's co-operation. Some judges have distinguished the *White and Carter* case by giving a wide interpretation to this restriction.[354] Secondly, Lord Reid's qualification of the claimant having 'no legitimate interest' in performing the contract or, as other judges have termed it, of the claimant acting 'wholly unreasonably',[355] has occasionally been given a wide interpretation, thereby enabling a different decision to be reached, where damages are adequate, than in the *White and Carter* case.[356] But, in general,[357] while accepting Lord Reid's qualification, the courts have applied the *White and Carter* case in substance as well as in form so that it is in extreme cases only that a claimant, who has refused to accept a repudiatory breach, will be denied the agreed sum.

4.176 It should be realized that the approach in the *White and Carter* case contrasts with the traditional approach to the remedy of specific performance in that, as we shall see below,[358] if damages are adequate, specific performance will not be granted.

(b) Award of agreed sums other than the price

4.177 Awards of agreed sums other than the price may be payable on breach or payable on an event other than breach. The former comprise 'liquidated damages and penalties'. They raise different questions from the agreed price in that they constitute the parties' own fixing of damages for breach of contract. Specific enforcement of a liquidated damages clause does not therefore require a defendant to comply with his primary duty to perform the contract;[359] rather the liquidated damages clause is itself a response to breach of that primary duty. The question at issue is whether the parties' own assessment of damages through that clause should oust the assessment of damages by a court.

4.178 The short answer is that the courts will award the agreed sum if it is liquidated damages. But if it is a penalty, the promise to pay is invalid and the courts will instead award normal (unliquidated) damages. Traditionally, liquidated damages are a sum which represents a genuine pre-estimate of the loss caused by the breach, ie, of what is needed to put the claimant into as good a position as if the contract had been performed. A penalty, on the other hand, is a sum which is greater than such a genuine pre-estimate. It is inserted to punish the other party in the event of breach and to pressurize him into carrying out his contractual obligation. The distinction was emphasized in Lord Dunedin's seminal speech in *Dunlop Pneumatic Tyre*

---

[354] See eg *Hounslow London Borough v Twickenham Garden Developments Ltd* [1971] Ch 233; *Attica Sea Carriers v Ferrostaal (The Puerto Buitrago)* [1976] 1 Lloyd's Rep 250, 256, CA.

[355] See *Gator Shipping Corp v Trans-Asiatic Oil Ltd SA (The Odenfeld)* [1978] 2 Lloyd's Rep 357 (*per* Kerr J). cf *Ocean Marine Navigation Ltd v Koch Carbon Inc, The Dynamic* [2003] EWHC 1936 (Comm), [2003] 2 Lloyd's Rep 693, at [22]–[23] (*per* Simon J). In *The Odenfeld* and in *Reichman v Beveridge* [2006] EWCA Civ 1659, [2007] 1 P & CR 20, Lord Reid's qualification was held not to be made out so that, applying *White and Carter*, the agreed sums claimed were awarded.

[356] See eg *Clea Shipping Corporation v Bulk Oil International Ltd (The Alaskan Trader)* [1984] 1 All ER 129 (*per* Lloyd J).

[357] See eg *The Odenfeld* [1978] 2 Lloyd's Rep 357; *Ocean Marine Navigation Ltd v Koch Carbon Inc, The Dynamic* [2003] EWHC 1936 (Comm), [2003] 2 Lloyd's Rep 693, esp at [22]–[23] (*per* Simon J); *Reichman v Beveridge* [2006] EWCA Civ 1659, [2007] 1 P & CR 20; *Isabella Shipowner SA v Shagang Shipping Co Ltd, The Aquafaith* [2012] EWHC 1077 (Comm), [2012] 2 All ER (Comm) 461.

[358] See 4.186–4.188.

[359] cf paras 4.06 and 4.166. Strictly speaking, therefore, the award of liquidated damages falls outside the main scope of this section. Nevertheless, it has been thought most convenient to deal with it here rather than in the section on compensation. Note also that, strictly speaking, the questions raised on liquidated damages concern the validity of the defendant's promise rather than the judicial remedy itself.

Ltd v New Garage and Motor Co Ltd.[360] In that case £5 was made payable for every tyre which the defendants bought from the claimant that was then sold or offered by the defendants in breach of their agreement not, eg, to sell the tyres to the public below list price. The House of Lords held that this sum was liquidated damages. Although there were several ways in which tyres could be sold or offered in breach of the agreement, the loss likely to result for any such breach was difficult to assess and £5 represented a genuine attempt to do so.

In *Phillips Hong Kong Ltd v A-G of Hong Kong*[361] Lord Woolf, giving the opinion of the Privy **4.179** Council in upholding as liquidated damages a clause in a road construction contract, considered that the courts should not be too zealous to knock down clauses as penal. It was stressed that a clause can be a genuine pre-estimate of loss even though hypothetical situations could be presented in which the claimant's actual loss would be substantially lower. To hold otherwise would be to render it very difficult to draw up valid liquidated damages clauses in complex commercial contracts. Moreover, it was thought acceptable to take account of the fact that, as matters had turned out, the actual loss was not much greater than the agreed damages. Although the issue must be judged as at the date the contract was made, what actually happened can provide valuable evidence as to what could reasonably have been expected to be the loss at the time the contract was made. More recently, the courts have applied an alternative test whereby a sum will be upheld if it is commercially justified and does not have the dominant purpose of deterring breach.[361a] There therefore appears to be a trend in favour of upholding agreed damages clauses rather than knocking them down as penalties.[361b]

Controversial issues on agreed damages under the present law include; first, whether the loss **4.180** that needs to be genuinely pre-estimated includes loss that is legally irrecoverable (eg, because recovery of the loss would be contrary to the claimant's duty to mitigate);[362] secondly, what happens where the agreed damages clause is a penalty but the claimant's loss turns out to be greater than that penalty;[363] and thirdly, whether a liquidated damages clause is valid if it seeks to underestimate and hence limit the claimant's damages.[364]

Agreed sums, other than the price, payable on an event other than breach have traditionally **4.181** been treated in the same way as an agreed price. This means that once the event has occurred the sum can be recovered without any type of liquidated damages/penalty analysis.[365]

(2) Specific Performance

Specific performance is an equitable remedy which seeks specific enforcement of a defendant's **4.182** positive contractual duty. It plainly protects the claimant's expectation interest.[366] Prohibitory

---

[360] [1915] AC 79, HL. See also, eg, *Bridge v Campbell Discount Co Ltd* [1962] AC 600, HL (penalty); *Wadham Stringer Finance Ltd v Meaney* [1981] 1 WLR 39 (liquidated damages); *Lordsvale Finance plc v Bank of Zambia* [1996] QB 752; *Murray v Leisureplay plc* [2005] EWCA Civ 963, [2005] IRLR 946 (liquidated damages). In *Jobson v Johnson* [1989] 1 WLR 1026, CA, the law on penalty clauses was extended to a clause to transfer shares rather than to pay money.

[361] (1993) 61 Building LR 41, PC.

[361a] *Lordsvale Finance plc v Bank of Zambia* [1996] QB 752, *El Makdessi v Cavendish Square Holdings BV* [2013] EWCA Civ 1539.

[361b] See also *Parkingeye Ltd v Beavis* [2015] EWCA Civ 402.

[362] See eg *Robophone Facilities Ltd v Blank* [1966] 1 WLR 1428, CA (Diplock LJ considered that liquidated damages could properly include loss that was irrecoverable because too remote).

[363] See eg *Wall v Rederiaktiebolaget Luggude* [1915] 3 KB 66 (penalty clause inapplicable even though lower than claimant's actual loss).

[364] See eg *Cellulose Acetate Silk Co v Widnes Foundry Ltd* [1933] AC 20, HL (valid liquidated damages even though seeking to underestimate, rather than pre-estimate, the claimant's loss).

[365] *Alder v Moore* [1961] 2 QB 57, CA; *Export Credit Guarantee Department v Universal Oil Products Co* [1983] 1 WLR 399, 402, HL.

[366] See 4.17.

injunctions also enforce contractual duties but differ in that the duties in question are negative. If what is in form a prohibitory injunction, in substance orders specific performance, or if the courts consider that in practice the injunction amounts to specific performance,[367] it is governed by specific performance principles and is dealt with in this section.

4.183 Strictly speaking, it is not an essential prerequisite of specific performance that the defendant is in breach of contract.[368] Rather an action for specific performance is based on the mere existence of the contract, coupled with circumstances which make it 'equitable' to grant a decree. But, in practice, it is a breach of contract, actual or threatened, that renders it 'equitable' to grant specific performance.

4.184 Specific performance, being an equitable remedy, may be granted 'on terms'. The most common example occurs where the vendor of land seeks specific performance against the purchaser and there is some non-substantial defect in the property; specific performance will be ordered 'with compensation', ie, subject to the vendor paying compensation to the purchaser to cover the defect.[369]

4.185 In contrast to damages, specific performance is not available for every breach of contract. Indeed, as in this section, specific performance is best approached negatively, that is by examining the numerous restrictions on its availability. Positively, it then follows that if the remedy is not barred by such restrictions, a claimant who applies for it will succeed.

(a) The primary restriction—adequacy of damages

4.186 Specific performance will not be ordered unless damages are inadequate. It is this that fundamentally distinguishes the approach to specific performance of the common law, from that of the civil law, which has no such hurdle. There are two main reasons why the courts may consider damages to be inadequate.

4.187 The first and most important reason is if money cannot buy a substitute for the promised performance: ie the non-availability of a substitute. Most discussion of this has been in relation to contracts of sale, where the issue has generally been expressed as being one of the 'uniqueness' of the subject-matter. So contracts for the sale of land have traditionally been specifically enforceable on the ground that each piece of land is unique and cannot be replaced in the market.[370] Similarly, contracts for the sale of physically unique goods, like works of art, ornaments and ships, have been specifically enforced.[371] In some decisions, but not all, it has also been accepted that specific performance can be ordered for the sale of commercially unique goods.[372] Goods can be said to be commercially unique (a term coined by Professor Treitel)[373] where, although the goods may not be physically unique, buying substitutes will be so difficult or cause such delay that the claimant's business will be seriously disrupted.

4.188 A second main reason why damages may be considered inadequate is because of the injustice that an award of nominal damages will cause where a contract has been made for a third party's benefit. The classic illustration is *Beswick v Beswick*.[374] A coal merchant transferred his

---

[367] But see 4.208.
[368] *Hasham v Zenab* [1960] AC 316, PC; *Zucker v Tyndall Holdings plc* [1992] 1 WLR 1127, CA.
[369] *Re Fawcett and Holmes' Contract* (1889) 42 Ch D 150, CA; *Shepherd v Croft* [1911] 1 Ch 521. For other examples of specific performance on terms see *Baskcomb v Beckwith* (1869) LR 8 Eq 100; *Price v Strange* [1978] Ch 337, CA; *Harvela Investments Ltd v Royal Trust Co of Canada Ltd* [1986] AC 207, HL.
[370] *Sudbrook Trading Estate Ltd v Eggleton* [1983] 1 AC 444, 478, HL.
[371] *Falcke v Gray* (1859) 4 Drew 651; *Behnke v Bede Shipping Co Ltd* [1927] 1 KB 649.
[372] Contrast, eg, *Sky Petroleum Ltd v VIP Petroleum Ltd* [1974] 1 WLR 576 with *Société des Industries Métallurgiques SA v Bronx Engineering Co Ltd* [1975] 1 Lloyd's Rep 465, CA.
[373] 'Specific Performance in the Sale of Goods' (1966) JBL 211.
[374] [1968] AC 58, HL.

business to his nephew, who in return promised that, after his uncle's death, he would pay £5 per week to his widow. The uncle died and his widow brought an action for specific performance of the nephew's promise, suing both personally and as administratrix. The House of Lords, upholding the doctrine of privity, held that while the widow could not maintain a successful action suing personally, she could as administratrix succeed in an action for specific performance because damages were inadequate. This meant that the nephew was ordered to pay the £5 a week to the widow in her personal capacity as promised. But why were the damages considered to be inadequate? The reasoning was as follows: if a party sues on a contract made for the benefit of a third party the damages, which are assessed according to his own loss, are often nominal; where this produces injustice, as in this case where the nephew had got the business and would end up paying almost nothing for it, nominal damages should be regarded as inadequate, thereby permitting specific performance to be granted to enforce the defendant's promise. It is noteworthy that all their Lordships, and in particular Lord Reid, explained the relationship between damages and specific performance not simply in terms of the inadequacy of damages but rather in terms of the appropriateness or justice of granting specific performance. One can interpret their Lordships as wishing to effect a radical change in the relationship between damages and specific performance. But even if this interpretation is correct, it has not been followed through in subsequent cases which have largely continued to talk, and think, in terms of whether damages are adequate or not.

(b) The constant supervision objection

Traditionally, specific performance has not been ordered where this would require constant supervision. What this means is that specific performance will be denied of a contractual obligation that demands continuous acts, on the ground that this would involve constant supervision by the courts: ie too much judicial time and effort will be spent in seeking compliance with the order.   **4.189**

A leading authority is *Ryan v Mutual Tontine Westminster Chambers Association.*[375] The lease   **4.190** of a service flat to the claimant lessee included an obligation on the part of the defendant lessor to provide a resident porter who would be 'constantly in attendance'. The lessor in fact appointed as resident porter someone who was absent every weekday for several hours. The claimant brought an action for specific performance of that obligation. The Court of Appeal held that specific performance should be refused because this would involve constant supervision by the courts.

However, in more recent times—and until the decision of the House of Lords in *Co-operative*   **4.191** *Insurance Society Ltd v Argyll Stores (Holdings) Ltd*[376]—there has been a movement against accepting constant supervision as a bar to specific performance. For example, in *Tito v Waddell (No 2)*[377] Megarry V-C was faced with the question whether specific performance should be ordered of a contractual obligation to replant land that had been mined. While ultimately refusing specific performance Megarry V-C thought that it was no longer a valid objection that the order involved constant supervision by the court. Instead he thought that, 'The real question is whether there is a sufficient definition of what has to be done in order to comply with the order of the court.'[378] Other older cases support the idea that it is the

---

[375] [1893] 1 Ch 116, CA.
[376] [1998] AC 1, HL.
[377] [1977] Ch 106.
[378] [1977] Ch 106, 322.

uncertainty of the obligation, rather than constant supervision, that constitutes the bar to specific performance.[379]

4.192   In *Co-operative Insurance Society Ltd v Argyll Stores (Holdings) Ltd* [380] the House of Lords controversially reaffirmed the constant supervision objection in overturning the Court of Appeal's order for specific performance of a covenant in a 35-year lease to keep premises open for retail trade during usual hours of business. Lord Hoffmann, giving the leading speech, said that there had been some misunderstanding about what is meant by continued superintendence. 'It is the possibility of the court having to give an indefinite series of rulings in order to ensure the execution of the order which has been regarded as undesirable.'[381] He added that it was oppressive (and, moreover, put the claimant in an undesirably strong position) to have to run a business under the threat of proceedings for contempt. His Lordship distinguished between orders to carry on activities and orders to achieve results (regarding, eg, building contracts as falling within the latter category), arguing that the possibility of repeated applications for rulings on compliance with the order which arises in the former type of case does not exist to anything like the same extent in relation to the latter type of case. His Lordship further thought that, in the case at hand, the order could not be drawn up with sufficient precision to avoid arguments over whether it was being complied with. With respect, Lord Hoffmann's reasoning is unconvincing. In particular, it is hard to see why the order could not be drawn up with sufficient precision; and nor is it clear why the constant supervision objection should be thought valid in respect of orders to carry on activities but not orders to achieve results. This is not to say that the decision in this case was wrong. To force a defendant to carry on with a business that is losing money may well fall foul of the severe hardship bar or a separate specific bar. But this should have been addressed separately rather than being confused with the constant supervision objection.

(c) Contracts for personal service

4.193   It is traditionally a well-established rule that the courts will not award specific performance of a contract for personal service, of which the prime example is the contract of employment.[382] One reason for this bar is that such a contract creates a relationship of mutual confidence and respect and where that has broken down, it cannot be satisfactorily rebuilt by a court order: on the contrary, to force the relationship to continue is only likely to lead to friction between the parties. Another reason is that where services are of an artistic kind, like opera-singing, it would not be possible to judge whether an order of specific performance against the employee was being properly complied with.[383] Perhaps the most fundamental objection to specific performance of a contract for personal service from the employee's point of view is that specific performance would result in involuntary servitude. Thus in *De Francesco v Barnum*[384] Fry LJ said that the courts were afraid of turning 'contracts of service into contracts of slavery'.[385] From the employer's side the analogous rationale, seemingly implicitly accepted by

---

[379] eg *Wolverhampton Corpn v Emmons* [1901] 1 KB 515, CA. See also, subsequent to *Co-operative Insurance Society Ltd v Argyll Stores (Holdings) Ltd* [1998] AC 1, *Rainbow Estates Ltd v Tokenhold Ltd* [1999] Ch 64 (specific performance can exceptionally be ordered of a tenant's repairing covenant: Lawrence Collins QC said, at 73, '[T]he problems of defining the work and the need for supervision can be overcome by ensuring that there is sufficient definition of what has to be done in order to comply with the order of the court').

[380] [1998] AC 1, HL. For an interesting contrast with the law in Scotland, see *Co-operative Insurance Society Ltd v Halfords Ltd (No 2)* 1999 SLT 685, OH.

[381] [1998] AC 1, 12.

[382] eg *De Francesco v Barnum* (1890) 45 Ch D 430; *Johnson v Shrewsbury and Birmingham Rly Co* (1853) 3 De GM & G 914.

[383] See *Giles & Co Ltd v Morris* [1972] 1 WLR 307, 318.

[384] (1890) 45 Ch D 430.

[385] (1890) 45 Ch D 430, 438.

the courts, is that as he has to organize and pay for the work the employer should have the prerogative to decide who remains employed by him.

As regards an employee being ordered to carry out a contract of service, the bar still applies **4.194** in full force, being enshrined in the Trade Union and Labour Relations (Consolidation) Act 1992, section 236. However, on the other side of the relationship, there has been some movement in the cases so that the bar is less absolute than it once was. For example, in *Hill v CA Parsons & Co Ltd* [386] the Court of Appeal confirmed the grant of an interim injunction which amounted to temporary specific performance of a contractual obligation to employ the claimant. The defendant employers had a closed shop agreement with a trade union and gave the claimant one month to join that union. When he failed to do so, he was given one month's notice of termination of employment. The court held that the defendants were in breach of contract by giving only one month's notice. The majority of the Court of Appeal (Lord Denning and Sachs LJ) held that the interim injunction sought should be granted even though this amounted to temporary specific performance of a contract for personal service. In a particularly influential judgment, Sachs LJ stressed that there was no breakdown in mutual confidence between employer and employee. Again in *Powell v Brent London BC* [387] the claimant was appointed principal benefits officer for the defendant local authority. A few days after starting work, she was told that her appointment was invalid because there might have been a breach of the defendant's equal opportunity code of practice in employing her. She sought an interim injunction requiring the defendant to treat her as if she were properly employed as principal benefits officer and, even though that would amount to temporary specific performance, the Court of Appeal granted it. Ralph Gibson LJ, giving the leading judgment, relied on *Hill v Parsons*, especially Sachs LJ's judgment, to justify a departure from the general bar to specific performance. He said that specific performance would be ordered where it was clear that, first, there was sufficient confidence on the part of the employer in the employee's ability and other necessary attributes for it to be reasonable to make the order; and, secondly, it was otherwise just to make the order. [388]

It should be noted that there are two other aspects of the law in relation to an employee's **4.195** rights which, while not directly infringing the rule against specific performance, do modify its ambit. First, office-holders (ie those in public employment) have always been able to gain a measure of specific protection of their positions through the application of public law principles. [389] Secondly, there is the statutory regime of unfair dismissal, embodied in the Employment Protection (Consolidation) Act 1978 which, while not protecting employees by any equivalent to specific performance, may make it expensive for employers to dismiss unfairly their employees. [390]

(d) Want of mutuality

Fry in his book on specific performance, first published in 1858, [391] stated a rule of mutuality **4.196** to the effect that a court will not in general order specific performance against the defendant unless, from the time the contract was made, he could have got specific performance against

---

[386] [1972] Ch 305, CA.

[387] [1988] ICR 176, CA.

[388] [1988] ICR 176, 194.

[389] See eg *Vine v National Dock Labour Board* [1957] AC 488, HL; *Malloch v Aberdeen Corp* [1971] 1 WLR 1578, HL; *R v East Berkshire Health Authority, ex p Walsh* [1985] QB 152, CA.

[390] Although, by ss 68–71 of the Employment Protection (Consolidation) Act 1978, reinstatement or re-engagement, rather than compensation, can be ordered of an employee who has been unfairly dismissed, non-compliance does not constitute contempt and is instead dealt with by an award of extra compensation.

[391] *Fry on Specific Performance* (6th edn, 1921) 219.

the claimant had the claimant been in breach. In the leading modern case on mutuality, *Price v Strange*,[392] the Court of Appeal rejected Fry's rule. The defendant was the head-lessee of some flats in a house. She orally agreed to grant the claimant a new under-lease of his flat in return for his promise to carry out certain repairs to the house. The claimant did half of the repairs but the defendant refused to allow him to complete them, had them done at her own expense, and refused to grant him the under-lease. The claimant brought an action for specific performance of the promise to grant the new under-lease. Specific performance was granted by the Court of Appeal subject to the claimant compensating the defendant for the expense she had incurred in having the remaining repair work done. The defendant had argued that, in accordance with Fry's rule, specific performance should not be granted because, from the time the contract was made, she could not have obtained specific performance against the claimant because his obligation to repair was not specifically enforceable. But Fry's rule was held to be wrong and as, on these facts, there could be no risk of the claimant not performing (the work had already been completed) specific performance was granted.

4.197   It was, however, left unclear what the correct rule of mutuality is. Perhaps most helpful was Buckley LJ's formulation of the true rule as follows: 'The court will not compel a defendant to perform his obligations specifically if it cannot at the same time ensure that any unperformed obligations of the plaintiff will be perfectly performed, unless, perhaps, damages will be an adequate remedy to the defendant for any default on the plaintiff's part.'[393]

(e) Other bars

4.198   In addition to the four main bars that we have so far looked at, there are other bars to specific performance. For example, specific performance will not be ordered if the terms of the contract do not allow a sufficiently certain order to be made.[394] There will be no specific performance of a contract made by deed or supported merely by nominal consideration (ie 'equity will not assist a volunteer').[395] Specific performance will be denied where the contract has been unfairly obtained.[396] Specific performance will not be ordered where performance is physically impossible or where this would require the defendant to do something he is not lawfully competent to do.[397] Specific performance will be refused where it would cause severe hardship to the defendant.[398] Specific performance will not be awarded where the claimant's conduct has been generally inequitable (embodied, eg, in the maxims 'he who comes to equity must come with clean hands' or 'he who seeks equity must do equity').[399] And specific performance will be denied because of delay (ie laches) by the claimant in applying for specific performance.[400]

(f) The trend in favour of specific performance

4.199   Having examined the various bars to specific performance, it can be seen that the general picture, despite *Co-operative Insurance Society Ltd v Argyll Stores (Holdings) Ltd*,[401] is one of a trend in favour of specific performance. In relation to several of the bars there have been modern cases favouring specific performance. It appears, therefore, that a claimant will now

---

[392] [1978] Ch 337, CA.

[393] [1978] Ch 337, 367–368, CA.

[394] *Joseph v National Magazine Co* [1959] Ch 14. See also 4.191–4.192.

[395] *Cannon v Hartley* [1949] Ch 213.

[396] *Walters v Morgan* (1861) 3 De GF & J 718.

[397] *Ferguson v Wilson* (1866) 2 Ch App 77; *Warmington v Miller* [1973] QB 877, CA.

[398] *Patel v Ali* [1984] Ch 283.

[399] *Lamare v Dickson* (1873) LR 6 HL 414; *Chappell v Times Newspapers Ltd* [1975] 1 WLR 482, CA.

[400] *Milward v Earl of Thanet* (1801) 5 Ves 720n; *Lazard Bros & Co Ltd v Fairfield Properties Co (Mayfair) Ltd* (1977) 121 Sol Jo 793.

[401] [1998] AC 1, HL. See 4.192.

find it easier than ever before to obtain this remedy. In this sense, English law has moved closer to the approach taken in civil law jurisdictions. However, the essential difference remains—and it is a significant difference—that a claimant in English law has to overcome the substantial hurdle of first showing that damages are inadequate before he will be entitled to specific performance. There is no such initial hurdle in civil law jurisdictions, such as France, Germany and Scotland.[402]

(3) Injunctions

An injunction is an equitable remedy. The special principles governing interim (ie, pre-trial) **4.200** injunctions will be examined in the last chapter.[403] We are here, therefore, solely concerned with final injunctions (ie, injunctions granted at the trial of the action or at another hearing in which final judgment is given).[404] Injunctions are of two main types: prohibitory and mandatory. Prohibitory injunctions seek to prevent the commission or continuation of a wrong by enforcing negative duties. Mandatory injunctions, which are less common, require the defendant to do something: they enforce positive primary duties (other than for breach of contract where the appropriate remedy is specific performance) or, in the form of a mandatory 'restorative' injunction, they require the defendant to 'undo' a wrong.

Both prohibitory and mandatory injunctions may be awarded '*quia timet*' where no wrong **4.201** has yet been committed but is merely threatened. Although there is no reason why a *quia timet* injunction cannot be ordered to restrain the commission of any wrong,[405] the commonest examples concern the tort of nuisance. In addition to the normal principles governing prohibitory and mandatory injunctions, a claimant seeking a *quia timet* injunction must show that the tort is highly probable to occur and to occur imminently.[406]

(a) Prohibitory injunctions

(i) Breach of contract

The prohibitory injunction is the appropriate remedy for restraining the breach of a negative **4.202** contractual duty. It therefore belongs on the reverse side of the coin from specific performance which enforces a positive contractual duty. However, in contrast to specific performance, and presumably because the law considers it less of an infringement of individual liberty to be ordered not to do something than to be ordered to do something, a prohibitory injunction is much easier to obtain than specific performance. In particular, while there is technically an adequacy of damages bar, it is very easily overcome. In other words, damages are in this context hardly ever considered adequate and one can rightly regard the prohibitory injunction as the primary remedy as against compensatory damages.[407]

To say that the prohibitory injunction is the primary remedy does not of course mean that it **4.203** will never be refused. Two main grounds for refusal are that the claimant has acted inequitably[408] or that he has acquiesced in the wrong.[409] But indisputably the most discussed

---

[402] See *Co-operative Insurance Society Ltd v Halfords Ltd (No 2)* 1999 SLT 685, OH.
[403] See EPL ch 22.
[404] eg summary judgment.
[405] But in relation to breach of contract, if one regards an anticipatory breach as a breach, even though unaccepted, it will never be appropriate to describe an injunction as being awarded '*quia timet*'.
[406] eg *Redland Bricks v Morris* [1970] AC 652, HL; *Hooper v Rogers* [1975] Ch 43, CA.
[407] *Doherty v Allman* (1878) 3 App Cas 709, 720, HL; *Araci v Fallon* [2011] EWCA Civ 668.
[408] eg *Telegraph Despatch and Intelligence Co v McLean* (1873) 8 Ch App 658.
[409] eg *Shaw v Applegate* [1977] 1 WLR 970, CA.

ground for refusal is that to grant the prohibitory injunction would amount to indirect specific performance of a contractual promise for which specific performance would not be directly ordered under the principles we have looked at earlier. This will now be examined in relation to express negative promises in contracts for personal service, which is the main area where the problem has arisen.[410]

4.204 The classic case is *Lumley v Wagner*.[411] Johanna Wagner undertook that for three months she would sing at Mr Lumley's theatre (Her Majesty's Theatre) in Drury Lane on two nights a week and not use her talents at any other theatre without Mr Lumley's written consent. She then agreed to sing for Mr Guy at Covent Garden for more money. Lord St Leonards LC granted an injunction restraining her from singing except for Mr Lumley, and considered that this did not amount to indirect specific performance of her obligation to sing for Mr Lumley, which he recognized could not be granted.

4.205 This approach was followed and explained further in *Warner Bros Pictures Inc v Nelson*,[412] where the film actress Bette Davis had agreed that she would render her exclusive services as an actress to the claimants for a certain period and would not during that time render any similar services to any other person. In breach of that contract she entered into an agreement to appear for another film company. The claimants were granted an injunction restraining her for three years from appearing for any other film company. Branson J reasoned that this did not amount to indirectly ordering specific performance of her contract with the claimants: for, while the defendant was being ordered not to work as a film actress for anyone else, she was left free to work elsewhere in any other capacity.

4.206 A different approach was taken in *Page One Records v Britton*.[413] 'The Troggs' pop group employed the claimant as their sole agent and manager for five years, and agreed not to make records for anyone else during that time. In breach of that contract they then entered into an agreement to be managed by someone else. The claimant sought an interim injunction to restrain this breach. Stamp J refused to grant it because he thought that it would amount to indirect specific performance of The Troggs' personal obligations. Although to grant the injunction would still leave The Troggs free to take up any other employment, they were wanting to continue as a pop group; and, therefore, preventing them taking on any other manager would 'as a practical matter' compel them to carry on engaging the claimant as manager.

4.207 The latter approach was preferred to that taken in *Warner Bros v Nelson*, on grounds of 'realism and practicality', by the Court of Appeal in *Warren v Mendy*.[414] This concerned a dispute over the management of the boxer Nigel Benn. The case differed from the usual restrictive covenant case in that the injunction being sought by the claimant was not against Benn for breach of contract but against another manager in a tort action for inducing breach of Benn's contract with the claimant. But the Court of Appeal felt that, as the claimant would seek an injunction against anyone who arranged to manage Benn, the same principle should be applied as if the injunction had been sought against Benn for breach of contract. The injunction was refused on the ground that to grant it would constitute indirect specific performance of Benn's contract to be exclusively managed by the claimant for the three-year

---

[410] For examples of the same issue in relation to contracts for the sale of goods, see *Metropolitan Electric Supply Co Ltd v Ginder* [1901] 2 Ch 799; *Decro-Wall International SA v Practitioners in Marketing Ltd* [1971] 2 WLR 361, CA; *Evans Marshall v Bertola SA* [1973] 1 WLR 349, CA.
[411] (1852) 21 LJ Ch 898.
[412] [1937] 1 KB 209.
[413] [1968] 1 WLR 157.
[414] [1989] 1 WLR 853, CA.

contract period. While disapproving the approach in *Warner Bros v Nelson*, the Court of Appeal thought *Lumley v Wagner* was a correct decision because of the short contract period involved, which did not make it unrealistic to see the injunction as distinct from specific performance.

In *LauritzenCool AB v Lady Navigation Inc*[415] the Court of Appeal, in upholding the grant **4.208** of an injunction to restrain a shipowner from breaking a time charter by employing the ship with any other charterer, distinguished *Warren v Mendy* on the grounds that the personal service element involved in a time charter is far less significant than in a close working relationship between, eg, a boxing manager and a boxer. That is no doubt correct but it is far from clear that it justified the grant of the injunction in this case given that it was accepted that specific performance could not be ordered. A controversial distinction was drawn between a prohibitory injunction that juristically would amount to specific performance (eg an injunction restraining the defendant from taking any step which would prevent performance of the contract) and one that *as a practical matter* would amount to specific performance. Specific performance principles were thought applicable to the former but not the latter.

(ii) Torts

While a prohibitory injunction can be granted in respect of any tort that can be continued or **4.209** repeated—prohibitory injunctions have been granted, eg, to prevent trespass to the person,[416] inducing breach of contract,[417] defamation,[418] infringement of copyright,[419] infringement of patent,[420] and passing off [421]—it has mainly been sought, particularly at the final rather than the interlocutory stage, to restrain torts protecting the claimant's real property rights, namely nuisance and trespass to land.

In relation to these two torts—and there is no reason to suppose that different principles **4.210** apply to other torts—it is clear that the prohibitory injunction rather than compensatory damages (which will usually be equitable damages awarded under section 50 of the Senior Courts Act 1981)[422] is the primary remedy. The leading case illustrating this is *Shelfer v City of London Electric Lighting Co.*[423] An electric housing station had been built next to a pub and the vibration and noise caused by the operation of the machine generating the electricity constituted an actionable nuisance to the lessee of the pub. The Court of Appeal granted the injunction and said that damages should only be awarded in substitution for an injunction: 'If the injury to the plaintiff's legal rights is small. And is one which is capable of being estimated in money. And is one which could be adequately compensated by a small money payment. And the case is one in which it would be oppressive to the defendant to grant an

---

[415] [2005] EWCA Civ 579, [2005] 1 WLR 3686.

[416] *Egan v Egan* [1975] Ch 218 (interim injunction).

[417] *Emerald Construction Co Ltd v Lowthian* [1966] 1 WLR 691, CA (interim injunction). The availability of the prohibitory injunction contrasts here with the reluctance to grant specific performance of positive obligations in the main contract.

[418] *Saxby v Easterbrook* (1878) 3 CPD 339; *Bonnard v Perryman* [1891] 2 Ch 269, CA (interim injunction). The desire to protect free speech means that the courts are reluctant to grant an interim injunction to restrain defamation: *Herbage v Pressdram Ltd* [1984] 1 WLR 1160, CA; Human Rights Act 1998, s 12(3).

[419] *Performing Right Society Ltd v Mitchell & Booker Ltd* [1924] 1 KB 762.

[420] *Coflexip SA v Stolt Comex Seaway MS Ltd* [2001] 1 All ER 952 (note), CA.

[421] *Erven Warnink v J Townend & Sons (Hull) Ltd* [1979] AC 731, HL; *British Telecommunications plc v One In A Million Ltd* [1991] 1 WLR 903.

[422] See paras 4.138–4.142.

[423] [1895] 1 Ch 287, CA. For recent illustrations see *Regan v Paul Properties DPF (No 1) Ltd* [2006] EWCA Civ 1319, [2007] Ch 135 (injunction granted to stop the construction of a building that would infringe the claimant's right to light: the principles applied were those for prohibitory injunctions albeit that the court referred to the injunction as mandatory); and *Watson v Croft Promosport Ltd* [2009] EWCA Civ 15, [2009] 3 All ER 249 (injunction granted to restrict use of a motor racing circuit that constituted a nuisance).

injunction.'[424] This statement has been applied many times since, a good example being in *Kennaway v Thompson*,[425] where the Court of Appeal awarded a prohibitory injunction to limit power-boat racing, the noise from which was causing the claimant a nuisance.

4.211 Naturally, this does not mean that damages will never be awarded instead of a prohibitory injunction. For example, the claimant's inequitable conduct may bar him from the injunction. There is conflict in the authorities as to whether a prohibitory injunction will be refused where the interference with the claimant's rights is trivial. On the one hand, there are cases such as *Behrens v Richards*[426] where, having decided that the defendants, local inhabitants, were trespassing on the claimant's land by crossing it to reach a beach, Buckley J refused a prohibitory injunction because the trespass was causing no real harm to the claimant. Nominal damages were considered sufficient. On the other hand, the Court of Appeal in *Patel v W H Smith (Eziot) Ltd*[427] preferred the view that an injunction can be granted irrespective of the harm suffered and *Behrens v Richards* was put to one side as an exceptional case.

4.212 But while the courts rarely refuse a prohibitory injunction to restrain a continuing tort, they do often suspend or restrict its operation, and it is through this power that some account is taken of the defendant's hardship or the public interest. So, eg, in *Pride of Derby and Derbyshire Angling Association Ltd v British Celanese Ltd*[428] an injunction restraining the defendants polluting a river with untreated sewage was suspended for two years. And the injunction granted in *Kennaway v Thompson*[429] is notable for its particularly detailed specifications of what was and was not permitted: eg, rather than being an unrestricted injunction, it was laid down how many days a week power-boat racing was to be allowed, when international events were to be allowed, and when club events were to be allowed.

4.213 Moreover, there have been cases that cannot be reconciled with the traditional approach affording the prohibitory injunction such primacy. The best-known example is the Court of Appeal's refusal to award an injunction against a cricket club in *Miller v Jackson*.[430] Most recently, the Supreme Court in *Coventry v Lawrence*[430a] has looked afresh at the award of damages instead of an injunction. The leading judgment was given by Lord Neuberger. His Lordship indicated that, at least in relation to the tort of private nuisance, the courts should be more willing than has generally been the case in the past to award damages in lieu of an injunction; and that the *Shelfer* criteria should not be rigidly applied. Furthermore, the public interest should always be a relevant factor in deciding whether to award damages, rather than an injunction, for private nuisance, as sometimes should the fact that planning permission has been granted to the defendant.

(iii) Equitable wrongs

4.214 A prohibitory injunction can be granted to restrain the continuation or repetition of any equitable wrong. There are numerous illustrations of injunctions being granted to restrain a

---

[424] [1895] 1 Ch 287, 322–323.
[425] [1981] QB 88, CA.
[426] [1905] 2 Ch 614. See also, eg, *Llandudno UDC v Woods* [1899] 2 Ch 705; *Armstrong v Sheppard & Short Ltd* [1959] 2 QB 384, CA.
[427] [1987] 1 WLR 853, CA. See also *Anchor Brewhouse Developments Ltd v Berkley House Docklands Ltd* [1987] 2 EGLR 173.
[428] [1953] Ch 149.
[429] [1981] 1 QB 88, CA. cf *Tetley v Chitty* [1986] 1 All ER 663.
[430] [1977] QB 966, CA. See also, eg, *Bracewell v Appleby* [1975] Ch 408. In *Dennis v Ministry of Defence* [2003] EWHC 793 (QB) a declaration (treated as equivalent to an injunction) was refused to restrain a private nuisance constituted by the noise from RAF Wittering where fighter pilots are trained. But the public interest invoked was particularly strong because it concerned the defence of the realm and, for that reason, one should perhaps not see the decision as departing from traditional principles.
[430a] [2014] UKSC 13, [2014] AC 822.

breach of trust. For example, injunctions have been awarded to prevent a trustee in breach of trust, from completing a detrimental contract for the sale of trust property;[431] or to restrain a proposed distribution of trust property contrary to the terms of the trust;[432] or to restrain a sale of trust property where the vendor was not complying with statutory requirements for the sale.[433] Prohibitory injunctions have also been commonly granted to restrain a breach of confidence;[434] or to prevent a defendant acting contrary to a claimant's rights acquired under the doctrine of proprietary estoppel.[435]

The same principles apply here as in relation to prohibitory injunctions restraining a tort (or **4.215** breach of contract). In particular, the prohibitory injunction rather than equitable compensation (or equitable damages awarded in substitution for the injunction) is the primary remedy.

(b) Mandatory injunctions

(i) Breach of contract

At first sight, one might expect that the mandatory injunction would be the appropriate rem- **4.216** edy to enforce a positive contractual promise. But, leaving aside interim injunctions, this role is entirely taken over by the remedy of specific performance.[436] This leaves for consideration here the mandatory restorative injunction, which is the appropriate remedy for undoing what the defendant has done in breach of a negative contractual promise.

A leading case is *Shepherd Homes Ltd v Sandham*[437] where what is being sought was an **4.217** interim mandatory injunction to remove a fence that the claimant alleged had been erected in breach of a restrictive covenant. Ultimately the injunction was refused, Megarry J stressing that the courts are particularly reluctant to grant interim mandatory injunctions and would not do so here, where it was unclear whether a mandatory injunction would be granted at trial, and where the claimant had delayed in bringing his application. In discussing the relevant principles Megarry J said that a mandatory injunction was not as easy to obtain as a prohibitory injunction. That is, damages (in substitution) are generally regarded as sufficient and are the primary remedy. Megarry J preferred not to try to particularize all the grounds upon which a mandatory injunction might be refused but he said that they at least included '. . . the triviality of the damage to the plaintiff and the existence of a disproportion between the detriment that the injunction would inflict on the defendant, and the benefit that it would confer on the plaintiff'.[438]

Of course this does not mean that a mandatory injunction will never be granted to remove the **4.218** effects of the breach of a negative promise. A good example is *Charrington v Simons & Co Ltd*[439]

---

[431] *Dance v Goldingham* (1873) LR 8 Ch App 902.
[432] *Fox v Fox* (1870) LR 11 Eq 142.
[433] *Wheelwright v Walker* (1883) 23 Ch D 752.
[434] See, eg, *Peter Pan Manufacturing Corp v Corsets Silhouette Ltd* [1964] 1 WLR 96; *Duchess of Argyll v Duke of Argyll* [1967] Ch 302; *X v Y* [1988] 2 All ER 648. Where free speech is in issue, the courts may be reluctant to grant interim injunctions to restrain breach of confidence: see *Woodward v Hutchins* [1977] 1 WLR 760, CA; *Lion Laboratories Ltd v Evans* [1984] 3 WLR 539, CA; *Cream Holdings Ltd v Banerjee* [2003] EWCA Civ 103, [2003] Ch 650; Human Rights Act 1998, s 12(3).
[435] *Ward v Kirkland* [1967] Ch 194 (injunction restraining the defendant interfering with the passage of water through drains); *Lim Ten Huan v Ang Swee Chuan* [1992] 1 WLR 113, PC (on a counterclaim, defendant granted an injunction, conditional on payment by defendant to claimant, restraining the claimant from entering land).
[436] See 4.182–4.199.
[437] [1971] Ch 340.
[438] [1971] Ch 340, 351. See also, eg, *Sharp v Harrison* [1922] 1 Ch 502; *Wrotham Park Estate Co Ltd v Parkside Homes Ltd* [1974] 1 WLR 798, CA.
[439] [1971] 1 WLR 598, CA. See also, eg, *Wakeham v Wood* (1982) 43 P & CR 40, CA.

where the Court of Appeal granted a mandatory injunction ordering the defendant to remove a tarmac farm road, the height of which contravened a restrictive covenant with the claimant.

(ii) Torts

4.219 Given the rarity of positive tort obligations, mandatory injunctions for torts are almost invariably mandatory restorative injunctions concerned to undo the tort.[440] The classic discussion of the general principle governing mandatory injunctions is Lord Upjohn's speech in *Redland Bricks v Morris*.[441] The injunction being sought was for steps to be taken by the defendants to restore support to the claimant's land. The House of Lords discharged the mandatory injunction that had been granted because it left as too uncertain what the defendants were required to do. Therefore uncertainty is a bar to mandatory injunctions as it is to specific performance and prohibitory injunctions.[442] But Lord Upjohn clearly accepted that the mandatory injunction is not granted as readily as a prohibitory injunction. He said, 'The grant of a mandatory injunction is, of course, entirely discretionary, and unlike a negative injunction can never be "as of course".'[443]

4.220 So it is the case that, while the injunction may be the better remedy for the claimant, damages (in substitution) are generally regarded as sufficient and are the primary remedy. It follows that no mandatory injunction will generally be granted where the tortious interference is merely trivial.[444] Furthermore, in contrast to a prohibitory injunction, the hardship to the defendant is a bar to a mandatory restorative injunction. In *Redland Bricks v Morris*[445] Lord Upjohn indicated that hardship can here be a very wide restriction since, even in contrast to specific performance, the test can be a relative one; ie, so long as the defendant has acted reasonably, albeit wrongly, the courts can weigh the burden to him against the benefit to the claimant. Applying this to the facts, it was held that a mandatory injunction ordering the defendant to carry out the restoration work, while probably overcoming the uncertainty objection so long as set out in detail, would impose an excessive burden on the defendant who had acted reasonably. Such work might cost £35,000 while the value of the claimant's land affected by the slip was only about £1,500.

4.221 On the other hand, Lord Upjohn made clear that no sympathy will be shown for a defendant who has tried 'to steal a march' on the claimant, or has otherwise acted 'wantonly and quite unreasonably'.[446]

4.222 It should also be noted that, while constant supervision has traditionally been a bar to mandatory injunctions,[447] recent developments in relation to specific performance[448] suggest that it may no longer be so regarded.

---

[440] Although conceivably a mandatory injunction could be granted to enforce a positive tort obligation, there is no obvious example of its having been granted.

[441] [1970] AC 652, HL.

[442] See also eg *Kennard v Cory Bros Co Ltd* [1922] 1 Ch 265, 274, [1922] 2 Ch 1, 13, CA.

[443] [1970] AC 652, 665.

[444] *Isenberg v East India House Estate Co Ltd* (1863) 3 De GJ Sm 263; *Colls v Home and Colonial Stores Ltd* [1904] AC 179, HL; cf *Kelsen v Imperial Tobacco Co* [1957] 2 QB 334.

[445] [1970] AC 652, HL.

[446] [1970] AC 652, 666. See also *Daniel v Ferguson* [1891] 2 Ch 27; *Colls v Home and Colonial Stores Ltd* [1904] AC 179, HL; *Pugh v Howells* (1984) 48 P & CR 298, CA.

[447] See *Powell Duffryn Steam Coal Co v Taff Vale Rly Co* (1874) Ch App 331; *Kennard v Cory Bros & Co Ltd* [1922] 2 Ch 1, CA.

[448] See 4.189–4.192.

(iii) Equitable wrongs

A mandatory injunction is the appropriate remedy to enforce a trustee's positive fiduciary duties.[449] Such an injunction has also been granted ordering a defendant to convey the fee simple[450] or grant a lease[451] to a claimant under the doctrine of proprietary estoppel. In principle, a mandatory restorative injunction can be granted in respect of an equitable wrong but no illustration of this in the case law has been found.   **4.223**

(4) Delivery Up of Goods; Delivery Up for Destruction or Destruction on Oath

Delivery up of goods is a remedy which, like the mandatory restorative injunction, compels a defendant to 'undo' a wrong. Delivery up for destruction or destruction on oath may, at first sight, be thought to have the same purpose: but in general a claimant is concerned not with the mere continued existence of infringing material but with the harmful use of that material so that the primary function of the remedy is best viewed as being to prevent acts infringing the claimant's rights.   **4.224**

(a) Delivery up of goods

This is the appropriate remedy for the claimant to recover his goods where the defendant is tortiously 'interfering' with them (whether by the tort of conversion or trespass to goods).[452] The power to order delivery up is enshrined in section 3 of the Torts (Interference with Goods) Act 1977. By the remedy the defendant is ordered to deliver the goods to, or to allow them to be taken by, the claimant.   **4.225**

There is no reason to think that the 1977 Act has affected the principles governing when delivery up will be ordered. The primary principle, deriving from the remedy's roots in equity, is that delivery up will not be ordered if damages are adequate. The same approach to adequacy has traditionally been adopted as for specific performance of a contract for the sale of goods and specific performance and delivery up are regarded as directly analogous remedies. It can therefore be said that delivery up will not be ordered for most goods on the ground that damages will enable substitutes to be bought in the market.[453] But delivery up will be ordered of physically unique goods[454] or 'commercially unique' goods.[455] Even where damages are inadequate, delivery up may still be refused. For example, given its equitable roots, the court may deny the remedy, while granting damages, because of the claimant's conduct, such as his acquiescence or 'unclean hands'. Like specific performance and injunctions,   **4.226**

---

[449] *Fletcher v Fletcher* (1844) 4 Hare 67 (trustees ordered to pay beneficiaries what was owing to them under a trust). Analogously, but going one step further, the court has jurisdiction to appoint a receiver to ensure that the duties owed by a fiduciary are performed: Senior Courts Act 1981, s 37(1); *Middleton v Modswell* (1806) 13 Ves 266.

[450] *Pascoe v Turner* [1979] 1 WLR 431, CA (note that it was ordered that, in default of conveyance by the defendant, the conveyance should be settled by the defendant's solicitors); *Voyce v Voyce* (1991) 62 P & CR 290, CA.

[451] *Griffiths v Williams* (1978) 248 EG 947, CA.

[452] An analogous remedy, for breach of confidence, is delivery up of material containing confidential information belonging to the claimant: *Alpteron Rubber Co v Manning* (1917) 86 LJ Ch 377; *Industrial Furnaces Ltd v Reaves* [1970] RPC 605.

[453] *William Whitley Ltd v Hilt* [1918] 2 KB 808, 819; *Cohen v Roche* [1927] 1 KB 169.

[454] *Pusey v Pusey* (1684) 1 Vern 273 (the Pusey horn); *Somerset (Duke) v Cookson* (1735) 3 P Wms 390 (antique altarpiece); *Fells v Read* (1796) 3 Ves 70 (ornaments); *Lowther v Lowther* (1806) 13 Ves 95 (a painting); *Earl of Macclesfield v Davies* (1814) 3 Ves & B 16 (heirlooms).

[455] *North v Great Northern Rly Co* (1860) 2 Giff 64. For 'commercial uniqueness' see 4.187. See also *Howard Perry & Co v British Rly Board* [1980] 1 WLR 1375 where interim delivery up under s 4 of the 1977 Act was ordered in respect of 500 tons of steel.

delivery up may also be ordered on terms, eg that the claimant compensates the defendant for improvements made to the goods.[456]

(b) The action for the recovery of land—a contrast to delivery up of goods

4.227 The common law action for the recovery of land (formerly known as the action for eject-ment) enables a claimant to recover possession of his land by ordering the defendant to give up possession. But it is not as such a remedy for the tort of trespass. So, eg, unlike a claim for that tort, the action for the recovery of land is necessarily available to an owner who is out of possession; and the limitation period is 12 years rather than six.[457] It follows that, in contrast to delivery up of goods, the action for the recovery of land has retained its identity as a remedy solely within the law of property without becoming dependent on wrongdoing by the defendant.

(c) Delivery up for destruction or destruction on oath

4.228 Where there has been a wrongful interference with intellectual property rights (whether by infringement of copyright,[458] patent,[459] trademark,[460] or design)[461] or a breach of confi-dence[462] the courts have an inherent jurisdiction to order the defendant to deliver up for destruction, to the claimant or the court, or himself to destroy on oath, articles made in infringement of the claimant's rights (or even in some cases the means of making those articles).[463] The remedy goes one step beyond, and protects the claimant more effectively than, a prohibitory injunction; and it appears that there is no power to order destruction where a prohibitory injunction has not been granted.[464] Of course just because an injunction has been granted does not mean that the courts will exercise their power to order destruction. If the claimant's rights can be effectively protected by ordering something less than destruc-tion, this will be preferred.[465] It is important to stress that this remedy is granted even though the claimant does not own the articles ordered to be destroyed.

4.229 Although this remedy is clearly ideally suited for the wrongful infringement of intellectual property rights, there are other torts for which one would have thought it would be equally appropriate.[466] The explanation for its non-availability beyond the intellectual property torts (and breach of confidence), although hardly a justification, is presumably that the intellectual property torts have their roots in equity and delivery up for destruction is an equitable remedy.

---

[456] As expressly laid down in s 3(7) of the 1977 Act.

[457] Limitation Act 1980, s 15(1).

[458] *Mergenthaler Linotype Co v Intertype Co Ltd* (1926) 43 RPC 381.

[459] *Paton Calvert & Co Ltd v Rosedale Associated Manufacturers Ltd* [1966] RPC 61.

[460] *Slazenger & Sons v Feltham & Co* (1889) 6 RPC 531.

[461] *Rosedale Associated Manufacturers Ltd v Airfix Products Ltd* [1956] RPC 360.

[462] *Prince Albert v Strange* (1849) 2 De G & Sm 704; *Peter Pan Manufacturing Corpn v Corsets Silhouette Ltd* [1963] 3 All ER 402; *Ansell Rubber Co Pty Ltd v Allied Rubber Industries Pty Ltd* [1972] RPC 811.

[463] By ss 99 and 230 of the Copyright, Designs and Patents Act 1988 (and see analogously ss 195 and 204 as regards a person's performer's or recording rights and s 16 of the Trade Marks Act 1994 as regards infringe-ment of trade mark), the courts have a specific statutory power to order delivery up of infringing copies or articles, or anything designed or adapted for making infringing copies or articles. Moreover, while the courts may require the material delivered up to be destroyed they can also simply order it to be forfeited, eg, to the copyright or design right owner. Delivery up and forfeiture may be regarded as occupying a mid-position between delivery up of (one's goods) and delivery up for destruction.

[464] *Mergenthaler Linotype Co v Intertype Co Ltd* [1926] 43 RPC 381, 382.

[465] eg in *Slazenger & Sons v Feltham & Co* (1889) 6 RPC 531 the defendant was ordered merely to erase the claimant's trademark from tennis racquets, rather than being ordered to destroy all racquets bearing the trademark.

[466] An obvious example is libel: a claimant who has obtained an injunction would be even better protected by the destruction (or erasing) of libellous material.

E. Declaring Rights

While all remedies impliedly declare what the parties' rights are, a declaration is a remedy, **4.230** generally regarded as statutory albeit with equitable roots, by which a court pronounces on, without altering, the rights (or even the remedies) of the parties.[467] Available in relation to any kind of legal right, a declaration can quickly and easily and without invoking any coercion, aid the resolution of a dispute or prevent one from arising.

Early last century it was thought that the discretion to grant a declaration should be exercised **4.231** with extreme caution.[468] There is no such reluctance in modern times so that a declaration is readily granted. It has also now been accepted that, while an unusual remedy, a negative declaration (that the claimant is under no liability) can be granted where it would serve a useful purpose.[469] This of course does not mean that a declaration will never be refused. The claimant must have a real interest in the matter and must not be merely an interfering busybody. Nor will a declaration be granted where no dispute or infringement of legal rights has yet taken place and the chances of that occurring are regarded as too hypothetical.[470] Moreover, there must be a dispute between the parties.[471] Given its equitable roots, it would also appear, although there is little authority on this, that equitable defences, such as laches, acquiescence and 'unclean hands', bar a declaration.

As a remedy for a civil wrong a declaration is generally concerned to pronounce authorita- **4.232** tively that the defendant's conduct did or does amount to a wrong. For example in *Harrison v Duke of Rutland* [472] the defendant, on a counterclaim, was granted a declaration that the claimant was trespassing when he rode his bicycle along the defendant's road as a means of interfering with the defendant's grouse shooting.

Two further points are noteworthy. First, in some cases the courts have found it useful to **4.233** be able to grant a declaration, while refusing or suspending the more drastic remedy of an injunction.[473] Secondly, the courts now have power to award an interim declaration.[474]

An award of nominal damages can also be regarded as having the purpose of declaring rights. **4.234** Nominal damages are awarded in respect of wrongs that are actionable without proof of damage. Where the court is satisfied that the claimant has not suffered any damage, the claimant is still entitled to damages for the defendant's wrong (eg, the defendant's breach of contract or tort actionable per se). Nominal damages comprise a trivial sum of money, usually about £2–£10. Nominal damages are therefore not compensatory and must be distinguished from a small sum of compensatory damages. Given that the remedy of a declaration is specifically designed to declare rights, it would appear that nominal damages are superfluous and could happily be abolished. Certainly there are no longer any practical consequences turning on whether an award of nominal damages has been made or not (eg, a claimant awarded nominal damages is no longer necessarily to be regarded as a successful claimant for the purpose of costs).[475]

---

[467] Declarations are to be contrasted with remedies by which a court pronounces on, and alters, the legal rights of the parties: see 4.06, n 18.

[468] *Faber v Gosworth UDC* (1903) 88 LT 539, 550.

[469] *Messier-Dowty Ltd v Sabena SA (No 2)* [2000] 1 WLR 2040, 2050 (*per* Lord Woolf MR).

[470] *Mellstrom v Garner* [1970] 1 WLR 603, CA.

[471] *Meadows Indemnity Co Ltd v Insurance Corporation of Ireland Ltd* [1989] 2 Lloyd's Rep 218.

[472] [1893] 1 QB 142, CA.

[473] *Llandudno UDC v Woods* [1899] 2 Ch 705; *Stollmeyer v Trinidad Lake Petroleum Co* [1918] AC 485, PC. See 4.212.

[474] CPR r 25.1(1)(b).

[475] *Anglo-Cyprian Trade Agencies v Paphos Wine Industries Ltd* [1951] 1 All ER 873.

INDEX

Printed and bound by CPI Group (UK) Ltd, Croydon, CR0 4YY